Discovering Washington's Historic Mines

Volume 2: The East Central Cascade Mountains and the Wenatchee Mountains

Northwest Underground Explorations
   Phil Woodhouse
   Daryl Jacobson
   Greg Cady
   Victor Pisoni

N W M P
L L C

Northwest Mining
Publishers, L L C

Northwest Mining Publishers, LLC
P.O. Box 386
Monroe, Washington 98272

ISBN 978-0-9822558-1-0

was

(ISBN 1-931064-04-0)

Printed and bound in the United States of America

First printing 2002
Second printing 2009

Copyright 2009 Northwest Mining Publishers, LLC

All rights reserved. No part of this book may be reproduced or transmitted by any mechanical or electronic means, including photocopying, scanning or digitizing, or any other means, without written permission from the publisher, except for purposes of critical review.

Manuscript Editor: Teri Kieffer
Proofreader: Jane Wyatt
Indexer: Julie Kawabata
Design: James D. Kramer design services, Everett, WA 98208
Production Editor: Lynda Rygmyr

We dedicate this book to Lawrence Kaye Hodges

In 1895 and 1896, the *Seattle Post Intelligencer* sent one of its reporters, Lawrence Kaye Hodges, into the mountains to cover mining activity between the Columbia River and the southern British Columbia Mining Districts. Hodges' reports subsequently appeared in the newspaper in a series of articles that by the end of 1897 had been combined into a book titled *Mining in the Pacific Northwest*.

The book was printed on standard newsprint paper, so unfortunately over the next few years most copies deteriorated to the point that few exist today. During the 1960s, Shorey's, a Seattle bookstore, obtained a loan of a copy of this rare work from the Seattle Public Library, and with the encouragement of several individuals, private groups, and government institutions was able to reproduce the entire book as a facsimile.

L. K. Hodges

The original text, now over 100 years old, is still considered the bible of the early hardrock and placer mining histories of the districts Hodges covered. Although not 100 percent accurate, it is by far the most comprehensive of any document on the subject printed at that time. Some of the book's inaccuracies appear to be the result of transportation difficulties of the era and Hodges' publishing deadlines. Almost all of the areas he wrote about were unsurveyed at that time, and because many of the mines were being heavily promoted, it's likely that he was misled by those who stood to gain from the development of some of the properties.

We don't know how Hodges got his information to his editors in Seattle. Transmission by telegraph could account for some of the errors. Moreover, upon reaching the desk of his editor, the information was no doubt condensed, which possibly caused some important omissions.

Today almost every serious miner, geologist, and prospector in Washington owns a reprint of *Mining in the Pacific Northwest*. We highly praise Hodges for his tenacity in writing it, we thank the *Seattle Post Intelligencer* for publishing it, and we commend Shorey's for reprinting it. Without this extraordinary document, a vast amount of our early history would be lost forever, and we, as authors on mining history, would have been denied this wonderful source of data and our readers deprived of much valuable information.

We don't know whether Hodges' original notes still exist. After completing his assignment for the *Seattle Post Intelligencer*, he moved to Portland, Oregon, where he wrote a book about politics.

We dedicate this book to Lawrence Kaye Hodges and to all those who've contributed to preserving his work.

Disclaimer

> In utilizing this publication, it is and should be understood that mines, mining, and mining claim locations can be dangerous with numerous natural and artificial hazards.
>
> By accepting and using this publication and the information contained herein, the user agrees to relieve the authors and Northwest Underground Explorations, its officers, and/or its assignees from any liability from the use of any information contained in this publication. The user also accepts responsibility for any liability incurred by family members or guests incurred from the use of any information contained herein.
>
> The authors and Northwest Underground Explorations do not encourage or condone trespass on private or otherwise restricted properties without express prior and proper permission from the rightful owners of said property.

Warning

> Besides its hardrock and placer mines, Washington State is also peppered with huge coalmines on both sides of the Cascade Mountains: Newcastle, Renton, Issaquah, Black Diamond, and Grand Ridge on the western side, to name just a few. On the eastern side, there are coalmines at Cle Elum, Roslyn, and Ronald, plus smaller prospects near Wenatchee. Should you happen across an open coalmine, do not enter it under any circumstances. Coalmines contain deadly and explosive gases, and most have been mined to the point of imminent collapse. Never linger near an open tunnel or airshaft, since gas escapes through these openings and can cause immediate death. Report open coalmines to the authorities.

Contents

Dedication .... *iii*
Preface .... *iv*
Acknowledgements .... *vii*
Introduction .... *ix*
The Law and You .... *xxv*
Preparing for a Mine Trip .... *xxvii*
Hike Ratings .... *xxix*

Stehekin Mining Area — 31
Chelan Mining Area — 43
Chiwawa Mining Area — 67
Chelan Butte, Entiat Mining Areas — 83
Wenatchee Mining Area — 91
Blewett Mining Area — 129
Swauk Mining Area — 167
Cle Elum Mining Area — 217

Appendix A *305*
References *310*
Maps *316*
Glossary *317*
Resources *325*
Index *327*

Acknowlegments

Books of this nature are seldom an individual effort. They come into being because many knowledgeable people have donated their time to provide almost-forgotten facets of history, which together supply a factual account of past events. We have found this to be especially true in the mining history of Washington State. For some reason, no one has ever undertaken this endeavor before, and certainly not since or on such a scale as the great work on the subject by L. K. Hodges over 100 years ago.

Our books are not intended to replace the works of Hodges or other authors on mining history. Our goal is to provide you with a thoroughly researched and updated version of what actually took place at various mines, highlighting the successful and unsuccessful attempts to reach into the depths of the earth and wrench minerals from it. We try to do this in a way that is fun to read and brings life back to the colorful characters involved, some good and some bad. We also explain how to get to the remote areas where the mines are located, so that you can also enjoy some of the most spectacular scenery to be found anywhere.

The mines are for the most part hardrock mines (mines tunneled into the earth to extract and recover minerals such as gold, silver, copper, zinc, and so on). We cover some placer mines too. Placer mines were generally located along recent and ancient stream channels, where mining was done by panning, sluicing, hydraulic/sluicing, and dredging. Some placer mines were also dug underground.

When we first entertained the idea of documenting Washington's mining history some years ago, we had no idea what a monumental undertaking it would be. Many of the mines described in this book as well as our other works literally had to be rediscovered. Portals sometimes had to be dug or blasted open, and water drained or pumped from the underground workings to allow exploration. Mistakes in formerly recorded elevation and location had to be corrected. In some instances, we spent weeks and even months searching the mountains to get them to reveal just a few of their secrets to us. When weather conditions and other factors prohibited us from actual hands-on exploration, we spent many hundreds of hours searching the back shelves of bookstores, the basements of historical institutions, and volumes upon volumes of technical data concerning the mines, the people who operated them, how they were financed, and what they produced, if anything. We logged thousands of miles driving to remote locations throughout the state to visit mine sites, conduct interviews, and search for even more data, photographs, and other mine-related information.

Special thanks go to several people, without whose assistance and cooperation we couldn't have written much of this book: Ann and Joseph Gaspers, two of a number of owners of the Lovitt property; James Marr Jr., a former Lovitt miner; Ed Lovitt Jr., the son of Ed Lovitt; Joe Carl, a former Cannon miner; Ben Guenther, a former superintendent of the Cannon Mine and general mining expert; and Oscar Thompson, the former superintendent of the Lovitt Mine.

We'd also like to thank Asamera Minerals U.S. for a guided tour of the Cannon Mine; Connie Manson, senior librarian for the Washington State Department of Natural Resources; the staff and librarians at the University of Washington; the Washington State Historical Society Research Center; and the Ellensburg Library; and in addition, we'd like to thank Grace (Browitt) Elkins and Erin Black of the Kittitas Historical Society in Ellensburg Washington.

We thank Mark Buhler and the staff of the North Central Washington Museum, the Erickson Logging Company, and Mr. and Mrs. Reed Brown and Bruce Butts, the owners of the Trinity town site. To Tom Marr, we give thanks for the music. To Bud, Ruby, Dan Corbaley, and Bill Priestly, we give thanks for their help and especially for the time they took to guide us through the mines of Blewett.

We thank Wes and Carole Engstrom, Liberty residents, historians, and experts on the region, for their generous assistance with the later history of Liberty and for sharing with us photographs, documents, and other reference materials from their private files. Many thanks go to Paul Heit, the grandson of Ralph Fackler, for sharing his knowledge of the region as well as showing us some of the mines around Liberty that we would never have found without his help.

Thanks to the late Jack Kirch, a long-time Liberty resident and miner, and to the late Ralph Fackler, who with his wife and others were instrumental in obtaining township status at Liberty after many years of battling just about everybody. Thanks to Joanne Roe for her help on the Trinity story, and to Patty Tappan and Cathy Holden for their help on the history of the Holden Mine and town site. Thanks too to Bruce and Joyce Osgoodby for introducing us to Ralph Fackler, who helped us get the ball rolling on information about the Liberty area. We thank Kelly, Lynn, Bill, Mike, Dell, Len, and all the wonderful miners of the Swauk for sharing with us their mines, milling facilities, and historical information. We also thank the many mine owners who have allowed us access to their properties, provided us with historical background and photographs, and helped us track down and separate fact from fiction. We also thank the paid and unpaid workers at the many historical institutions throughout the state, who have taken their valuable time to aid us in our enterprise.

Last, to all of the wives, girlfriends, and mothers who have, over the last 20 years or so, had to put up with us being gone every weekend; living with piles upon piles of reports, maps, documents, and technical data we litter our homes with; and most of all for worrying about us, our safety, and our sanity when we go exploring underground.

Our deepest apologies to anyone we have forgotten to mention.

Introduction

Artifacts

By definition, just about anything you find at a historic site could be classified as an artifact. Whether it's a rusting relic of mining machinery or an old pop bottle, you should leave it where you found it. Some people seem compelled to salvage, damage, or destroy things they find in the hills. Some take them home as souvenirs only to discard them later, while others like to shoot holes into stuff.

In the U.S. forests, you get slapped with a big fine, plus jail time, for removing, damaging, or destroying any artifact. If the judge happens to be an environmentalist, you might find yourself in federal prison. Leave all artifacts alone so that others can enjoy them too.

Up to a $5,000 reward is awarded to anyone who turns in violators of these laws upon conviction.

Mining: A Short History

Mining dates back to prehistoric times. Gold was washed from gravel, and copper was mined and reduced from ore before recorded civilization existed. Tools made from flint have been found alongside the bones of Paleolithic man, who lived some 450,000 years ago. Underground mining was accomplished using picks, hammers, and wedges made from rocks, wood, and the horns of animals.

The earliest recorded production mining was done by the Egyptians in the turquoise mines on the Sinai Peninsula, where sandstone cliffs are inscribed with pictorial representations—dating to about 3400 B.C.—of their expeditions. Silver is mentioned in an inscription on a granite obelisk discovered at Susa, the capital city of Elam, which was captured by the Babylonians around 3500 B.C. Iron, zinc, and lead have been found at the ruins of Troy, establishing a date of about 2500 B.C. Mining has undoubtedly been a greater factor in the development of the world than we often realize.

When we think of mining, the gold rushes of the Klondike in 1896, the discoveries in California in 1848, and the rush to Nome in 1900 generally spring to mind. Perhaps some think of the huge open-pit strip mines of the Midwest. Although some groups seem opposed to any form of mining, it doesn't take much to realize what life would be like without the products that wouldn't exist without mining. It has often been said, "If it isn't grown, it has to be mined."

Mining and agriculture are the two basic industries upon which modern civilization developed. Agriculture gives us food, medicine, and wood for construction. Mining supplies us with structural materials, such as clay, glass, stone, and the ingredients for making cement. It provides us with gasoline, natural gas, coal, and other petroleum products. It also supplies abrasives such as garnet and corundum, and fertilizers such as potash, phosphates, and nitrates.

Mining gives us substances for industrial use such as sulfur, graphite, and borax, and metallic minerals, like gold, silver, copper, lead, zinc, iron, and aluminum (to name just a few). The precious stones diamonds, rubies, and sapphires are all mined. The list is almost endless.

Early mining in Europe was fairly easy, because most of the deposits were at or near the surface of the Earth. Miners, at least those who owned and operated the mines, were among the most respected and wealthiest people in their areas. After all, they had what everyone needed. As surface deposits became depleted, miners had to dig deeper and deeper into the soil and rock for their commodities. This required crews of workers. Thus the mining industry was born, and it consisted of an elite owner/management class and a worker/miner class that did the digging and hauling of the ores to the surface. The terrible ways that the miners and their families were treated during the Industrial Revolution, and well into the twentieth century are legendary. Our hats are off to their heroic and often tragic efforts to create the civilization that we know today.

Present consumption of minerals in the United States requires that we locate and mine, per year, 100 million tons of iron ore, 150 million tons of copper ore, 25 million tons of lead, 20 million tons of zinc, 10 million tons of molybdenum, and 40 million tons of phosphates. Yes, even the chip in your computer was mined.

Like it ore not (pun intended), without mining the world today would not exist as we know it.

This was one method of hauling steel mine rails up to their destinations in the mountains. One would simply attach one rail to each side of a horse and drag them up the trail to the mine. (*Pioneer Days in British Columbia,* 1977)

Gold

In our first book, *Discovering Washington's Historic Mines, Volume I,* we discussed how the mountains were formed and how the *big* gold rush in Western Washington during the latter part of the 1800s came about. We talked about the fictional character Goldfinger and his love for gold because it gave him power over others. For the most part, the mines in east central Washington were gold producers; even the two major copper mines there extracted a considerable amount of gold.[1] Let's take a moment now to look at what this amazing metal actually is, where it hides, why it is considered so valuable, and how it is recovered from the Earth.

Of all the world's precious metals, only gold combines lustrous beauty, easy workability, rarity, and virtual indestructibility. Not even diamonds possess these four characteristics. Throughout the ages, men and women have cherished gold, and many have had a compelling desire to amass great quantities of it. So compelling is gold, in fact, that the frantic need to seek and hoard it has been aptly named "gold fever."

Gold was among the first metals to be mined because it commonly occurs in its native form—that is, not combined with other elements—because it is beautiful and imperishable, and because exquisite objects can be made from it. Artisans in ancient civilizations used gold to lavishly decorate tombs and temples, and gold objects made more than 5,000 years ago have been found in Egypt. The most noteworthy were those discovered by Howard Carter in 1922 in the tomb of the boy king, Tutankhamen. The Egyptians believed that the gold and other valuables would be transported, along with the king, into the next world. King Tut died in 1350 B.C., yet the golden chariots, chests, crowns, bracelets, anklets, rings, collars, amulets, the famous facemask, and the gold coffin were just as beautiful when they were found as they were the day they were buried. Over 4,000 Egyptian slaves[2] were needed to mine the gold found in just this one tomb. When the King Tut Exhibit toured the U.S. not so long ago, over seven million people turned out to view his treasures.[3]

About 15 years ago, some of the ancient mines from which the Egyptian gold was extracted were discovered. To the astonishment of experts who visited these properties, there was evidence that the mining techniques used were virtually identical to those used in modern mines. The adits, drifts, crosscuts, stopes, and raises demonstrate a high degree of sophistication. Oil lamps that lit the miners' way still sat where they had been last used.

---

[1] The mines at Holden and Trinity.
[2] Not only slaves worked in the mines. Those convicted of criminal activities of certain types, *and their families,* were often sent into exile to work the mines for extended periods of time.
[3] All of ancient Egypt's gold was declared the royal property of the Pharaohs. Because of its brightness and glow, Egyptians linked it to Ra, the god of the golden sun. Many of the goldsmiths of this time were regarded with the same respect and stature as that awarded the high priests and other dignitaries.

Ancient civilizations seem to have obtained their supplies of gold from various deposits in the Middle East—chiefly, mines in the Nubian Desert. When these mines ran dry, deposits elsewhere, possibly in Yemen and southern Africa, were exploited. The gold in the Aztec and Inca treasures of Mexico and Peru is believed to have come from Colombia, although some undoubtedly was obtained from other sources. So much gold was stolen from the Aztecs that in one raid alone, after they had killed 50,000 indigenous people, it took 580 Conquistadors three full days to divide it up.

Many nations today use gold as a monetary standard. A large part of the gold stocks of the United States are stored at the Fort Knox Bullion Depository near Louisville, Kentucky.[4] Gold is measured by the karat.[5] In its purest state, it contains 24 karats, which is far too soft to be used in jewelry or most anything, for that matter. By mixing, or alloying, gold with other metals, its hardness can be increased and its color modified. The term *karat* is used to determine the amount of pure gold in an alloy, 24 karat being the purest, or about 100 percent gold. Eighteen karat is 18 parts gold and six parts other metals. Fourteen karat is 14 parts gold and 10 parts other metals, and so on. In the U.S., 10 karat is the legal minimum standard accepted for gold. In France and Italy, it's 18 karat. England accepts nine-karat gold, while some countries accept a standard as low as eight karat.[6]

When other metals are combined with gold, its color changes. Combined with copper and silver, it retains much of its natural yellow shade, but with copper alone it takes on a pink or reddish tint. Green gold can be created by the addition of silver, copper, and zinc. Combination with copper, nickel, and zinc results in white gold.

After the United States deregulated gold in the 1970s, its price increased markedly, briefly reaching more than $800 per ounce in 1980. Since the 1980s, the price has remained in the range of $250–$450 per ounce. The rapidly rising prices of the 1970s encouraged both professional and amateur prospectors to renew and expand their searches for the yellow metal. As a result of these efforts, many new gold deposits were located and several mines were opened. Later in this book, we will take you through some of these mines.

Gold is a noble metal (an alchemist's term) because it does not oxidize or combine with other elements under ordinary conditions. Its chemical symbol is Au, which derives from the Latin word *aurum*, meaning gold. Tracing the word's origin back even further, it appears that its first use may have come from Aurora, the Roman goddess of the shining dawn.

Pure gold is relatively soft, the most malleable and ductile of metals.[7] The specific gravity or density of pure gold is 19.3, compared to 14.0 for mercury and 11.4 for lead. This means that pure gold weighs almost 20 times more than a quantity of water of equal volume. Impure gold, as found in most lode deposits, has a specific gravity of 16 to 18, whereas the associated waste rock, or gangue, has a specific gravity of about 2.5. This difference in density is what enables gold to be concentrated by gravity and permits the separation of gold from clay, silt, sand, and gravel by various agitating and collecting devices such as the gold pan, rocker, or sluice box.

In the early days of mining in the Pacific Northwest, ingenuity was a requirement among mine operators. In this photograph, a surface haulback tramway has been fashioned using readily available logs as tracks. (*The Mining Journal-Press,* 1925)

---

[4] The first known use of gold coinage was by King Croesus of Lydia around 560 B.C.
[5] Not to be confused with "carat," a unit of measurement for gems.
[6] Interestingly, in some parts of Europe garnets qualify as rubies. Many uninformed tourists have purchased what they thought was fine jewelry overseas, only to find upon return to the States that all wasn't what they believed it to be.
[7] Gold is so soft and malleable that one ounce can be stretched into a wire an incredible 50 miles long, or hammered into a sheet so thin it covers 100 square feet.

Mercury (also known as quicksilver) has a chemical affinity for gold. When mercury is added to materials containing gold, the two metals form an amalgam. In other words they are chemically bonded together, almost like a solution. Mercury is later separated from the amalgam by retorting, or cooking off, the mercury in a sort of still. Extraction of gold and other precious metals from their ores by treatment with mercury is called *amalgamation,* a process used in the early arrastres (drag-stone mills) as well as modern mills throughout the world. Amalgamated silver has also been used for many years as filling for dental cavities.

Gold dissolves chemically in only one acid, aqua regia (royal water), a mixture of three parts concentrated hydrochloric acid and one part nitric acid, to form chloride acid. The only other commercial solvents that dissolve gold are dilute solutions of sodium, potassium, or calcium cyanide. Potassium or calcium cyanide is the base for the cyanide process that is used to recover gold from low-grade ore and tailings. Utilizing the cyanide process, auriferous rocks carrying as little as one part gold to 300,000 parts of worthless material can be treated successfully. This method is called *cyanide leaching,* and it has created some environmental concerns in the Southwest, as well as in eastern Washington and other parts of the world.

Gold is relatively scarce on Earth, but it occurs in many different types of rocks and in many dissimilar geological environments. Though rare, gold is concentrated by geological processes to form commercial deposits of two principal types: lode (primary) deposits and placer (secondary) deposits. There is a third and extremely rare occurrence of gold in what is called a pocket. Several pockets were discovered around the Liberty area, for instance. The pockets contained very large nuggets as well as crystalline wire gold. Some are still being discovered today.

Lode (primary) deposits are the targets of the hardrock prospector seeking gold at the site of its deposition from mineralized solutions. Placer (secondary) deposits represent concentrations of gold derived from lode deposits by erosion, disintegration, or decomposition of the enclosing rock, and subsequent concentration by gravity. These are usually found in or near water or along ancient stream channels.

Gold is extremely resistant to weathering and, freed from enclosing rocks, is carried downstream as metallic particles consisting of dust, flakes, grains, or nuggets. Gold particles in stream deposits are often concentrated on or near bedrock, because they move downward during high-water periods when the entire bed load of sand, gravel, and boulders is agitated and moving downstream. Fine gold particles collect in depressions or in pockets and cracks in sand and gravel bars where the stream current slackens. Concentrations of gold in gravels are called *placer pay streaks,* and are recovered by panning, dredging, and sluicing.

In gold-bearing country, prospectors look for gold where coarse sand and gravel have accumulated and where *black sands* have concentrated and settled with the gold. Magnetite is the most common form of mineral in black sand, but other heavy minerals such as cassiterite, monzanite, ilmenite, chromite, platinum-group metals, and some gemstones may be present. Garnets are the most common gemstones found in black sand in Washington State.

Consumption of gold in the United States ranged from about six million to more than seven million ounces per year from 1969 to 1973, and from about four million to five million ounces per year from 1974 to 1979. Since 1980, consumption of gold has been nearly constant at between 3 and 3.5 million ounces per year. Mine production has increased at a quickening pace since 1980, reaching about nine million ounces in 1990, and exceeding consumption since 1986. Prior to 1986, the balance of the supply was obtained from secondary (scrap and import) sources.

It is estimated that only 88 million tons of gold have been mined, and about two-thirds of this in the last 50 years. More steel is poured in just one hour than all the gold poured since the beginning of gold mining. If all of this gold could be contained in one single cube, it would measure 18 by 18 yards in size. Even the most profitable mines now in operation require several tons of ore to produce even one ounce of gold. It is also estimated that 10 billion tons of gold (100 thousand times more than we have managed to mine from the Earth) is suspended in the world's oceans.

In many areas, Chinese miners were the first to sample the streams and hills for mineral wealth. This is a drawing of a Chinese camp in the very early days of the gold rush in the United States. (*The Gold Rush* by Liza Ketchum, 1996)

As of this writing, the largest gold mine in the United States is the Homestake Mine at Lead, South Dakota. It is over 8,000 feet deep and has accounted for almost 10 percent of total United States gold production since it opened in 1876. Reserves at the site as of 1997 exceed 40 million ounces.[8] In September 2000, we learned that the Homestake was about to be closed down. It will not be abandoned but rather will be closed in an environmentally sensitive manner, through a process requiring 18 months. The mine will essentially be mothballed, which will permit its reactivation if and when the economic climate becomes more favorable.

Gold can also be found in seawater, as mentioned above. Experts estimate that for every inhabitant on the globe, over $50 million worth of gold resides in the Earth's oceans and seas. Many efforts have been made to tap this vast treasure, but no commercially practical process has been discovered yet.

In 1934, President Roosevelt issued an order limiting the amount of gold any American could own to 200 ounces. In 1942 (during the Second World War), the War Production Board issued its famous L-208 order that literally closed down every gold and silver mine in the country, deeming them nonessential to the war effort. As you can well imagine, these two events alone severely impacted the precious-metal mining industry in America. It wasn't until March 17, 1968, that the federal government discontinued the buying and selling of gold and locked the price at $35.00 per ounce. Finally in December 1974, the 200-ounce-per-person limit was lifted as well as the locked rate, and the price of gold shot up as it floated on the world market. Within five short years, its price had climbed to over $600.00 an ounce, and the industry again began to flourish. During the late 1970s, the price of gold reached a brief high of just over $800 per ounce. Professional and amateur prospectors throughout the west, where most of the deposits are, reactivated many of the old and previously closed mines and began searching for new low-grade deposits that could be profitably exploited.[9]

Even though the price of gold has dropped considerably since the 1970s, it has somewhat stabilized at around 8 to 10 times the $35.00 per ounce rate as of this writing.

In the past three decades, low-grade disseminated gold deposits have become increasingly important. More than 75 such deposits have been found in the Western United States, mostly in Nevada. However, one very large deposit was located in east central Washington, the Cannon Mine, and the story of its discovery will be told later in this book.

You have no doubt heard that the price of gold changes constantly, and perhaps wondered why this happens and who controls it. Twice daily, at 10:30 A.M. and 3:00 P.M. London time, representatives of the five internationally respected member firms of the London Gold Market gather at the Rothchild Bank to determine the price of gold worldwide. When a determination is made, it is referred to as "the fixed price."

---

[8] South Africa is the world's top producer of gold. Some of the mines there reach depths of over 11,500 feet below the surface and contain more than 600 miles of tunnels.

[9] Large, low-grade deposits were preferred over small, high-grade deposits because concentrating mills could be constructed and long-term mining could be carried out.

The price is based on buy and sell orders that have been placed by customers with each of the member firms. This serves to establish a price at which both supply and demand are balanced. This fixed price is then communicated to all parts of the world for use in commercial and investment transactions.

Since 1991, the United States has been the second-largest gold producer worldwide (South Africa being number one), surpassing the Soviet Union for the first time in over 50 years. In 1999, Nevada produced three-quarters of gold domestically, the remaining share coming from 11 other states, mostly in the West but with one producer as far east as South Carolina. Of these mines, 120 were lode mines and about 15 were large placer operations located in Alaska. In addition, a small amount of domestic gold was recovered as a byproduct of base metal mining, mainly copper. In the recent past, open-pit mines produced the majority of gold. However, estimates by the Gold Institute speculate that during the year 2000, 33 percent was expected to come from underground mines.

Gold in Washington

The earliest reported gold find seems to have been along the Yakima River in 1853, when a small amount of placer gold was recovered. By 1855, miners were swarming to an area near Colville, where more placer gold was being reported. Placer gold was discovered along the Similkameen River in 1859. At Mount Chopaka, lode gold was discovered in 1871. About this same time, lode and placer gold was being mined in the Blewett and Swauk Districts.

Reported gold production in Washington between 1860 and 1952 amounted to 2.57 million ounces, valued at $68,705,393. Until 1984, 97 percent of all recovered gold came from three mines, all of which were located in Eastern Washington: the Holden, Lovitt, and Knob Hill Mines. Between 1985 and 1995, the Cannon Mine near Wenatchee was the highest producer, bringing in over 1.25 million ounces alone. "How do I find some," you may be asking. Well, the heavy, yellow metal has been sought worldwide; wars have been fought over it, empires have risen and fallen because of it, and many people have turned immoral from the lust for it.

Ore Theft/High Grade

The term *high-grading* has two meanings in the field of mining. It can mean that the method of mining removes only the highest grade of ore from a mine. It also refers to the theft of valuable minerals. Let's first discuss the latter.

Rich ore and minerals can sometimes invite theft, especially if the miner is morally weak. Whenever miners see minerals so valuable that just a small piece represents money, there can be the temptation to steal. Greed sometimes overcomes conscience. The theft of gold and silver from mines is nothing new; even in ancient times mine workers sometimes disregarded the law. This became so rampant that severe laws were enacted to protect mine owners from thieves. For example, the Vipascan law, in effect at the Roman mines in Spain during the reign of Emperor Hadrian, specified that if a slave stole ore, the prosecutor was to have him whipped; and whoever sold or bought stolen ore was to be put in chains for life.

Many means of removing high-grade ore from mines throughout history have been quite imaginative. In 1902, the owners of a silver mine in Mexico knew that some of the miners were stealing ore but couldn't figure out how they were doing it. The mine foreman did notice an unusual increase in the demand for candles, however, without a corresponding increase in the demand for kerosene used in the oil lamps. He also noticed that a number of miners had long, oily hair. He ordered the men shampooed, and low and behold discovered their hiding place. Several ounces of powdered silver ore were recovered from the miners' hair.

In 1915, a law passed that required all purchasers of ore to have a license and to record where the ore had been mined. If the seller didn't own a mine, the fact that the ore had been stolen became obvious.

But this didn't stop some thieves. The Sheep Ranch Mine in Calaveras County, California, even closed down because its ore was stolen on such a grand scale. The theft made the difference between profit and loss to the owners, and the crooks won out. Thievery was such a problem that in 1936, by virtue of the Gold Reserve Act, the federal government began to require licensing in addition to an affidavit accompanying any transaction over five ounces in the form of bullion, retort, or precipitate. The affidavit had to specify where the material had been mined and when, together with the tonnage or yardage of rock or gravel from which it was extracted.

The owner of the Black Oak Mine thought he know how to prevent stealing. He paid the miners 50 cents an hour over the prevailing wages, bought health insurance for them and their families, and gave them a yearly $200 bonus. Nevertheless, an investigation disclosed that $60,000 in gold had been stolen. Nearly the entire work force was arrested, 26 in all. Seventeen pled guilty and received sentences of five years' probation, restitution, and 90 days in jail. The others stood trial, were convicted by a jury, and were sentenced to 1 to 14 years at San Quentin.

In many states, when stolen ore is traced from the mine to an unprincipled buyer, the owner of the mine may bring a civil action against the buyer for the value of the gold, plus seven percent interest. This is done by the common law called "conversion," whereby one cannot transfer a title to stolen property even though it is bought in good faith.

Stealing from mines was rampant, but it didn't always work out very well for the thieves. Mr. Arthur Foote, the former owner of the Tightner Mine, received a letter in 1931 with a return address that read, "A. Man, Sacramento, California." Enclosed was $2700 in cash and a note that read, "The enclosed money was borrowed from the Tightner Mine in the years 1914–1915. Divide it among your stockholders, and it is hoped that none of this will bring the misery it has brought to me." The note was signed A. Mistake.

Another thief got a dose of his own medicine in this story: During the operation of a mine in Idaho some years back, a miner had been stealing high-grade ore for many years, so much that he had acquired a large pile in his back yard. Upon retiring from the mine, he contracted with a trucking company to haul the ore to a smelter and then sat back to await the check in the mail. After a week or two, sure enough the check arrived and he looked at the figures in the pay box, over $1 million. With a big grin on his face, he handed the check to his wife, but she noticed something that he'd overlooked. The check was payable to two parties, him and the mining company he had stolen the ore from. It seems that the smelter "recognized" the ore and knew exactly where it had come from.[10] Not only was he out the million dollars, but the weight of the high-grade ore had also cost him extra in shipping expenses.

Theft from mining operations was not limited to gold and silver. In 1925, the Kimberly Diamond Mine in Africa caught a miner who had swallowed a diamond as big as a chestnut and weighing 152 karats.

Even as late as the 1980s, high-grading was taking place in Washington State at the Cannon Mine in Wenatchee. A bucket of high-grade gold and silver ore was discovered hidden away and ready to be smuggled off the property. This led to an investigation, which resulted in the exposure of a large conspiracy in which

Two placer miners examine their find along a creek bank. Early miners often began this way, and some never stopped. When the color played out in one area, they would simply move on to a new, yet unpanned locale. (*Western Trail Magazine,* December 1899)

---

[10] Many ores are highly recognizable. Even some members of Northwest Underground Explorations who have a very limited knowledge of geology can look at a chunk of rock and tell you exactly which mine it came from. The Nuggets recovered from the Swauk Mining District in Eastern Washington are another good example of this: The gold in Williams Creek was found to have less silver content and is more "rounded" than that found in Swauk Creek, making it very recognizable to those in the know about the geology of this region. The reason for this is that the gold traveled farther from its source and erosion caused the changes.

mill workers on different shifts had, over a period of time, been removing large amounts of high-grade ore from the property. It is presumed that the company lost several hundred thousand dollars as a result of these thefts.

Earlier we mentioned that the term *high-grading* has two meanings. The other usage refers to the removal (mining) of only the highest grade of ore from the mine. This is usually done when the market price for the extracted metal is low and long-term mining of the lower grade ore is not economically feasible or when transportation of large amounts of ore is not practical. Many mines subcontract to smaller or independent operators on a percentage basis of what is sent to the mill.

The Flip Side

There is also a flip side to miners' attempts to steal valuable minerals from their employers, which is called *salting*. Unscrupulous owners of mining properties have *salted* mines they're trying to sell for a high price. In other words, they created the illusion that a mine was more valuable than it actually was by concealing valuable minerals inside it and letting the prospective buyer find them. One of the most popular of these methods was actually quite simple. The seller would take a shotgun shell and remove the pellets, replacing them with gold dust. Firing the gun into the working face of the mine would impregnate the worthless rock with gold.

Most mine speculators quickly became aware of salting, so sellers had to come up with better ideas. One of these was to actually let the unsuspecting buyer salt the mine. The seller would tell the buyer that gold could be found anywhere in the mine, and that the prospective buyer could pick a spot to examine. The seller would bore the drill holes and allow the buyer to set off the charges. Low and behold, any rock exposed by the blasting would reveal rich deposits of gold. But the seller had previously packed the gold dust into the explosives, so when the buyer fired them, the mine became salted.

The Sperry/Iverson Mine in eastern Snohomish County was reportedly the site of a salting incident. Dick Sperry and his cohort Iverson bored a tunnel just off the rail line of the Monte Cristo Railroad, right where it could be clearly seen by trains arriving at Silverton. Outside the portal of the mine, they piled large amounts of rich ore. We don't know whether this helped them to scam investors into buying any stock, but we do know for certain that the ore hadn't come from that tunnel. It had been purchased from the owners of the Jackson/St. Louis Mine farther up the road.

These morally reprehensible practices have over the years given the mining industry a bad reputation. We have even heard some describe a mine as "a hole in the ground with a liar standing next to it."[11]

We will refer to two types of gold in this book: free-milling and non–free-milling. Free-milling gold has not chemically bonded to other elements or minerals. All gold found in rivers and streams is known as free-milling placer gold. Lode gold, which can sometimes be free-milling, is the kind usually associated with hardrock mining and is for the most part non–free-milling. It is mined as an ore.

Unless you own an ore concentrator and a smelter, as well as a gazillion dollars to throw at your project, non–free-milling lode gold should not be too high on your list of things to mine. However, the first rule in hunting down native gold deposits is that gold is almost always found where it has been found before. Although just about every year we hear of fabulous gold discoveries, with a little research you will undoubtedly find that they actually are not discoveries at all, but rather extensions of previous deposits. The chances of finding a new mother lode are extremely rare because prospecting has been ongoing since long before our time, and just about every rock has been turned over at least once.

This is not to say that you can't make new discoveries using modern prospecting methods and devices, but unless you plan on spending a ton of money and going into competition with the huge mining companies, this shouldn't be your goal. Let us give you an example of what we mean.

---

[11] After nearly 30 years of dealing with miners and mines in Washington State, we have found very little dishonesty among the real miners. Like any industry, however, there are always a few who try to live by wit rather than sweat.

When Asamera Minerals opened the big Cannon Mine in Wenatchee in 1984, it had already spent over $62 million *before* mining its first ounce of gold. The Holden Mine cost three million dollars to get up and running, and that was way back in 1938. It is interesting to note that the Cannon Mine was not a new discovery either; gold had been found in that area many years before.

Before you commit any capital to the development of a lode deposit, consider the following:
- Total value of the ore body
- Cost of benefaction and treatment of ores
- Availability of market
- Transportation costs
- Availability of cheap electric power
- Environmental concerns and permitting
- Reclamation bonding
- Professional services such as geologists and assayers
- Core-drilling and blocking-out costs

Unlike placer mining, lode mining falls under the jurisdiction of the Federal Mine Safety and Health Administration, MSHA, and you will be regulated by its rules, especially if you plan to hire employees.

Now, let's talk about the explosives and chemicals you will need to extract and treat your ores, plus housing and milling facilities, and the handling and disposal of waste water and other materials. Let's be realistic; only a large and well-financed company or corporation can afford such an enterprise, and many of those have tried and failed.

There is a more pleasant and positive side to all of this, however. If you have discovered a good ore body and are considering mining it, file a claim and make sure that you are the one in control of the minerals at the site. Then consider contacting one of the major mining companies and have its geologists look over your discovery. The company may pay for the development costs (i.e., surveys, core-drilling, underground exploration, and permitting). If it finds a large enough ore body, it might lease or even purchase the property from you, giving you a percentage of what is mined. Don't overlook anything in your quest for minerals; they are out there and they are needed in larger quantities every day.

Besides those large, low-grade ore deposits, you can find free-milling gold in either placer deposits or unmined lode deposits. Let's examine what free-milling gold actually is and find out how it behaves.

To understand gold, we have to study a little geology and chemistry. Don't let this scare you; remember that many old prospectors had limited knowledge of these subjects but still were usually able to locate some gold.

One of the most popular methods of locating lode gold deposits used by old prospectors and new is very simple; it's called looking for the *float*. Float is the term given to ore minerals that have outcropped to the surface of the Earth, broken off, and either slid or been washed down a mountain. The prospector would simply walk around the bottom of a mountain, keeping a close eye out for the float, and once having found loose minerals at the bottom, climb up and locate the outcrop. It was by this method that the famous prospector Alex Barron located the Eureka Lode, near Harts Pass, whose glory hole yielded $120,000 during its first two seasons of operation.[12] This was a good deal of money in 1893.

Chinese miners carry buckets of water to wash the gravel for gold. They are using a riffle box to separate the heavier metal from the lighter sand and gravel. (*Cariboo Yarns* by F. W. Lindsay, 1963)

---

[12] Located in eastern Whatcom County and most easily reached via Harts Pass.

Dangerous Critters Some of God's little creatures can turn a good day into a miserable one in no time. If you're a "wet-sider," you should be aware that the Central Washington countryside is home to a variety of living threats to people, which are not found on the cool, damp west side of the mountains.

Ticks thrive in the dry, warm climate of Eastern Washington, and they are most active from late spring into midsummer. These critters live in brush and trees and can easily hop undetected onto a passing human or animal. During, and especially after, trips into the country, it is important to check yourself and your animals carefully for ticks. Contact your local doctor or emergency room for how to remove the little hitchhikers. Not only can ticks cause infections, they also carry diseases transmittable to humans and animals such as Lyme disease or Rocky Mountain spotted fever.

Common to the lower elevations (below about 3,000 feet), as a general rule, is the Pacific rattlesnake. Although its bite is seldom fatal, the strike, as well as the experience of it, can be traumatic. The bite can be extremely painful and can cause permanent numbness, while the venom causes swelling and even the loss of use of a finger or toe, if that's where the fangs have penetrated. Rattlesnakes are generally on the move in the warm weather of mid-to-late spring to mid-fall. They are most active in the evening around and after sunset, often near water, where they hunt for small rodents and birds. When the temperature drops as the evening wears on, snakes tend to move to warm rocks or pavement. Watch where you step or put your hands in this country, and *never* turn a rock or log over with your hands or foot. Use a long stick. Snakes often hide under rocks and logs because they provide shelter from the hot sun. Don't panic if you are bitten, but seek immediate medical help.

The black widow and brown recluse spiders also make their home here. They prefer dark, out-of-the-way spots such as the undersides of old boards, root cellars, and abandoned outhouses, barns, or other buildings. A bite from one of these critters can be very uncomfortable and long lasting. Again, watch where you put your hands and feet, and if you are bitten, see a doctor.

The native scorpion spider is another arachnid that frequents the arid and semi-arid areas of the state (yes, Washington boasts two different species of scorpion). Its sting is much like that of a bee, but if you happen to be allergic to it the venom can cause you some real problems. It's better that you avoid the little guys altogether. Just like you would to steer clear of snakes and spiders, watch where you put your hands and feet, keep your eyes and ears open, and seek immediate medical help if you are stung or bitten.

Although bats are relatively rare in most of the mines we have explored, occasionally they are encountered. Usually they will leave you alone if you don't bother them. They can, however, carry disease. Bats are the leading spreaders of rabies in Washington State, for example, so beware.

Another popular method involved climbing to a high ridge and scanning the neighboring mountains with binoculars, looking for reddish stains called *iron cap* or *gossen*. These stains suggest that minerals have reached the earth's surface and are undergoing oxidization. It was by this method that Joe Pearsall discovered Monte Cristo in 1889.

A less-used method of locating lode gold deposits is known as *pocket hunting*. The prospector would usually start by locating an area on or near a river or stream that had once been a good placer deposit. Knowing that the gold had to have come from somewhere, the prospector would begin to work back up the waterway, taking panning samples along the way. When no color remained in his pan, he would dig down into the earth to locate the gold's source, or pocket. This method was widely used in the Swauk Mining District in eastern Washington. Local geology will determine your prospecting technique.

Locating gold in streambeds and river placers can be a lot trickier and requires some knowledge of how the mineral behaves when combined with water. The first thing gold usually does when it encounters water is sink to the bottom, where it is slowly carried downstream. Now, let's see what we are looking for.

Chemistry lesson number one: gold is bright yellow when pure, but its color intensity becomes lighter or darker depending on the amount of silver or copper present. Gold is very heavy and soft and is the most ductile and malleable of metals. It is a good conductor of heat as well as electricity, and it is extremely inactive. It also amalgamates (bonds chemically) with mercury.

> **Warning** Mercury vapor can destroy your nervous system and kill you. Do not attempt to retort mercury unless you have been properly trained and know exactly what you are doing.[13]

Panning, sluicing, and dredging are the most popular methods of recreational prospecting.[14] The old saying, "Gold is where you find it" is a pretty general statement, but to examine it in the context of the modern weekend prospector requires some explanation. You will often see these weekend adventurers along highways and back roads, sluicing, dredging, or panning in creeks and rivers for the elusive grains of gold, and often in the same areas. This is especially true in the Swauk/Williams Creek and Peshastin/Shaser Creek areas, where most of the choice spots are under claim by individuals and prospecting clubs.

The hobby of prospecting can be interesting and rewarding for the entire family, maybe not for the fortune in gold you'll find (or likely not find), but just in plain recreation and enjoyment. The whole family can enjoy the activity together in the crisp, mountain air amid beautiful scenery.

Before You Start Your Search

First, it is important to consult the local Forest Service and Department of Natural Resources Offices where you'll be prospecting. This will allow you to determine ownership, area prospecting closures, updates to fire dangers, and other possible limitations. Also, a current copy of the *Gold and Fish* book is absolutely mandatory if you plan to prospect in or near water. You must have a current copy of it *on the job site* when engaged in prospecting or mining activities. This publication is available from the Department of Fish and Wildlife, 600 Capital Way North, Olympia, Wash. 98501. You can also check the telephone book for local offices.[15]

You'll be dealing with a number of agencies once you begin prospecting, among them the Bureau of Land Management, U.S. Forest Service, U.S. Army Corps of Engineers, National Marine Fisheries Service, U.S. Fish and Wildlife Service, and the National Park Service. On a state level, these agencies will come into play: Washington Department of Ecology, Department of Natural Resources, Washington State Office of Archaeology and Historic Preservation, Washington State Parks and Recreation Commission, and local government entities such as cities, counties, municipalities, etc. Don't forget about tribal governments if you're prospecting on or near tribal lands.[16]

Metal Detecting

Are there laws regulating the use of metal detectors? Yes! On National Forest and other federal land, you must get a special permit. Wilderness areas, U.S. Parks, and federal recreation areas are generally off limits.

Shorelines and lakes are regulated by the Corps of Engineers, and metal detecting is allowed only in predisturbed areas such as public beaches and attached swimming areas. On Bureau of Land Management land, some are open and some are not. The same is true of state parks and other state-controlled land. Most city and county parks are open unless posted otherwise. All historically marked sites are out. Always check first.

---

[13] Under Washington State law, mercury (quicksilver) is not allowed on a prospecting job site. If it is recovered from aggregate or collected in concentrators, it is to be disposed of as a dangerous/hazardous substance, as specified by the Department of Ecology.

[14] You may notice that some dredging operations use skin-diving and SCUBA equipment. These operations require special training, and you can endanger your life if you don't know the proper safety measures. Exhaust fumes from gasoline-powered dredge motors sucked into the lungs is instantly fatal. *Danger looms everywhere when one is seeking gold rather than thinking safety.*

[15] This department enforces the Hydraulics Code (RCW 75.20.100). You must obtain a Hydraulic Project Approval (HPA) when prospecting in or near any river or stream. Always consult with the proper agencies before disturbing any water or land within the state. In 1997, the Washington State Legislature passed House Bill 1565 (Chapter 415, Laws of 1997). This law defines small-scale mining and prospecting, and you must know its contents with regard to permits, regulations, and rules concerning the recovery of minerals within the state.

[16] Some hardrock mining operations may fall under the jurisdiction of the Mine Safety and Health Administration—MSHA, the "Federal Mine Police." You may be wondering what in the world the U.S. Army Corps of Engineers has to do with prospecting for gold way up in the mountains. Under the Federal Clean Water Act of 1977, the Corps may require suction dredge operators to obtain a Section 404 Permit. The Washington State Department of Ecology oversees the Shoreline Management Act and has the authority to prosecute those who degrade water quality. In some situations, you will be required to post a reclamation bond. Check *Gold and Fish* for more information.

Filing and Retaining a Claim

The problem with describing how to file and retain a claim is that by the time this ink is dry the ever-changing laws, rules, and regulations governing claims will no doubt be out of date. The Mining Act of 1872 is now in a constant state of flux, and even many of the longtime miners we know are not sure what they can and can't do on a daily basis. The best advice we can give is that you contact the jurisdiction that you are dealing with for the latest rules, the Department of Natural Resources, the BLM, or the Forest Service. And don't forget the Hydraulic Project Approval (HPA) if you're planning on panning, sluicing, or dredging in or near water.

A Word about Silver

Between 1933 and 1963, the U.S. Treasury was the largest buyer of silver in the United States for use in coinage; worldwide, the largest current user is the photographic film industry. In January 1967, the Treasury Department passed legislation to eliminate the use of silver in coins and began to hold weekly auctions to sell much of the 3.5 billion ounces of silver-containing coins it held. About 165 million ounces were kept for Defense Department uses and another 35 million ounces for the minting of the last silver dollar, the Eisenhower, which contained 40 percent silver.[17]

When the government got out of the silver business, the price of silver per ounce dropped considerably. During the 1970s, the famous Hunt brothers attempted to corner the silver market. Toward the end of the 1970s, the price of gold had begun to skyrocket, and silver gained in value as well, briefly reaching around $40.00 per ounce. When the price of gold fell, it brought silver down with it, and many investors lost money. As of this writing, silver is at an all-time low, selling for about $3.00 to $4.00 an ounce.

In the mines of Eastern Washington, silver was quite commonly extracted in combination with gold, copper, lead, and zinc. Up until 1950, the Knob Hill Mine was the top silver producer, followed by the Holden, Bonanza, Lovitt, and Grandview Mines.

The three major mines in Chelan and Kittitas Counties, the Holden, Lovitt, and Cannon, had a combined silver recovery of around 4.5 million ounces.

Mining Districts

The mines covered in the following pages are listed by area, which characterize the mines by geographical location. Mining *districts*, which you'll also see mentioned, were more than just the geographical areas where mining took place. Let's take a quick look at early mining law in the United States, why and how these districts were established, and what role they played in the overall picture of mining in eastern Washington.

As early as 1849, during the California Gold Rush, some means of regulating mining was needed. The federal government had no hard and fast rules or laws regarding mining operations on public land, so miners themselves had to come up with some form of orderly regulation.[18] Districts were formed around the mining camps to settle claim disputes; define boundaries; and determine the size, manner, and means of recording claims. Every claim holder was allowed one vote, and questions were settled by majority rule in mass meetings. As federal, state, or territorial governments enacted mining laws and effectively took over control from the mining regions, the functions of the mining districts were steadily diminished. Eventually, the mining district existed in name only.

The first attempt at establishing mining laws by the government occurred in the early 1800s. These laws addressed three issues: they sanctioned the miner's right to trespass on federal land for the purpose of locating and exploiting minerals; they recognized regulations set down by the local mining districts; and

---

[17] Silver was also used in the Kennedy half-dollar.
[18] Just how many people made the "rush" to California in the first few years can be estimated, at best. The figures show that around the end of 1848 California had a population of about 20,000, not counting Native Americans. By the end of 1849, it was nearly 100,000, and in 1852 the census showed over 225,000. Many of these gold-seekers were Latin American, French, German, English, Mexican, Australian, and Chinese.

Most of the areas that early miners explored and worked in lacked even the most rudimentary trails. This scene of a prospecting party picking its way across uncharted rock was typical: rigors confronted early miners at every turn.
(*Handbook for Prospectors and Operators of Small Mines* by M. W. von Bernewitz, 1943)

they established a procedure for obtaining a title to lode claims, the patenting of land. But these laws didn't address the issues of placer miners. It wasn't until May 10, 1872, that the government passed an act to govern and regulate all mining in the United States.

The 1872 Mining Act limited the size of claims to 600 by 1500 feet (20 acres), and required the claim holder to perform annual assessment work and improvements to the property, specifying the manner in which the work and claims had to be recorded. Failure to follow these guidelines rendered a claim invalid. The Act also addressed the issue of placer claims.

The first mining district in the Wenatchee Mountains was the Swauk District, formed in 1873. It was reorganized by John Black, Tom Meagher, and others on May 7, 1884. The old local laws regarding the registering of claims were revised, but it appears that the primary reason for the meeting was to exclude Chinese miners from the district. Article four of the minutes (printed from a certified copy of the meeting) reads as follows: "Resolved that all Chinaman [sic] within the boundaries of Swauk Mining District shall leave and shall not be allowed to work or hold any mining ground in the District and that no Chinaman [sic] shall hereafter be allowed to come into the same for the purpose of mining, and that a notice be served on those now in the limits of the district to leave it at once." The resolution was carried unanimously. There was no provision made in the district for the enforcement of this rule, and it appears that many of the Chinese were tolerated despite it.[19]

In 1905, A. F. York, a Swauk miner and county surveyor, platted the Swauk Mining District boundaries. They ran from the mouth of First Creek (at its confluence with Swauk Creek), eastward along First Creek to its headwaters southeast of Lion Rock, and then north along Table Mountain to Swauk Pass. From Swauk Pass, they extended west to Teanaway Ridge and then turned south along the ridge, returning to the confluence of Swauk and First Creeks.

Mining communities seemed to attract a great number and wide range of people, some good citizens and some not. It was common to see ministers and rogues working side by side at their sluice boxes, or southern planters turned miners swinging their picks beside Yankee abolitionists. These were the hard workers. Early mining also attracted another element, those who planned to live by their wits rather than by labor. Also present in great numbers were those who came to "mine the miners": saloon owners, gamblers, con artists, prostitutes, gunfighters, moonshiners, robbers, bandits, cattle rustlers, and horse thieves. Many had drifted north from the mining towns in California after the gold strikes there began to dwindle, or they had been forced to leave when law and order was established. Others were fleeing from the law and thought the newfound gold fields in Washington Territory would be an ideal place to ply their trades on greenhorn miners. Some of these people got rich, but the majority died with their boots on.

In the uncommonly decent society of the Wenatchee and Cascade Mountains Mining Districts the respectable people outnumbered the undesirables. Aside from mild contempt toward the Chinese, it appears that the early miners were more good-natured than bad-tempered.

---

[19] In all our research on this topic, we have not found a single "recorded" incident of violence among white and Chinese miners in the Swauk Mining District. This is not to say that there were no problems, only that tolerance seems to have prevailed. The fact that as early as 1870 Chinese miners in Eastern Washington out-numbered white miners two to one is of interest in this discussion as well. We believe that in many cases an employee/employer relationship may have existed between the two groups, but we can't verify this.

Days of Discovery

Over the past 100 years, many books, newspapers, geological reports, and theses have discussed mining in the Northwest from boom to bust. However, the true plight of the men and women who made these discoveries and set the stage for this famous period of Washington's history remains vague and is often forgotten. Their deeds, and the reasons for doing them, have been pushed aside in favor of stories about the great mines and the accomplishments of the companies that developed the claims into financial success stories.

As westward movement extended the boundaries of the U.S. across the Missouri River, over the plains, and into the Rocky Mountains, prospectors began the long and dangerous task of combing the hills, canyons, and mesas in Colorado, Utah, Montana, and Idaho in search of precious minerals that would bring wealth to themselves and prosperity to the country. Gold in California had packed that state with hungry, greedy people looking for their El Dorado.

What the prospectors found were small, sometimes overburden-covered veins of quartz and sulfides containing small quantities of low-grade gold, silver, copper, lead, and other valuable minerals. Although these discoveries at first appeared to be of "poor man's quality and quantity," prospectors soon realized that the deeper they dug into the ore body, the richer and more abundant the minerals became. Therefore, a small strike could open up a great gold rush that would last for many decades.

The problem of developing these mines was not only one of weather, moving equipment into the area, and dealing with the local Native Americans who may not have taken favorably to the operation; it was also the immense amount of money needed up front to finance the project through the first few months or years of development until the mine was deep enough to strike the richer deposit well below the surface. The preponderance of poorer ore near the surface in the Rocky Mountains and Sierra Nevadas, while much richer ore could be found at depth, was due to *secondary enrichment*. Secondary enrichment is a process whereby minerals are carried downward from original veins over millions of years by descending water that percolates through the rock. When the water reaches the water table and ceases descending, the minerals are redeposited. The upper, leached veins are depleted, while the lower, secondary deposit ore bodies are enriched. The longer the process, the greater the disparity.

"Go West Young Man"

Horace Greely's word began to resonate once nearly all the mountain areas of the Rockies had been explored, and the rich areas had been claimed and were under development. Hungry adventurers began to look to the Northwest. Whispers of rich gold, silver, copper, and lead deposits lying right on the surface of the ground, just waiting to be picked up and hauled off, began to circulate throughout the country. Some claimed that nature itself had already done the mining, that descending glaciers had sheared off the overburden from cliffs and canyon walls and eroded them, exposing rich ore bodies. This was quite a turnaround from what experienced miners in other parts of the West had seen.

Prior to the turn of the century, no reputable geological survey had ever been made of Washington, and prospectors had to choose between figuring out the geology themselves or relying on unproven theories. It was widely known that the Cascade Mountains were mainly formed of granite, syenite, diorite, and kindred rocks. But broad belts of gneiss,[20] schist, slate, shale, and sandstone, along with dikes of porphyry and limestone were deposited among these rocks. The same formation was reputed to range eastward into the foothills of the Rockies. The mineral ledges occurred mostly in fissures in the granite, syenite, diorite, and slate, often cutting though several of these rocks, but was also in contact between one of the granite rocks and a dike of porphyry or limestone. A heavy capping of oxidized iron or magnetic iron (iron cap),[21] often of great width and thickness, generally indicated the presence of such a ledge. This ore was almost always low grade and not free-milling, with the exception of the Slate Creek area of the extreme north central Cascade Mountains in Washington State. However, most ore deposits did contain minor amounts of free gold near the surface, which quickly turned to sulfide ore as depth increased.

---

[20] Strongly metamorphosed, layered rock, pronounced "nice."
[21] Iron cap is a rust or orange oxidized coloring often seen on Cascade Range mountain slopes in Washington State.

Beginning the opening of a stope. The quartz vein is clearly visible along the ceiling of the tunnel. The stoping drill is anchored on the floor and driven upward into the vein. Longer and longer steels (bits) would be used as the vein material was extracted. Eventually, either a wooden platform would be built and the process begun anew, or, in shrinkage stoping, the extracted material would be left on the floor and used as a base for boring the stope ever higher. Then the extracted ore would be removed as the final step in the process. (Victor Pisoni collection)

The sulfides were mostly iron and copper pyrites, arsenopyrite, chalcopyrite, pyrrhotite, galena, tetrahedrite, gray copper, or zinc blende. The pyritic ore usually carried gold and some silver but contained so much copper that it was ultimately mostly mined as a copper proposition.

The prospectors found that a mineral belt of gold and copper seemed to run from about 200 miles northwest of Vancouver, B.C., across the Skagit Valley between Hamilton and Marblemount, across the Stillaguamish River east and west of Silverton, through Sultan Basin and Silver Creek, into the Index area and to the Miller River and Monéy Creek Districts, then on through the Snoqualmie and Cedar River watersheds. Another belt ran farther south and along the western edge of the Cascades to Mount St. Helens. On the east side, a similar belt was discovered in the Palmer Mountain, Methow, Chelan, and Cle Elum Districts.

Even with the wide-eyed excitement of the experienced early Colorado and California prospectors who'd made some of the first discoveries here in the 1860s, 1870s, and 1880s, the experienced mining outfits in the Rockies and California who had finances to develop the ore deposits were hesitant to put the money forward on such unproven properties. They believed the ore was too base and low-grade to make treatment worthwhile and that it was too broken, making the vein impossible to follow from the outcropping to any considerable depth.

To add to this, local investors already had lost money on mining ventures that were too remote, contained no ore, or failed because there were no suitable treatment methods or equipment to process the ore once it had been mined. These local investors were more suited to backing farms or manufacturing and professional services. They were merchants and business owners, not miners or geologists.

Thus the speculation that a few investors had engaged in early on the strength of a little free gold found near the surface opened the door for unskilled miners to operate machines they knew little about, and which were not suited for the ore found at depth. Stamp mills were installed without concentrators or reasonable knowledge of the proper operating procedure for them. Tales of outright fraud soon spread throughout the region as less-than-reputable speculators took advantage of uninformed folks who had big dreams and little experience.

However, despite intense interest, mining lagged behind other industry and commerce in the state though the 1880s and early 1890s. The exception was at Monte Cristo, where the powerful John D. Rockefeller–backed Colby-Hoyt Syndicate moved in machinery and built a railroad despite problems in the local economy.

The economy worsened in 1893 when the great silver panic placed a stranglehold on all commerce in the state. Companies folded or tightened their belts, laying off many workers in the process. Jobs were hard to find, so when laborers, merchants, and entrepreneurs began to hear that high-altitude mining was enjoying some success in Monte Cristo in Washington and in the Trail Creek and Slocan Districts in British Columbia, they began to look to the mountains for their livelihood.

These rookie fortune seekers took up where earlier miners had given up. They located outcroppings high on mountain ridges and deep in nearly vertical canyons, unfortunately miles from railroads or decent wagon roads, which made development too expensive. To add to the problem, most of the claims were no more than small pockets of low-to-medium-grade ore, which was of little value. The claims did have resale and sucker value, however. Assays were generally high, so with a little luck some poor soul from the city could be enticed to dump a few dollars into the project, staving off creditors and stockholders a little longer.

It wasn't long before seedy con artists reappeared to again trick unsuspecting investors out of their bank accounts, convincing the lowly claim owner that the property would soon become a bonanza. Because of the dire economic conditions, a general lack of knowledge about mining, and the desire to keep from starving, it was seldom much of a task to win the investor over. With the basic claim papers in hand, stock certificates in pocket, and just a few dollars from some local believers, a train ticket back East, a fine hotel, and good food could be procured. With all the excitement of the mining boom in the West, it was fairly easy to entice money from investors of means who knew little or nothing about the Pacific Northwest but plenty about other famous regions such as Cripple Creek, Colorado, Virginia City, Montana, and Bodie, California. With investment money in hand, commonly acquired with the use of phony geology reports, overstated assays, and big promises, the price of the stock would be driven up and the swindler would sell off his stock, which he had obtained free for coming on board as consultant and mining engineer. This left everybody else holding the bag with near-worthless claims and lost money. Some promoters were known to obtain the title to the mine they had just defrauded and start the whole thing all over again with the same property under a new name.

The Law and You

As you enter the mining areas, you may wander onto federal land managed by the U.S. Bureau of Land Management (BLM) or the U.S. Forest Service (USFS), land owned by the state of Washington, or privately owned land. The Mining Law of 1872 (amended-30 U.S. Code 22-54) grants United States citizens the right to explore for, discover, and claim valuable mineral deposits on federal lands. It also grants statutory authority to the BLM to administer the law. Certain federal land is not available for claiming, for example, national parks, national monuments, designated wilderness areas, and administrative areas such as campgrounds.

Normally, under the Mining Law, a citizen can obtain either a patented claim or an unpatented claim. A patented claim is one in which the federal government has given a deed, or passes "actual title," to an individual as long as that individual has claimed the land within the parameters set by the law. The land is then treated like any other private land and is subject to local property taxes and laws. At the time of this writing, however, the government has placed a moratorium on granting patented claims.

An unpatented claim is one in which an individual, after locating valuable mineral deposits, as defined in the law, has been granted the right by the federal government to extract and remove the minerals from the land. The individual receives *only* the right to remove locatable minerals, *not* full title to the land. The land remains under the legal jurisdiction of the federal government.

Washington State–owned land is held in trust by the state for the people of Washington. Mineral extraction rights are sometimes leased by the state to certain individuals who meet qualifying criteria. The proceeds of these leases go to various state trusts, such as the State School Trust. The lands are *not* available for patented claims.

Mining leases on Washington State–owned lands are regulated by the Washington State Department of Natural Resources (DNR). The regulations include the Mining Law of 1872 and state laws and restrictions. You can find these laws and restrictions in the Washington Administrative Code (WAC 332-16) and the Revised Code of Washington (RCW 79.01). Additional information can usually be obtained from the DNR, from state geologists, from geological surveys, and from state mining departments.

So, how does this affect you? If you plan simply to go hiking and probably won't look for a site to stake a claim on, you may still be interested in collecting a few mineral specimens or maybe even doing some prospecting with a gold pan along the way. Can you collect or not?

On federal lands, you may come across a patented or unpatented claim. The law requires the owner of the claim to properly mark its boundaries with visible monuments and to post a "Notice of Location" at the discovery site. You may also find signs indicating a mining claim and an *ORMC number*. This is a serial number assigned to the claim by the BLM when the filing of the claim is recorded. If you happen upon one of these monuments or claim sign, it probably indicates that the claim is active. *Do not*, under penalty of law, remove any mineral specimens or prospect at these sites since the rights to the minerals are owned by someone else and may be very jealously guarded by that individual. If you would like to obtain permission from the claim owner to do some collecting or prospecting, we suggest that you write down the ORMC number and contact the county assessor's office in the county where the claim is located, or the Oregon/Washington State office of the BLM in Portland (they won't give you any specific information over the phone, so you'll probably have to write or visit the office in person). It will also be helpful to know the meridian, township, range, and section(s) numbers of the claim location. You can get this information from a geological survey map of the area. Both the county assessor and the BLM offices maintain records of mining claims, and these records are available for public inspection. You can often find the name and address of the owner of the claim you're interested in among those documents.

If the spot where you want to collect or prospect is not under claim or in a restricted area such as a national park, the Forest Service has no objection to your picking up a specimen or two, as long as you are sensitive to any impact the activity might have on the environment. This being the case, mineral and fossil collectors are usually allowed to remove small quantities of materials, as long as the specimens are to be used for private collections or educational purposes. You are allowed to remove these specimens *only* from the surface of the ground or by panning the present-day stream gravels. You are *not* allowed to pan gold on *any* stream in an area administered by the National Park Service. You are also *not* allowed to remove any vegetation or operate any power equipment for the purpose of excavation.

> **Note** The Forest Service may have closed some areas to prospecting or mineral collection. There are many reasons for this, not the least of which is environmental impact, so be safe rather than sorry. If you are unsure about the status of a particular area, contact the nearest Forest Service or BLM office and ask about it.

Rockhounding is reportedly allowed on state-owned lands, as long as you do not disturb the surface of the land and the area is not currently under mineral lease. Gold panning is not allowed unless you have a placer mining contract for the parcel of land you want to prospect. These contracts are negotiated with the Washington State Department of Natural Resources. The State has been trying to institute a recreational rockhounding permit system, but at the time of this writing it was not yet in effect. If you have any questions regarding rock collecting or gold panning, you should contact the Geology and Earth Resources Division of the DNR in Olympia at (360) 902-1450, from whom you can also get printed materials about rockhounding and prospecting that are free for the asking and very informative.

Washington State–owned lands may not always be marked by boundary signs or otherwise identified. To learn whether a particular parcel of land is state-owned, you will need to get ahold of the geological survey description, including the meridian, township, range, and section number(s). You will then have to contact the Land Records Office located in the basement of the DNR Building in Olympia, Washington. If you can provide the accurate location, they can tell you whether the land is state-owned and whether there are any existing mineral leases on it.

One last caution! The Washington Department of Fish and Wildlife (DFW) is responsible for protecting fish and wildlife in the state of Washington. Any recreational activity that might affect these resources or their habitat is of vital concern to this agency. Therefore, the DFW has prepared a pamphlet called *Gold and Fish*, which was designed to protect our streams and rivers from disturbance, especially during sensitive periods when certain fish species are in their spawning cycles. This publication tells you which streams and rivers are open to prospecting, when they are open, and what equipment you may use. You *must* have a copy of this booklet on any site where you are panning for gold.

Finally, please respect the rights of private landowners. *Always* seek prior permission before entering private land, and *never* remove anything from private land without obtaining the express consent from the landowner.

Good luck, and enjoy your outing!

Preparing for a Mine Trip

Many of the mines described in the following pages are located in remote, mountainous regions, and reaching them requires that you park and leave your vehicle. Never leave valuables where they can be seen. Lock them in your trunk or, if possible, take them with you. If you come to a locked gate or a cable across a road, be sure to park so that you're not blocking access to it. These closed roads are often used for fire control or search-and-rescue operations. Blocking an emergency road will not only get you a fat ticket, but your vehicle could be impounded as well.

As of 1998, the U.S. Forest Service charges a fee to park at or near trailheads. These trailhead passes can be obtained at district offices and usually from some local businesses located near the trailheads.

When traveling in the mountains and forests, always let someone know exactly where you are going and when you expect to return. Then stick to those plans.

If you're planning on going "mine hunting," whether to rockhound, prospect, or just take in some scenery, we have found that an altimeter comes in just as handy as your compass; we list many of the mines by elevation. United States Geological Survey (USGS) maps are almost mandatory for traveling in the mountains. They contain elevation gains, contouring information, roads, and trails, plus sections, townships, and ranges. Many of the computer-mapping programs on the market (such as *TOPO!*) are also useful for planning a trip into the backcountry.

Weather can change without warning in the mountains. Warm, sunny weather can suddenly give way to thunderstorms or torrential downpours. It gets dark faster in the mountains than in the city, especially in the valleys and forests. Rivers and streams are deeper in the afternoons than when you cross them in the morning. Be prepared. Always carry the 10 essential items when traveling in the backcountry.[22]

Although we do not recommend that you enter the mines listed in this book, we know that some of you will feel the urge to do so anyway. This section will help you prepare to go underground as safely as you can. Remember that there are as many different safety concerns as there are mines. The conditions differ from mine to mine, and a lot of common sense is required to understand each one. Some mines were dug in hard rock and present relatively little danger to the explorer. Some are in decaying, crumbly mineralized rock and can be very, very hazardous. Some mines are partially caved at the entrance, and sliding down the backside of the collapsed material into the tunnel may land you in water as deep as your armpits. Some mines contain winzes, shafts that are bored straight down from the horizontal tunnel. A step into one of these could be your last. It is particularly hard to avoid underwater winzes when you are wading through a tunnel. Some tunnel ceilings are low and you must squat to get through them, while other tunnels are spacious.

Exploring stopes—cavities from which ore has been removed—can present a whole new set of dangers. Stopes are very irregular in shape, and they follow whatever angle the ore lay at in the vein. They can be enormously wide or tortuously narrow, and they can lie at shallow or very steep angles. The air in both tunnels and stopes may be low in oxygen or contain noxious gases. The human biological system is used to breathing air that contains 20.8 percent oxygen. Air containing 16 percent oxygen can cause a person to become disoriented, and air containing 14 percent oxygen can cause unconsciousness due to oxygen deprivation. If any of this scares you, it should. Entering mines is a risky business.

But, if you've decided that you're going in anyway, you can prepare for the experience. First, forget any notion that you may have gotten from watching movies or TV of what a mine is like. There is no light in a mine. It is a totally dark, stygian, black hole in the ground. You can't go in without light, and if you lose your light inside, chances are you're not coming out. The rule of thumb for exploring underground is to carry three independent sources of light at all times. Make certain that batteries are fresh and carry a spare set. A spare bulb is not a bad idea either. (You can often carry one inside the lamp behind the reflector, depending on the make and model of lamp.) Even candles can serve as an emergency light to get you out in

---

[22] According to The Mountaineers, the 10 essential items are extra clothing, extra food, sunglasses, knife, fire starter, first-aid kit, flashlight, waterproof matches, map, and compass. We also recommend extra fully charged flashlight batteries and bulbs, whistle, altimeter, clothesline, duct tape, florescent flagging tape, and a good two-way radio with a range of at least a mile.

a pinch, but remember to bring dry matches or a reliable lighter. A headlamp is your best bet, because it leaves your hands free to do the exploring that you want and the light is always pointing where you are looking. Handheld lights do well also, but they somewhat inhibit your ability to examine and explore.

Personal protection should be your next consideration. First in this category is a hardhat. It won't save you if the mountain caves in on you, but it will protect you from small rocks that tumble down from high places such as shafts or stopes. It will also serve you well if you accidentally bang your head into a very solid chunk of mountain. We have had our hardhats firmly slammed down around our ears on many occasions. The hat should fit firmly—it should not fall off if you tilt your head side-to-side or front to back—but not too tightly. Mounting the headlamp on the hardhat is the best of all possible worlds for underground travel, because you have your light where you need it and you are protected as well.

Footwear is your next concern. Many mines contain water at varying depths. In most cases, a pair of 10- or 12-inch–high rubber pacs or dairy boots will serve, while other mines may demand either hip or chest waders for entry.

> **Warning** If you enter mines requiring these last items, remember the winzes discussed above!

Often you must visit a mine more than once to fully explore it. A first trip allows you to assess the situation and determine just what you will need to enter. You can enter and explore it on subsequent trips. If you plan to do technical climbing in a mine, the rubber boots may not suffice; climbing boots may be your best solution.

Mines are usually cool, remaining at about 45 to 50 degrees Fahrenheit all year long. Air sometimes flows through mines, causing them to get very cold in the wintertime and sometimes form ice that can complicate exploration. In any case, you will want to bring warm clothing for your underground excursion, be it in summer or winter.

Wear thick gloves. They can be of use if you have to make your way through sticker-infested brush while hiking to the mines, and when you explore the mines themselves. If there are several people in your group, walkie-talkie radios with at least a mile range can add to the safety and enjoyment of the trip. Keep in mind that walkie-talkies will *not* allow you to communicate with the outside world, only among yourselves, and under some conditions not even that. This brings us to the issue of bringing cellular phones in case of an emergency. Unfortunately, cell phones work only when they are in an area, or cell, that is covered by a computer-controlled transmitter/receiver. Several recent Cascade Mountain rescues that involved cell phones were a fluke, because the accidents occurred near Snoqualmie Pass and Index where there are active cells. In virtually all mountain areas mentioned in this book, cell phones are useless. Moreover, carrying one might give you a false sense of security and possibly embolden you to overextend yourself beyond your capabilities. Don't do anything that you will not be able to walk away from.

Whenever you leave for a mine-exploration a trip, be certain that you let someone know where you are going and when you will be returning. Bring along the same 10 essential emergency items that you would take on any hiking/climbing trip. If something unforeseen happens to you or your party, you may be out in the wilds longer than you expected.

The mines mentioned in this book are hardrock[23] mines that were dug in search of metallic minerals. The state of Washington is also peppered with coalmines. Do not enter coalmines under any circumstances! They may contain methane gas (explosive), carbon monoxide (a very toxic and deadly complex asphyxiant), and carbon dioxide (a simple asphyxiant). *Be certain of the type of mine that you are entering.* Report all open coalmines to local law or fire departments, or to the Bureau of Surface Mining in Denver, Colorado.

---

[23] The term "hardrock" does not imply that a mine is necessarily safe. Some hardrock mines are bored into very unstable, crumbly material. Be cautious at all times.

Hike Ratings

It is difficult to know the abilities of each and every person who may wish to partake of the activities listed in this book. For this reason, we have rated the hikes according to the system noted below. Although we rate the hikes on a scale of A through E for distance, and 1 through 5 for difficulty, it is not in any way to be confused with the mountaineering scale, which is similar. If you are familiar with the mountaineering scale, do not compare it to the one used in this book.

Rating Distance
- A Less than ¼-mile from your vehicle.
- B Between ¼-mile and 1 mile from your vehicle.
- C Between 1 and 2 miles from your vehicle.
- D Between 2 and 4 miles from your vehicle.
- E Greater than 4 miles from your vehicle.

Rating Difficulty
- 1 A very easy walk from your vehicle. Little uphill hiking is involved.
- 2 A more difficult walk than #1. You may encounter muddy or rocky trails, with elevation gains of up to 500 feet.
- 3 This level may require you to do some rock scrambling, with total elevation gains of up to 1,000 feet. Some scrambling may be off-trail, requiring some elementary route-finding skills.
- 4 This level may require you to do some precipitous rock scrambling and other hiking on steep rock slopes. Elevation gains may be as much as 2,000 feet. Some off-trail hiking may be required. Good route-finding skills are required. Serious missteps on trips with this rating could be life-threatening.
- 5 The most difficult rating. On hikes with this rating you will often be required to climb steep and loose rock and talus slopes. Off-trail hiking is required, which may lead you through heavy brush. Good route-finding skills are mandatory. Elevation gains in excess of 2,000 feet and up to 4,000 feet will be required. Life-threatening possibilities abound, so be prepared.

These ratings are only a guide. If a hike appears to be too much for you before you reach your goal, it is always safer to turn back and save yourself for another day. Also make sure you leave time to get back to your vehicle while there is still plenty of daylight. Remember that it is far darker in the forest, and that darkness comes earlier than in open country.

Stehekin Mining Area

The Stehekin mining area is one of the few that cannot be reached by motor vehicle. Encompassing the area that lies to the north of Lake Chelan, and continuing up the Stehekin River Valley to its headwaters at Cascade Pass, this is one of the most awesomely rugged regions in the lower 48 United States. Often referred to as the American Alps, it contains peaks such as Sahale, rising 8,425 feet above sea level. From the flank of Sahale juts Ripsaw Ridge, whose jagged edge leaves no doubt as to what inspired its name. Storm King Mountain, at 8,515 feet in elevation, and McGregor Mountain, at 8,122 feet, retain the winter's snow long into the summer months. Many of the mountain slopes in this region sport glaciers, making them a challenge to climbers and hikers alike. Often, where the glaciers have receded, the rock is bare, revealing mineral veins in cross-section.

Tributaries of the Stehekin River such as Park Creek and Bridge Creek further subdivide the mountainous terrain. At one time, two roads actually traversed the region. The best of the two ran over Cascade Pass from the town of Marblemount, and the other traveled up the east side of Lake Chelan to Stehekin and then on into Horseshoe Basin, where many of the mines were located. These were little more than horse trails, nothing like roads today.

> **Warning** There are many rattlesnakes in this area, so beware. Do not place your feet or hands anywhere out of sight. You may startle a basking snake, inviting a nasty bite.

History

As in many parts of the Cascade Mountains, the first visitors of European origin to the Stehekin area were trappers. The earliest recorded trapper to travel through the Stehekin Valley was a Scottish fellow named Alexander Ross, who in 1814 ascended the steep slopes to what later was called Cascade Pass. He must have chosen one of the Northwest's gray, lugubrious, rainy days for his climb, considering how he described the scene: "Country gloomy, forest almost impervious with fallen as well as standing timber. A more difficult route to travel never fell to man's lot. And the rocks and yawning chasms gave to the whole an air of solemn gloom and undisturbed silence. My companions began to flag during the day."

Other trappers found the route difficult as well. When the Gold Rush of 1849 drew thousands of prospectors and would-be prospectors to California, many began to move northward from stream to stream to seek their fortunes. In 1858, just north of the Stehekin area, gold and "rubies" (actually, garnets) were found in a stream that was later named Ruby Creek, and a gold rush in the North Cascade Mountains was on. The strike was not as rich as first hoped, and the difficulty of accessing the region dampened the hopes of all but the hardiest prospectors. Over the next 20 years, the stream of gold-seekers diminished to a trickle.

Another brief rush occurred a few years later, but it was over by 1880, when the strike again proved disappointing, as one record recalls: "On July 4, 1880, a miner's meeting was held at Ruby City. Around 4,000 men were in attendance at this meeting. Speechmaking and receiving reports from the various districts were the order of the day." But the meeting only painted a dire picture of future mining prospects in the area, so "abandoning their tools and other belongings, the next morning found 5,000 disheartened miners on the trail."

In the mid-1880s, a Methow Indian named Captain Joe, who served as a guide on a government expedition, stumbled upon a ledge of gold in the area. He collected a sample, which he told the other members of the troop about soon afterward. They returned to the area the next day but were never able to relocate the ledge. Later, when the sample was displayed in Portland, Oregon, it created such excitement that a gold rush to the area resulted in 1887 and 1888.

In 1896, a board of examiners decided that the route over Cascade Pass was the most feasible way to provide access to this remote region. Again, due to the area's inaccessibility and the lack of supplies, little progress was ever made on the road.

Gradually, some prospects were recorded, and a few mines were established, mostly in the higher basins above the upper reaches of the Stehekin River. The small community of Stehekin was founded at the northern end of Lake Chelan, which served as a supply station for the scattered population. Supplies were shipped 55 miles up the lake from the town of Chelan at its southern end. Families like the Buckners and the Courtneys settled into the region, rejecting the hurry and scurry of the outside world. They cut their own wood, set up a one-room log schoolhouse, and were largely self-sufficient.

Viewed from the southern flank of Sahale Peak, Ripsaw Ridge presents an awesome scene as it connects with Mount Buckner in the distance. The vast scree slopes below the mountain and ridge mark the upper reaches of Horseshoe Basin, where some of the Stehekin mines are located. This picture is a testament to why this area is called the American Alps. (Phil Woodhouse photo)

Today descendants of the early settlers are still there; the one room schoolhouse is too, but it is only open to visitors, since students now travel to Chelan for school. Stehekin is the gateway to the North Cascades National Park, in which most of the mining properties reside. Motor vehicles still can't reach the area, and residents intend to keep it that way. The American Alps will not be trampled by the motorcar.

What to See

Soaring, snow-capped mountains, from which melt water drains into myriad sparkling streams, characterize the area. High mountain cirques, many with attendant lakes, are spread like jewels throughout the alpine region. You can visit for a day, a week, or a month, if you wish. There are accommodations at Stehekin, or you may want to stay at one of the campgrounds along the Stehekin River. If climbing and hiking are your wont, the many peaks and high lakes will not disappoint. You can travel by Park Service shuttle bus almost to Cascade Pass at Cottonwood Campground, or see magnificent Rainbow Falls on a day's stay, just a short distance from the dock at Stehekin. You can also visit in the wintertime, but plan ahead; the weather can be bitterly cold and the snow deep.

The forests are dense and grand in the valleys, with Engelmann spruce growing near the streams and rivers. At higher elevations, lodgepole pine appears, and still higher, subalpine fir, mountain hemlock, and white-bark pine predominate. Finally, there are no trees at all as you climb into the raw, glacial crags of the high country. In the spring at this altitude, the bear grass, with its bushy head of white flowers, competes for dominance with the avalanche fawn lily. Later in the year, purple mountain gentians decorate bare patches of soil, while showy cliff penstemons sprout from cracks in the rock that seem an unlikely spot for plant growth.

Getting There

The best way to get to the Stehekin area is by first driving to Chelan. If you are traveling from the western side of the Cascades, the trip takes roughly three and a half hours. From the Puget Sound basin, drive east either on I-90 or US 2. If you take US 2, continue until you reach Wenatchee. From I-90, take exit 85 (US 970) just beyond Cle Elum, and travel over Swauk (Blewett) Pass until you reach US 2 near the town of Cashmere. Turn right (east), and drive to Wenatchee.

Upon approaching Wenatchee, take the very tight off-ramp to the right to US 97 northbound to Entiat and Chelan. After about ½ mile, take the US 97 Alternate exit, also to the right. Drive along the Columbia River and Lake Chelan until you reach the town of Chelan.

If you are planning to take the boat trip up the lake, you can either begin at Chelan very early in the morning, or you can catch it at Field's Point Landing. If you want to do the latter, do not take the US 97 Alternate all the way into Chelan. Instead, look for the Navarre Coulee Road that switchbacks up the bluff on your left. This is SR 971, and it will take you to Lake Chelan State Park on the lake's shore. Bypass the park by turning left, and drive along the lake's shoreline until you reach Field's Point, and the boat landing there. There is ample parking for boat passengers.

To get to Stehekin at the lake's northern end, you must travel by either boat or plane. The National Park Service provides a shuttle as far as Cottonwood Campground on the Stehekin River, near the Cascade Pass and Horseshoe Basin areas.

To determine the schedules and fares for taking the boat up the lake, you can visit www.ladyofthelake.com or call the Chelan Chamber of Commerce. There are several boats to take you up, some that travel at a brisk 50 miles per hour and others that move at a more leisurely pace. The schedules vary depending on the time of year. If you plan to stay in Stehekin, be certain to make arrangements beforehand, because it is a very popular destination and space is limited.

An aging miner's cabin in the Stehekin area. A blacksmith's bellows rests against the wall. Notice the finely fitted corners of the building. (*Up and Down the North Cascades National Park,* by Allan May, 1973)

Geology

The majority of the Stehekin mining area is underlain by pre-Upper Jurassic gneisses, many migmatic in nature. To the northeast of the Stehekin River lies an exposed, narrow band of pre-Upper Jurassic metamorphic rocks, running from southeast to northwest. The headwaters of Bridge Creek rise in Tertiary-Cretaceous, intrusive, igneous, granitic rock that contacts the gneisses along a broad zone in the region of the McGregor Mountain ridge. The mineral-bearing zones were found throughout the gneisses and along the contacts between dissimilar rocks. The area is not heavily mineralized, and with few exceptions, mining never really gained a foothold there. Several of the properties assay highest in gold or silver, but by far the majority assay highest in lead.

The Mines

> **Note** Locating properties in this area is very challenging due to several corrections in the ranges located east of the Willamette Meridian. Several east-west shifts occur in the alignments of ranges 13, 14, and 15. On the Forest Service map for Wenatchee National Forest, range 15 no longer exists north of the 8th standard parallel. The locations given in Huntting's *Inventory of Washington Minerals* appear to have been based on an earlier interpretation of these shifts. Where *Inventory* describes a property in R15E, the newest National Forest Service maps place it in R14E. This book uses the latest National Forest Service map for the Wenatchee National Forest to obtain these figures.

Davenport Mine

Rated at E-5, the Davenport Mine is located in the upper end of Horseshoe Basin in Section 29, T35N, R14E. Horseshoe Basin is a breathtakingly beautiful, double-level, high mountain cirque nearly at the upper end of the Stehekin Valley. This is some of the most rugged backcountry in the state. Weather can change with almost no notice. At one time, there was a road from Stehekin to the basin, but it is no longer there. Keep in mind that many of the mines and prospects on this property are under current claim or are deeded.

Development

The mine, consisting of over 500 feet of tunneling, was located in 1891 by Morrison M. Kingman and his brother-in-law, Lloyd Pershall. It operated during 1907 and 1908 under the Cascade Copper Company and around 1949 under the Horseshoe Basin Mining and Development Company. The mine produced lead, copper, silver, and gold. A 230-pound chunk of silver ore extracted from this property was sent to the World's Columbian Exposition in Chicago in 1893.

Production

Records indicate that only one ton of ore was shipped from the property. Given the remoteness of the area and its general lack of transportation, this isn't surprising.

Black Warrior Mine

Rated at E-5, the Black Warrior Mine is also located at the upper end of Horseshoe Basin at an elevation of 3,900 to 4,725 feet (in the northeast ¼ of Section 32, T35N, R14E). The mine was accessible at one time by road from Stehekin. It sits on three patented claims: the Black Warrior, Blue Devil, and Golden Gate; and three unpatented claims: Waterfall #1 and #2 and the Campsite.

Development

The original claims were staked in the late 1880s by M. M. Kingman and William Pearshall of Chelan. The Black Warrior, the Blue Devil, the Doubtful, and the Quien Sabe were the original claims. In 1891, the Black Warrior Mine was sold to a Pennsylvania company, George Markle Mining, for the amazing sum of $30,000.[1] Word of this transaction started a small gold rush into the Stehekin area, and many small mining claims were staked, most of which have been forgotten.

The new owners hoped that a spur line of the Great Northern Railway would be built over Cascade Pass, right beside Horseshoe Basin. The spur line never arrived, and the property lay idle until after World War II. In 1946, two men, named Gans and Harris (backed by Frank Funkhouser, a Spokane businessman) formed a corporation, came to Stehekin, and began developing the site. In 1947, they acquired a bulldozer and punched a rough road into the property. A 1948 flood washed out the road, but they managed to rebuild enough of it to get a large air compressor and three drilling machines to the mine.

By 1949, they had drilled over 200 feet of tunnel as a crosscut and had drifted right and left along the vein, exposing minerals of iron, copper, and lead. The problem was that the ore was very low grade and required the construction of a mill nearby. By the end of 1949, the company had realized that building a mill, a mining camp, and other support facilities nearby was not feasible. The winter avalanches that roared down Horseshoe Basin and the whole of the upper Stehekin Valley routinely covered not only the mine but also the whole valley below it.

Sporadic mining continued on a small scale into the 1950s, but eventually the terrain won out and the operation was closed.

Production

There are no known production records.

Horseshoe Basin Mine

Rated at E-5, the Horseshoe Basin Mine is located in the north ½ of Section 29, T35N, R14E at an elevation of from 6,600 to 7,000 feet. The mine workings were accessed by trail and road from Stehekin at the head of Lake Chelan. The property consisted of 22 unpatented claims and three mill sites.

History

The mine was operated from 1946 to the early 1950s by the Horseshoe Basin Mining and Development Company of Bremerton, Washington.

Development

The mine workings were pretty extensive and consisted of over 1,000 feet of crosscutting, which accessed another 1,000 feet of drifting. Other development consisted of a 7,000-foot aerial tramway and cook and bunkhouses.

Production

The mined ore contained lead, copper, zinc, silver, and gold, but the highest assays were in copper. We have been unable to locate records of ore shipments, though we assume that the operators sent *something* down the long aerial tramway. The terrain won out in this case too.

---

[1] Some accounts put the selling price at $40,000.

How did they get items like great lengths of cable into mines like those in remote areas like Horseshoe Basin? This picture shows an example of the great ingenuity of the early miners. Rather than leave the cable coiled on a spool, they have removed it and spread the load among many pack horses. A few coils of the cable were assigned to each animal to distribute the weight as evenly as possible. (*Pioneer Days in British Columbia, Volume I*, Heritage House, 1977)

For the Rockhound

As mentioned earlier, literally hundreds of small mining claims and prospects were located between Cascade Pass and Stehekin. Most of these are pretty difficult to find, but should you choose to visit some, we will give you what information we have. Remember to check first to see whether the property is privately owned or whether wilderness or other restrictions apply.

> **Caution** Most of these properties lie within the North Cascades National Park. Check with the rangers before you take samples; most, if not all, national parks forbid the removal of anything from the premises.

Speaking of rockhounding, some of the following properties have produced among the finest-quality specimens to be found in Washington State.

> **Warning** Remember that this is very rugged territory. *Never* enter these areas during avalanche season, and always sign in at the trailhead boxes.

Prospects

(No hike ratings are given to prospects)

Cascade Consolidated Company

Cascade Consolidated Company operated a silver property (Section 31, T31N, R14E).

Clagstone Prospect

Located at an elevation of 5,200 feet and reachable by 12 miles of trail from Bridge Creek (in the southwest ¼ of Section 30, T35N, R16E). Development consisted of three short tunnels and one open cut. Prospectors sought lead, silver, gold, and zinc from this site.

Doubtful Prospect

Doubtful Prospect was another lead property (Section 31, T35N, R14E) south of the Quien Sabe property and north of the Falls Prospect. Two adits are on the claim, one 30-footer and one that is 100 feet long. This is part of the Black Warrior Group and might be private property.

Falls Prospect

Also a lead prospect and located in the same section as the Doubtful, it can be reached via about two miles of trail from the end of the Stehekin road. There is one small open cut at this prospect.

Galena Prospect

Another lead prospect, located in Section 29, T35N, R14E, adjacent to the Quien Sabe. Ore is exposed for 250 feet along the surface. An open cut only seven feet long is the extent of the development.

This is the view from Sahale Arm, above Cascade Pass, in the vicinity of the Belcher Prospect and looking east across Doubtful Lake at the mine dump of the Quien Sabe Prospect (arrow). This tunnel also shows as an adit symbol on the USGS 7.5 Minute Series map for Cascade Pass. The Franklin Prospect was probably located in the first major gully to the north (left) of the Quien Sabe. (Phil Woodhouse photo)

Panama #2 Prospect

Located somewhere within upper Horseshoe Basin, a short adit and one open cut make up the only attempt to develop this site.

Quien Sabe Prospect

The Quien Sabe Prospect is located (Section 31, T35N, R14E) on the east side of Doubtful Lake Basin. Ore minerals contained lead, silver, gold, and copper. A 250-foot drift is the extent of the workings. This prospect is part of the Black Warrior Group and might be private property.

Franklin Prospect

Located just north of the Quien Sabe Prospect (Section 30, T35N, R14E), the Franklin produced a small amount of silver and lead. The extent of development is not known.

Rouse Prospect

Located on a small stream that drains Doubtful Lake (in the southwest ¼ of Section 31, T35N, R14E). Lead, silver, and gold were the values sought here. This prospect is located on private property.

Spokane Boy and Girl Prospect

A copper property located high in Horseshoe Basin.

Belcher Prospect

This is likely one of the prospects that is situated high on the top of Sahale Arm (Section 36, T35N, R13E), the southern arête connecting Sahale Peak with Cascade Pass. One of us ascended Sahale Arm, and imagining having been one of the first people to climb this difficult-to-reach location, was shocked to come upon a shaft of unknown depth and a small quantity of cast iron debris lying scattered about. Lead and gold were the principal values found here.

Summit Prospect

A 45-foot–deep shaft (beware) is the only development. The prospect adjoins the Marlin Claim (in the northeast ¼ of Section 36, T35N, R13E). This is private property. Access is via about three miles of trail from the end of the Stehekin River road. Claimed in 1910, this property had showings of lead and gold.

Homestake and Star Prospect

Located across the canyon from the Isoletta Claim (Section 5, T34N, R14E). The ore body is reported to be four feet wide. The development consists of a 30-foot open cut. Silver and gold were the primary metals located.

Isoletta Prospect

This property actually shipped 2,200 pounds of silver ore. It is located in Section 5, T34N, R14E. The development consists of 215 feet of tunneling.

Flamingo Prospect

Possibly located in the Trapper Lake Basin (Section 9, T34N, R14E). This was a copper prospect, with low values in gold and silver.

Lottie S. Prospect

This prospect adjoins the above-mentioned property. No development information is available. Assays high in silver and low in copper were obtained.

Minneapolis Prospect

This 40-foot tunnel produced a small amount of lode gold, silver, and some copper (Section 32, T35N, R14E).

Silver Jack Prospect

Located at the head of Bridge Creek (in the northwest ¼ of Section 30, T35N, R16E). Development consisted of a small open cut containing lead.

Tommy Jack Prospect

Located a few hundred feet to the south of the North Fork of Bridge Creek (in the southeast ¼ of Section 30, T35N, R16E). An 85-foot tunnel on this spot produced some gold. Elevation at the property is 4,450 feet.

Lake Shyall Prospect

Located on the shoreline of Trapper Lake (in the northwest ¼ of Section 16, T34N, R14E). The ore contained copper, gold, and silver.

Marlin Prospect

Found northeast of the Quien Sabe Prospect (near the northeast corner of Section 36, T35N, R13E). This was another patented claim with a quartz vein containing copper, gold, and silver.

Ombompo Prospect

Located high on the divide between Doubtful and Boston Basins (in the east ½ of Section 36, T35N, R13E), this property consists of one patented claim with a three-foot vein of gold ore.

Logan Prospect

Located 600 feet south of Park Creek Pass (in the north ½ of section 26, T35N, R14E), one shaft and four adits—25, 75, 150, and 190 feet long, respectively—make up the workings at this site. The ore contained lead, zinc, silver, copper, and gold.

Defender Prospect

Located on Grizzly Creek (in the northeast ¼ of Section 28, T35N, R16E), the ore contained copper, silver, and lead.

Butte Prospect

Located on Bridge Creek, about 25 miles from the head of Lake Chelan, the Butte Prospect was claimed between 1902 and 1907, and was located on two veins. Two tunnels, one 56 feet long and the other 42 feet long, were bored into the lode. Ores reportedly contained copper, gold, and silver.

Blankenship Prospect

Located at the mouth of Agnes Creek (Section 10, T33N, R16E), this prospect is very near to the High Bridge Campground on the Stehekin River Road. Seven claims and one mill site formed the property. There are no records of production.

Sunset and Mountain Sheik Prospects

We include these two properties together because it is possible that they are one and the same. Both are said to be located on Flat Creek (in or near Section 24, T34N, R14E), and both were owned by the same person. The ore was gold with some very high assays.

Tiger Prospect

This is another Bridge Creek property located on Memaloose Ridge (Section 4, T34N, R16E). Seven claims were filed in 1897 (a very popular year for prospecting near Stehekin). Gold, lead, copper, and silver were the minerals sought. Development consisted of several open cuts and a shallow shaft. Very high assays were obtained.

Gray Eagle Prospect

Also located on Bridge Creek, near its head, the exact location of this prospect is unknown. High assays were obtained in silver, with some gold also showing.

Texas Jack Prospect

The Texas Jack is located in upper Horseshoe Basin (Section 29, T35N, R14E), two miles by trail from the end of the Stehekin road. Some copper and silver were produced in samples.

Twin Falls Prospect

Located under the falls of Horseshoe Creek, directly below the Black Warrior Mine, this prospect was claimed in 1949. Assays showed a little copper.

Kingman Prospect

Located at the very head of lower Horseshoe Basin and adjoining the Black Warrior property on the east (Section 32, T35N, R14E), the ore deposit here is most likely an extension of the Black Warrior vein. Production unknown.

Mayflower and East Side Prospect

Located on Bridge Creek in 1897, the exact location of these prospects and whether they produced any ore are unknown.

Two turn-of-the-century miners use a star drill bit and double-jack a hole for blasting the beginning of a tunnel in the Stehekin area. (*Reflections of Lake Chelan,* a U.S. Forest Service booklet)

Chelan Mining Area

The Chelan mining area extends as far south as the town of Chelan, where it meets the Chelan Butte/Entiat mining area. Its northern boundaries extend to the town of Stehekin at the northern end of Lake Chelan.

The rolling hills surrounding the resort community of Chelan give little hint of the magnificent views offered by this fjord-like lake, which for most of its length lies in a valley that is twice as deep as the Grand Canyon. At the upper end of the lake are the communities of Holden, Lucerne, and Stehekin, but no roads connect them to the outside world. The remoteness and the spectacular setting of this area have prompted federal protection for much of the district. Portions of a national park, two national forest wilderness areas, and a national recreation area encompass much of the Chelan drainage.

Lake Chelan, the deepest lake in the state, was measured at 1,548 feet in depth by echo soundings in 1966. Wire soundings in the mid-1980s proved the actual depth above Twenty-Five Mile Creek to be 1,642 feet. The lake is roughly 51½ miles long. The widest part, near Wapato Point, is just under two miles wide, and the narrowest, near Slide Ridge, is less then ½ mile wide. Before the lake was dammed and raised 21 feet in 1928, it was about one mile shorter. As of this writing in 2000, there has been some talk of removing the dam.

According to speculation, Lake Chelan was formed in a very unusual way. Glaciers could not have carved the lake's canyon to its measured depth. But the enormous continental glacier formed during the last several ice ages covered the plateau east of the lake to a great depth. It is thought by some that the tremendous weight of the ice depressed the Earth's crust and caused it to split along the glacier's western flank, creating the valley. When riding the boat up and down the lake, look carefully for cliffs on either side of the lake that match like a jigsaw puzzle. The theory of the crust cracking open seems very plausible when you witness these phenomena in person.

The Chelan mining area is divided down the middle by Lake Chelan, and the mines in this region will be described as westside and eastside properties.

History

An astounding amount of game occupied the Lake Chelan area in the early days. Grouse, deer, mountain goat, bear, and cougar were often seen. Grizzly bear weighing up to 800 pounds were fairly common. Mountain sheep are depicted in Native American paintings found on cliffs along the lakeshore. Prior to the turn of the century, mountain goats were so plentiful that people came on safari from as far away as Egypt and London to hunt them for their hides. The first settlers in the region reported many bands of these mountain goats, with some herds numbering in the hundreds. Today Lake Chelan is home to several types of fish, the largest of which is bull trout. Rainbow trout are plentiful, and the streams feeding the lake reportedly contain large numbers of brook trout.

The earthquake of December 14, 1872, that threw Ribbon Cliff into the Columbia River, temporarily blocking its flow, also opened up many fissures around the lake that spewed odorous sulfur water for many years.[1] The quake cracked the lake bottom too, causing a huge geyser at Chelan Falls that lasted several months. In 1790, a volcanic ash fall on Lake Chelan occurred alongside a powerful earthquake, which

---

[1] The blockage was said to have dried up the Columbia River as far south as Wenatchee. If this was indeed the case, where were the Entiat and Wenatchee Rivers that entered the Columbia *below* the blockage?

shook the lake violently. Two inches of volcanic ash—most likely originating from an eruption of Glacier Peak, located about 20 miles to the west—fell on the region. The ash could also have been ejected from one of several cinder cones situated near the Cascade Mountain crest.

At one time, mainly during the 1880s, Stehekin River County Road #21 connected Chelan to the mines in Horseshoe Basin. This road was declared a public highway in 1892, but actually it was nothing more than a narrow trail, not even capable of accommodating a wagon. Access into the remote upper Lake Chelan area was improved by the 1897 construction of the new Cross-State Wagon Road, which extended from Marblemount over Cascade Pass down to Stehekin, up Bridge Creek, down the Methow to the Columbia River, and from there on to Wenatchee.

The original Chelan town site had an interesting beginning. In July 1889, a judge named Ballard laid out and staked the lots at what had formally been an Army base called Camp Chelan. Before that, the land had been part of the Columbia Indian Reservation.[2] In 1886, it was made available to homesteading, but its title was not clear. It took an act of Congress in 1892 to clear the title, and by this time over 1,000 lots had already been sold at a price of $5.75 each.

Today you can reach Stehekin by boat, trail, or floatplane. A small grass airfield is also located near the town.

> Native American paintings have been found at Stehekin, Domke Falls, and Meadow Creek. "Stehekin" is the Skagit word for "the way through." Artifacts leave no doubt that Native Americans, as far back as prehistoric times, used Rainy Pass and Cascade Pass to cross the mountains. It is also believed that they used Ross and Suiattle Passes. A smallpox epidemic around 1830 wiped out almost every Native American in the area. By 1883, there were only nine survivors out of a once–fairly-dense population.

What to See

The upper Lake Chelan area and the mountains north of Stehekin have been called the American Alps. Those who have ascended the peaks and trails in the area fully understand why. It abounds with glaciers, tarns, alpine basins, and meadows. As you ascend the mountain slopes, valley pine gives way to subalpine fir and white-bark pine in the upper basins. In season, avalanche fawn lily pushes its head through the melting snow. Later showy, purple cliff penstemons soften the often-stark rocky escarpments. The boat ride up the lake exceeds anything that a theme amusement park could offer. At one time, the company operating the lake boats would do "whistle stops," beaching the boats at the bow to discharge and pick up passengers. (They were specifically designed to beach without suffering damage.) Nowadays, the boats will often throttle down when a herd of mountain goats is sighted high on the cliffy banks so that passengers can get a good look.

On the boat, with the mountains rising over 8,000 feet above you and the bottom of the lake almost 2,000 feet below the boat's keel, you will find yourself in a two-mile–deep canyon. Or you can charter a floatplane to fly into Stehekin. If the weather allows and the pilot flies high enough, the true grandeur of the area will take your breath away.

Fishing, water sports, hiking, technical climbing, mineral exploration, and just taking a tour on Lake Chelan's boats provide activities for every taste and budget.

Getting There

The first leg of your journey to this area will usually entail a drive to the town of Chelan. If you are traveling from West of the Cascades, you have roughly a 3½-hour trip ahead of you. From the Puget Sound basin, either drive east on I-90 or US 2. If you take US 2, continue to the city of Wenatchee. If you are driving I-90, take the US 970 exit just beyond Cle Elum, and travel over Swauk (Blewett) Pass until you reach US 2 near the town of Cashmere. Turn right (east), and drive to Wenatchee.

---

[2] At one time, this reservation extended east to the Columbia and north to the Canadian border. Once it was closed, Native American residents were given a choice of either remaining in the Chelan area on an allotment of land or moving to the Colville Reservation. This is why even today several small sections of land surrounding Lake Chelan are still Native American lands.

One of the original Lady of the Lake boats, perhaps THE original that ferry passengers and goods up and down Lake Chelan. Today's high-powered catamaran Lady is a far cry from this early steamboat. (From *Up and Down the North Cascades National Park*, by Allan May, 1973)

As you approach Wenatchee, take the *very tight* off-ramp to the right to US 97 north toward Entiat and Chelan. Within about ½ mile, take the exit to US 97 Alternate, also to the right. Drive along the Columbia River and Lake Chelan until you reach the town of Chelan.

If you are planning to take the boat trip up the lake, you can either begin at Chelan very early in the morning, or you can catch it at Field's Point Landing. If you want to do the latter, do not drive US 97 all the way into Chelan. Instead, look for the Navarre Coulee Road that switchbacks up the bluff on your left. This will be SR 971, which will take you to Lake Chelan State Park on the lake's shore. Bypass the park by turning left, and drive along the shoreline until you reach Field's Point and the boat landing. There is ample parking available for boat passengers.

Years ago, you could make arrangements beforehand with the Lutheran Church to take its bus up Railroad Creek from the boat landing at Lucerne to Holden, now a church camp and retreat. As of this writing, it is unclear whether this is still an option. If you take a boat or fly to Stehekin at the lake's northern end, the National Park Service provides a shuttle to as far as Cottonwood Campground on the Stehekin River, near the Cascade Pass and Horseshoe Basin areas.

To determine the schedules and fares for riding the boat up the lake, you can visit www.ladyofthelake.com, or call the Chelan Chamber of Commerce. There are several boats to take you up, some fast (50 miles per hour) and others that travel at a more leisurely pace. The schedules vary depending on the time of the year. If the boats no longer make whistle stops along the lakeshore, you may have to charter a boat or floatplane to access the mines located on the eastern side of the lake.

Geology

Lake Chelan lies in an area composed of metamorphic and igneous rocks. The oldest of these are of metamorphic origin, and they are cut by younger granitic rocks. These in turn are traversed by dikes of andesite, diorite porphyry, and quartz porphyries. The principal ores sought by prospectors and miners in this area contained copper, gold, silver, molybdenum, and lead, with some zinc thrown in for good measure.

Literally hundreds of small mines and prospects were located in the district. We will describe some of the smaller prospects and claims first and then proceed to the larger mines. This area contains one of the largest copper mines in the state of Washington—the mine at Holden. Enormous amounts of copper and silver were extracted from this property, which is located on the side of, appropriately enough, Copper Mountain.

The Mines

West Side of Lake Chelan

Marcus Stein Mine

Rated at C-3. This property is located along the banks of Wilson Creek, a tributary of Railroad Creek (northeast ¼ of Section 17, T31N, R17E), which flows into it from the south. The Marcus Stein is only a mile downstream from the famous Holden Mine. The Marcus Stein miners missed the mother lode of copper by very little. The ore minerals are pyrargyrite and pyrite, which produced silver and gold.

Raymond Mine

Rated at C-3, the Raymond is adjacent to the Marcus Stein. Again, the miners missed the copper lode, but came up with ore containing some silver and gold.

Silver Trail Mine

Rated at E-4 from Holden. This property is located on Railroad Creek, near the Crown Point Mine, about six miles west of Holden (Section 8, T31N, R16E). It consisted of 36 claims with values in copper, gold, silver, lead, and zinc. The development and production of this mine are not known.

Crown Point Mine

Rated at E-5 from Holden. The Crown Point Mine is located in a cirque basin southwest of Hart Lake, at the head of Railroad Creek (in the northeast ¼ of Section 8, T31N, R16E). The elevation at the mine is 4,300 feet.

The property can be reached by taking the boat to the village of Lucerne, traveling by bus to the old town site of Holden, and then going by foot six miles up to the mine. The trail to the property was very brushy in the summer of 1998. A considerable amount of large machinery is at the site, which brings us once again to that old haunting question: "How did they get all this heavy junk up here?" To which the answer is, "Nobody told them that they couldn't, so they just did it." The property dates back to 1900 when the Crown Point Mining Company began development. The mine was operated off and on by various owners until around 1924.

The ore mined was molybdenite. Underground workings consisted of two tunnels containing more than 400 feet of drifts and a lot of stoping.

Production

It is amazing that, as remote as this property is, the operators were able to ship any ore at all. Somehow they managed to ship almost 25 tons of "moly" off that mountain and down to the smelter.

For the Rockhound

Some of the finest molybdenite specimens on display in museums all over the country came from this property. In the long adit, 200 feet below the molybdenite outcropping, is a vuggy zone containing clusters of quartz crystals, some of which are an amazing two inches long.

Holden Mine

Rated at A-1 to B-5 from Holden. The Holden Mine is located on the west side of Lake Chelan on Railroad Creek, about 12 miles from the boat landing at Lucerne. The mine area can be reached via boat from the town of Chelan, to the village of Lucerne, and then by truck road to the town site of Holden, which is now a retreat owned by the Lutheran Church.[3]

Ore Deposit Geology

The Holden ore deposit occurs in an apparent shear zone in metamorphic rocks that are evidently a roof pendant in intrusive granodiorite. The ore body has a strike of north 23 degrees west and dips southwest between 60 and 70 degrees.

The deposit is irregularly tabular. The portion of the fractured zone impregnated with the sulfides varies from 30 to 100 feet in width. It was mined longitudinally for a distance of over 2,000 feet, and to a depth of over 1,700 feet below the outcrop.

The nature of the ore body, and the hardness of the country rock, was very conducive to low-cost mining, since the mine required almost no timbering except in a few badly fractured areas. The ore itself was low grade, containing chalcopyrite, pyrite, pyrrhotite (which produced primarily copper), and smaller amounts of gold and silver.

History

The Holden Mine was located on July 24, 1896, by John Henry Holden, who was born in Springfield, Massachusetts, and migrated west at the age of 19. After working for a short time in the mines of Nevada, he moved to the Seattle area where he met and became friends with Victor Denny, one of the sons of Seattle pioneer David Denny.

The Dennys hired Holden to work part-time at their home in Seattle and at their ranch at Licton Springs located north of the city.[4] After about a year, Holden moved to Port Angeles, where he began prospecting in the Olympic Mountains. He reportedly also served as judge and coroner in the town of Dungeness. In 1893, he returned to Seattle and was rehired by the Dennys to work at one of their mines near Snoqualmie Pass, the Esther Gold and Silver Mine.

A 1909 photograph of the Holden Mine "family". On the far left is Harry Holden after which the place is named. Grover Kelly and John Falleto are also pictured. The log structure belies the fact that lumber was not easily available in 1909 at the mine. (From the Long Collection, North Central Washington Museum, Wenatchee, Washington)

---

[3] Overnight facilities are available.

[4] This spot is now a city park, located around 97th and Ashworth Avenue North. Two mineral springs are on the premises, and it was developed as a health spa during the 1930s and 1940s. The history of this property actually predates the Dennys, when local Native Americans used the water for medicinal purposes.

The mine dump of the Holden Mine in 1909. While the discovery outcrop was far up on the side of Copper Mountain on the left, this haulage crosscut tunnel had been driven to tap the vein at depth to allow mining in earnest. (From the Long Collection, North Central Washington Museum, Wenatchee, Washington)

Holden and Victor, along with three other men, worked the property. Heavy snow caused them to close the mine in June 1893 and return to the Seattle area.[5] On July 6, 1893, the Dennys sent Holden to Lake Chelan to make preparations for a family camping and prospecting trip. It was during this period that he heard the Great Northern Railroad was sending engineers and surveyors to an area near the head of the lake to see whether a route through the Cascades at that point would be feasible. Somehow Holden got word that they had found some rich mineral outcroppings, and he became fascinated with the area almost to the point of obsession. This region would later be named Railroad Creek because the Great Northern began to survey a line along it that would possibly cross the Cascade Mountains via this route.

On April 4, 1896, Holden hooked up with Victor Denny at the Lakeview Hotel in Chelan and took him to the Railroad Creek area. They didn't find anything worth claiming, and Victor called it quits and returned to Seattle, leaving all the camping and prospecting equipment with Holden. On July 13, 1896, Holden hired W. P. Robinson to pack the equipment to the Railroad Creek area in another attempt to find minerals. To finance this trip, Victor Denny again loaned him money. On July 24, 1896, while hunting game for lunch, Holden found an outcropping and located four claims. He sent samples to a Seattle assayer and got back some very favorable results. He again borrowed money from the Dennys and returned to Seattle.[6]

Men and women gather for their picture at the adit of one of the tunnels at the Holden Mine in 1909. Notice the bottle resting on the mine car. It has a candle pressed into its top. Mines can be spooky when carrying electric lights, and downright terrifying by candlelight. (From the Long Collection, North Central Washington Museum, Wenatchee, Washington)

---

[5] Heavy snow at Snoqualmie Pass in June? It must have been one heck of a winter.

[6] Holden either worked off or paid back in cash the money he had borrowed from the Dennys. But there is some dispute about the fate of the cash he obtained from others in the Chelan area.

An early air compressor at the Holden Mine, c.a. 1909. The log cabin building was typical for the time period because of the remoteness of the site. Compare this picture to the photo of the later compressor building at the Holden Mine. (From the Long Collection, North Central Washington Museum, Wenatchee, Washington)

The compressor house at the Holden Mine in its halcyon days of operation. The drills, muckers, and underground locomotives were all powered by compressed air, making this facility the real powerhouse of the mine. (From the Chadebourn Collection, North Central Washington Museum, Wenatchee, Washington)

For the next two years, Holden worked for the Dennys back at the Seattle properties but dreamed of returning to the Chelan area. In April 1895, he packed up and headed over the pass to the town of Chelan, where he acquired provisions, hired a boat, and set off for the area around Meadow Creek and Railroad Creek near the head of Lake Chelan. On this trip, after failing to locate any minerals, he returned to Chelan and borrowed money from some local friends. He again set out for Railroad Creek but still failed to locate anything.

After acquiring an additional grubstake, Holden returned to the Chelan area, recorded several more claims along the outcrop, and set about developing the property. He formed the Holden Gold and Copper Mining Company, sold stock shares, and spent over $100,000 grading the area along the lake to the prospect with the intent of eventually building a railroad.[7] The railroad project was supposed to connect the prospect with Refrigerator Harbor located some 12 miles away. By the end of 1901, only five miles of roadbed had been completed and the project was abandoned.

By this time, stockholders had poured nearly all of their available money into the deal. This left Holden with five well-developed tunnels, sizeable ore dumps, thousands of railroad ties, and several bridges, along with a few permanent buildings.

---

[7] For a more detailed look at the mining operations during this period, see *The Holden Mine from Discovery to Production* by Nigel Adams, 1981.

In 1907, the Grandby Company, which had mining operations in British Columbia, took up an option on the mine and did extensive underground exploration for almost two years before turning the mine back over to Holden. At that time, there were six tunnels, with over 2,000 feet of workings on three levels.[8]

In 1922, the Chelan Copper Company was organized, apparently for the sole purpose of selling more stock, and again the property lay idle for some time. Railroad Creek is a very remote and rugged area; it would eventually require millions of dollars to develop a producing mine there.

Development

In August 1928, the Howe Sound Mining Company of New York—which was located near Britannia Beach on Howe Sound, north of Vancouver, B. C., and had extensive holdings in British Columbia—leased the property with an option to buy. Actual work didn't begin until May 1929,[9] most likely due to heavy snowfall during the previous winter. The company brought in a workforce of 105 and conducted extensive drilling and tunneling operations to define the extent of the ore body. In June 1930, the Chelan Copper Mining Company (whose postmark was CHELCOP) was formed as an operating company for the Howe Sound Company, and development work continued at the mine.

The operation was suspended in 1931 because of the Great Depression, but the company had no intention of abandoning the mine. It finalized the purchase in 1933 and sat back to see what the world's economy would do. By 1937, copper prices were again on the rise, so permits for the construction of a power line from Chelan Falls to the property were filed. As soon as the snow melted in the spring, the company planned to commence full-scale development. Howe Sound announced that it was ready to spend $3 million to put the mine into production.

The first order of business was to subcontract the construction of a power line from Chelan Falls to the mine, build a mill, and organize shipping and trucking systems.[10] The next step was to bring in compressors, air line, pumps, lumber, rails, a caterpillar tractor, a 180-horsepower diesel engine, a 37.5-kilowatt alternator as a backup electrical source, and a portable American sawmill. A large dock was also built and a tug and

The assay office and laboratory at the Holden Mine. All of the facilities were state-of-the-art at the time of their installation. Here, the core samples and other samples from the mine were assayed to determine their value. (From the Chadebourn Collection, North Central Washington Museum, Wenatchee, Washington)

---

[8] John Holden ultimately had a difficult time establishing ownership to the mine claims on Railroad Creek. Victor Denny sued him for money he had loaned Holden to help him establish his claim. Too late, Victor realized the value of the property and attempted to obtain half the profits. His efforts failed, even after a lengthy legal battle.

[9] In 1929, when the first crews working for Howe Sound were doing exploratory work in Copper Basin, a large forest fire broke out, burning 600 acres. The Forest Service was planning on arresting the men and fining the company $50,000 for the suppression of the fire when it was discovered that the burn was caused by a bolt of lightning hitting a snag. It is entirely possible that Howe Sound would have pulled out of the operation if it had been to blame.

[10] The construction of the mill required 740,420 tons of steel. The total roof area of the mill, dry rooms, assay office, warehouse, and compressor room was 75,946 square feet, or about 1.7 acres.

Dormitories and staff houses at Holden in 1939. The Holden mine spared no expense in providing the best living conditions for its people. The site was remote, and any amenities were welcome. (Larry Penberthy photo, North Central Washington Museum, Wenatchee, Washington)

barges brought in. The tug had a steel prow that enabled it to bash through the ice in the event that Lake Chelan should ever freeze over, which it never did. The tug, the *E. B. Schley*, is still alive and well and moored near Portland, Oregon, on the Columbia River as of the year 2000.

Meanwhile, at the town site of what would become Holden [11] construction of buildings to house up to 450 people continued apace. This included four bunk houses that would each sleep 50, guest house, staff house, 10 family homes, a school, and a mess hall capable of feeding up to 265 people.

Also added were a hospital, complete with dentist office, and a recreation hall with a four-lane bowling alley, barbershop, pool tables, library, movie theater, and a multipurpose gymnasium for sports, church services, dances, meetings, plays, and other events.[12] The next order of business was the installation of fire hydrants, a water system, and a sewage system. A second town site, Winston Camp, sprang up to house the workers who had families.[13]

Startup costs had now reached the $3 million mark, and the Holden Mine and town were a showpiece of modern mining technology and employee comfort. They had everything except a saloon, but drinking establishments could be found in Chelan, Lucerne, and Stehekin.

Mining and Milling

In the first week of April 1938, the mill was put into operation.[14] By the end of May, it had exceeded all expectations and the decision was made to increase capacity from the original 1,100 tons per day to over 2,000 by the addition of another ball mill, classifier, flotation cell, and filter. All equipment brought to the property was the most modern available.

---

[11] The movie *Lassie Come Home*, starring Liz Taylor, was filmed at Holden.

[12] The hospital included the dental office (a dentist came from Chelan once a month) and apartments for the resident doctor and nurse.

[13] Howe Sound intended Holden to be a single man's camp. The homes at Winston Camp (west of the town site) were not built by the company, but by the workers who wanted to bring their families to live at Holden. The company assisted these families by platting home sites and putting in roads, sewers, water lines, and electrical wiring. It also offered loans of $2,500, which were repaid via deductions from the worker's pay. When the mine was closed in 1957, the people living in beautiful Winston Camp were moved out by the Forest Service and the town was razed because it presented a potential fire hazard.

[14] The mine and mill operated three shifts, 24 hours a day. Day shift was from 7:00 A.M. until 3:00 P.M., swing shift was from 3:00 P.M. until 11:00 P.M., and graveyard ran from 11:00 P.M. until 7:00 A.M. The crews worked 12 days on with two days off so that they would have time to make a trip to the outside world of Chelan.

When a large crew of men were engaged in heavy work such as mining, food was of paramount importance. The dining hall served a hearty fare that kept the mine in operation. All food had to be barged the 50 miles up Lake Chelan to the mine. (From the Chadebourn Collection, North Central Washington Museum, Wenatchee, Washington)

Another point of interest was the mill's conveyor belt system. There were six conveyor belts in the crushing plant system. Each was electrically interlocked to the feeders and crushers ahead of it so that if any belt stopped, all equipment ahead would also be stopped. A magnetic head pulley and two suspended magnets removed any tramp iron (pieces of drill steel, bits, nails, or other metal objects) before the ore entered the crushing circuit. The plant was also equipped with a dust-collecting and air-washing system, thus minimizing the hazard of silicosis.

Recovery of copper averaged around 94 percent. Gold recovery presented some technical problems due to its super-fine nature, and recovery was limited to around 85 percent.

The concentrates were loaded into steel containers, each holding five tons of concentrate. The containers were trucked the 12 miles down to Lucerne and from there by company barges and tug 40 miles down the lake to Chelan where they were off-loaded and then reloaded aboard trucks for a four-mile trip to the Great Northern Railroad siding at Chelan Falls. All loading stations and transfer points were equipped with large cranes for rapid handling of the loaded containers as well as the returning empties.

The first barge, loaded with 200 tons of copper, gold, and zinc concentrates arrived in Chelan on April 9, 1938. The containers traveled 238 miles to the American Smelting and Refining Company smelter (ASARCO) at Ruston, near Tacoma, Washington.

The tailings from the mill were impounded in a 10-acre area near the mill site. All water used in the processing system was pumped back for reuse even though it contained no detectable traces of reagents that might contaminate the water of Railroad Creek, a favorite fishing stream and tributary to Lake Chelan.

The mill buildings of the Howe Sound Mine at Holden in 1938. This view is looking up Railroad Creek. (From *The Miner, Chemist and Engineer*, November, 1938)

Even though Howe Sound had met some very stringent environmental requirements, local fishers were not convinced that the milling process would not affect the fish in Railroad Creek. As a test, the company installed two small tanks and stocked them with fish. One tank was intentionally contaminated with milling regents, while the other contained fresh water. Although the fish in both tanks gradually died off, the loss in the contaminated tank was no higher than that in the fresh water tank. Howe Sound also contributed $5,000 to the construction cost of the Beebe Springs Fish Hatchery at Chelan Falls.

About 40 men were employed at the mill. While miners were paid $4.60 per day, laborers received $4.00, and both paid the $1.20 room and board per day. Many of the workers spent at least some of their pay in a never-ending poker game. When one person was finished, there was always another waiting to step in. Because the mine and mill operated around the clock, there was always something going on in the town. This game was just one of the goings-on in this round-the-clock community.

Because of the remoteness of the Holden Mine's operations, they had to be self-sufficient in almost everything. To this end, the operation had a top-notch machine shop on the site. This allowed them to repair and/or manufacture most of the machinery that was used in the everyday operation of the mine. (From the Chadebourn Collection, North Central Washington Museum, Wenatchee, Washington)

Workers at Holden Mine were usually tolerant of pay and conditions, but during the summer of 1939 they went on strike over the issue of low wages. Many of them took to the woods around Domke Lake and along Railroad Creek, where they lived off the land while waiting out the strike, which lasted about a month.[15]

Holden was frequently honored by visits from company officials, stockholders, and other dignitaries, and the miners were encouraged to be cleanly dressed when coming to town. One of the people we interviewed said that in that era Holden looked more like San Francisco than a mining town in the middle of nowhere.[16] Nonetheless, it remained primitive in many regards. For instance, early-morning radio listeners in Holden sat up sharply on Monday, January 26, 1948, when the news commentator announced that Holden had been functioning for 10 years without law enforcement. In a news article the same day, Chelan County Commissioner K. P. Sexton described this as "the most unusual situation ever to confront the County Commissioners." R. S. Brown and N. E. Sims were sent from Holden to Wenatchee, where they were appointed justice of the peace and constable, respectively.[17]

Strangely, the town seemed to have found a way to police itself up to this point. For example, some of the more resourceful of the miners' children got a real racket going at one point. The tavern down at Lucerne was closed on Sundays, so on Saturday nights the miners would buy their stashes of beer and liquor

---

[15] Domke Lake was originally called Crane's Lake in honor of a member of the Great Northern Railroad survey party that came through the area in the mid-1880s. The name Domke is a misspelling of "Henry Dumpkey," one of the first white settlers in the region.

[16] The miners at Holden worked every day in a dirty, harsh, and dangerous environment. When the whistle announced quitting time, the married men ran for home and many of the single miners ran for their boats and headed uplake to a place called Edgemont. This is where the whorehouse was located; the area was better known to the locals as "Pecker Point." Some men purportedly wore their oars out rowing to Edgemont and back.

[17] Shortly after Sims was sworn in as constable, someone burglarized the recreation hall. In the morning, Sims followed footprints leading up Railroad Creek where, under a bridge, he located the missing loot. The thief was in such a hurry to hide his ill-gotten gains that when he emptied his pockets his brass ID tag fell out. The fellow wasn't hard to locate.

for the next day and hide them somewhere in the nearby woods or along Railroad Creek to be retrieved the next morning. The children caught onto this and began to keep an eye on the tavern on Saturday nights, following the men to their hiding spots. The kids would confiscate the booze, put it in a safe spot, and retire for the night. The next morning they would sell the men their own hooch back, which seemed to work, since none of them wanted to have a dry Sunday.

Mining Methods

The primary mining method used at Holden was called *shrinkage-bulldozer chamber*. We have also heard it referred to as *block caving*. First the ore body was undercut and a series of finger raises were bored upward from below. At the bottoms of the raises, rooms called *bulldozer or bulldozing chambers* were created. The ore was blasted from above, whereupon gravity took over and it fell down to the bulldozer chambers below. At that point, it was mucked through grizzlies, down the finger raises to the main haulage, and taken to the mill. The upshot of this type of mining method is that once the undercut had been completed, no one entered the stope again.

Instead, the stope expansion was accomplished using a method known as *powder drifting*, which the miners called *coyote holing*. Raises were bored upward on both sides of the ore body, and then the powder or blasting drifts connected with each raise about 35 feet above the back (top) of the stope. All along the drifts, three-by-four–foot pockets or coyote holes were bored, which were loaded with explosives and blasted to bring down the ore. The hardness of the rock at Holden was a great advantage in this type of mining because the stopes required almost no timbering support.

Buckskin Mountain forms a backdrop to the Holden Mine's mill building. Typical of mine mills, it is built on a mountainside to take advantage of gravity in the process wherever possible. For an explanation of the mill's operation, with equipment photos, see Appendix A. State-of-the-art when first built, the mill was in desperate need of upgrading when the mine closed in 1957. (From the Chadebourn Collection, North Central Washington Museum, Wenatchee, Washington)

Miners in the Holden mine prepare to set an explosive charge to loosen some recalcitrant ore above one of the bulldozer rooms at the base of the main stope. (From the Chadebourn Collection, North Central Washington Museum, Wenatchee, Washington)

The Holden Mine Isometric

While not depicting the actual mine, this drawing illustrates the technique that was used to mine the vein in the Holden Mine. The shrinkage stoping technique used in the Holden Mine was unique in the area. First a series of "bulldozing chambers" were formed along the ore body. These were conical in shape with the apex pointed downward like a funnel. At the base of each was a grizzly screen that allowed up to 28 inch-sized ore to pass. Each chamber was accessible via a service drift that ran along the ore body. Below each grizzly was a finger raise that connected with other such raises and a haulage tunnel below. Once this configuration was established, no one even needed to enter the stope again.

Miners would break up the ore in the bulldozer chambers to allow it to pass through the grizzlys. Once cleared, the stope was ready for its next stage. While the ore was being broken and dropped down the finger raises to the haulage tunnel, other miners were boring the powder drifts and coyote holes about 35 feet above the ceiling of the stope. The coyote holes were packed with explosives, about 0.7 pounds for each ton of ore to be brought down. The explosives near the center had a shock-front velocity of 19,000 feet per second, while those near the walls were 10,500 feet per second. Once the charges were set, the mine was completely cleared of personnel. After everyone had been accounted for, the charge was detonated, and the 35 feet of ore above the stope ceiling was brought down. The bulldozing then began anew, as did the digging of the next set of coyote holes. By this method the ore was removed ever higher in the stope, and no wooden falsework had to be constructed.

It has been said that the most explosives ever set off at one time weighed 7,000 pounds. By the formula given above, that would mean that roughly two million tons of ore would have been brought down in that single blast.

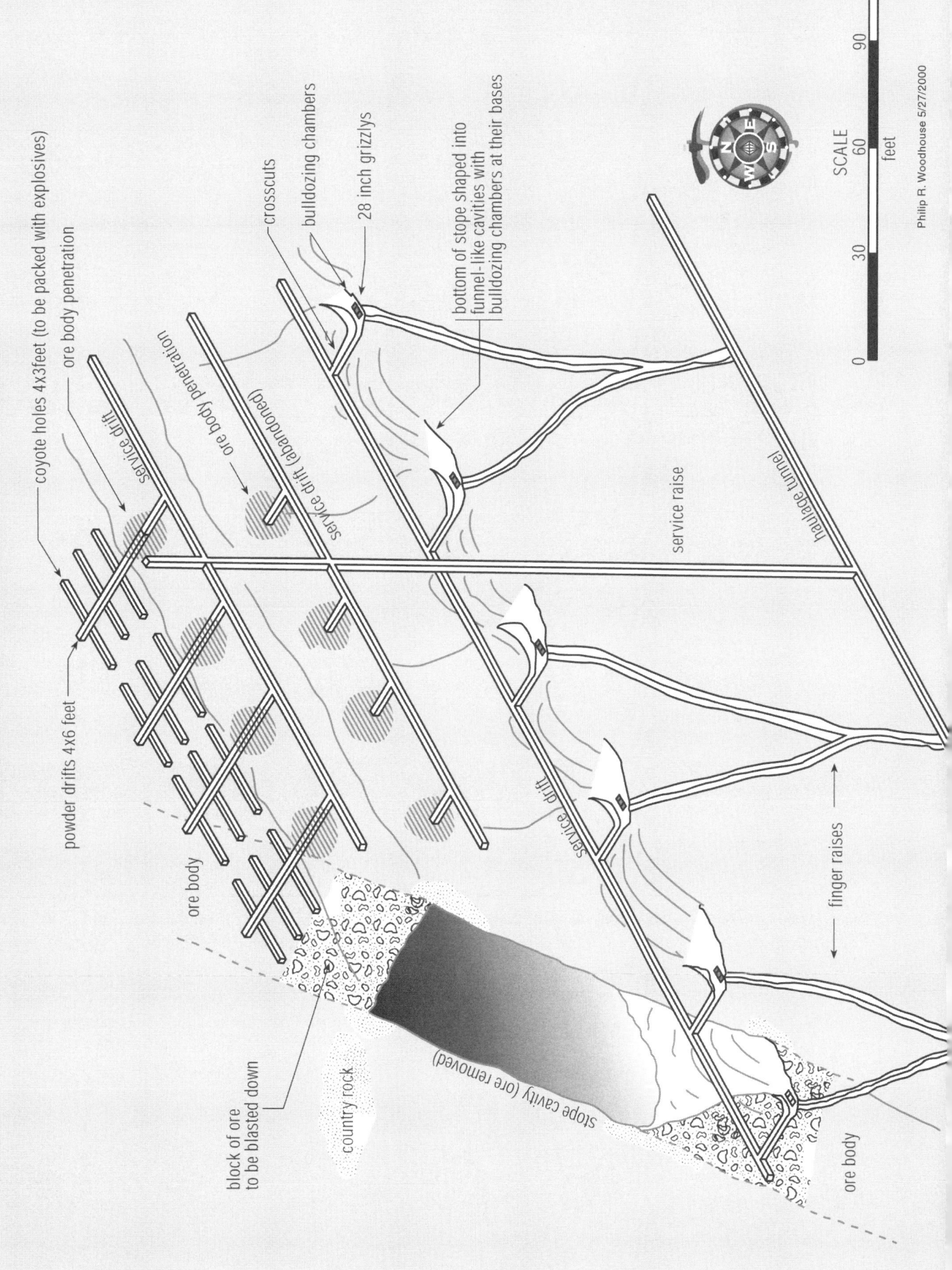

Drilling in the Holden Mine. The drill is the large cylinder on the left with air and water hoses attached. Notice the timber jack being used to stabilize the roof of the tunnel and as a mount for the drill during the drilling process. (From the Chadebourn Collection, North Central Washington Museum, Wenatchee, Washington)

What was it like working deep in the Holden Mine? Jim Marr Jr. told us a story that still makes us shudder:

My father, James Marr Sr., worked as a miner at Holden. He was one of the highest paid because he worked as a coyote holer, drilling small tunnels just big enough for him and his drill, off a drift high above the stopes. He had an assistant called a nipper, *a young man whose job it was to keep the miner supplied with drill steel and explosives.*

One day Dad sent him down to get more steel and was very surprised when he returned so quickly and announced, "Mr. Marr, the drift is gone." Crawling out of the hole and looking the situation over, he saw that indeed something strange had happened. The whole back of the stope had given way, leaving them trapped hundreds of feet in the air.

Dad realized that they had to do something soon, as the area around them was beginning to disintegrate as well. He saw that there was only one way they could save themselves, and that was to go hand over hand across the open stope, on the air line that supplied the compressed air to the drill, to reach the ledge some 80 feet away. The young man argued with Dad that he couldn't do it, and that nothing he said was going to get him on that air line.

Arguing with my Dad was never a winning proposition, and he knew that if they were going to live they had to go for it now. Dad reached up, took hold of the air line, and began going hand over hand across the abyss. He told me that when he was about 30 feet out from what was left of the drift, he felt a tug on the line, looked over his shoulder, and saw that the nipper had listened to him and was right behind him. They both reached the other side safely and were met by applause from a group of miners, including the mine foreman, who had been summoned to mount a rescue.

Here is another story about the working conditions at Holden, as told by Leonard Lynch:

I arrived at Holden on June 1, 1947, with Bob Marsh, Harry Stine, Ben Snyder, and Don Duncan. We had been working in the copper mines at Sheridan, Montana, and thought we would come out west for a change of scenery. The Holden Mine was a pretty good place to work in the summertime, but in the winter it got really cold and snowfall of 15 feet or more was not uncommon.

My job at the mine was loading the explosives used in blasting the stopes and drifts, and seeing to its delivery to the powder monkeys, whose job it was to actually fire the charges. Mining back in those days was a little different than it is today. For instance, blasting underground in today's mines takes place only after **everyone** *is out of the mine and accounted for. Back then, production was considered more important than safety. (A mule was said to be worth five miners. The mine owners had to buy the mules, but miners were waiting in line for jobs.) You had better know who was doing what and when because explosives were going off around the clock.*

Since the mine at Holden was unionized early on, some of the miners were paid a base wage and then would bid on contracts for taking on a specific job, for instance driving a winze, manway, or ventilation raise. They were called contract miners.

This scene is typical of a mucking operation in one of the crosscut or drift tunnels that were driven to access the main ore body at the Holden Mine. The rock, once blasted down, had to be "mucked" or loaded into cars for transport to the surface. The scoop device seen here is called a mucker. (From the Chadebourn Collection, North Central Washington Museum, Wenatchee, Washington)

The rock in the Holden Mine was very hard, and the miners had to use a lot of drill bits and dynamite to make a reasonable living. I remember that we were also given tins,[18] because there was no bank at Holden and almost everything was owned by the company. Tins were 50-cent pieces in $5.00 bundles, which were used in lieu of money. Employees and their spouses could also sign receipts at the company store, recreation hall, and commissary. Tins were also accepted at several Chelan Taverns.

*Around the end of August, the days became shorter, and it started to get very cold at night. It began to snow the first week of September, and Holden began to look like pictures I had seen of Switzerland. The company installed ultraviolet lights in the dry rooms, and the miners were working in three shifts, 24 hours a day. Everyone looked so white. In fact, **everything** was white.*

Some of the fellows had been hearing about a big dam project down on the Feather River and how they were hiring miners and powder men like me. California was beginning to sound pretty good too. We got together one day and decided to head down there and see what that job had to offer. All the men I had come to Holden with, with the exception of Don Duncan, who had fallen for a girl who worked at the café, left Holden to try our luck at dam building.

The End

By the mid-1950s, the mill, very modern in its day, was about spent. It desperately required modernizing, but with copper prices in a slump there was no extra money to pay for improvements. The company assayed samples of its tailing pile, now so large that light aircraft could land on and take off from it, and found a substantial amount of gold. Plans to establish a cyanide plant to extract gold and silver from the tailings, with the proceeds to be used to rebuild the mill, were drawn up. But the Forest Service, fearing an ecological disaster should the cyanide solution spill into Railroad Creek and thus into Lake Chelan, nixed the project.

In 1957, a 40-cent drop in the price of copper proved to be one fluctuation too many, and Howe Sound closed the mine. The copper deposit was very nearly exhausted by this time, and operating costs had reached an all-time high.

The company left over 247,566 feet of drifts, crosscuts, and raises; 231,922 feet of core drilling; and a tailing pile over a mile long and 150 feet deep. There are about 40 miles of tunnel inside that mountain, which gives you an idea of how enormous this operation was.

---

[18] This was similar to, but not the same as, the scrip money used earlier in the mining towns of Colorado and elsewhere. Tins were issued to employees and their spouses as an advance on paychecks. Groceries could be ordered from stores in Chelan and were brought to camp by the returning barges once a week. A portion of one of the dormitories was converted into a private grocery store and operated by a fellow named Price. After the Price store opened, the commissary area became a small, privately owned shop that carried small appliances, hunting and fishing gear, etc. No liquor was sold at Holden, but folks could take the bus to Lucerne to buy it.

Miners in the Holden Mine driving a core drill into the adjacent rock structure. The drill used industrial diamonds for the rock-cutting material. The hollow-stem bits and steels allowed a hole of several hundred feet in length to be bored. The cores extracted from the bore were sent to the assay office and examined. By this method, the rock structure could be examined for mineral value without the expense of driving tunnels. (From the Chadebourn Collection, North Central Washington Museum, Wenatchee, Washington)

Production

For 19 years, the Holden Mine held the state record for copper and gold production.[19] The mine produced a total of 10 million tons of ore, from which 212 million pounds of copper, 40 million pounds of zinc, two million ounces of silver, and 600,000 ounces of gold were extracted. This would be worth over $550 million at 2000 prices.

Between 1958 and 1960, the town was abandoned and vandals took over. Howe Sound tried to sell the property as a mountain resort, promoting it as the "Switzerland of America." The asking price was $100,000, but there were no takers. Instead, Howe Sound gifted the property to the Lutheran Bible Institute, and later that year a watchman was sent to the site. Holden became Holden Village, funds were raised, volunteers recruited, and a massive cleanup of the site ensued.

In the 1980s, the Clean Water Act and other laws were enacted that required that any company causing damage to a waterway—provided that the company is still in business or its successor corporation is still in business, whether or not the company followed all the laws in effect at the time of the damage—pay for the cost of cleanup. Pechiney Corporation, the successor to Howe Sound, therefore received a bill from the Forest Service for $4 million, and was informed that more bills would be forthcoming. As of this writing, several lawsuits involving the government, mining company, and insurance companies are pending.

Loading the explosive charges into drill holes in the breast or face of a tunnel at the Holden Mine. The blast would drive the tunnel farther into the mountain. (From the Chadebourn Collection, North Central Washington Museum, Wenatchee, Washington)

---

[19] During the Korean War years, the U.S. government purchased 50 percent of the copper mined at Holden. It paid 32 cents a pound.

While the main adit of the Holden Mine was sealed in 1965, some of the ancillary tunnels remained open. This portal is one of the many used to wrest the copper from the depths of Copper Mountain at Holden, Washington. (Phil Woodhouse photo)

The irregularly-shaped rail seen here is called a camel back or camel hump. This served as a camming mechanism that would automatically tip the side-dumping ore cars as they were driven through the facility. (From the Chadebourn Collection, North Central Washington Museum, Wenatchee, Washington)

Howe Sound did comply with all the laws, rules, regulations, and so on that were in effect at the time the mine was operated. It received full approval from the Washington Water Pollution Control Commission,[20] and it conformed with all Forest Service regulations.

All that is left of the old Holden is a reunion that several of the miners and townsfolk who lived and worked there put on every few years. They bring their children and grandchildren to this beautiful place to visit the museum, to hike to the lakes and streams where they once camped and fished, and to discuss the good old days.

The Mines

The Eastern Side of Lake Chelan

The Meadow Creek mining area is located above the east side of Lake Chelan, directly across from Railroad Creek. The mines range in altitude from near the shoreline at 1,100 feet[21] to as high as 6,000 feet. This area is part of the Chelan/Sawtooth Wilderness. Minerals are no longer claimable, and you should check with the local rangers about other regulations.

---

[20] The Washington Water Pollution Control Commission later became the Washington State Department of Ecology.

[21] Several small prospects that were once at or near the shoreline of Lake Chelan are now underwater. The construction of the Chelan Dam raised the level of the lake by several feet.

In 1965, the remains of the Holden Mine were quickly deteriorating. This locomotive has been vandalized and cannibalized to the point where little remains. The remnants of the mill building forms the backdrop. (Phil Woodhouse photo)

The topography is, in a word, rugged. The nearest road ends high above Safety Harbor, about 12 miles south of Meadow Creek. Hike ratings range from A-1 through E-5. This area can be reached only by boat, floatplane, or Trail #1247, which runs along the eastern shore of the lake beginning at a point near Prince Creek.

The geology is essentially the same as the Railroad Creek area, and the ores sought contained copper, gold, zinc, and silver.

Blue Jay and Blue Jay Extension Claims

Rated at B-3 from the shore of Lake Chelan. This property, once consisting of more than eight claims, is situated along the east bank of Meadow Creek (in the south ½ of Section 1, T31N, R18E). At least two adits of unknown length are on the property. Assays show values in gold, silver, and copper.

Emma Lee Prospect

Rated at B-3 from the shore of Lake Chelan. This prospect lies on Meadow Creek, near the Blue Jays, and has values in gold, silver, and copper.

Gem Claim

Rated at B-3 from the shore of Lake Chelan. This claim lies east of the Blue Jays (in the northwest ¼ of Section 12, T31N, R18E). It produced showings of copper, gold, and silver.

Grace mine

Rated at B-2 from the shore of Lake Chelan. This property, which once consisted of six or seven claims, has two adits, one 146 feet long and the other 13 feet long. It is located on Cascade Creek (in the southeast corner of Section 1, T31N, R18E). The amount of production is unknown. Values were in copper, silver, and gold.

Hunter Claims

Rated at A-1 from the shore of Lake Chelan (in the southwest ¼ of Section 12, T31N, R18E). These claims are just north of the mouth of Cascade Creek. They produced showings of silver, gold, and copper.

By 1965 the Holden mill was quickly succumbing to the elements. Much of the structure has been removed as salvage, and not much remains. The classifier vat still rests on its foundations in the foreground. (Phil Woodhouse photo)

The mill tailings at the Holden Mine in 1965. The surface is so large that light aircraft use it as an airfield, both landing and taking off from its surface. It is estimated that millions in gold and silver lie trapped within the tailings. The Forest Service will not allow a cyanide plant to be operated due to the obvious risk. (Phil Woodhouse photo)

Idaho Prospect

Rated at C-5 from the shore of Lake Chelan, this prospect, consisting of two claims, is situated at 6,330 feet elevation (in Section 1, T31N, R18E), on the upper reaches of Meadow Creek. If you want to undergo the punishment required to reach this site, you will find a 73-foot adit, which produced samples of ore containing values in copper, gold, and silver.

Orphan Boy Mine[22]

Rated at A-1 from the shore of Lake Chelan. Located adjacent to the Hunter Claims (in the southwest ¼ of Section 12, T31N, R18E) at the mouth of Cascade Creek, this property sports a 50-foot adit and a 10-foot incline. Ore samples produced showings in gold, silver, zinc, and copper.

Hidden Treasure Prospect

Rated at A-1 if the logging access road is still usable. This property is just west of the Chelan-Methow summit at nearly 6,000 feet in elevation (in the northwest ¼ of the southwest ¼ of Section 17, T30N, R21E). The 1997 Forest Service map of the Wenatchee National Forest indicates that it is not far from Road #8200. A 20-foot shaft on the property produced ore samples that had values in gold and silver.

King Solomon Mine

Rated at E-5. Don't confuse this mine with the other one of the same name in the Cle Elum mining area. The mine workings are located in the southeast ¼ of Section 36, T32N, R18E, between the elevations of 5,000 to 5,800 feet. They can be reached by trail starting at the mouth of Meadow Creek on the shore of Lake Chelan. These are patented claims. The ore mined was mainly copper, with small amounts of silver, gold, zinc, and cobalt.

Development

The underground workings consist of one 832-foot adit, two caved adits of 200 feet each, and a 10-footer. The mine operated during the late 1940s and early 1950s. No production records have been found.

Around 1955, King Solomon Mines Inc. held claims to various unpatented mines in this area. Among these were the Bismarck Prospect, located about 0.8 mile due east of the old Meadow Creek Lodge at an elevation of 2,300 feet; the Blue Jay Prospect, located 0.6 mile north and 65 degrees east of the lodge at an elevation of 2,400 feet; and the Grace Prospect, located about 1½ miles east of the lodge at an elevation of 4,000 feet. The Blue Jay and the Grace Prospects, mentioned above, are located several thousand feet to the south of the creek.

The company also owned the Moscow Prospect, which is ¼ mile east of Round Lake at 4,300 feet and has a 20-foot and a 10-foot adit, plus the Nebraska Prospect, with a 36-foot adit (Section 35, T32N, R18E). The company also owned mining properties at Wauconda, Washington, and uranium properties in Wyoming and New Mexico.

Sunday Morning Mine

Rated at B-3. This mine was located at the shoreline of Lake Chelan (in the southwest ¼ of Section 2, T31N, R18E), at the base of a cliff. The property consists of one claim that was mined during 1897 by J. R. Moore. The deposit contains a quartz vein one to five feet wide with a two-to-four-inch pay streak of ore. The main minerals contained copper, silver, lead, and gold. Production records indicate that about 4,600 pounds of ore were shipped from the mine. The area can be reached only by boat.

---

[22] There was a cabin on this property in 1947.

Copper King/ Safety Harbor Mine

Rated at E-4. The Copper King Mine is located in the southeast ¼ of Section 31, T31N, R20E. The mine workings are about 15 miles east of the summit of the Cascade Range and about four miles northwest of South Navarre Peak. South Navarre Peak is on Sawtooth Ridge, which runs southeast from the summit of the Cascade Range.

The mine can be reached by 5½ miles of steep trail from the end of Safety Harbor Creek in Miner's Basin. Road #82 on Green Trails Map #115 reaches the South Navarre Campground. If the road is not washed out or gated at some point, you can save several miles of steep hiking by taking it as far as you can.

The mine workings are all located at elevations above 6,000 feet and are on Forest Service property. (Some of the workings may be in wilderness area.)

History

The Copper King ledge was discovered and located by Harry H. Hunt and Peter Rabicharid (Hunt spells it "Robischaud" in the *Inventory of Washington Minerals, Vol. I*) on August 3, 1897. They named the claim the Alpha Quartz.

In 1898, Rabicharid sold his interest in the property to Hunt, who worked the claim until 1917 when he sold out to Crooker Perry. Perry later became involved in the Holden Mine and owned several small mining prospects near the town of Chelan.

We don't know whether any development work was done on the property between then and 1931 when a small stamp mill was installed and operated during the summer and fall. A small amount of copper-gold concentrate was extracted, but research proved that commercial production was not warranted. No amalgamation took place, and it is doubtful that any commercial quantity of ore was shipped, due to the remoteness of the area.

Development

Development work done on the claim consists of several hundred feet of trenching, as well as a few open cuts.

The underground workings amount to two tunnels dug by Hunt, one containing about 360 feet of crosscutting and 200 feet of drift, and another with about 150 feet of crosscutting. One is at an elevation of 6,000 feet, and the other is 6,166 feet above sea level.

The Perry workings consist of one tunnel about 120 feet long at an elevation of 6,115 feet, and many drill holes at various elevations throughout the property.

> **Note** Department of Natural Resources unpublished data files indicate that around 1955 the Western States Uranium Company held six claims in the same area as this property, so they may have been one and the same as the Perry workings.

Production

We have found no record of production and assume that the only ore removed from the property was small samples for assaying purposes.

Other Mines and Prospects

The Meadowlark is located at lake level, around 1,100 feet. The Meadow Creek Strike and the Phyllis Prospect lie along the creek at somewhat higher elevations.

Around the turn of the century, hundreds of small mining claims were located in the areas above the Holden Mine, near Stehekin, in Horseshoe Basin, and above Safety Harbor. This is really rugged territory requiring good route-finding skills and plenty of common sense.

Remember that our hike ratings are only a guide, not to mention that spring runoff and avalanches can change trail conditions, if there are trails at all. The trails to many of these properties are now either overgrown or have slid down the mountainsides. Before setting off to any of these locations, always let someone know *exactly* where you are going and when you will be back. Check with local ranger stations for weather reports and trail information. If there is a trailhead box, be sure you sign in. There is a Forest Service shelter located at the southern mouth of Meadow Creek that can be of assistance if you run into trouble.

Chiwawa Mining Area

The Little Wenatchee, White, and Chiwawa Rivers drain into the Chiwawa mining area. It is bounded on the west by the Cascade Mountain Crest, on the east by the Entiat Mountains, on the north by Railroad Creek, and on the south by Miners Ridge. Elevations range from about 2,000 feet to over 8,000, and while summer temperatures get up into the high-80s to mid-90s, winter brings below-zero cold and heavy snowfall from November to late April. Light brush and abundant ponderosa pine predominate in the lower elevations, western larch and lodgepole pine in the medium elevations, and subalpine fir higher up in the hills and valleys.

History

Prior to the turn of the century, placer mining was common in and around the Phelps Creek area. In 1892, a five-foot vein of chalcopyrite ore was discovered in Una Basin north of what is now Trinity. The Una Basin Mining and Milling Company formed to explore and develop it. However, the value of the ore was found to be mostly in copper. Gold values, which were mainly of interest, showed from $2.75 to $275.00 per ton near the surface but quickly diminished to almost nothing as depth increased.

In 1901, another large, low-grade copper deposit was discovered by pioneer prospector J. J. Ross on Red Mountain, so named for its color, and the North Star Mining Company was formed.[1] But the only mining the company did was along Phelps Creek 4½ miles above its confluence with the Chiwawa River, at workings called the Leprechaun tunnel, located west of the confluence of Leroy and Phelps Creeks.

In 1905, the Chelan Consolidated Copper Company was organized and capitalized at $12 million by eastern investors who had gained a controlling interest in these mining claims and to others to the south of the Leprechaun workings adjacent to Chipmunk Creek. In 1906, the new company began driving a tunnel on the southern claims and proposed building a railroad from the Great Northern tracks to its claims at Red Mountain, hinting that it would possibly extend over the mountains via Buck Creek Pass and continue down to Darrington on the west side. Although this railroad never materialized, a wagon road was completed to the company's mine in 1907, mostly along the path of the current road. Also that year, a 40-horsepower water-powered air compressor was installed to run an Ingersoll air drill.

Fifteen men worked to drive the tunnel around the clock. But the mine never paid off, probably because there were no funds to build a suitable camp and crosscut tunnel to the lode in a safe location. The camp had been set up in an area of serious avalanche activity, and mining the property on a year-round basis, necessary for the operation to make a profit, would have been impossible at this site.[2] In addition to the geographic precariousness of this enterprise, we believe that the Chelan Consolidated Copper Company had overextended its resources at that time because it was also involved financially in the Sunset Mine near Index in Snohomish County. This combination of unfortunate circumstances forced the termination of all the company's mining activities in the Chiwawa District.

Around 1910, Father Francis J. Naughten, a Catholic priest[3] from Hornell, New York, decided to look into the mining potential of the property. (Naughten had previously been an investor in the North Star Mining Company and in the Chelan Consolidated Copper Company.) He hired a mining engineer by the

---

[1] We have been unable to determine the amount of development North Star did, but it held the property until 1905.

[2] Moreover, there was considerable water in the tunnel, making the sinking of shafts or underhanded stopes from this level very unfeasible.

[3] The involvement of Father Naughten probably explains the Christian names associated with this operation.

name of Phillip Lonergan to make an exhaustive examination of the Red Mountain area, with the assistance of a crew that included Naughten's brother James. The examination and surface prospecting cost Father Naughten $15,000, but it also convinced Lonergan that a marvelous and minable ore body was there.

In 1914, the Royal Development Company was formed from the old Chelan Copper Company.[4] In 1918, work was rekindled on what we believe may have been the old Chelan tunnel, and the mine was renamed the St. Francis. While work progressed on the St. Francis tunnel, where the chalcopyrite was said to look like a band of brass around the tunnel, work had already begun at the nearest suitable spot for a town site, soon named Trinity (nicknamed Trinity Camp).

Because of the steep terrain and severe avalanche danger in the St. Francis area, as well as the steep road grade to the site, it was decided to relocate the camp. The new town site and mill were moved near the confluence of Phelps Creek and the Chiwawa River below the southeastern flank of Red Mountain (Phelps Ridge) on a relatively low and safe slope. From this location, a crosscut tunnel to tap the ore body at depth would be driven.

Over the next decade, a 25,000-foot-per-day sawmill, hydroelectric power plant with diesel backup, mess hall, commissary, clubhouse, laboratory, dry house, cool house for perishables, blacksmith, stables, barn, and other buildings necessary to house up to 300 people were built. The town also boasted modern houses and cabins to accommodate married men and their families.[5] In all, the settlement amounted to about 40 buildings. The company also had plans to increase the size of the town to accommodate over 1,000 people.

For whatever reason, all the buildings in the town were painted battleship gray. Not only was the color unusual, but just the fact that buildings in a mining camp were painted at all was surprising. By the beginning of 1927, nearly $372,000 had been spent on claims, roads, building construction, and equipment. Unlike most remote mining camps, the miners living in the bunkhouse enjoyed electric lights in every room and above each bed. They slept in beds, rather than bunks, and had access to hot showers at all times and plenty of the very best food money could buy. For entertainment, a 500-volume library, a talking machine, hundreds of records, and a powerful radio were on site, along with card games and a pool table. To publicize the mine, a paper called *The Royalist*, which described the work and fortunes of enterprise, was occasionally printed.

The company's plan called for boring a long crosscut tunnel from the new town site for a distance of over 11,000 feet to a point under the St. Francis ore body. From there, a raise would be driven upward, using gravity to assist in the removal of ore. This tunnel would also serve as a haulage way into the mine for workers and equipment and a way out for ore and waste rock. Once the St. Francis lode was reached, the crosscut would be extended another 36,000 feet to explore other suspected ore bodies under Red Mountain.[6] The company believed that just the gold and silver in the mountain would pay for all mining operations, and the copper value, running as high as 40 pounds of copper per ton, would be pure profit.

The work on the Trinity tunnel began in September 1923. The money for this development came from the sale of stock to several New York investors, who were friends and relatives of Father Naughten. The par value of the stock sale was then invested in federal, state, and municipal bonds, which were held in the company treasury, while the extra above par cash and the interest from the bonds were used to develop the property. Net worth was around $4 million, represented by an equal amount of stock shares at $1 par value. To augment the company stock when it was decided to drive the long Trinity tunnel, the company introduced another form of financing called "Participating Contracts and Royalty Certificates." These units called for the holder to receive a royalty of 20 cents a share on every ton of ore extracted from the mine. They were expected to yield the investor about 15 percent per annum. (Although several shipments of ore were made from the mines, it's unlikely these unit holders ever received much, if anything,

---

[4] During the operation of the company, Reverend Naughten was president and Lonergan was chief engineer, while James Naughten served as superintendent.

[5] Some of these houses were built as sturdily and were as comfortable as most homes in larger cities, with modern bathrooms, electrically heated hot water, and lights. Several of the houses are in good condition and were still in use in 1998 by the current owners and the caretaker.

[6] The proposed extension beyond the St. Francis was never undertaken.

This picture of the Royal Development Mine at Trinity was taken when the main crosscut tunnel had been driven only 5,000 feet toward the ore body. The tunnel ultimately was run 11,000 feet before it reached its goal. The adit is directly in front of you as you look at the center of this photo. (*Mining Truth* magazine, August 2, 1926)

from the receipts.) Although the venture appeared safe because of the bonds backing it, some people felt it was still a risky proposition because there was no guarantee that the St. Francis ore body would extend to the depth of the Trinity tunnel.

In the 22nd Annual Report of the U.S. Geological Survey 1900–1901, published in 1902, Josiah E. Spurr threw a big wrench into the entire Cascade Mountains mining scene when he stated that the nature of the ore bodies was such that they would decrease in value as depth was attained. This report caused many investors to strongly doubt that the St. Francis lode would be struck 1,000 feet below by the Trinity crosscut. In addition, only the par value of the stock ($1.00) was backed by the bonds, not the price most investors actually paid for it. These risks were enough to cause the fledgling company a lot of problems later, since the funds had been spent on developing the camp and the Trinity crosscut tunnel. The meager, token production began to aggravate investors.

The property consisted of 112 claims, 22 of which were patented, including the town site, and another property called St. Ann's, located at Chikamin Creek some 12 miles downstream from Trinity. At this location, there was a large halfway cabin, and the construction of a smelter was planned.[7] This big building was a welcome sight for travelers crossing the great expanse of backcountry between Leavenworth and Trinity, especially during the long, cold winters when snow drifted and piled up many feet high. The company also owned about 25 acres in Leavenworth for loading sites. It obtained power station water rights from the Wenatchee River, plus a tract in Wenatchee near the Great Northern right-of-way and a lot in Seattle.

The 11,000 foot crosscut tunnel that ran from Trinity to the St. Francis workings contained an electric railway, and was single track most of the way. To allow trains to pass, every few thousand feet the tunnel widened and a siding, as seen here, was used. The electrical trolley wires can be clearly seen in this photo, as a load of rock is hauled past. (The Trinity collection, North Central Washington Museum, Wenatchee, Washington)

---

[7] A railroad was planned to connect the two sites.

The powerhouse at the Royal Development Mine at Trinity, Washington. The water wheel, located in the far casing, was built by the Pelton Company. The AC generator, the larger machine on the near end of the assembly, is a General Electric unit capable of producing 250 kilowatts. Between the two is a flywheel that absorbs any sudden load changes. The small machine nearest to the viewer is the exciter that produced the direct current for the field coils in the generator. The complicated-looking piece of machinery, driven by the flat belt and located between the penstock valve and the Pelton wheel, is the fly-ball governor that would maintain the rotation of the shaft at a more or less constant speed. This power plant is still in operation in 2000, and is reportedly the longest continuously operating hydroelectric plant in Washington State. (The Trinity collection, North Central Washington Museum, Wenatchee, Washington)

The mine workings included the St. Francis tunnel on the east slope of Red Mountain, at an elevation of 3,000 feet; the old North Star Companies; the Leprechaun workings farther up Phelps Creek; and the Trinity tunnel 850 feet below the St. Francis workings. An option held by the old Chelan Mining Company on claims at the headwaters of Phelps Creek (east of Spider Gap) in the Spider Meadows area, owned by "Red Mountain Ole," was also exercised for an undisclosed sum.[8]

What to See

A long, dusty road takes you to where mountains rise thousands of feet from open, wooded valleys, which remain draped in winter snow long into the summer months. Fortress Mountain (8,674 feet high), Buck Mountain (8,573 feet), Carne Mountain (7,085 feet), and Chiwawa Mountain (8,459 feet) grace the surrounding ridges. In the middle of it all, between Phelps Creek and the headwaters of the Chiwawa River, lies Red Mountain, 7,600 feet high. Trails to Buck Creek Pass and Red Mountain offer the outdoor enthusiast ample opportunity to sample the terrain up close and personal. The forests are open, with little brush to impede the explorer's way. The creeks and rivers that flow through the area offer little in the way of rafting or other action water sports, but the fishing can be rewarding.

---

[8] Red Mountain Ole (John Smith by name) was an old prospector and trapper who prospected in the Chiwawa District and had a cabin there beginning in the late 1880s. His best-known claim was the Galena Claim in the Spider Meadows area, which he continued to work by lease after selling it to the Royal Development Company.

Getting There

To get to the Chiwawa District from the Seattle area, take US 2 east from Everett, cross Stevens Pass, and travel down the other side to the Lake Wenatchee exit at Cole's Corner. Follow the signs to the Goose Creek Campground, and take the road up the Chiwawa River to the Trinity town site,[9] which is located near the conjunction of Chiwawa River and Phelps Creek, and where the portal of the main haulage tunnel is located. The mine itself is inside Red Mountain almost two miles away.

The road splits to the left and right just before reaching Phelps Creek. The left branch takes you to the Buck Creek Pass trailhead, while the branch to the right will take you to the locked gate at Phelps Creek. Beyond this gate is private property. Do not proceed without permission. You will be able to see the remaining buildings on the Trinity town site from this point. The mountain just to your right is the end of Phelps Ridge, also known as Red Mountain.

To reach the St. Francis workings on Phelps Creek, turn around at the gate and drive 0.8 mile back down the road to a branch road that goes uphill to your left. Drive about two miles or so to where the road is washed out or gated. Park and continue on foot.

The road is in excellent condition beyond the washout, and mountain bikes should work well there. Walk or ride a mile or more along the road until you notice an old roadway dropping to your left toward Phelps Creek. Upon reaching the creek, you will see the workings on the opposite bank. You might also see what's left of a couple of railroad flat cars that were once used for a bridge to the workings. Avalanches over the years have twisted them beyond repair, mute testimony to the forces of nature. The St. Francis workings are on private land, so don't trespass. A timber company owns the claims as of this writing. Get permission before entry.

Geology

Although relatively small in area, the Chiwawa Mining Area consists of several geologic units. The largest of these contain pre-Upper Jurassic gneisses and quartz diorites. It is through this unit that Phelps Creek flows. On a line that runs east to west along the course of Phelps Creek, there is a narrow band of Mesozoic granitic rock that contacts the Jurassic gneiss for several miles. The Mesozoic rock also occurs elsewhere throughout the eastern portion of the district in the Jurassic gneisses. The Chiwawa River, flowing along the southern side of Red Mountain (Phelps Ridge), begins with its headwaters in the pre-Upper Jurassic gneisses and quartz diorites that Phelps Creek also flows through. Once the river joins with the waters of Buck Creek, it flows along the contact zone of the Phelps Creek unit and pre-Upper

Deep inside the Royal Development Mine, miners set shoring into place in one of the stopes. (The Trinity collection, North Central Washington Museum, Wenatchee, Washington)

---

[9] The Trinity site is privately owned and so is the mine, but not by the same people. The area is not open to any type of prospecting, and trespass is not tolerated.

The Trinity powerhouse as viewed from the sawmill. The power plant is located at the near end of the building, while the remainder of the facility contains the woodshop and other repair shops. (The Trinity collection, North Central Washington Museum, Wenatchee, Washington)

Jurassic metamorphic rock that consists largely of schists and silicates. The latter unit lies south of the river. The Royal Development Mine is centered in a breccia pipe, situated immediately west of Phelps Creek about 1½ miles north of the southern end of Red Mountain. Breccia pipes often originate deep within the Earth's crust, where extremely high temperatures and pressure cause the formation of minerals not often found on the surface. The formation of the pipe can sometimes allow these unusual minerals to reach the surface. (The Kimberlite Pipes of South Africa carry diamonds to the surface, for example.) It may have been partly for this reason that such interest was shown in the primary mine of the Chiwawa District, the Royal Development Company's mine at Trinity.

The Mines

Royal Development Mine/Trinity

Rated at A-1 to B-3. The first attempt at mining the ore in Red Mountain by Royal Development was to develop the St. Francis ore body high on the east side of the mountain where the body outcropped. The engineers and geologists believed that the ore body would increase in size and quality the deeper they went.[10] The plan for the success or failure of the Royal Development Mine hinged on two questions: whether the long Trinity crosscut tunnel, bored from the town site, would reach the St. Francis ore body at depth, and if so whether the zone would be large enough and rich enough to be profitably mined over a long period of time.

The Trinity tunnel was the main haulage and exploration tunnel, and it was driven from the southeastern end of Phelps Ridge, near the town site, northeast for over 11,000 feet (which took several years) to reach the zone directly below the St. Francis workings. The tunnel contained fresh air and compressed air and water lines for the drills, plus a series of fans and trolley tracks, and it was completely outfitted with

---

[10] They hoped that the ore body would be like the one then under development at the Holden Mine.

electricity.[11] Again, due to the dangerous avalanche conditions in the St. Francis Mine area, all work there ceased in inclement weather, whereupon all attention was directed toward the Trinity tunnel. This was one of the largest mining enterprises to be undertaken in the state up to this time, and all eyes in the mining community were watching.

Mining at the St. Francis workings consisted of about 750 feet of crosscutting and 300 to 400 feet of drifting. (Exact measurements can't be taken because the St. Francis tunnel is now caved a few hundred feet in, and digging past it has been deemed too dangerous.)

Mining at the Trinity tunnel began at the end of the long crosscut at a point where the tunnel encountered the lower portion of the St. Francis ore body. This is over two miles from the portal. There, a raise was driven and eventually connected to the upper workings at the St. Francis level, 836 feet above. This raise was completed on August 8, 1936. The ore found in this area was very low grade, not what the operators and investors had hoped to find.

Exploratory work was also done around and beyond the raise on the lower and intermediate levels, from several exploration drifts and inclined raises. In fact, the Trinity tunnel,[12] after reaching the St. Francis ore body, swung in a large loop through the workings, which allowed for the consist of ore cars to make a circle through the mine rather than having to be loaded and then turned around—an interesting innovation.[13]

By 1927, the company began construction of a mill (250 tons per day) at Trinity for concentrating the ore, but it was not completed until 1931.[14] Meanwhile, plans were made to build a smelter at the St. Ann town site, several miles down the Chiwawa River from the mine—a rather ambitious undertaking for a mine that was so unproven and contained so little known ore. In 1928, news reached Wenatchee and Spokane that indeed the St. Francis ore body had been reached in the Trinity tunnel and ore shipments would begin soon. An article in the November 1928 *Mining Truth* magazine adamantly disputed this story and indicated the information was premature and of unknown origin. It went on to say that ore had been struck in the tunnel, but it was not the St. Francis ore body.

Mining at Trinity was conducted in a very relaxed way, and the miners were paid good wages. One of the newspapers in the Chelan area reported that "the Royal Development Mine is not hiring, and just about the only way to get a job up there is to have some-one [sic] die."

With the problem of this remote mining town being located some 50 miles from the nearest liquor establishment and a camp full of imbibing residents who would often disappear with their paychecks for a few days to satisfy their thirst, the company managers decided to bring alcohol into Trinity for the craving populace. Once prohibition came along, moonshine became the drink of the day and the law was on the

Skiers pose for a picture at St. Ann on Chikamin Creek located 12 miles downstream from Trinity. (The Trinity collection, North Central Washington Museum, Wenatchee, Washington)

---

[11] This is one of the longer mine tunnels in the United States: the Sutro tunnel in Nevada is 22,000 feet long, the Snake Creek tunnel in Utah is 14,000 feet long, the Elton tunnel, also in Utah, is 24,000 feet long, and the Argo tunnel in Colorado is 22,000 feet long.

[12] In several places, the Trinity tunnel was made double-wide to accept two side-by-side tracks. This allowed mining trains to pass each other in the long bore.

[13] The ore car train was powered by electricity transmitted through the workings on overhead wires.

[14] Mill construction was delayed because the mill had to be designed for the particular ore that is to be concentrated. So, until the ore body was reached and samples taken, the proper equipment could not be procured.

lookout for moonshiners as well as bootleggers.[15] This created a distribution problem until a man and woman dressed as a priest and nun were able to pass a load of White Lightning undetected and without suspicion though the countryside. On another occasion, a driver apparently died of alcohol poisoning on the road while delivering a load of spirits.

When we last visited the mine, the area beyond the crosscut in the Trinity workings was flooded to a depth of around 2½ feet, and a good portion of what was once the roof of the tunnel was on the floor and underwater, making exploration past the inclines extremely dangerous.

> **Warning Bad Ground!** Please do not enter the crosscut in the Trinity workings. In addition to being private property, this area of the mine is one of the most dangerous places we have ever explored. The current owners of the town site have told us that they are considering damming the Trinity tunnel at the portal, allowing it to become flooded, and using it as a water source in the event of forest fires. This sounds like a *very good* plan to us.

It looks like most of the copper that was taken from the mine came from the upper and intermediate levels, since little stope work was done at the Trinity level, or on the much-less-worked Leprechaun tunnel farther up the mountain. The money was there, but the huge, low-grade ore body was not.

By 1938, the company realized that further mining was futile. The mine was shut down, and the disposal of the property was left to the New York investors.[16]

Production

In October 1929, the first carload of unconcentrated ore was shipped from the mine, but there are no production records for that year.[17] *Inventory of Washington Minerals, Vol. I*, indicates that in 1930 and 1935 the mine shipped 10,000 tons of ore. In 1936, 5,825 tons were shipped, and in 1937 only 12 tons went to the ASARCO smelter in Tacoma, Washington.

The Mill

During the summer of 1930, much of the milling equipment was hauled into Trinity on large trucks. One piece of equipment, the Symons cone crusher, weighed over 11 tons.[18] The large ball mill had been positioned in front of the company office in Leavenworth at 10:00 A.M. on Saturday, August 16, 1930. By 5:30 P.M. of the same day, it was sitting at the mill site 42 miles away, quite a task for 1930-era trucks. Two 40,000-gallon oil storage tanks and two giant diesel engines were also delivered. In all, 1.78 million pounds of machinery and building supplies were moved during the summer of 1930 from Leavenworth to Trinity, and not a single piece was broken.

Ore from the Trinity Mine was said to average from two to eight percent copper, with some gold and silver present. The ore from the mine was taken to the crushing plant where it was dumped into a 350-ton coarse ore bin and through a 24-inch Webster-Brinkley traveling apron feeder and conveyor to a Union Iron Works shaking grizzly. From there, it was moved on to a Traylor 15×30 crusher set to three-inch size, whereupon it went by belt conveyor under a 30-inch magnet to a #4 Symons cone crusher set to ½ inch.

---

[15] In 1916, Washington State voters passed a law prohibiting the buying or selling of alcoholic drinks, which lasted until 1932. The federal government's prohibition was in effect from 1919 until 1933.

[16] In late 1997 while doing research on a different project, we came across a small pamphlet on a dusty back shelf of a Seattle bookstore: *The Miner, Chemist, and Engineer, Vol. 2 #5*, Nov. and Dec. 1940. It contains an article describing how in 1939 the Royal Development Company decided by a unanimous vote to dissolve the mining company and sell the mill and machinery, water rights and other properties, and cash in the U.S. Bonds. It also mentions that the company did this against the recommendations of its geologists and engineers, who had suggested additional core drilling.

[17] The concentrating mill had not yet been completed.

[18] The top of the crusher measured 14 feet above the road. Another piece weighed 14 tons, measured 8½ feet by 24 feet, and stood five feet high.

The bunk houses, commissary, cook house and shower house as seen from the power plant building at Trinity. (The Trinity collection, North Central Washington Museum, Wenatchee, Washington)

Standing on the road to the main crosscut tunnel of the Royal Development Mine, you would have seen this view of the Trinity town site, with the Chiwawa River valley beyond. In the foreground is the sawmill, and to the right the powerhouse. The bunk house, cook house, and shower houses are on the far left, while individual residences are in the distance. (The Trinity collection, North Central Washington Museum, Wenatchee, Washington)

The winding mechanism for the cage that ran the length of the raise between the crosscut haulage tunnel and the upper workings of the St. Francis tunnel 800 feet above. (The Trinity collection, North Central Washington Museum, Wenatchee, Washington)

From this unit, a long Webster-Brinkley 24-inch conveyor belt lifted the ore from the crushing plant to a separate building where the ball mill and flotation cells were located. There it was deposited into a 300-ton fine ore bin. Between this bin and the 8×48 Union Iron Works ball mill, there were a Harding constant-weight feeder, a Merrick Weightometer, the dry and wet reagent feeders, and a Geary Sampler. The ball mill product passed into an eight-foot Dorr Classifier and then to the 18-inch, 13-cell Union Iron Works flotation cells. The primary concentrates passed though a Wiffley pump to a 10-foot McIntosh cleaner cell, and then returned by the Union Iron Works pump to the ball mill or classifier as desired. The concentrates from the cleaner passed into a Dorr thickener, and the excess moisture was removed by a six-foot three-leaf American filter.

The Beginning of the End

Not long after the concentrating mill was completed in 1931, the company was thrown into receivership in Hornell, New York, where the Royal Development treasurer's office was located. This occurred because the company had technically violated its own by-laws by going into debt. It's likely that the newer improvements added to the property prior to full-scale production led the company to borrow against the property or to redeem some of the bonds held in trust, which were said to amount to $1,793,400.[19]

Whatever the reasons, the Royal Development Company was able to dodge the bullet for a while by leasing the mine to a Canadian concern that operated it on a small scale from 1931 to 1936. The action was taken by Waldo Longwell of Elmira, New York, a past company officer, who had filed a lawsuit to recover money that he had invested in the stock of the company.[20] The company countered by agreeing to suspend sale of stock until a competent engineer could make a study of the property, and declaring that for every share of stock issued, the par value of $1 would be invested in bonds. The annual income derived from those bonds amounted to approximately $60,000.00, which was sufficient to maintain the property and to retire the company debts by the coming spring (1932).

To add to the problems, the copper industry was not producing favorable financial results in the early 1930s as the Great Depression tightened its grip on the nation, and the outlook for low-grade deposits such as the Royal Development's was in question. The litigation continued through the 1930s, characterized by friction between the eastern stockholders and a group of western investors. By 1940, the much-heralded mining endeavor was all but finished. The mine had been shut down since 1937, and only a handful of people remained to watch over the lonely, little town. In the beginning, it had been promoted as "the one and only foolproof mining venture," given that its unique capital structure was so different from other companies. Nothing was ever supposed to happen to this mine in the way of litigation, court battles, or loss to the stockholders. But the Royal Development Mining Company ended the same way as thousands of other mining companies had.

---

[19] The Great Depression was then in full swing, and the panic it caused may have been a factor in the litigation.
[20] A similar suit was filed by James G. McLaughlin, also of Elmira, New York.

Miners in a cage in the Royal Development Mine at Trinity. It appears that the winding equipment was located at the crosscut, or lower, level and the cable was run under the sheave at the top of the picture, then up to the top of the shaft, over another sheave, and back down to the cage. (The Trinity collection, North Central Washington Museum, Wenatchee, Washington)

The bonds and most of the equipment were sold, the proceeds distributed to the stockholders at 85 cents on the dollar to cover the promised "par value" of $1.00 per share. The shareholders who had paid as much as $5 a share lost out as well as the holders of the Participating Contracts and Royalty Certificates, worth about $1.35 million, who likely lost everything despite a lawsuit to collect. In 1946, the property, buildings, and 102 mining claims were sold to Jesse Smith for $10,000.

Trinity Today

After Royal Development sold the property, it became a resort for a short time. The owners even installed a bowling alley in the old machine shop. The powerhouse at the town site still works. It is alleged to be the longest continually running water-powered electrical source in the United States—truly a marvel of early engineering.

Keefer Brothers Mine

Rated at E-5. The Keefer Brothers Mine is located on the west slope of Red Mountain, near the headwaters of the Chiwawa River, about one mile south of Lyman Glacier. It can be reached via seven miles of trail up the Chiwawa River from near the Trinity town site.

The property consisted of several unpatented claims ranging in elevation from 6,200 to 6,800 feet. Operations were sporadic between 1918 and 1948. We have never visited this property because of its remoteness and high elevation. Although the mine never produced anything of commercial value, it is worthy of mention because of the many different minerals that were found there.

The main ore sought contained molybdenum, but also present in varying amounts are copper, gold, silver, tungsten, uranium, lead, zinc, nickel, cobalt, antimony, and chromium. *Inventory of Washington Minerals* shows some extremely high assays, and we assume that mining never took place because the high altitude and remoteness of the site prevented the operators from constructing a mill nearby. Several hundred feet of underground workings are reported to be on the property, which consisted of numerous unpatented claims. This should be another good location for rockhounds.

Una Claims

Rated at C-4. These consist of several claims in the Spider Meadows area toward the head of Phelps Creek. When we visited the Trinity area in 1995, the road leading to Spider Meadows and up to the mine was closed to vehicles near the St. Francis workings about two miles off Trinity Road.

The main buildings in Trinity. The structure on the far left is the bunk house/commissary, the building in the center is the cook house, and on the right is the bunk house/shower house. Notice the large amount of cordwood stacked on the porches. These buildings are now gone, but some houses remain and are now a private resort. Electricity from the hydroelectric plant is so plentiful that heaters under the metal roofs keep the snow off today's houses without shoveling. (The Trinity collection, North Central Washington Museum, Wenatchee, Washington)

Linston Mine

Rated at E-5. To reach the Linston Mine, located high above Spider Meadows at the headwaters of Phelps Creek, drive to the Trinity town site. Turn around at the gate and drive 0.8 mile back down the road to a branch road that goes uphill to your left. Drive about two miles or so to where the road is washed out or gated. Park and continue on foot. The road is in excellent condition beyond the washout, and mountain bikes should work well there. Walk or bike along the old road until it ends. Hike from there to Spider Meadows. You will be about five miles from your car at this point.

Continue, crossing Phelps Creek to the remains of Ed Linston's cabin as you ascend the side of Red Mountain. You will encounter a fork in the trail. Take the left fork and make the exhausting climb to the base of Spider Glacier. Ascend the rock spur to the east of the snowfield to 7,100-foot Spider Gap. The rock in this area consists of a spider web of white granite laced through a groundmass of dark gneiss. The white granite also contains lenses of the darker material. From here, you can look north down to Lyman Lake and 9,511 foot Bonanza Peak, the highest nonvolcanic mountain in Washington State.

From Spider Gap, a ¼-mile trail *ascends* to Ed Linston's mine tunnel. The machinery that he laboriously hauled to this lofty site litters the area. We are not certain that the mine was actually named the Linston, though it belonged to him. At one point, Ed was injured in a dynamite explosion at the mine. His brother helped him down off the mountain, where he ultimately recovered, going on to spend many years exploring the Cascade Mountains. He died in 1969 at the age of 82.

Drilling deep inside the Royal Development Mine at Trinity. The drill is attached to a jack that holds it in place, and driven forward with a hand screw. (The Trinity collection, North Central Washington Museum, Wenatchee, Washington)

> **Warning** Most of the mines in this district are located at high elevations in areas that are associated with *extreme* avalanche danger.[21] They are to be avoided during the spring and early summer months.

Georgie Smith Mine

Not rated. Located at the head of Deep Creek (Section 17, T27N, R18E) and accessible by trail. The property consisted of nine claims owned by the Monterey Gold and Milling Company (1897). Developed by only 40 feet of crosscut tunnel, gold values were reported to be very high.

The majority of these properties are now abandoned because the ores mined required that milling facilities be located nearby. But because of heavy snowfall, avalanches, and a short operating season, this never proved to be feasible. As luck would have it, many of these sites contain some of the finest mineral specimens in the state. Some of the mines were patented and some were not. Check to see which are private and which are public.

Other Operations

In the fall of 1907, the Chiwawa Mining Company began driving a tunnel on a vein of galena and silver, located on the east side of Phelps Creek opposite the St. Francis workings. This drift was said to have been bored a distance of 1,300 feet straight into the mountain using a 25-horsepower water-driven air compressor, supplying power to a new machine drill.

The camp was built on the banks of Phelps Creek 300 to 400 yards from the portal. It consisted of a comfortable bunk house, cook house, office building, power house, blacksmith shop, and assay office, all sturdily built using hewn logs. The actual location of this mine is unknown at this time.

On Rock Creek, eight miles below Trinity and ½ mile from the confluence with the Chiwawa River is the P I Prospect, with its 60-foot adit. Another claim located about a mile up Rock Creek from its mouth and on the left bank 500 or more feet above it is said by local miners to be haunted. Check it out yourself, if you dare.

The Rock Creek "Ghost" photo as mentioned above. Use your own judgement as to what you see in the photo. (Jim Marr Jr. collection)

---

[21] As of this writing, the U.S. Forest Service backcountry avalanche forecast can be reached at (206) 526-6677. The mountain pass report: (206) 434-7277, and U.S. Forest Service campground information: (800) 280 CAMP. The Chelan County Ranger District: (509) 682-2576, and the Lake Wenatchee Ranger District: (509) 763-3103.

We have heard reports of strange happenings from latter-day prospectors as well as people who have camped overnight near the site. These folks have experienced eerie feelings and have heard and seen figures resembling Native Americans and Spanish Conquistadors. There are rumors that a battle involving Native Americans took place in this area possibly during the 1700s, and others have said that the area may contain a Native American burial ground.

In September 1999, we were given a copy of a photograph taken at Rock Creek in the mid-1970s when a group of Yakima prospectors and miners were conducting core drilling and other prospecting activities at a claim called the Gossen 4. They told us that for several days two dogs they had brought along had been acting very strangely. The dogs would be sleeping, but then would suddenly wake up and start to bark at the ground and neighboring hillside, seemingly at nothing. The wives of some of the men felt "creepy" at the site too.

Several photographs were taken of the mining operation, and clearly evident in the pictures are a face in the rocks and what appears to be a human skull, as well as a figure that looks like a priest or monk wearing a long, black robe with a high upturned collar, among other strange things. Most people who look at the photo without our telling them anything about it ask who the "three" people are, not knowing that only "two" are human. (One strange object or face would be interesting in itself, but *several?*) It is our sincere belief that this photo has not been altered or otherwise tampered with and that it is authentic. Examine it yourself and draw your own conclusions.

The property was believed to have been worked by Chinese miners many years ago. It consists of two tunnels, one about 150 feet in length and the other about 60 feet long.

To visit the place where this picture was taken, proceed as if traveling to Trinity until you reach the Chikamin Creek Campground and the Rock Creek Horse Camp. Follow the old mine road until you reach a hard switchback to the left marked Estes Butte. At a point about two more switchbacks up, turn right (east) and enter a draw. At this point, you should see two mine tunnels. The area where the photo was taken is 200 feet above the portals and will be recognizable from the evidence of core drilling. You'll be dealing with some steep and rugged terrain here, so be careful. During our examinations of this property, we noticed many signs of bear, so exercise caution.

On Maple Creek in Section 10, T29N, R16E, near its mouth is the Champion Prospect. The claim has two reported tunnels, each about 300 feet in length. Aside from that, only a couple dozen prospect pits and short adits remain in what was once said to be the most promising district in the state.

Chelan Butte and Entiat Mining Areas

Chelan Butte lies almost directly southwest of the city of Chelan, between Lake Chelan and the Columbia River. Its highest point is a lookout tower at 3,835 feet above sea level.

Some of the mines here are located on private property, so get permission before entering them. We rate the hikes in these areas between A-1 and B-3.

> **Warning** Watch out for rattlesnakes.

The Entiat Mining Area is located just to the north of the Wenatchee Area. The only recorded production in the district came from the Rex Mine. The amount of free-milling gold taken from placers along the Entiat and Columbia Rivers during the early 1870s, when white as well as Chinese miners prospected and mined this area, was not recorded. The heart of the area is easily accessible by taking US 97 Alternate north from Wenatchee up the Columbia River to the Entiat River Road. Drive this road to the Crum Canyon Road, and turn east into the canyon to visit the sites of the hardrock mines in the area.

You may find that the USGS 7.5 Minute map of the Ardenvoir Quadrangle comes in handy, especially if you try to navigate the maze of roads winding through the canyons. Some of the properties are on state land (DNR) and some are on federal Wenatchee National Forest land. Also remember that getting to the Crum Canyon area will require you to travel on private property. Please respect the signs and watch for snakes.[1]

History

The Chelan Butte Gold Rush

Although mining dates back to the 1800s, on April 19, 1907, the *Chelan Leader* newspaper announced that free gold had been discovered on Chelan Butte. This set off a small gold rush in the area. On May 3, the paper reported:

Local interest in the gold discovery shows no sign of lagging; on the contrary, it seems to grow more intense with each day's developments.

Sunday, the big hill was literally peopled with men, women and children, all eagerly seeking the shortcut in the road to wealth. "On May 17, the paper did a story on a ledge so rich in the yellow metal that experienced miners were predicting assays as high as $10,000 and $20,000 to the ton. On August 27, the Chelan Leader reported that gold had been found in chicken gizzards: "Poultry grown at the base of this hill [Chelan Butte] continues to yield returns of placer gold whenever a bird is killed. One bird alone was reported to contain some 20 or more nuggets the size of BB shot.

The gold rush largely died in the following year, but minor prospecting continued through 1935. In 1926, when the Washington Water Power Company bored a tunnel under Chelan Butte to carry water from Chelan Dam to the powerhouse on the Columbia River, the old prospectors eagerly examined the rock that was blasted from the mountain. They found no gold.

---

[1] We have been told that many years ago a Native American trail led from the Entiat District all the way to Cascade Pass through this region.

What to See

The Chelan Butte and Entiat areas transition from dry, desert brush along the Columbia River to open pine forest at higher elevations. The blue of the river contrasts strikingly with the muted reds and browns of the surrounding land. If you climb onto the southern flanks of Chelan Butte, you will be rewarded with views of the Columbia River. If you ascend the northern side, you will see breathtaking scenery along Lake Chelan. The Entiat area takes you deeper into the highlands and the pine and tamarack forests. It also, unfortunately, has been ravaged by several forest fires over the last decade.

Remember, this is hot, dry country in the summertime. Be very careful with fire, and take plenty of water along. Think "desert" when hiking here in the summer, and wear appropriate head cover. A broad-brimmed straw hat works well.

This is mostly hiking and climbing country, although hunting in season may also be an option. The lake and river provide fishing as well.

Getting There

You travel to this area by taking the route to Chelan. Drive to Wenatchee and take US 97 Alternate north first to Entiat, and then to Chelan Butte. From the north, drive down US 97 until it splits into US 97 Alternate. Take the Alternate through Chelan to Chelan Butte, and then to Entiat.

Geology

Most of the gold that was recovered in the Chelan Butte area seems to have been free-milling and was carried in quartz. However, a small amount of ore was shipped to the Tacoma smelter from various mines in the early 1900s. Wire gold was also reportedly found here.

The oldest rock in the Entiat mining area is known as Swakane gneiss and is believed to be pre-Ordovician in age. It is intruded by Chelan granodiorite. Free gold, the chief metal, occurs with quartz in veins cutting the Swakane gneiss. Native silver, cinnabar, ilmenite, and nickel-rich pyrrhotite occur in the ores in varying amounts. There is lots for the rockhound to explore.

Before the construction of the dams along the Columbia River, two large rapids in this area caused havoc for travelers, the Entiat and Methow rapids. Entiat means "fast waters" in the local Native American language.

At one time, Entiat was the state's largest mining district in the area, occupying 790 square miles but boasting only one productive mine. As mentioned earlier, a good deal of placer mining took place all along the Entiat River, but no records were kept of that production. Chinese prospectors were known to have mined all along the Entiat River between the Columbia River and the town of Ardenvoir during the mid-to-late 1800s.

Chelan Butte Area Mines

Gold Mine Gulch

Almost all of the mining done on Chelan Butte occurred in an area referred to locally as Gold Mine Gulch. This is a rugged canyon running from near the summit of the butte down its northeast side to the Columbia River. The gulch is about 2½ miles long and drops almost 3,300 feet.

In the gulch near the summit, the Lost Vein or Higgins Mine is reportedly located. Its tunnel is said to be in the west wall, with the mine dump forming a dam across the canyon. There was a stamp mill located near the portal, as well as a panning table for separating free gold from ore before packing it down the hill for shipment to the smelter. A bunkhouse, cook house, and other buildings that served the mine were built at the base of the canyon.

The mine is reported to consist of several hundred feet of tunnel and a winze or underhanded stope of unknown depth. Another mine, possibly the Pigeon Wing Mine, is above the Higgins Mine and on the north side of the canyon near the saddle.

Mr. M. M. Kingman reportedly brought out (salvaged) by horse sled a Star engine, compressor, drills, and other mining tools by going up and over the saddle and down the north side of the Butte to Lakeside. He then placed them in the old Ferguson tunnel, wherever that may be. Another mine tunnel is reported to be east of Butte Road from Lakeside, at the foot of the Saddle.

If you study the current USGS 7.5 Minute Series map for Chelan, you will find a canyon on the southern side of Chelan Butte that is composed of two gullies near the crest of the butte. The eastern branch begins just below the summit, while the western branch starts just below the ridge top about ½ mile south of the summit. These branches join to form the lower Gold Mine Gulch. Homestead Canyon, to the west of Gold Mine Gulch, is named on the map. The map shows that there is a prospect on the east wall at the head of Homestead Canyon. This places it in the center of Section 28, T27N, R22E. Another prospect is located in the south ½ of the south ½ of Section 27 at an elevation of 2,160 feet, high up a gully off the roadway.

Gold Bug Mine

Rated at A-3. The Gold Bug Mine was located in the head of Saddle Valley on the west face of what is referred to locally as "Huni Hogback." The description of this property matches the first prospect mentioned above. While we have not been to this location to verify its identity, you can obtain a copy of the Chelan USGS map and judge for yourself.

The extent of the mine workings is unknown, and its portal was reported to be collapsed in the early 1930s. However, a pocket of wire gold, reportedly worth $2,000, was taken from this property by M. M. Kingman and his partner, Mr. Pershall. This property might be the same as that mentioned in *Inventory of Washington Minerals* (See "Other Mines" below.)

The two-stamp mill used at the Rex Mine mill in Crum Canyon above the Entiat River. The slanted openings at the base of the mill were fitted with screens that would allow only the finely crushed ore to exit from the stamp chamber. The ore was mixed with water and introduced to the mill from the rear (left). The rotating flywheel drove a cam shaft whose cams alternately lifted and then dropped the stamps upon the ore. The resulting slurry that exited through the screens was collected in troughs and directed to riffle tables or other devices that separated the heavy gold from the base rock. The stamps usually dropped about 50 times a minute, or almost once a second. You can imagine the noise created by such a mill when in full operation. The flywheel was driven directly by a flat belt. (Victor Pisoni photo)

Butte Mine

Rated at A-3. The Butte Mine was located in Sections 25 and 26, T27N, R22E. It appears that the mine dates back to 1898, but that most of the work was done between 1909 and 1915, while the Chelan Butte Mining Company owned it.

Records show that the ore mined was gold, but no information has been found on how much, or whether it was free-milling.

Other Mines

Several other mines are reported to be on the butte, but information is very sketchy. The Cook Mine is supposedly somewhere in Section 25. The Keeler Mine is said to be in Homestead Canyon. The Deefy Lowe Prospect is reported to be on "one of the toes of Huni hogback." Another prospect called the Jumbo is

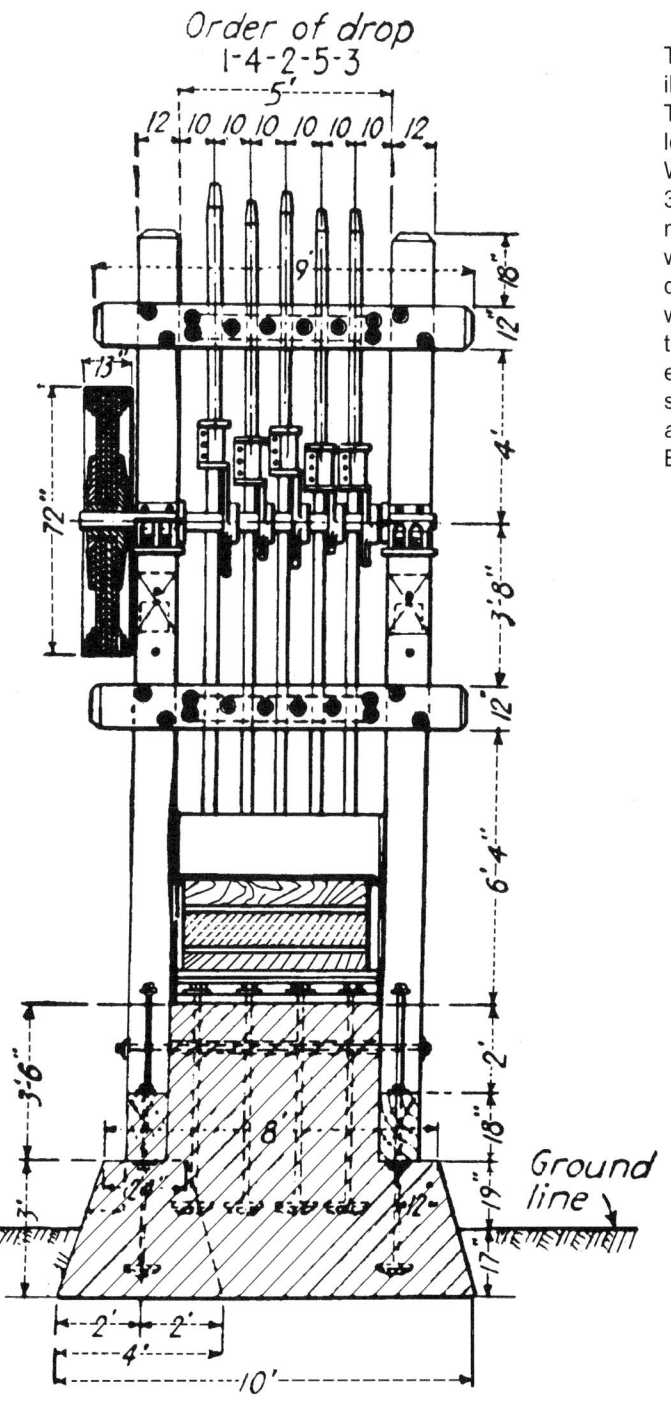

This diagram of a Joshua Hendy 5-stamp mill illustrates the basic construction of these devices. This one is very similar to the stamp mill that was located at the Rex Mine near the town of Entiat, Washington. In this model, each stamp weighed 300 pounds and could be dropped 40 to 50 times a minute. Ore was introduced to the cast-iron mortar with water, and the stamps caused to repeatedly drop upon it. The exit from the enclosed mortar was covered with a fine mesh screen so that only the pulverized ore could escape. Gold was then extracted by amalgamation, riffle tables, or other suitable devices. (From *Handbook for Prospectors and Operators of Small Mines*, by M. W. von Bernewitz, 1943)

somewhere on the Butte. The Kingman and Pershall Mine is mentioned in *Inventory of Washington Minerals* on page 114, but no location is given. Production was $15,000 in the 1890s.

No one has ever found the mother lode on Chelan Butte, but year after year claims have been filed on everything from silver, gold, and uranium to even quicksilver.

The Chelan Butte mining area is an interesting place to rockhound, do a little prospecting, or just plain gather in the history of this lesser-known region. Undoubtedly, some of the mines located here are on private property, so be sure to get the owner's permission before going there.

Entiat Mining Area Mines

Rex (or Rogers) Mine

Rated at A-1. The Rex Mine is located in the north center of Section 36, T26N, R20E. To reach this property, take US 97 Alternate to a point just south of the town of Entiat. Turn on the Entiat River Road (as of this writing, County Road #371), and travel a little more than seven miles. The Crum Canyon Road will head up to your right (as of this writing, it was County Road #301). Take the Crum Canyon Road approximately two miles until you come to a fork, where you can either continue straight ahead or take a right-hand turn. Take the turn and begin traveling downhill, eventually swinging to the right and crossing a small stream. Continue for another mile, and at an elevation of 2,100 feet, you're there.

The mine site is on the hillside just to the left of a wooden structure containing the remains of the stamp mill. On our visit to the site in 2000, we were amazed to find the two-stamp mill in such good condition, because it is several decades old. Just about everything was there except the motor. With a power source and a little WD-40, you could be stamping away by morning.[2]

The diggings consisted of several (we counted seven) short tunnels and two open pits, of which we could find only one.[3] Most of the tunnels were caved at or near the portals, with the exception of one across from the pit that was heavily shored and went in about 250 feet, and another, which had a door on it that extended about 50 feet in. (Jim Marr Jr., who once examined the property, remembers a tunnel leading off into the hill from the bottom of the open pit.) *Inventory of Washington Minerals, Vol. 1* lists three adits and 500 feet of tunneling. During our investigation of the property, nothing like this was in evidence.

Production

Although the Rex Mine dates as far back as 1906, records of production are pretty sketchy, though DNR documentation does indicate that prior to the year 1930 the mine produced $170,000. Most of the development was done between 1906 and 1922 by the Wenatchee Gold Mining Company.

This is the total recorded production for the entire Entiat Mining District. Even though the other lode mines were active over short periods of time, no production records exist for them.

Combining the district's placer mining with the recorded lode mine production, a good guess is that production amounted to less than 10,000 ounces of gold.

Sunshine Mine

Rated at A-1. This mine is in Section 36, T26N, R20E, and consists of 40 acres of leased state land. The elevation at the mine is 2,170 feet. It was said to have a 100-foot–deep shaft and a 730-foot–long tunnel.

When we visited the site in October 1997, the current lessors had erected two large ponds lined with carpet for collecting the free-milling gold. A large air compressor and other mining equipment were also there.

---

[2] It is a rare pleasure for us to come upon such an impressive artifact and not find it shot full of holes or otherwise vandalized—testimony to the integrity of the locals as well as previous visitors.

[3] On the USGS map of the area, there appears to be another large pit in the canyon to the east of the Rex Mine at an elevation of 2,400 feet.

The current lessors of the property told us that two brothers operated the mine sometime in the past. They did a considerable amount of tunneling before encountering a very high-grade vein of gold ore. An argument ensued, and one of the men reportedly blasted the workings shut. They did a pretty good job of it because as of 1998 the current operators had been unable to reenter the old workings.

You can find the mine easily by first driving to the Rex Mine stamp mill. Turn right just above the mill and follow the road to its end.

Savage Mine

Rated at A-2. The Savage Mine is located in Section 36, T26N, R20E. It is reachable via a short, steep road from the Sunshine Property. The property consisted of four claims, held under state land lease in 1918 by Mr. G. S. Savage. Development consists of a 100-foot–deep shaft and several short adits. The ore was said to contain free gold and free silver.

Pangborn Mine

Rated at A-1. The Pangborn Mine can be found 1½ miles south of the Rex Mine (in Section 36, T26N. R20E). Originally, the mine consisted of 80 acres leased from the State in 1938 by Mr. P. C. Pangborn. Development is a 180-foot tunnel, a 60-foot shaft, a 40-foot shaft, and several open cuts. The ore was free-milling gold and silver in several quartz veins, ranging in width from three inches to three feet. No production records are available.

Northwest Underground Explorations investigated the 40- and 180-foot adits that are located on the hill just above Sunshine Camp. They are situated to the west of the camp and up a rough dirt road. The 40-foot lower adit lies along the road and cannot be missed, but it is in a state of collapse and is of little interest.

The second adit, which represents the main workings, is located above and to the right of the lower tunnel. It can be reached by following the road around and over the hill to where it splits near a gully that drops down toward the Sunshine Camp below. Follow the road about 150 feet to the portal.

This mine is interesting in that the first 40 feet or so were dug by hand with a pick. To take a close look, stop about 15 feet inside, drop to your knees, turn around, and look up at the ceiling. Notice the miner's fine workmanship in the nicely rounded curve of the tunnel top, which was shaped using only a pick. Continue to the intersection where the left tunnel begins a 40-degree decline. Observe the old windlass station and the wooden roller just down the shaft where it turns back toward the right. This old roller was positioned to allow a skid to be drawn up the decline without jamming against the corner. If you descend farther into the decline, a stope, open to the upper level, will reward you with a view of a very rare, hand-built windlass that was used to lift ore and waste rock from the depths, probably before the decline was completed between the first decline and the top.

The upper tunnel leads to the remains of a collapsed stope, with stulls and platforms still intact. Although there is no known record of production from this mine, the stopes indicate that at least one carload was shipped from it. Outside the portal, you'll see the collapsed remains of yet another adit to the left. This tunnel is about 50 feet long but does not access any ore. The property includes another tunnel that is reportedly several hundred feet long but completely closed by rock and debris. The Pangborn is owned by the same people who own the Sunshine, and trespass is not permitted. Please seek permission from the owners before visiting. Their name and address can be found at the Washington State Department of Natural Resources in Olympia.

Dick Mine

Rated at A-2. The Dick Mine is located on the north side of Winesap Canyon, also known as Oklahoma Gulch (Section 9, T26N, R21E). This is also private property, so get permission before visiting. A range fire devastated this entire area in the 1990s.

History

The mine was located in 1898 by Mr. Condi Dick. It is not known what work was performed during the time he held claim, but it must have been enough to allow for the patenting of 80 acres. The mine was worked from 1942 to 1946 by a company out of Yakima, which we believe did most of the underground exploration.

Development

The mine workings consist of four adits, some trenching, and several diamond drill holes bored by the Bureau of Mines, which totaled over 1,000 feet. The ore mined contained nickel, cobalt, copper, and wire gold. This is one of the very rare nickel properties in Washington State.

The deposit is a body of peridotite about 400 feet long and 100 feet wide, enclosed in quartz diorite and gneiss, containing primary and secondary ore minerals. It is believed that the ore zone extends to over 50 feet in depth.

This mine, and the area surrounding it, deserves to be looked at by not only rockhounds but also the serious and professional prospector. Wire gold has been found in Winesap Canyon.

> **Warning** There are rattlesnakes throughout this region. Don't put your hands or feet into any enclosure. There could be a rattler sunning itself in any hidden spot. If you startle it, it will defend itself by striking at you.

Winesap Canyon Prospect

Rated at A-2. This small mine is located near the head of Winesap Canyon (in the southwest ¼ of the northwest ¼ of Section 5, T26N, R21E). It consisted of one unpatented claim. The ore was thought to contain uranium. The development consists of two caved adits and numerous open pits and trenches. Radioactivity occurs throughout this entire area. With a Geiger counter, who knows what you'll find? A great rockhounding area.

Winesap Nickel Prospect

Rated at A-2. This property can be reached by driving 0.8 mile up Winesap Canyon (Oklahoma Gulch) and following the deteriorating mine road about ½ mile up the hill on the right to the main tunnel, which is at an elevation of 1,450 feet. Now in a state of collapse, the workings penetrate the mountain for approximately 360 feet, including two drifts and the main tunnel. Fifteen feet from the portal, there is a winze that is 8 to 10 feet deep. Extra caution should be exercised here because the roof of the mine is in the process of coming down. It's best to stay out of this one altogether. The large dike that the miners were exploring is visible as you look up the gulch.

Returning along the mine road, you will encounter another caved adit 120 feet in length that we have not explored due to its condition.

Farther down the road at the next switchback, you can take a side trip for a couple of hundred feet up the mountain in a down-canyon direction to two other mine adits, which are both caved. The upper adit penetrates the mountain for a distance of 110 feet, and the lower one contains 240 feet of workings. It's possible that the adits are connected by raises below the surface. Above and around these two workings are numerous prospect pits and trenches, including a now-caved 25-foot–deep vertical shaft.

For the Rockhound

Many samples of malachite, bornite, nickel, and possibly pitchblende can be found in the dumps.

Wenatchee Mining Area

This chapter is dedicated to the memories of Howard Zude, John Porter, John Husband, and George Duncan.

The Wenatchee mining area lies in east central Washington State. It occupies approximately 320 square miles in southeastern Chelan County. Kittitas County is on its southern boundary, and the Entiat Mountains are on the northern boundary. The line between Ranges 18 and 19 East separates the Wenatchee District from other districts to the west. This is one of the least rugged mining districts, although elevation gains of 6,000 feet occur between the Columbia River and some of the highest peaks. The Columbia River divides the towns of Wenatchee and East Wenatchee and is also the dividing line for Chelan and Douglas Counties.

The climate is semi-arid, with average annual precipitation of nine inches and annual extremes in temperature ranging from -10 to 110 degrees Fahrenheit. A portion of the area south of Wenatchee is desert, with rolling hills populated by an abundance of rattlesnakes. The relatively mild climate, plentiful water (from the Columbia and Wenatchee Rivers) for irrigation, and fertile soil have contributed to the development of Wenatchee as a major agricultural (fruit-producing) center. The city prides itself as the "Apple Capital of the World."

History

The Native Americans

The history of the clash of cultures between immigrants of European and Asian origin and Native Americans is a sad and sometimes grim tale. In the early days of the Pacific Northwest, newcomers were called pioneers or settlers. By 1850, there were 13,000 white people and several thousand Native Americans living in the Oregon Territory.[1] Each had different lifestyles and very different religions.

After many skirmishes, the leaders of several tribes came to the inevitable conclusion that to fight the whites would be a losing proposition. They agreed to meet with a fellow named Isaac Ingalls Stevens at a great council near Walla Walla, Oregon Territory, to discuss treaty arrangements in the summer of 1855.

Stevens was a very ambitious young man. At 35 years of age, he stood only 5 foot 3, yet he held the posts of territorial governor, secretary of Indian Affairs, and head of the railroad survey expedition.[2] Stevens County is named in his memory.[3]

Realizing the futility, and knowing that many people would die on both sides if war broke out, the chiefs reluctantly signed with their marks. But the ink wasn't even dry on the treaty documents before things began to go wrong. Stevens was good at making promises but not very good about keeping them. Moreover, what Stevens and other people of European origin didn't understand was that, as far as the Native Americans were concerned, their Chief's signing of a document meant only that the chiefs had to abide by it; the other members of the tribe did not!

---

[1] In the 1840s, the area was first defined as the Oregon Territory. In 1853, the region now called Washington State, along with Idaho and part of Montana, was carved from it and named the Washington Territory. In 1859, the remainder of the territory became the state of Oregon. Washington became a state in 1889.

[2] Stevens sent Army Captain George McClellan to Snoqualmie Pass to see whether a railroad could be built over it to the Puget Sound. McClellan got as far as North Bend, where he ran into a group of Native Americans who told him there were over 25 feet of snow on the pass. He returned to Olympia and informed Stevens about the problem. Soon after, a party of men arrived in town after crossing the pass from the east, and told Stevens that there were only seven feet of snow and that it would make a great pass for a railroad. The government chose to believe McClellan's version over Steven's, and that's why it took so many years to get the railroad to Seattle.

[3] Some people think that Stevens Pass was named after him. This is incorrect. In 1884, Major A. B. Rogers located the right-of-way for the Great Northern Railway through the Rocky Mountains and on to the Pacific Coast. About this time he was severely injured in a fall from a horse. An engineer named John Stevens took over the work; Stevens Pass was named for him.

There also may have been a misunderstanding, partly because Stevens insisted that the negotiations be conducted in Chinook Jargon, which was essentially a trade language that almost all Native Americans and whites could understand. But it consisted only of a small number of words extracted from several local native dialects, English, and French, and no exact grammar. Even those who spoke Chinook Jargon very well could not express complicated ideas such as those involving land trades.

Problems escalated when the gold deposits in California become depleted and the transcontinental railroad was almost completed.[4] These two events alone put thousands out of work. Rumors of free gold brought droves of these and other people to the Northwest in search of the yellow metal. Then gold was discovered near Colville in northeast Washington, which resulted in a gold rush stampede across Native American land to reach the bonanza. Word spread quickly, even back then, when it came to new gold finds. By 1863, the population of eastern Washington was three times larger than that of the Puget Sound coastal lowland to the west. The reason, of course, was GOLD!

The Chinese section of a mining town in the American West. While often thought of as simply camp follows as indicated by the laundry on the right, many of the Chinese were skilled and able miners in their own right. (From *The Gold Rush*, by Liza Ketchum, 1996)

The natives soon noticed that whites were arriving in large numbers and were stealing their horses, food, and women. This quickly led to hostilities. At one point, 80 miners were attacked near the present city of Wenatchee. Several of the miners were killed, and the skirmish went on for some time until the arrival of an old Wenatchee chief on a large red horse. He raised his hand in peace, and the fighting stopped on both sides.

This peacemaker was Skamow, one of the tribal leaders among the Wenatchee who were friendly to the whites. Quiltenenock, the leader of the raid on the miners, was determined to finish the job he'd started, no matter what. Not receiving support from his brothers, he took after the miners by himself. The miners realized what was up, and in an ambush they shot and killed him at a place called Twin Rocks, which is located just southwest of the present-day town of Wenatchee. The death of Quiltenenock left the leadership of the tribe to his younger brother, Moses, who later became a chief.

The war between Native Americans and whites lasted many years, and though they tried, the former were unable to unite and fight as one nation. These battles were not confined to eastern Washington. Chief Leschi of the Nisquallies launched several raids against settlers in the West, and he even led an unsuccessful attack on the city of Seattle.

By 1858, it was over. Native Americans on both sides of the Cascade Mountains were no longer a free, independent, and sovereign people. They were now "wards" of the United States and subject to laws enacted by a distant and white Congress, which were executed by the Bureau of Indian Affairs. Their lives would never be the same.

---

[4] On May 10, 1869, Central Pacific's locomotive, Jupiter, rolled over the last-laid rails near Corinne, Utah, to meet Union Pacific's loco #119—a great moment in American history. In one day, between 7:00 A.M. and 7:00 P.M., 4,000 Chinese had laid 10 miles and 200 yards of track. But the completion of the railroad put hundreds of people out of work in the middle of nowhere. Also during this period, many Chinese placer miners were literally driven out of California, and they came north following the white prospectors.

Several incidents later resulted in deaths on both sides. Despite the earlier treaty, these wars continued off and on until the final battles between the Army and the Nez Percé, led by the great Chief Joseph (whose native name means "Thunder Rolling in the Mountains." Those who have heard thunder in the mountains can appreciate the power that this name evokes).

Afterward, Chief Joseph and his people cleverly eluded the U.S. Army for almost two years. Slipping away just as the Army thought they were trapped, the Nez Percé retreated from their ancestral lands in Oregon to a spot in Montana, which they believed placed them safely in Canada. Unfortunately, they had stopped several miles short of their goal. In 1879, after a battle in which many Nez Percé men, women, and children were killed or injured, the embattled chief declared, "Hear me, my chiefs, I am tired. My heart is sick and sad. From where the sun now stands, I will fight no more, forever." Why did the Army track Chief Joseph so relentlessly? Perhaps, in part, because they were jealous. When the Nez Percé rode into battle on their Appaloosa horses, which they bred especially for their own use, they lived up to their reputation as the "finest light cavalry in the world."

The Chinese

In 1848, three Chinese men arrived in San Francisco aboard the American sailing ship *Eagle*. During the next 34 years, over 300,000 others would follow, fleeing China and hoping to escape chronic famine, floods, and wars in their homeland. They came in search of a better life in the American West, but they were greeted with prejudice and hatred.

Beginning in the early 1850s, eastern Washington received its first influx of immigrants. Following closely behind the whites came the Chinese prospectors, many of whom had previously worked in areas that required large labor pools such as road building, mining, agriculture, and railroad construction.[5] Many Chinese placer miners in California were forced to leave when that state passed the Foreign Miners License Tax, which had been aimed originally at Mexicans but was used almost solely against the Chinese. Tax collectors reportedly brought in $5 million between 1850 and 1870. They applied the tax to all Chinese, miners or not. The Chinese had no voice in government during that time. With the mineral discoveries along the Columbia and Fraser Rivers, white placer miners poured into those areas, and the Chinese miners followed closely behind but carefully avoided any competition with their white counterparts. Prejudice ran strong, and many of the citizens felt that the Chinese were infringing on their employment possibilities.[6]

The white placer miners didn't stay very long in any one area because they always wanted to be the first to get to the next bonanza. Grab the easy pickins' and move on was the white miner's philosophy.[7] When they had abandoned a placer deposit and moved on to the next, the Chinese would move in and patiently rework the deposit for any missed gold, which as often as not turned out to be worth their while. Chinese miners were extremely industrious; a story that came out of the California Gold Rush illustrates this. Several white placer miners had worked their claim out and were moving on. They put their rude cabin up for sale for the then-princely sum of $25. It was sold to four Chinese men, who paid full price. The miners went on their way, laughing about how they had cheated the Chinese by selling them a cabin that was not worth even $10. The new owners quietly and meticulously dismantled the cabin and then panned the dirt that had sifted through cracks in its floor over the years. It was the Chinese who had the last laugh when they panned $400 worth of gold that had slipped past the white miners. Not a bad return on their money and efforts!

Physical violence was always a threat to the Chinese miner as well. During the Nez Percé War in the late 1870s, Chinese were often attacked or murdered by bands of roaming miscreant Native Americans as well as white outlaws.

Some adventuresome souls may wish to explore areas well known to the Chinese. The Columbia River, downstream from Wenatchee was well known as a "hot pocket" for the early Chinese who pros-

---

[5] Groups of Chinese also worked in such industries as fishing, canning, road building, agriculture, and lumbering.

[6] In fact, so many Chinese were in eastern Washington by this time that they outnumbered the whites two to one. In 1852 alone, 18,400 Chinese were admitted to the United States.

[7] In the earliest days of the gold excitement, the true-blooded white placer prospector was always ready to drop whatever he had in hand to follow the news flashes of the "golden dream," wherever the rumor may take him.

pected the Inland Empire prior to the turn of the century. What is not commonly known is that their diggin's were about 15 miles below Wenatchee and on benches about 400 feet above the water. Some of these spots were very good paying sites and some were never completely worked out. These high benches represent the old channel where gold was deposited as the river a few million years ago and many times larger, dug deeper into the earth leaving gold high and dry on the banks. It is said that this bar produced a great many thousands of dollars in coarse placer gold, and we know the Chinese worked this bar with the use of water from a creek that, at that time, descended the hillside near by. In several places along the river, and high above it one can still see the early Chinese writings. Later Chinese visitors have not quite been able to decipher the faded scripts, but it has been determined that the writing was about gold along the river. Large Chinese camps were also located at the present location of the Rock Island Dam and on the west side of the Columbia where the Burlington Northern-Santa Fe Railroad bridge spans the river. In pre-Rock Island Dam days, on a bar about 150 feet above the Columbia River in East Wenatchee, chickens often had gold in their crops when dressed, which of course came from the old river gravel bars. The Chinese were also known to work the Columbia River Bars as well as the Wenatchee River near Leavenworth, with several paying placers near the towns of Cashmere and Peshastin.

Mining

The mining history of this area is typified by an early discovery near Squilchuck Creek just above its confluence with the Columbia River. This dates back to around 1867 when Chinese prospectors in the region dug free-milling gold from the nearby cliffs (later known as the D Reef), containing rhyolite porphyritic sandstone.[8] The ore was packed down to Squilchuck Creek, where it was pulverized and panned out.

In 1884, a man named Frank Morris acquired 80 acres along Squilchuck Creek, which included this property. He made a deal with the Gold King Mining Company and an investor named V. Carkeek, and they staked two claims there, one named the Golden King and the other the McBeth. Both claims were subsequently patented.

In 1894, they erected a five-stamp mill and began drifting on the property. A 60-day run at a rate of four tons per day netted them only $1,600. In October of that year the operation was shut down.

Between 1895 and 1910, a judge by the name of McIntosh held title to the claims, and it is not known whether any additional work was performed on the property.

What to See

The Wenatchee area stands in stark contrast to the western side of the Cascade Mountains. Small groups of pine trees gather on the higher elevations, while deciduous trees and scrub brush predominate in the lower regions. The Columbia and Wenatchee Rivers flow through the area, with the Columbia making a grand turn at the city of Wenatchee. Fruit orchards carpet the hillsides where irrigation is available, and many use large propeller fans that stir the air on chilly fall evenings to prevent the nearly ripe fruit from freezing.

Water sports on the rivers include boating and fishing, and hikers have their choice of trails higher in the hills. The internationally renowned Ohme Gardens occupy this area, punctuating, along with the orchards, the otherwise arid landscape. Often when it's wet on the west side of the Cascade Mountains, it is warm and pleasant in Wenatchee. In winter, the Mission Ridge Ski Area draws devotees to its slopes from all over the state.

Rocky Reach Dam, located a short distance to the north of Wenatchee, is also worthwhile to visit. There is an interesting museum there, not to mention fish ladders with built-in viewing windows. In the spring, the view of water thundering through the open floodgates is spectacular.

---

[8] Some of the ladders they constructed remain today directly across from the old offices of the Lovitt Mine on Methow Street. These ladders are over 100 years old; it's amazing that they still exist.

Getting There

It is easy to get to Wenatchee[9] from the Seattle area by taking US 2 east from Everett. It's about a two-hour drive over Stevens Pass, depending on weather and construction conditions. You can also take I-90 over Snoqualmie Pass to a point east of Cle Elum, and then travel via route US 97 over Swauk (Blewett) Pass to US 2, and from there east to Wenatchee. From the central part of the state, simply drive to the Columbia River and go north or south as appropriate to reach the city.

Geology

Besides placer mining by the early prospectors and the Chinese, the Wenatchee Mining District was fortunate to have had two major lode gold and silver production mines, the Lovitt Mine and the Cannon Mine. Both of these mines were located so close to the city of Wenatchee that they actually had street addresses and mailboxes. No hike ratings are given for these two mines because both are on private property and off limits. However, some prospects lying above the main workings are rated at B-2.

> **Warning** This is rattlesnake country, so be alert. The ones that warn you with their rattles are the good ones. Some don't warn, so be vigilant.

The geology of the area surrounding the Lovitt and Cannon Mines is essentially the same, with the exception that the ore bodies at the Cannon reached much greater depths. (Water encountered in the lower workings at the Lovitt Mine required pumping, while the Cannon Mine was essentially dry).[10] The ore bodies at the Lovitt Mine were of a much higher grade than those of the Cannon Mine, but the Cannon ore bodies were much larger and deeper.

The major areas of mineralization stretch several thousand feet to the west of Squilchuck Canyon, just south of the town, to an area known as the NORCO Well, on Compton's Knob. The NORCO Well project resembled something that Howard Hughes might have been involved in. NORCO stood for Northwest Oil Research Corporation, and its plan was to bore a hole down through Compton's Knob, where there was believed to be a "dome" containing oil, or at least some natural gas.

From September 1933 until the hole was capped in 1942, the company went down some 4,900 feet but never hit petroleum. The project was fraught with problems from day one, including a continual lack of funding and geologic difficulties such as loose sand and cave-ins. Over 1,000 people invested in the venture, which eventually ate up around $80,000. The derrick stood for several years, finally collapsing in the mid-1950s. Although the drillers never found the dome of oil and gas, core drilling in the 1990s has revealed a sizable deposit of minerals at depth. Two six-foot beds of good sub-bituminous coal were encountered at a depth of 2,000 feet (though this was too deep to be commercially mined.) On the west side of Squilchuck Canyon, the minerals trend north-northwest to an area slightly south of #2 Canyon. This zone is about 850 feet wide.

A small amount of coal was mined near the corner of Squilchuck Canyon and Pitcher Canyon,[11] a project that was run by the enigmatic N. W. L. Brown. It seems that Brown was a close buddy with Robert Woodruff, the president of the Coca-Cola Company, and when Woodruff would visit the Pacific Coast aboard his private railroad car, he would send for Brown. Their relationship was always shrouded in secrecy. Brown led a very solitary lifestyle while in Wenatchee, seldom leaving his mining prospect. When he did go to town for supplies, he hitched a ride from the locals.

---

[9] Population: 60,000

[10] Some water was encountered at the Cannon and allowed to drain by gravity to the lowest workings, where a sump was located. From there it was pumped to the surface.

[11] Besides the coal mining activity in Dry Gulch, silica sand of the Wenatchee Formation was quarried from there for many years. This activity was discontinued when Asamera abandoned the Cannon Mine in 1995.

The coal extracted was said to be of very low grade, possibly lignite, or extremely sub-bituminous. The same is believed to be true of that mined over the hill, west of Wenatchee Dome, in Dry Gulch. These are most likely extensions of the same seams, which were said to be only about four feet wide.[12]

Microscopic particles of gold and silver were found in the silicified sandstone formations that stand above the surrounding hills in long, east-west–tending ridges known as *reefs*. Some of the reefs also extend several hundred feet underground. The rock that comprises the reefs is more weather-resistant than the surrounding rock, allowing the harder reefs to rise above the countryside. The highest amount of silica occurs at D Reef. These reefs are identified as follows by the different companies who prospected or mined them:

- A Reef contained the Gold Knob, Anaconda, and Cannon Prospects.
- B Reef hosted the Anaconda, Lovitt, and later the Cannon Mine sites.
- C Reef held the Anaconda and Knob Hill Prospects.
- D Reef became the site of the Lovitt Mine.
- E Reef was the Charlotte Prospect.[13]

The very early Chinese miners took some of the first free-milling gold from D Reef. At that point, the reef is cut by Squilchuck Creek, which essentially cross-sections it. The ore deposits occur in dike-like bodies that are cut by innumerable small quartz veins carrying pyrite. Many carry valuable minerals. The reefs are inter-bedded with other sediments, are substantially tilted and fractured, and lie in a down-faulted geologic structure.

During the formation of the Earth, the silica solutions, which were discharged from volcanoes and magmatic upwellings, carried with them the gold, silver, and other minerals. The sandstone was so porous that it acted like a sponge, soaking up the silica solution. The solutions cooled, leaving behind the mineral deposits. Over millions of years, sediments covered these deposits. Eventually, the sediments eroded, leaving the silicified reefs above as well as below the ground. The deposits in the Wenatchee Valley were laid down in the Eocene Epoch, which began about 58 million years ago and lasted about 22 million years.

Small pockets of extremely high-grade, malleable gold were also found in and around the upper B, C, and D Reef areas, and wire gold was recovered at the Lovitt Mine. The Cannon Mine was more of a huge, deep, low-grade ore deposit.

The chief ore values at the Lovitt Mine were in the silicified parts of the hanging wall. A cobble conglomerate is prevalent on the footwall side of a fault that dips to the southwest. The same relationship exists over at B Reef: the ore is on the hanging-wall side of the footwall fissure, and the conglomerate is on the footwall side. Neither the footwall fissure nor the conglomerate are present at A Reef, suggesting that the fault either is northeast of A Reef or has been offset by another right-lateral fault. The ore in the Wenatchee mines is very similar to that found in the hardrock mines around Liberty.

Several studies of the geology of the Wenatchee Heights area are available at the Department of Natural Resources office in Olympia,[14] as well as at the University of Washington, in the form of mining theses.

The Mines

Lovitt Mine

No rating. The Lovitt Mine is located near the mouth of Squilchuck Canyon on Methow Street, just southwest of the Wenatchee city limits. This is private property and is posted with "No Trespassing" signs. The Chelan County Sheriff patrols here regularly, and trespassers *are* prosecuted. The site should be considered extremely dangerous. Some of the open stopes on this property are several hundred feet deep.

---

[12] A four-foot bed of bony coal, bone, and shale was mined around 1934. It produced about 1,275 tons.

[13] Other reefs in the area are designated F, G, and H. These were core drilled, but not much was found and no tunneling took place other than on a stub tunnel at G Reef. These are all located to the northwest of B Reef, and they extend north to an area near #2 Canyon.

[14] See Asamera's Cannon Mine files, Geology and Earth Resources Library in Olympia, which contain all of the core-drilling data on this area.

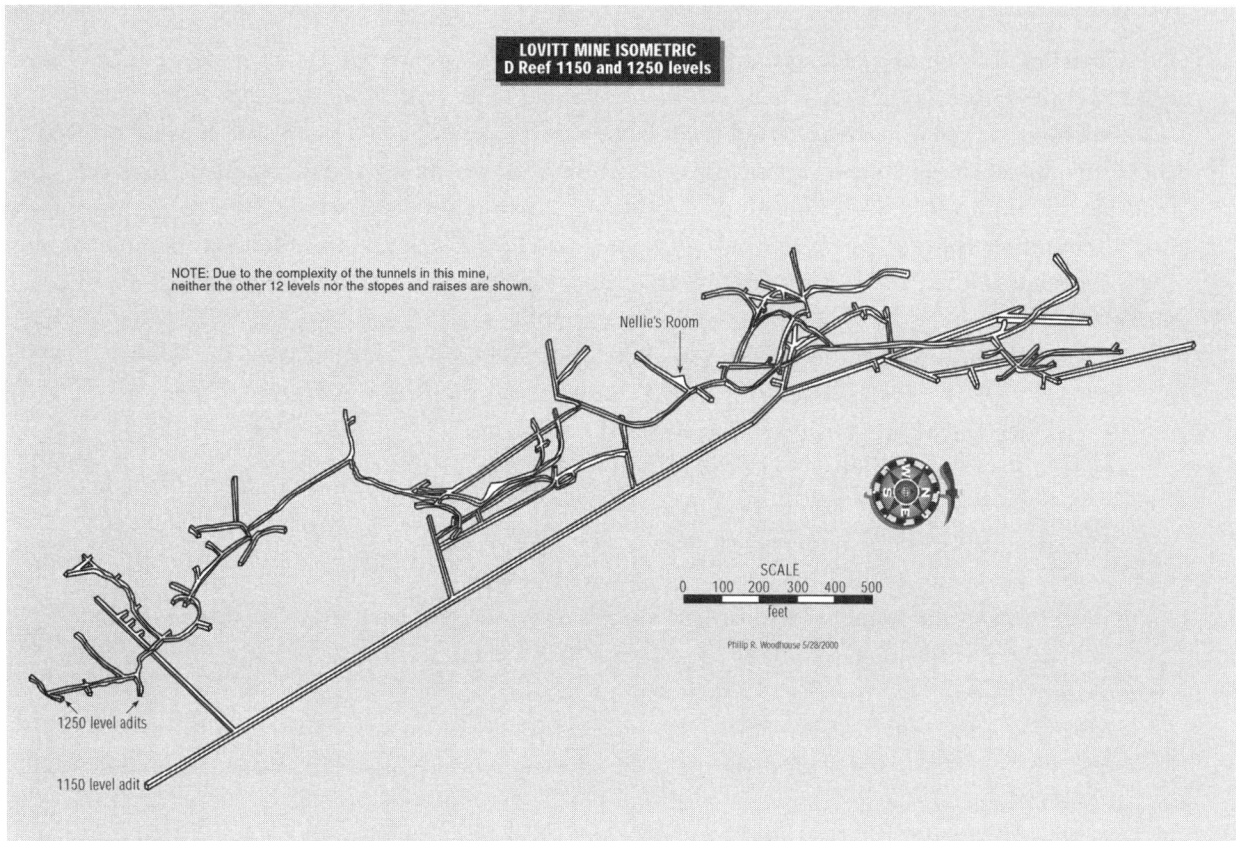

Northwest Underground Explorations visited the mine in the summer of 1997, with permission from the owners and the Sheriff's Office. Many of the mine buildings and much of the equipment still remained, even though the mine had not been actively worked in over 30 years. The mine office, mill building, ore bunker, grizzly, assay office, dry rooms, and compressor house, including the huge Ingersoll-Rand air compressor, all remained somewhat intact, despite obvious attempts at destruction by vandals.[15]

Note In mid-2000, all of the adits and other accesses to the Lovitt Mine have been blasted shut. This was done for the safety of the inquisitive public. Although the mine has been physically closed, the property remains off limits to the public, and *no trespassing* is allowed.

The tailings dam, which stretches several hundred feet to the southeast of the property, is up Squilchuck Canyon from the mine buildings. The towering formations that make up the D Reef loom to the northwest of the buildings. They contain many of the mine's portals and glory holes, as well as the massive mine dumps that are visible.

The only structure that was obviously missing was the head-frame and hoist house that once stood high above the inclined shaft.[16] This shaft was dug in the 1950s, and it accessed several sub levels. The sub levels encountered water and had to be constantly pumped. The stopes from these lower levels extend upward hundreds of feet through the reef, and "daylight" near the top of the reef.

After obtaining permission to examine the property, we began our surface exploration. Our first order of business was to locate and identify the mine's entrances, or portals. The lowest and the earliest was the 1100 level. This tunnel ran directly to the northwest of the mine office complex under Methow Street. It accessed the lowest of the mine's workings, other than the flooded workings below the long-gone incline shaft. We found that the 1100 level portal was wide open, but a cave-in at around 50 feet

---

[15] During the summer of 1999 many of the aforementioned structures were removed by the owners of the property, including a bridge spanning Methow Street used for transporting ore from the grizzly to the ore bunker.

[16] The head-frame and hoist house were removed in the 1990s when Asamera was doing exploration at the site. The incline was covered over, and a large core-sample storage building was built over it.

The Lovitt Mine Isometric As opposed to the Cannon Mine, which used modern methods to locate the ore bodies and then drove large tunnels directly to them, the Lovitt Mine evolved in a more traditional way. Tunnels were driven along veins or stringers until an ore body was located, and then the body was stoped until the ore was removed. Because the gold in the D Reef lay in a complex, random pattern, the tunnels were equally complex and circuitous. The Lovitt Mine Isometric drawing renders only two levels of this complex mine. The 1250 level (all levels were numbered by their elevations above sea level) was one of the more productive in the mine, but it was far from the only one. The 1190, 1150, 1100, 957, and 850 levels lay below it and the 1315, 1350, 1400, 1440, 1480, 1550, 1595, and 1625 lay above it. The 850 and 957 level quickly flooded when they were abandoned.

The 1150 level was bored as a haulage tunnel. Notice that its lateral tunnels have been placed to run beneath the 1250 (and higher) tunnels in the areas of the greatest ore body locations. So complex is the mine that any attempt to depict the other 12 levels would result in a hopeless mass of images that would be difficult to decipher. The stopework in the mine is very extensive, and numerous raises and manways connect the various levels. These too have been omitted from this isometric. We in Northwest Underground Explorations refer to the tunnel drawing from which this rendering was made as the "spaghetti drawing" because of its complexity.

The stopes in the Lovitt Mine were built without woodwork: As the stope was opened, anchors were set into the ceiling of the stope, to which cables were connected to support a catwalk. As additional anchors were set from the end of the catwalk, it was extended farther into the stope. Once the catwalk was complete, the holes for explosives were bored into the ceiling of the stope. The explosives were loaded, the charge set off, and the top of the stope dropped to access rooms below. Then the process began anew.

Before every workday, the miners would meet and lay out each crew's duties for that day. Every miner knew the location of every other miner in the operation. There could be as many as 16 miners working at one time or as few as one, depending on the fortunes of the company. With each person understanding the location and the actions of all the miners, there was less chance for them to affect, or injure, each other. Partly because of this close coordination, there was only one fatality at the Lovitt Mine during its operation.

blocked the way. Just inside the portal, we came across the huge air receiver tank, which had stored the compressed air to power the drills far inside the mine. The air header, or supply pipe, between the receiver and compressor is 12 inches in diameter. We found another entrance about 100 feet to the north of the caved portion in the form of a trap door and ladder leading down to the adit level. A strong, cool breeze was flowing from the hole, indicating this tunnel connected with workings higher up in the reef.

The 1150 level portal was located about 200 feet farther north, 50 feet to the east and 50 feet higher in elevation than the 1100 portal. This was the main haulage tunnel, which connects via raises, stopes, drifts, and manways to all underground workings. The portal was caved, and water was coming from under the cave-in on our visit. There are well over 3,000 feet of tunnel on this level alone. The 1150 level is inaccessible from this portal.

We located the two portals of the 1250 level 150 feet higher and to the west of the 1100 foot level. These were in such good condition that we embarked on most of our underground exploration from this level. The huge, open stopes were above the 1250 level at elevations between 1,350 to 1,625 feet. These were opened when the east side of D Reef collapsed during the 1960s.

The Chinese were often early to the digs, and they taught their European counterparts some of the finer points of mining. A group of four Chinese miners show three Europeans the methods of operating a long tom and gold pans. (California State Library #912)

Warning These stopes are wide open and are several hundred feet deep. A fall into one would be instantly fatal. Even coming close to the edge of one of these stopes could cause the ground to collapse under you. While exploring underground in the upper tunnels, we found a large fracture indicating that another collapse is imminent. *Stay off D Reef.*

History

From 1910 to 1928, the Wenatchee Mining Company extracted a small amount of silver and gold. Between 1928 and 1942, the American Smelting and Refining Company (ASARCO, the smelter near Tacoma) had a contract with J. J. Keegan, the owner of the mine. After shipping several tons of low-grade material, the option was dropped, most likely due to the outbreak of World War II.[17]

Between 1943 and 1946, the Knob Hill Mining Company prospected on the property. The company hired two brothers from Wenatchee, Chuck and Dick Stumph, to do some drilling and ore sampling at the site. The company shipped 6,200 tons of low-grade ore to the Tacoma Smelter but then eventually lost interest in the site and pulled up stakes.

In the mid-1800s, when the Chinese first discovered gold outcroppings on the end of what later became known as D Reef, they built ladders to more easily access the ore. They would climb onto the face of the reef, remove the ore, and then carry it down to Squilchuck Creek, where they'd pulverize and pan it. They didn't get rich, but they didn't do too badly either. Only later, when tunnels were driven into D Reef, was the true value of the ore realized, when Ed Lovitt's savvy located many rich pockets, some of which yielded wire and sheet gold as well as nuggets. (Paul Smith photo)

---

[17] During World War II, all gold and silver mines were closed because they were deemed nonessential to the war effort.

C. E. Cockle, a Montana mining engineer, and J. J. Keegan, owner, sample ore from the Gold King Mine. This later became the Lovitt Mine, one of the major producers of gold in the area. (From *The Miner, Chemist and Engineer* for March 1940)

In 1948, a group of Wenatchee business developers became interested in the property. Wanting a new, fresh, and independent opinion on its mining potential, they contacted Ed Lovitt, a successful mining engineer in British Columbia, and asked him to examine the D Reef to see whether it could be profitably mined.

After a careful study, Lovitt concluded that by using a selective mining method known as *shrinkage stoping*[18] the ore bodies inside D Reef could be successfully and profitably mined. Lovitt was so impressed with the D Reef property that he went back to Canada, sold a number of his mining holdings, and returned to Wenatchee with a plan.

Development

Lovitt formed the Lovitt Mining Company and the Wenatchee Mining Partnership, eventually buying out Keegan in 1951. He sold shares to various investors but retained 51 percent interest for himself. He then set about putting the mine into full production, installing electric lights in some of the tunnels, bringing in modern ore cars, along with two donkeys to pull them, and putting together a topnotch crew. Lovitt also brought his friend and longtime partner, Vere McDowall, down from Canada to look at the operation. McDowall, who was also an experienced mining engineer, was impressed with what he saw, but was obligated to return to British Columbia to finish up some mining business and couldn't return to Wenatchee until 1953.

Later in 1951, Lovitt signed a $1 million option with the Anaconda Copper Mining Company of Butte, Montana, giving the company the chance to take over the mine if it could define a large enough ore body. Anaconda brought in its own crew and began doing exploratory work on the property to determine the exact extent of the ore body. Its focus was on development and exploration rather than production.

Anaconda dug an incline shaft 500 feet under Methow Street, drifting on several sub levels, as well as crosscutting on the 1150 level to create a haulage and main exploration tunnel, and bored a tunnel at the 1250 level. The company did some core drilling around the upper areas of D Reef, and crossed over the hill to the B Reef, blasting a drift along an outcropping from which a 600-foot incline raise was bored for about 100 vertical feet.[19]

In March 1953, Anaconda brought in its top geologists and engineers. The $1 million had been spent in just three years, but the company had failed to define the ore bodies. By April 1953, further exploration plans were abandoned and Anaconda turned the contract back over to Lovitt, leaving all of its machinery and supplies at the mine. As we will see later on, Anaconda was simply looking in the wrong place.

---

[18] Shrinkage stoping is a very inexpensive method of mining steep or narrow ore bodies. For a more detailed description, see the Glossary.

[19] Anaconda had previously done work under an option with Keegan at Saddle Rock, boring several hundred feet of tunnel and a deep winze into the southwest side of A Reef. Silica ore was found but deemed too low-grade to mine.

Ed Lovitt (on the left) with Vere McDowall in the early days of their mining careers. This was taken while they were still in Canada. (Ann Gaspers photo)

This was probably the best thing to ever happen to the mine, because it left full control of the property to Lovitt, plus all the machinery, tools, rail, tunneling, and piping Anaconda had used on the project. With the mining giant out of the picture, Lovitt could begin doing what he did best: mine gold and silver.

Realizing that he needed both help and more funding, Lovitt again contacted his partner, Vere McDowall, who returned to Wenatchee to oversee the development, operation, and expansion of the mine. Both men felt that the D Reef had tremendous potential, and their determination to mine it would ensure them an eventual place in northwest mining history.[20]

McDowall was not only an expert mining engineer but also a "working man's boss." He understood the needs of those he supervised, and the pay and working conditions at the mine were the best in the industry over the next few years.[21]

Ann Gaspers, Vere McDowall's daughter, remembers living near the mine as a child. When the kids would visit the property, they would sometimes ride the empty ore cars into the mine while being pulled by one of the donkeys. She recalls, "There were two donkeys and their names were Jenny and Johnnie. One day they were caught by the mine inspector and that was the end of that. Later, when the animals were replaced by a motorized trammer, Johnnie lived out his days playing with the horses and a pony we had."

The Lovitt Mine immediately flourished under McDowall's leadership and soon became the tenth-largest gold producer in the United States. The work was going well at the mine. A case in point: The smelter at Tacoma, owned by ASARCO, went on strike just about the time Lovitt and McDowall's miners discovered Nellie's Room,[22] a high-grade pocket of ore valued at well over $1 million in one of the 1250 level drifts. When the strike was finally over and the ore had been processed, the Internal Revenue Service sent agents to the mine offices to make sure that Uncle Sam got his cut.[23]

It was during this time, 1954, that the mine experienced its only fatality. Howard Zude was fatally wounded while installing shoring in the 1150 level crosscut. Five tons of rock broke loose from the ceiling, killing him instantly.

Warning Another fatality at the mine happened long after the operation closed. Evidently, a man removing stone near the top of the mine backed a Trojan rubber-tired loader off the cliff. Mine sites contain as many dangers above ground as they do below. You can observe the portal of the mine and enjoy the ambience, but you cannot go on the property or enter the mine.

---

[20] Vere McDowall and Ed Lovitt had been partners for many years and had worked together with the Geological Survey during the 1930s.

[21] He also owned many shares of stock in the mine and was the company vice president and public relations man.

[22] No one seems to remember who Nellie was, or whether there ever was a Nellie. We have looked at the room and it isn't all that big, maybe 15 by 15 feet.

[23] The take from Nellie's Room was split evenly, with each of the miners receiving somewhere around $100,000. A couple of them quit the mine and ended up drinking themselves to death. Lovitt felt terrible about this and vowed to never let it happen again.

Over the next several years, the mine produced a record amount of gold and silver ore containing a high amount of silica, and brought thousands of dollars of income to the Wenatchee area. (Silica ore helps in the separation of the metals from the concentrates.) Because of the high silica content, ASARCO paid Lovitt a higher than normal price per ton of ore shipped.

Vere McDowall passed away in 1961. His duties were assumed by Oscar Thompson, who had been with Lovitt Mining since 1953 as head of underground operations. One of Oscar's functions at the mine was to determine how much ore each individual miner mined, since all the miners at Lovitt were paid on a contract basis.[24] Contract miners had to lay their own track; install air and water lines; do whatever timbering was necessary; and drill, load, blast, and muck their workings.

Later that year, Day Mining of Wallace, Idaho, expressed an interest in the mine. (Day Mining already owned several mining properties in both Idaho and eastern Washington.) On December 1, Henry L. Day and Ed Lovitt formed a joint venture, the Lovitt Mining Company and Wenatchee Partnership, which owned a 70 percent interest in the new venture; Day Mining held 30 percent. The company was renamed L & D Mining (but for the sake of continuity we will continue to refer to it as Lovitt Mining except in direct quotes).

The new company's first order of business was the construction of a 300-ton-per-day flotation mill, the installation of a huge air compressor and receiver tank, and the replacement of the donkeys with a motorized trammer. Henry Day oversaw the operation of the new mill, while Lovitt ran the mine itself.

The mill turned out its first run of concentrates in July 1962, and the underground crew was increased to over 16. After 1962, some of the concentrates were shipped to a smelter in Idaho, and the shipments to ASARCO were concentrates rather than ore. (ASARCO had imposed a 400-ton-per-day restriction at that time.)

According to James Marr Jr., a former Lovitt miner, the stopes in the mine were so large by this time "that they could hold the nine-story Wenatchee West Coast Hotel Building," and the mine was being worked on 14 different levels.[25] Jim also describes how several of the miners had quit smoking cigarettes and taken to chewing tobacco. "When climbing a raise or manway you had to watch where you put your hands, as that was a favorite place to spit."

Sometime during the early 1960s, the Civil Defense Department came up with the idea that the Lovitt Mine would make a good atomic bomb shelter, or emergency hospital, in the event of nuclear war. They filled two drifts in the 1250 level with war rations, including many cans of drinking water, boxes of crackers, toilet paper, and other essential items. (These goods were still in the mine when we visited it in the summer of 1997).

Five principals of the Lovitt Mine pose with the Squilchuck Canyon behind them. The fellow second from the left is probably Ed Lovitt, mine owner. (Ed Lovitt Jr. collection)

---

[24] Oscar Thompson also came down from Canada to join Lovitt and McDowall in mining D Reef. Oscar told us that fresh out of mining school, he was hired by a placer operation in British Columbia. A tour of the various properties the company owned led him and his guide to a huge pit. In Oscar's words, "I looked down into the hole and saw hundreds and hundreds of empty dynamite boxes. When I asked my guide, 'Why all the dynamite boxes,' he laughed like hell and said, 'Boy, you are a young one!' They turned out to be whiskey boxes. This was during prohibition in the United States (1919–1933), and Canadian booze was being smuggled across the border near the mine."

[25] Once we obtained the mine's plan map, we soon began to refer to it as the Spaghetti Map. The tunnel system inside D Reef resembles a large platter of spaghetti, with its over 14 different levels containing manways, huge stopes, raises, and a labyrinth of drifts.

Hauling material from the 1369 level at the Lovitt Mine. Squilchuck Canyon can be seen in the distance. The rocks of the reef rise above the softer country rock. (Ed Lovitt Jr. collection)

Clearing the adit of the 1369 level at the Lovitt Mine. The serpentine tunnels in the mine contained many stopes extending among the 14 levels. (Ed Lovitt Jr. collection)

Over this period, the Lovitt Mine was producing so much ore that some of the contract miners were taking home larger paychecks than the owner. Lovitt was paying himself $2,500 a month. Times were good, but the boss, though a great miner, was also pragmatic. Jim Marr remembers one incident:

One day when we were working in the mine, one of the miners found a chunk of ore about the size of a softball containing the most beautiful crystalline wire gold any of us had ever seen. As we stood there passing it around, Ed Lovitt happened by. He asked us what was so interesting, and one of the fellows handed him the specimen. Well, ol' Ed rolled it around in his hands for a couple of seconds and then said "Yah! This looks pretty good." Then, to the amazement of all of us, he casually reached over and tossed it down the ore chute with the rest of the rock that was destined for the mill. To Ed, gold was gold.

Another event around this time also showed how dangerous mining could be. Lovitt had decided that more ventilation was needed in the upper levels of the mine, so he told the men to blast a *small* hole through the west side of D Reef near the 1350 level. A short drift was driven to the face and explosives, perhaps too many, were set in place. It seems Mrs. Lovitt was having a few of the ladies to her home, which

The buildings of the Lovitt Mine as seen from high on the gold-bearing reef in May 1955. The tunnel from which the rails are extending is the 1250 level of the mine. The Squilchuck Canyon stretches away in the background. (Ed Lovitt Jr. collection)

was located just southwest of the mine, for tea that day. Promptly at 2:30 in the afternoon…BOOM! the explosion occurred, shattering several windows in the house. The tea parties were held elsewhere after that. As the story has it, Ed really caught hell when he returned home that night.

B Reef Project-Dry Gulch

By 1965, the known ore reserves at D Reef were beginning to reach depletion, some of the stopes were mined to daylight,[26] and some had collapsed. So Lovitt sent his number-one prospector, Bill Lancaster, over to the other side of the hill to search for another ore body in an area known as B Reef, located in the mouth of Dry Gulch. This would later be the site of the famous Cannon Mine. Anaconda had done some digging here in the 1950s on the lookout for a large, low-grade ore body but hadn't found anything.[27]

Lancaster, well known for his expertise in long-hole drilling, brought back samples that, after assaying, convinced Lovitt that B Reef had good mineral potential.[28] Lovitt then sent two of his miners, Chuck Stumph and Clarence Reeves, and they extended the tunnels that Anaconda had started, bringing the B Reef workings to a total of around 3,000 feet of tunneling.

---

[26] The stopes were mined right to the surface, creating a yawning pit.

[27] Anaconda wanted a large low-grade ore body because mining high-grade ore is almost certainly a short-term proposition. However, a large, low-grade deposit, practically guaranteed that a mill could be constructed and long-term operations conducted. In mining and milling high-grade ore, a mill constantly required adjustments. Milling is done with the aid of gravity, and the specific gravity of higher-grade ore caused what is called "sliming," in other words the gold and silver passed through the process with the useless gangue and end up in the tailings.

[28] Strangely, Lovitt wouldn't spend the extra money to do diamond core drilling, and Lancaster was forced to do his explorations using long holing.

The Lovitt Mine's office buildings are seen at the lower left, and the decline head house is beyond. (Ed Lovitt Jr. collection)

They discovered a vein of gold that assayed at between three and eight ounces per ton. Parts of this high-grade vein are still in the B Reef tunnels, according to a reliable source. After about a year, the money for the project ran out. The main ore body was nowhere in evidence, and the site was once again abandoned.[29] Knob Hill, Anaconda, and even Lovitt had all missed it. The project cost $133,260, of which $66,630 was obtained from a mineral exploration loan.

D Reef

Meanwhile, back at the Lovitt Mine, they were *pulling the pillars* just to keep the hungry mill operating. It ate 300 tons of ore per day, but the end was near. The known, minable gold in D Reef had finally "pinched,"[30] and in March 1967 Ed Lovitt and Henry Day announced that the mine would be shut down, ending one of the most fascinating and successful chapters in Northwest mining history. Several of the miners wanted to keep the mine open, and they approached Lovitt to try to make a deal of some kind. But Lovitt, not in the best of

Ed Lovitt, the mining engineer from Canada, who visited the mine, realized its potential, moved to Washington State, purchased the property, and successfully operated the mine for many years. (Ed Lovitt Jr. collection)

---

[29] The low price of gold was another factor that made mining B Reef uneconomical.

[30] Pinching out describes a condition in which the vein becomes too narrow or too low-grade to profitably mine.

health at the time, was concerned about the collapse of some of the major stopes and wouldn't let them work the mine any further. Jim Marr Jr. tells the story of the great collapse that eventually occurred:

One day I was working at the 1150 level grizzly, where we were trying to break up some of the larger pieces of ore so they could pass on down to the mill. All of a sudden, I heard a loud roar coming from the hillside behind me. As I turned to see what was happening, I saw a large pine tree near the top of D Reef suddenly disappear and the whole side of the hill was collapsing down toward us. We quickly realized what had happened; the huge stopes above us had broken loose from the mountain around the 1625 level. We also knew that there was a crew of men working in the 1450 level. As we ran toward the road leading up the hill, we saw them emerge safely from the portal. It seemed like it took forever for the rocks to stop rolling and the dust to settle, and when it did we looked up to see that what had once been the east side of D Reef was now a cliff with a small hole in it that used to be a drift leading into the stope.

The miners had been aware that something was about to happen in the upper tunnels. Cracks had been appearing in the walls for several days. At the end of every day, they would drive wedges into the crevices, but when they returned the next morning many of the wedges had fallen to the tunnel floor. When we explored in the tunnels above the 1250 level, several large cracks in the ceilings were visible, despite the fact that a good deal of new shoring had been installed by Asamera during its investigations of the mine in the 1990s. We chose to back out of some of these tunnels, deeming them to be bad ground.

Production

During its last 16 years of operation, the Lovitt Mine produced 1,036,572 tons of ore, from which 410,482.5 ounces of gold and 625,849.0 ounces of silver were extracted. It is also interesting to note that under Lovitt and McDowall's leadership the mine produced a higher tonnage per day, per miner, than any other hardrock mine in the U.S. The daily average was 33 tons per man shift.

Although the Lovitt Mine did not produce any ore after 1967, neither did it just fade away. During the 1980s and 1990s, Asamera Minerals U.S., the operator of the Cannon Mine, did extensive core drilling and spent a lot of money reshoring and rock bolting on the 1250 and the 1350 levels. It mined a small amount of very high-grade ore from around the area of Nellie's Room. (A short tunnel leads off Nellie's Room for about 40 feet to another room of nearly the same size. This second room does not appear on maps predating 1986, and the method of roof control in this area was obviously Asamera's rather than Lovitt's).[31]

The mine was also featured in the action/adventure movie *Surviving the Game*, starring rap music's Ice T. A close look at the film footage shows that the 1150 level adit was wide open at the time the movie was made.

As for the core drilling done by Asamera during the 1990s, we once asked a member of its exploration team what was found, and his reply was, "Not much. Old Mr. Lovitt must have been one hell of a miner."[32]

Charlotte Prospect/E Reef

The Charlotte Prospect is located about ¼ mile west of the Lovitt Property. A small, by comparison, tailing pile can be seen about 300 feet above Methow Street, and an old ore bunker or other mine structure is also visible from the road. The property was owned and operated around 1897 by Mr. Bigelow, Thomas Groves, and F. M. Scheble. The ore extracted was gold and silver, with assays as high as $6.00 to $8.00 per ton. No production records have been found, and it must be assumed that only a small amount of high-grade ore was taken from the property because core drilling in the later years proved unfruitful. This is believed to be the same property described in *The Geologic History of the Wenatchee Valley and Adjacent Vicinity*, by Charles Mason. Mason indicates that the visible structures were part of a short-lived quartz mining operation: "The quartz was believed to be pure enough for the manufacturing of glass. Several loads were shipped to Seattle for that purpose, but were found to contain too high an iron content for such usage, and the mine was abandoned."

---

[31] Lovitt used rock bolting and steel strapping, whereas Asamera used rock bolting with steel mesh.

[32] Every person we interviewed who had worked at the Lovitt Mine told us the same thing: "It was the best job I ever had."

The surface facilities of the Lovitt Mine in April 1966. The sloping building in the distance is the head house for the decline that accessed the two lowest levels of the mine. The covered shed-like structure on the far right is a roof over the grizzly screen through which the ore was dropped to a crusher, and then carried via conveyor belt over the road to the mill on the far left. The office buildings and compressor house can be seen just over the conveyor housing. (*Wenatchee World* newspaper photo, Ed Lovitt Jr. collection)

The Lovitt Mine's decline headhouse is central to the picture, while the end of the reef appears at the far right. It was in this portion of the reef that Chinese prospectors extracted the first gold in the middle of the 19th century. The remains of their ladders can still be seen. (Ed Lovitt Jr. collection)

Gold Knob Prospect / A Reef

The Gold Knob Prospect is located in Sections 16 and 21, T22N, R20E. It occupies all of Section 16 and 20 acres of Section 21. This is the area known as the A Reef, also referred to locally as Saddle Rock. The property was held by state land lease during the late 1930s and early 1940s by J. J. Keegan, who subleased to the Anaconda Mining Company, which conducted most of the exploration at the site.

The easiest way to reach the property is to take Circle Street past the former Cannon Mine offices to the end of the road. There, you will find a locked DNR cable across the road.[33] This is public land, but you can walk from here. Our tunnel maps show three portals to the A Reef workings, as well as several hundred feet of tunneling.

Development

Although the Gold Knob never produced any ore, it is worth mentioning because of the great amount of money spent in trying to locate an ore body here similar to the one in the nearby Lovitt Mine.

Anaconda bored over 800 feet of crosscut tunnel, sank a winze almost 100 feet deep into the ore body, and spent thousands of dollars core drilling at the site, but it never got assays high enough to justify mining.

Asamera's tunnel maps also show that during the operation of the Cannon Mine (1985–1995), a long crosscut was extended north under the A Reef area and some stope work was done on the 520 and 460 levels.[34] When Asamera Minerals closed the Cannon Mine in 1995, it also dynamited shut the A Reef portals bored by Anaconda years before. The portal of the lowest tunnel is located about 200 feet up the road from the gate. The largest of the tunnels is located another 200 feet higher and ¼ mile up the road. It will be obvious because of its rather large dump. Because it felt like around a million degrees Fahrenheit the day we were there, we did not look for the third portal.

James Marr Jr., on the right, poses with Oscar Thompson, a former superindentent, at the Lovitt Mine. D Reef is in the background. This is the geologic feature in which the Lovitt Mine was dug. The two men are standing in front of Oscar's home, which was once occupied by the Lovitt family. (Greg Cady photo)

For the Rockhound

The A Reef area is open public land, however the mineral rights are probably leased by one of the many mining companies involved in the mineral exploration of the Wenatchee region. It is doubtful that they would object to your picking up a sample or two, or even picking through some of the dumps, as long as you don't set up a mill and start processing ore. Remember that the wire gold was found at the highest elevations on the reefs. It might be interesting to run a metal detector up there. Bring your camera, because A Reef affords a spectacular view of the Wenatchee Valley and the Columbia River.

Warning Beware of rattlesnakes on A Reef.

C Reef Prospect

The C Reef formation is directly to the north and above the Lovitt Mine workings when viewed from Methow Street, and is referred to as Rooster Comb. During our examination of the Lovitt Property, we located a heavily shored caved portal near the top east side of C Reef. We believe this to be part of the exploration tunnels bored by the Anaconda Company while it held an option on the property in the 1950s. There has been so much drilling and tunneling at these sites that it is hard to say exactly who did what when.

---

[33] In 1997, we contacted the Eastern Washington Department of Natural Resources office and were informed that there were no "cabled" roads in the Wenatchee area. Take a look at the lock for yourself; it has a big "DNR" stamped on it.

[34] The Cannon Mine's stopes are about 600 feet lower in elevation than the Anaconda workings.

Relatively early in the Lovitt Mine's operation, one of the adits has an air receiver tank and a mobile compressor to power air drills in the mine. (Ed Lovitt Jr. collection)

Our maps show a tunnel system containing around 750 feet of crosscutting and 100 feet of drifting. The tunnels are now most likely in a very bad state, considering the number of faults that crisscross these workings.

Geologic reports indicate that the silica at C Reef was so low that mining it was deemed not worthwhile.

> **Warning** During our exploration of the Lovitt Mine, we found a full box of dynamite in a stope below the 1250 level. It was exploded the year after our visit. This explosion, as well as the collapsing stopes, makes further entrance into this mine extremely dangerous. We discourage further underground exploration at D Reef. Also remember that the mine is on private property.

Cannon Mine

Bonanza! The Cannon Mine was by far one of the largest and most profitable mining operations ever to be conducted in Washington State. We in Northwest Underground Explorations were very fortunate to have been given a guided tour of the mine in 1991 and to have interviewed several people who worked there.

When we first heard of the Cannon Mine, we were struck by its location in the middle of an apple orchard. We wondered whether there could be millions and millions of dollars in gold and silver under the apple trees and rattlesnakes, within a rock's throw of downtown Wenatchee.

We also knew that no matter what great geologists Ed Lovitt and Vere McDowall may have been, the Big Guys—i.e., Anaconda, ASARCO, and Knob Hill—had already examined this property and deemed it not profitable. Something changed all of this negative thinking, leading the operators of the Cannon to mine 500 ounces of gold a day (not counting the silver).

Getting There

The Cannon Mine site is just south of Wenatchee, where north-south Miller Street ends, at 1001 Circle Street. It sits at an elevation of 1,021 feet, in the mouth of Dry Gulch, under B Reef. The mine was closed in 1995, all its portals were sealed, and most of the stopes were backfilled. Today there is almost nothing remaining to indicate that one of our nation's largest gold producers once inhabited this spot. The only structure that is left, the old mine administrative building, now houses the local school district offices.

Deep within the Lovitt Mine is an underground lunchroom. A radiant heater was placed at the back to dispel the cold and damp often present in the mine. Overhead heat lamps helped as well. On the left are Jerry Bainard and E. H. Hall. On the right is foreman Chuck Stumpf. (*Wenatchee World* photo, Ed Lovitt Jr. collection)

At the east end of the property, you will find an old ore car and a bronze plaque. The ore car was a gift to the mining company from a powder company and was not used at the mine, since the Cannon was trackless. The bronze plaque is a memorial to two of the miners who died in accidents while employed.

Look directly behind the ore car in the side of the rock formation (locally known as Wenatchee Dome), and you will see the huge sealed portal that was once the entrance (called the main decline) to the mine. Now turn around and look at the very top of the flagpole in front of the building. That brass ball is actually a toilet bowl float, believe it or not. The B Reef tunnels were located under the small rock formation directly behind the school offices and slightly to the southwest of the building. They were also sealed when the mine closed.

These are the only reminders of what once was an extremely productive, active, and profitable mining operation. During its operation, the Cannon Mine brought millions of dollars into the Wenatchee area, and a large percentage of locals worked there. The mine was named in honor of longtime Asamera executive Donald G. Cannon, who first brought the Wenatchee property to the company's attention and urged them to pursue it. [35]

The workers at the Lovitt Mine proudly pose with the sign attesting their safety record. From the left are Gerald Bainard, Don Reeves, Don Kalma, Robert Reeves, L. H. McGuire of the U. S. Bureau of Mines, Bureau of Mines instructor John Conrad, Clarence Reeves, J. A. Reeves, Chuck Stumpf (pointing), D. W. Mays, and Newton Sloan. (Ed Lovitt Jr. collection)

---

[35] During our research, we tried unsuccessfully to locate Mr. Cannon.

The Lovitt Mine and the Squilchuck Canyon in the 1950s. (Ed Lovitt Jr. collection)

The mine's underground workings range in depth from 1,021 feet above sea level at the portal of the main decline and at the B Reef portal, to 70 feet above sea level in the deepest workings, called the Lower B-Neath Zone. From the administrative offices on Circle Street, the workings went south to the base of Dry Gulch, and to the north under the Appleatchee Stables, with a long crosscut extending northwest under A Reef, the area known as Saddle Rock. There are 22 levels of stopes, one above the other. Several miles of tunnels comprise the mine complex.

The property was held under several leases, and royalties were paid to the property owners during the mine's operation.[36] Asamera Minerals, the operator of the Cannon Mine, set aside $2,500 a month for its employees to donate to the Wenatchee community. It went to food banks, women's shelters, and other charities, and 560 jobs in the Wenatchee area were supported by the operation of the mine.

History

In the early 1950s, Anaconda Copper Company, working under an option with the Lovitt Mining Company, did some exploratory work in and around B Reef. Earlier than that, Knob Hill and ASARCO had both examined it. No one found enough ore to make the property marketable, and the workings, which subsequently became flooded, were abandoned.

During the 1960s, Ed Lovitt spent almost $134,000 doing exploratory drifting as well as metallurgical test work directly under B Reef. Unfortunately, he wasn't able to define the extent of the ore body either, even though he found some very high-grade veins of gold, and once again B Reef was abandoned. Low gold prices at the time didn't help.

During the mid-1970s, when the price of gold began to skyrocket, Cyprus Mines Corporation assembled a large land package in the Wenatchee area and conducted explorations (did some core drilling) at B Reef and D Reef (the old Lovitt workings). This led to the discovery of the B West ore body.[37]

In 1981, Goldbelt Mines and Asamera Minerals U.S., Inc., a subsidiary of Asamera Canada, obtained a working option from Cyprus and began investigations on the B Reef property. In 1982, Breakwater Resources Ltd., another Canadian company, acquired control of Goldbelt. Diamond drilling later that year confirmed the quality and quantity of the ore reserves at the B and B West ore bodies. The companies defined a total of 1.5 million tons of ore, with an average grade of 0.15 ounces of gold per ton. It was during this year that the mine experienced its first fatality. A contract miner from Idaho was working in the recently de-watered B Reef tunnels and was killed by a rock fall.

---

[36] By 1994, Asamera had paid property owners over $14 million in royalties and exploration agreements.

[37] On the last day of drilling and with the last core extracted, they hit it. The company was in the process of dismantling the drills and laying the crew off when the phone call came from the executives. They said, "The assay is good. Stay put in Wenatchee, we're on our way."

The surface workings of the Cannon Mine. The city of Wenatchee is located off to the right of this picture. The buildings were deliberately placed behind the ridge to mask their presence from the town. The mine was located just outside the corporate boundaries of the city. The long, narrow buildings in the distance belong to a horse stable facility. (Ben Guenther collection)

In early 1983, the higher-grade B North ore zone was located. Full-scale development began in 1984, and more diamond drilling confirmed and expanded the known ore bodies. A feasibility study was completed, and environmental permits for construction of facilities were filed. Thirty-five separate permits were required before mining could start, one specifying that all surface structures be removed at the end of operations. Another permit forbade that any water be discharged from the property. The city of Wenatchee also requested that all structures at the mine remain "out of sight" from the city.

Tenneco Minerals also discovered the B-Neath ore body during this period and completed 18,200 feet of core drilling. The B-Neath and the Lower B-Neath were the lowest ore bodies to be mined, and they were also some of the richest.

In the early operation of the Lovitt Mine, ore was handled by front-end loader and dump truck before the concentration mill was installed at the site. (Ed Lovitt Jr. collection)

By the end of 1984, more drilling had established ore reserves of 5.27 million tons, with an average grade of 0.214 ounces of gold per ton, making the B-Reef Mine one of the most significant discoveries in North America. Asamera and Breakwater committed $62 million to the project, and the B-Reef Mine was renamed the Cannon Mine. Contracts were signed with several companies to bore the main decline tunnel, construct a tailings dam, and assemble a mill. Mining and milling began on July 15, 1985.[38]

Development

The Cannon Mine was serviced by both a vertical shaft and decline ramps. The shaft was concrete-lined, 18 feet in diameter, and 620 feet deep, over 30 feet deeper than Seattle's Space Needle is tall. The shaft contained the skips used in bringing the gold and silver ore to the bunkers above. The decline ramps were over 9,000 feet in length, and they spiraled downward for 1,000 feet at a 15 percent slope. The main decline was 15 feet high by 12 feet wide and served as the principal entrance and exit for the mine. Traffic and ventilation in the main decline were controlled by a series of stoplights and air doors. It also intersected with the workings Anaconda and the Lovitt Mining Company had driven earlier (the B Reef tunnels) and used them as one of its emergency escape routes. Until 1992, these tunnels housed the huge ventilation fan for the mine.[39]

The other emergency escape consisted of a 10-foot–diameter ventilation raise, which had been bored between the 820-foot level near the top of the mine, to the B-Neath ore zone at the 200-foot level. This raise was known as VR5. In case of fire, explosion, cave-in, or other emergency, fresh air could be directed to flow down into the B-Neath zone from the top of the mine, out into the 200 level near the bottom of the mine, and then up the vertical shaft at the 620 level to the surface. This raise was also equipped with an Alimak U600 service cage, which provided the powered escape way mandated by Federal Mine Safety and Health Administration regulations. Landings were placed at the top (820) level, and at every other level of the mine other than the 500 level. This escape route proved workable, after a propane explosion near the portal of the main decline in the 1990s. Miners were evacuated via VR5 to the B Reef tunnels. One of them told us it was "a long, ugly journey to the surface."[40] The vertical shaft was equipped with an enclosed ladder, and in the event of a major disaster, a ride to the surface could also be obtained in one of the ore skips.

Ed Lovitt (left) and one of his miners, "Shorty" Tibbs, pose with their "pay dirt" at the Lovitt Mine. (*Wenatchee World* photo, Ed Lovitt Jr. collection)

---

[38] In October 1985, Asamera Inc. greatly enhanced the Cannon Mine's economic potential by acquiring all of the property interests in the Wenatchee area belonging to Tenneco Minerals Company, Houston Oil and Minerals and Exploration Company, and United Mining Corporation. The purchase price was $12.5 million. Prior to the Cannon Mine project, Asamera was primarily involved in crude oil exploration in the North Sea near England, in South Sumatra, in Colombia, and in Italy.

[39] The fan was later moved to a side tunnel just inside the portal of the decline ramp.

[40] Propane fueled a large heater that warmed the mine during the winter months when temperatures in Wenatchee drop below freezing.

A radio system linked various areas of the mine to the mine foreman, shops, offices at the surface, and several mine vehicles. Telephones were also located at several points throughout the workings. The main decline ramp also served the machine shops, crusher room, backfill plant, conveyor to the shaft, and the mine sump, and it was the primary access to the working drifts and stopes. The shaft was used to move the crushed ore, via two counter-balanced seven-ton–capacity skips, to the bunkers at the surface where the mill was located.

In a review of MSHA accident reports, we came across two interesting incidents regarding traffic problems in the main decline, the first of which is referred to as "Bill Holland's Wild Ride." Holland was driving a truck down the decline's 15 percent grade when its brakes failed. Fortunately, no one was hurt, but what a ride he took. Also, a fellow parked at one of the air doors was awaiting the upcoming traffic to pass when he was rear-ended by a runaway L.H.D. (huge, earth-moving front-end loader). He wasn't hurt either.

While a memento of the Cannon Mine uses a rail ore car as its symbol, the mine did not use such equipment. Wheeled and caterpillar tracked equipment was used in this trackless mining operation. (Greg Cady photo)

Operation

Mining was conducted in four phases: drilling, blasting, mucking, and roof control. The latter was accomplished using Shotcrete, wire mesh, and rock bolting as needed to protect against collapse.[41]

Because of the mine's proximity to Wenatchee, and permits that required no surface subsidence, it was mandatory that the operators backfill much of the underground workings. This was fairly easy to do because the Cannon Mine used sublevel bench (cut) and fill, overhand cut and fill, room and pillar, and vertical crater retreat (VCR), which allowed for total support pillar recovery and caused no problem above ground. If you didn't know that the Cannon Mine was there, you might not be aware of it at all, because there were no large tailing piles or mine dumps. The offices, mill, tailings thickener, and head frame were just about the only visible surface structures.

Underground

The access drifts were 15 by 15 feet in size and driven along the strike at 50-foot levels off the decline ramps. Then, 24-foot–wide parallel production stopes were laid out on 48-foot centers and were generally developed level with the access drifts. Hydraulic drills carrying $1^7/_8$-inch drill bits were used in development drifting, producing a blasting area 10 feet deep. This would get the miners to the spot they wanted to stope. Then, 15 by 24–foot sill drifts were driven across the ore body, and slot raises between levels were drilled

---

[41] Resin-grouted rock bolts and Swellex Bolts were used to hold up the wire mesh, like chain link fencing, in the underground workings requiring support. Rock bolts are 6 to 10 feet long and hollow, with a slot down one side. They are slightly larger in diameter than the drill holes and are compressed by being driven into the holes and allowed to expand, holding the wire mesh in place.

The main adit to the Cannon Mine in Wenatchee, Washington. Today this portal is sealed with Shotcrete, and entry is not possible. (Greg Cady photo)

The headframe of the Cannon Mine. This stood on top of a shaft in which a skip hoist that hauled the ore to the surface ran. (Greg Cady photo)

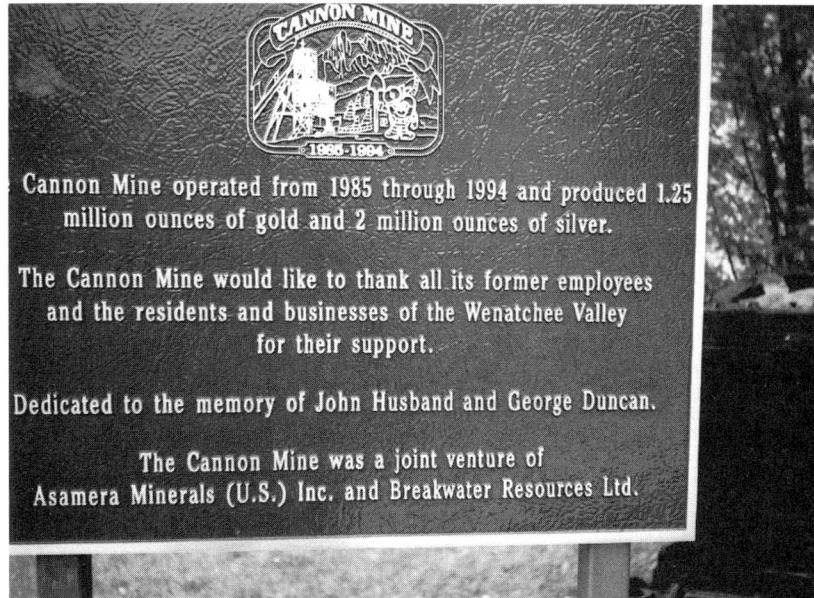

Near the sealed adit of the mine is this plaque memorializing the mine and its operation. The headquarters building of the mining company is now occupied by the local school board. (Greg Cady photo)

and shot from above. The 35-foot-plus sill benches between the superimposed sill drifts were drilled vertically using single-boom-track–mounted hydraulic drills with 2½-inch drill bits. This allowed the ore to drop into the previously dug lower sill drifts (see Cannon Stope Isometric #1).

Ore was mucked from the lower sill drifts using remote-controlled LHDs (Load-Haul-Dump vehicles, which are like front-end loaders with a low profile). The LHDs loaded 26-ton trucks that hauled the ore to a vertical ore pass. The ore pass fed the underground jaw crusher, and from there the crushed ore was transported to the shaft station ore bin by a conveyor belt, where it was hoisted to the surface in the two skips.[42]

Stopes were mined and then backfilled in 50-foot vertical increments, up to a total of 200 feet high. High-strength concrete fill permitted subsequent mining of the 24-foot alternate stopes, or pillars.[43] Sand, water, and cement were fed into the mine via three vertical bores to the surface near the mill. The entire concrete mixing plant was located underground.

"Anfo," an explosive containing ammonium nitrate and fuel oil (thus the acronym), was mainly used. The shots were fired using millisecond time-delay detonators tied to a detonating cord bus. When blasting was underway, only slight vibrations could be felt at the surface, much like what you would feel if you were inside a house and someone shut the front door forcefully.

Following a fatal accident in 1994, a centralized electrical blasting system was installed and the shots were fired from a blasting station located near the portal of the main decline ramp. Electrical charges were not used from the get-go because it was feared that lightning, which occurs frequently in the Wenatchee area, could cause a detonation. The centralized system had a 15-foot shunt just beyond the portal to prevent this from happening.

> **Warning** The very last place you want to be in an electrical storm is near the portal of a mine. Lightning, always seeking the lowest ground, has been known to follow metal pipes, wires, rails, and ventilation equipment deep into underground workings. During the 1980s, a mysterious electrical problem plagued the computer-operated equipment in the mill. It was finally traced to static electricity in the cement drop hole liner pipe. Static electricity is another constant problem in underground workings.

A single-boom Jumbo drill working in the Cannon Mine. The drill was positioned by a diesel engine, but the drilling was actually done hydraulically, with an electric motor powering a hydraulic pump. This unit drilled 10-foot–deep holes, 1⁷/₈ inches in diameter. (Ben Guenther collection)

---

[42] The ore was reduced to less than five inches by the jaw crusher, and the conveyor belt was 900 feet long.

[43] After filling the alternate stopes with the high-strength concrete, which was allowed to harden for two months, the intervening stope areas were mined and then filled with waste rock.

A 5-cubic-yard load-haul-dump (LHD) machine in the Cannon Mine. Since the mine was trackless, all equipment was either tracked or rubber-tired. The LHD is a low-profile front-end loader, and some of them were operable by remote control to allow the operator to stand a safe distance away while the LHD was working in unstable conditions. (Greg Cady photo)

After the centralized system was installed, blasting was never undertaken until everyone was out of the mine and accounted for. A large board in the Lamp Room with an *IN* side and an *OUT* side made this practice possible and is now standard operating procedure for all mines in the United States (not to mention that it's an MSHA-mandated regulation). At the Cannon, the board held a hook on which hung two tags that both contained the employee's number. Before going underground, the employee would remove both tags from the *OUT* side of the board, place one tag on the *IN* side of the board, and carry the other tag in a pocket. (This told operators that the employee was inside the mine.) Upon leaving the mine, the employee would replace both tags on the *OUT* side of the board. This procedure was known as "brassing out" or "tagging out."

If blasting was to take place and a tag was not located in its proper spot, mine officials would search for the missing person, usually a mining engineer or geologist (according to a well-informed source). Only when the person was found would the explosives be fired.

The Lamp Room furnished all who entered the mine their hardhats, recharged headlamps, and self-rescue units. The self-rescuer was a rebreather device that was worn on the belt, which provided a limited amount of oxygen through a mouthpiece. The rebreather has been required by federal regulation ever since the Sunshine Mine Disaster in 1972, in which 91 miners suffocated to death. When we visited the Cannon in 1991, we were trained and certified in the use of this device prior to going underground.

A shrinkage stope in the Cannon Mine is being mucked by a 5-cubic-yard LHD. The machine is being operated by remote control by the fellow at the top of the ore pile in the stope. This stope is 24 feet wide and 65 feet high. The average stope in this mine was 100 feet long, and 7,000 tons of ore were extracted from each. (Ben Guenther collection)

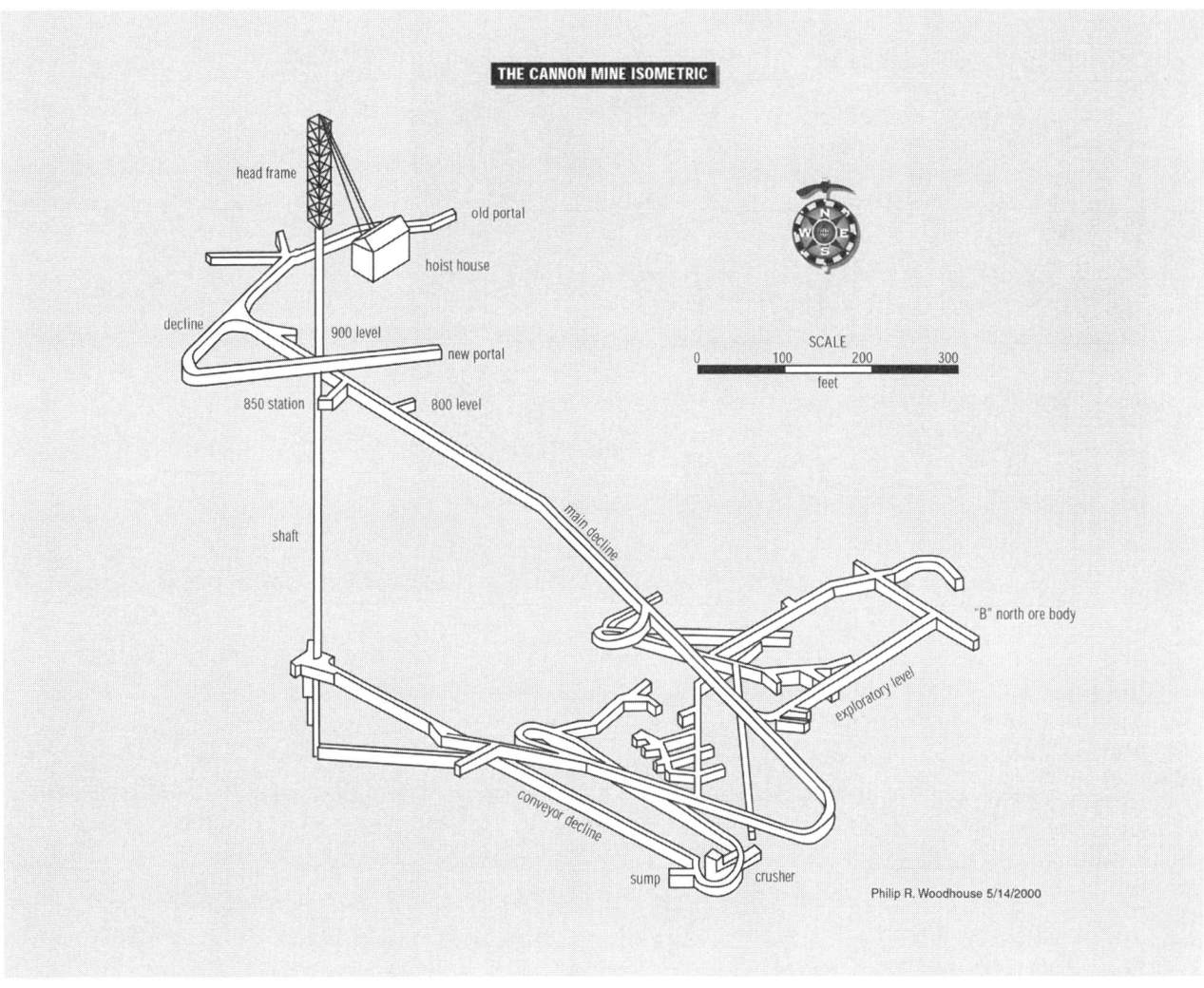

Cannon Mill

The Cannon mill was purchased in Arizona. It had been designed originally as a copper concentrator for a company called Oracle Ridge Partners. This purchase included everything except the building, conveyer, tanks, and pumps. The only major change involved converting one of the ball mills to a rod mill.

The mill was equipped to handle up to 1,500 tons of ore per day.[44] Mined ore passed through the milling process after being surfaced. Due to the refractory nature of the carbonaceous ore, cyanide leaching was not feasible and flotation was chosen as the best concentration process. A lot of thought and testing went into the operation before the mill began functioning. The cyanide, pressure oxidation, and ore-roasting methods were considered but rejected because of low silver recovery in the two latter cases.

At the mill, the ore first went to the cone crusher, then to the rod mill, and last to the ball mill, where it was ground to 200-mesh, like a fine powder. It was then sent to the flotation circuit as slurry. By agitating the ore slurry in the presence of air and chemicals, the gold- and silver-bearing minerals attached to the air bubbles and floated to the top of the flotation cells, in much the same way dirt sticks to soap bubbles. The resulting black concentrate was refloated to remove as much waste as possible, and then skimmed off and squeezed to extract residual liquid.

---

[44] Originally a 2,000-ton-per-day mill was planned, but the tonnage was changed to 1,500 to allow for more time in concentrating the ore, which would result in a purer product.

A 5-cubic-yard LHD is being used to load a 26-ton truck in the Cannon Mine. As clearly seen, the mine operated completely without trackage of any kind. (Ben Guenther collection)

About 100 tons of concentrates were produced from each 2,000 tons of ore processed. Recovery of gold and silver averaged about 85 to 86 percent. The concentrates were then hauled by truck to the Columbia River, Appleyard Siding, where they were loaded aboard rail cars, sent to Vancouver, Washington, and then barged to a smelter in Japan and other smelters in the United States.

The tailings were pumped to the impoundment area high in Dry Gulch where the dam was located. The dam is 6,000 feet from the mill and is 600 feet higher in elevation. The tailings dam is still the largest earthen structure in the state of Washington. It is 300 feet high, 980 feet wide on top, and 1,600 feet long. The dam contains three million cubic yards of material. Over $20 million of the $62 million *start-up* costs for the Cannon Mine were spent on the dam's construction.

During its operation, the Cannon Mine employed an average of 175 people, 86 of whom worked underground. The hoist for the mine's vertical shaft was capable of lifting at a rate of 1,000 feet per minute. The ventilation fan was 96 inches in diameter and was run by an 800-horsepower electric motor, exchanging 450,000 cubic feet of air per minute. The mine used over 350,000 tons of cemented backfill per year, and over 1.5 million pounds of explosives were used on the project.

Looking into the main adit of the Cannon Mine in Wenatchee, Washington. It is difficult to judge the size of the tunnel, but suffice it to say that a full-size dump truck could easily fit into the bore. (Greg Cady photo)

An explosives carrier in the Cannon Mine. Explosives are always dangerous to handle, but every precaution is taken here to avoid a mishap. (Greg Cady photo)

The underground repair shop in the Cannon mine where equipment could be fixed without having to be taken to the surface. (Greg Cady photo)

Mysteries, Rumors, and Secrets

During our exploration of the Lovitt and Cannon Mines, we came across several mysterious clues, one during an expedition into the 1250 level of the Lovitt Mine. We noticed electrical wires coming from the back of the mine rather than from the portal, as would normally be the case. We followed the wires to a point where they disappeared into a backfilled drift. Where did they come from, we asked ourselves? Who put them there, when, and why?

We began to wonder whether the Cannon Mine connected underground with the Lovitt Mine. With hearts racing, we immediately got out our map of the Cannon Mine tunnel system, and closely checked the area around the B Reef workings. The map shows a 500-foot tunnel called 940 BRAD (940 level B Reef Access Drift), which connects to the main decline ramp and then angles southwest under the tailings thickener, in the direction of the Lovitt Mine.

Another question presented itself in the form of the huge ventilation fan, which had been housed 100 feet down inside B Reef, but had for some reason been moved to the decline ramp. It occurred to us that this move had been done to help ventilate a tunnel between the Cannon and the Lovitt Mines. To further make us wonder, we found that the Cannon miners had extended a crosscut under the A Reef and had done a minor amount of stoping in that area. Did they do the same with the D Reef?

Our Cannon Mine maps were made in 1993, but the mine did not cease operating until 1995. So we also knew that our maps were out of date. During the missing two years, lots of tunneling could have been done.

For many years, a rumor had been going around the Wenatchee area that the Cannon Mine operators (Asamera) had somehow discovered a huge deposit of high-grade gold and silver directly under Wenatchee High School. Our maps did not show any crosscutting in that direction (east of the B Reef workings) other

One of the large, semi-automated drilling machines used in the Cannon Mine. Called a Tamrock 2-boom electric-hydraulic drill jumbo, it could drill blasting holes at a great variety of angles and distances. The large tunnels in the trackless mine couldn't have been bored without it. (Greg Cady photo)

To ventilate a mine the size of the Cannon, large air-moving equipment was required. Made by the Joy Company, this 96-inch–diameter fan was powered by the 800-horsepower motor seen in the foreground. The unit moved 450,000 cubic feet of air per minute through the mine. (Ben Guenther collection)

than the mining that was done under the Appleatchee Stables. Moreover, a search of Asamera's records didn't show core drilling anywhere near the high school. So where did this information come from? If it was true, why didn't Asamera mine it?

That was when another story surfaced. Reportedly, the city of Wenatchee heard of these great ore deposits and had put a stop to permit applications to protect students from mine gases, collapses, or explosions.

No one we had interviewed so far could answer our questions, so we decided to find the person who would know all the answers: Ben Guenther, the former superintendent of the Cannon Mine. It had been over two years since the mine had closed, and we were told that Mr. Guenther might be in Elko, Nevada, where many of the former Cannon miners were now employed. We contacted him there, and he said that he would gladly answer our questions. Here are his answers, in his own words:

Q. Did the Cannon Mine tunnels intersect with the workings of the Lovitt Mine?
A. No.

Cannon Stope Isometric #1

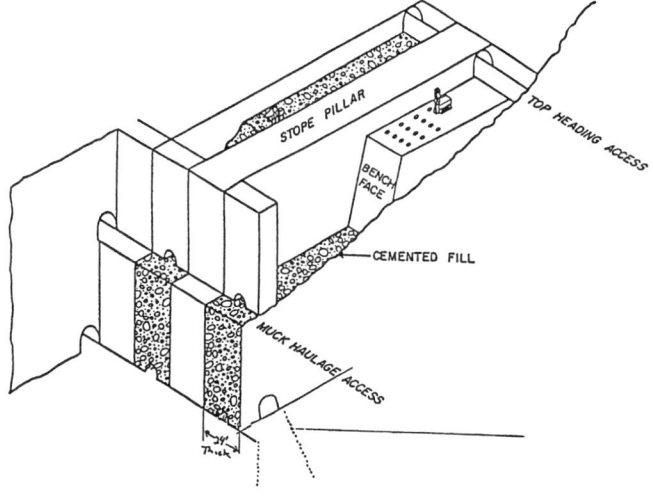

Before visiting the Cannon Mine, Daryl Jacobson, on the right, a Northwest Underground Exploration member, gets last-minute instructions. Any visitors to this mine had to learn to use an escape pack self-rescue unit before entering, and, of course, adequate lighting equipment had to be worn. Notice the banks of headlamps on their battery-charging equipment. (Greg Cady photo)

Strapping on the equipment belts and self-rescue units prior to entering the Cannon Mine in 1991. (Greg Cady photo)

Q. Why was the ventilation fan moved?
A. To allow for mining in the upper B West and B Reef. The fan was too close to these areas and could have been damaged.

Q. Did Asamera Minerals discover a huge body of high-grade gold and silver under the Wenatchee High School? If so, why wasn't it mined?
A. No, not even close. There was no mining within the Wenatchee city limits, and no permits were ever applied for.

Q. Why are there electrical wires in the 1250 level of the Lovitt Mine, coming from the rear rather than from the front of the mine?
A. Electrical wires were used by Asamera for underground diamond drilling in the Lovitt Mine. The electrical wire remaining was possibly a portion not removed after diamond drilling ended.

Q. In your opinion, if gold prices reach another high, as they did in the 1970s and 1980s, do you think that the Cannon or Lovitt Mines would ever be reopened?
A. Ever is a long time, and anything is possible.
Ben Guenther, 1998

Cannon Stope Isometric #2

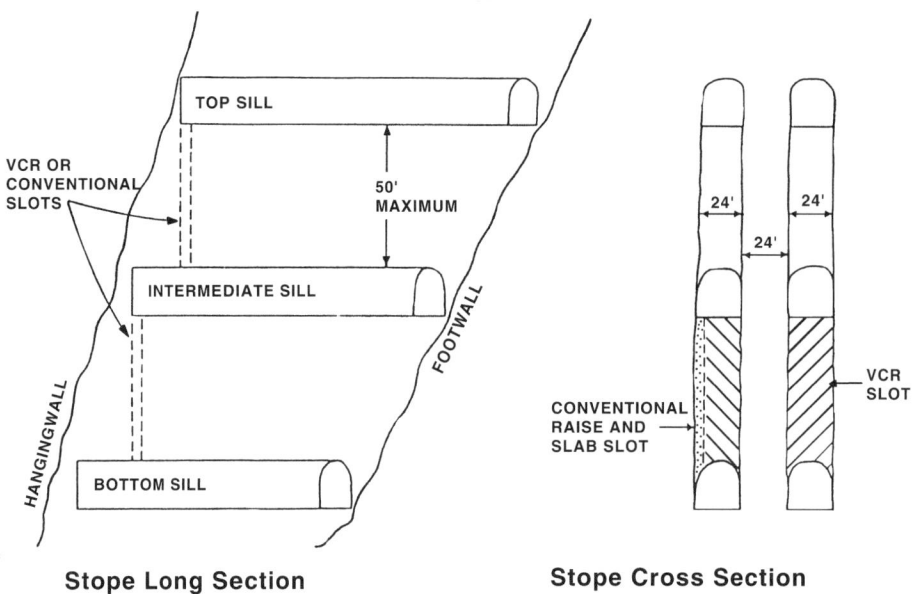

Stope Long Section   Stope Cross Section

Cannon Fatalities

Three men were killed while working at the Cannon Mine: John T. Husband and George C. Duncan, who were Asamera employees, and John M. Porter, who worked for another company.

On May 8, 1982,[45] John Porter, a 29-year-old employee of the Wallace Diamond Mining Company of Idaho—with 10 years of mining experience—was doing mucking and barring-down work in the 840 track drift of the B Reef workings before installing drilling stations. A large slab of rock, weighing about five tons, fell from the side of the drift, killing him instantly. The official cause of the accident, according to MSHA, was "failure to detect the loose slab, even though the rib (side) and back (ceiling) had been checked and obvious loose rock had been barred down. The B Reef tunnels had just been de-watered, after having been flooded for about 20 years. As the rock in the tunnel dried, a slaking action occurred, and a hairline fracture may not have been noticeable."

On February 12, 1987, John Husband, a 34-year-old miner with considerable experience in the mines, three years of which were at the Cannon Mine, was killed when he fell 50 feet down into the 650 D45 stope while in the process of setting off explosives. According to MSHA, the official cause of the accident is as follows: "Since there were no eyewitnesses to the accident, it can only be assumed that for some unknown reason the victim went too close to the edge of the bench in 650 D45, which either collapsed out from under him or he slipped and fell off the edge of the bench, or both, before the blasting took place."

On August 11, 1994, George Duncan Sr., a 55-year-old miner with 32 years of mining experience, the last two years and nine months of which he worked at the Cannon Mine, was killed by a rock fall. The official cause, according to MSHA, is as follows: "It appears that the accident resulted from blasting earlier in the day that caused a large slab of rock to loosen, finally dislodge, and then fall from the stope back. The victim was exposed to this hazard when he entered the roped-off location which had been tagged as [bad ground]."

---

[45] This was before the mine was officially known as the Cannon Mine. It was still in the exploration phase and was known as the B Reef Mine.

Cannon Mill Concentrator

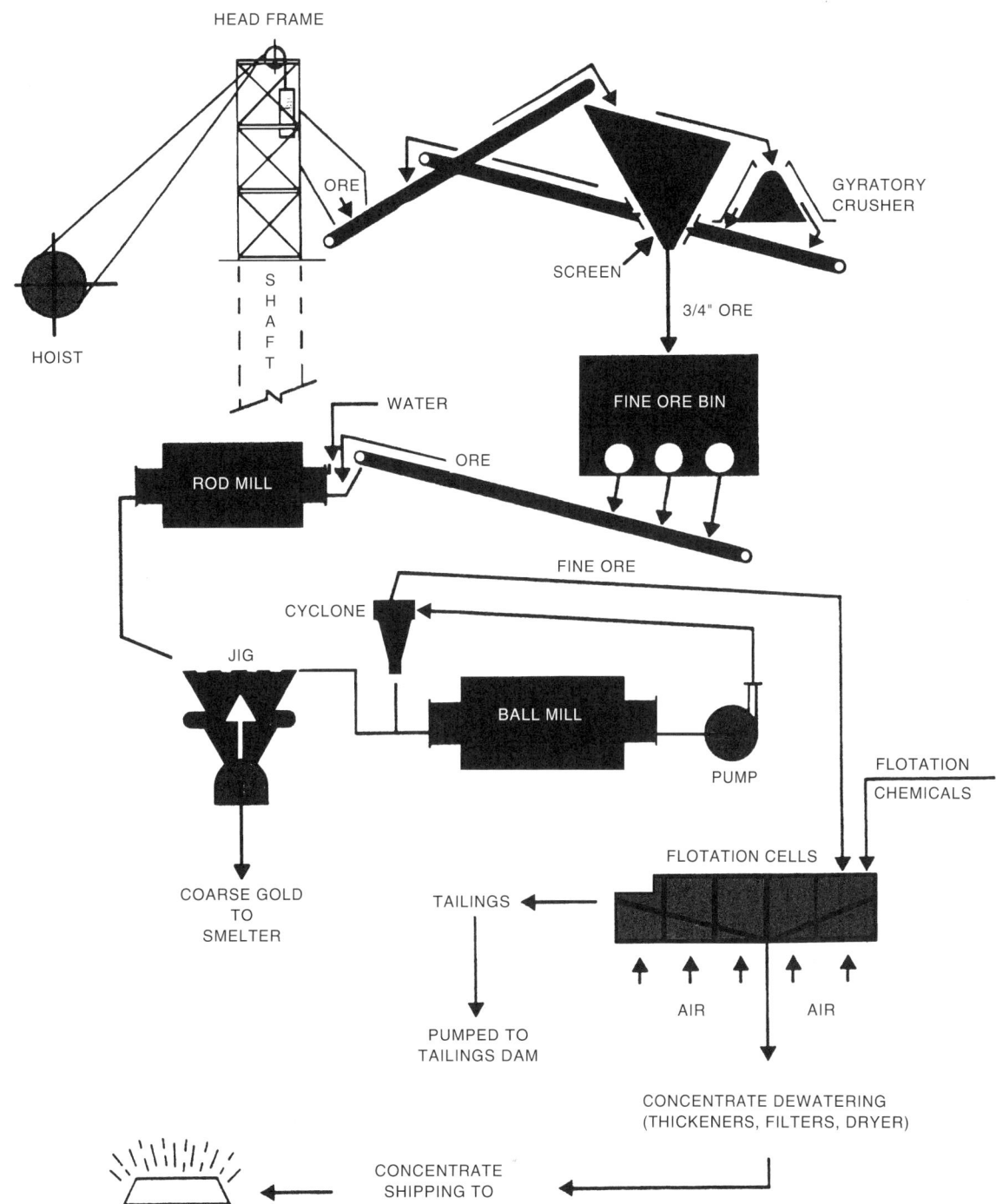

During our tour of the Cannon Mine in August 1991, members of Northwest Underground Explorations ride the rubber-tired jitney down the spiral decline toward the workings below. (Greg Cady photo)

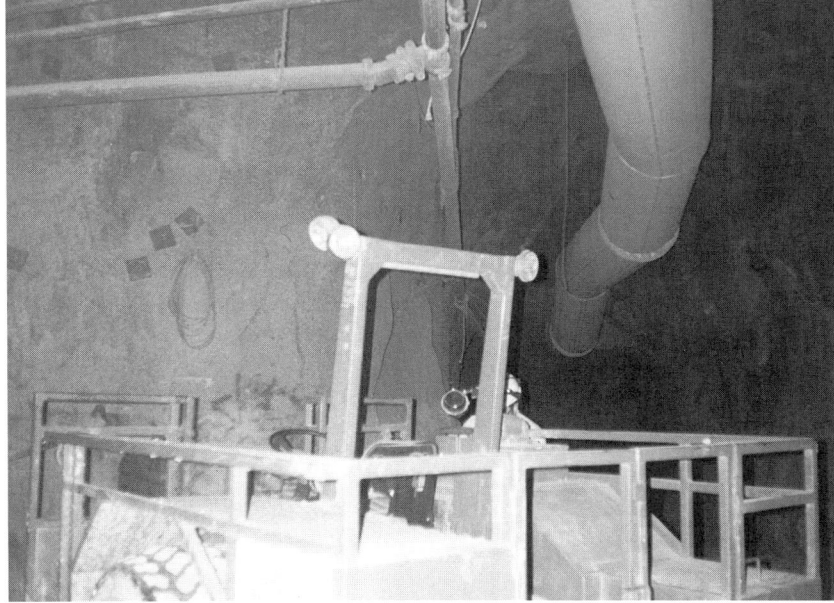

The jitney that carried men and equipment throughout the Cannon Mine. Notice the large ventilation pipe overhead. (Greg Cady photo)

Note We mention these accidents to illustrate how very dangerous this line of work can be and to emphasize that, even when great safety measures are taken, underground workings are not forgiving. Please stay out of the mines.

Production

The Cannon Mine produced an average of *500* ounces of gold *per day*. Between 1985 and 1994, the miners extracted 1.25 million ounces of gold and over two million ounces of silver. It was the second-largest gold producer in the United States during its period of operation.[46] The operating cost to mine one ton of ore, including supplies, salaries, electricity, fuel, and explosives, was $49.00. Add to this the shipping and smelting costs of $163.00.[47]

---

[46] The Homestake Mine at Lead, South Dakota, came in at number one.

[47] The mine's payroll was approximately $8 million per year.

The percentages that each individual reef supplied to the total production areas follow:

A-Reef	1 percent
B-Reef	1 percent
B-West	12 percent
B-4	12 percent
B-Neath	35 percent
B-North	39 percent

The closure of the Cannon Mine in 1995 brought an end to lode-gold mining in the Wenatchee area for the time being. As of this writing, it doesn't seem that gold prices will ever reach the all-time highs of the late 1970s. The Lovitt and Cannon ore bodies are essentially mined out, and although many thousands of dollars have been spent on modern prospecting in the Wenatchee region, nothing has been found that could be profitably mined at today's gold prices.

An examination of several geological reports and visits to the Wenatchee area indicate that another large ore body similar to the B Reef does exist to the northwest of A Reef, extending under the Wenatchee city limits.[48] Other indications of silicified ore are visible across the Columbia River in Douglas County. Core drilling at Compton's Knob south of the Lovitt Mine has revealed gold ore at great depth. A final geological report on the Cannon Mine states: "Significant resources of sub-economic mineralization remain in B-Reef, B-West, and B-North, at mine closing."

Hundreds of thousands of dollars' worth of silver and gold ore are estimated to remain in the Lovitt Mine's dumps and tailings. It would not be surprising if Wenatchee hosts another major mining operation sometime in the future.

Just a Reminder The fatalities that occurred at the Lovitt and Cannon Mines happened to experienced miners who had a total of nearly 80 years of combined underground experience, and were working under federally mandated safety conditions. Mining, mine sites, and especially underground exploration can and most often do contain hazards at every turn. Again, please stay out of the mines.

Big Ed and a Word About B Reef

One of the most amazing and interesting results of our research on the Lovitt Mine and the surrounding area was the discovery of a mining thesis written back in 1967 by Thomas Charles Patton. Patton wrote about a conversation he had in June 1967 with Ed Lovitt, in which he asked what Lovitt thought about the future of gold mining in the area around the now-closed L&D Mine. Ed said, "Economic gold deposits have been found at B Reef. There is enough gold at A Reef to suggest that exploration in the valley between these two silicified areas might reveal a sizable deposit at depth." Lovitt had predicted the existence of the huge Cannon Mine ore bodies *15 years before* their discovery by Cyprus Mines and Asamera Minerals. We guess someone should have listened when he said, "Dig here."

---

[48] *The Cannon Mine and Its Surface Outcrop*, Wenatchee, Washington. Donald Cameron, August 1994.

Blewett Mining Area

Peshastin and Negro Creeks

This famous district is located near the geographic center of Washington State. It runs along the north slope of the southeast-to-northwest–trending Wenatchee Mountains, which rise from an elevation of about 1,000 feet near the Columbia River on the east to the 9,415-foot summit of Mount Stuart on the west near the range's junction with the crest of the Cascade Mountains. This very bold and rugged mountain landscape is typical of the eastern slopes of the Cascade Range. Barren rock faces are common at higher elevations, whereas heavy overburden and brush abound in the lower valleys and steep canyons.

Several varieties of trees are common in the district, including tamarack, yellow pine, and red fir. The main tributaries from south to north include Tronsen Creek, Shaser Creek, King Creek, Culver Springs Creek, Negro Creek, Ruby Creek, and Ingalls Creek, all of which run into Peshastin Creek, the main drainage for the area. The winter climate is characterized by cold, snowy winters and temperatures below zero degrees Fahrenheit. Summers are warm and dry, but seldom are as hot as just 20 or so miles to the east. The heart of the district is at the mouth of Culver Gulch, along US 97, 11 miles south of US 2 and 32 miles north of Cle Elum.

History

In 1860 or so, during the very early days of mining in Washington Territory, prospectors began returning from the Okanogan and Fraiser River areas. They paused long enough to work the placer deposits along the creeks, recovered some gold, and then moved on. The first reported gold discovery was made by members of the Mortimer Robertson prospecting party in 1858. Robertson himself apparently washed a dollar's worth of gold from the gravel bedrock in his bare hand near the camp,[1] and another $1.50 worth from a single pan as he backtracked upstream from the camp to a point believed to be near the mouth of Shaser or Scotty Creek.[2]

Later, probably around 1874 or 1875, a black man named Antoine Etienne (nicknamed "Big Antoine")[3] was said to have recovered about $1,100 from the gravel of the creek that was later named Negro Creek because of his discovery.[4] Although Antoine was born to slave parents, he had attended the school of his white master, where he learned to speak French and proper English. Etienne went west following the Civil War and joined the Army as an interpreter. Along the way, he also picked up several Native American languages. In his post-mining years, Etienne became locally famous for his peach, grape, and cherry crops. In 1907, he died on a trip to Vancouver.[5]

---

[1] The location of this camp was said to be 12 miles from the mouth of Peshastin Creek, which would put it at about the old Blewett town site.

[2] As you'll read a little later, discoveries may have been made as early as 1855, before the Indian/White wars in 1855-1856.

[3] Cattleman Andrew Splawn had heard of Etienne while traveling through Native American country along the Columbia River. Splawn ran into Indians with "attitude" not to his liking while driving cattle through the Entiat area in 1868. Etienne was mining gold a short distance up the Entiat River, and was in good with the indigenous locals. He could speak several of their languages, and he told them to make it difficult for those traveling to and fro in the area. Splawn discovered the source of his problems: the "border ruffian" as he called Etienne. Meeting with him face to face, he said if he ever heard of Etienne causing more harassment to travelers, he would take him to task. The troubles ceased.

[4] All the old maps use a now socially unacceptable word for the creek's name, which was in common usage back then.

[5] We don't know whether it was Vancouver, Washington, or B.C.

Chinese miners aim a monitor nozzle to direct water for sluicing a placer deposit. (*Idaho, an Illustrated History*, 1976)

For the next 15 years, placer mining seemed to wax and wane until the loose gold became more and more elusive and prospectors turned instead to hardrock gold. Chinese miners, however, continued to work the gravels of the area's creeks. In 1874, pioneer prospector Samuel Culver located and claimed a ledge of free-milling gold on the left side of the gulch that bears his name. He named the claim the Pole Pick. Culver was soon followed by another prospector by the name of John Shafer who located and staked the Culver Claim high on the divide between what is now known as Culver Gulch and Negro Creek. Soon after that, Culver located the Humming Bird Claim farther down Culver Gulch. Then the rush began in

In the last part of the 19th century, Blewett residents built their homes using local materials. The sturdy log cabin was common at that time because logs were plentiful and the area was too remote to allow the shipping of lumber from distant sawmills. Here a Blewett family relaxes on the front porch of their home, perhaps on a Sunday. (The Burmeister collection. North Central Washington Museum, Wenatchee, Washington)

earnest as prospectors such as James Lockwood, John Olden, Sylvester Cover, Jack Brusha, and Peter Wilder began locating hardrock claims. The Fraction and Little Culver became two of the next claims in this young district, and several arrastres were built in the area.

In 1877, James Lockwood, his son E. W. Lockwood, and Harbin M. Cooper acquired all the claims except the Pole Pick and Little Culver and set up a six-stamp mill with one Frue vanner. It became the very first stamp mill in Washington Territory. The mill was operated by waterpower and could pulverize eight tons of ore in 24 hours. The cleanup for the first nine days of operation was said to be $2,100. The

An early cabin near the town of Blewett, Washington. This is most likely its builder sitting on the porch. Notice the cordwood stored, ready for the cold winter months. (Wes and Carole Engstrom collection, Liberty, Washington)

partners also ran an arrastre with a daily capacity of 1,000 pounds. Its output averaged about $70.00 a day. This mine and mill ran for several years before being sold to Thomas Johnson, who soon shut the operations down for reasons that are unclear.

The first wagon road into the area was completed in 1879. It connected the booming little mining camp with Cle Elum some 32 miles to the south. All heavy supplies and equipment had to be hauled into the area over this road on wagons, horses, or mules. The packers were paid about $60.00 a month. In 1891, the property owned by Thomas Johnson was sold to the Culver Gold Mining Company. This new company erected a 10-stamp mill with four Woodbury concentrators and installed a bucket tramway that ran for one-fifth mile from the mine to the mill. In 1892, the property again changed hands to the Blewett Gold Mining Company, which comprised a group of Seattle investors, including Edward Blewett, a well-known mining investor, and H. C. Henry, who had built the Henry Building in Seattle. This new company went right to work developing the mine and mill. The mines began producing, and values in free gold were reported at anywhere from $8 to $20 per ton, with pockets reaching as much as $700 per ton. Unfortunately, as the tunnels obtained depth, free gold values diminished.[6]

The original Blewett schoolhouse was sturdily built out of logs from the surrounding forest. The schoolmaster and teacher pose with their pupils between 1892 and 1894. The first motion picture in the region was shown here, and it created quite a sensation. (The Burmeister collection. North Central Washington Museum, Wenatchee, Washington)

---

[6] This is typical of the geology in the Cascade and Wenatchee Mountains.

The new owners soon erected a 20-stamp mill, with room for an additional 20 stamps to be added later,[7] at the mouth of Culver Gulch. The mill also had four Woodbury concentrators and many labor-saving appliances. The bucket tramway was extended to the new mill, and a 10,000-foot-per-day–capacity saw mill was erected three miles south, on what is now known as Scotty Creek. This mill supplied lumber for the stamp mill buildings and bridges, over which much of its new machinery was transported.

By 1892, the camp had a store, barbershop, and blacksmith shop, and a saloon was under construction. Later in the fall of 1892, a doctor and lawyer were brought in by the company and a minister agreed to make bimonthly visits to the camp from Leavenworth.[8] On January 9, 1893, the first post office was established at the little mining camp, and the camp's official name became Warner, after Mr. Warner, the general manager of the Blewett Gold Mining Company. The first postmaster was Ella I. Dodge. The camp's name was changed a few months later to Blewett.[9] In addition to the post office, Blewett had grown to accommodate three stores, two restaurants, two boarding houses, a saloon, and a dozen homes.

In 1894, a town hall was built using donated materials. Some of the miners volunteered three day's labor to build it. The town hall also served as a school. The mine and mill had been operated as a single unit by the owners until 1894, when they decided to lease out portions of the mine to independent miners. They felt that the miners took more interest in the ore they mined and were a bit more careful in sorting when they held an actual interest rather than just working for wages.[10] The miners who continued working for the various companies received about $2.00 per day, plus room and board for their sunup-to-sundown workday, and in some cases also got a grubstake to prospect for themselves in their free time. The company contin-

The clapboard Blewett schoolhouse that replaced the older log building. The school marm, on the left, poses with some of her charges. (The Burmeister collection. North Central Washington Museum, Wenatchee, Washington)

---

[7] This was said to be the largest stamp mill in the state at the time.

[8] The doctor arrangement apparently didn't last long because it was said that the place never had a doctor of its own.

[9] Nobody seems sure whether the town was named after Edward Blewett, a Seattle mining engineer who had extensive holdings in the area, or his brother Bill, who lived nearby and also had some mining holdings there.

[10] Most likely this was because the earth was so fractured and faulted that true veins were impossible to follow and no real geological principals could be employed to seek out the pockets. This made mining in the area a hit-or-miss prospect, so it was cheaper to let independents spend their own money on exploration, which also eliminated the problem of high grading.

ued to run the mill, charging royalties and a milling charge graduated up to a certain value of the ore. In full production, the mine and mill employed about 60 men. Under this system, the Blewett Mining Company produced about $60,000 in bullion in 1896.

The operation was not without problems, though. For example, arsenic in the ore caked the quicksilver on the plates, which prevented it from catching the gold, and much of the fine copper sulfides escaped in the slime as foam. For this reason, the mill tailings were retained in dams until a suitable process to deal with the loss problems could be devised. In about 1899, a small cyanide plant that separated the minerals from the country rock more efficiently was built near the mill.

In spring 1896, the Blewett Mining Company sold the old 10-stamp mill to Thomas Johnson, who had been using it for milling ore from the Pole Pick Claim.[11] The property changed hands again later that year, when the Warrior General Company purchased the mill and mines for $3,500.00. A short time later, the Warrior General Company changed to the Chelan Mining and Milling Company. Under the new organization, the materials left in the old ore dumps were run though the mill. At about the same time, King County Assessor T. A. Perish acquired the Peshastin Claim in Culver Gulch and drove an 85-foot tunnel, striking an ore chute that became known as the Perish Ore Chute. From this operation, 2,000 tons of ore was run though the Chelan Mining Company Mill, producing about $13.00 to the ton, along with several tons of concentrates of unknown value.

A young boy stands before his log cabin in Blewett. The little home was most likely built with hand-hewn logs and hand-split cedar roofing shingles. (The Burmeister collection. North Central Washington Museum, Wenatchee, Washington)

As it became available in Blewett, sawn lumber began to replace logs for construction purposes. A family poses in front of their clapboard home. (The Burmeister collection. North Central Washington Museum, Wenatchee, Washington)

---

[11] By this time, several arrastres had also been built and were in use in the area.

The Blewett post office around the turn of the century. Lingering winter snow is indicative of the harshness of the weather. (The Burmeister collection. North Central Washington Museum, Wenatchee, Washington)

In 1898, the 18-mile–long wagon road from the town of Peshastin, located to the north in the Wenatchee Valley, was completed to Blewett.[12] This proved to be a major benefit to the miners at Blewett because the Great Northern Railway passed though Peshastin, enabling them to transport bigger and heavier equipment and livestock into the area. Almost immediately, tri-weekly stage and mail service began. Extensive development in the district ensued, and an old saloon in Blewett was even converted to a stage station.

A series of crosscut tunnels were driven on the Peshastin ore bodies from the Culver Gulch Mines to the vein, in which rich ore pockets were encountered. The Blewett District became very active at this time. In 1905, the Chelan Mining and Milling Company merged with the La Rica Mining Company to become the Washington Meteor Company.[13] It was estimated that from 1870 to 1910, $1.7 million was mined from the Blewett area, including both placer and quartz, with the majority coming from the mines in Culver Gulch.[14] Ore values varied widely, but the median range was between $3 and $10 per ton, plus some occasional shoots ranging as high as $10,000.00 to the ton. Silver was prominent in the mines here, but gold was of primary interest.

The Genesis of the Gold Bond Mining Company 1934–1974

Changing of claim names and groups, and consolidating solo claims into groups, has caused old and new groups to overlap, as evident from the following data.

In 1937, Company President J. F. Hocking stated the mines were ready to ship 30 tons of ore daily. Company holdings included the Blinn Claims, which include the patented Shafer, Olympia, Pole Pick No. 3, Seattle, and Vancouver. The Wilder Mine claims were the Ivanhoe, Kennilworth, and Amber Glee, situated on the north side of Culver Gulch and over the divide down toward Negro Creek and the Johnson-Davidson property. A 20-man crew was employed at these properties.

C. P. Davenport was in the process of driving tunnels on the Blinn and Wilder Mines from the Negro Creek side. Some high-grade ore was taken down Culver Gulch by Pack animal at first. Then new roads were built to the mine's ore bins. Harve H. Phipps was secretary and general manager at the site. He ordered deeper tunnels and a mill to treat the lower-grade ore. H. B. Stoner became mine superintendent. He hired the Brand, Sullivan, and Carson Company of Seattle to expand the Pole Pick tunnel and also had the Pole Pick mill reconditioned. Two thousand feet of tunnel and shafts were developed on the properties.

In 1938, George, H. Lewis was contracted to install a tramway from the portals of the Negro Creek tunnels to a mill site. By 1941, the Gold Bond Mining Company was under lease: Karl Fackler served as general manager, J. W. Hatley as president, and Harve Phipps as secretary. Gold and silver ore was produced at irregular intervals.

---

[12] It would be many years before the road from Peshastin to Cle Elum would be anything but a very crude, dangerous, and at times impassable wagon road.

[13] The La Rica Mining Company operated the Peshastin and Keynote Claims and later acquired the famous Blackjack property.

[14] This figure would not include the placer gold removed by the Chinese and other one-and two-man operations that sold their gold elsewhere.

And just what did the good folks do on a Sunday after Church in the mining towns like Blewett? Often they would pack their picnic baskets and pay a visit to the nearby mines. That is probably what is happening in this picture. Everyone is dressed in their Sunday best. (Grace Browitt Elkins collection)

In 1949, Frank Lily wrote the "Gold Bond Report and analysis," a promotional piece on the Gold Bond mining company. The report mentioned C. P. Davenport, Antone Neubauer, and Charles E. Marr, all respected men of mining and engineering knowledge and experience. These mentions were meant to promote the property.

From 1950–1955, the Gold Bond Mining Company was in operation again after a few years of inactivity. Ore was being produced from the Pole Pick lower property on the Peshastin vein via the Olympia tunnel. Frank Lily became the company president during this time.

By the early 1960s, Hadley Hackney had risen to vice president, and J. J. Jutzy was consulting engineer. A tramway connected to the upper tunnel of the Olympia transported ore down Culver Gulch to the Suckling mill, located between the Pole Pick Claims.

In 1963, Arthur H. Ellis filed a complaint in Superior Court asking for an appointment of receivership against the Gold Bond Mining Company. Lily was named as a codefendant with Gold Bond. He was enjoined from disposing of or secreting company books. Harm H. Schlomer was named temporary receiver. Ellis alleged that Lily had no list of shareholders, that he held an unknown majority of company shares, and that there had not been a shareholder meeting since Lily started the company in 1949. In fact, the last meeting of directors had been held in 1947. The judge ordered that a stockholders' meeting be held.

Thirty shareholders attending the meeting elected a five-man board to whom Lily gave a weak and unconvincing testimony. Willis R. Priestly said that he and his father, who had formed a partnership known as NW Mining Ventures, planned to start mining and milling gold from the company's Pole Pick Claim that spring, continuing from development work they had done the previous fall under contract agreement with Lily. The company's new board elected Ellis as president. Mrs. Corliss Stewart was elected vice president, Mrs. Marle Meyer was secretary, Archie Stewart treasurer, and Fred F. Woeppel company attorney.

In 1964, Priestly continued to operate the Pole Pick properties on a contract basis. He had seven men mining, milling, and doing exploratory work. Attempts in the 1970s to reestablish interest in the properties via nickel exploration and continuing pursuit of gold and silver faded, and by 1974 the only reported values were coming from the Priestly operation.

About 1912, litigation put the Washington Meteor plans on hold until 1918, when the Amalgamated Gold Mines Company took over the operation with plans of reopening the old workings, which were in a very bad state of collapse. The company managers also planned to remodel the Blewett Mill, much of which had been dismantled except for the battery of 20 stamps. They wanted to first do a little experimenting by placing only five stamps in operation and an amalgamation process, followed perhaps by shaker tables and flotation concentration.

Also in 1912, Frank S. Earnest (son of John Earnest, Pole Pick No. 2's original owner in 1874) and other Spokane, Washington, men took over three of Culver Gulch's top producing claims. This was on a five-year lease, capitalized as the Consolidated Gold Mines and Refining Company. The company put a six-stamp mill and a six-tank cyaniding plant on the Golden Eagle property. It had a capacity of 50 tons of ore per day. Three shifts of eight men were put to work under the management of F. S. Earnest. But by 1925 the mines and mill were once again idle, and except for an occasional spurt of interest they have remained inactive since.

What to See

This district, accessible via US 97, offers a pleasant Sunday's drive for the casual traveler. For the more adventuresome, the side creeks and hills present a challenging and sometimes dangerous escape from the workaday world. The altitude gain in the Swauk Pass area usually keeps the summer's heat at bay, but temperatures in the 80s and 90s can be expected here in July and August. Winter weather piles snow and ice on the region, making travel treacherous at times. Many babbling brooks and streams that quickly dry up as summer approaches accompany springtime in the area. The rock is often reddish in color. The foliage is generally rather sparse, with pines, deciduous trees, and light brush predominating. The scenery consists of steep, rolling hills, with spectacular mountains (the Stuart Range) rising beyond. Mount Stuart is the second-highest nonvolcanic mountain in Washington State, and its gullies remain snow-covered until the later summer months. In the fall, when the leaves on the deciduous trees and brush turn color, this is a beautiful area to visit. Mine tunnels can sometimes be glimpsed from the highway, as well as some of the placer tailings that remain from dredge mining.

Getting There

The Blewett District can be reached from the Puget Sound area via either Snoqualmie Pass or Stevens Pass. Take I-90 east to the US 970 (Wenatchee) exit just east of Cle Elum. Travel several miles to the junction with US 97, and continue north over Swauk Pass toward the Peshastin Creek valley. Or, if you prefer, take US 2 east through Leavenworth. Turn right just east of Peshastin onto US 97, and follow it south toward Swauk Pass. From Wenatchee, go west on US 2, the Stevens Pass highway, to the above-mentioned exit east of Peshastin. Continue as stated above. From Ellensburg, travel east on I-90 to the US 97 (Wenatchee) junction, and continue as stated above. The heart of the district will be very apparent when a roadside sign alerts you to the historic marker just ahead. The marker is the site of what was once Blewett and one of the many arrastres in the area.

Geology

One of the most important factors associated with the final uplift of the Cascade mountain mass was the differential warping of the raised dome, which in this particular portion of the Cascades resulted in the formation of the Wenatchee Mountains. The upward movement caused drainage gullies to adapt themselves to the new conditions. Streams such as Ingalls Creek and Peshastin Creek developed as a result. As the Wenatchee mountain mass kept rising, the grade of the newly developed streams increased. Their accelerated flow rapidly cut into the rock below, which possessed differential resistance. The small, lateral streams excavated their channels into rock that offered the least resistance, giving rise to such streams as Negro Creek, Ruby Creek, Shaser Creek, and Tronson Creek. This carving of the land increased until the present topographical features developed. Glacial action played little part.

The oldest rock formation in the district consists of a lower series of quartzites, slates, quartzite-conglomerates, and cherts, overlaid apparently unconformably by an upper series of brecciated lavas and tuffs, together with massive igneous rocks. There's been no fossil dating to determine the age of the rocks because no fossils have been found. After they were deposited, they underwent deformation, resulting in their current morphism. Great intrusions of peridotite and other associated basic igneous rocks that were later more or less altered to serpentine accompanied the deformation. Erosion and deformational movements warped the rock, allowing great drainage basins to form. Sandstone and shale belonging to the Swauk formation accumulated to a thickness of 5,000 feet, in some spots, in the great drainage basins caused by this warped rock.

Numerous diabase dikes leading up to and connecting with the surface lava flows of the Teanaway basalt cut though the Swauk sandstone. Plutonic masses and sills of gabbro are intruded into the Swauk and the older rocks as well; they were probably injected either just before or at the same time as the diabase. Later sedimentary lake deposits known as the Roslyn formation are overlying this. There are still-younger sediments, lavas, and tuffs above these, but no rocks younger than the diabase occur within the Blewett District proper, with the exception of Quaternary gravels and alluvium. Rocks in the area are pre-Tertiary metamorphic and igneous formations and Tertiary sedimentary, intrusive, and volcanic assemblages.

Gold-bearing quartz and carbonate bodies occur as lenticular veins in serpentine zones within a peridotite mass. Ore was mined from four veins with westerly striking, steeply dipping fissures: the Ivanhoe, Peshastin, Pole Pick, and North Star (north to south). It appears that the ores mined in the past were of the free-milling variety, with values averaging in the $15 to $50 per ton range, and some high-grade pockets averaging as much as $63,000 to the ton (based on a $35.00-per-ounce price). Most of the production was from the Peshastin vein, where about 90 percent of the ore removed contained gold that was later extracted.

The Mines
Ingalls Creek

Ingalls Creek defines the northern boundary of the Blewett mining area. Although little serious mining activity was ever carried on here, it is the centerpiece of one of the most interesting lost gold mine stories in Washington. The legend of Captain Ingalls's lost gold strike has been told in many variations, and theories abound as to the true nature of the cache and its actual location. The generally accepted version is that a U.S. Army captain, Ben Ingalls, became separated from his detachment while on patrol in the Wenatchee Mountains sometime prior to mid-December 1872. As dusk deepened, he began to search for a suitable spot to camp for the night, since making contact with the rest of the soldiers that night would be out of the question. From a ridge overlooking a deep valley, Ingalls spotted a series of three lakes nestled snugly in the valley below. He believed that the area around the lakes would make a comfortable camp spot, and water was readily available, so he descended into the beckoning valley.

When he arrived near the middle lake, Ingalls noticed a crumbling rotten quartz vein laced with abundant native gold. He remained in the area long enough to spend the night and draw a crude map to his newfound fortune, and then he started down the stream (now known as Ingalls Creek), expanding his map as he traveled. He hid the map near the mouth of the creek at its junction with Peshastin Creek, along with a few chunks of the booty he had packed down as evidence of his find. As the story goes, Ingalls later confided his secret in letters to his old friend John Hansel, also revealing the map's hiding place. Ingalls was later killed, leaving Hansel as the only benefactor to the map. But Hansel couldn't find the map or the three lakes Ingalls had mentioned. Folks presumed that the large earthquake on December 14, 1872, that had completely blocked the Columbia River between Wenatchee and Chelan, and formed Ribbon Cliff, had also covered the three lakes and the map's hiding spot, which were many miles from the quake's epicenter.[15] However, this popular theory lacks continuity with several established facts.

Daniel Meschter, from Wenatchee, has spent a great deal of time researching this story and the one told by Kate Bailey,[16] both of which put another spin on the facts. The first question is, who was Captain Ingalls? Of the half-dozen or so Ingallses in the Oregon Territory at the time in question (1871–1872), none

---

[15] Although the big Ribbon Cliff Quake was enough to rattle teacups in the Walla Walla area, it would certainly not have been enough to cover three lakes completely, more than 30 air miles from its epicenter.

[16] Kate Bailey was a well-known and respected historian and natural weather forecaster with a reputation for correctly predicting the weather up to a year in advance. Kate spent a portion of her childhood in Blewett.

could be traced to an Army captain who would have been stationed anywhere near Peshastin. This also includes members of the Oregon Volunteers. And did the events happen in 1871–72 in the first place? Probably not. Miner and prospector Charles Splawn, whose version likely comes closest to the truth, places the discovery during the 1855–56 Indian/white wars. But there is still no record of a Captain Ingalls in uniform in this area. Although several soldiers by that name were stationed at Fort Vancouver, none had a military job that would have put him in the Peshastin area.

A civilian by the name of Dewitt Clinton Ingalls, from the Willamette Valley, did pass though the area in the late 1850s, with a Native American companion named Colawash, on his way to the gold fields of the Similkameen. This Ingalls was not a military man but may have acquired the title of captain because he had operated a river ferry near his Willamette Valley home. Or possibly he served in the Volunteers during the Indian/white wars in southern Oregon prior to that time. It's also possible that he possessed an honorary title of some kind.

The true story will probably never be known unless the Ingalls/Hansel letters are found. It is a known fact that D. C. Ingalls was killed in an accidental shooting while guiding a party of prospectors along the banks of the Wenatchee River in February 1860 en route to the Peshastin area to reclaim his rich gold strike. The prospecting party included John Hansel. Hansel later brought his family and built a home north of Hansel Creek (Bonanza Creek in Hodges) near the confluence of present-day Hansel Creek and Peshastin Creek, in the southeast ¼ of Section 24, where he spent years searching for the elusive map. Meanwhile, he worked the three Hansel mining claims on the southern slopes of Long Ridge, located to the north of his property.[17] To this day, no gold cache or series of three lakes have been found in the Ingalls Creek Valley.

If you try to solve this baffling mystery for yourself, you may want to heed the story told by Kate Bailey. Bailey claims to have known two prospectors in the early 1900s who worked their way down Ingalls Creek from the headwaters. Along the way, they spotted three small lakes far below, but were unable to descend because the cliffs in the area were too steep. They made plans to return the following year with rope ladders, but the next spring when they returned they were unable to locate the lakes. This suggests that the lakes were covered that spring by a large slide, or maybe a natural dam gave way, emptying them out. The prospectors did mention that the stream emitting from the trio of lakes entered a steep, narrow, impassable canyon and that the hillside they were on was free of rattlesnakes. According to Bailey, there are no snakes on the south side of Ingalls Creek. We haven't verified this, but it does mean that either Bailey is right or the area the prospectors were referring to is too high for rattlesnakes, who prefer the warm, dry climate below 3,000 feet elevation.

> **Warning** There is a fine hiking trail if you turn right at Ingalls Creek intersection and then left at the first intersection. But be aware! This is rattlesnake country, so be careful of the little critters.

Using the most current USGS maps, we have been able to locate only one string of three lakes that seems to match the sketchy descriptions at hand. Kate Bailey mentions that one of the lakes at one end of the string had a fishhook-shaped crook. Consulting the USGS 7.5 Minute Series map for the Enchantments, you can see that three of the Enchantment Lakes lie on a bench at roughly the same altitude, near 7,000 feet—Leprechaun Lake, Lake Viviane, and Temple Lake. Leprechaun is indeed fishhook-shaped. The drainage stream from the lakes is not only accessible, however, but it also drains to Snow Lake rather than into Ingalls Creek, plus there is a trail along its length. If you observe the lakes from the ridge above at certain locations, they appear to lie in a string.

These lakes are situated high on the north side of Ingalls Creek, along with the many other Enchantment Lakes. The gullies that descend from the Enchantments into Ingalls Creek are very steep, and though some are forbidding and inaccessible, they do not serve as a drainage creek to the three lakes. If Ingalls had hiked up to Prusik Pass from the Shield Lake Valley, he would have been looking directly down at the three

---

[17] In 1897, Hansel had a placer claim (the Ingalls Creek Placer) located in Section 25, T23N, R17E, on Peshastin Creek at the mouth of Ingalls Creek.

lakes in question. Were these Ingalls's lakes? We will probably never know, but if you want to check them out, the trip is rewarding. The Enchantment Lakes area is one of the truly spectacular spots in the Stuart Range—one you will never forget, even if you don't find Ingalls's gold.

It's also possible that Captain Ingalls made his discovery in a nearby valley, such as Negro Creek, or in the upper reaches of the Cle Elum or Leavenworth Districts. Over time, the location could have become confused with the present-day Ingalls Creek Valley. If this were the case, the three lakes could very well have been simply the result of natural debris or snow slides that produced temporary dams. Many of the valleys in this area are steep and narrow, given to such temporary lakes and ponds. Ingalls's find may have been at the very location of some of the many mines and prospects that today dot the upper Cle Elum, Leavenworth, and Blewett areas. If so, it may already be mined out. However, there is enough evidence in the historic record, that at some point in time, a Captain Ingalls did locate a rich deposit of gold ore somewhere in the area. Good luck on your search.

Garnierite Group (nine claims), 1942

East of the confluence of Hansel and Peshastin Creeks, there is a feeder stream that flows west into Peshastin Creek from the southwest ¼ of Section 19. Along its steep slopes is a ledge of garnierite in serpentine. Garnierite is a very poorly defined hydrated magnesium nickel silicate, hence the mine's name. Harry J. Hood had a 110-foot adit, in which less than one percent nickel was found in any one of 10 samples taken, ending further development.

Ingalls Creek Mines

Boston Group (four claims)

Rated at D-2 to D-4. The claims are located in the southeast ¼ of Section 27 and northwest ¼ of Section 26, T23N, R17E, on the USGS 7.5 Minute Series map of Blewett. The lowest claim in elevation (2,400 feet) is two miles from the mouth of Ingalls Creek, at stream level. From there the claims ascend end to end in a northeast direction, cutting through the middle portion of Agnes Creek (unnamed on the map) to an elevation of about 3,800 feet. Information on this property comes from a map, with no accompanying data for development or production.

Velma Claim

The Velma is located in the southeast ¼ of Section 29, T23N, R17E, on the south side of Ingalls Creek, about two miles upstream from the Boston Claim. In 1951, Wenatchee resident L. G. Olds had five claims. Mercury was the main mineral sought, with gold, silver, and copper following in value. A nickel ledge had a pay streak of quartz, carbonates, and cinnabar one to three feet wide. Olds stayed on site during mining season in a well-built cabin. Development consisted of several open cuts.

Lynch Group and State Group of Properties

Rated at E-4 and located in T23N, R16E, on the USGS 7.5 Minute Series maps of Blewett and Enchantment Lakes. These 14 claims are located 5½ miles from the mouth of the creek, and start to appear south of the area marked "falls" on Falls Creek, printed on the map. The four claims are located in the northeast ¼ of Section 31, at around 4,400 feet, through west of center. The site extends into the southwest ¼ of Section 31 (four more claims), as high up as 6,300 feet between the "Y" of two of the Falls Creek streams. From there, four more adjoined claims continue northwest through Falls Creek in a northwest direction into the northeast ¼ of Section 36. The property ends down at 4,000 feet elevation. The last two claims are separate and south 500 feet from the last four claims, and go west through a feeder stream, which is located in the northwest ¼ of Section 36 at about 4,500 feet elevation. One look at those areas on the map, and you will wonder how these claims could have been located by anyone who wasn't at least half mountain goat.

Owners John and William Lynch had two parallel nickel dikes on claims that were each 60 feet wide. It appears the Lynches did a lot of prospecting, and claimed areas that showed potential in hopes that development would encourage production. There are no records to this effect, which indicates that no further production occurred.

Bonanza and Deadwood Claims

Rated at E-4. The claims are located in the southwest ¼ of Section 1 and the southeast ¼ of Section 2, T22N, R16E, following north to south on the section line. On the east and west sides of the easternmost feeder stream paralleling Falls Creek trail, about one mile south of the Lynch/State Claims. The claims lie at an elevation of between 5,400 and 6,000 feet. Our rating is C-3 should you prefer to approach from the Negro Creek side. The only other known information about these claims is that Charles Newberry and W. F. Peterson owned them.

Nickel Plate Group (12 claims)

The Nickel Plate Group is located in the northeast ¼ of Section 2, adjoining the west boundary lines of the Bonanza and Deadwood Claims. This block of claims goes west off the point, where three forks of the headwaters of Falls Creek join together, and then up the slopes over an unnamed mountain ridge to Cascade Creek. The Lynch Brothers were in pursuit of another nickel-bearing formation with these claims, which they tracked from the Negro Creek side, over the Falls Creek divide. The ledge was 60 feet wide. Development consisted of multiple prospect holes. There was no production.

Negro Creek

Our next stop will be Negro Creek, 9.2 miles from US 2. At this point, we can look across Peshastin Creek on our right and see the long-forgotten abutment of the Old Blewett Pass highway bridge that once crossed Negro Creek at its confluence with Peshastin Creek. By crossing Peshastin Creek on the north side of Negro Creek, you can attain the old road that at one time paralleled Negro Creek. Or you can continue up US 97 for about 0.8 mile to the junction of the old Blewett Pass highway and the new. Turn right, proceed north 0.3 mile to the end of the drivable road, and park. Continue on foot along the old road for ½ mile, and descend to Negro Creek. (A footbridge built in 1999 makes for a dry crossing.) Negro Creek Road is on the other side. Be on the lookout for rattlesnakes, especially in the lower reaches of Negro Creek. The road is no longer drivable but is great for foot traffic. From here, we rate the hike at E-3 to E-4, depending on whether you take extra side trips

Historic Cedar Grove Campground Site

The Cedar Grove Campground area is located about one mile from the mouth of Negro Creek. On the USGS map for the Blewett quadrangle, it is about 500 feet east of the adit symbol (a small arrow, and the only visible sign of the old War Eagle Mine) under the printed word "Restricted" (northwest ¼ of Section 2). There was a building on the grounds in 1902, and "Cedar Grove Campground" can be found on maps well into the 1950s. These days, all that remains are the memories of those who enjoyed this out-of-the-way spot.

Along the course of the valley, many of the deserted mine sites contain old equipment and relics of bygone mining days. There are considerably more sites that are completely undetectable because of rockslides and rapid advancement of undergrowth.

Queen Bee Mine

Rated at C-2. The first tunnel you may want to visit is 1.6 miles from the mouth of the creek. It is shown as an adit symbol on the USGS 7.5 Minute map. Find a path up the hillside that leads to an outcrop of rocks. The adit can be found about 60 feet from the trail. The tunnel is approximately 60 feet long, and a one-foot–wide vein is most evident about 20 feet into the mine. Another 600 feet up the road, and then 60 to 70 feet off it by trail, is another adit consisting of about 100 feet of workings that contain a few quartz stringers and a pack rat, complete with nest. A five-foot–wide white quartz vein shows at the top of a portal another 700 feet up Negro Creek on the south side (at the center of Section 3 and marked as a prospect). This well-preserved but flooded adit shows vein material for 100 feet, which disappears from sight as the tunnel turns to the southwest.

One thousand feet upstream, an old wooden bridge leads to an open area at the base of a new tailing pile. This was an attempt to crosscut under a much older mine tunnel located about 200 feet above this one. Rusting mining equipment can be found scattered around.

Barkdull Mine

Rated at D-3. The Barkdull Mine is 2.3 miles from the mouth of Negro Creek, at an elevation of 2,500 feet. The workings intersect a complex of three different formations. Serpentine is the dominant rock throughout the workings. The miners encountered two dikes here while tunneling in two main fault systems/shear zones. The ore depositions—green and brown nickel silicates in tunnel #1 (30 feet long), #2 (350 feet long), and #3 (60 feet long)—are all located on the south side of the creek. On the north side, adit #4 (50 feet long) was driven into a 12-foot width of mineralization, but it is now caved.

Adit #5 (50 feet long) is 500 feet downstream (east) of #4 about 100 feet north of the creek. This tunnel is barren, perhaps due to a dislocated/faulted block that could have dropped or pushed the mineral lead out of line with the strike of the ore located on the creek's south side. Adit #3 (60 feet long) is 450 feet southeast of adit #4 and 250 feet south of the creek. A very narrow, mineralized fault extends all the way through the dig.

The 30-foot–long #1 tunnel is 100 feet southeast of #3. This adit encountered highly altered siliceous-carbonate rock containing green and brown nickel silicates. The 300-foot–long #2 adit is 30 feet southeast of #1. The portal enters the hill on a southwest heading and cuts 100 feet of serpentine. Then it enters into a gabbro dike and again encounters serpentine for another 60 feet. It penetrates 50 feet of acid dike (dacite porphyry, a possible extension of the Mount Stuart granodiorite formation), and finally another 60 feet of serpentine to the end of the tunnel.

Caldo Mine

The patented Caldo Claim is around 2.5 miles from the mouth of Negro Creek. An old miner's cabin, occupied by prospector Jim, is visible south across the creek at this spot. Jim has spent the last 15 summers up here, and he is a living volume of history and information on Negro Creek. As soon as the snow is gone in the early summer, he makes his way to his mountain home for a season of prospecting and solitude in this beautiful valley.

Two hundred feet northwest and across the creek from Prospector Jim's cabin, an area obscured by brush and small trees contains a storage shed, covered electric generator, ore car, and mucker. A mining company that pulled out of the area left these artifacts behind. The caved mine portal is just up the hill to the north from the machinery. The creek has eroded the tailings considerably, masking the fact that this mine comprises a considerable amount of underground workings.

Big Antoine's Tunnel

Rated at B-3 from Jim's cabin. A multi-switchback caterpillar road begins north of the mining equipment mentioned above and the collapsed adit across from Jim's cabin. A strenuous ½-mile hike to an elevation of 3,800 feet leads you to an adit (symbol shown on local USGS map). Jim's dad, an old miner who worked many years in the Negro Creek area, claimed this was the tunnel of Big Antoine for whom Negro Creek is named. The digs are on the north side of the road and caved, almost obscured by rock. A few timbers lying around the workings are evidence of them. Jim's dad was getting fine gold from this property. We saw evidence of sulfides in the tailing rock, along with some interesting decomposed quartz.

Chinese Digs

Not rated. Prospector Jim told us in September 1999 about an old Chinese dig about 1,500 feet north to northeast of his cabin near Negro Creek (northwest ¼ of the southwest ¼ of Section 3), at nearly 3,400 feet in elevation. As of 2000, searches on this precipitous peak of uncooperative rock outcrops have failed to give up its location.

More prospects and history can be found beyond Jim's place, but records of the area are vague at best, and this remains one of the most mysterious mining regions in the state. We spent a good part of three summers exploring the rugged Negro Creek area, only uncovering a fraction of the mining past. Much more remains to be found.[18]

Upper Negro Creek

Tip Top Claim (Gold Creek Basin)

Rated at B-3 if you have an off-road vehicle, motorcycle, or mountain bike; E-3 if hiking is your chosen mode of travel. From US 97, take the North Shaser Creek road about two miles to gated Road #400, which allows all but passenger vehicles to pass through. The next six miles is steep, winding up and over Iron Mountain Pass and then down into upper Negro Creek (west-trending Road #400).

To locate the area, use USGS 7.5 Minute Series maps for Blewett and the Enchantment Lakes, and Green Trails maps of Liberty and Mount Stuart. Go to the end of Road #400, where unmarked Trail #1211 (there is no sign, use maps to locate it) goes to Gold Creek Basin, located in Section 6. The unmarked trail starts at 5,000 feet elevation, and goes for 0.8 mile to 6,000 feet (a 1,000-foot gain in altitude) on a scenic high-country trail centered in the Three Brothers Mountain Range.

The predominant rock is serpentine, some weathered to a bright, rusty-red color due to iron minerals that have leached out to the surface. A stream of water flows from an unseen source in the steep ridge, and down the basin wall—clear and cool as late in the summer as September, as in 1999 when we passed through on a 70-degree T-shirt day.

At the end of an east-heading switchback, the tunnel's tailing pile appears. About 100 feet higher and west of the trail is the cabin site. Broken, rusting artifacts are scattered about. From here, you can hike to the trail's end (an additional 1,000-foot elevation gain) at the top of a 7,169-foot peak, which offers a great photo opportunity of all the surrounding mountains. Or you can contour across the slope to the Tip Top Mine tunnel. Enjoy views of Iron Mountain Pass, Miller Peak to the south, Navaho Peak to the southwest, and the remainder of the Three Brothers Mountain Range to the west as you go.

In September 1999, we found the 570-foot tunnel in as good shape as the day it was dug. Although the mine is in Gold Creek Basin, available information showed it was mined for silver, with a very poor showing at that. The adit was driven on the east basin wall into a 10-foot horizontal ledge that cuts north/south. Above the portal, the rock is stained with streaks of an oxidized black mineral, which could be where the silver values came from.

---

[18] This valley at one time held promise of large amounts of cinnabar (mercury ore), as well as gold and silver.

The tunnel goes in for 100 feet and then curves slightly to the right at its end. The miners were following a three to four–foot vein of calcite with black minerals in the matrix. Usually, the floor of a tunnel is packed down from foot traffic, but in 1999 it looked to have been dug up in conjunction with drill holes that were patterned to blast the end of the dig. The drill holes at the breast (end) showed serpentine (the rock the vein was in), indicating that the vein might have been displaced by geological movement that was so common in this once often-heaved region, that an effort had been made to relocate the values.

Outside the tunnel (10 feet to the north), there are bits of spent coal and slag, a sign of blacksmithing. There were also some hand-forged artifacts around the tailing pile.

For the Rockhound

This area is remote, so you can occasionally find one- or two-inch flat rectangular calcite crystals in the mine tailings.

Negro Creek (Davenport) Claim

Rated at B-3 from Road #400. This claim is located south of Gold Creek Basin about one mile in the south ½ of the southwest ¼ and north ½ of the southeast ¼ of Section 7; the northwest ¼ of the southwest ¼ of Section 8; and the southeast ¼ of the southeast ¼ of Section 12. Basically, from where Gold Creek flows into Negro Creek, the claim stretches 1.6 miles west along Negro Creek. The north/south boundaries extend to an elevation of 4,100 to 4,800 feet off both sides of Negro Creek.

In 1944, these four claims were prospected for iron and nickel by Cliff Davenport. Sedimentary iron beds were exposed in three areas. The total amount of iron ore in exposed, probable, and possible locations was estimated to be about 540,000 tons. A 75-foot adit and several open cuts were the extent of the development.

In 1942, Washington State geologists reported that the gravel in this same stretch of Negro Creek contained a small amount of platinum.

Copper Queen #1 and #2 (Negro Creek Chromite Claim, 1942)

Rated at C-4 from the end of Road #400. To locate this site, use the USGS 7.5 Minute Series map for the Enchantment Lakes. Trail #1210 starts in the southwest ¼ of Section 7, where Road #400 heads northeast to Gold Creek Basin. The elevation gain is 2,000 feet for the two-mile hike to the Copper Queen Prospects.

In 1942, pieces of nearly pure chromite float weighing up to two pounds were found in a narrow serpentine gulch 400 feet below the pass and one mile southeast of Navaho Peak, at an elevation of about 5,800 feet. The gully is a feeder stream to Negro Creek near its head. The source of the chromite was not located. These days, there are a three-foot snub tunnel and 14-footer at the claims, which were run along a shear zone of serpentine and granodiorite. The miners followed a five-foot–wide quartz-carbonate vein, with less than five percent sulfide minerals showing.

Negro Creek Milepost Four Cabin and Tunnel

Rated at B-2 from Road #400. To find this property, use the USGS 7.5 Minute Series map of Blewett. The site is in the southeast ¼ of Section 5 at the end of east-trending Road #400, downstream from the Negro Creek (Davenport) Claim. The milepost four cabin is printed on the map.

The cabin is located in a level, forested meadow. Original and add-on sections enhance the present makeup of the building. Northeast of the cabin, the Negro Creek trail leads to a nearby creek crossing, and then follows the south side of the creek downstream 0.7 mile to a washout. You will find several additional tunnels and prospect digs printed on the USGS map. Most are now caved, although we found unnamed, short adits on both sides of the creek (not noted on the map) that were still open.

A Northwest No Name Prospectors Club member told us there was once an 80-year-old-plus prospector who requested a ride to the milepost four cabin so that he could camp and reminisce about his past days of mining in the area. When the return ride came for him a few days later, he had already departed, spiritually speaking.

The trail to the "Cabin Adit" (it doesn't have an official name) starts west of the cabin. An aging 20-foot snag marks the trailhead leading from the main road. Against the snag, there is a signpost that lists the names Don, Doug, and Jon. At the 0.3-mile point, the trail crosses a feeder stream. Gray sediment covers the rocks and gravel with an obvious mix of calcite, sandstone, and so on. This sediment resulted from heavy rains in the summer of 1999 that saturated the south side of a ridge on the Three Brothers Mountain Range, causing a very large portion of the north gully to slide into the stream. We were at Jim's cabin that day as the waters of Negro Creek transformed from clear to a flow of liquefied sediment that passed by the cabin down to Peshastin Creek for a period of three days. Any fish fortunate enough to survive are now likely suffering from terminal cases of aquatic silicosis.

Go another 0.4 mile along a climbing and dipping trail to the tunnel. In September 1999, the portal was caved, and a "rat hole" (of squeeze-through size) was the only access to the digs. A cave-in at about 60 feet stopped us. Although the tailing pile indicated a 300-to-400–foot mine, we didn't see any sulfide ore or quartz of collectible worth in the tailings.[19] Years ago, Negro Creek Jim looked this dig over. He reported that it became an incline tunnel that later flooded. Fractured, crumbly serpentine and granodiorite make this a very dangerous place to be, so do not enter it. Enjoy the safer outside adventures.

To read about the mines beyond the upper Negro Creek area, see the chapter on the Cle Elum Mining Area. The area beyond upper Negro Creek is easier to access from that end.

Ruby Creek

At 8.7 miles from US 2, Ruby Creek Road leaves the highway to the left. Only a few hardrock prospects are hidden in the steep canyon, but placer gold is present in the creek. Keep on the lookout for mining claim markers and notices in this area. Much of the creek region is recorded under mineral claim.

Ruby Creek Placers (1897)

This group of six claims ran in a line from the mouth of Ruby Creek upstream. Located in Section 36, T23N, R17E. The claims were owned by James and Thomas Lynch, Riley Eisenhour, and Thomas Medhurst.

Warning You are still in rattlesnake country.

Johnson Property

Rated at B-4. The USGS 7.5 Minute Series map of Blewett shows this property to be located in the northeast ¼ of Section 1, about ½ mile from the historic Blewett town site. An east-trending horseshoe bend in Peshastin Creek at BM2268 (as seen on the map) is the start of the three Johnson claims, which lie to the east toward the 3350T elevation on Windmill Ridge.

The first claim to the east off Peshastin Creek is the April Fool. The tunnel was 100 feet long on a vein of quartz that is pitched almost vertically. The Venus dig is next, with a 115-foot tunnel that is driven north, 20 degrees west. No vein was found here. The last claim was the Donaldson. Its east claim line reached the top of Windmill Ridge. Two tunnels were developed: one, 195 feet long, headed east to a diabase dike 60

---

[19] Two caved adits, 200 feet east and 50 feet higher did show copper values in the tailings.

feet from the portal; the second tunnel was 80 feet long and headed north 40 degrees east. On Windmill Ridge, we found a four-foot vein in a trench that exposed decomposed calcite and quartz. Sulfides were also present. Both walls consisted of serpentine. We weren't able to locate these tunnels.

Blewett

At mile 10.7 from US 2, on the right of the highway, the crumbling remains of the old Blewett 20-stamp mill stand starkly against the hillside. The Blewett historical marker is a good place to begin your tour, just up the road at mile 10.8 and on the left. Plenty of off-road parking is available here. Most of the Blewett business district, as well as the main street, stood at this point. Known as "The Camp," this was said to be the most violent mining town in Chelan County, because of its high number of shootings and knife and fist fights. Most fights were initiated by claim boundary disputes, ownership disputes, and greed, all of which were exacerbated by liquor consumption.

Blewett's sometimes dusty, sometimes muddy streets, lined with false-front buildings and log cabins, were typical of small western mining camps of the period. Kids played while old, well-worn prospectors and miners discussed the day's events and exchanged their thoughts on the porch of one of the town's two saloons. Weekend dances and celebrations were common here, along with the sounds of dynamite exploding in the hills above and the big stamps hammering to pulverize the ore. People worked hard to glean just enough to stay alive, while the dreams of the riches they would find occupied their imaginations. Their work and their very existence in this remote part of the frontier were dangerous.

Blewett never did have a resident doctor. When someone was sick or injured, the nearest doctor in Leavenworth, 20 or more miles away, had to be fetched. And with the winter snows and spring freshets often wiping out the road and trails that led to civilization, quite often the patient had to be treated on the spot by ladies in the town. Everything from chicken soup to the local "cure 'em or kill 'em" remedies were used.

By 1964, the old Blewett stamp mill had been reduced to its foundation and main structural timbers. The trees and brush have quickly begun to take over the scene. This photo looks west toward Culver Gulch. (The Burmeister collection. North Central Washington Museum, Wenatchee, Washington)

The old town site of Blewett in 1895, looking south up Peshastin Creek toward Swauk Pass. The large building on the right is the 20-stamp mill. The little roof just above the right-hand roofline is the aerial-tramway receiving station for the ore that was trammed down Culver Gulch, located off the picture to the right. The stacked material in front of the mill is the cordwood required to keep the fires in the mill's boilers lit. The line running along the hillside just beyond the mill's main roof peak is the water flume. The roof in the lower lefthand corner belonged to the cyanide plant, while the structures to its immediate right were office buildings. Above the office buildings were the general store (with the low roof) and the town's hotel, which was three stories tall. Just behind the hotel is the roof of the schoolhouse. The Black Jack Mine building is far off in the distance, up Peshastin Creek. (The Burmeister Collection. North Central Washington Museum, Wenatchee, Washington)

If you cross the road at the Blewett historical marker, watch out! There is no crosswalk and certainly no traffic light. Vehicles travel at a good clip, and sight distance is limited. Once across, turn left and walk a short distance until you come to a stairway leading down to Peshastin Creek. At the edge of the water, you'll see one of the old arrastres that served the very early hardrock miners. Notice its large circular ring and the Mexican sombrero–shaped center knob. This arrastre is especially interesting in that there is no central pivot point on the center knob, suggesting that it did not operate like the more common arrastres used throughout the Americas. Instead, it appears that the dragstone was suspended from an overhead frame anchored on the sides of the dish.

We don't recall seeing any other operation like this one in our many years of research. Three large rocks weighing about a half a ton each were dragged around the top of the well-rooted rock until the deep groove was formed. Then roughly 50 pounds of high-grade ore at a time, along with quicksilver (mercury), was placed in the groove. The three large rocks, powered by a large water wheel, were pulled around the groove again until the ore was pulverized to the desired consistency. The gold amalgamated with the mercury and settled into the groove, while the country rock was washed away by water flowing into and out of the trough. When sufficient ore had been processed, the amalgam of gold and mercury was removed and retorted (distilled) to separate the two.

Now hike back down the road and take a look at the old stamp mill. Standing at the top of the massive timber and stone walls of the structure, imagine the heavy ore coming down from the mine to the mill via a 4,000-foot–long Hallidie Aerial Tramway, in buckets that held 250 pounds each. This tramway consisted of a 12,000-foot–long cable on which iron hooks had been attached 120 feet apart. The ore was dumped into sacks and hung on the iron hooks for the trip to the mill, where it was dumped into two receiving bins with a capacity of 400 tons each. Later, self-dumping buckets replaced the hooks.

The tram was gravity-powered—the weight of the loaded buckets or sacks descending from mine to mill pulled the empty buckets back up. When supplies or timbers were needed above, they were placed on the empty returning buckets or hooks. This was said to be the first bucket tramway erected in Washington State. The 2,197-foot–long span between the upper tram station and the first tram tower was the longest clear span of cable in the world at the time. The cable itself weighed about six tons, and the tram could carry 4½ to 5 tons of ore at a time. The ore was then dropped onto a grizzly (which allowed only a predetermined size of ore to pass though), while the large chunks were broken up by a hardy soul with a large (and heavy) sledgehammer.

From the grizzly, the ore was dropped into the crusher and passed into one of the four Fraser and Chalmers automatic feeders that discharged the desired amount of ore into the stamp shoes, where it was pulverized. The stamps were arranged into four sets of five stamps each. They weighed 950 pounds each and were equipped with chrome-steel shoes and dies that dropped 6½ inches 90 times per minute.

The resulting silt was then mixed with water, screened though diagonal slot screens equivalent to 50-mesh, and then dropped on copper plates four feet wide and 10 feet long, which were set at a slope of 1½ inches per foot. The lower plates were silvered, 14 feet long, four feet wide and they fell two inches per foot. Four Union tables then received the silt, after which the slime passed over canvas tables with a three-inch fall. The canvas was swept, and the remaining fines were saved in settling boxes four times over a 24-hour period.

Under earlier ownership, much of the excess mill waste that had been deposited in the creek carried several dollars' worth of gold. Outside parties became aware of this loss, and to counter it they built a small cyanide plant with two tanks next to the mill. The cyanide plant processed

In the 1890s, acquiring power was catch as catch can. This large water wheel may have been used to power an arrastre or perhaps an air compressor. Notice the fellow and young boy posing on a pulley at the center of the wheel. (*A Pictorial History of Kittitas County, Volume II*, 1989)

The 20-stamp mill at Blewett. Although once powered by water, the mill is clearly being run by steam at the time of this picture, circa 1906. Notice the cord wood stacked in front of the mill. Notice also the structure emerging from Culver Gulch high to the left and descending to the back of the mill. This appears to be some device for the delivery of ore to the mill from a mine high up the gulch. We are not certain if it is a pipe, open flume, or some other conveyance. (Grace Browitt Elkins collection)

about 10 tons per day, recovering a considerable amount of gold that had previously been lost.

The mill was powered by two wood-burning boilers measuring 4 feet by 12 feet and used alternately to furnish steam to power a 50-horsepower Corliss steam engine. A 500-foot–long flume brought water from farther up the creek to a large tank set 20 feet above the stamp battery to feed the boilers and the mill. When adequate water was available, it was also used to power the mill via a vertical water turbine[20] located 40 feet below the mill building. Remains of the old flume trench can still be seen along the hillside upstream from the mill.

After the milling process, the small gold bars, each about the size of a bar of soap, were loaded onto a wagon at the mill and hauled to the railroad at Cle Elum. This was done at unannounced, unpredictable times to help prevent robberies.

Today you can take a walk up Culver Gulch. Find the dirt road just south of the mill and follow it up to the gate. At the time of this writing, the property owners had posted No Trespassing signs at the gate. Please respect their wishes and don't trespass if signs are posted. When we visited the property, we had full permission of some of the mine owners and the guidance of their representatives so that we were able to give you the following descriptions.

> **Warning** Mines and mine-related structures are *never* safe. This is especially true in the Blewett area, where much of the rock is cracked and crumbly and most structures date back at least 75 years. Stand back, enjoy the view, drink in the history, and live to visit again. Please stay out of the mines and buildings!

Matwick Mine

Rated at B-1. The short adit not too far inside the gate on the left is the Matwick (elevation 2,380). It is a 175-foot–long, very uninteresting tunnel with no stoping or drifting. This is reportedly the Lower Matwick; the Upper Matwick is located about 250 feet east of the Meteor at the elevation of the Meteor portal.

Meteor Tunnel

Rated at B-1. The Meteor tunnel, located on the Peshastin Claim (elevation 2,475), is just up the road from the Matwick and on the same side. This was one of the major workings in the district and is connected underground to several other mines in the area, all of which are caved at some point and inaccessible.

---

[20] Conflicting information describes the power unit as both a vertical turbine and a Pelton wheel. Reportedly it's still there under 40 feet of soil.

This unusual photo is a view of the backside of the Blewett 20-stamp mill. The small canopied building seems to contain some manner of winching or winding device. This is where the ore from the mines up Culver Gulch would be delivered for milling. We are not certain whether an aerial tram or other such device was used for this purpose at the time of the photo, circa 1906. (Grace Browitt Elkins collection)

A former owner and a couple of former Blewett residents told us a funny story about this mine. Some years ago, possibly in the 1970s or 80s, a contractor was doing some core drilling and exploration in the mine for the owners when a large bear decided that the dark recesses of the workings would make a great place to spend the winter. The miners, good citizens and humanitarians that they were, did what they felt was right—they called in the State Fish and Game people to remove the intruding bruin.

Surely and confidently, the two agents arrived at the portal ready to perform their worthy deed. While the miners waited outside the adit in great anticipation, the officers, tranquilizer gun at the ready, began their slow journey into the dark, subterranean depths of the mine. A hundred feet or so into the trek, the two men realized with a thud that the tranquilizer darts take at least five minutes to put a bear out. The two quickly reversed their direction and headed for the sunlight. Back at the mouth of the mine, they promptly informed the owners that this was their mine, their bear, and their problem and quickly departed. The bear ultimately decided it didn't like the sound of dynamite going off in the area, so it disappeared in search of a more comfortable and quiet place to hibernate

Draw Tunnel

Rated at B-2. Several hundred feet up the gulch to the left of the adit is the caved portal of the Draw tunnel (elevation 2,579). The Draw workings connected with the Meteor, Peshastin, and Sandell Mines underground. This mine is completely collapsed as of this writing and very uninteresting, though several large and rich ore bodies were worked from it at one time.

Peshastin and Sandell Mines

Rated at B-2. As we continue up the increasingly steep road, we pass the caved adits of the Peshastin[21] (elevation 2,565) and Sandell Claims[22] (elevation 2,708) across the creek to the left. The original owners of the Sandell in 1874 were John Olden and Peter Wilder. Production from the Meteor, Draw, and Peshastin Mines was about $60,000 by 1902 and 22 tons in 1940. Production from the Sandell tunnels is unknown.

---

[21] The Peshastin is a crosscut tunnel extending from the center of Culver Gulch south 300 feet, where it intersected the vein. Drifts ran east and west for a total of 1,000 feet, and there is a rise that connects to the Sandell.

[22] The Sandell tunnel is also a crosscut extending 300 feet to the south, where it cuts the main Peshastin lead 180 feet higher than the level of the Peshastin tunnel and consists of a series of drifts on the vein.

Golden Eagle and Lower Hummingbird Mines

Rated at B-3. The Golden Eagle stamp mill, operated by Charles Fackler in the 1930s, was located where the road turns sharply uphill to the right. Its six stamps crushed the ore from the now-caved Golden Eagle Mines several hundred feet up the hillside.

If you continue straight ahead instead of following the road as it turns, you'll find the portal of the Lower Hummingbird Mine (elevation 2,881).[23] Production for this mine is unknown. Continuing up the road as it switches back over the old stamp mill location in a downvalley direction, you'll see above you the tailing pile of the collapsed Golden Eagle Mine lower adit (elevation 2,942). Production was reported to be about $2,000.

Below the pile, the road again turns upvalley and continues to a level area at the base of a large draw. On the hillside to the right, you might see the remains of the old Suckling Mining Company's modified ball mill scattered down the hillside. Some of the old machinery is well worth a closer look, but please be careful and leave relics and artifacts where they lie. It has been reported that the equipment never worked properly.

One of the old aerial tramway towers still stands in 1997 as mute testimony to the activity that once flourished in Culver Gulch above Blewett. (Victor Pisoni photo)

---

[23] At one time, this crosscut tunnel went south 150 feet, where the same vein as the Sandell and Peshastin intersected on which 500-foot drifts had been run. Production is unknown. When we visited these workings in 1991, the portal was open but just inside the stope was collapsed, and more material threatened to come down. Please stay out! This mine is extremely dangerous.

Top: The 20-stamp mill at Blewett, circa 1910. The boiler room was on the left. This scene looks west, with Culver Gulch ascending in the distance. (Washington Geological Survey Bulletin #6, *Geology and ore deposits of the Blewett Mining District*, Charles Weaver, 1911)

Middle: A group of people rest beneath an ore bunker, possibly the ore bunkers at the stamp mill at the mouth of Culver Gulch, Blewett.. (The Burmeister Collection. North Central Washington Museum, Wenatchee, Washington)

Bottom: A general view of the Meteor Mining Company's operation at Blewett, circa 1905. Culver Gulch is visible beyond the mill building. This is where the mine's tunnels were bored. (*The Westerner* magazine, November, 1905)

The Meteor and Peshastin mine tunnels in Culver Gulch above Blewett, circa 1910. (Washington Geological Survey Bulletin #6, *Geology and ore deposits of the Blewett Mining District*, Charles Weaver, 1911)

Golden Crown Mine

Rated at B-3. This tunnel is located about 1,000 feet northeast of the Golden Eagle at 3,200 feet elevation. We didn't see a trail leading to the property. We found this dig during a cross-country hike and scramble leading to the center of Section 2, where we accidentally stumbled upon the mine. The solid but flooded tunnel heads northwest for about 100 feet, where it curves to the west out of sight of "we want to keep our feet dry" observers. The tailings are spread far and wide down a very steep slope below the portal, making it difficult to notice if approached from below. The Golden Crown is private property, so please keep out.

Bobtail (Wye/Amber Glee) Mine

Rated at C-2. At the landing above the old suckling mill, there are a couple of unnamed caved adits. The Bobtail is located up the gulch, to the west of the Hummingbird at an elevation of 3,046 feet. The owners of the Bobtail Mine had planned to bore directly under the famous No. 9 workings and tap that zone at depth, but apparently the work was never completed. Production is unknown.

Upper Hummingbird Mine

Rated at C-2. To your left, you can see the Upper Hummingbird adit (elevation 3,012). Production is unknown.

Pole Pick Mines

Rated at C-3. The road again swings in a downvalley direction along the south side of Culver Gulch as it gains altitude, and then turns sharply upvalley to the remains of the Pole Pick Mines (elevation 3,216). The Pole Pick No. 2 claim was located in 1874 by John Earnest and later sold to John Shoudy and resold in 1906 to Thomas A. Parish, who organized the Alta Vista Mining Company. Production for these mines was extensive. Signs of more recent mining activity are present from the Montana De Oro Mining Company activity in the 1980s. The company worked this adit and the Ellinor and Fackler #2 tunnels above. There is quite a bit of mining machinery and equipment present, which is still under ownership. Again, please just look and leave it for others to view and enjoy.

The Ellinor Mining Company ran a tunnel off the Pole Pick to the west until it contacted the vein. Turning east for 100 feet, the company stoped up and took out over a million dollars in gold. They tunnel is now caved where the stope went to the surface.

A convenient method of transporting goods to a mine that was located high on a mountain, and bringing ore down, was by aerial tramway. The one shown here uses a single span between the lower and upper terminals. Often the builders placed support towers along the way to handle the cable's load and to lift the tram over terrain. (*Pearson's Magazine*, April 1903)

As you hike up the road, check out the several A-frame ore bucket tram towers that have toppled or are near collapse.

The #9, #9½, and #10 Mines

Rated at C-3. From the Pole Pick camp, the road turns north and climbs to an intersection with another road. Below the intersection is the #9 adit (elevation 3,211), the #9½ (elevation 3,188), and the #10 (elevation 3,132) mines. Production was extensive.

In the early days, these mines showed the most promise and underwent the most activity of all the area mines at the time. They were leased by the Alta Vista Mining Company from the Washington Meteor Mining Company, with the plan of extending the #9 tunnel a great distance to undercut other ore deposits in the area. As work progressed, the #9 tunnel was extended into the Culver Claim and across the south line of the Culver into the Pole Pick #2 at the northeast corner of the claim. In this area, a 266-foot raise was made to the Blewett tunnel, which continues up to tunnel #6. The nearby landing was the upper station for the tram that delivered the ore down to the old stamp mill at Blewett.

The #8 Adit

Rated at C-3. Turning sharply left at the intersection and proceeding southeast, you pass the #8 adit (elevation 3,282). There was no known production. This short tunnel failed to strike ore and today is of little interest.

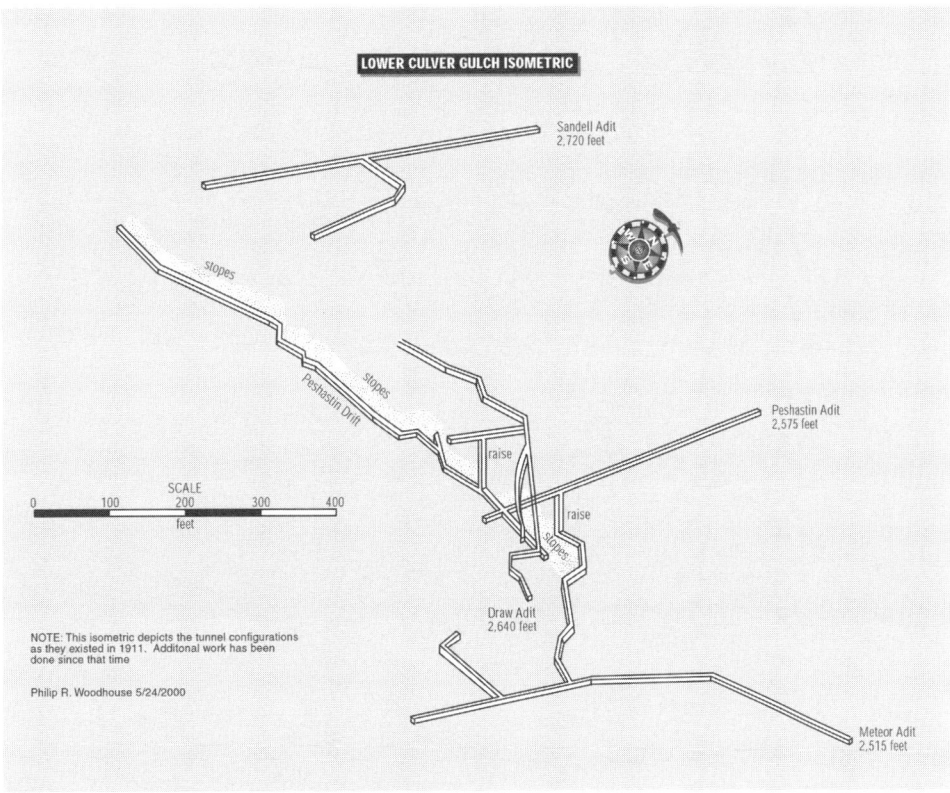

The #6 and #6½ Tunnels

The #6 tunnel was driven westerly on a vein. Tunnel #6½ was below #6 and was also driven to the west on the vein and connected to #6 with a raise. Tunnel #6 is connected to #5½ by a raise and in #5½ there is a raise up to #5. Both were driven on the vein. Tunnel #5½ extends to the diabase dike, where the vein is cut in two by the dike intrusion. The ore between #9 up to #5 was stoped out and sent to the stamp mill at Blewett by bucket tram. Part of the work was done by leases from 1894–1900.

Ellinor Tunnel

Rated at C-3. At the next road junction, continue south as the road again turns sharply left and passes the caved portal of the Ellinor tunnel (elevation 3,351). There was some good production here. During its construction, the workers who were driving the Ellinor encountered a valueless vein of unknown source. Farther in, a tunnel wall with water seeping through fissures had gangue material that contained 2½ ounces of gold per ton. Stringers of quartz found in the main tunnel were devoid of value. Passing beyond a place where a small waterfall eminates from the tunnel wall, rock that didn't match anything in the area was exposed. Elsewhere, in a drift 600 feet from the main adit, gold ore ran 18 ounces to the ton and was four feet wide at that level. These areas are now blocked by cave-ins.

The Fackler concentrator, named for the Fackler family who operated it in the 1940s, is just past this on the left side of the road.[24] This mill was later reconditioned by the Montana De Oro Company while it worked the nearby mines.

As of 1999, this mill was in a bad state of disrepair and under private ownership, so entrance should not be attempted under any circumstances. Remember, there is quite a bit of heavy machinery on three different levels ready to come down on some poor unsuspecting soul who may be careless enough to step inside.

---

[24] In 1940, the Gold Bond Mining Company of Spokane, Wash., held the deed to the Pole Pick Property. Charles Fackler of Yakima, Wash., leased it from Gold Bond. Charles was building a trail across the claim, and while scraping he had exposed a "blanket" lead of ore four to six feet wide, and of varying depth. He sent $3,000.00 worth of this high-grade free-milling gold ore to the Tacoma, Wash., smelter. Fackler then used an "Allis Mill" to treat future shipments.

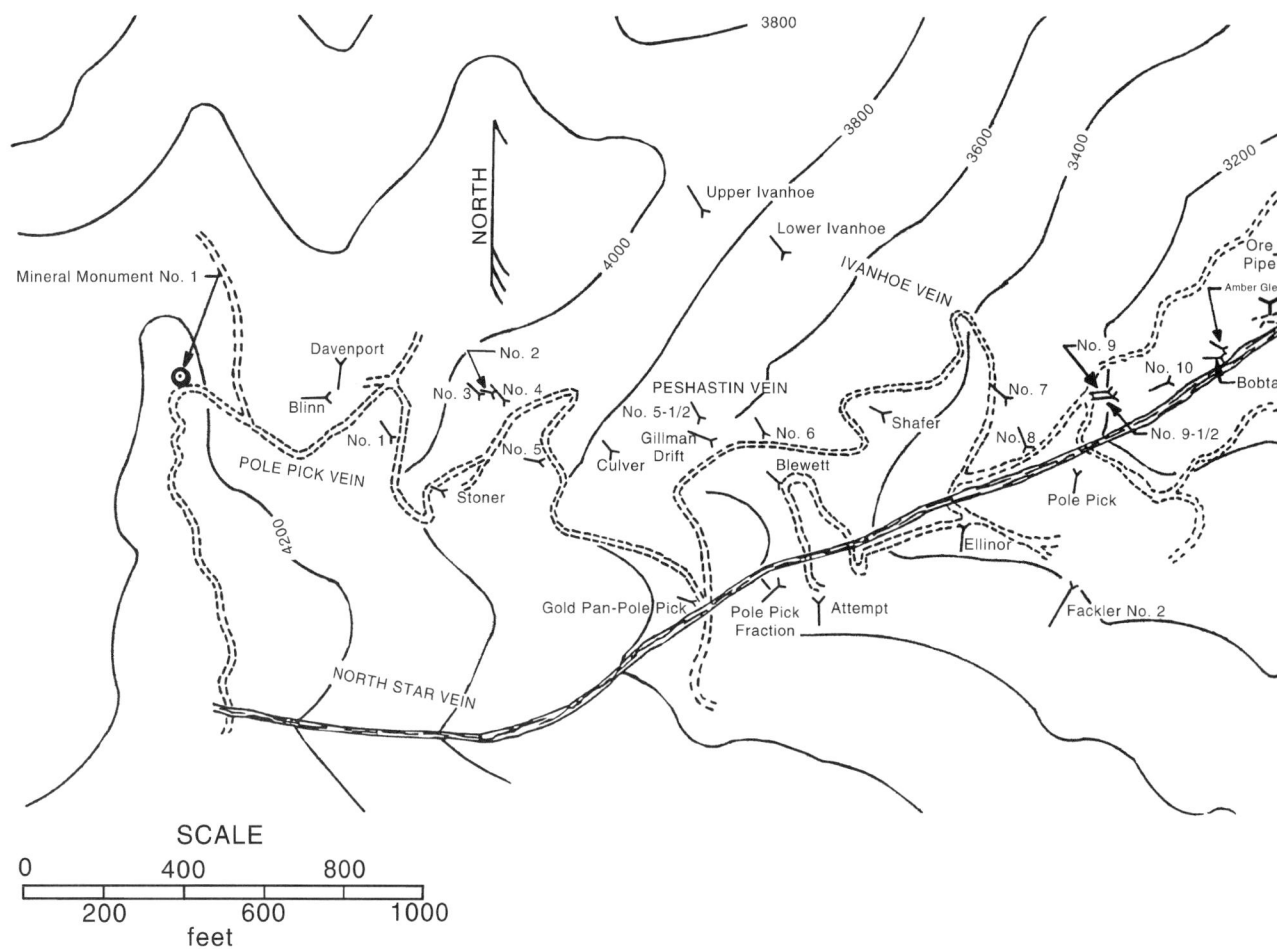

Fackler #2 Adit

Rated at C-3. The Fackler #2 adit is at the end of the road. In 1964, Karl Fackler and Tommy Smith ran a drift with a 50-foot raise. They got three ounces of gold per ton from this new area.

In 1980–81, Bill Priestly and his underground miner Tommy Smith attempted to crosscut to the Pole Pick #1 vein and blast a raise into it. Priestly also planned to make contact with the Fackler #1 by a raise, which if completed would have defined the vein. The contacted vein was narrow, but it produced several tons of good ore, which was run through the mill. In 1984, they dropped back to the main tunnel and drove west to strike the vein at a lower elevation. Here a raise went into low-valued sulfide ore. The gold ore 120 feet above that place was a very good grade. It was sent down an ore chute to the main tunnel and then to the mill for processing. When Priestly drilled 80 feet trying to contact the Pole Pick #2 vein, three stringers of quartz carrying very high-grade sulfide ore indicated the main vein was near.

Gold Finger 2001 (formally known as Big Mouth)

This claim is located 100 feet south of the Fackler #2 property, at the end of the road. The owners of this patented property are in the process of cleaning up debris and developing the mine's internal workings. This includes a 50-foot tunnel heading south from a secured portal to an intersection. Here the tunnel continues south for another 150 feet, with drifts that define value-carrying ore. Back at the intersections and to the west is a 50-foot drift with a 60-foot stope. All reworked areas show pay dirt in the veins and pockets that have been exposed, as of 2001. This tunnel was originally an attempt to reach the vein in the Pole Pick's west extension.

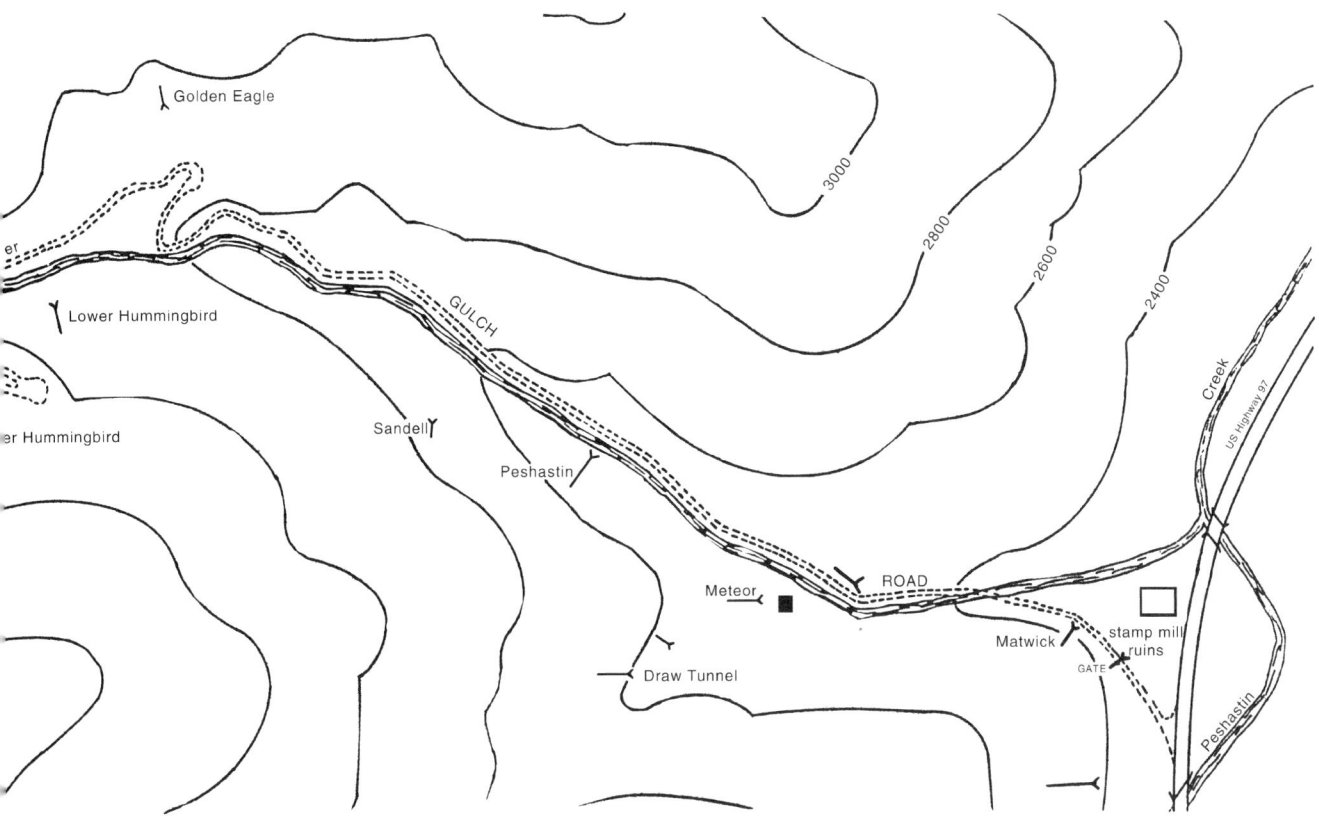

The Pinnacles

From the Fackler #2, go back to the intersection. Five hundred feet to the north, the road turns upgrade and heads southwest. There is another narrow byway leading north off that turn. It goes 800 feet to the center of Section 2. Located at 3,400 feet elevation on the ridge saddle is a formation of valueless, iron-stained, quartz-veined dolomite known as The Pinnacles. In 1893, this area was known as the Providence Claim. Around the rust-colored rock is a 2½-inch–diameter cable. This cable runs under a large (now collapsed) 20×50–foot ore bin, which we examined. We looked over and excavated a bucket tram bull wheel three feet in diameter. It had a braking system consisting of a long handle (rotted away), with a concentric hand-forged cam at the base attached to a steel band that would constrict around the wheel, stopping the carrying cable as pressure was applied. The square-set tram tower timbers we found downslope showed this to be a Bleichert tram.

We followed the 2½-inch double support cables downslope 1,000 feet to Negro Creek and found the remnants of a late 1890s mill site. On the USGS Minute Series map of Blewett, "prospect" is printed 1¼ inches directly north of the ridge saddle. Presently a backhoe, small cabin, and trommel machinery are situated there. The old mill site is out of sight, 300 feet to the southwest. Although there are no reports of this setup, it seems conceivable the mines in Culver Gulch and the ridge claims on the north could have had easy access to the tram and mill. Perhaps the mill on Negro Creek was the reason the full 40-stamp capacity of the Blewett Mill was never used. To date, this question goes unanswered.

Wheelbarrow Mine

In the area of The Pinnacles ridge, there apparently is a lost claim. We were told that an old miner had a good gold-producing claim here. He was using a trail just wide enough to haul ore out by wheelbarrow. The claim looked so promising that he went back east in pursuit of financial backing to expand his operation. While there, he passed away. Secrecy must have been his modus operandi, because the dig location has never been found. So it is told…very interesting.

Returning to the last road junction, follow left and begin climbing north. You are now entering the area where the first claims were staked many years ago.

Shafer Tunnel, Blewett Workings, and Culver Mines

Rated at C-3. Use the map to get to the Shafer adit (elevation 3,456), Blewett workings, (elevation 3,524), and Culver Mines (elevation 3,755). Production was spotty. Again, please stay out of the workings.

Stoner and Phipps Crosscut Tunnels (1938)

A contractor named Stoner, under lease for the Gold Bond Mining Company, blasted a tunnel from the Culver Gulch side, 50 feet lower than the Phipps adit. It was developed to remove ore uncovered by the Phipps crosscut to the old Blinn vein. The Blinn is 50 feet above the Phipps portal, which is situated on the Negro Creek side. The Phipps crosscut showed five feet of barren, white quartz in serpentine and two inches of gouge seams on either wall. Where the crosscut hit the vein at 150 feet, the ore was 43 inches wide. A 40-foot stope was constructed at this spot, and then an 80-foot drift was driven. There, ore was mined from a stope that went 40 feet up and 60 feet down. Twenty feet past the stope an incline shaft was put in to haul ore down to the Stoner tunnel. Ore minerals taken were free gold, pyrite, and arsenopyrite.

Blinn Workings

Rated at D-4. From the U.S. Mineral Monument (elevation 4,211), walk east about 250 feet to the old Blinn workings. These workings consisted of one long adit of unknown length and 1,000 feet of shorter tunnels.[25] These are believed to be the very oldest hardrock mine workings in the Blewett area.[26] Production is not known, but ore was removed in 1880, 1936, and 1937.

Thad Neubauer, a Blewett resident and mining speculator who lived in the town around the turn of the century. (The Burmeister collection. North Central Washington Museum, Wenatchee, Washington)

Olympia Claims

In 1938, the Gold Bond Mining Company was in possession of this claim. It was located about 600 feet due west of the U.S. Mineral Monument at the top of Culver Gulch. The tunnel was driven as a crosscut through serpentine rock. Thirty-seven feet into the adit, a shear zone is cut and then followed for 870 feet. Two raises 50 feet and 60 feet in length have exposed lenses of quartz 1½ feet wide by 3 feet long. Ore minerals present were pyrite, arsenopyrite, and chalcopyrite. No other minerals were found in the remainder of the tunnel.

---

[25] Some of these shorter ones could include the Blewett and Shafer digs.

[26] A point of interest is the old ore bin south of the landing/tailing pile of the Blinn dig. It has fallen with the downhill slope, spilling high-grade ore before it could be sent below to the mill. You can examine the ore to see what the miners believed to be of production quality.

Summit Workings

The Summit workings are also known as the Summit pockets. These various digs comprise tunnels 1, 2, 3, and 4, on the west side of a big basaltic dike. The Summit pockets lie in a rich oxidized zone, with a high occurrence of gold. Toward the top of the gulch, the vein repeatedly splits and then coalesces. Some of the richest ore came from this area; it was said to have yielded up to $60,000 per ton. General J. D. McIntire operated these properties for years, and produced approximately $1.2 million from gold ore.

Summit Workings Update

The main source of the following general information is from the 1960s via conversations with Cliff Davenport.

Miner Bill Lamar trenched the area of the ridge separating Culver Gulch and Negro Creek. The gold-bearing quartz was exposed from the upper south side to north of the gulch ridge. An 80-foot shaft was dug and ore was mined. The shaft was then filled with dirt and rocks. Tunnels were later driven under the trenched ground. At one time, signs were posted for all the names of the ridge-top workings. Now most claims are unnamed and caved, and the cabins have collapsed. Large chunks of white quartz are scattered throughout the area.

In 1940, Karl Fackler, using a D-6 cat, bulldozed the roads for the Gold Bond Mining Company. This exposed numerous quartz deposits via trenches all along the ridge top and slopes east of the balsaltic dike to the north and along the Culver Gulch road to the south. In one of the roadbeds, Fackler exposed a blanket lead of gold bearing ore four to six feet wide at varying depths. The ore taken from that find was worth $3,000.

Anton Neubauer, an active resident in the Blewett area around the turn of the century. (The Burmeister collection. North Central Washington Museum, Wenatchee, Washington)

Lucky Queen Mine

Rated at B-2. Returning to the town site at the highway, turn your attention down the road to the north. Ascend the hillside on the east side of the highway to a point where you can traverse the terrain above the cliffs along the edge of US 97, to the north. Travel a safe distance above these cliffs for about ¼ mile, and you'll come to the lower adit of the Lucky Queen Mine (elevation 2,300), which was opened in 1894.

The name of this mine was born from a lucky hand at poker. As the story goes, Henry Ernest owned a mine and had a love for draw poker. In a game with fellow Blewett area residents Thad Neubauer and Pete Anderson, Ernest came up short on chips. Not wanting to fold and call it a night, he put his mine up as stakes in the game. Ernest himself dealt the cards for the hand.[27] Neubauer had been dealt a broken flush, consisting of an ace, king, jack, and 10. Neubauer called for one card, which Ernest quickly dealt to him. Low and behold, the card was a *queen*. Neubauer took ownership of the mine, naming it for the improbable but "Lucky Queen." Neubauer, along with his nephew, Antoine, worked the mine for years afterward.

The workings consist of two claims, the Lucky Queen and Queen Bee, containing one principal vein with a number of intersecting veins that had pockets of ore. They sported two, now-caved, adits, the Lucky Queen with 545 feet of underground workings and the Queen Bee with 412 feet. The Lucky Queen had a raise of 328 feet from the portal that exposed a gold-rich talc vein. Production was about 20 tons of ore worth at least $1,000.

---

[27] Henry Ernest was one of the first miners to stake claims in the Blewett area in 1894. He was also the first to be buried at the Blewett cemetery. This end-all event occurred in 1897. Old Henry was working his noisy ore-crusher near Peshastin Creek, within sight of two six-year-old twins, Roy and Ray (sons of Peter, who had the Ray & Roy, Twins, and Sandell Claims) Wilder. After shouting greetings to each other across the creek, Henry turning back to his business, tripped, and fell headfirst into the pit where the large grinding machinery was crushing ore—and the life out of Henry.

Key Note Tunnel

Rated at A-1. Return to the town site and walk south along the west side of the highway. The Key Note adit is on the west side of Peshastin Creek, on the hill above the arrastre you visited earlier. This prospect penetrates the mountain for a considerable distance but fails to strike a paying ore body.

Blackjack Mine

Rated at A-1, this mine was opened in 1890. Continue up the road (south) from the arrastre, about 50 feet, and peer across the creek to the now-caved Blackjack Mine (elevation 2,340). The development here consists of one 1,300-foot–long adit, complete with winzes and raises. Production is reported as having been $30,000 by about 1900, and an additional $4,000 in 1940.

There is an old story about some miners who worked in this mine. Because the ore was found in pockets as opposed to veins, when they found one of these small pockets, the men made a habit of covering new discoveries with heavy shoring and lagging to conceal them. The following night, they would sneak back into the mine, remove the rich pocket of ore behind the timbers, and sell the booty themselves.

Lone Rock Mine

Rated at A-2. On the hill across the highway from the arrastre is the Lone Rock Mine (elevation 2,600). The adit is visible from the road, and an overgrown trail up the side of the hill near the historical marker leads to it. It consists of about 100 feet of tunnel. This mine has a very low ceiling, so watch your head if you enter.

Golden Cherry (Golden Chariot) Mine or Eureka Mine

Rated at A-1. Continue to walk up the highway (south) from the historic marker on the east side roughly ¼ mile, where you'll see a storm drain next to the road at the base of the cliff. This storm drain empties into the Golden Cherry Mine, also known as the Golden Chariot or Eureka Mine (elevation 2,400), and flows under the highway into Peshastin Creek from a pipe that has been placed at the mine's portal. The portal is no longer evident. This tunnel consists of about 970 feet of underground workings and is not accessible due to the drain. Production is unknown.

Tip Top Mine (1883)

Rated at C-3. This property is located in the southeast ¼ of Section 1 at an elevation of 3,500 feet. The 2½-foot–wide vein is an extension of the vein on the Eureka Mine and is situated in an east-trending gulch above the mine. The first workings were a 75-foot shaft from which two crosscuts were driven. A 380-footer cut into the ledge, as did the lower 400-foot crosscut. Free-milling gold ore was stoped out of these levels and run through an arrastre that was supplied with waterpower via a 500-foot–long ditch. The ore paid an average of $40.00 (to a high of $90.00) per ton.

In 1883, Mose Bollman, whose family operated a boarding house in Peshastin where the miners stayed, ran a tunnel above the Tip Top ledge. An article from the *Kittitas Wua-Wua* (Vol. 1, No. 2) states that Bollman extracted $1,521.00 worth of gold in a mere five hours. Mose refuted the story and later abandoned what he called a barren mine to build roads. Mose's post-Blewett days found him in the Liberty area, locating a mine or two and living in Ellensburg. He said that prospecting was a disease and he couldn't help doing it.

The Tip Top Mining Company quit the claim in 1888, and T. J. Vinton picked up the property in 1889, which he worked until 1895. Jack Kirk then leased the mine from Vinton and got a large amount of ore, extracting an average of $22.00 per ton in gold at the Blewett Mill.

A group of miners pose for the camera in front of their mine at Blewett. This may be the Black Jack Mine on Peshastin Creek just upstream from the town. Notice that many of the men are holding fresh candles. This indicates that they were preparing to enter the mine, because candles were the only source of light in the mines in those days, and they were issued before each shift began. (The Burmeister collection. North Central Washington Museum, Wenatchee, Washington)

Sometime during the early years, a 600-foot tunnel was developed at the mine. From this tunnel, plus earlier workings, the property produced $10,000 in ore. George Porter took a lease on the claim after Vinton and got 60 tons of ore, which yielded $10.00 a ton.

Black and White Mines

Rated at B-1, this property consisted of 12 claims. The mines are located farther up the road (south) and on the east side, just off a secondary road that parallels the highway, at the old Blewett town site (elevation 2,400 feet). All are now caved, but at one time they consisted of a vertical shaft and three adits comprising about 850 feet of underground workings, including stopes and raises.

In 1936, one-eyed John White (a.k.a. Blackie) was president of the Black and White Claims. Blackie and a miner named Herman Whitley, one of the mine's trustees, lived in a shack that was half-buried in the ground at the old Blewett town site.

In 1940, Percy Pangborn of Wenatchee reopened these old workings[28] and installed a pilot mill to treat the ore in preparation for installation of a bigger mill that would use a chemical process to extract the values from the ore. Pangborn hoped the process now would produce remarkable returns for the operators of the pilot mill. But after only cleaning out the tunnels and sinking a shaft on the property, he abandoned the operation.

Back on the other side of Peshastin Creek, you'll find more operations along a trail that passes by the Key Note tunnel and parallels it just above the old water ditch that brought water to the big 20-stamp mill. Most are caved and uninteresting. Some 300 feet beyond (south of) the Blackjack Mine and on the same side of the creek lie the remains of the old Blewett cemetery, where a dozen or so early residents were laid to rest. The site is about 935 feet south of the old Blewett historical marker on the west side of Peshastin Creek. It is heavily overgrown, and the graves are not recognizable. Several individuals and organizations have made plans to restore this old cemetery, but as of summer 2000 nothing had been done, and only close inspection and a little imagination hints to the cemetery's presence.

Look for mining activity as you travel south along US 97, particularly on the west side. King Creek, 1½ miles up the road, has seen its share of both placer and hardrock mining in the past, and to this day claims are held there.

---

[28] Several other Black White Mine officers apparently kept up the assessment work and other maintenance on the property until Pangborn took over the mines.

King Creek

Tillicum Gold Prospect

Rated at D-4. Use the USGS 7.5 Minute Series map of Blewett, and find this property in the southeast ¼ of Section 10. It is located at an elevation of 3,800 feet at the head of King Creek. The King Creek road (which is gated) begins 1.2 miles south of the historic Blewett town site. The hike up comprises 2.8 miles (one way) of good dirt road and presents some fine photo-op views as you gain the 1,400 feet of elevation to the site.

Hike the road for 1.8 miles to 3,600 feet in elevation (you'll be at the center of Section 11). Head southwest on a good dirt road (not shown on the map), continue for about 0.7 mile, and watch to the right for the area that is level with the road. Search around to find the cabin site. Follow the shallow gulch to the northwest. The caved adits and prospect holes are within 600 feet of the road.

We haven't located an adit that is said to be south of a cliffy area in the northeast ¼ of the southeast ¼ of section 10. Finding it would involve a cross-country trek requiring route-finding expertise and the ability to scramble up steep, dangerous areas.[29]

Gem Claim

Not rated. This property is located in Section 11. Gold and silver ores were taken from a five-foot–wide vein here. The claim consisted of a 20-foot adit and a 60-foot crosscut. As of the year 2000, we haven't found them.

Culver Springs Gulch Creek

Culver Springs Mining Camp Claim (1897)/Spring Pheasant Claim (1893)

Rated at D-4. Use the USGS 7.5 Minute Series map of Blewett to locate this claim in the northeast ⅛ of the northeast ¼ of Section 10, at the head of Culver Springs. Its elevation is 4,400 feet. To access this old camp/claim, use the King Creek road. This entails a 3.2-mile hike one way.

The tunnel to the digs is open, but it's not visible, even though it is a mere 150 feet from the road. The entry angle of the portal prevents you from spotting it. The tunnel runs north 20 feet to a drift, which heads left for 30 feet to flooded workings at the tunnel's end. It's not clear whether this is a winze or an underhanded stope. At any rate, its depth is unknown. There are three building sites (all collapsed), two north of the adit, which is only about 100 feet east of the road. The third and largest was destroyed when the King Creek road was connected to the ridges above Culver Gulch and Culver Springs Creek.

This is the main adit of the Tip Top Mine near the town of Blewett. Written on the photo; "take out here $20,000." The young person in the photo is Tracy. (Grace Browitt Elkins collection)

---

[29] We have been in pursuit of a number of these "said-to-be" tunnels. Some simply don't exist, some are a gulch off the present descriptions, and some are off in elevation into by hundreds of feet.

A worthwhile four to five-mile hike can be arranged by a group of hikers with two vehicles at their disposal. Park one vehicle at the Blewett town site, and drive the other car to the King Creek road to start. Hike the road to the top of Culver Gulch and down the steep gulch road through all the historic mine sites, ending back at the Blewett town site, where the second vehicle awaits.[30]

Remember, many of the properties that you will be passing in this area are private. Respect this privacy, and do not enter without the owner's permission.

Alternate Hike for Experienced Bushwackers

Warning Do not venture beyond road trips if you are inexperienced or not in very good physical shape. Even going downhill is demanding off trail.

At the head of Culver Springs Creek, follow the south side of the creek down to its mouth at Peshastin Creek (US 97). Watch for signs of old workings as you descend. Some of the mines you will pass on the way down follow:

Ruby Tunnel

Rated at D-4. The Ruby tunnel is located in the southwest ¼ of the southwest ¼ of Section 2, down creek from the Culver Springs tunnel. At the 3,600-foot level and 80 feet above the creek, the 30-foot-long Ruby tunnel was driven into a rock outcrop in a northeasterly direction. The tunnel contains a 1 to 1½-foot-wide white quartz vein. The end of a road that starts from the King Creek area is 600 feet south of and across from the tunnel. A shaft lies near the end of the road at the base of an outcrop of serpentine. These appear to be the only prospects.

Prospect Claim (1911)

Rated at B-3, when descending from the north slope of the ridge top. The site is located on the north side of Culver Springs and extends to the creek, and down to Peshastin Creek. The property consisted of five claims: the Sunset, Sunset Extension, Red Jacket, Lone Star, and Katy. All contained free-milling gold that was treated in its early development with an arrastre. The veins were oxidized and located in quartz, calcite, and talc within serpentine outcrops. We found several caved snub tunnels in 1999.

Golden Wedge #1 and #2 (1948)

Rated at B-3. This spot is downhill from the Prospect Claim on Culver Springs Creek, ¼ mile from the mouth of the creek. In 1948, H. A. Searles and Ernie Rubin were the owners of these workings.

The lower tunnel, at creek level, was cut north from the creek into the slope to an east-west-running quartz vein, which dips 67 degrees south to north. The quartz vein was drifted six feet east and six feet west from the adit. Pyrite and scattered blebs of chalcopyrite are the minerals. An assay showed $11.20 in gold per ton.

The upper adit is about 200 feet above the creek adit. At 37 feet, an east-west vein three inches to eight inches wide was encountered. The quartz was infused with calcite, pyrite, and scattered chalcopyrite, and was inferior in value to the vein material in the lower adits. The country rock differs from that in the lower digs. It is fine-grained granitic rock to the northwest and dense, light grayish-green rock on the east. It is possibly part of the Hawkins formation. The veins in the two tunnels may be the same, but their respective country rock is quite different.

---

[30] We highly recommend this route for a great mountain bike tour that starts from the Blewett town site, goes up King Creek to the ridge above Culver Gulch, continues down through all the mining areas, and finally winds up back at the car.

Homestake (1911)

Rated at B-2 from Peshastin Creek up Culver Springs Gulch. This property, owned by John Olden, was located in the southeast ¼ of Section 2 as seen on the USGS 7.5 Minute Series map of Blewett.

The remains of a cabin and other small structures can be found 400 feet up on the south side of Culver Springs Creek. There are two caved adits, with a total of 165 feet of digs, on either side of the creek. The longest was run on a quartz vein leading north into an iron-stained serpentine deposit that was laced with calcite seams. The assay, from the face of this tunnel, ran 0.4 ounce of gold and 0.2 ounce of silver per ton. The vein could be an extension of the Pole Pick vein.

Iron King Mine, 1934 (Rothert)

Rated at A-3 with steep slopes. This property is located in the southeast ¼ of Section 13, T22N, R17E, as seen on the USGS 7.5 Minute Series map of Blewett. Two and a half miles south of the old Blewett town site, US 97 cuts through two of the claims on the eastern end of the property, as does Tronsen Creek. The remaining claims are located west of Tronsen Creek. The six mineral lode claims are the Magnetite #1, Magnetite #2, Venue, Apollo, Magnetite, and Blue Rock formation.

The steep slopes where the altered serpentine rises are dominated by iron deposits. Fifty to a hundred feet above these slopes, the deposits expand to a width of from 50 to 600 feet or more. The iron formation can be traced for over a mile and was once the pebbly beach of an old lake bed. If you backtrack down US 97 to the north a short distance, you can turn left (west) onto the old Blewett Pass Highway scenic drive. On the west side of the iron conglomerate, you'll see small, round, water-worn rocks, ranging from pea-size to one inch in diameter, that have been altered to magnetite.

Most of the work consists of open cuts and short tunnels. One 70-foot tunnel had a three-foot-wide vein of talc ore that carried 0.2 ounce of gold per ton. Assays from most of the digs showed hematite, magnetite, manganese, and chromium.

Shaser/Scotty Creeks

Rated at A-1 to B-3 from the start of the hike. About ¾ mile from US 97, the Shaser Creek road branches to the right from the old Blewett Pass Highway. The creek is named for Daniel Shaser, an early teamster and miner in the area.[31] Only a small amount of mining took place along this valley, but some people do have claims here, so be careful if you plan to try your hand at prospecting. If you continue along Peshastin Creek on the old Blewett Highway, in little more than a tenth of a mile past the Shaser Creek turnoff, the Scotty Creek road branches off to the left (east) and quickly crosses the creek, past more former diggings, to the site of an old grave on the right of the road. The wooden head marker reads, "Pat King, killed September 23, 1892. Gone but not forgotten." According to local folklore, Pat King was a teamster who was delivering supplies to a remote camp when one of his wagon wheels broke. Using a large pole to lift it high enough to change the wheel, poor Pat positioned himself under the heavily loaded wagon, whereupon it slipped off the pole and killed him. He was buried on the spot.

---

[31] In 1879, Shaser was a 17-year-old chief packer. The pack train was made up of 14 packhorses, led by a rider/pack boss. Several areas of trail along the canyon shelf were dangerously narrow, and many pack animals fell off it to their deaths. It took three days for a round trip: two days with a full complement of goods and a day back to Ellensburg. Packers made $60.00 a month, with room and board. This was similar to combat pay, and considering the dangers involved, was required to attract men willing to do this work. The push for a "good road" began when an intolerable situation occurred: the lack of whiskey and tobacco. Enter Mose Bollman, who saved the day a year later with what the miners called a "really good road."

As in the case of the Shaser Creek road, mining seems to have waned after that junction. Still, it doesn't hurt to snoop around as long as you respect the rights of others, including active claim owners. This road does continue up Peshastin Creek, then turns up Scotty Creek and eventually emerges back onto US 97 at Swauk Pass. Whether it is passable by vehicles or not will have to be determined at the time of your visit.

For the Prospector/Rockhound

Historically, placer gold has been found along nearly the entire length of Peshastin Creek to the Wenatchee River, and down to the Columbia. However, most of the promising grounds are along the Peshastin from Shaser Creek to Ingalls Creek. As luck would have it, most of this ground is under federal mining claim, making it off limits to the casual prospector. The good news is that many of the claims are held by prospecting clubs, and membership is open to anyone willing to pay membership dues and follow the clubs' very reasonable rules. Some of the clubs are listed in the back of this publication under "Resources."

If you're willing to devote more to your search for gold, it has long been believed that a lot of the precious metal can be found in the ancient creek channels that run both parallel with, and across, Peshastin Creek. The best hunting ground for these old channels is in the canyon between the Blewett town site and Ingalls Creek. Scan the hillsides for a distance of up to 30 feet above the water for the old channels. This is where early placer miners worked these channels using hydraulic operations. They succeeded in washing many a good nugget for their trouble.

This entire area can provide the rockhound with more than just gold. Many deposits of agate nodules and stringers produce abundant specimens. These range from banded and fortification agates to geodes that contain quartz and amethyst (and sometimes smoky quartz crystals). Euhedral calcite crystals can often be found in these geodes as well. Most of the quartz-related deposits seem to be at just about 5,200 feet in elevation along the flanks of Red Mountain, above Ruby Creek and Table Mountain, above the town of Liberty. Other areas, such as Crystal Mountain, also have produced fine samples.

Swauk Mining Area

The Swauk mining area is located in low, mountainous country near where the rugged, east-trending Mount Stuart Range in the Wenatchee Mountains blends in with the backbone of Washington State's Cascades. The Swauk area lies along either side of Swauk Creek and its tributaries, on the southern side of Swauk and Blewett Passes. The area is characterized by mostly open pine forest and relatively sparse plant growth.

The winters are cold and the summers hot. Many of the streams in the area are seasonal, drying up late in the summer months as the searing heat takes hold. Foothills as opposed to craggy mountain peaks predominate in this area, and the entire locale is easy to access without climbing gear or other technical equipment. Elevations run from about 2,500 to 6,000 feet at the summits of the highest mountains. The only town in the area is Liberty, originally called Meaghersville, which is 26 miles northwest of Ellensburg. Liberty was once the hub of mining activity in this area.

US 97 cuts through the Swauk region. It is commonly called the Blewett Pass Highway, although it doesn't go over Blewett Pass. It did at one time, and old-timers have many a harrowing tale of near misses while driving the sinuous, narrow road. Big rigs and commercial buses plied the highway in those days, along with hapless, private cars. Today US 97 goes over Swauk Pass at the head of the Swauk Creek Valley. It is steep in grade, and caution must be exercised, especially in winter. But it is wide now, and driving it is much less of a white-knuckle experience than it once was. You can still drive to the old Blewett Pass from the south side of Swauk Pass via Forest Service Road 7320. Road 7320 can also be accessed where Peshastin Creek and Tronsen Creek merge on the north side of Swauk Pass. You can glimpse portions of the old highway high on the hillsides on the northern side of Swauk Pass along Peshastin Creek, parallel to where the new part of US 97 runs.

History

It is generally accepted among the historians of the Swauk region that the first gold placer discovered by whites was in 1867 when a party of prospectors, headed up by the Goodwin brothers, were making their way up an Indian trail along Swauk Creek on their way to the Blewett and Peshastin gold fields.[1] The most common version of the story is that in 1867 Newton and Benton Goodwin, two of the three Goodwin brothers, and others had stopped to cook a meal about ½ mile north of the present-day Liberty access road on Swauk Creek. Benton either went to the creek to get water or to do some panning—the story varies—but he *is* credited with finding the first Swauk gold. The party named the location of the find Discovery Bar.[2]

The amount of gold the Goodwins found at Discovery Bar was not enough to impress them nor to compel them to stay and continue their search, and the find lay undisturbed until 1873 when the Goodwins revisited the spot. This time their efforts were rewarded with a very rich strike. When word of this bonanza leaked out, a gold rush to the Swauk Creek area ensued, resulting in a population increase of several hundred people. In 1874, G. W. Goodwin (Newton and Benton's uncle) formed the Discovery Company, along with several other partners.

---

[1] It is possible that Chinese miners were working this district prior to the arrival of the white miners. We have been unable to verify this.
[2] Some sources refer to the brothers as Thomas and Benton Goodwin. This area is now known as the Burcham Tract. It is about ½ mile north of Williams Creek on the eastern side of Swauk Creek. Benton was reportedly a deaf mute.

Many who came to the Swauk in search of the yellow metal were very ill-equipped, and it wasn't uncommon to see some of them using kitchen utensils in lieu of mining tools, panning with frying pans and digging around with butcher knives and forks. Prior to 1890, the area was mainly a placer gold producer, but after 1891, lode mining greatly increased. Tunnels and shafts peppered the hills throughout the vicinity. These underground diggings required shoring and the cutting of timber, which necessitated the eventual construction of two sawmills.

The Discovery Claim produced an ounce of gold per day for each prospector during the following mining season, but once the richest ground had been worked out the claim was abandoned. By 1876, most of the miners had left the Swauk area, headed for the more lucrative districts in Colorado, Idaho, and Utah.

Meanwhile, a miner named Gus Nelson, or Nilson,[3] was at work developing a mine on the north side of Baker Creek.[4] The way this story is usually told, one day he rolled over a large boulder, picked up a nugget, and what a nugget it was. It weighed 67 ounces! The nugget most likely was made up of wire gold, not a true nugget.

During the winter of 1892, the smaller mines were temporarily shut down due to severe weather conditions; heavy rain, snow, and hail pummeled the area. But the biggest problems were the resulting road conditions. The miners proposed that every man in camp donate three or four day's labor if the county would do the same. The county seemed to have other priorities, however, and road conditions deteriorated until the Culver Mining Company of Blewett needed to move some heavy equipment to its mines, at which time the improvements were made without the county's help.

A post office was also established in 1892 on the east side of Swauk Creek, just south of its confluence with Williams Creek. Gus Nilson was the first postmaster. The name Swauk Camp was being used, but there was already a "Sauk," and the Post Office Department, always fearing confusion, objected. Nilson invited the miners down to the building and told them, "You're at liberty here, boys; sit down, lay down, or do as you please." When the postal inspector requested a different name, all agreed upon "Liberty."

In early 1902, the Cedar Valley Gold Mining Company of Spokane formed and sold $50,000.00 worth of stock to do placer mining in the Swauk District. We have been unable to determine where or for how long the company operated.

The histories of the individual claims, prospects, and mines throughout the region will be provided as the properties are described.

One way to high-grade a placer deposit is shown here. The gravel is dug from the bank and panned in a wash tub. This was handy if no stream was immediately available, or as is often the case in the Liberty area, the streams would dry up during the summer. (Grace Browitt Elkins collection)

---

[3] His actual name was Gustaf Nilson, but for some reason Nelson appears on almost all of the old maps and records. We determined his true name from a certified copy of the miner's meeting held at Meaghersville on June 28, 1897, attended by 49 miners, including Tom Meagher, John Black, J. K. Morrill, and other notables. Nilson signed the document in three separate places, and the spelling is without a doubt "Nilson."

[4] Nilson also developed a large underground placer mine on the east side of Swauk Creek just north of Williams Creek during 1881-1882. We investigated this property in 1994 and found that it contained over 1,000 feet of tunneling. Since almost no shoring was used, these tunnels are extremely dangerous and should not be entered. Nelson Bar (Nilson) is under mineral claim as of this writing.

The Discovery Mine at T. I. Meaghers' property on Williams Creek in the vicinity of the present-day town of Liberty. Everyone in the area must have turned out for this photo opportunity. (Ellensburg Public Library collection)

What to See

The Swauk area has numerous back roads and hiking trails for those seeking outdoor adventure. Because of the relative dryness of the area, water sports are not an option here. Hikes along the many creeks and streams (which are often dry) can provide a pleasant day's journey, especially if you also make a few discoveries of old mine sites and mining artifacts. Agate and geode hunting sites abound for the rockhound. There are mountains to be climbed, most of which require a simple walk to the top. The hiker is rewarded with views of the spectacular Stuart Range to the northwest and, far in the distance, snow-capped Mount Rainier.

In the fall, driving US 97 can provide an autumn foliage tour. Folks from Seattle can do the loop—crossing Snoqualmie Pass, Swauk Pass, and Stevens Pass in turn—or traveling the route the other way around. In late September and early October, the colors are often grand and well worth the trip. Columbia Basin residents also find this to be a worthy jaunt for viewing fall colors, either by driving a loop through Vantage, over Swauk Pass, and back through Wenatchee, or vice versa.

Getting There

Visiting the Swauk mining area makes for an interesting day tour that will loop you through some of the most beautiful scenery that the Central Cascades and the Wenatchee Mountains have to offer.

If Seattle is your starting point, drive east on I-90 across Snoqualmie Pass to Cle Elum. (You can either enter town and follow the main street east or stay on I-90.) Roslyn and Ronald, two neighboring towns, are just a short drive away. Cle Elum, Roslyn, and Ronald were once the hubs of coal

A close-up of a cradle in action. Notice the riffle plate on the right where the useless rock is being rocked out onto the ground, while the riffles, hopefully, retain the gold. (Grace Browitt Elkins collection)

The original town of Liberty located at the confluence of Swauk and Williams Creeks. The town moved two miles up Williams Creek in 1916, when the Liberty post office moved to Meaghersville. The original town then slowly faded away, leaving no trace of its existence today. This view is looking to the northeast up Williams Creek from the west bank of Swauk Creek. The broad ridge seen against the skyline is Table Mountain, while nearer Flag Mountain can be seen just beyond the shoulder of the descending ridge on the right. (Grace Browitt Elkins collection)

mining in Eastern Washington. In Roslyn, be sure you visit the Brick Tavern, the site where the television show *Northern Exposure* was filmed and also the oldest saloon in the state. The town has a wonderful museum as well.

Leaving Cle Elum, take US 970 to its junction with US 97 (the Blewett Pass Highway). From there, it's a short drive to the Liberty turnoff (a well-marked road). Turn right (east) onto the Liberty Road, cross Swauk Creek, and follow the road into town.

After visiting Liberty, you can either return the way you came by going back to US 97 and turning south, or you can continue the loop by turning right (north) onto US 97. The journey north will take you over Swauk Pass. Then head down the mountain to the junction of US 97 and US 2. Turn left (west) on US 2, and the road will take you through the Bavarian village of Leavenworth, a tourist stop with many small, interesting shops to explore. Stay on US 2 and you will cross Stevens Pass and eventually pass through Monroe. Continue and follow the signs to Everett. Once you reach Everett, turn left (south) on I-5 and begin the relatively short drive back to Seattle.

From Eastern Washington, take I-90 west to the US 97 cutoof to Blewett Pass and drive north to Liberty Road, located three miles north of the US 970 junction from Cle Elum. From US 2, turn south, travel over Swauk Pass to the Liberty Road, and turn left.

Geology

Liberty, which is almost the exact center point of the state, sits atop the Swauk formation,[5] a Cenozoic-era structure that developed in the Tertiary period and is generally considered the oldest Eocene unit in the central Cascade Range. It is 39 to 55 million years old and is composed of arkosic sandstone, conglomerate, and shale—mostly carbonaceous with occasional fossil vegetation, which suggests rapid erosion, transportation, and deposit. The Swauk basin shows no record of glaciation or prior presence of ice, as associated with the Pleistocene ice age. This nonglaciated area aggregated large streams, leaving terraces above some of the present creeks and feeder streams.

The Teanaway lava flow in the Swauk District can be identified by its reddish-brown color, although some outcrops are dull to jet-black. Iron in the rock and soil oxidizes to a rust color. Northeast-trending diabase and basalt dikes, exposed throughout the Swauk basin, were fed from the Teanaway lava flow, and were intruded into the Swauk sandstone formation, which dominates the southern slopes of the Swauk District. So many dikes populate the area that it is often referred to as the Teanaway "dike swarm."

---

[5] "Swauk" in the local Native American language means "a good hunting place."

An arrastre in the Liberty area. Water was conducted to the site via an overhead flume, it was then directed down the large wooden column and shot through a nozzle to power the horizontal undershot water wheel (it looks like a merry-go-round). A rock-lined tub was situated in the center of the water wheel (not visible) and the wheel dragged a stone around to crush the gold ore. Mercury was used in the bottom of the tub to recover the gold. The wheel was not operating when this photo was taken so the water was simply left to flow off the end of the flume. (Wes and Carole Engstrom collection)

The sandstone is one of the largest sedimentary formations in the state (adding to the geological nonconformity of the area). Recent sediment measurements near Liberty were found to be about 5,000 feet in depth. One phase of the Swauk formation occurred when bedrock from three feet to one foot thick formed ripples in the stream bottom, which acted as a natural riffle box and trapped gold.

Shale is an important substance in the Swauk Mining District, a favorable host for incoming mineral solutions, which found many cracks to flow into. Shale also weathers more rapidly than sandstone or conglomerate and reveals its treasures sooner. Where the shale is cut by dikes, it often holds pockets of gold, and crevices in the shale streambed hold the gold in place. Occasionally, veins form that are entirely enclosed in dike rock.

The gold of Swauk's placers is believed to have originated in the Table Mountain area on the east, and Teanaway Ridge on the west. It is found most prevalently in the bars that cover old creek channels along the banks of Baker, Williams, and Boulder Creeks. The same can be said of Swauk Creek between Baker and First Creeks, a distance of three miles north and south and about the same east and west.[6]

Essentially, a river ran through the area millions of years ago. The gold was carried downstream and lodged in the bedrock of the ancient streambed. No one has ever found the true source of the Swauk gold. Many of the miners who worked the area called it "freak geology," a phrase coined by an old miner named Clarence Jordin. Perhaps somewhere in those mountains hides the mother lode.

An ore called *Bird's Eye Quartz* is peculiar to the Swauk area. Typical specimens consist of small fragments of dark rock scattered almost evenly throughout a calcite and quartz matrix in a brecciated vein. These bits are mostly angular diabase (a dark-colored igneous rock), most commonly the size of a bird's eye but also occurring up to an inch in diameter. Drusy quartz crystallizes as a coating around each fragment, with slender crystals pointing outward. Cavities lie between the coatings of adjacent particles; the quartz masses almost grow together. The gold found in Bird's Eye Quartz is not evenly distributed. The local miners say only the iron-stained deposits carry gold.

---

[6] One of the earlier theories was that the entire Swauk District was a crater like that of Cripple Creek, Colorado. It is interesting to note that after the Swauk formation was created, there existed a basin-like depression 12 miles west of the district. Then the Rosyln sandstone formation filled the sunken area with clay and sandstone to a depth of about 3,500 feet, extending east where an outcrop of Roslyn sandstone 200 feet thick and ½-mile long now appears on the western slope of Table Mountain.

When we visited, we saw mineralization that showed gold quartz veins in narrow fissures accompanied by calcite and talc. Calcite gangue as a host in veins encourages the deposit of crystalline pocket gold. This is due to the gold-carrying solutions not having undergone pressure to deposit in tight places as in quartz veins, allowing the gold to form more of its natural art. Some digs had sandstone or shale for wall rock, sometimes one on one side and the other forming on the opposite wall. Other workings had basalt for one wall, and either sandstone, shale, or diabase rock forming the wall across from it. The sandstone, often seen in bedded planes, sometimes had stringers of quartz between the stratified formations. Miners familiar with the ore mined at Wenatchee have found several similarities between it and the Swauk ore.

Liberty The dictionary defines liberty as, "The condition of being free from restriction or control. The right to act, believe, or express oneself in a manner of one's own choosing. The condition of being free from confinement, servitude, or forced labor. Freedom from unjust or undue government control." The story of the town of Liberty and its people demonstrates what life in America is all about—freedom.

The present-day town of Liberty lies nestled on the banks of Williams Creek two miles east of US 97, at an elevation of 2,650 feet. As you drive the short road from US 97 to the town, you will see the remains of mining equipment and machinery from bygone days scattered amidst the wild growth along Williams Creek. Most of the machinery along this portion of the road is rusted and unusable now—a silent reminder of the dreams of the miners who searched for the elusive wire and nugget gold that has made Liberty world-famous. The hills around Liberty contain many miles of mine tunnels and shafts.

Liberty was not always in its current geographic location. At one time, it sat at the confluence of Swauk and Williams Creeks, where Thomas Meagher, a local miner and store owner, originally lived. Local residents were trying to decide on a new name for the town. Gus Nilson had invited the townspeople to a meeting and announced, "You're at liberty here." Eventually, the name of Liberty was chosen. But Meagher no longer lived in the town. He'd built his residence about two miles up Williams Creek at the New Yakima Campsite. Later, the population in the area around

Meaghersville (later Liberty), Washington, as it appeared in 1896. The two-story building on the left was the hotel, while the building in the trees on the right was the schoolhouse and community hall. Only the hotel remains standing today. (Wes and Carole Engstrom collection)

The John Flodin family and Archie Morrison (on the left). The child is Frank Flodin. The Flodin's were long-time miners in the Liberty area. (Wes and Carole Engstrom collection)

Meagher's place grew, and the spot became known as Meaghersville. Meanwhile, Liberty had begun to fade away. In 1916, when the post office was moved from Liberty to Meaghersville, the town of Liberty and its name moved with it. Today there is a two-story house located at the eastern end of Liberty that was once the Meaghersville Hotel, where four guests could stay at a time. Narcissa Needham-Stonebraker ran the place, cooking for up to 20 people per meal. The fee was $3.75 per week for room and board, but the miners or drifters who stayed there would occasionally depart without paying. Pat Jordin, Ollie Jordin's nephew, rented the house in 1970.

Over the past 20 years, our group has explored several mining districts throughout the Pacific Northwest, but we have never seen anything that compares with the Swauk District. The massive amount of tunneling that was done there is almost incomprehensible.

The gold rush days of Liberty are long gone, but the town still boasts a number of permanent residents and quite a bit of present-day mining activity. Every summer weekend during the season, you can hear the sounds of recreational dredge motors alongside the road. In the hills and valleys above and around the town, heavy machinery still grinds away at the earth in search of the elusive yellow metal. A general store, the last business in town, closed its doors in July 1998.

During the warmer spring and summer months, tourists, hikers, would-be prospectors, and other adventurous souls frequent the town. In the Northwest Forest Plan, the entire Swauk drainage basin around Liberty is set aside for wildlife, and fall brings hunters who scout the area for the abundant deer, grouse, and elk. In the winter, Liberty is a popular mecca for snowmobile driving and other winter sports.

Despite its remoteness, Liberty is unique in another way. The town was never incorporated or properly platted. It is situated on a mine claim called Fraction Placer (later renamed the New Discovery Placer), and was never chartered by the county, state, or federal governments. Much of the town's history has been turbulent as a result: for example, for an extended period the federal government, working through the Forest Service, tried to disband Liberty and throw its inhabitants out of their homes.[7] Many of its residents were born, grew up, worked their whole adult lives, and retired there, so the thought of being uprooted from the only home they knew was a terrible proposition.

A group, possibly members of the same family, poses in Liberty with what may have been their most prized possession, their automobile. (Wes and Carole Engstrom collection)

---

[7] Around 1925, the Salem Mining Company acquired the unpatented claims upon which the town of Liberty was situated. In a court ruling, prescriptive rights to the land surface was granted to the townspeople. In the 1960s and 1970s, Nugget Properties, Inc., Gold Placers, Inc., and Golden Thunderbird Mining Company also attempted to remove the residents from the property after obtaining mining rights to the land.

Ralph Fackler (Nov. 12, 1909–Mar. 13, 1998) in his Liberty home in early 1998. His father established many of the early mines in the Swauk and Blewett areas. Some of the Culver Gulch mines carry the Fackler name. (Victor Pisoni photo)

The entire population battled the bureaucracy, engaging senators, representatives, and presidents of the United States in their efforts. In 1966, following a bitter lawsuit, the judge in the case surprised everyone when he ruled in favor of the Liberty residents, stating that they had established a prescriptive right to the use of the surface of the land in question. In a title decree, the mining claim location rights were upheld except the land the town sat on. The court also warned both sides not to interfere with the other. The Forest Service as well as the Golden Thunderbird Mining Company were caught off-guard by this ruling. They were certain that the court would find the residents in trespass and order an eviction.

On October 15, 1974, after considerable legal wrangling, Liberty residents succeeded in placing the town site on the National Register of Historic Places. Relations with the Forest Service also started to improve around this time. In 1976, the Forest Service decided to help the homeowners clear their titles to the land. It suggested applying for a new township under the old township laws, as had been recommended to them 68 years earlier. The homeowners agreed, and the Forest Service assisted in preparing the application. Kittitas County Superior Court Judge W. R. Cole agreed to act as trustee, and the townspeople deposited $5,000 in trust with him to cover the cost of the land at $2.50 per acre, plus the cost of a survey and other legal fees. The application was submitted on July 4, 1976, as part of Liberty's celebration of the nation's bicentennial.

The issue appeared to be on its way to a resolution until October 1976, when Congress passed the Federal Land Use Management Act. This Act, among other things, repealed homestead and town site laws, including the one Liberty had filed under. (The rifles and shotguns didn't come out, but the Rolaids and Maalox sure did.) The application was now in limbo, and no one knew whether it could or would be processed under the old law. It took until May 1977 for a decision to be made: the Department of the Interior rejected the application, claiming that its authority to create town sites had been repealed and that the new Federal Land Use Management Act also did not provide a grandfather clause for applications that were not yet acted upon. To make matters worse, the new Act did not contain provisions for creating any new town sites, only a provision to add to existing town sites. Things looked pretty gloomy for the residents. They wondered if they should finally throw in the towel and give it up. "Hell, no!" was the answer they agreed on.

The Forest Service consented and suggested that the best way to proceed was to have a special-interest bill passed by Congress to create a new town site. Not knowing just how difficult something like this would be, the townsfolk went ahead and did it. It helped that their attorney, Jack McSherry, was a high-school buddy of Washington State Senator Henry M. Jackson and that Congressman Mike McCormick was a longtime friend of the Liberty cause.

Senate Bill S. 2033 was passed by Congress and signed by President Jimmy Carter as Public Law 95-310 on June 30, 1978. A dispute over the rights of counties to dispose of government lands in Washington again delayed resolution, but a special bill finally passed in the Washington State Legislature that allowed the townspeople to obtain ownership of the land they and their forebears had lived on. On December 22, 1981, Liberty residents became the official owners of their land after nearly 70 years of battle.

A view of Liberty, looking east up Williams Creek. (Wes and Carole Engstrom collection)

The Mines

Because of the geology of the Swauk Mining District, many shafts are present on the claims. They vary in depth from shallow to hundreds of feet deep. Be aware of this danger. Some might be flooded and others not. A fall into one of these old workings would most likely be fatal. We have listed the ones we know about, but without a doubt there are many more. Beware!

Diamonds

Diamonds have been recovered in gold placering operations at various locations in the area. Diamonds are usually found in kimberlite, and though there is no kimberlite in Washington State, there are other peridotites that could contain diamond crystals. We have yet to find one. The most sought-after mineral in this region is, of course, gold.

Free-milling gold has been found in Swauk, Baker, Williams, Boulder, and other area creeks. The Swauk area is famous for its huge nuggets and beautiful examples of crystalline and wire gold usually found in isolated pockets. Gold has been found in the district's lode-gold deposits, as well as in underground placers (into which tunnels are dug in the same manner as lode mine adits). The placer mines show stains indicating that minerals such as iron and manganese oxides exist in sufficient amounts to act as a cementing agent, keeping some of these ancient stream-channel bed tunnels solid today, unsupported though they are (except for unmined pillars that hold up the larger dome-shaped areas). Miners in the vicinity report that the lode gold is usually in the pockets in shale in shear zones. It has also been found in veins of quartz and calcite. Although most of the area is under claim, there are still places where you can pan for gold. The rules for panning and other gold-gathering activities are constantly changing. Get a copy of the Washington State Department of Fish and Wildlife's *Gold and Fish Booklet* to keep up on current changes, and remember to carry it with you always; otherwise you could get ticketed. *Remember to respect the rights of existing claim and private-property owners.*

H. C. Dennett Placer Claim, 1898

Rated at A-1. In 1956, this claim was known as the Collins Placer. The property is located in the southeast ¼ of Section 10, T20N, R17E, off the side of US 97. It is 0.2 mile south of the Deer Gulch Pond Road, where the remains of the once active gold dredge are located. See the USGS 7.5 Minute Series map of Swauk Prairie.

The USGS map shows an adit symbol to mark the workings area. A 1920s gold-dredge company map specifies the location of four placer tunnels along the ¼-mile strip of private land. Presently, two open tunnels exist. The owner gave us a tour of one tunnel. Only an invitation will get you anywhere near this site.

The grand celebration of July 4, 1916, brought people from all over the region. The Wild Cat Dance Hall, which probably rang with music that night, is on the right. Everyone dressed in their finest, and the latest-model automobiles were shined up for the occasion. (Wes and Carole Engstrom collection)

The placer tunnels had been dug through the Swauk Creek watercourse, first by whites and then by Chinese miners. The Chinese were very thorough in gleaning the gold that the previous miners had missed. They stacked the large rocks out of the way while reworking the bedrock, lining either side of the tunnels in what appears to be added support with a touch of artistic masonry, so tight and well jointed was their work. The tunnels accessed hundreds feet of meandering workings into the hillside.

Livingston Placer Tunnels

Rated at A-1. Also known as Livingston Bar, this property is located in the northwest ¼ of Section 15, T20N, R17E, about 1 mile south of Liberty Road on the west side of Swauk Creek. See the USGS 7.5 Minute Series map of Swauk Prairie.

In 1885, Dave Livingston took up residence at Liberty with his Native American wife. Dave ran the town store and post office up until 1916.[8] During those years, he wrested $60,000 worth of gold from three placer tunnels dug into the old Swauk Creek channel. Dave's sons, Jim and Tom, continued to work the placer claims, and also labored at their Homestake Hill Mine (one of the first hardrock quartz digs in the area) until the late 1880s. Tom and Jim reported obtaining $50,000 worth of gold for their efforts. They spent their old age in Ellensburg.

The present site is privately owned. Conservatively, we estimate that about two acres are honeycombed with tunnels.

A scene of the Fourth of July celebration at Liberty in 1916, with the Wild Cat Dance Hall serving as a backdrop. The event was sponsored by Cascade Pride, a popular malt liquor of the time. Both coffee and beer sold for 5 cents a glass. (Wes and Carole Engstrom collection)

---

[8] Samples of calcite and quartz with free-gold protruding were on display at the store.

A group poses in front of the post office at Liberty. This photograph may have been taken on the Fourth of July, 1916. (Wes and Carole Engstrom collection)

Homestead Lode Claim

Rated at A-1. This property is located in the south ½ of Section 10, T20N, R17E, along the centerline area, west of Swauk Creek, across from the Dennett Mine placer tunnels, which are below Deer Gulch. See the USGS 7.5 Minute Series map of Swauk Prairie.

The claim comprised three tunnels of undetermined length. In 1882, owner William Pennell sold 750 feet of the Pennell quartz vein on the Homestead Lode to Louis Quietsch (a Swauk miner who held multiple claims) for $1. The vein adjoined Quietsch's claim on the south, where Louis had run a not-so-profitable 125-foot placer tunnel. So he quit placer mining to pursue his new lode property. Dredge miner Frank Bryant later acquired this same property and owned it into the 1950s. It remains private land.

Homestake Claim

Not rated. Not to be confused with the Homestead Lode Claim, this property was located in the southwest ¼ of the northeast ¼ of Section 10, T20N, R17E. See the USGS 7.5 Minute Series map of Swauk Prairie.

This historic mining claim was north of the Deer Gulch Dredge pond east of the mouth of Deer Gulch. This is possibly the same ground where the Livingstons had located their Homestake Hill Quartz Claim.

During a miner's rodeo at Liberty, two men compete in a double-jacking contest. One miner holds the drill bit while the other drives it with his sledge. (Wes and Carole Engstrom collection)

People gather in front of the Liberty general store during the 1916 Fourth of July celebration. The structure peeking out from behind the left side of the store is the schoolhouse. (Wes and Carole Engstrom collection)

Deer Gulch Dredge Pond

Rated at A-1, it is located in the northeast ¼ of Section 10, T20N, R17E. See the USGS 7.5 Minute Series map of Swauk Prairie.

About ½ mile south of the Liberty road, there is an east-trending road that goes 0.2 mile to the dredge pond, as shown on the map. The dredge was attempting to work its way up the gulch, but it ran into a mess of problems. It is now rotting away. The best time to check it out is in the late summer when low water allows for a more exposed view of the hull remains. As of 2000, a gate has been installed on the road and it might be closed and posted.

US 97 Tourist Tunnel

Rated at A-1, this tunnel is located in Section 3, T20N, R17E, on the west side of US 97 at a roadside turnoff. It is about ½ mile north of the Liberty access road. This 50-foot tunnel, run along a contact zone, offers you the chance to experience being inside a relatively safe tunnel, creates a rare photo opportunity, or may wind up afflicting you with a new phobia.

Several folks pose for their picture on a splendid, sunny day on the porch of the Liberty General Store. (Wes and Carole Engstrom collection)

The grocery store at Liberty, circa 1915. (Wes and Carole Engstrom collection)

Ben Killson stands on the porch of his typical, sturdy clapboard house in Liberty in the early part of the 20th century. (Wes and Carole Engstrom collection)

Four folks pose in front of a Liberty building, sometime between 1910 and 1920. (Wes and Carole Engstrom collection)

Fraction Placer Claim

Rated at A-1. This claim is located in the southwest ¼ of the northwest ¼ of Section 1, T20N, R17E, as seen on the USGS 7.5 Minute Series map of Liberty.

In 1893, J. K. Morrill located the claim where most of the cabins of Liberty now stand. The area was home to several businesses, and the name of the site was New Yakima. Thomas Meagher jumped Morrill's claim in 1897, retaining the Fraction #343 name for the ground but renaming the town site Meaghersville. Meagher and Charles Bigney formed a mining company and controlled most of the placers along Williams

Top: Three children play with their little (red?) wagon in this timeless Liberty scene. (Wes and Carole Engstrom collection)

Center: Five people with a horse and buggy pose for a photo in front of the store in Old Liberty in 1903. (Wes and Carole Engstrom collection)

Bottom: The town of Meaghersville prior to 1917. In 1916, the post office moved here from Liberty, which was located two miles down Williams Creek at Swauk Creek. The post office carried the Liberty name with it, and Meaghersville ceased to exist. Looking east Flag Mountain graces the skyline just right of the street, while snow-covered Table Mountain is is the distance. (Grace Browitt Elkins collection)

A number of pupils and their teacher stand on the porch of the Liberty schoolhouse. (Wes and Carole Engstrom collection)

and Boulder Creeks. Bigney held the claim directly to the east of the Fraction #343. Called the #342, Bigney drove 2,800 feet of tunnel along the bedrock on the property. Thomas transferred the #343 over to his son, Martin Meagher, who failed to do the required annual assessment work. William Anderson reclaimed the Fraction #343, naming it the New Discovery.

Williams Creek Placer Tunnels

Rated at A-1, these tunnels are located in the northeast ¼ of Section 10, and northwest ¼ of Section 11, T20N, R17E, as seen on the USGS 7.5 Minute Series map of Swauk Prairie. These placer tunnels are situated between the mouth of Williams Creek at Swauk Creek, and a point ½ mile up the Liberty Road. The tunnels pass under the Liberty Road, entering from below the south side of the road grade at its base and then bearing north. Curious folks can easily wander into nonposted land in the area and see where these adits began their meandering quest over thousands of feet of gold-laden bedrock. Ownership and claim names have changed over the past 100 years. The lineage of owners and the history of these properties are presented below.

Andrew Flodin began with a 400-foot placer tunnel on the first claim above the mouth of Williams Creek. Upstream from Flodin, Thaddeus Neubauer and H. C. Jones dug a number of adits. Jones had two more claims in partnership with a man named Steel, which were located on Swauk Creek between Williams Creek and Deer Gulch. During the late 1800s, the Green Tree Mining Company had four claims along and near Williams Creek. Twelve hundred feet of Williams Creek and Liberty Road were covered by the width of two of the claims. Flodin's original workings lay within the Green Tree property boundaries at a later date.

The next property upstream was one of John Black's many mine holdings; he also had a creek/high bar claim called the Blackjack. This was located about one mile from the mouth of Williams Creek where Pine Gulch Road bears south off Liberty Road. His two properties could actually be one and the same. A north-trending tunnel was driven into the property. The Blackjack shaft is located in a private field at the northern end of the connected workings.

The aforementioned "under the road" tunnels have cut into the Blackjack system of digs. Local miners have been known to exit via this shaft after following a maze of tunneling unrelated to the Blackjack. The high bar (ancient creek bed of Pleistocene gravel) on Black's land was developed using a hydraulic plant. This washed a 25-foot–high creek bank, directing the resultant slurry through six Hungarian riffles in a 30-foot sluice box. Immediately east of the Black property lay the Mountainside and the Morning Star digs.

Northwest of the placer tunnels listed above are the thousands of feet of Gus Nilson's historic tunnel workings. The present owners continue to extend these digs, and they have broken into the "under the road" tunnels, which probably means that all of these properties have now been interconnected.

There was a flurry of mining activity in the later years from the ½-mile point up Williams Creek to Boulder Creek, which obliterated much of the early historic mining excavations. The land is now owned privately, and public intrusion is restricted. As for the claims, do not attempt to enter any of these digs. Not only are some being actively mined, but the tunnels are also unsafe in certain sections. That, along with the fact that they comprise a network of confusing, intersecting drift tunnels, makes them extremely dangerous. *Do not enter.*

Blackjack Mine

Rated at A-1. This property, still active and privately owned, is located along the north side of the road that runs from Swauk Creek to Liberty, about one mile after the turnoff onto the Liberty Road. Jack Kirch worked it upon his arrival at Liberty in 1928. We visited this mine with the permission of the present owner. It consists of a crosscut tunnel under the road used for drainage, and an 80-foot–deep shaft that accesses the working drifts. Do not enter this property without the owner's permission.

The cradle rocker shown here is a simple riffle device. The ore and water were introduced via the hopper at the left side. It is worked down the slanted riffle plate when the operator rocks the cradle using the provided lever. The riffles will retain the heavy gold, while the waste rock is washed out the end to the right. (Grace Browitt Elkins collection)

Dixie Claim

Gus Nilson had the Dixie Claim, and the shaft he drove on it was called the Nilson Shaft. The exact location is unknown, but it is reported as being in Deer Gulch.

Ace of Diamonds

Rated at A-1, this property is accessible by Road 114 on the Green Trails Map of Liberty. It is located in the northeast ¼ of Section 6 on Snowshoe Ridge, in T20N, R18E, at an elevation of 3,800 feet. This spot also can be found on the USGS 7.5 Minute Series map of Liberty.

In the Dennett Placer tunnel, the rocks that were hand-stacked by the Chinese miners as they worked the bedrock for the residual gold can be seen. They were almost artistic the way they removed the rocks from the floor and stacked them along the walls of the tunnel. (Greg Cady photo)

In one of the flooded Dennett Placer tunnels, a pillar stands at the intersection of two diverging bores. While it appears that this is simply a tunnel intersection, you can walk all the way around the pillar in the center of the photograph. (Greg Cady photo)

The remains of the old Liberty dredge that operated on Deer Gulch. The wooden barge that carried the dredge has succumbed to the ravages of time. (Victor Pisoni photo)

On the patented Elliott Claim in the 1930s. Connected to the east side of the Bigney property. Water was transported to the workings via this wooden flume. (Wes and Carole Engstrom collection)

Clarence Jordin bought and operated the mine and in 1932 made a 120-pound gold strike (worth $40,000), including two seven-pound chunks of wire gold. Junior Jordin, Clarence's son, worked the mine during the 1950s and 60s using an old backhoe to excavate several open cuts.

Miner Jon Vauthiers leased the claim from Junior Jordin in the 1960s and 1970s. He hired two men and in six months had driven a 100-foot shaft. When we visited the site, it was in a state of disrepair. The original workings consisted of a vertical shaft connected with several hundred feet of drifting. What appear to be a glory hole and a horizontal adit are also in evidence. Both were flooded, so we didn't do any exploring.

Anna May

Rated at A-1. This property adjoins the Ace of Diamonds' north property line on Snowshoe Ridge, and probably dates to around the same time period. When we visited the mine in 1998, a very well-built cabin, minus the windows, was still standing. Development work seemed to be fairly consistent with that of the neighboring Ace of Diamonds. In other words, there are a lot of surface diggings and some underground workings in this immediate area.

We found a flooded, well-shored incline shaft near the county access road. A local story about this shaft reports that a married couple had just purchased the property and was conducting an inspection tour of the workings. The woman entered the incline first and was followed closely by her husband. Suddenly he stopped, looked down at the floor of the tunnel, and exclaimed, "They missed it; it's right here, I can smell it!" Digging down a few inches below the surface, they found a large deposit, or pocket, of wire gold.[9] Remember, there is no shortage of stories in a mining district. We have heard "smell" stories before. It is not that a person can sniff out gold, but rather that one might be able to sense the geology that tends to accompany it. Or maybe we simply lack this olfactory ability.

One other item of interest about this property was that sometime during the 1920s a Canadian mining company decided to undercut both the Anna May and the Ace of Diamonds Claims. A long crosscut tunnel was bored below a neighboring hillside to the south of the claim. Amos Jordin remembered working on the project, but he could not recall the name of the company nor the exact year the tunnel was dug. It appears that they were able to go for about 900 feet before encountering an area of loose, wet clay.

---

[9] Wire gold is found in tunnel digs and placer mining. It forms as felted, tangled masses of curved, angular wires, each up to five inches long. There were many interesting natural wire gold patterns found. Miners called it fly-leg gold, hair-root gold, and fern gold, indicating its wide variety of shapes.

When Liberty resident Paul Heit examined the large, smooth tunnel in the 1980s, it was open a few hundred feet to where the wet clay caved, blocking the remainder. Paul noticed steel strap on top of wood rails that once served as ore cart tracks. In 1998, we found the portal caved, barring access.

Cougar Claim

Rated at A-2 to A-3. This property consists of a single placer claim located in the northwest ¼ of the northeast ¼ of Section 36, T21N, R17E, at an elevation of 3,000 feet. This placer was claimed and developed by the State of Washington Mining Company (1915), Cougar Gulch Mining Company (1934), and the Washington Gold Mining Company, Inc. (1938).

Numerous prospect pits, caved digs, adits, and the outlines of old cabin sites lie just off (west) Cougar Gulch Road, and up to the ridge top in Sections 25 and 36. Bird's Eye Quartz float can be found scattered near and around the tunnels and other digs.

There are game trails and old miner's trails you can use when searching the hillside for these historic workings. As you explore the old claims dotting the west side of Cougar Gulch, the newer (nonposted) claims you traverse will be the properties of the American Nickel and Copper Company, claimed in 1980 by a party from Wheat Ridge, Colorado.

American Nickel

Rated at A-2 to A-3. The American Nickel Claim has three caved adits and several open cuts. We couldn't determine the extent of the original digs from the newer developments, because of nature's way of quickly reclaiming shallow surface workings. This property overlaps the north line of the Cougar property described above. The flurry of mining activity during the Depression years to the present also makes it difficult to identify some of the original claims.

Francis Girard Quartz Lode, 1990

Rated at A-1 to A-2. This property, consisting of two claims, is located in the northwest $\frac{1}{8}$ of the northwest ¼ of Section 36, T21N, R17E. This places it west of Cougar Gulch Creek next to the American Nickel Mine, and adjoining the Betty Lou Two on the south. Records describe it as consisting of a discovery shaft and a tunnel (supposedly caved). We found two adits, each 80 feet in length, both of which have obviously been reopened in the last several years.

Betty Lou Two Group of Claims, 1984

Rated at A-1 to A-2. Located in the southeast ¼ of Section 25, T21N, R17E, the two claims of the Betty Lou Two, the Ace of Hearts, and Honey Do #2 were claimed first. They adjoin the Francis Girard's north claim line, and the east claim boundary of all properties is Cougar Gulch Creek. The Medicine Boot, Little Poland, Two Bit, and Emma came later, crossing over several old workings on the hillside.

Brown Bear Group

Consisting of two claims, this property is reported in two different locations: one at the head of Cougar Gulch and the other on the ridge between Cougar and Lion Gulches.

In the late 1890s, North Yakima residents K. W. Dunlap, Mrs. M. A. Chapman, Whitson and Parker, Vestal Snyder, and Matt Bartolet had a three-foot ledge with a 45-foot shaft into gold-bearing ore.

Jennifer Ann (Taft) Mine

Rated at A-1. The property is in the southwest ¼ of Section 35, T21N, R17E, as seen on the USGS 7.5 Minute Series map of Liberty.

The Kittitas Gold Mining Company's dredge in a pond near Livingston Bar. This machine required 18 railroad cars to transport it from where it had been purchased in Oregon. The digging ladder was 100 feet long, could remove material from 30 feet below the water line, and contained 65 manganese steel buckets, each capable of raising 7.5 cubic feet of gravel. The device ran at 21 buckets per minute, and the material it raised was run across sluices consisting of 42,000 square feet of riffles. One of the difficulties of the operation was that no petroleum-based lubricant could be used, because any gold coming in contact with it would not be caught by the riffles, but instead flushed out the back of the dredge with the rest of the waste rock. This meant that excessive wear plagued the operation. Only three years after it started work in 1926, following a series of mishaps, the company ran out of money. (Asahel Curtis photo, negative #50183, Washington State Historical Society)

An unmarked road leaves the Lion Gulch Road to the left, in the northeast ¼ of Section 26, 2.5 miles north from the beginning of the Lion Gulch Road, heads south about 2.5 miles, and crosses an unnamed seasonal feeder creek that flows east into Lion Gulch Creek. The claim area lies south of where the creek cuts the road, and southwest of the road itself. A vague trail starts near the seasonal creek, passing near two old (possibly original) caved tunnels. Portal timbers show above the rock and dirt. A rock outcrop with recent development sits 100 to 150 feet southeast of the adits, and there is some mining gear lying around. We saw two types of ore at the site: Bird's Eye Quartz and dark gray slate, with stringers of quartz running throughout. The trail goes on up the ridge from the digs, following mineralized rock in a series of pits striking southwest to the top of the ridge, and a peak 3,943 feet in elevation.

Red Mine

Not rated. In 1889, George Hampton located the Red Mine on the hill between Cougar Gulch and Lion Gulch. Gold-bearing sulfides were worked from a three-foot ledge. There were two shafts, 75 and 50 feet deep, and a 200-foot crosscut. Fifty tons of ore was taken out, mostly sulfides averaging $16 per ton in gold.

Ewell Claim

Not rated. The Ewell was located in the northeast ¼ of Section 1, T20N, R17E, on the USGS 7.5 Minute Series map of Liberty. The map shows a shaft and a prospect in the area. This claim was worked in 1952 by William Ewell and in 1953 by E. Lamb of Cle Elum. Lamb put in a 10-ton mill.

Virden Mine (George Virden)

Accessible by road, this property is very difficult to locate without a guide. It lies in the northwest ¼ of Section 32, T21N, R18E, at an elevation of 4,200 to 4,500 feet. Use the USGS 7.5 Minute Series maps of Liberty and Swauk Pass.

This area had the last five adjoining placer claims on Williams Creek above the Alley Ranch, which were sold in 1891 to a group from San Francisco for $20,000. Virden was one of the earliest miners in the Swauk area.

Virden took some of the richest ore in the Liberty area from the Gold Vein and the Badger Vein. Both properties are extensions of the Wall Street Mine's series of veins. Material taken from tunnels 80 and 100 feet in length and a shallow shaft averaged $30 per ton, although some pockets ran $1 a pound; several thousand dollars' worth was extracted from one run of milled ore. There is a very well-constructed cabin on the site, although it has been heavily vandalized. The remains of Virden's arrastre, which reportedly could crush about 500 pounds of ore per day, has also suffered vandalism. We were told that he might have added a stamp mill on the claim in the late 1890s as well. The last claim he owned was the Summit Quartz Claim. In 1892, he milled $10 a day using one of the first stamp mills in the area. He made his big strike working gold at the Virden hardrock claims.

The mine portal is located above the building sites and was easily found by following a trail up and to the left. Another tunnel, 200 feet to the right, is a short dig containing a wheelbarrow. The underground workings we saw were about 200 feet in length. Virden, with the aid of his small crew, was able to remove a considerable amount of free-milling gold from this mine. This very low tunnel makes a brain bucket, or hardhat, a "must have."

In 1990, a small washing plant was in service on the site. The operator was after leaf-type gold specimens.[10] The gold was very light yellow, indicating a high silver content. People familiar with the local geology told us that this mine still contains extractable gold and is one of the better properties in the district. A resident miner now operates this claim.

Wall Street Mine

Rated at A-2, this mine is accessible by road and trail, but it's hard to find. We were very lucky to have someone along who was familiar with the area when we visited the property. It's located in the northeast ¼ of Section 30, T21N, R18E, as seen on the USGS 7.5 Minute Series maps of Liberty and Swauk Pass. This places the mine 5½ miles up Cougar Gulch from Liberty.

History of the Wall Street

In 1897, John H. Price had six claims, with a creek cutting through them. There were three ledges, one of which was six feet wide and contained sulfide ore that carried free gold in a 60-foot drift and a 40-foot shaft. Another ledge, 30 inches wide, was the location of an 18-foot shaft. The third ledge, five feet wide, contained a 145-foot crosscut tunnel that exposed quartz stringers two inches to two feet wide.

The Wall Street Mining Company worked the mine from 1909 to 1915. William Newstrum, George Radabaugh, and George Sides of Roslyn had formed this partnership to dig a shaft on a steep hillside in Cougar Gulch. A tram carried the ore to a mill built on the creek below. Several hired men worked on the property. The Newstrum family reported seeing two gold bars, both three inches long, and a large bowl of fine gold during those early years.

Hydraulic mining used large nozzles (called monitors) to propel water at the loose soil of the stream bank. The gravel washed from the bank was conducted through a series of riffles to trap the gold. Powerful pumps or a sizable head of water conducted from far upstream was required to achieve the necessary pressure and flow. (Wes and Carole Engstrom collection)

---

[10] Leaf gold is found in irregular masses; some are thin fragments connected at various angles, as if the material that molded it had disappeared, leaving the gold in that particular form. No apparent crystal form arrangement is evident other than the occurrence of imperfect octahedral shapes end to end in ½ to 5-inch-long wires.

Hydraulic mining in Kittitas County. This was possibly along Swauk Creek where Sawpit Gulch and Swauk Creek converge. Water was collected far upstream and conveyed in pipes to the mining site. The pressure created by transporting the water to the lower elevation provided the velocity required to wash the gravels from the stream banks. The sand and gravel was then run through a long tom or other riffle device to separate the heavy gold from the waste rock. The nozzles used to project the powerful stream are known as monitors. (Grace Browitt Elkins collection)

But in 1915 the three owners were forced to close the Wall Street when the head miner, who operated the works for them, ran off with the gold that had been accumulated from the mine. The thief was caught two years later and jailed in San Francisco, but the damage was done: the gold had been spent.

Production

References list the workings as 900 feet of tunnel connected by a raise with a 306-foot adit 260 feet above the lower tunnel. Production values between 1909 and 1935 amounted to $50,000 in gold.

Several different groups or individuals attempted to extract gold from this claim, living in the property cabin while mining it. In 1934, Billy Newstrum, sole owner, hired Jack Jordan (his son-in-law) to work the Wall Street. Jack Jordan and Tom Livingston spent two years cutting a tunnel into the base of the hill, trying to connect with the original shaft, but they never succeeded.[11]

Newstrum later sold the Wall Street to Ed Lannigan of Roslyn. Jack Jordan worked with Ed until the spring of 1935, with no profit to show for their effort. There was a disagreement between the two, and Jack left. Many attempts at mining met their end in this way during the Depression years. By 1941, F. Fry had acquired the Wall Street.

We were able to locate the lower tunnel, and we found it to be considerably longer than 900 feet. The tunnel had several side drifts, but no sign of a raise. We encountered bad ground at the back of what was believed to be the last working drift, and it is possible that at one time a raise was located in this area. Several minor stopes are present in the workings. We also noticed sulfides, but no sandstone with silicified fracture zones, such as those once mined for mineralized gold. Our geologist was very impressed with what he saw on the site.

We also located some tunnels above the Wall Street workings, which are known today as the Three Joes Mine. The portals are now caved, and digging in would require a major effort. It is entirely possible that these portals are the ones referred to in *Inventory of Washington Minerals* as the upper Wall Street.

---

[11] Jack Jordan reconstructed the old stamp mill, which he put into operation while he worked the claim. Its remains are located about 200 feet south of the main adit, just east of the property road.

Not rated. The history of this site tends to get a little confusing. Gus Nilson, also known as Nelson, had several mines in the Liberty area: the Nelson Shaft on the Dixie Claim in Deer Gulch; a mine north of Baker Creek in the southwest ¼ of Section 34; a ledge of quartz up Mill Creek, which he bonded to a party from Tacoma; another property, the York and Linden Claims; plus two men worked for him on his Boulder Creek Claim. By far, the largest of these was an underground placering operation near the confluence of Williams and Swauk Creeks[12] in the northeast ¼ of Section 10, T20N, R17E, (Nelson Bar).

> **Note** The USGS 7.5 Minute Series Map of Swauk Prairie is also called Blewett Pass in some references. This can lead to confusion.

We visited the mine in 1994 and found that the underground workings were quite extensive, with possibly as much as 4,000 feet of tunneling. The aggregate into which it was dug is very shaky and very wet. The miners crosscut and drifted in whatever direction the pay streak led them along the bedrock of this ancient streambed, extracting several hundred ounces of free-milling gold and silver in the process.

Gus also owned the properties that were later worked by Frank Bryant of dredging fame. Nelson Hill, located between upper Williams and Cougar Creeks, is northeast of Liberty. Many prospects exist up in this area.[13]

Nelson (or Nilson) Hill

Rated at A-1 from the 4WD roads: see the USGS 7.5 Minute Series map for Swauk Pass. This property is located in Section 30, T21N, R18E, at about 4,000 feet elevation. The northernmost prospect appears to be a mined outcrop of Bird's Eye Quartz. Quartz rocks up to 50 pounds lie around the site and are scattered east down the ridge slope.

There must be something about prospecting and mining that leads to longevity. Jack Kirch, a long-time prospector and miner in the Liberty area, was 98 years old when this picture was taken in 1998. In 2000, he was feted at a grand party in honor of his 100th birthday. Jack passed away on February 1, 2001. (Victor Pisoni photo)

The next prospect south on Nelson Hill is a caved shaft of unknown depth. There are two short tunnels about 50 feet long each, and an unmarked adit near Williams Creek at about the 3,000-foot level, with various items of mining equipment in the area. As of this writing, all claims are active. The two westernmost prospects on Nelson Hill are no more than shallow trenches meant to define the ledge that runs north in line with the Gold Leaf Mine, which is at the southwest end of Nelson Hill.

At about 4,000 feet elevation, east of the upper Nelson Hill Prospect, and on the west side of the 4WD road (the southeast slope of Nelson Hill), lies a caved shaft. The items we saw here—a 30-gallon ore bucket (with hand-forged hardware) and two heavy timbers with lead bushings that once held thick hoisting axles.

A partly caved tunnel that crosscuts east toward this dig sits downslope 200 feet to the west of the shaft. The slate rock that the shaft was dug in carries widely disseminated gold that was not worth mining. (Or, more likely, pockets of gold were mined, and the lesser values were left behind.) There is another caved tunnel 300 feet downslope. You can see its portal timbers through the rubble. Clarence Jordin was working this tunnel around 1950 when it collapsed, trapping him inside until he could be dug out. The rock above and to the southeast of the portal has been worked along a fault contact in an attempt to define a possible vein.

On the east side of Nelson Hill, there is a 50-foot tunnel driven west in the direction of the previously mentioned quartz outcrop area, quartz boulders, and caved shaft. This adit is about 150 feet down the hill. There is a flooded pit at the end, with evidence of more recent activity. We didn't notice an obvious vein, but we saw several fault fissure lines in the rock.

---

[12] The mine is currently active, and the land it occupies is privately owned. Do not enter without prior permission.
[13] We have found numerous unnamed digs from long ago. Their original names have often been replaced with present-day claim titles, which sometimes makes it difficult to identify them.

South of the hill, and west of the fork in the road that leads to the Alley Ranch, there is a caved adit with a homemade shaker table and other inventive mining devices. Some trench work has been done above the adit.

About ¼ mile north of the Gold Leaf Mine, there is a newer prospect called the White Lighting. It lies west of an eroding claim access road. This spot affords some interesting calcite patches and stringers on an area of outcropping rock.

Sonny Brown Mine (on Nelson Hill)

Rated at A-2 from 4WD roads, and accessible by bad 4WD roads from the Cougar Gulch side (Road 9712), this mine is located on Nelson Hill in the northeast ¼ of the southeast ¼ of Section 30, and the southeast ¼ of the northeast ¼ of Section 30, T21N, R18E, at an elevation of 3,200 to 3,600 feet. Use the USGS 7.5 Minute maps for Liberty and Swauk Pass. (The Swauk Pass map has four prospect locations printed on Nelson Hill.)

Nelson Hill is composed of sandstone and shale, cut by various diabase dikes thought to be connected with the mineralization of the area—quartz veins in shale-diabase contacts and Bird's Eye Quartz. A. R. Jordin and E. K. (Sonny) Brown located five claims in 1932, running north to south: the Sonny Brown #3, Sonny Brown #2, Sonny Brown, Sonny Brown Annex, Sonny Brown Lower Annex, and Sonny Brown Mill Site. The group of claims lay in a northeast-to-southwest direction, joining one another continuously on one side, and covered most of the south side of Nelson Hill. The mill site was at 3,800 feet, and about 150 feet south of the southmost claim on the North Fork of Williams Creek.

Eleven veins on the property had millable values in free gold and some silver. The main vein was the Gladstone, which showed a width of up to eight feet. The other 10 veins varied from 20 inches to five feet wide.

Amos and Mae Jordin, residents of Liberty, pose for their portrait around the turn of the century. (Wes and Carole Engstrom collection)

Liberty Mine[14]

Rated at A-1 to A-2, this site is accessible by driving 3½ miles up Lion Gulch Road 9712. (Primitive byways connect the various digs on the claim.) In the summer of 1998, the cat road was regraded to the digs. You must get permission before visiting this active claim.

The property is in about the northwest ¼ of the southwest ¼ of Section 19, T21N, R18E, and the east ½ of the east ½ of Section 24, T21N, R17E on the USGS 7.5 Minute Series map of Liberty, at an elevation of 3,600 feet (at the main adit, about 100 feet above the creek) to 4,000 feet at the two upper tunnels. When you're ¼ mile past the old rock quarry, search on the right for a road leading down to the creek. Park here and descend to creek level. Cross the creek, and ascend the hill straight ahead. You will quickly come across a very large tailing pile (the mine dump) and the main portal. This tunnel is a crosscut that undercuts the ore body of the two upper tunnels (one is known to be 200 feet long), which are now both caved. They are located several hundred feet directly above this lower adit at the head of a shallow gulch.

Liberty Mine Geology

The rock walls of several tunnels in this area are composed of sandstone or slate members of the Swauk formation. The fissures were clean cut, and walls, where exposed, are smooth and unbroken. Various vein materials between the walls range from four to nine feet wide at the face. They are made up of quartz, with talc and calcite running off the main vein in quartz stringers.

---

[14] The Liberty Mine, as of 1998, is a vestige of what it was in 1936, when it was promoted as a multiclaim property. We located the main tunnel, the two caved adits at the head of a gulch, several older and newer pits and open cuts above the caved digs, plus a shallow trench prospect north of the main road, across and up the ridge slope from the main adit. The prospect in 1998 was known as the Bobcat Claim.

A member of Northwest Underground Explorations peers into the shaft of a modern mining operation near the head of Cougar Creek above Liberty. The head frame is covered, perhaps to allow operations to continue during winter months. (Vic Pisoni photo)

The gold can be found in fine grains within the quartz, next to the slate or sandstone. Bird's Eye Quartz is present in two tunnels[15] and several of the open cuts. Most of the gold is free milling, and there is a small amount of sulfides. The original claims covered a surface area of about 220 acres[16] and were exposed along a strike of visible outcroppings.

History

Liberty Mines Inc. was organized in August 1933. At that time, the officers were C. A. Pelland, president, and William H. Fowler, manager. Oscar Roseland became vice president in 1936, while H. A. Stucky was manager in 1936. E. B. Olmsted took over as vice president in 1937.

Property

Property improvements for the year 1937 consisted of the construction of three cabins, a root cellar, a mill building, a tool shop with tools, a compressor, ore carts, trucks, a garage, an ore bunker, and a 15- to 25-ton mill.

The Liberty Mining Company was an amalgamation of properties that had been owned by William Fowler: the Contact, Contact #1, Oro Grande, and Oro Grande #1. The rest of the digs were sold[17] to William Fowler, who served as the buyer for the company. Fowler bought the Big Boy #1; Big Boy #2; Big Chief #1; Big Chief #2; Golden Eagle; and a placer claim, the White Fir, from Roy T. Pease. The property was in the development stage, and a mill was set up to test and determine ore values in the gold quartz on a tonnage basis.

Claim Development

The purpose of the development was to expose the ore bodies, their diameter, and continuity of their strike, and to determine the type of ore. By 1937, total workings of old and new claims amounted to the following, by claim:
- Contact: 300 feet of tunnel, a 150-foot open cut, and a 60-foot shaft
- Contact #1: a 200-foot open cut and a shaft
- Oro Grande: a 135-foot tunnel and a 150-foot open cut (this claim had a 1,800-foot–long vein)
- Oro Grande #1: a 150-foot open cut
- Big Boy #1: a 25-foot tunnel, 375-foot open cut, and 20-foot shaft showing part of a 1,400-foot–long vein
- Big Boy #2: a 300-foot tunnel, a 200-foot open cut, and a 15-foot shaft, all exposing a 600-foot vein
- Golden Eagle: a 20-foot tunnel
- Big Chief: a 247-foot tunnel that crosscut four veins, a 30-foot open cut, and a 40-foot shaft

The Golden Eagle Fraction, Big Boy Extension, and Big Chief #1 were in the early stages of preliminary and assessment work. The Sunset Claim, established later, eventually boasted a 30-foot tunnel.

---

[15] We visited these tunnels in 1998. Bird's Eye Quartz was scattered around the pits, open cuts, and caved upper adits. We did see different types of rock in the main adit. Most of the tunnel was solid except for a two- to three-foot vein of slate that cut horizontally through the workings, which has created bad ground prone to collapse, as indicated by the slate and rock debris already on the tunnel floor.

[16] Fully a third of a section in 1936, as opposed to the Liberty Claim of today (600 feet wide by 1,500 feet long), showing that numerous individual claims within the surrounding area of the Liberty Mine of today were consolidated to form the Liberty Mining Company of 1936.

[17] The sellers were George, Ted, and A. L. Mercer (Marcear?), A. R. Jordin, and G. A. Bloomquist.

Liberty Mines Inc. sent invitations to potential stockholders and friends to attend a test run on September 27, 1936, of company ore from all exposed veins on the property. At this time, common stock numbered a million shares at 10 cents par value each.

According to reports, test ore was taken from the Big Boy #1 and #2 digs, it was run and cleaned, and one ton of ore from the Oro Grande was tested. The combined gold produced was 10 ounces of gold, or 0.3 ounce per ton from 33 tons run through the mill. An undated report showed that 60 to 80 ounces of leaf and wire gold, embedded in quartz, came from a surface open cut and a tunnel on the Oro Grande Claim. Several separate veins cross the properties. The contact vein was said to be over 3,000 feet long.

T. W. Melrose, Director of Mines for Washington State, reported corresponding for the last time with Liberty Mines Inc. while it was in active development in June 1938. The company failed to pay its incorporation fees in 1940, so it was stricken from the records. Companies are usually allowed three years to pay annual dues before they are dissolved, but Liberty failed to comply.

Flodin Mine/Morrison (True Fissure Gold Mine)

Rating: easily reachable from Liberty via Cougar Gulch Road 9718. This property lies in the lower southwest ¼ of the northeast ¼ of Section 25, T21N, R17E and the upper digs in the northwest ¼ of the southwest ¼ of Section 30, T21N, R18E, as seen on the USGS 7.5 Minute Series map of Liberty.

Andrew Flodin was involved in developing several early claims in the Swauk District. He reportedly had the first claim above the mouth of Williams Creek, on which a 400-foot tunnel that followed a pay streak of gold was run on bedrock. Then in 1891, Flodin located the First of August in the area of the present Flodin workings. On the claim, there was a four-foot ledge of Bird's Eye Quartz between solid slate walls. He hit a pay streak 13 inches wide via a 96-foot shaft, and drove a 240-foot crosscut tunnel in an attempt to strike the ledge at 140 feet.

In 1894, Flodin built a water-powered arrastre on Williams Creek, which had the capacity to run 3,200 pounds of material per day. The average pay for a ton that year was $21.23. On a southwest extension of the same ledge, Andrew drove three crosscuts, the longest of which struck the ledge at 85 feet. Encouraged, he sank another shaft on the same claim to define the ore in black, carbonaceous slate veined with quartz. The main vein was named the Gladstone vein, and high-grade ore was taken from it. It was also reported to have produced an impressive number of quartz crystals. Andrew's grandson, John Flodin, has reported that one of the tailing piles is missing—possibly reworked for its gold and crystals. In 1897, a ball mill was bought in New York for $40,000, shipped, and placed on the claim site. The building that housed the machinery was 50 feet square.

Despite his many mining endeavors, Andrew still found time to enjoy playing his guitar at the local dances. In 1895, he became road repair and construction supervisor for the district. A 1901 report specifies that A. B. Morrison and Daniel Morrison were running a tunnel on the Livingston ledge that adjoined Flodin's First of August Claim on its northeast edge. Flodin's aunt was married to a Morrison. The three men apparently had worked the ledge together for the previous several years with good results.

A group of people visiting a mine near Liberty. The manufacturer's name is emblazoned on the car, along with a list of the patent numbers applied to it. Notice the wooden chute dropping toward the portal from the upper right of the photo, which was probably used to drop ore from a higher tunnel. (Wes and Carole Engstrom collection)

Flodin was still working his claim in 1903. He passed away in 1905. From 1905 to 1928, the Morrison brothers took control of at least a portion of Flodin's claim and added a few others to their holdings, which they called the Morrison Quartz Claim. Before 1928, development had expanded to a 260-foot shaft, a 288-foot adit, and a 140-foot crosscut, with 159 feet of drift tunnel. The ore mined from the oxidized area of the workings produced several thousand dollars of profit. The mine was also operating in 1928 (in part) as the True Fissure Gold Mine (possibly on lease). By 1936, Andrew's son Frank had possession of the six claims comprising the Flodin workings. Frank sold them that same year.

This property is presently under claim by two individual miners. One claim in Section 25, at an elevation of 3,000 feet, has a wood-cribbed and somewhat protective wood-collared shaft of unknown depth that is now flooded. A tunnel 40 yards to the southeast was reopened, but we did not enter because it seemed on the verge of sloughing in or caving. There is another open shaft 200 feet down the road, over the hill, and southeast of this tunnel; this one is very dangerous because it has no cover. On the west side of the road, 100 feet southwest of this shaft, there is a caved adit that is visible from the road. It's only a few yards away from the storm ditch.

The claim, in Section 30, is about one mile away and at an elevation of 3,600 feet. The current owners have bored several new tunnels. Most are relatively short, less than 100 feet long. One of these adits contains a fairly large, underhand stope about 20 feet inside the portal. A dog took a fall here several years ago, so be aware. Better yet, stay out of all the mines in this district. Almost all are old, in a state of decline, and could collapse at any time without warning. If you enter anyway, you may get slapped with a trespassing charge, depending on the mood of the local authorities.

Dandy Claim

The Dandy is located below the Flodin Mine, on Cougar Gulch. Louis Quietsch had located a six-foot–wide ledge with a mineralized stringer, and in the late 1890s he mined it using a 25-foot tunnel, running the ore through an arrastre and earning $20 to $25 per ton.

Morning Claim, 1896

We are uncertain of the location of this claim. Dr. O. M. Graves of Roslyn had two ledges of Bird's Eye Quartz on this spot. A 50-foot tunnel was driven on the larger four-foot–wide ledge, cutting two blind feeder veins. Graves had a single 750-pound stamp mill to service the property.

The old Virden arrastre near Liberty. (Wes and Carole Engstrom collection)

Vic Pisoni, author and Northwest Underground Explorations member, poses at the adit of the Nelson Hill workings #1 site. (Vic Pisoni photo)

Bunker Hill Mine

This mine is an extension of the Morning Ledge that was traced on both sides of Cougar Gulch, and over the ridge (we don't know whether to the east or west). Owner Louis Quietsch found veins of free-milling, gold-bearing Bird's Eye Quartz, ranging from seven inches down in size. He ran a 35-foot tunnel on the widest vein.

Great Western Group

The location of this site is unknown. The property consisted of two claims owned by Gus Nilson, Evan Strander, and Charles Kineth. The mine consisted of one 14-foot ledge carrying high values in sulfides, with some free gold in a four-foot vein crosscut by a 50-foot tunnel. A second four-foot ledge with a one-foot vein of free gold was cut by a 16-foot shaft.

Great Wonder

The location of this property is unknown. Two claims lay on this spot, owned by Gus Nilson and H. C. Condon. They sunk a 29-foot shaft down to a two-foot vein of ore in a ledge, to which they ran a 42-foot crosscut tunnel on one claim. On the other claim, an 18-foot shaft cutting an 18-inch cross-ledge vein was reached via a 22-foot tunnel. They processed the ore through a one-ton arrastre. Nilson, E. Strander, and O. Kineth later owned these claims. They worked the ledges with a 16-foot shaft and a 52-foot crosscut tunnel.

Cascade Chief Mine (Morrison Gold Quartz Mine)

Rated: no public access. This actively mined property is located in the southwest ¼ of the northeast ¼ of Section 25, T21N, R17E and northwest ¼ of the southwest ¼ of Section 30, T21N, R18E. Use the USGS 7.5 Minute Series map of Liberty. The elevation of these five claims varies from 3,400 to 3,700 feet. You can access the spot via a three-mile drive on Road 1918 (which was in good condition when we were there) up Cougar Gulch to the Cascade Chief mining area.

A 1934 report, by J. B. Mason, states that the original 1894 discovery was made by panning the gold trace up the gulch to the point where vein #1 was found, about 150 feet above the bottom of the gulch. An open cut on the hill exposed where the vein was crosscut, and surface drifts were run for 20 to 25 feet on each side. The ore value and vein width were determined, and a 90-foot shaft was sunk on the vein. Two arrastres produced about $20,000.00 in gold. Later a crosscut tunnel (#2) was driven into the mountain to the vein 214 feet from the portal. A raise was worked into the ore 22 feet, connecting with the shaft. Ore was then stoped from 25 feet of the vein to a height of 60 feet. The stope was open at the time of the report. From where the ore was worked, a drift was run 182 feet, showing good ore all the way to the face. A drift dug in the hanging wall for 156 feet showed very little of the vein. Four cuts on the surface showed good gold values all the way.

Tunnel #3 (a crosscut) is about 380 feet northeast of #2 and about 60 feet higher. Tunnel #3 cut the vein 25 feet from the portal. A drift ran southwest for 15 feet and encountered gold ore. Tunnel #4 is 50 feet east of #3, and slightly higher. It missed vein #1 but cut vein #2 with a cross-formation tunnel of 50 feet. Surface cuts showed this vein to be four to six feet wide.

Tunnel #5 is in the Gladstone Claim across the gulch and north of #4. In 1934, this 225-foot adit was caved. Cuts on the hill over the tunnel exposed a vein six feet wide that showed good values in gold. The #1 adit is 400 feet west of #2 and 100 feet lower. It is a 290-foot crosscut aimed at the #1 vein. The summit of a hill lies on the west end of the Uncle Sam Claim. On this property, 10 cuts have been made across four veins that show high values in gold. In 1936, the only work being done was on the 250-foot–long Tunnel #3. A 15-ton mill and a small smelter were also operating.

Ellensburg attorney A. K. (Sonny) Brown acquired the Cascade Chief in 1941. His Sonny Brown Claim and the Cascade Chief adjoined each other. Assays at that time reported ½ ounce of gold per ton.

The State of Washington Mining Company appears to have controlled the properties briefly in 1915, prior to the Cascade Chief Mining Company's acquiring control. Its activities on the site and motive for obtaining it are absent from the records, however.

There were five quartz claims on the Cascade Chief property at its start in 1934, all located on the strike of the vein system, which ran for 6,000 feet. Four parallel veins exposed Bird's Eye Quartz and slate with quartz stringers. The five claims were the Gladstone, First of July, First of August (previously Andrew Flodin's claim), Fourth of July, Uncle Sam (a former holding of A. F. York), and one placer, the Cougar.

Twelve ore samples taken from four adits, one open cut, one outcropping, one tunnel dump, and one crosscut assayed and gave values ranging from 0.11 ounce to 8.46 ounces of gold per ton.

The main tunnel is now caved, and the most recent data shows over 1,800 feet of old, inaccessible workings.

Golden Fleece Mine (Mercer, T-Bone)

Rated at A-1. The Hurley Creek Road (Road 9711) is in good condition in 2000. It travels through the center of the workings, which are located in the northeast ¼ of the southwest ¼ of Section 13, T21N, R17E, on the USGS 7.5 Minute Series map of Liberty, at an elevation of 3,400 to 3,600 feet.

The property consisted of three claims and five mill sites and was operated off and on from 1934 to 1941 by Liberty Mines Inc. A 100-foot adit worked a mineralized shear zone vein about four inches wide that cut into beds of carbonaceous shale similar to that in the Liberty Mine, and open cuts exposed Bird's Eye Quartz on an outcropped ridge spine. This whole zone reportedly contains fine gold, the larger part occurring with pyrites in shoots separated by barren spots.

In Hurley Creek Road's cut, on the west side, there is a 20-foot adit. Two shallow, caved shafts lie 40 feet above it. There are remnants along the creek of what appear to be concrete foundations, possibly debris remaining from the old mill site. Across from the 20-foot adit, 200 feet to the east, there is an overgrown mining road, the location of a caved tunnel with portal timbers showing. To the east of the caved adit, a rock spine outcrops between the road and the top of the ridge. There are several open cuts and pits exposing Bird's Eye Quartz. In the 1930s, a reported $30,000.00 was taken from the claims.

Southern Star Mining Claim

Rated at A-2 to A-3, this claim is located at an elevation of 3,600 to 4,000 feet, in the southeast ¼ of southeast ¼ of Section 13, and the northwest ¼ of the northeast ¼ of Section 24, T21N, R17E, as shown on the USGS 7.5 Minute Series map of Liberty. At 0.2 mile east of the Golden Fleece Mine, travel on a southeast-bearing 4WD road (121) with an unlocked gate (no low-clearance cars should attempt this steep, twisting, deeply rutted road) ½ mile, and watch to the north. There is a caved shaft 200 feet up on the open hillside (it is labeled as "X Prospect" on the map); a sign identifies it as the Southern Star shaft.

Across the road, south of the shaft, you'll see an outcropping ridge running southwest down to a feeder stream that flows into Hurley Creek. Exploring the rock spine will turn up several open cuts south of the ridge crest. Near the base of the ridge (150 feet above the feeder stream), there are a caved adit and a big tailing pile. Below and southwest of the caved adit lies a deteriorating building with an interior, overshot water wheel about eight feet in diameter. There is a 60-foot tunnel 100 feet upstream from the building, which runs east on a ledge that shows stringers of quartz. A sign at the building site indicates the claim originated in the late 1890s.

Hurley[18] Creek Claim (Nairn)

Rating: Road trip. This claim is situated 2.4 miles east of the Golden Fleece Claim on Hurley Creek Road 9711. It is located in the center of the north ½ of Section 18, T21N, R18E, on the USGS 7.5 Minute Series map of Liberty.

Nairn had possession of this property in 1938. The gold was mined from charcoal-black carbonaceous shale and sandstone averaging four feet wide, with mineralized, white quartz stringers. An adit 170 feet long, two shafts about 40 feet deep, and some open cuts were developed.

As of 1998, the location of the workings is unknown.[19] It is possible that the records are incorrect. This has been the case in other sources, as it was for the Cascade Chief. It has been suggested that the Nairn Claim and the Southern Star are one and the same.

Gold Leaf Mine

Rated at A-2. At present, this is a private claim, located in the northwest ¼ of Section 31, T21N, R18E, at the end of a 2½-mile road, ½ mile southwest of the Nelson Hill Prospects.

This early mine, consisting of two ledges, was worked by W. A. Seaton in 1892. One six-foot vein lay in sandstone and shale, and the other vein, of unknown width, was in a large diabase (basaltic rock) dike. Gold and silver were taken via two main digs: a shaft that went down 60 feet on a ledge of free-milling gold that was intersected by a 60-foot tunnel, and another adit 40 feet long that tapped a ledge four feet wide at a depth of 50 feet. A third tunnel ran 100 feet on a ledge. We weren't able to identify the ledges on our visit. Early production is shown as six tons of ore, averaging $40.00 per ton in gold, with high silver content, all of which was processed by a one-ton arrastre. Some of the free gold occurred as perfect octahedral crystals lying on the ends of quartz crystals.

A 1900 mining report states that L. F. McConihe[20] had sunk a 33-foot shaft on the Gold Leaf Group of claims. Clarence Jordin Jr. and others later worked this ridge, as indicated by trenches, pits, a shaft, and two adits just over the ridge on the east side of the rock outcrop. The present owner contemplated calling his claim "The Buzzard" when he discovered a nesting downy-white buzzard chick having a hissing fit at the end of the east-trending portal tunnel.

Fairy Queen

The Fairy Queen was located about 700 feet east of the Gold Leaf Mine. In 1891, J. R. Love of Ellensburg had a 40-foot tunnel driven into a serpentine formation on a strong ledge that showed an assay of $37.00 in gold and $3.50 in silver per ton.

---

[18] It is not clear whether Pat, George, or both staked the original claim. The only record of Pat Hurley describes him as living in the Liberty area in 1892, when all his cabin windows were broken by a vandal. George Hurley, on the other hand, has a long and respectable (not that Pat was not respected, himself) list of honors.

George J. Hurley (1859-1921) came from Ellensburg, and he prospected in the Liberty area. After the Hurley Claim was sold to Mr. Nairn, George headed for the Okanogan country where he became a store clerk at the Ruby Mining Camp. He was later named county commissioner, and he participated in creating Okanogan County. He served several terms as mayor of Ruby City, and he was also editor of the *Ruby Miner Newspaper* at one time. His highest achievement was election to the Washington State Senate.

[19] We could be misinformed about this claim. The descriptions of the Hurley Creek Mine and the Southern Star workings resemble one another so much that they could be one and the same.

[20] McConihe also mined in the Cle Elum District around 1897, as half owner of the John C. Claim on Red Mountain, near the north end of Cle Elum Lake. He had an interest in the Princeton Bar Placer on Little Boulder Creek, which flowed west into the Cle Elum River as well.

Even today, innovation in mining knows no bounds. This is the discharge end of a homemade rod mill at the Nelson Hill Mill. The five-framed area is fitted with fine mesh screens. The ore exits the mill once it has been pulverized to a size that fits through the screens. The drum contains several steel rods that crush the ore as the unit rotates. (Vic Pisoni photo)

Little Gem, Accident, Arabian Knight, and Buckeye Claims, 1891

These free-milling gold properties were, according to a vague report, located in the vicinity of the Gold Leaf and Fairy Queen Mines. A party of mostly Seattle men did little work on the digs, other than some gophering to show mineralization in the ledges.

Hope Quartz Claim, 1912

The Hope Quartz formerly belonged partly to Seaton's Gold Leaf Group of claims, but which part is not known. Owners Charles H. Powles and Mrs. M. A. Pool took over the property after McConihe tried to extract values from what turned out to be barren rock. A stamp mill on the claim was removed after the quartz operation went broke.

Afterward, others demonstrated that Powles and Pool had missed a chute of gold on an unworked outcrop 400 feet in length.

Ollie Jordin Mine

The history of the Ollie Jordin is also hazy. We have straightened out as many of the contradicting facts as possible. This mine was owned by another longtime local miner and prospector who had several properties in the area. He was in on numerous multipartner properties, and at one time owned 11 claims and two sandstone quarries.

During the Depression, Ollie and his brothers made strikes. He was reportedly still taking gold out of his Flag Mountain tunnel in 1932. Ollie's most well known operation was located 1.9 miles from Liberty, in the northeast ¼ of Section 1, as found on the USGS 7.5 Minute Series map of Liberty, in T20N, R17E. From the beginning of the Cougar Creek road sign, go 0.9 mile and turn right. At 1.2 miles, turn right on Road 117. Stay on the left fork of the road at 1.4 miles. At 1.8 miles, turn right and then drive one-tenth mile to the tunnels. They might be posted against trespass to uninvited people, since this is an active claim.

Ollie bought this mine from Roy Lilne. After the sale, Roy went to Liberty and joked about the lemon of a mine he sold. Ollie went mining and SHAZAM! He hit a pocket of gold worth $5,000. Ollie soon went to town and shoved 27 pounds of gold under Roy's nose, stating, "I picked these lemons out of your old mine." Within 300 feet southeast of these digs are five other tunnels, two of which are caved at the portals.

Here Jordin and Miss Allie Blissett mined in excess of 500 tons of ore. These mines also contained very rich pockets of wire gold that were taken from a 170-foot adit. About $20,000.00 in gold was produced from 1932 to 1934. One of these digs (the Mountain Daisy) is located somewhere in Section 1 (Liberty map, in T20N, R17E), of which he was the lessor in 1934 to 1938.[21] He still had control in 1952.

Ollie and Jon Vauthiers worked these claims in the 1950s. Ed Miner used a bulldozer to develop the property in the 1960s and had the good fortune of exposing a surface pocket of gold while pushing dirt around.

---

[21] In September 1938, while Ollie was asleep, within hearing and gunsight, a robber stole $1,500 from his arrastre. With a growl or two, he accepted the loss as a matter of course and resumed his pursuit.

Boulder Creek Claims

These claims are generally located on the USGS 7.5 Minute Series maps for Liberty, Swauk Pass, Swauk Prairie, and Reecer Canyon. Boulder Creek and its feeder streams meander in and out of the adjoining corners of these four maps in Section 1, T20N, R17E and Sections 5, 6, 7, and 8, T20N R18E. For a general but less defined look, use the Green Trails Maps of Liberty (#210) and Thorp (#242).

In 1891, W. R. Hart was the first to strike placer gold on Boulder Creek. He dug his shaft down to bedrock, on which he ran a crosscut, and found gold in small nuggets.[22]

By 1896, partners Thomas Meagher, A. F. York,[23] and J. B. Morrison were working ground up Boulder Creek. Their strike caused a rush of miners to the area. Unconfirmed data reports that Boulder Creek was to have had a town site platted, surveyed, and divided into lots for sale, but nothing further developed to consolidate this short-lived nonevent.

Bertha Claim

Miners Whitaker, Meagher, and York had two rich placer claims on a gulch running down into Boulder Creek. The Bertha was on a ledge of porphyritic quartz five to six feet wide. They stripped four- and six-inch quartz stringers from a ledge studded with small gold nuggets. They also dug up a dinner-plate–size nugget worth $840.00.

North Star Claim

The owners of the Bertha also had a three-foot ledge on the North Star Claim, across the gulch from the Bertha.

That same year (1896), C. C. Whitaker, A. F. York, and Meagher had a three-claim property called the Trilby Group that they cleaned up on, finding gold worth $4,000.00. They then sold the Trilby Group to the Swauk Mining Company. The new owners outfitted the digs with hydraulics (under local guidelines and restrictions). The company had a setback when a fire broke out, which set off six sticks of dynamite, destroying the shaft house and the blacksmith shop and putting 10 hired men out of work.

Josie Claim

The Josie is located on the ledge above the Bertha Claim. Owner/miner Albert Talli cut into two narrow seams of ore, in which he found a pocket of small nuggets. Talli also ran ore in an arrastre.

Golden Eagle Placer (1921)

Rated at B-2. Located in the northwest ¼ of Section 6 and the southeast ¼ of the southeast ¼ of Section 1, T20N, R17E (Trilby Gulch area) on the USGS 7.5 Minute Series maps of Liberty and Swauk Prairie.

To get to the area, go through Liberty and travel a half mile south onto the Boulder Creek Road. Trilby Gulch runs southwest from Flag Mountain and will be on your left.

This claim ran southwest to northeast mainly along Trilby Gulch. There are two tunnels in the gulch: one is 170 feet long, and the other is 20 feet long and has a flooded shaft near the face. In 1985, Virgel Hiner, an old miner, located the Bald Eagle Lode Claim for Gold Placers Inc. by staking over the Golden Eagle Placer Claim and a portion of the southwest slope of Flag Mountain.

---

[22] The Livingstons later prospected the Hart Claims, finding moderately coarse gold from two feet below ground level downward.
[23] That same season, York dislocated his shoulder while struggling with a tree stump that suddenly broke loose, throwing him down a creek bank.

Nugget Placer (1921)

Rated at B-2, this property is located in the southwest ¼ of the southwest ¼ of Section 6, directly south of Trilby Gulch.

Boulder Creek ran northeast to southwest through this patented claim. Within the claim boundary, south of the creek, there is a 50-foot tunnel, 200 feet west of Robinson Gulch Road and 50 feet above the creek. An incline shaft lies east of Robinson Gulch Road near the road's start and across from a cabin that is located west of the shaft.

Gold Bar Placer (1921)

Rated at B-2. This placer is located in the southeast ¼ of Section 6. This claim extends east off of the Nugget Placer on Boulder Creek.

Two branches of upper Boulder Creek flow southeast to northwest across the claim and into the main stream of Boulder Creek. There are three adits and three open cuts on the property. All have been located, but are caved.

Boulder Creek Placer (1921)

Rated at B-1. Located in the southeast ¼ of Section 1. The waters of Boulder Creek, south of Trilby Gulch, flowed through the southeast corner of this property.

Boulder Creek 2001 Update

Rated at B-2. Located in Section 1, T20N, R17E, and Section 6, T20N, R18E, on the USGS 7.5 Minute Series maps of Liberty and Swauk Prairie.

To get there, go to the east end of Liberty and turn south on the Boulder Creek Road. A new cat road goes north for about 200 feet to an open cut. Above the open cut there is a very old caved tunnel. Two more caved adits that appear to be attempts to cut into the old tunnel are just east of it. Less than 100 feet to the east, the start of a dry flume ditch contours south at 3,000 feet elevation, along the slope for a half mile to its source at the mouth of Trilby Gulch. The flume ditch passes through several active mining claims with buildings and tunnels. At the beginning of Trilby Gulch there is an incline shaft covered by a building that is identified as the Lucky Day. Multiple adits on both sides of Tribly Gulch, from bottom to the top of the ridge on Flag Mountain, all are a part of the Lucky Day property. Some are open: others are caved. From Trilby Gulch south, there are a number of open and caved shafts and tunnels at varying elevations for the next half-mile on the south slope heading east to northeast toward Snowshoe Ridge.

The interior of a homemade rod mill. The drum was rotated and the ore, mixed with water, was crushed by the rods. Once it had been crushed finely enough, it passed through fine mesh screens in the five openings at the far end. (Vic Pisoni photo)

Mountain Beaver #1 and #2 Placers, 1954

This property is located in Section 6, T20N, R18E, and consists of 18 acres along Boulder Creek.

Andrew M. Lechman had located the old channel south of the present creek. The main digs were connected by an incline shaft, where several drifts follow bedrock and several crosscuts were also dug. This mine was active as far back as 1922 when R. F. Rupert sold his half to Lechman.

Robinson Gulch

Located in Sections 12 and 7, T20N, R18E and 17E, respectively, this property runs south to north into Boulder Creek, as shown on the USGS 7.5 Minute Series maps of Liberty and Swauk Prairie.

Red Jacket Mine

This mine is located in the southeast ¼ of Section 36, T21N, R17E, and northeast ¼ of Section 1, T20N, R17E, on the northwest foot of Flag Mountain.

Naneum Creek Placers

Rating: Various, depending on which area you want to access. This property is located east and north of Table Mountain. The main branch of Naneum Creek begins at Upper Naneum Meadow (Section 12) and heads south through Section 13 at Haney Meadow, to Section 23 where the main creek meets with the West Fork of Naneum Creek in Naneum Meadow. From there the creek flows through Sections 26, 35, and 36, increasing in volume, from several feeder streams that merge with it, and goes east into Section 31.

See the USGS 7.5 Minute Series map of Swauk Pass (T21N, R18E). Elevations vary from 5,800 feet at Upper Naneum Meadow, down to 4,800 feet in Section 36.

A 1912 report indicates several placer miners were active on Naneum Creek east of Table Mountain, but no specifics were available. Roads and trails allow entry into most traversable areas. The sweeping vistas provide a grandiose photo opportunity from the top of Table Mountain.

Sylvanite Mine

Rated at A-1. The Hovey Creek Road goes directly to the claim, an easy walk. The site is located in the southeast ¼ of the southwest ¼ in Section 10, T21N, R17E, (on the north side of Hovey Creek and one mile southwest of the historic Mountain Home site). These can be located on the USGS 7.5 Minute Series map of Liberty.

Drive about 0.2 mile west of US 97 and park anywhere before the bridge. Walk north on the road nearest the east side of the creek. At 300 feet, the workings will be obvious. Free gold was extracted at 0.4 ounce per ton from the fractured Swauk sedimentary rock, which has been hydrothermally altered. No production data has been found.

In 1900, the Sylvanite property, was known as the Greater New York Claim and was owned by F. M. Graham. The Greater New York Claim was the only claim, out of six others in the Utla Group, that underwent any development. In 1933, a fire destroyed the ore roasting plant, but Graham soon had it rebuilt.

Records show that D. H. Gayre was serving as mine and mill manager in 1934, and a 16-man crew was working the property. Gold-bearing arsenical sulfide ore was treated at the stamp mill, and loaded aboard a railroad car and sent to the Tacoma smelter. The latest data for the Sylvanite shows miners were working with free gold.

A 1934 report shows that the Sylvanite comprised 400 feet of tunnel and workings. The owner in 1936 was Bill Hawks, who sold to Earl Eyler. Earl owned and worked the mine from 1936 to 1946. Dave Sayers is also recorded as a more recent owner.

The beginning 15 feet of tunnel ran through soft dirt and had to be lagged with timbers. This tunnel extended into several feet of shale 30 degrees to the northwest. The adit continues 35 feet more through shale 30 degrees to the northwest. The next 40 feet goes in the same direction into diabase, and on for 50 additional feet in basalt, where the tunnel hit sandstone on the east side and ore on the west (where a drift heads northeast into the ore deposit). The main adit goes past the drift northwest for 50 feet into shale, but no ore was struck. The drift splits at about 25 feet, and the other tunnel heads north for 60 feet; the tunnel showing ore runs northeast to east. A 50-foot–high raise was dug between the wall of the two drifts. Its width and length were about 10 and 15 feet, respectively. The ore was concentrated in an area about 100 feet long and 20 feet wide, but it was extracted only from the raise that is surrounded by the lower-grade rock.

We visited in 1998 and found the main tunnel caved. The mill site was 300 feet south of the portal. There is some debris 200 feet southeast of the mill site near several building sites. If you look closely, you can find the remains of an old water-wheel frame.

We spotted some unrecorded workings and a trench cut into the rock that outcrops about 100 feet above the portal over the mined ore deposit of the stope. Several open cuts continue around the ridge to the southeast, to a tunnel just off an old road. It starts as a 15-foot trench heading north where a five-foot prospect was dug westward into the rock. The tunnel at the end of the north-heading trench was caved, but it has been reopened along with the main adit, and is active as of our 2000 visit. We noticed very few sulfides in the tailings of any of the workings.

Zerwekh Mine/Big Z Mine

Rated at A-2; the elevation of this property is 3,500 feet. It is located in the northwest ¼ of the northwest ¼ of Section 8, T21N, R18E, which can be found on the USGS 7.5 Minute Series map of Swauk Pass.

Take the Pipe Creek Road (140) south off US 97. You get to the prospect printed at the northwest corner of the map via a 0.3-mile walk south from Pipe Creek down a road running south and parallel to the east side of Swauk Creek. This is an open 80-foot tunnel run on a seven-foot vein of chalcedonic Bird's Eye Quartz. The south wall is slate, the other sandstone.

Samples in the digs and near the portal were of sandstone with quartz stringers up to one inch in width. There were also some connecting Bird's Eye Quartz veins up to two feet wide. Two open cuts and a cabin site sit above the workings. The other prospect, marked on the map, (0.2 mile up Pipe Creek Road) is on the west side of Pipe Creek and is visible from the road. Watch for an indistinct trail headed toward it. This prospect appears to be the back side of the ledge that the 80-foot prospect tunnel was driven on. Two barren open cuts are located above this prospect. An unvisited, caved 207-foot tunnel was driven west into the ridge.

Another prospect about ½ mile east of the above is no more than a caved pit 15 feet in diameter. Vernon Zerwekh operated this unpatented property during 1950. The following minerals were reported at this claim: gold, silver, molybdenum, vanadium, and titanium. The region contains mostly gold and silver. If the other minerals are present, they do not seem apparent upon inspection at the property. There are signs that the tunnel has been worked within the last few years.

Two more prospects trace the ledge across (northward) US 97 in the southwest ¼ of the southwest ¼ of Section 5. The workings farthest north are dug into a sandstone outcrop showing no appreciable mineralization. The 10-foot roadside adit (dangerously close to caving) is visible as you drive by. In actuality, it is a stope at the end of a tunnel that was eliminated in the construction of US 97. The highway now lies where the tunnel once did.

The 1872 Robinson Gulch Earthquake/Landslide During the gold-mining era in the Swauk District, there was renewed interest in an old story told by Yakima Indians of geological occurrences related to the regional earthquake of 1872, which was corroborated by local miner, John Robinson. There had been a landslide in the Swauk area, of which Robinson found proof in the discovery of an old piece of manmade iron similar to an old-fashioned gunlock lying on bedrock 90 feet underground in his mine shaft.[24] It could be that a Native American acquired the gun (likely through trade), brought it into the area to hunt, and lost it in the earth-moving event.[25] Robinson also uncovered a section of an alder tree with its bark still intact.

There was talk of sending the iron object to the Smithsonian Institution to see whether additional analysis could unravel the mystery. Other interests must have prevailed, because no follow-up was reported.

Hard Hat #1 Mine

This property is located in the northeast ¼ of Section 15, T21N, R17E, at an elevation of 3,000 to 3,200 feet. This places it about 0.3 mile south of Iron Creek Road at milepost 158 on US 97, east of Swauk Creek and up a gulch. The last owners to work this claim were John Newman and J. Godwin.

Float from the tailing piles is apparent at the beginning of the gulch. At 100 feet, watch for a sloughed-in open cut heading north into the crest of rock that goes to the top of the ridge.

A 20-foot shaft with vein material showing lies 50 feet northeast of the open cut. The vein trends into the hill where a 50-foot tunnel picks up and follows a four-to-six-inch vein of what looks to be gray sulfides and quartz ranging from hard to decomposed. There is an outcrop of mineral-bearing rock, with a 20-foot tunnel following a weak vein 150 feet up the east-running gulch.

Back down on the flat area east of Swauk Creek and about 300 feet south of the gulch lies a cabin site marked by a stand of alder trees. Later, when the timber railroad was run up to the Swauk Pass area, the cabin became a depot. The train track was also used to carry skiers to Swauk Recreational Lodge, which was located in the northeast ¼ of Section 12, T21N, R17E situated east of US 97, across from the Swauk Campground. Today there is no evidence the lodge ever existed, because it was moved to its present location as the Mineral Springs Resort Restaurant (in the southwest ¼ of Section 22). In the early 1940s, it was built as the Swauk Recreational Lodge, 4¼ miles north of its present location. The fireplace had a 10-foot firebox with both sides open and a chain-driven pulley moving the logs through as they burned. It then became the Swauk Lodge, a home for Boy Scouts and Camp Fire Girls. From 1954–1959, it operated as the Swauk Ski Bowl, with rope tows for downhill skiers. In 1961, it was cut into three sections, moved to its present location—replacing the old restaurant and grocery store—and renamed Mineral Springs Resort. A unique indoor stone fountain was put in the center of the restaurant. The Rock Hounds of America and other groups donated agates from here and beyond the USA. These now decorate the tops of tables in the dining room and the agate room. A local Liberty miner, Larry Brighton, donated the gold nugget that is circled by chips of Ellensburg Blue in the bar top. Ask the owner about the ghost that occupies the old lodge structure.

The now-defunct Mineral Springs Campground, across from the Mineral Springs Resort, is the site of real, live mineral springs, which are now capped. Before there was a road to the Red Top Mountain fire lookout, longtime Liberty resident Ralph Fackler used to pack supplies or firefighting equipment by horse via a trailhead near Mineral Springs for the several-mile journey (one way) when necessity demanded it.

---

[24] Lowland, or valley fill, to a depth of 120 feet (deposited before whites entered the area) was found in other old mine shafts as well, indicating that it covered some of the valuable gold properties. Williams Creek flows on alluvial deposits rather than on bedrock, a condition that suggests that the material comes mainly from Pleistocene deposits, and more recently from erosion and slide occurrences.
[25] Hopefully that was all that this gun owner lost in the slide.

The Old Indian Trail To locate this trail, use the USGS 7.5 Minute Series maps for Swauk Prairie and Liberty. This ancient Native American trail went from the Kittitas Valley (east of Ellensburg) through the Swauk Mining District to the Wenatchee area. You can visualize the trail best by using the maps to plot the route the travelers took, and perhaps to plan a visit to a point of interest, or to hike a section. The trail itself is no longer recognizable, so relocating portions of it will be a challenge. But the pursuit alone can be worth the effort because the areas you'll hike are enjoyable. Today roads follow along parts of the trail.

To get a feel for the direction of the trail, follow a route starting from the historic Yakima Indian summer encampment area in the Kittitas Valley east of Ellensburg. Using the USGS 7.5 Minute Series map for Swauk Prairie, locate the Green Canyon Ranch (in Section 6, T19N, R18E) on Green Canyon Road. Follow the road north to the end of Section 30, and follow the bottomland creek in Section 19 north to its top center. There the trail heads northwest, away from the road, above a feeder stream (Section 18).[26] Then head west to the two unnamed lakes in the area located in the southeast ¼ of Section 13, T20N, R17E. From here the trail goes down Deer Gulch (Section 11) and crosses over to Pine Gulch and north to Williams Creek.

Using the USGS map of Liberty, follow it to Liberty (Section 2). From there, it goes north up Lion Gulch (Sections 2, 35, 23, 26, and 24). Where the map indicates a quarry (Section 24), the trail went up and over the lowest saddle between Lion Gulch and Hurley Creek. From the low saddle, it goes down a feeder stream, passing the Southern Star Property, to Hurley Creek and then follows Hurley Creek (Sections 14 and 11) to US 97.

The historic Mountain Home site is across from the mouth of Hurley Creek. This site was a hunter/gatherer campground used by the Yakimas long before the fur traders, and later the miners, came into Swauk. On the site, there was an area designated as a dumping place for all the animal hair scraped off the hides. For some time after the camp was abandoned, a 12-feet–wide by 3-feet–high pile of animal hair served as a landmark for travelers. Local residents report that there were two Native American sweat lodges in the Mountain Home area. A look around might turn up evidence of them.[27]

From Mountain Home, the trail went directly north up an unnamed feeder creek (Sections 1 and 2) to Blewett Pass. There were paths leading off into various other places, but the main trail to the Wenatchee area took the route of the old Blewett Highway, north down Peshastin Creek (through the Blewett Mining District) to the lower valley and bottomlands.

Peak 4047T Adit (Orion Claim)[28]

Rated at C-3, this tunnel is located in the northwest ¼ of Section 15, T21N, R17E, on the USGS 7.5 Minute Series map of Liberty, at about 3,800 feet in elevation.

The trail (a former 4WD road) to the tunnel starts 0.4 mile north of Durst Creek on the west side of US 97. A road to the Washington Department of Transportation Iron Creek Stockpile Site is located here. This road leads a short way to the road-material staging area, but don't park on the site. At the west end of the site, there is a concrete block building. The unmarked west-trending trail starts across from the structure behind a berm of dirt, on the north side of a stream that originates east and near the summit of Peak 4047T. A hike that takes you 1.2 miles and 1,000 feet up on this easy-to-follow byway will pass below the adit. When you get near the adit, watch to the right (north) of the road as you ascend. There is no trail, but only about 100 feet down the road the obvious gray tailings will alert you to the tunnel's location. From here, scramble 200 feet up the steep slope to the top of the tailings.

At the portal, a rest and the view of the high ridges and distant mountains to the northeast, east, and southeast will help quiet your climb-induced rapid pulse. This is a great photo op. A look to the east reveals a peak 4,006 feet high. Just to the north (left) of Peak 4,006 is the northernmost end of Table Mountain and a flat lava formation named Diamond Head. The Wenatchee Mountains dominate the background from northeast to southeast. Turn 180 degrees, and you'll see the tunnel.

---

[26] A sharp, prominent notch in the mountains is visible when you approach from Ellensburg toward Green Canyon.
[27] In later years, Mountain Home was the location of a stagecoach station that served the Ellensburg/Wenatchee run.
[28] This claim was not listed in the *Inventory of Washington Minerals,* leading us to believe that the tunnel was started after the book's publication in the late 1950s.

Peak 4047T is on the easternmost edge of Teanaway Ridge and is composed of Teanaway basaltic rock. The workings were driven into barren-looking basalt on a northwest course. At 150 feet, this untimbered tunnel cuts a 10-to-20–foot vein of carbonaceous slate, with calcite stringers laced throughout. The dig ends here in the slate vein area. There are no mineralized areas on the slopes or outcrops of the peak. A shaft on the ridge slope above the adit prompted the most recent working.

For the Rockhound
We didn't notice sulfides in the observable rock.

Durst Creek NW #1 Lode

Rated at A-1, this property sits in the southwest ¼ of Section 14, T21N, R17E, at an elevation of about 3,600 feet. See the USGS 7.5 Minute Series map of Liberty.

To get to this lode, turn east off US 97 onto Forest Service Road 9705. There is a "Y" in the road after about one mile. Continue straight ahead (east) for another mile of twists and turns. As the road heads south and cuts an outcrop at 3,600 feet elevation, there is an unmarked (almost hidden) 4WD road that drops south down the side of a ridge top. Park off to the side of Road 9705, and hoof it 0.2 mile to the mine tunnel.[29] This adit has 230 feet of workings into sandstone where the miners were seeking out a vein of quartz. This vein is defined by a trench cut into the ridge directly above and west of where the tunnel has been run. The portal is in a state of ongoing collapse and is posted to keep you out, so don't even entertain the thought of entering. This is an active dig, and you can't get permission to enter.

Bloomquist Brothers Mine

Rated at A-1. This mine is located in the northwest ¼ of the southwest ¼ of Section 22, T21N, R17E, on the USGS 7.5 Minute Series map of Liberty.

About 0.2 mile west of US 97 on Road 9738 (Blue Creek Road) lies an old cabin. There is a tailing pile leading to a caved shaft 150 feet northeast of the building. About 150 feet northwest of the shaft, a west-trending incline tunnel was driven into a rock outcropping, which is 25 feet long until the spot where it is caved.

Area Geology
The makeup of the low-gold–content ground north of Baker Creek is different from the higher, gold-bearing quality of the channel-wash downstream. Hill-wash prevails above Baker Creek. Even the gold from the Baker Creek area is lower in quality because of its higher silver content. This made it worth $2.00 less per ounce than the Williams Creek gold.

Medicine Creek Claims

Not rated. This site is located in the southeast ¼ of Section 21, T21N, R17E. Medicine Creek flows east from its feeder creeks in Sections 20, 21, 28, 29, and 30 into Swauk Creek. Use the USGS 7.5 Minute Series map of Liberty.

Take Blue Creek Road 9738 for 0.2 mile past the Bloomquist brothers cabin, and turn south on Road 9702. Go 0.6 mile to the Medicine Creek Road, and drive west 0.2 mile, watching for a vague dirt road that goes up and along the north side of the creek. At the end (300 feet), park and beat feet across the water. Search the creek bank for the old digs. We haven't been able to find the names of the old historic claims.

---

[29] The original (caved) adit is on the opposite (west) side of the ridge from the newer dig. It is directly under the newer NW #1 Lode, which is 100 feet higher, and was driven west over the original, in search of the vein.

Research has shown that W. A. Ford, William Kaup, and T. W. Smith worked a series of claims together and separately on Medicine Creek: the Oro Fino, Big Blue, El Dorado, Little Joker, and St. Patrick, all prior to 1891. They had sold off the properties by the end of 1891. John Black picked up the St. Patrick at that time.

The three men then went on to discover a good ledge, which they named the Buckhorn, located above the Hampton ledge. By 1893, the Buckhorn Mine, owned by Ford, Kaup, and Smith, was one of the four mines in the Swauk Mining District attracting attention because of its impressive gold output. A company from California was interested enough to help the Buckhorn place a five-stamp mill on the claim. In 1898, the three partners bonded the Buckhorn Mine to an Idaho man for $24,000.00.

As of 1998, we have located some old workings in the southeast ¼ of the southeast ¼ of Section 21, and the northeast ¼ of the northeast ¼ in Section 28, located south of the creek. They consist of two six-by-four–foot holes recently dug in the waterway of a seasonal runoff gulch. We also came across two caved adits and two caved trenches at creek level just downstream from the runoff gulch. There are four open pits north of these digs that have been dug at 150-foot intervals from the road up to the ridge top. We haven't found any Buckhorn tunnels or ledges.

For the Rockhound

Before roads existed up Medicine Creek, which drains from the well-known agate-producing Red Top Mountain, old prospector August Draft investigated this creek. He found color (gold) in a number of places while working his way upstream. More importantly, for the rockhound, Draft also noted masses of water-born blue agate in the creek bed. Boulders in the creek were found to have jasper, mossagate, and other minerals included within them. Using the proper tools, Draft removed the gem material from the matrix.

In the summer of 2000, a group of rockhounders who were camping at Mineral Creek showed us impressive amounts of blue agate nodules, along with some red jasper gem rock. One agate was the size of a fist. One of us even took home a sample of a blue agate nodule.

Lib Group, Seven Prospect Claims

Rated at A-3, this group is located in the southeast ¼ of Section 20, and northwest ¼ of Section 29, T21N, R17E. They run along Peak 4028T, as seen on the USGS 7.5 Minute Series map of Liberty.

The group of claims runs north-south, three-wide from Medicine Creek to the ridge top, with a solo claim running off the north center claim downslope to the north toward Blue Creek. We saw numerous prospect pits along the ridge outcrops and just off either side, not to mention well-developed Bird's Eye Quartz in some of the digs. The workings showed no sign of mineral content when we examined the rock unmagnified. This appears to be another area to not get too excited about. Then again, if you like ridge running, this is the place. The ridge top puts you on even ground with surrounding peaks and ridges, and the Red Top Mountain lookout is visible to the north. A golden eagle resides in the vicinity, and you can often catch a glimpse of it against a backdrop of blue sky or forested hills.

Properties Between Medicine Creek and Baker Creek

These properties are generally located west of the portion of Swauk Creek that flows south from Medicine Creek to Baker Creek. This spot is in Sections 27 and 34, T21N, R17E, as found on the USGS 7.5 Minute map of Liberty.

The adit shown on the map, which is now caved, lies in the northwest ¼ of the southwest ¼ of Section 27, at the end of a short road. The portal timbers are visible in the sloughed-down dirt and rock. Above the adit, there is an open cut, and a prospect pit sits 100 feet north of the tunnel.

A claim marked the Merry Widow is located in the northwest ¼ of Section 34, but we didn't see any visible workings there. A thousand feet south of the Merry Widow, there is a caved adit on the Norway claim.

Baker Creek Claims

Not rated. This property is located in the southwest ¼ of Section 34, the southeast ¼ to northwest ¼ of Section 33 (North Fork), and the center of Section 33 through Sections 32 and 31, T21N, R17E. These are shown on the USGS 7.5 Minute Series map of Liberty. We haven't been able to uncover the names of the nine workings printed on the map along Baker Creek.

Traveling 0.4 mile downstream from the Norway (west of Swauk Creek), you'll see two caved adits 0.1 mile west from the start of Baker Creek Road, and up the north bank about 150 feet. The various mines we visited were a mix of reopened original placer and hardrock properties. A very old arrastre site with parts of the handmade artifacts still intact stands at the end of an overgrown ¼-mile road located about ½ mile up and north of the Baker Creek Road.

Potato Patch[30]

Not rated. This property, also located along Baker Creek, was originally called Tweet's Pocket. It was named for Torkel (Tom) Tweet, who worked the property along with Bill Johnson in the summer of 1897. They found wire gold on the site.

When they made their discovery, Tom and Bill declared a holiday and invited every miner in camp to come down to Cle Elum to celebrate. Upon their arrival in the big city, they sold the gold and went to every restaurant and saloon in town, telling the owners to furnish food and drinks to all, as long as the money held out. Three days of partying ensued, and it's been said that Cle Elum has never seen anything to rival those days before or since. After returning to Baker Creek, the two partners built an arrastre and ended up mining over $100,000 from their claims.[31]

This is private property and is still actively mined today. Do not trespass.

The Potato Patch Mine. Known for the large size of its nuggets, this mine was a major producer of gold in the Swauk area. (Victor Pisoni photo)

---

[30] Named for the size and shape of the nuggets found here.
[31] In 1897, there were eight arrastres operating in the Swauk Mining District. Around 1900, stamp mills began to replace them, though one arrastre operated into the 1930s. The price of gold in 1900 was $20.00 per ounce, and the common laborer earned $2.00 a day.

Early History of Baker Creek

The exact locations of the following claims have not been determined.

Little York/Phoenix/Settler Claims

These claims are located in the northeast ¼ of Section 3, T20N, R17E, on the USGS 7.5 Minute Series map for Liberty, on the southwest slope of unnamed Peak 3943T (locally known as Liberty Peak), 2,800 feet up Jack Gulch. As you stand facing the main tunnel on the Phoenix, the Little York will be above you and to your left.

In 1887, Norwegian Torkel (Tom) Tweet and Swede A. W. (Billy) Johnson had a bonanza of a gold claim across from the mouth of Baker Creek, east of Swauk Creek. They were busily mining wire gold and nuggets from broken quartz.[32] In the first 60 feet of tunnel, the miners followed numerous quartz stringers to a vein, but they didn't locate a ledge.[33]

In 1891, Torkel Tweet and Ole Peterson ran an arrastre, getting one ounce of gold per man each day. In 1892, Tweet was living part-time with A. F. York and Ole Peterson, until their cabin burned down. Later, Tweet and Johnson owned three quartz claims: the Little York, Phoenix, and Settler. This mining union produced a pocket of gold worth $65,000.00, and another one gave up $10,000.00 in gold. They made several more gold finds, which produced 145 ounces of gold amalgam worth $2,320.00 in a two-week period. A display of their better gold nuggets was sent to the 1893 Columbian Exposition World Fair in Chicago. One winter they must have gotten cabin fever, because they had completed 180 feet of tunnel on the Phoenix Claim by the following spring.

By 1894, Tweet and Johnson claimed they were taking out $100.00 in gold per ton, but we haven't determined how many tons they extracted.

Little York and Phoenix Claims, 1974 Update

The following information from a sampling report verifies the mineral wealth and validity of the two properties. Local miner and Liberty resident, the late Jack Kirsh participated in taking the samples. Wallace Rutherford had leased the claims from owner Signa Lauch, and was actively mining. Wallace had a portable mill that included a jaw crusher and a grinding mill located on the dump of the Little York Claim.

Little York

In 1974, the lower tunnel on this claim was 500 feet long, and it ran through both claims. It originates on the Little York Claim, but the greater part of the tunnel passes under the Phoenix property. It is about on line between the Little York Claim to the west and the Phoenix land to the east and follows a course a little north of due east.

Fifty feet into the tunnel, then 20 feet north (left) on a drift that follows a prominent vein structure, and east again for 10 feet is a winze. The winze measured 10 feet, 4 inches deep. The opening at the top was six feet six inches long (north to south), and four feet four inches wide (east to west). The adit is 150 feet north of a cabin with a rock cut leading to it. The tailing dump is 150 feet west of the portal, and the top is level with it. Some discarded rock that probably originated in an ancient river delta fills the natural slope of the downhill terrain. At one time, a mill stood on top of a flat area that was large enough to use for parking and as an equipment yard.[34]

---

[32] Billy was careful about holding onto his earnings. Torkel preferred to live it up, as evidenced at his death in 1940 when all that remained of his wealth was $500.00 in gold nuggets and gold dust.

[33] A quartz ledge was later found that extended from one mile above the mouth of Baker Creek at a heading of northwest/southeast, across Swauk Creek, through the hills to Cougar Gulch, and then cutting through Williams and Boulder Creeks. It contained free gold in Bird's Eye Quartz and blue quartz.

[34] It was common practice to dump possibly valuable mineral rock to one side of the tailing pile for possible recovery later. Rockhounds today can take advantage of this old-time practice.

Perhaps their Settler Claim adjoining the Little York and Phoenix Claims has the adits we couldn't find.

Phoenix Claim

The Phoenix has a caved 200-foot (upper) tunnel located 200 feet southeast and uphill from the portal of the Little York. The Phoenix adit tailing dump is a flat-topped pile of broken rock extending from the portal west and downhill.

The cave-in at the Phoenix portal appeared to be blocked by at least 50 cubic yards of rock debris and dirt. Water may be dammed up behind the blockage.

Johnson Pocket

This pocket of ore was in an irregular-shaped rock cut about 24 feet long, and 10 to 15 feet deep, which is now sloughed in with fill material. It is located about 75 feet above and northeast of the Phoenix adit.

A short adit 15 feet long was dug 20 feet vertically below the north end of the Johnson pocket, and aimed to go under the dig. There are quartz-calcite stringers in these workings, but they appear to be devoid of value. This property was reportedly mined out long ago.

The rock on this dump is mainly diabase or basalt, with some slate and sandstone. There is rock with calcite veinlets and calcite druse on the broken surfaces. We came across miscellaneous digs just above the Little York tunnel that we couldn't identify, plus there was evidence of numerous other old excavations across the hillside near the unknown drift.[35]

Samplings showed that the gold values were limited to discontinuous quartz-calcite veins, and the wall rock was essentially barren of gold. The claims were recorded as not worth developing, and that limited deposits were of an exploratory nature. (The 1970s were peak years of contention between miners and Forest Service personnel trying to shut down mine claims.) However, in 2000 the claim was active.

Baker Creek/Early Claims (1896)

Green Horn

Owned by F. N. Watson, this claim is located one mile above the mouth of Baker Creek. Watson took "round shot" (pin head nuggets) and free-milling gold from a three-foot ledge between iron rock and porphyry on this site.

Bob Tail

The past owners of the Bob Tail were Irvine Liggett, Isaac Zeran, and H. B. Runnels. The claim is located on a north extension of the Green Horn ledge. Ligget, Zeran, and Runnels drove a 20-foot shaft in 20 inches of ore, similar to that of the Green Horn claim.

Maryellen

The owners, the same people who owned the Bob Tail, sank a 20-foot shaft into a ledge 14 inches to two feet in width at this site.

A display of nuggets from the Swauk district. This picture was taken in 1904, and at the going rate for gold at that time, the large nugget in the center was worth $1,105. Publicity like this prompted people to pour into areas like the Swauk to seek their fortunes. (*Wilhelm's Magazine, The Coast,* March 1904)

---

[35] Tweet and Johnson reported having driven considerably more footage in the original tunnels than were found during the 1974 report.

Big Bear/Little Bear

F. D. Wilson and E. J. Young owned this claim, which produced coarse and flake gold from a ledge that was traced for 3,000 feet.

In 1903, Lars Halverson was working on drifting into a bank at the mouth of Baker Creek. Lars and Tweet also drove a crosscut that year to tap a quartz ledge that they had located extending through the Little York and Phoenix Claims.

A vague reference refers to a high bar worked by Gus Nilson on the northernmost placer claim up Swauk Creek, north of the mouth of Baker Creek, where he was tunneling on bedrock.

J. C. Pike had a 37-acre claim off one of the sides of Baker Creek, but our source didn't specify its exact location. Pike's biggest nugget paid him $745.00. The ground Pike worked had 10 to 18 feet of dirt over bedrock, but once he had reached it, he pulled out an ounce of gold a day.

W. A. Ford took over the Pike properties, running a 196-foot tunnel west into the old channel. Ford also outfitted the claims with hydraulic monitors and found nuggets worth $5.00 to $300.00 on bedrock. James Boxall was also doing some mining in a tunnel in the same area around this time.

Mother-in-Law Group

In September 1900, the Teanaway Mining Syndicate was incorporated to promote the Mother-in-Law Group of claims. A sum of $250,000.00 in capital was divided into five million shares worth 5 cents each.

Less than ¾ mile up Baker Creek, from its mouth, lay the company's 110 acres of mineral-bearing land. Five claims were included: the Mother-in-Law, Wife, Daughter, The Boys, and Dudland, with a mill to service the three distinct veins of ore. A tunnel ran south from a gulch into the hillside on the Mother-in-Law Claim, and three shafts were sunk that year (1900). One shaft was on The Boys Claim.

The trustees of the company included a dentist, two publishers, a manufacturer, an engine builder, and two mine owners, G. M. Radabaugh[36] and Roy A. Barry,[37] who were promoting the sale of stock. When the smokescreen cleared, so did any sign of further development.

Mill Creek/Mill Gulch Claims

Not rated. These claims are located in Sections 3, 4, and 5, T20N, R17E, near where the Mill Creek Road meets US 97 just north of Liberty Road. See the USGS 7.5 Minute Series maps of Liberty and Swauk Prairie. In 1896, Gus Nilson discovered a quartz ledge, from which he extracted 30 pounds of gold-bearing ore worth $60.00. He then bonded the claim to a Tacoma businessman for $5,000.00.

In August 1896, Mill Gulch claimed the life of Ben Twiss. He was lowered into a 70-foot shaft that had previously been tested and found to contain bad air. Nonetheless, Ben had himself lowered to the bottom, where he filled a bucket full of ore. On ascending with the bucket toward the top, Ben lost consciousness and fell into the shaft. Miner Joe Anderson descended to rescue Ben, but was also overcome by bad air. Joe was still in the bucket when his limp body was brought up. Ernest Wheat happened by and revived Anderson, but it was too late for Ben Twiss. The only thing to do was ship his body home to Centralia.

The Potato Patch Mine got its name from the size of the nuggets it produced. In this picture, the coin is a U.S. half dollar, and the three nuggets being compared to it for size live up to the mine's name. (Vic Pisoni photo)

---

[36] George Radabaugh was one of three partners in the Wall Street Mining Company in Cougar Gulch in 1909.
[37] By 1901, Barry was in charge of developing the Mother-In-Law Group of claims.

Fanny Edell, 1903

Lars Halverson worked this quartz claim, which is located at Mill Gulch. It later became part of the Hellen holdings.

Hellen Mining Company/Syndicate, 1904 –1909

Rated at A-2, this area was located in Section 4, T20N, R17E, and the southeast ¼ of Section 33, T21N, R17E, north of Mill Creek. The year 1904 saw the beginning of an aggregated group of nine claims eventually covering 520 acres, which A. D. Hellen accumulated from other miners. Shares were sold until 1909. The company claimed to have thousands of tons of free-milling gold ore in sight.

The Fanny Edell Claim was showcased (how much of the reported development belonged to Lars Halverson was not noted). The Hellen Mining Company developed a tunnel in which it sank a shaft in what was called the lower tunnel. A 100-foot upper tunnel had a vein of ore 8 to 24 inches wide. A shaft started on the vein widened to five feet across at 40 feet of depth.

By 1909, five ledges had been added to the properties. The Hellen Mining Syndicate (as it was then called) had expended all available capital on the Fanny Edell. The company's crosscut tunnels had been extended to the ledge to ascertain how far the ore went down. Tunnel #2 was connected to Tunnel #3 by an incline shaft.

Records show that somewhere along the way, the company removed some hanging wall rock in a blind drift run under a surface pocket of gold. The blind drift disclosed a rich gold vein that opened up a short distance away into another pocket of gold just as rich as the upper deposit. The two gold occurrences were 45 feet apart and separated by almost barren rock. An eight-stamp mill was erected with a capacity of 40 tons per day. A boiler and engines ran an air compressor and power drills.

The White Rose Mine (on the far south end of the Fanny Edell Claim, an extension from the Fanny Edell ledge) had exposed that same ledge for 175 additional feet. The ore on the White Rose was a silicious and porous quartz.

Other claims on the Hellen Mine property where main leads were opened up were the Bonanza and Washington Claims on outcroppings varying from three to eight feet in width, with a northeast-to-southwest strike. Shortly after 1909, the whole promotion slipped into unrecorded obscurity.

In 1999 we did an extensive search in Section 3 at the areas of the ridge marked elevation 3258T, running northwest to southeast, and all the surrounding slopes. We also examined the ridge marked 3492T in the southeast ¼ of Section 33 and down Baker Creek. All of these areas showed signs of numerous mining digs, new and historic. About one mile up Mill Creek, a dam still stands, evidence that a mill once operated there. Just downstream from the dam, on either side of the creek, there are two adits, 20 and 30 feet long. Upstream about 0.2 mile from the dam is a private claim beyond a gated road. Several open and caved adits lie on the south and southeastern slope, north of the Mill Creek Dam Road, scattered over the hillside up to 3,000 feet. The shaft in which miner Ben Twiss died is located just off the ridge, about where you can see "Section 3" printed on the map.

The area around elevation 3492T was once quite actively mined, as noted by the many old pits, trenches, and caved tunnels. The tunnels of the open claims are posted or sealed with plywood. *Never* enter these digs without prior permission.

Red Hook Claim, 1987

Rated at A-2. The original 1800s name for this claim is not known. The trail leading to it is difficult to locate, but the property is in the southeast ¼ of Section 5, and northwest ¼ of Section 9, T20N, R17E, at an elevation of 3,700 feet. See the USGS 7.5 Minute Series map of Swauk Prairie.

We found these old workings while trying to locate physical evidence of another 1800s dig. We crossed a trail in the southwest ¼ of Section 4 (east of a flat peak marked 3729T) while dropping off Mill Creek Road and heading north. About 200 feet beyond the road, we came upon the old route, which contours west about 300 feet to a cabin site. You must look upslope 50 feet to be able to see the two remaining four-log–high corners of the building. We saw artifacts from the 1800s in the form of rusting kitchen tools, buckets, and cast-iron stove parts, along with other stuff. A piece of stove showed a date of 1887. Another 100 feet of travel will bring you to rock debris from an outcrop and several prospect pits. Contouring 100 feet farther, there is a caved tunnel. Metal ore car track strapping, shovels, and the portal head beam are in evidence. From here, a quick, steep ascent south and over the rock outcrop containing the tunnel will take you back to the road.

Wind Fall Lode Claim

This property is located in the Boulder Creek area. Frank Bloomquist[38] recorded the Wind Fall Claim in 1932, two years after it was initially discovered. Frank named the claim after an incident in which he checked out a fallen tree that had crystalline wire gold entangled in its roots. He went into a grubstake agreement with Mr. and Mrs. Benson[39] in 1949.

Frank Bloomquist was an outstanding old-time prospector who lived, worked, and mined in the Swauk most of his life. He was known to be especially good at pocket-gold hunting. He passed away December 29, 1962.

In February 1963, the Wind Fall Claim was renamed the Black Eagle. In March, the Benson family purchased the Wind Fall from Bloomquist's heirs. Claim jumpers litigated in court with the Bensons for several years before giving up.

Mr. Benson died in 1966. Bertha Benson had acquired extensive mining knowledge over the years working with Frank Bloomquist and her husband. She used this experience in what she considered challenging and interesting work. Living in the natural peace and quiet of the mountains also made it more than worthwhile to stay. Besides, she knew that the price of gold might go up in the near future. Bertha was able to pursue this lifestyle for several more years. Three cheers for her!

Deer Gulch Dredge Pond

Rated at A-1, this pond is located in the northeast ¼ of the southeast ¼ of Section 10, T20N, R17E. See the USGS 7.5 Minute Series map of Swauk Prairie.

About ½ mile south of the Liberty Road, a road takes you 0.2 mile to the dredge pond, as shown on the map. The dredge attempted to work its way up the gulch, but it ran into a series of problems along the way. The keel and floor of its hull is now rotting away. The best time to check this site out is in the late summer, when lower water levels allow a more exposed view of the hull's remains. A shaft about 200 feet south of the pond reportedly belonged to Frank Bryant. As of the year 2000, a gate had been installed, and it might be closed and posted now.

Hiking and Touring

Maps

For maps of this area, use Liberty Green Trails Map #210, and the USGS 7.5 Minute Series maps of Liberty, Swauk Prairie and Swauk Pass.

---

[38] Frank's father John arrived with his nephews (the Jordin brothers) in the initial rush to the Swauk in 1874. John Bloomquist and the Jordins located claims at the mouth of Baker Creek. They started for the area the same day that the Goodwin brothers reported their gold discovery. John later had the first sawmill on Williams Creek, followed by one at Swauk Creek, which he operated for several years. John stayed in the Swauk until his death in 1906.

[39] Bertha Benson put in endless time and effort over the years to complete an alphabet of mined natural wire gold forms.

Recommended Drives and Hikes

Road conditions vary from year to year, so getting to some trailheads might require high-clearance or 4WD (four-wheel drive) vehicles. Driving up an unmaintained 4WD road can be a creative outing in itself. Some of these former roads are no more than glorified trails today, but they allow you to traverse into worthwhile hiking country, so plan your trip well. The better byways give you access to panoramic heights such as Table Mountain and Lion Rock. For 4WD buffs, there are plenty of roadways lacing the ridges and mountains, and exploring them can take up most of a day. You can enjoy a variety of natural art in the form of spectacular viewpoint vistas and rock formations. The Swauk area is friendly to outdoor enthusiasts in winter and summer.

Table Mountain Hike #1368

Rated at C-2. Use Green Trails Map #210 of Liberty. This hike is 2.6 miles round trip.

Take Cougar Gulch Road 2120 (which is 4WD for the last ½ mile). At about one mile, watch for a road going east, which in 2000 was marked with bright-orange arrow cards. Find Road 114 on the map, and follow it over Snowshoe Ridge, which connects with Road 3507 (an improved road). Go ½ mile to an east-trending, unimproved (4WD) road for about one mile to a tight turnaround at the #1368 Trailhead. Hike a short, steep stretch of an old 4WD road turned trail. Starting at 5,300 feet elevation, go 0.6 mile to a spring-fed area (the head of one of the feeder streams to Williams Creek). Follow the trail northeast for 0.7 mile. The last 0.3 mile is very steep. The trail crosses Table Mountain Road 35. The hike is 1.3 miles one way, and the view is worth it.[40] From the top of Table Mountain, there are several moderate hikes to choose from in the Owl, Drop, and Nealey Creeks area, all of which empty into Naneum Creek. If you hike this popular hunting area in the fall, be sure to wear hunter orange to preserve your visibility, and possibly your life. When the snow is deep, the Swauk area is a mecca for winter sports enthusiasts because of the considerable amount of road available for these activities.

Wildlife

In the Swauk area, it's not unusual to come upon the tracks of wild critters throughout the year. During the summer, turkey buzzards, having returned from their wintering grounds, can be spotted, along with red-tailed hawks, golden eagles, bald eagles, and a wide variety of other birds. As late as 1929, wolf, coyote, cougar, lynx, and bobcats were sought for bounty.

No one we've talked to knows of any wolf or lynx being in the Swauk since that era, but one way to familiarize yourself with the tracks is by engaging in slow-paced winter sports such as snowshoeing or cross-country skiing. It is amazing how the snow reveals otherwise unseen critter traffic. Near river and stream banks where animals must go to get water in the dry season, you can also find tracks. Obtaining a booklet on wild animal tracks will help you identify them and evolve into a keen-eyed track spotter.

For the Rockhound

Fossils

Plant fossil remains can be found in this region where shale is exposed in certain road cuts. Palm leaves are abundant, along with oak, poplar, and maple. All told, there are 25 species of plant fossils in the Swauk shale.

Agates and Geodes

Blue agates and quartz-lined geodes have been found at elevations between 5,000 and 5,200 feet in the Table Mountain and Lion Rock area within the headwaters of Williams and Boulder Creeks. These sites are located about three miles northeast of Liberty (as the crow flies). Rockhounders who have hunted in this

---

[40] Hikers have been known to park one vehicle at one end, drive a second to the other, and hike one way, up or down.

Dredge Mining Using dredges to mine can be thought of as either placer mining on an industrial level or placer mining on steroids. When we think of normal placer mines, we picture a person with a gold pan, washing out the color or perhaps using a cradle or riffle box to extract the gold. Dredging scales up this process, sometimes by several orders of magnitude.

It begins with the digging of a pond large enough to float the dredge, which can be very small or very large. The larger dredges were placed on barges. A crane-like digging device was suspended by cables from the front of the barge. This could be a suction tube, rotating digger, clamshell, or whatever was suitable for the local soil. The digging device swung from side to side to dig a swath in front of the dredge.

Once dug, the material was brought on board the dredge by a conveyor or some other suitable method. Once aboard, the gravel and rock were run through a series of classifiers and riffles to separate the heavier gold from the gangue rock. The gangue spoils were then dumped off the rear of the dredge. As the dredge progressed, the pond expanded in front of it and was filled behind it. The dredge would slowly move along, laying waste as it went. Rock piles similar to dredge tailings can be seen along US 97 near Liberty, and in the valley of Williams Creek at Liberty itself.

The dredges were completely self-contained and very efficient, with all of the engines, pumps, and power machinery on board required to accomplish its task. Some of the mining companies that used dredges in the Swauk area were the Cascade Dredging Company and the Swauk Dredging and Mining Company.

---

basaltic belt that passes south of Liberty in an east/west direction through Crystal Mountain have found chalcedony (agate) nodules and fluorescent rock crystals at Lion Rock. Use your map to plan a trip; the right choices could put you in the right place at the right time. Rock on!

First Creek

Rated at D-3. Use the USGS 7.5 Minute Series map of Swauk Creek. The area is located in the southeast ¼ of Section 23, and southwest ¼ of Section 24, T20N, R17E.

The starting point for this road hike is a small parking area off US 97, east of the confluence of First and Swauk Creeks. Duck under the gate and follow the recently graded (late 1990s) dirt road, which parallels the north side of First Creek for 2.2 miles. At the end of that stretch, the road swings north at an elevation of about 3,000 feet.[41] Searching the slope off the road (west) will reveal numerous new and old rockhound digs. From there up to 3,600 feet, you can traverse this very steep area in a meandering hunt for banded agates, the elusive Ellensburg Blue Agate, or geodes. This lesser-known area has been dug for as many years as the Red Top Mountain agate beds, and is still a good producer. Crosscountry and scrambling abilities are required for this outing. Put on your best goat feet and enjoy!

Crystal Mountain

Rated at B-2, this area is located on the USGS 7.5 Minute Series maps of Liberty, Swauk Pass, Swauk Prairie, and Reecer Canyon. Green Trails Maps for Liberty #210 and Thorp #242[42] are also useful. The area is located in the north ½ of Section 18, T20N, R18E. The unnamed peak printed on the map as 5020T is Crystal Mountain.

For the most direct and best-maintained road to Crystal Mountain, go north from Ellensburg up Reeser Creek Road four miles, which turns left into a multi-switchback road (do not take Road 35 to Table Mountain). Three miles up Road 3507, there is a dirt road leading west off Road 3507.[43] Park here and hike 0.2 mile on the west-heading 4WD road. At a crossroad, bear north for 0.2 mile, and go west again up a

---

[41] Unlike most agate digs, which occur at around 5,000 feet, these grounds show their stuff at about the 3,000-foot mark.
[42] This route requires more driving but affords a shorter and less strenuous hike than other routes.
[43] Or take a network of twisting, interconnected (a mix of maintained and unmaintained) roads from Liberty that heads toward Road 3507, and go south. This is the adventurous, high-clearance or 4WD part of the trip.

The dredge in operation near Liberty, Washington in the 1920s. (Asahel Curtis photo, Washington State HIstorical Society)

steep jeep road to the top of flat-ridged Crystal Mountain. There is a view of Table Mountain to the northeast. This site has produced boulder agate, colorful red jasper, calcite crystals, petrified wood, and drusy quartz. To get at it, you'll need a hammer, chisel, and eye protection.

> **Warning** Keep children away from the cliffy north side of the ridge. In fact, leave them in the car with the dog. (Don't forget to roll the window down a few inches.)

For the Rockhound

The best areas to collect are along the east/west–running spine of mineralized rock that protrudes through the topsoil. At the far west end of the ridge top, there is an old claim marker, and all around that zone there is an abundance of collectibles. For another grand vista, look to the west.

Red Bluff[44]

This area is located in the southeast ¼ of Section 20, T21N, R18E, as shown on the USGS map of Swauk Pass, at an elevation of 5,500 feet. To reach this area, begin where you see "Nelson Hill" printed on the map, and go about 0.5 mile on the 4WD road. In season, there is a seep spring on the south slope of the wooded hill. There is no trailhead, and the trail leading to the bluff is obscured from view by fallen trees and thick underbrush. It begins behind the fallen trees beyond the spring. After gaining the trail, you'll climb steadily for 0.4 mile to the bluff.

---

[44] This region is most noticeable when the sun shines on it directly from the west, accentuating the iron-stained rock at the moment when it shows the most reddish hue. You have to be on top of Nelson Hill headed east on the ridge top road. At any other time, the bluff blends right into its surroundings. We refer to it as Red Bluff.

For the Rockhound

If you search the north top of the bluff first, you'll see two four-inch–wide seams of moss agate cutting through the north/south–trending bluff on an east/west strike. The top of the bluff is grass-covered, and it gently slopes to the east into the trees. The easiest way to work the bluff is to go from north to south over the top, rounding the south end and keeping close to the base of the cliffy south, then covering the west side of the bluff as safety allows. When you search the debris along the bottom of the bluff, you'll see rockhoundable minerals in the form of boulder agates (in boulders and those that are scattered on the ground from erosion). Also look for calcite crystals in the talus along the base of the bluff. There are geodes up to the size of softballs available to those who have the stamina to beat on the very hard rock that contains them. Even if you get started on one, though, chances are it will shatter from the hammer blows.

> **Big-Time Warning** The rock on the sides of the bluff is in a constant state of erosional flux. Rock can, and probably will, come down on you if you pick the wrong place to pound. Wear a hardhat, gloves, and eye protection, bring along any tools needed, and apply a good dose of rock savvy for added safety. In other words, you'll be in trouble if the big ones cut loose and start to fall down on you. Unlike Crystal Mountain, this is no place for children.

Red Top Mountain/Agate and Geode Beds

Rated at B-1. This is a wonderful area for family activities located near the Red Mountain Fire Lookout in the northwest ¼ of Section 19 and southwest ¼ of Section 18, T21N, R17E, on Teanaway Ridge. Use the USGS 7.5 Minute maps of Red Top Mountain, and Liberty and Green Trails Maps of Mount Stuart #209 and Liberty #210.

The Mineral Springs Campground is three miles north of the Liberty Road, on US 97 (west side of the highway). About 0.3 mile north of the campground, you'll run into Blue Creek Road 9738. Go 2.8 miles and take a left to Road 9702. At 4.7 miles lies the Red Top Mountain Lookout and parking area. Hike north past the lookout for ½ mile on Trail #1364 to the popular Red Top agate beds.

Geology of Red Top Mountain

The summit of Red Top Mountain is partly made up of the Teanaway basalt formations—lava flows with interbedded tuffs. The lava is black and vesicular (containing many volcanic gas holes). In some areas, these cavities are very large. The holes, or vesicles, hold both the fine, solid-blue agates and quartz crystal–lined geodes that percolating water has deposited. Every agate you find will by no means be blue. Most are colorless, while others are gray; the hard-to-find blue agate is actually rarely dug up.[45]

The agate beds cover a large area, and there are signs of former mineral hunters all around. Many small, shallow digs are in evidence. Broken geodes and fragments of agates used to be common, but not so these days. In shallow digs, water seeps into hair-fine cracks in the agate and expands with the winter's cold, breaking the mineral. Digging deep, long, and often is the only way to a rewarding mineral find. *Remember to backfill your holes.*

Red Top Mountain provides adventure *and* scenic grandeur. Looking out from the agate and geode-bearing ridge, there is a sweeping semicircle of individual mountains and mountain ranges to the west, the Stuart Range to the north, and Table Mountain to the east. There are few places where you can find a better one-day outing or vacation area, combined with the chance of collecting some choice minerals.

---

[45] One look at a true Ellensburg Blue Agate at a local rock shop gives some folks agate fever, which can be just as intense as gold fever.

Cle Elum Mining Area

The Cle Elum mining area covers a large portion of the southern slopes of the Wenatchee Mountains, beginning near the upper reaches of Ingalls Creek to the north and continuing south to the towns of Cle Elum, Roslyn, and Ronald. On the west, it is bounded, roughly, by the Cle Elum River and on the east by the ridge between the Cle Elum and Teanaway Rivers. The area's flora ranges from sagebrush and grasses in the lowlands, to pine and tamarack forests at the higher elevations. Most of the mountain slopes are open and relatively free of brush, which makes exploring easy, as long as you're in good physical condition.

Among the many mountains in the district are Ingalls Peak, which rises to an elevation of 7,662 feet, and The Cradle, the summit of which reaches 7,467 feet. The mountain slopes tend to be very steep and composed of loose, unstable rock. Mountain climbers consider the peaks in this region challenging, especially Mount Stuart, which is immediately north of the district, along Ingalls Creek.

Since the weather gets quite hot during the summer months, many of the pristine streams and creeks that are rushing with water in the springtime are dry in early fall.

The tamarack, or larch, trees that grow at higher elevations are unique. They look like evergreens, sporting needles like the pine trees they intermingle with. In the fall, however, the tamarack's needles turn yellow and eventually drop off. The turning leaves of the trees can create quite a sight in the late summer and early fall months—a mosaic of bright yellows and greens against the mountainsides. Unfortunately, many people who are unfamiliar with these trees think that they are dead or dying when they shed their needles, and cut them down for firewood. This is so common in some areas that campfires have been banned.

History

Because of the size of this district, it would be difficult to include all of its history in a single section, so we will detail the history of each region within the Cle Elum District as we address it. Some brief descriptions of the early settlers in the area around Cle Elum Lake are described below.

Cle Elum Lake Pioneers, Homesteaders, and Miners in the 1880s and Later[1]

Mill Creek

Very early on, numerous homesteads and cabin sites existed along the east shore of Cle Elum Lake. The homestead of Mr. and Mrs. Henzer lay at the southeast end of the lake. Later, a sawmill was built on the Henzer property and operated by Joe and Dick Welsh, with the Davis brothers as partners. It was located on Mill Creek.

---

[1] According to Robert Bell Sr.

Spring Creek

Spring Creek Hill was about a mile north of Mill Creek, on the main road. A steep road went to the top, and on the right side of the drive there were two homesteads: those of John Brown and Mr. and Mrs. Harrington. A man named Wilson married a Brown daughter, and they also settled there.

Bear Creek

Tom Ambers's cabin was located up the road, just before Bear Creek. Ambers was one of several African-American residents living in the Cle Elum area at the time.

Davis Creek

Cap Davis had a cabin near Davis Creek. When Cap died, his brother took over the homestead and lived there until the government bought all the land along a lakeshore that would eventually be covered by water from the first dam (at the south end of the lake), which was built in 1905–1906.

After passing the Davis Ranch (as it was later called), the road headed down to the lakeshore. The homestead of the A. W. (also known as Dick) Denny family was one mile up the shoreline road. Dick had a tame bear that attracted an audience from time to time. The bear liked the attention, and would climb up a pole with a platform on top and stand on his head, to the delight of onlookers. But the bear did not like being manhandled into a crate on the day the Dennys tried to carry him to a new residence. The group of men left standing in bloodied, torn clothes once their task was completed were a testament to how much he didn't like it.

Newport and Bell Creeks

The road up Newport Creek led next to Newport Hill and then over to the homestead of Jim Bell on Bell Creek.[2] The Bell family had a large, four-room log cabin that was visible from the road. A sign on the building read, "The Travelers Rest." Jim ran a stage line from his place to Fish (Tucquala) Lake and down to Roslyn and Cle Elum, hauling anything the rig would hold. Jim and his brother Con (Cornelius) had blasted a tunnel into solid rock, which had double doors and served as a food cellar.

Jim's wife died in 1885. In the spring of 1889, Jim and Con left for Alaska. The five Bell children were sent to stay with relatives or friends. The one girl, Mary, was the first white girl born at the north end, the original shoreline, of Cle Elum Lake. The local Yakima Indians liked Mary and called her "Queenie."

The Yakimas used to travel their old trail every season to hunt the area and pick berries each fall. The Bell children would sit and watch caravans (up to a mile long) of Yakima braves and their families pass by. At these times, Mary's brothers were told to keep an eye on her, fearing she would be picked up and led away because of the Yakima's fondness for her.

A quarter mile north of the Bell homestead, on the west side of the main road, sat the cabin of a bachelor named Mulser. The Pete La Caff homestead was a half mile beyond Mulser's place, on the east side of the road. Ed Buhrn had a cabin across the road from La Caff. Ed was a fine cook, and he always had fresh bread and cinnamon rolls handy for visitors.

Morgan Creek

The Morgan homestead/ranch was up the main road from La Caff and Buhrn. Mr. and Mrs. Morgan had two sons and three daughters. They were the last to move from their homestead after selling to the government. The Morgan place was used by the first forest warden in the upper Cle Elum, Giddings, who stayed there until the rising lakeshore forced him out.

---

[2] The original north shoreline was where Bell Creek now enters Cle Elum Lake. After 1906, it covered several homestead sites. The present dam was constructed in 1934, extending the present north shore to the Thorp and French Cabin Creek area.

John La Bonn had built a home east across the Cle Elum River and at the top of the original north lakeshore. He eventually left his homestead to the rising lake, headed to town, and became the operator of a Roslyn hotel. A man named Welch lived in a cabin a short distance up the Cle Elum River, on the same side as La Bonn. Welch was remembered for his love of hunting up a meal of black squirrel using his muzzle-loading shotgun.

French Cabin Creek

Ben French had a trapper's cabin on the first bench above the Cle Elum River, where the creek and river join together.

What to See

The Cle Elum District has much to offer the outdoors enthusiast. Hiking and climbing immediately come to mind. Fishing and hunting, in season, are also worthy pastimes. When you come to this area, remember that the summers tend to be hot in the lowlands and very warm even at higher altitudes, so dress accordingly. The temperature also tends to plunge in the evenings, so don't get caught off guard. There are many spectacular hiking trails along the Cle Elum and Teanaway River valleys. Many take the traveler to, or near, mining properties. Even if the mines are not your ultimate goal, a hike like one from the end of the North Fork Teanaway Road, over Ingalls Pass, to Ingalls Lake is sure to take your breath away. The best time to do this is in the early fall before the first snow flies and after the summer's heat has dissipated.

Cle Elum, Roslyn, and Ronald are old coal-mining towns, and the legacy of this past can be seen everywhere. The large mine dumps near the old portals bear testimony to a vibrant past when coal was king and the steam engine powered the land.

Getting There

This section will describe how to reach this general area. Several of the subsections in this chapter contain more detailed information for reaching specific areas within the district.

To get to this region from the western side of the Cascade Mountains, take I-90 over Snoqualmie Pass. To reach Cle Elum, take the US 970 exit, cross over the freeway, and turn left. This road will take you into town. If you wish to go directly to Roslyn and Ronald, take the earlier Roslyn exit. This also puts you on the road to Cle Elum Lake, the Cle Elum River, and Salmon La Sac.

To reach the Cle Elum area from the lower Columbia Basin area, drive I-90 west to the US 970 exit, and turn right and then immediately left into Cle Elum. The highway to Roslyn, Ronald, and points beyond can be followed after passing through the town.

To reach Cle Elum from the upper Columbia Basin, take US 2 west from Wenatchee to the turnoff for US 97, and drive over Swauk (Blewett) Pass. At the Ellensburg turnoff, take the right-hand fork. After the road turns to the west, it will take you directly into Cle Elum and points beyond.

Geology

The Cle Elum District is exciting geologically, which probably accounts for the extent of prospecting and mining throughout the area. The town of Cle Elum is situated at the boundary of the valley alluvium deposits and Eocene nonmarine rocks that carry the many coal seams that drove the early economy of the region. The Eocene rocks extend up the valley of the Cle Elum River to about a mile above the outlet of Cle Elum Lake. From that point, Paleocene-Cretaceous rocks predominate until about five miles above the upper end of the lake. These are often intruded by Tertiary dikes, sills, and small bodies. Just north of the upper end of the lake, two small intrusions of Miocene-Pliocene rock occur, while along the northeastern shore of the lake, there is an intrusion of basic rocks, primarily consisting of gabbro and some serpentine.

Farther up the Cle Elum River, beyond five miles above the upper end of the lake, pre-Tertiary, ultrabasic intrusive rocks predominate, consisting of peridotite and pyroxene, often altered to serpentine. There are also smaller areas of pre-Tertiary andesite and basalt with greenstone, along with Tertiary granitic rocks such as quartz diorite and granite.

Farther upstream in the Tucquala (Fish) Lake area, the eastern side of the river is composed of Mesozoic granitic rock with granite and quartz diorite, which extends east to the Paddy-Go-Easy Pass and Cradle Mountain areas. The Van Epps Pass region hosts a contact between the pre-Tertiary ultrabasic rocks mentioned above and pre-Tertiary andesite, basalt, and greenstone.

The variety of different rocks, each carrying minerals and all interbedded throughout the region, has created a great number of contact zones. These zones provided ripe hunting grounds for the riches that prospectors sought. Many of the prospects and mines in this district were claimed in or adjacent to these zones of contact. When molten volcanic rocks are intruded—or forced under enormous pressure—into cooler, native rock, a chemical exchange of the two takes place. Accelerated by the heat of the molten component, the exchanged chemicals cause new minerals to form. If the intrusion takes place deep below the surface, it may take millions of years to cool. This causes the exchange of chemicals to migrate deeply into the two rock masses, creating extensive contact zones.

The thermal action in these zones can cause metals and minerals that would otherwise be trapped deep within the Earth's crust to rise higher through the hot zone. Millions of years after the intrusive rocks cool, via the weathering of the surface as it is uplifted through an orogenic (mountain-building) process, these treasures are laid bare.

Background Information

We'll begin our study of the Cle Elum mining area by examining mineral properties at the district's south boundary, working up the Cle Elum River to the east or west of the waterway, or as the workings are encountered. The data has been derived from geologist's field notes, Northwest Underground Explorations outings, conversations with people who have knowledge of the region's historical past, and published or unpublished information accumulated from the Department of Natural Resources library in Olympia, Washington.

L. K. Hodges named 92 claims in the Cle Elum Mining District in *Mining in the Pacific Northwest*, written in 1897.[3] Most turned out to be no more than prospects. Progress on claim and tunnel development was current in Hodges' book only up to 1896. We found considerably more tunneling and building sites on certain workings, obviously done after his reporting ended. Numerous workings were driven up to 125 feet or less by miners or prospectors who were trying to define a ledge or vein or locate rich ore for assay, with which to promote the mining claims. Often the tunnels were short because they had been blasted to a point at which the powder fumes (which caused long-lasting headaches) and dust inspired the immediate need to bring fresh air from outside to the breast of the adit so that work could continue in a speedy and cost-effective manner. Lack of funds, minerals, or both also explain the abundance of short tunnels and shafts.

Some of the creek, river, and lake names in the district have been changed since the 1800s, so we've had to do some sleuthing to make sense of it all. These inconsistencies will be noted as they come up in the text and the old and present names correlated. Original claim names sometimes disappeared with new ownership, so we'll match current and old names when possible.

Where they make sense, we'll provide hike ratings. The ratings are meant to be a guide only. It is your responsibility to judge the circumstances and decide whether to embark on a particular hike. A planned outing to try locating a certain claim can become even more rewarding when you come across a cabin site or tunnel unexpectedly, adding one more piece to the puzzle, or making a new find altogether. Even if you never find a mine site, these areas make for some very scenic hiking, more than compensating for an

---

[3] Hodges received much of his information through word of mouth from mine owners and prospectors, each promoting their properties. Descriptions drawn from his writings were not always proven to be correct but in many instances led us to investigate until we found the truth.

otherwise unfulfilled adventure. Considering the amount of mining and prospecting done in this region, it is not unusual for a trail to pass within a few feet of an adit obscured by underbrush—often the one obstacle to discovery.

Many pioneers and area founders participated in mining above and beyond their regular work. Their names appear frequently in association with mining history, creeks, rivers, lakes, and mountains. Hiking to a historic mine site also gives you the chance to rockhound the workings' tailing piles and find crystals or other attractive minerals, or perhaps chip at a well-exposed vein sample from an interrupted mining operation.[4]

Roads marked "4×4" on maps might be original mine-to-market access roads serving one or more claims. Erosion has rendered some of them impassable, even to four-wheel drive (4WD) vehicles. When you reach the end of such a road, you will have to hike to the mineralized areas. There might be an old dig in the form of a trench, pit, or adit with tailings where exposed minerals can be collected. When you leave any area, no trace of your passing through should be visible. Make sure you backfill your dig. Some places you come across will seem too remote for visitors, but rock-framed fire rings prove otherwise.

Finding a wilderness lake on a hot, sweaty hike can be very rewarding in itself. Add to it the discovery of a nearby mineralized area, and go for it! Keep in mind that weathering exposes new minerals yearly. We have found this to be true, especially in remote areas where there is little possibility of recent activity.

If you're planning to collect field samples for grinding and panning at home, bag and mark the location of the find. We were once involved in a frustrating situation in which several samples were taken (nice, rough gold flakes were found once the samples were panned at home), but the spot couldn't be found again.

Trails and Roads

To be fully prepared for hiking in the mountains and among the mines of the district, you will need the best maps available: Green Trails maps for Stevens Pass #178, Chiwaukum Mountains #177, Kachess Lake #208, and Mount Stuart #209. In addition, USGS 7.5 Minute Series maps of Davis Peak and Mount Stuart are essential for more precise location finding. Among the many Forest Service trails that traverse the region, there are numerous open ridges and low hills, with some well-worn game trails that are scenic and worth following, provided you know your limits. Some of the most noteworthy trails lead to mountains west of the Cle Elum River: Red Mountain, Davis Peak, Goat Mountain, and Cathedral Rock. East of the river are Jolly Mountain, Sasse Mountain, Koppen Mountain, Esmeralda Peak, Hawkins Mountain, Ingalls Peak, Huckleberry Mountain, and various trails along the extensive Wenatchee Mountain Range. The secondary road system will allow you to travel a short distance from the main road, but every year more are gated and most of the 4×4 roads have eroded into wide trails.

The Mines
Miscellaneous Mineral Locations Outside the Cle Elum Mining Area

Introduction

We have not visited these prospects or claims. We will provide locations, but you as a hiker, history, or rockhound aficionado will have to plot your route and check access to properties (remember to get permission if the property is privately owned). No hike ratings are available.

Economic depression was setting in for the Cle Elum and Ellensburg area by 1891. Mining activity was again accelerating as old digs were reclaimed and new property recorded. Unfortunately, the rush to wealth was slowed in places by conflicts or court litigation between corporations and individuals over property titles.

---

[4] Gold and silver mining was halted by the U.S. government during World Wars I and II. All mining efforts were geared toward acquiring strategic metals such as antimony, chromium, copper, iron, molybdenum, tungsten, titanium, zinc, etc. Some mines never reopened, waiting to be relocated, perhaps by you.

Big Creek Mining District
South of Easton

Big Creek Claim

This is located on the USGS 7.5 Minute Series Easton and Blowout Mountain map. The claim is said to be five miles southeast of Easton. That is all the information we have. Happy hunting.

Grand Entry

The original owner of the Grand Entry was Patrick Twomey.[5] After leading a solitary life of nomadic prospecting over several decades leading up to this 1891 iron discovery, Twomey had worked his way from the mouth of the Teanaway River, up the Wenatchee Mountain Range, over Easton Ridge, followed Cabin Creek and Little Creek. In 1891, he became the owner of the promising Grand Entry Iron Mine. Thomas Johnson of Seattle bought the mine from him in 1892.

Negro Baby Iron Lode

Discovered by D. W. Hill in 1888, this iron lode is located near the Grand Entry.

Ellensburg Improvement Company

Hill had sold the Negro Baby Iron Lode to the Ellensburg Improvement Company by the end of 1892. The company was working the Negro Baby and the Iron Heart, Iron Crest, Uncle Sam, and Brother Jonathan Claims. Two railroad cars full of ore were mined from the Uncle Sam and Brother Jonathan iron veins. Red and gray hematite ore was blasted off the ledges in blocks and sent to the Tacoma Chamber of Commerce. A Mr. Michals delivered several specimens, taken from an immense deposit in the Big Creek district, to Tacoma for assay. The hard ore was black streaked with white and wine-colored crystals, and it took a high polish. Peter Nelson showed Big Creek ore around the town of Cle Elum. The samples from his claim were black and red hematite.

The location of and directions to the Grand Entry and Ellensburg Improvement Company are vague. According to 1891 information, the trip to the mines begins about two miles west of Cle Elum where the Cle Elum River flows into the Yakima River. Turn south up Summit Creek (which we assume to be today's Tillman Creek) one mile, and then go along the Iron Mountain Gulch trail (not on recent maps) to the mines.

Red Rock Mine

Located in the northwest ¼ of the northwest ¼ of Section 20, T19N, R15E, as seen on the USGS 7.5 Minute Series maps for Ronald, Cle Elum, and Frost Mountain.

This mine is somewhere within the above-mentioned area. Red Rock was listed in 1942 as a nickel and chromium mine.[6] The property had six claims (possibly the Grand Entry and the five Ellensburg Improvement Company claims). Owner R. H. Turton worked some open cuts and two adits driven into a nickel ledge 100 to 500 feet wide in graphite schist overlain by continental sediments.

---

[5] Also spelled "Twomey" in early records.
[6] Many of the iron mines never panned out but were sought as a source for strategic World War II minerals, such as nickel and chromium.

Claims Southwest of Ellensburg

Taneum Iron Claim

This deposit of iron ore is said to be 10 feet thick and is located 12 miles southeast of Easton on North Fork Taneum Creek.

Manastash Creek Claim

This claim lies at the headwaters of South Fork Manastash Creek.

Frost Mountain Agates and Geodes

Use Green Trails maps of Thorp #242, Cle Elum #241 and Easton #240 to access the areas. For a closer view of the exact site within a section, use the USGS 7.5 Minute Maps of Frost Mountain adn Quartz Mountain.

From Cle Elum (on I-90) go about 20 miles to exit 101 (Thorp map #242). Drive west ½ mile to the Thorp Cemetery Road, turn right and drive five miles, where the same road becomes Road 33. Referring to the Cle Elum map #241, drive five more miles on Road 33 and you will arrive at Taneum Campground. Continue three more miles to the Ice Water Campground. From this campground, follow the south trending serpentine Road 3330 for eight miles to Road 3100, go another four miles west on Road 3100 (refer to Easton map #240) and you will arrive at the Frost Mountain area.

South Fork Manastash Creek Gold Placers

Located on the USGS 7.5 Minute maps for Frost Mountain and Quartz Mountain. This gold panning site starts west of Frost Meadows and parallels along the south side of Road 3100 (refer to the lower ½ of Section 7 and Section 8, T18N, R15E, on the USGS Frost Mountain Map) for about one mile up the creek in Frost Meadows, and toward Taneum Lake. Check your *Gold and Fish* booklet regarding any water you pan.[7] No production information is available.

Agates

Millions of years ago, erupting volcanoes sent red-hot lava across the countryside, which hardened into basalt. As the lava cooled, gas bubbles formed inside it and then remained in the solid rock. After a long period of time, silica (glassy mineralized dust or sand suspended in water) seeped through the basalt and deposited in the gas bubbles. As the basalt weathers away, the nodules, or agate-filled gas bubbles, are exposed. Different minerals in the silica cause the variety of colors you see in agates. Manganese salts make beautiful silhouettes on cut and polished surfaces, which are known as *picture agates.*

Geodes

The term *geode* dates back to 1619. "Geo" is the base Greek word for geode, meaning "earth" or "round." A geode is a hollow ball of agate that has not completely filled with silica. Instead, the interior is lined with crystals. From the outside, geodes are nothing special to look at; but inside they sometimes sparkle with indescribable beauty. Less common are those lined with white or bluish-gray, grape-like chalcedony (a smooth form of opal-like quartz), or colorless crystals of calcite, which has many and varied crystal forms. More exotic geodes might have crystals of lead (galena), zinc, iron sulfide, or numerous other minerals. You might even find one containing water that has been sealed in for millions of years. Geodes come in all sizes and shapes. Around Cle Elum and Ellensburg, they are usually pea- to egg-size, occasionally ranging up to six inches in diameter.

---

[7] Good maps along with written directions make locating much easier. USGS 7.5 Minute Series quadrangle maps are best. Rock and gem shops, rockhounding clubs, and the Chamber of Commerce in the areas you visit have useful information. The *Gold and Fish Book* can be found at your regional Washington Department of Fish and Wildlife office.

At Frost Mountain lookout, hike southeast below the bluff. In the basalt, hammer and chisel (using eye protection) for the quartz and calcite-lined geodes. Search the talus for blue-gray agates.

Manastash Ridge Pack Trail Mineral Sites

Between Quartz Mountain and Mount Clifty, there are several comparatively new mineral-collecting digs. Calcite crystals in association with coarse quartz crystals and zeolites (whitish silicate minerals usually discovered in lava cavities) have been found in holes up to eight inches wide. Red jasper and green chalcedony can be taken from veins up to six inches in width. The area is heavily volcanized, allowing for a wide variety of minerals.

This property is located on the USGS 7.5 Minute Series maps of Quartz Mountain and Mount Clifty. Park at the end of Quartz Mountain Road (Quartz Mountain Campground). On the pack trail (1388) toward Mount Clifty, go 1½ miles to find a group of six digs in the northeast $1/8$ of Section 5 and southeast corner of Section 32 on its south section line of the USGS map for Quartz Mountain. Two miles up the trail, the first of five more sites is located to the left of the elevation printed on the map (5762x). The "X" marks the spot to the left of the trail on the USGS map for Mount Clifty. The others (this is a guesstimate) are spread north along Section 30's north/south centerline.

You will need expert cross-country skills from here, because there is no trail on the map. From the "X" to the next dig site is about 600 feet and left of the line. Six hundred feet north and also left of the line is the third area. The next is approximately 800 feet up and on the centerline, where the word "North" appears on the map. The last site is near the "o" in North. If you plan an over-nighter, the Taneum shelter across North Fork Taneum Creek will accommodate you. Check with USFS.

Cascade Mining Company

There are no indications of what kind of ore the owner of this property was prospecting. No minerals show, and only a little fractured quartz appears on the face. This property is located on the USGS 7.5 Minute Series map of Frost Mountain, in Section 26, T19N, R15E, three miles west of the Taneum Creek campground. The portal is at the road, on the north side of Taneum Creek, and driven in Easton schist. Its length is unknown.

Silver Tip Mine

Located in the southeast ¼ of Section 28, T19N, R15E, as seen on the USGS 7.5 Minute Series map of Frost Mountain.

Owners V. C. Denny of Ellensburg and T. F. Gannon of Seattle's Ballard area had a mercury mine tunnel located on a hill 250 feet north and above the South Fork Taneum Creek. The workings start in the Manastash formation, continuing for 300 feet to a contact with black, carbonaceous, highly sheared Easton schist, and

Reported to be the first building in Ellensberg, the Robber's Roost was a typical small log cabin. Similar buildings would have been built just to the west in Cle Elum in the early days. (*Wilhelm's Magazine, The Coast,* March 1904)

into the schist 100 feet. At the contact area, two drifts were driven 150 feet in either direction. A zone 12 feet wide carried cinnabar and native mercury. Assays showed low-grade ore. Five tons of ore is recorded as having been shipped out.

H-O-M-E Mining Company (Silver Tip), 1943

Located on the USGS 7.5 Minute Series map of Frost Mountain, two miles west of the Cascade Mining Company claim area.

Denny and Gannon sold to H-O-M-E in 1943. H-O-M-E in turn expanded to 27 claims within Sections 26, 27, 28, and 34, T19N, R15E, of which five claims were patented. The two principle producing claims were the Gold Crown and Silver Tip. Their tunnels reportedly shipped 9.5 tons of ore. A thousand feet of adits and shafts were the extent of development.

Burbank Valley Gold Panning, 1922

In Kittitas Canyon, 15 miles south of Ellensburg, prospector and homesteader Jack Lyon reported gold in paying quantities. Jack's residence was near the town of Roza, according to a short news column from *The Pacific Mining Journal*. Burbank Valley is the target area for your exploration.

Magpie Canyon

Rated at A-2. This property contained one lode gold claim located in the northeast ¼ of Section 34, T19N, R17E, on the USGS 7.5 Minute Series map of Thorp. It sits seven miles north of Ellensburg where a seasonal run-off creek, coming from the center of Section 27, follows Magpie Canyon to the northeast corner of Section 34 and continues toward (and ends at) a canal flume, the Yakima River, and US 97.

Rockhounding in the Cle Elum and Ellensburg Areas

Ellensburg Blue Agate

In about 1930, this unusual blue agate caught the attention of rockhounders in general, but its existence was first announced in 1913 by Ellensburg jeweler J. N. O. Thomson. Thomson had befriended Yakima Native Americans, who showed him samples of the blue agate and described where it could be found.[8] One well-known Yakima Indian woman, Cecelia, told Thomson to walk with the sun over his left shoulder, which would help him locate the agate in its natural, earth-tone state.

Thomson sold blue agate jewelry, "Ellensburg Blue,"[9] in his store up to the time he retired in 1941. His son, John Prentiss Thomson, wrote a great deal about the geological history of Ellensburg, including a booklet titled *Ellensburg Blue*.

The current popular hunting areas for these semiprecious stones are Reeser Creek, Dry Creek, Green Canyon, Horse Canyon, First Creek, and Red Top Mountain. Some of the old digs are now on private land, so ask permission before hunting, and obey any posted signs.

A less strenuous way to search out the blue agates is to walk the power lines indicated on USGS 7.5 Minute Series maps of the lowlands. The best time is after the frosts have worked their yearly process of raising rock material to the surface. Domestic cattle and other hoofed animals sometimes help the rockhounder by dislodging the agates. You can find lots of varieties of minerals in the mountains, hills, and

---

[8] An Ellensburg Blue agate was found in 1958 that weighed 21½ ounces and was worth $1,500 at that time. The only other place in the U.S. where you can find blue agate is the Mojave Desert region of California, but its best does not match that in Kittitas County, Washington.
[9] The Ellensburg Blue and crystal-filled geodes originated in the Teanaway basalt, which then weathered to rusty-red soil that held the gems until they were found.

valleys around Ellensburg and Cle Elum. Many of the tailings outside hardrock mining tunnels can be dug up and screened.[10] Cle Elum and Ellensburg Chamber of Commerce, the area's rock shops, and local gem and mineral clubs are some sources of information about rock- and gem-hunting areas.

Teanaway Valley and Headwaters Area Geology

This region includes areas in and near Ingalls Creek; Turnpike Creek; De Roux Creek; the North, South, and Middle Forks of the Teanaway River; and as far south as Yellow Hill. The entire region is almost completely underlain by greenstone and serpentine. A spot in the lower southwest section of the valley consists of Teanaway basalt. Teanaway basalt is reddish in color and has vesicular[11] flow tops. In some places in south and southwest Teanaway country, Columbia River basalt can be identified by its mostly gray to black appearance.

At the northwest reaches of the Mount Stuart batholith,[12] the rugged and spectacular peaks of the Stuart range stand out—the result of glacially eroded batholithic granite. The area was formed about 88 million years ago, in the Cretaceous era. Subducted rock to the south of the Stuart batholith has greatly deformed slabs of ancient ocean coastal-plain crust (most of the rock is serpentine that formed when peridotite reacted with water), adding to some of the Ingalls formation of the metamorphic complex. These large volcanic masses folded and intruded into other sedimentary rocks at their contacts. In the Teanaway Valley, the most abundant rock is basalt, which forms the dark rock outcrops that exist today.

Teanaway-Swauk Prairie Cemetery

This cemetery is located above the Ballard schoolhouse on the USGS 7.5 Minute Series map of Swauk Prairie, in the northwest ¼ of Section 29, T20N, R17E.

In 1884, a group of early settlers—George Virden, Jesse Evens, and Ed Allen—gathered in a committee to select the site of the cemetery. In about 1889, A. F. York, county surveyor, platted the land. The five-acre area was bought from the Northern Pacific Railroad.

Teanaway Valley Mineral Claims

Yellow Hill Red Agate and Jasper Claim

Rated at A-2 to A-3, this site is located in the center north ½ of Section 21, T21N, R15E, as seen on the USGS 7.5 Minute Series map of Teanaway Butte. The Green Trails map of Mount Stuart #209 also shows the area. Road access begins at the Teanaway town site (USGS 7.5 Minute map for Teanaway). Take US 970 northeast for four miles. Head north following the Teanaway Road 5½ to 6 miles to Teanaway Campground (on the USGS 7.5 Minute map of Teanaway Butte). Follow the Middle Fork Teanaway River Road to a gate about 1½ miles from Teanaway Campground. Drive two miles to Indian Camp Campground. A road that varies in condition from year to year winds its way into the northwest ¼ of the northeast ¼ of Section 21, T21N, R15E. Here the road ends, and Trail #1222, on Green Trails Map #209 of Mount Stuart, begins. A ridge deposit lies 500 feet up the steep trail at 3,200 feet. Use an altimeter to keep track of your elevation. The claim has a 15-foot adit and a bulldozed area to search through. You can also dig through the nearby canyons.

William Cumby of Tacoma and Earl Waddell from Cle Elum, who had found jasper-agate in Teanaway basalt, leased this claim from the Northern Pacific Railroad in 1955. Jasper-agate occurs in veinlets and irregular lenses or pods along shear planes that strike and dip in various directions. The

---

[10] The minerals that rockhounds seek have often been cast aside by miners. In taking ore, they often discarded quartz crystals, jasper, agates, chalcedony, and quite a bit of high-grade ore because they were careless or couldn't see it in the low light of the mines. Check rust-colored rock by hammering; it could be beautiful high-grade ore, waiting for a good home.
[11] Containing many small cavities created by trapped gases.
[12] A mass of igneous rock intruded into older sedimentary or volcanic formations that often create large landmasses.

Settlers in Teanaway Valley Agriculture, raising livestock, timber harvesting, and some mineral prospecting "as time allowed" were among the occupations of the early settlers in the Teanaway Valley and its tributary creeks.

In the lower Teanaway Valley, area records show that in the early 1880s Theodore Cooper (son of Harbin Cooper, a prospector and regional businessman) and wife, Mary, settled on one of the largest ranches in Teanaway Valley.[13] Several Cooper grandchildren were known to still be living in the Cle Elum area into the 1950s.

The James Masterson family, brother of Bat Masterson of old west fame, came to the Teanaway-Swauk area via Snoqualmie Pass in 1878.[14] They had a place in the Swauk District, but moved shortly after Yakima Indians killed the Perkins family, who had lived nearby. The Mastersons took refuge in a fort at Ellensburg. After a year, they returned to the Swauk for a time and then moved closer to Cle Elum. Masterson Road, leading to the farm site, exists today in Section 33, T20N, R16E, as seen on the USGS 7.5 Minute Series map of Teanaway. One of their three children, Hattie Masterson, was the first schoolteacher in Teanaway. Hattie's brother Harry ran the family farm until the mid-1950s. Harry's son Bat took over after Harry's death.

Around the turn of the century, Miles and Minnie Ballard homesteaded a 320-acre ranch. They sold and traded their garden produce and livestock to miners and other locals. Timber from their trees was cut into ties for the Casland Railroad around 1911 to 1915.[15] When it came to gaining a profit, Miles was known in the valley as the best horse trader. The Ballards later homesteaded another quarter section of land on which they raised 3,000 head of cattle. In 1905, they bought the old Knight homestead, which became the Ballard Ranch at the south end of Teanaway Valley (Section 30, T20N, R17E on the USGS map of Teanaway) just north of the West Ballard Hill Road. An old store on the Ballard place was used as the first church in the valley. It later burned down in a prairie fire.

---

largest lens was 12 inches wide, in a mineralized vein inside the 15-foot tunnel. Cumby and Waddell took a few hundred pounds of the agate material, which had good color. The remaining face of the vein is white, colorless chalcedony.

Within a radius of about 300 feet from the adit, several other stringers and lenses up to 12 inches have been exposed, all showing good color. Some of the land in the area is administered by the Bureau of Land Management and open to collecting. As of 1998, the claim was inactive, although the railroad might have its land posted. If this is the case, you must get permission before entering. Much of the land is used to graze cattle, so when in the area close all gates behind you as you pass through them.

Other Rockhounding Sites

You can find a variety of agates in the Teanaway basalt across a large area that includes the ridge between Easton and Cle Elum Lake, Yellow Hill, Casland, and north and south of the Red Top Mountain area. Ellensburg Blue is mostly found in the Ellensburg formation (north of Ellensburg in Horse and Green Canyons). This area is covered in alluvium left by the erosion of the Teanaway basalt. Apparently you can find small, stout amethyst crystals in a canyon on the east side of the Middle Fork of Teanaway River, roughly two miles from the Teanaway River Road, but explicit directions to this spot are not available.

---

[13] The lower Cooper ranch was cleared by Chinese laborers.
[14] The Masterson brothers were involved in gold mining in the Swauk Mining District. In 1879, they were hired by several Chinese to pack gold (in large sacks) to Ellensburg. In 1881, they employed Chinese workers to dig four miles of irrigation ditches on their ranch.
[15] Casland was a semipermanent base for the Teanaway Valley logging operations.

Mine Claims in the Upper Teanaway Valley

Keystone Group of Claims

These properties are located in the southeast ¼ of Section 6, to the north ½ of Section 8, T22N, R15E, as seen on the USGS map of Mount Stuart.

The original Keystone Group of six claims, consisting of the Keystone, Nickel, Cottontail, Keystone Fraction, Clawson, and Green Bear, was owned by the Washington Quicksilver Mining Company, Incorporated. Adolph Elsner Sr., John Grosso, and John Somers from Cle Elum and Ellensburg held these properties. Gerritt D'Ablaing, Charles Flummerfelt, and Cornelius J. Vanderbilt appear as part owners in an undated report. Elsner later became sole owner.

The main ledge was reported to be from 20 feet to 110 feet wide, carrying cinnabar assaying from eight to 23 percent mercury, and $2.40 to $15 per ton in gold. The claims were prospected and exposed by several open cuts and short tunnels.

Skookum Copper Mining Company, 1903

Rated at D-3. A scenic, physically demanding seven-mile day hike (round trip) will take you to this property located in the northwest ¼ of the southwest ¼ of Section 9, T22N, R15E, as seen on the USGS 7.5 Minute Series map of Mount Stuart (elevation of 4,500 feet). It lies west of a pack trail (#1393 on the Green Trails map for Mount Stuart) and south of a seasonal creek gulch that flows east into the Middle Fork Teanaway River. This property is on the south end of the Keystone Group.

In 1908, George Koppen was president of the Skookum Mining Company, whose miners and road crew were getting the camp and roads cleared of winter debris. Avalanches, floods, and wind were destructive forces to be dealt with yearly.[16]

Skookums' Snow Avalanche

Inclement weather was responsible for an incident on Saturday, March 5, 1910. Ed Simmons, Skookum mine superintendent,[17] was fast asleep at 4:00 A.M. when a slide caused by heavy snowfall roared down the gulch that contained the Skookum surface buildings and other mine structures. The office in which Ed was sleeping was hit and pushed off its foundation. Sixteen men were asleep in the bunkhouse when it was slammed by the avalanche, but none were hurt. When a crew of men found Simmons, his body was at room temperature. He hadn't been hurt, but the shock of the slide had caused him to have a fatal heart attack. It took a party of 10 men from Roslyn all weekend to retrieve Ed's body because of deep snow, high water, and clogged roads.

The office of the Skookum Mine was this unimposing clapboard building. It somehow escaped the snow damage that was inflicted on many of the other mine buildings in the winter of 1915-16. (Grace Browitt Elkins collection)

---

[16] The large number of local stockholders would anticipate how much money was to be used before production could start each season.
[17] Formerly a foreman at Coal Mine #5 in Roslyn, Washington.

The remains of the Skookum Mine's bunkhouse in 1916 following the devastating avalanche that swept it away the previous winter. The mine's office building can be seen at the far right. (Grace Browitt Elkins collection)

The Skookum Mine bunkhouse in 1915, the year before an avalanche destroyed it. On the far left is the mine's office building that was spared from the avalanche's fury. The building was occupied at the time of the disaster, and the occupants were swept down the valley to the mine's office. (Grace Browitt Elkins collection)

In 1916, the Skookum Mine's mill shows the ravages of the snows that badly damaged it during the previous winter. (Grace Browitt Elkins collection)

As interest in mining waned and ownerships dissolved, Adolph Sr. dropped the Keystone Group of claims while retaining his 1880s Elsner Mine (north of and on the Keystone Group's north boundary line). He became sole owner of the Skookum Mine until he passed away in February 1919. His son, Adolph Jr., then acquired the two mines. Adolph Jr. evidently reacquired the Elsner Claim after O. F. Fry gave up the Nickelodeon #1 and #2 Claims (Elsner) in 1939. Jr. worked the mines off and on in his spare time, holding the claims until his death on December 1, 1981, at the age of 83. The properties were mined for, or noted as containing, quicksilver, gold, copper, and nickel deposits.

This remote area sees the occasional hiker or horseback camper. In the 1920s and 30s, there was a U.S. Forest Service shelter near the Skookum Mine (southeast ¼ of the southeast ¼ in Section 9, T22N, R15E, on the USGS map for Mount Stuart).

Getting There

Take the Teanaway road from Swauk Prairie seven miles to the North Fork road that follows the Teanaway River. De Roux Campground is 12 miles farther. At this point (with maps in hand), leave De Roux Campground via the De Roux Creek trail. After 0.3 mile (five minutes), a bridge (though there was no bridge in 1999) crosses over the creek. Follow Trail #1392 (Green Trails map of Mount Stuart) for 0.8 mile (roughly 30 minutes). Here the trail goes through the creek. Five hundred feet farther is the start of a 1.2-mile, 28-corner switchback trail (#1392), with an 800-foot elevation gain (from 4,200 feet up to 5,000 feet), which takes about 45 minutes to hike. Go northwest through a pass to start down a five-switchback hill to Trail #1393 (20 minutes). Go south on this Middle Fork Teanaway River trail for 0.6 mile (25 to 30 minutes). This is the Skookum Mining Camp area.

The mill at the Skookum Mine in 1915. Dumps of the mine's adits can be seen in the foreground. This was just prior to an avalanche and heavy snows that severely damaged the building. (Grace Browitt Elkins collection)

One of the three adits of the Skookum Mine in the Teanaway Valley. This may be the tunnel closest to the mill. Notice the timbers stacked just outside the portal. (Grace Browitt Elkins collection)

The building to the right is the mill of the Skookum Mine in the Teanaway Valley of the Cle Elum mining district. The building, just left of center, is the sawmill. The mine's three adits bore into the ridge just off this photo, to the right. All are now collapsed, but an interesting feature of the mine dumps is that each dump displays a completely different type of mineral. (Grace Browitt Elkins collection)

The first indications that the claim site is near are the items of mining debris along the trailside: riveted pipe, hand-forged artifacts, etc. The present trail avoids the mining camp, where slight traces of the old path can be seen. To find the mill site, at 0.6 mile, go about 100 feet west (uphill) of the new trail. The claim has three adits, the closest of which is 100 feet west of the mill site. Water drains from its collapsed portal. The tailings show this to be about 100 to 200 feet of tunnel. The main tunnel is 200 feet northwest and above. Three tailing piles spread from tunnels to the edge of the mill area. The rock nearest the ore-processing works is pinkish-brown and was reduced to grit sand for shipment to the smelter. The second pile of rock is serpentine, and the other is sandstone. No significant sulfides are visible. The 100-foot–long discovery tunnel is 200 feet above the main adit, and is open but in unstable condition at the portal. Although this is a copper mine, its lack of sulfides in obvious amounts is a puzzle.

This remote mine offers a scenic but hard hike (66 switchback corners roundtrip), so be prepared.

Hiking Suggestions

This region has several fine hikes to choose from, depending on your ability and physical condition. Check out the Green Trails map of Mount Stuart #209, and go for it!

Brown Bear Mining Company, 1896

Not rated. This property is located at the headwaters of the Middle Fork of the Teanaway River. The only mention of a Brown Bear Claim in the upper Teanaway Valley is an undated reference about the Cle Elum Mining District. The company's principal owners were three men from Roslyn: George Koppen, a Mr. Hardman, and August De Roux.

George Koppen has a mountain named for him; Mr. Hardman had his 15 minutes of fame; and a creek was named after De Roux, evidently for infamy, as the following look into De Roux's personal life revealed in a 1907 *Cle Elum Tribune* newspaper:

November; for several months a moving spirit into mining ventures took place near the Mt. Stuart area. De Roux had been developing copper propositions. He convinced a number of locals of his wonderful copper mine. Many bought stock. Others he persuaded to work as miners. Samples of copper ore that De Roux brought to Cle Elum seemed conclusive, and he had little trouble securing investors' confidence, plus all the help and credit needed. The true condition of things relating to De Roux and his character were exposed when miner Dan Cammeron's paycheck bounced at the Cle Elum State Bank. A warrant was sworn out for De Roux, and the marshal brought [him] to Cle Elum. De Roux insisted everything would be straightened out. He paid Cammeron a portion of the owed paycheck, which caused Cammeron to withdraw the charge against De Roux. The next day, De Roux was not to be found.

A steam-powered air pump (compressor) lies among the remains of the Skookum Mine's mill site. These devices were in common use on the steam locomotives of the day, but they were seldom found at mining sites. Steam pressure drove the pistons at one end, which were directly linked to the air cylinders at the other. (Victor Pisoni photo)

On January 2, 1909, August De Roux was hauled before Judge Willis for a different offense. A warrant had been issued against him on a forgery charge. It was shown that De Roux had given as security for $5 and a quantity of liquor some 105,000 shares of illegally issued mining stock for an unknown mine. De Roux had forged the signature of the mining company's treasurer on the certificates. The court placed $1,500 bail against him for an appearance before the Superior Court, and in default of those bonds he was put in the county jail. The past associates he had stiffed lost all confidence in him. Following the date of this final event, De Roux's name disappears from Kittitas County records.

Beautiful Snow Prospect[18]

Not rated. The ore from this property was said to contain a trace of gold and silver, as shown in a 1989 report. The prospect is located approximately midway up the centerline of Section 3 (west line for the northeast ¼), T22N, R15E, on the USGS 7.5 Minute Series map of Mount Stuart. It lies at an elevation of about 4,800 feet.

The prospect consists of a discovery pit in serpentine with highly altered white rock showing an irregular vein varying from 4 to 10 inches wide. The vein follows the foliation of serpentine rock that is sheared.

Lake Ennis Prospect

Rated at A-2. Ore samples from the open-cut area carry traces of gold, silver (1.7 ounces), copper (2.2 percent), and a trace of lead. The prospect, also known as the Gallagher Head Lake Prospect, is located in the southeast ¼ of the northeast ¼ of Section 33, T23N, R15E, at an elevation of 6,000 feet on the USGS 7.5 Minute Series map of Mount Stuart.

The sawmill at the Skookum Mine in 1916 shows that it escaped the damage that ruined other buildings at the mine during the previous winter. (Grace Browitt Elkins collection)

---

[18] The Beautiful Snow Prospect is located in the area originally occupied by the Chesapeake Group of five claims, established in 1896 by John Mulligan. Mulligan reported an assay of $13.00 in gold per ton from surface ore.

For easy access, travel via the Cle Elum River Road, up to the South Fork of Fortune Creek, and then via the 4×4 road to Gallagher Head Lake. Park at the south end of the lake and hoof it 400 feet up the west slope of Peak X6765T. Using an altimeter, start looking at the 6,000-foot level, where you'll see greenstone and an open cut dug in iron-stained irregular zones.

Tip Top

Rated at D-4. The ore contains gold, silver, and copper. The property, also known as the Grizzly Bear #1 and the Surprise #1 and #2, lies at an elevation of 5,200 to 6,000 feet in the southwest ¼ of Section 27, and southeast ¼ of Section 28, T23N, R15E, on the USGS 7.5 Minute Series map of Mount Stuart, and the Green Trails map of Mount Stuart #209. Two hiking trails approach this area (check the maps); take your pick.

The Ballard Gold Mining and Milling Company was the original claimant and developer of this property. It includes a 35-foot shaft and an adit (now caved) driven into a pyritized fracture zone in dacite porphyry–intruded serpentine rock. Ore was recovered from the claim, as indicated by tailings from a small, primitive mill constructed on the site. Samples of these minerals were tested in 1989, and they indicated the presence of gold (0.34 ounces per ton), silver (1.0 ounce), and 0.02 percent copper.

Lake Ann Prospect

Rated at C-3, this prospect was located in the center of the southwest ¼ of Section 22, T23N, R15E, on the USGS map of Mount Stuart.

The hike and chance to camp at Lake Ann are more compelling reasons to take this trail than the prospect itself. The workings are off the trail on the mountain slope at 6,000 feet. There, a shallow pit waits to be admired by those who are easily amused. There is no gold, only a trace of silver, and minimal copper. The area has a variety of serpentine rock types, some quartz, and barite veinlets in some of the highly altered serpentine. This is an interesting place for the geologically minded, but too far to go just to rockhound.

Joe J. Morris and Hope Claims

Rated at D-4, the ore in these claims assayed in silver. The claims are located in the southwest ¼ of Section 25, and northwest ¼ of Section 36, T23N, R15E, south and southeast of Long Pass. Use the USGS map of Mount Stuart and the Green Trails map of Mount Stuart #209.

The Joe Morris Prospect has a shallow pit on a ridge and a 150-foot adit running into serpentine rock (but no minerals in sight). The serpentine rock on the Hope Claim has veins of quartz and calcite, and only a trace of silver is visible.

South Mount Stuart Prospect

Rated at E-5 (this site is remote) and containing ore that assayed in gold and silver, this property is located in the northwest ¼ of Section 30, T23N, R16E, on the USGS 7.5 Minutes series map of Mount Stuart and the Green Trails map for Mount Stuart #209.

The claim has a shaft and two adits that are presently caved. There is only a trace of gold and silver.

East Section Teanaway River/Ingalls Creek Area

Grandview Copper Claim

Rated at E-5 (remote). The ore in this claim contained copper. The Grandview is located in the southwest ¼ along the north/south line of Section 33, T23N, R16E, at 6,000 feet elevation, and south of Peak 6417T. Use the USGS 7.5 Minute Series map of Enchantment Lakes.

In 1889, Will Johnson, E. Connell, and Jack Griffin of Cle Elum had three miners at work driving over 100 feet of tunnel that was expected to strike a solid ledge. These three owners bonded the claims to L. F. McConnihe of Roslyn, who was a representative for some eastern copper men. The 1897 Hodges report lists the owners as Paul Gaston, J. T. Hamlin, and Dr. R. C. Corey.

They ran a tunnel into a 10 to 12-foot outcrop ledge with a pay streak 12 to 48 inches wide. They mined native copper surrounded by black oxide. A crosscut tunnel was headed toward the ledge, which they hoped would tap it at a depth of 140 to 150 feet.

By 1900, the Grandview was producing some high-grade ore. Several chunks of native copper weighing 100 pounds were mined from the digs. In 1948, L. H. West of Cle Elum became the property's owner. He listed copper, gold, and nickel as the ore minerals that he sought.

The claim area at present has four adits ranging from 13 to 113 feet long, some pits, and a trench 40 feet long exposing felsite lenses in serpentine rock. Cuprite, chalcopyrite, magnetite, chromite, and pyrite were found in branching shear zones from six inches to six feet wide. Sampled ore was recorded at up to 11.6 percent copper, with a trace of gold and a trace of silver.

For the Rockhound
Interesting peridotite with scattered specks of copper has been found in this area.

Getting There
Three routes lead to this spot, and none are easy. Use the aforementioned map, and choose your course.

Copper Glance/Clean Sweep Prospects

Rated at E-5, the ore from this property contained copper and silver. It is located in the northwest ¼ of the northwest ¼ of Section 4, T22N, R16E, on the USGS 7.5 Minute Series map of the Enchantment Lakes.

The original owners in 1889 were Judge Gamble, Pat Twomey of Cle Elum, and George Sloan of Roslyn. They had a day shift and a night shift working on a tunnel that was in 30 feet, following solid copper glance carrying 57 percent copper. The ledge was four feet wide.

A 1989 report of these two prospects revealed a 47-foot adit in a shear zone about five feet wide in serpentine. Ten percent of this shear zone is lenticular pods composed of chalcopyrite, pyrite, magnetite, and cuprite. The prospect had a stockpile of ore that showed 13.2 percent copper and 0.7 ounce of silver per ton.

Upper Teanaway Valley Iron Claims

Iron Peak Deposits

This area is bordered by Eldorado Creek on the west, Beverly Creek on the east, and the southeast-flowing North Fork Teanaway River across the south. The deposits are located in portions of Sections 7, 11, and 12, T22N, R16E, as seen on the USGS 7.5 Minute Series map of Mount Stuart, and the Green Trails map of Mount Stuart #209.

In 1944, E. K. "Sonny" Brown (a prominent Ellensburg attorney) and A. R. Jordin (a renowned Swauk Mining District miner) had three iron ore deposit properties. The Iron Peak area was the westernmost claim among the prospective digs. The deposits are concentrated in seven areas covering a two-mile portion in Swauk peridotite contact from 3,700 to 5,900 feet in elevation, and ranging 150 to 2,350 feet above the major valley bottoms. No development work has been done on any of these deposits, except for a few old open cuts.

Area 1

Hiking is not recommended here because the claims are on undeveloped terrain and there are no trails. The Beverly Creek Trail #1391 passes west of the area's east line 1½ miles from the end of the Beverly Creek Bridge at the end of Road #2324.

The area is located 700 feet west of Beverly Creek in the southwest ¼ of the southwest ¼ of Section 7, T22N, R16E, and the southeast ¼ of the southeast ¼ of Section 12, T22N, R15E, extending from 200 feet above the creek to 800 feet higher on the ridge top. The iron beds show in the gully 400 feet above Beverly Creek to the top of the ridge. The iron bed is cut by 15 large (mostly vertical and northeast-trending) dikes and various faults.

Area 2

Not rated. This is remote country with no trail access. Area 2 is adjacent to the west end of Area 1 in the southeast ¼, of the northeast ¼ of the southwest ¼, and the southeast ¼ of the southwest ¼ in Section 12, T22N, R15E, at an elevation of 4,600 to 5,900 feet.

The Swauk peridotite extends west on the south edge of the area where nine iron beds, averaging nine feet thick and 580 feet long, contain the bulk of the Iron Peak reserves. The ore is in small, scattered bodies, is structurally complicated, and shows no indication of larger underground reserves.

Area 3

Not rated. This is remote country with no trail access. The location is just west of Area 2 in the southwest ¼ of the southwest ¼ of Section 12, and in the southeast ¼ of the southeast ¼ of Section 11, T22N, R15E, at an elevation of 4,300 to 4,800 feet.

Area 3 has five fine-grained iron beds. The largest bed is in the southeast corner of the area and is exposed in three outcrops. The bed is 410 feet long and five feet thick.

Area 4

Not rated. This is remote country with no trail access. Located 400 feet north and just west of Area 3 in the northeast ¼ of the southeast ¼ of Section 11, T22N, R15E, at an elevation of 4,400 feet. Five exposures show in one outcrop on a bed 280 feet long and averaging four feet in depth.

Area 5

Not rated. This is remote country with no trail access. It is located 400 feet west and north of Area 4, in the southwest ¼ of the northeast ¼ of Section 11, T22N, R15E, at an elevation of 4,600 feet. Five small exposures of fine-grained iron appear near the center of the area. There are two more outcrops of ore, one in a westerly position, and both are in a 250-foot iron bed up to one foot thick.

Area 6

Not rated. This is remote country with no trail access. Located in the southeast ¼ of the northwest ¼ of Section 11, T22N, R15E, 600 feet west and 500 feet north of Area 5, at an elevation of 4,100 feet. In the center of the area are two small outcrops about six feet wide extending 50 feet to the southwest.

Area 7

Rating: remote area with no trail, although North Fork Teanaway River Road #232 parallels the west line of Area 7. It is located 500 feet west of Area 6 in the northwest ¼ of the northwest ¼ of Section 11, T22N, R15E, at an elevation of 3,700 feet.

No iron beds were exposed in Area 7, but a small, buried bed 220 feet long and one to two feet thick was indicated in magnetic readings. The area is cut from its southwestern corner to the midway point of the east line by Eldorado Creek, which extends to the northwest of the North Fork Teanaway River.

Bean Creek Iron Deposits

Area 2

Rated at B-3 to B-4, this area is the first that you'll encounter and is located 1,800 feet west of Bean Creek in the northeast ¼ of the northwest ¼ of Section 17, T22N, R16E, as seen on the USGS 7.5 Minute Series map of Enchantment Lakes, and the Green Trails map of Mount Stuart #209.

Take North Fork Teanaway Road #232 to Beverly Creek Road #232A, and drive to the end. Go north for 0.3 mile on Trail #1391 and follow northeast-trending Bean Creek Trail for about a mile. Here the trail cuts across the southeast corner of Area 2, at an elevation of 5,100 to 5,500 feet.

In the southeast corner, there is a 190-foot iron bed that is terminated at its east side by a nearly vertical fault, and at the west end by a Swauk-peridotite contact. A search of this prospect showed nothing more than a one-foot–thick layer of iron ore, so it would not have been worthwhile to put a road in to develop the deposit.

Area 1

Rated at B-4. This area is located about 0.3 mile east, past Area 2 where the trail crosses northeast at the tip of the northwest corner of Area 1, in the northeast ¼ of the northeast ¼ of Section 17, T22N, R16E, at an elevation of about 5,400 feet. Here three exposures in outcrops covering a distance of 100 feet don't appear to contain minable iron ore.

Stafford Creek Iron Deposits

These iron deposits lie in two areas about 4½ miles above the mouth of Stafford Creek. There is a 5,000-foot belt of Swauk peridotite contact, in which the areas are located at 4,000 to 5,100 feet elevation, and 200 to 1,300 feet above Stafford Creek.

Area 1

Rated at E-3. This area is located 600 feet west of Stafford Creek in the northwest ¼ of the northwest ¼ of Section 14, T22N, R16E, at an elevation of 4,000 feet. Use the USGS 7.5 Minute map of Enchantment Lakes, and Green Trails map of Mount Stuart #209.

Head northeast up Road #2226 (Bean Creek Road) to Stafford Creek Trail #1359 for 4½ miles to Area 1. Several open cuts expose four places where fine-grained iron runs a distance of 750 feet. There were estimated to be 51,000 tons of iron ore in this bed, but great depth was not expected.

Area 2

Rated at E-3. At 0.8 mile west on Trail #1359, you'll find west-trending Trail #1369 at 0.6 mile, the location of Area 2 (at the end of the switchback portion of the trail, and south of the pack trail printed on the map). It is located in the northeast ¼ of the northwest ¼ of Section 15, T22N, R16E.

Area 2 is directly west (as the crow flies) a half mile from Area 1. Two small, undeveloped outcrops occur in the northwest corner of the area. This bed of iron is only 130 feet long and less than three feet thick.

In the eastern half of the area, there are two small iron beds 250 feet apart, and each 200 feet in length. The true contents of the deposits are undetermined.

Prospects of Navaho Peak

Geology

The predominant rocks in the Navaho Peak area are metavolcanic, serpentinized peridotite, and anorthositic gabbro (coarse-grained, dark igneous rock). The shear zones and rock contacts are the most highly mineralized, with the veins at most contacts and shear zones containing quartz, carbonates, talc, bornite, pyrite, minor chalcopyrite, and magnetite.

Many creeks originate on the slopes of Navaho Peak. Cascade and Falls Creeks flow north for two miles to Ingalls Creek. The area's north sentinel is the several miles of the Stuart Range spread east to west. The Navaho Peak's south and southwest slopes contribute to the North Fork of the Teanaway River by drainage via Stafford Creek's northmost feeder stream. On the southeast, Navaho Peak is the water source that feeds Negro Creek. Neighboring mountains in the Navaho Peak area are Earl Peak, on the Wenatchee Mountain Range, two miles to the southwest, and the Three Brothers, which start a half mile east of Navaho Peak and range eastward toward the Blewett area. Navaho Peak's 7,223-foot summit is the point of reference for wilderness boundaries and serves as county line for Kittitas on the south and Chelan County on the north.

Workings South of Navaho Peak

Not rated (remote area).[19] The ore contains gold, silver, and copper. The location lies on the USGS 7.5 Minute Series map of Enchantment Lakes, and Green Trails Map #209, Mount Stuart. One pit is at 6,400 feet, in the southeast ¼ (where the corner lines meet) of Section 3. One pit is at about 6,100 feet, in the northeast ¼ (where the corner lines meet) of Section 10. Three pits and a caved adit sit at about 6,200 to 6,400 feet, in the northwest ¼ of Section 11, T22N, R16E.

There is one pit north of Trail #1226 on the Green Trails map; the other workings lie south of Trail #1226, which is along a copper-bearing shear zone. Some of the digs revealed black serpentine. The development in Section 11 showed a zone of limonite/malachite stains in irregular exposures. Layers of fine-grained magnetite comprise about 10 to 40 percent of this zone. The zone showed traces of gold and silver, 2.24 percent copper, and some nickel and chromium. The caved adit is in a shear zone, with 10 to 20 percent quartz lens masses six inches to one foot wide containing arsenopyrite, pyrite, and chalcopyrite. Some of the more massive layers of pyrites are from four inches wide, expanding wider in places. Weathered rocks on the dump are stained by malachite and azurite from sulfide minerals in the material.

The pit had a trace of gold, less than an ounce of silver, and 1.2 percent copper.

Getting There

There are several ways to access this area via good trails, but from any direction Navaho Peak is a tough and long haul.

---

[19] Although this information appears in the Teanaway Valley section, it falls within the Blewett Mining Area. It can be accessed via the upper Teanaway trails, but can also be reached via a hike up Negro Creek on Trail #1210 off Road #400.

Starlite Prospect

Rated at E-5 (remote area). The ore contains gold, silver, and copper. The prospect is located in the southwest ¼ of the northwest ¼ of Section 3, T22N, R16E, one mile west of Navaho Peak. It lies at an elevation of about 6,200 feet. Use the USGS 7.5 Minute Series map of Enchantment Lakes and Green Trails Map #209, Mount Stuart.

The Starlite Prospect lies about 1,500 feet west of the Green Trails map's Trail #1217. An adit of unknown length was driven into slightly sheared greenstone and altered dikes of granodiorite. Gold, silver, and copper were taken from these contact zones.

Ball Eagle

Rated at E-5 (remote area, see previous footnote). The ore in the Ball Eagle contains gold, silver, and copper. This property is located on the USGS 7.5 Minute map of Enchantment Lakes and Green Trails Map #209, Mount Stuart, in the southeast ¼ of the northwest ¼ of Section 11, T22N, R16E, at an elevation of about 5,600 feet.

Stafford Creek, Green Trails map Trail #1359, is the nearest route to the Ball Eagle Prospect area. There is a peridotite dike within the claim area containing stringers of pyrites in lenticular deposits. Values were found in gold, silver, and copper.

Cle Elum District Hardrock Mines

St. Luke and St. John

Rated at B-3. This property is located north of Thorp Creek in Section 18, T22N, R14E, and can be found on the USGS 7.5 Minute Series map for Polallie Ridge. It is at an elevation of about 5,100 feet.

The St. John and St. Luke workings were on a ledge 18 feet wide. Owners William (Cascade Bill) McKasson[20] and John H. Corbins, the only black miners in the Cle Elum Mining District, worked these claims in the 1890s.[21] The St. John and St. Luke are on the northeast ridge of Red Mountain. The location of the claims is marked on the map as "xx Prospects."[22]

To get there, go two miles north of Lake Cle Elum, and cross the bridge over the Cle Elum River heading west on Road #46 toward Cooper Lake. At three miles, Section 7 on the Polallie Ridge map, there's a dirt road headed toward the workings. Use the map to find your way. These roads could be gated and locked at any time or impassable due to seasonal washouts. The alternative is the two-mile–long Red Mountain Trail (#1330 on the Green Trails map of Kachess Lake, #208). The trailhead is at top center in Section 17, T22N, R14E, as seen on the USGS 7.5 Minute Series map for Davis Peak. The ore sought here contained gold, silver, and copper.

Thorp and John C. Claims[23]

Rated at B-3. These claims, later named the Extension #1, Whistler Badger, and Star Lode, are located in the northwest ¼ of Section 29, on the southeastern side of Red Mountain (about 3,500 feet south of Peak 5085T), in T22N, R14E, as shown on the USGS 7.5 Minute Series map for Cle Elum Lake.

---

[20] In a late fall snowstorm in 1933, Cascade Bill died on a trail in the mountains.

[21] In 1888, a large population of black miners migrated from Illinois to work the Rosyln coal mines as strike-breakers. They were the majority ethnic group in town for two years following the end of the strike.

[22] McKasson and Corbins also had a placer claim located a mile north of China Camp (now named China Point). At these digs, they had a blue flag sporting the silhouette of a battle axe, also the name of their property. The bedrock adit floor of a 20-foot tunnel produced fine gold. These workings were driven in pursuit of the old river channel believed to be in the area.

[23] Present-day maps and accumulated data show these claims to be separated by a considerable distance from the St. John/St. Luke Properties. All are not on the northeast ridge of Red Mountain as mapped in L. K. Hodges' *Mining in the Pacific Northwest*. His text places the Thorp/John C. on the southeast slope, but his map doesn't. New information indicates the southeast slope as the location of the Thorp/John C. Claims.

To access these workings, cross the bridge ¼ mile north of the Cle Elum River Campground, and head west. This is the French Cabin Creek Road. At ⅛ mile, turn right (north) on Road #4309. Drive 0.7 mile to Thorp Creek, cross the bridge, and go 2.2 miles on this main road. At this point, there is what appears to be a dry, seasonal drainage stream entering the road from the west, but it's actually the first 200 feet of the washed-out portion of a mine road that heads 1,000 feet west to a ridge overlooking Thorp Creek. The road turns north and upslope here, but a miner's trail goes upward along a steep-sided stream gully for 1,500 feet to an elevation of 3,700 feet. Iron-stained rock dominates the claims area. The workings lie southeast to northwest through the portion of the map where "USTM4" is printed, in the northwest ¼ of Section 29. A more recent map showed the area reclaimed as the Star Lode, Whistler Badger, and Extension #1 Claims, all at the same location as the Thorp and St. John workings.

The Jones brothers first recorded mineral properties in this area in 1887. Claims nearby were listed under the names of a Mr. McManimie and Ed L. Simmons (both Roslyn residents). Elvin A. Thorp shows up in 1892 as a claim owner on Red Mountain. His mine was recorded as containing gold, silver, and copper. Thorp sold his claim to Edward Pruyn and J. B. Davison of Ellensburg. A 240-foot tunnel was reported to be in the workings under the red iron cap and into a 12-foot–wide ledge of iron pyrite. Credit for construction of the adit goes to the original owners.

The John C. Claim is the northeast extension of the Thorp. Lucien F. McConihe[24] (McConihe was part-owner of a Roslyn restaurant in 1895) and Jacob Welsh purchased this property from John Corbins. A general description of the Red Mountain Prospects area is that its red staining runs from light to heavy in the upper part and south side of the east ridge. Mineral inspection of two pieces from the region revealed pyrite, pyrrhotite, and minor amounts of chalcopyrite scattered along the grain boundaries in rather coarse quartzite. The rocks are interbedded silty slates, quartzite, arkose, and possible diabase sills. This was not a potential source for production-quality sulfides. In 1951, there were several open cuts and adits, but all of small extent. The bulk of the work was on the southeast ridge. The ore sought contained gold, silver, and copper.

For the Rockhound

The above-mentioned minerals are there to collect. Gear up in goggles, rock hammer, or hammer and chisel, gather your samples, take them home, and enjoy.

At this point it's helpful to consider one of the discrepancies in L. K. Hodges' *Mining in the Pacific Northwest*. His Cle Elum Mining District map has Big Salmon La Sac and Little Salmon La Sac Creeks entering from the west side into the Cle Elum River, whereas modern maps show these creeks draining from the east side into the river. Three situations could account for this: the names could have been reassigned by modern state and regional authorities, as so often occurred with rivers, lakes, and creeks; Hodges geographical layout was inaccurate; or the printer made a mistake. On the Hodges map, Parish Creek is up the road. Its present-day map designation is Paris Creek. Hodges' maps do give helpful directions in locating claims and in determining correct lineal accuracy in general, however.

Howson Creek Claims

Rated at C-4. These claims are located in Sections 33 and 34, T22N, R14E, as seen on the USGS 7.5 Minute Series map for Cle Elum Lake.

The Howson Company owned 36 claims in 1896. William Campbell and John McDonald, who incorporated them into the Morning Star Mining Company for $1 million, bought them from the Howson Company. This included seven claims on three ledges. J. B. Cain, superintendent, recorded quartz assays from $10 to $50 per ton of ore in gold and silver. A 16-foot ledge had a 100-foot tunnel showing minerals in gold, silver, and copper all the way to the end of the adit. Miners went in 15 feet with another tunnel. Minerals of white iron sulfides carrying gold were present there. Another snub tunnel was driven into ore

---

[24] McConihe also ran a placer operation in 1897 at Princeton Bar, located on Little Boulder Creek.

A shaft at the Morning Star Mine on Howson Creek. This property was later operated by the Golden Gate Mining Company. These shafts pop up unexpectedly almost anywhere, so you must exercise extreme caution when exploring in any known mining area. (Victor Pisoni photo)

and silver. Twenty-eight Howson Group claims were renamed the War Eagle Property. At that time, there were a 60-, 30-, 15-, 10-, and two 40-foot adits being worked and extended. The ore contained gold, silver, and copper.

Golden Gate Mining Company

In May 1906, the Morning Star Mining Company was bought and named the Golden Gate Mining Company by the Gallagher brothers. G. W. Gallagher was the company president; Ed D. Gallagher was vice president and manager;[25] and J. S McManimie (previously mentioned in the Red Mountain claims data), secretary. General Clarence M. Buel, a mining engineer, was inspecting the properties. Buel estimated the company to have 50,000 tons of ore in sight.

In June 1906, the company struck galena ore in a quartz gangue while sinking a shaft. Several small veins were found, but not an ore body. Clinton Fletcher, of Fletcher Investment Company (from Cripple Creek, Colorado), arrived to investigate and invest in the Golden Gate Mining Company. After two days, he was impressed and went back east to pique investors' interest in buying a large block of the mines' stock, even going so far as to remark that the area could become another Cripple Creek.

At the Yakima State Fair in September 1906, the Golden Gate Mining Company won first place for its exhibit of galena ore taken from the property's upper tunnel. Another display, this one consisting of free-milling gold from a big ledge at the face of a 50-foot adit, attracted much attention as well. Assays of the ore showed $16.22 in gold per ton and 42 cents in silver. After the fair, another stock promotion began. C. E. Price, a mining engineer with over 25 years' experience (seven years with the Check Mate Mining Plant in Coeur D' Alene, Idaho) gave high praise to the Golden Gate Mining Company's potential and the mining district in general.

A large log building 80 feet long by 30 feet wide, including a porch that went around one side and one end, was put up for workers and visitors. Other structures on site consisted of a kitchen with hot and cold running water, a connecting dining room, an office building with laboratory, a bunkhouse big enough for 60 miners, a blacksmith shop containing over $500 worth of tools, and a barn for eight horses. Several thousand dollars were spent on the complex.

That same year, 1906, the Water Reclamation Service entered the picture. For the price of $47 thousand, it built the first dam (1905–1906), thereby raising Cle Elum Lake and placing the north shoreline at the edge of the Golden Gate Property. This dam was lost to the winter floods of 1906–07 but later was repaired. In 1912, the dam was reinforced. The present dam (constructed in 1934) measures 1,150 feet in length and 20 feet wide at the top. It stands 125 feet above the riverbed.

---

[25] The Gallagher brothers also employed 50 miners at the Busy Bee Coal Mine (1918 to 1930, when it closed) about one mile north of the town of Ronald. The Busy Bee Mine is located in the northeast ¼ of Section 12, T20N, R14E, on the USGS 7.5 Minute Series map of Ronald.

Prior to the W.R.S.–built dam, the original structure was a low-crib dam 223 feet long, made of timber, rocks, boulders, and fill (no concrete). The Yakima real estate firm Lombard and Horsley had constructed it to assure a source of water to irrigate land it owned south of Yakima at Union Gap (the original site of the town of Yakima). Farmers in the greater Yakima Valley took exception to this stored water at Lake Cle Elum. Tempers flared in the dry summer of 1905 when the Lower Yakima Valley was getting only a trickle of the water needed and harvest was near. Litigation ensued.

Walter Granger, an irrigation engineer from Montana (the man hired to turn the desert in the Yakima Valley into a flourishing crop-producing region), sent Ross Tiffany, Joe Driscoll, and four hired men to the Lake Cle Elum crib dam to blow it up. Without being seen they placed the first of three planned charges (about half a box of dynamite per blast) near the top center of the dam. The explosion lifted timbers, boulders, and rock in a huge geyser of water, leaving a 20-foot–wide gap and discharging 1,500 to 2,000 cubic feet of water per second.

Cle Elum Deputy Sheriff Haight arrived at the scene and quickly arrested Tiffany and Driscoll. Joe presented the Yakima Valley Farmers' plight for the needed water and requested that he be allowed to set off the second blast. The sheriff was not amused.

The two men went to court and were fined $400.00 (paid by Granger and the Yakima Irrigation District). Tiffany and Driscoll had eliminated the dam, and also assured future water rights to lower valley farmers because of the attention and action the crisis kicked up. The water set free by the one-hole shot served its purpose, giving the Yakima area an extra two weeks of irrigation water and saving most of the crops.

In 1906, the Northern Pacific Railway was extended to the south shore of Lake Cle Elum. The Golden Gate Mining Company planned to have its team of horses cart ore four to five times each week to the company's small steamboat at the north shore.[26] From there, it was shipped to the south shore, where it would be loaded on railroad cars. Also underway was a steam hoist for the shaft on the Galena Claim.

E. H. McCurdy, a mining engineer from British Columbia, visited the Golden Gate Claims on behalf of eastern investors interested in buying some of the company's mining stock. He inspected the 60-foot tunnel of the Dolly Varden Claim. The whole face showed free gold and a shaft down 58 feet in a ledge 12 inches wide, which produced ore averaging $16.20 a ton. Various stockholders also viewed the development, resulting in the sale of more stock.

The election of new officers, from the ranks of stockholding residents from Ellensburg, North Yakima, Thorp, and Seattle, took place in January 1907. J. D. Medill of North Yakima was named president, George F. McAulay of North Yakima vice president and legal counselor, and J. S. McManimie secretary-treasurer.

While searching out these workings, we located several open cuts and tunnels (caved and otherwise), along with a multi-building campsite and isolated cabin sites throughout the claims area. You can get to this area via the new Howson Creek Hiking Trail #1439. The trailhead (elevation 2,447 feet) starts east of the Cle Elum River Campground. It follows northeast for a half mile, on what appears to be the property's old mine-to-market road. Here the road/trail splits. A sign points to the northeast-trending Howson Creek Trail, and the road continues up 0.2 mile to some mine digs. It crosses Howson Creek (elevation 2,600 feet) at about 0.2 mile from where the trail leaves the road on its course up Sasse Mountain.[27]

The workings on the old claims consist of a 30-foot snub tunnel located on the north bank of the creek and within 100 feet of the trail's creek crossing. South of the adit, on the opposite bank, there is a 40-foot open cut. An old campsite, containing the remains of several cabins, lies 50 feet southwest of the open cut. The old-mine-to-market road, which splits from the trail, is 200 feet south of these building sites. Between, there's a path running north/south that passes a lone cabin site whose remains are visible, along with an open cut. Fifty feet past and south of the old road, there is a flooded 200-foot shaft (at about 2,600 feet elevation). Tailings surrounding the shaft show its location. Other uninteresting pits and a trench lie south of the shaft area.[28]

---

[26] Roslyn businesses purchased a 15-passenger pleasure boat from Seattle to serve sightseers and campers visiting the Lake Cle Elum area.
[27] This new trail does not appear on the current Cle Elum Lake map. Contact the Forest Service headquarters in Cle Elum for more recent information.
[28] A more recent southeast corner claim marker shows the digs to be the Sasse Claim located for the Pyro-Metric Company by C. A. Carr on July 5, 1968.

The road passes the shaft, goes east and up a mountain slope for several yards, and then turns southeast toward a talus area 200 feet away. A tailing pile shows on the talus. Two hundred feet of steep scrambling offers a solid 65-foot tunnel you can check out. About 30 feet into the dig, there is a one- to two-inch vein of gray, decomposed mineralization on the left side. Looking west from the portal, the view of Red Mountain is worth a moment's pause. From here, you can see ledges and outcrops of minerals on Red Mountain that are not visible from the valley.

To get to the other tunnels and surface digs, go from the Howson Creek Trail creek crossing. Hike the steep switchback trail about 0.8 mile to where the trail crosses a gulch (at about 3,500 feet in elevation). South of the trail and on the west side of the gulch, there are four uninteresting open cuts. A flooded 50-foot tunnel lies above the trail. Three-tenths of a mile around and downslope, southeast to the 3,150-foot level of Howson Creek, there is a 75-foot tunnel that was driven in 20 feet, turned left 45 degrees for another 20 feet, and continued 35 feet to the face. Some quartz with small blebs of arsenopyrite is in evidence in the tailing pile.

This tunnel is hidden by brush and trees, so it's difficult to see even when you're standing 20 feet away in the creek. Sticking to the upper nearby off-trail workings will satisfy most historic-site–seeking hikers and rockhounders.

Mineral Creek Claims

Properties along this creek are rated at B-2 to the claims, or off trail, B-3. Located in Section 6, T22N, R13E, the workings' elevations vary from 2,800 to 4,200 feet. The USGS 7.5 Minute Series maps for Pollalie Ridge and Chikamin Peak will show the area.

Durrwachter Property

Situated in the northeast ¼ of Section 6, the property's south boundary is Mineral Creek. To reach this property, start on the Cooper Lake Road #46, as you did to approach Red Mountain. Cooper Lake was named for Harbin M. Cooper, a freight pack-train operator, miner/prospector, and prominent Kittitas County businessman. He hauled the first stamp mill to the Peshastin Mining District, where he worked one of his mines. He also found placer gold about one mile above the mouth of Williams Creek in the Swauk Mining District. This ground was later to be included in Thomas F. Meagher's old river channel property, in which Meagher had about 3,000 feet of placer tunnel. Mose Splawn (a member of Kittitas Valley's founding

Though not often seen, bats do roost in drier mines. This picture of a bat flying directly at the photographer appears to allow a glimpse of light from the adit through its wing membrane. This effect, however, is a result of the camera's slow shutter speed. (Victor Pisoni photo)

Splawn family, and one of the first miners to discover gold in Boise Basin, Idaho, in 1862) and Cooper traveled through the mining districts together. Splawn honored Harbin by recording the lake in Cooper's name after they had camped there on a trip through the mountains.

Pass the Cooper Lake entry road, continue to Cooper Pass and go four miles to the end of the road in Section 8 as shown on the Chikamin Peak map. Take the Mineral Creek Trail (#1331, Green Trails map of Kachess Lake #208) for about one mile to the prospect and adit symbols area printed on the USGS 7.5 Minute Series map of Chikamin Peak. Determine what your off-trail skills are in relation to the surrounding topography. The final judgment and responsibility to explore are up to *you*.

Charles[29] and Ernest Durrwachter started their digs prior to 1920, shipping 20 tons of copper ore as the Mineral Creek Copper Company (1917–1926). One thousand feet of tunnels and shafts were dug in 25 different workings. In about 1920, a mill was processing 25 tons of ore a day for the Durrwachters.

Geology in the volcanic rocks shows extensive alteration 1 mile wide and 1.5 miles long. The areas that have been studied have granitic rock intruding schist, arkosic sandstone, and andesite flows that underlie Mineral Creek.

At creek level in hard granodiorite, at an elevation of 2,850 feet, there are two main adits about 30 feet apart. The one to the east has been partly covered with slide rock at the portal. This adit was 248 feet long on mineralized rock. Drifts were driven and a small amount of ore was shipped. The western adit is open, with a flooded, 50-foot shaft just inside the portal. Exposed pyrite as disseminations and veinlets in granodiorite are evident. An old adit, 200 feet above the creek and $\frac{1}{8}$ mile down Mineral Creek from the two main digs, showed a three-inch fracture in medium-grained granodiorite with stringers of pyrite and minor chalcopyrite. About 130 feet east of the main tunnels, there is a three-inch fracture filled with vuggy quartz. The ore at this site contained copper. If you're not into scrambling up loose rocks and boulders, this is a good area to stay in. By the time you're done exploring at creek level, most of the day will be gone.

Copper Queen #1, #2, and #3

This mine is located in the southeast ¼ of Section 6, T22N, R13E, at an elevation from creek level (3,000 feet) to around 3,800 feet. The Copper Queen Properties are across from and southwest of the Durrwachters' mill site, south of the creek at creek level. They were mined by the Mineral Creek Copper Company (1917–1928) and the Cascade Gold Mining and Milling Company in the early 1950s.

The rock in the Copper Queen area consists of andesite, felsite, felsite breccia, and basalt, cut by dikes and shear zones. This prospect contains less than five percent sulfide minerals, except for a place of intense mineralization, a breccia and andesite contact. It is pipe-shaped, outcrops 45 feet wide by 60 feet long on the surface, and is 300 feet deep. A shaft running through the upper and lower tunnels defines the pipe. The site contains copper and silver.

Unlisted workings around Three Queens Mountain show almost entirely pyrite. On the north slope of Box Canyon Ridge, about 600 feet above creek level and a half mile west of the Copper Queen area, is a strongly brecciated zone at the contact of the Teanaway basalt and Kachess rhyolite. The breccia zone has been traced for 3,000 feet, but only a short distance was exposed. Two adits and several open cuts are in the area.

For the Rockhound

Glaucophane has been collected here. It is of metamorphic origin, occurring in medium- or low-grade schist. Colors can be bluish, gray, streaked gray-blue, black, pearly, or lavender-blue. Glaucophane fractures unevenly, splinters, is brittle, and is translucent. It is characterized by slender-bladed prismatic crystals and a diamond-shaped cross section, occurring in fibrous to column-shaped masses. These traits make it easy to find and collect ore rock samples.

---

[29] In 1895, Charles and Ernest were partners with three other men as owners of the Roslyn Brewing Company. Charles was also Roslyn's postmaster. In 1908, Charles had a crew of men do assessment work on his Cougar Gulch property near the town of Liberty in the Swauk Mining District.

During hiking season, you will encounter folks who have come 15 miles over the Pacific Crest Trail from the Commonwealth Basin area at Snoqualmie Pass to reach the point to which you traveled one mile. One member of our group was at the properties on an outing and found himself answering questions about why he was so lightly equipped at that point on the trail. At least you can count on being a subject for conversation.

Salmon La Sac

This area is four miles north of Cle Elum Lake on the Salmon La Sac Road. Salmon La Sac is generally known for its convenient and comfortable state-run camping facilities. These include clean restrooms, tent sites, and utility hookups for trailer camping. From here, the pursuit of various outdoor sports begins.

Little Salmon La Sac Creek

Little Salmon La Sac was once under the sole control of Native Americans as an important salmon-fishing location. When the first miners or settlers appeared, fish were purchased or traded from the indigenous locals and taken away in a little gunnysack, or so the story goes. Thus the creek became known early on as Little Sack Creek.

Big Salmon La Sac Creek

The same name-of-origin story applies here, but at this creek bigger sacks were used.

Native Americans used to spear salmon below where the present-day Salmon La Sac Bridge now stands. French capitalists are credited with the "sac" spelling of the current creek names. The French were attracted to the area when the hardrock mines in the Cle Elum District began getting attention and were being promoted. They were in the area because they'd just set up the Kittitas Railway and Power Company in 1911 (which was intended to be an electric railway) to serve passengers and haul freight.

Waptus River Falls was selected as the location for the company's power plant. The present building on the right side of the road just before you cross the bridge over the Cle Elum River leading to the campground was built in 1911 to serve as the proposed railway depot, but the French discontinued further pursuit when news of impending war in Europe was announced. The company went into bankruptcy, besides the fact that it owed a fine for having cut timber without a permit. The Forest Service later accepted the log structure as payment for the fine. The building was used as a Forest Service district headquarters from 1915 until the 1980s, followed by several years of disuse and deterioration. After reinforced foundation work and a facelift in the past few years, it is now on the National Register of Historic Places.[30]

Unpublished data reports several workings around the Big Salmon La Sac Creek area. The condition of the digs tells us that these prospects were dug very early on; they're the kind that get discovered as a matter of course by hunters or bushwhacking hikers. We don't know where the prospects are located.

Miners R. Dewitt and William Taylor had a placer claim in 1897, on which they constructed a wing dam and a tunnel at the confluence of the Cle Elum River and Big Salmon La Sac Creek. It was built to divert water flow through their property, which was known to have shown pay dirt.

Trail Creek Prospect

Rated at E-3. This prospect in the Waptus Lake area is located in the northwest ¼ of Section 18, T22N, R14E, as shown on the USGS 7.5 Minute maps of Polallie Ridge and Davis Peak, and the Green Trails map for Kachess Lake #208.

---

[30] In the 1920s and 1930s, there was a large lodge in the Salmon La Sac area that also rented cabins and horses. It was built by Ben Foster. Ben sold to Louis Davis and Roland Briggs of Ronald. By 1941, owners McDonald and Rice had the place.

The trailhead for Trail Creek Prospect begins at the Salmon La Sac Campground area and is indicated by posted signs. This hike is about seven miles one way, with a 400-foot elevation gain that follows the Waptus River.[31]

About seven miles up the Waptus River Trail (Trail #1310 on the Green Trails map of Kachess Lake, #208), Trail Creek Trail #3122 leads northeast up Trail Creek. Go 0.2 mile beyond Trail #1322 to the confluence of the Waptus River and Trail Creek. The prospect is about 300 feet east of this junction, near the creek. There, a 10-foot adit has been driven into quartzite, exposing a 3½-foot–wide shear zone. Another shear zone about 1½ feet wide is reported to be in the same area. These shear zones are east-trending and show one to five percent sulfide minerals, along with minor amounts of chalcopyrite. Minerals taken from the workings turned up a trace of gold (under one-sixteenth ounce) and minimal amounts of silver and copper. The ore is said to contain gold, silver, and copper.

China Camp, 1873

This claim, today known as China Point, is one mile north of the Salmon La Sac Forest Service station, on the Cle Elum River Road. Its name indicates that it was a Chinese placer camp, or that it was near the original China Camp, at the time the Chinese mined in the Cle Elum District.[32] In the early years of China Camp's history, the camp could be seen from the Cle Elum River Road just before it goes along the first outcropping of rock that is 300 feet straight down to the river. China Camp was located between a spot on the river then known as China Falls and the main road. Private property now occupies portions of this historic site.

The Chinese were the most prominent of the nonwhite pioneers; they were particularly resourceful and adaptable to the circumstances they lived and worked in. After the 1873 gold rush, if there was placer gold to be found, sooner or later the Chinese would be there to work the ground, or more often to reclaim placers after white miners had skimmed the easy finds and rushed off to newer and easier workings.[33] Unlike most miners, if the winter was mild the Chinese would tough it out to work the claims. Otherwise, they would gather at a winter camp with other groups for the safety, commerce, and social advantages that large numbers provide.

Prejudice toward the Chinese ran high. They were constantly suspect when claim jumping and sluice box theft occurred, though white miners were sometimes responsible for their claims getting jumped because they didn't do the assessment work necessary to hold their workings. The Chinese would relocate a claim, the former claimant would eventually return, litigation would ensue, and because it was difficult to prove a property had been abandoned the court would find for the previous owner.

When the Cle Elum Mining District was organized in 1883, the Chinese were expelled from their holdings for the most part. After interest in the claims from which they had been expelled waned and the other miners drifted away, the Chinese settled back in until the next mining boom in 1893 brought another expulsion.

That the Chinese were treated unfairly by other nationalities was amply illustrated in an 1880 incident in which Yakima Indians massacred 25 Chinese who had been brought in to placer-mine gold for white miners who owned river claims in the Salmon La Sac (China Camp and present-day China Point) area. The Yakimas saw the Chinese during the day as they mined the river. After dark, they entered the camp and killed all but one man, Charlie Sam, who later operated the New York Café in Ellensburg. Charlie reported that he ran all night, stopping to rest only a few times. Shortly after dawn, he sighted a bear smelling its way along his track/scent. He set off at top speed toward civilization.

---

[31] Picturesque Waptus Lake is recommended as an overnight camping area 1.3 miles beyond the Trail Creek Prospect. A trail runs along the east shore for the lake's 1.5-mile length. This is Trail #1329A and #1310 on the Green Trails map.

[32] Sometimes also referred to as Celestials or Mongolians by the other miners and local press, they were considered immigrants, while miners from non-asian countries were elevated to the status of frontiersmen, pioneers, or settlers.

[33] The Chinese were the first to use mercury for the recovery of fine flake and flour gold. This, along with the sloppy manner in which other miners took the most visible gold and hurried off, helped them do well in the cleanup of smaller finds.

Indian Pete and his wife pose for a photograph near their Cle Elum home in 1904. Many of the miners in the Cle Elum area interacted with the Native American population in the early years of mining. (*Wilhelm's Magazine, The Coast,* April 1904)

In 1886, Andrew Jackson Splawn met up with two Chinese men who were traveling with pack animals at mid-trail on one of his horse-trading trips. The two packers took the opportunity to hire two riding horses from him so that they wouldn't have to walk. While riding together, the three came upon two Native Americans (Chief Moses and an unidentified companion). Moses approached Splawn while the other man began beating the Chinese travelers with the elk horn handle of his riding whip. Chief Moses grabbed the bridle of Splawn's horse. The horse was forced back on its haunches, almost dismounting Splawn. But Splawn was courageous in such situations. He jumped off his horse and shoved a gun into Chief Moses's side. At that point, the Chief backed off, claiming he had been only joking. Moses and the other brave departed at gunpoint, leaving the two Chinese men only badly bruised. The next day, after arriving at their camp, they paid Splawn in gold dust for the hire of the animals. They added an extra ounce for saving their lives.

The Chinese miners were generally afraid for their safety in those days, as evidenced in an incident in which a party of drunken men left from Roslyn for their camps, traveling north through the mining district and yelling in intoxicated exhilaration. The Chinese, thinking they were being driven out, left the area in great haste.

The Chinese were also very protective of their claims, fearing they'd be forced off them if the claims were deemed valuable. The standard answer given to an inquiry of their digs was usually something like, "Oh, sometime two-bittee (25 cents a day), sometime four-bittee, heap plenty for Chinaman." At the risk of losing a good claim, they were reluctant to give out encouraging information. Rarely considered a crucial part of the mining district socially, the Chinese were an important element of mining history.[34]

China Camp Placer (China Point)

Rated at B-2. This placer is located on the Cle Elum River in the southwest ¼ of Section 3, the southeast ¼ of Section 4, the northeast ¼ of Section 9, and the northwest ¼ of Section 10, T22N, R14E, as shown on the USGS 7.5 Minute Series Davis Peak map.

Owners Theodore Cooper,[35] James Wright, and John Lind (all from Roslyn) had a gold and platinum low-bar placer. They claimed to have taken $400 in coarse gold in 1885. By this time, the Chinese were gone from the camp. The area was still producing gold two years later when another party of men from Roslyn

---

[34] In 1891, Cle Elum businessman August Sasse and Chung Yune were involved in a lawsuit brought to court by two Cle Elum residents. Yune and Sasse had a herd of pigs that had damaged the two property owners' gardens. Sasse and Yune paid restitution for the swine trespass.

[35] Theodore was Harbin Cooper's son. He had a permanent residence in the Teanaway Valley, one of the largest ranches in the region, located 7½ miles east of Cle Elum.

located and commenced placer mining at the China Camp placer. They were said to be making cleanups of as much as $144 a day. No data was found to back up this statement, although the placer was a minor producer for some time early in the district's history.

For the Rockhound
You might be able to find flour gold, tiny crystal grains, and nuggets of platinum in placer deposits or ultramafic rocks.

Upper Cle Elum Iron Deposits

Geology
The iron deposits are located along and on either side of the Cle Elum River Valley. The area starts one mile above the mouth of Paris Creek at the outcropping iron deposits in the mountains, and continues west across the lake from the former Fish Lake Guard Station site.

All the rocks in the iron deposit region are metamorphosed and intensively intruded by large masses of peridotite, which has altered into serpentine. The iron is a product of the decaying serpentine. This changes to laterite (red, residual soil) by removal through downward leaching, where a very porous blanket of limonite[36] has formed. A sea covered the deposit at one time (this area was once coastal land). Layers of sandstone then covered the limonite. The pressure from faulting, along with metamorphism and hot water pressing heavily on the laterite, turned much of the soft limonite into magnetite (a source of iron).[37] Earth movement then elevated and bent the flat-lying iron deposits onto newly formed mountainsides embedded in dense rock. Some tilt at steep angles, while other deposits remain on the valley floor in layered masses. Erosion has exposed various iron deposits, leaving all types of iron zones throughout the district. The resulting iron ores are a mix of hematite and magnetite that also contain nickel, chromium, and traces of titanium and manganese.

The iron occurs in three forms as layers, oölitic being the top, laminated in the middle, and laterite at the bottom. Oölites are small, conspicuous, nodular masses resembling concretions. Leaching action at the top gives them a lighter color than the remaining layers. The laminated middle level is due to a slight orientation of minerals caused by geologic pressure. It is not confined to specific horizons, nor is it in the nature of sedimentary bedding planes. Laterite is generally dense and massive; it develops on flat or slightly sloping surfaces.

Cle Elum Iron Claims
There have been several periods of high interest in the iron ore of the upper Cle Elum—from 1837, when fur trappers reported spotting it in the "Cle Elum," to the 1960s, when a study was done on nickel-bearing iron, the last of the serious exploration in the iron zones for these two metals.

Shortly after the discovery of minerals in the Cle Elum, Jacob Higson of Manchester, England, a consultant for the Elbow-Vale Steel and Iron Company of Wales, inspected the iron ore deposits west of Fish Lake and estimated the quantity of ore above water level to be in the millions of tons (these glowing initial reports came before extended reality kicked in). Eighteen sacks of iron ore were analyzed at Columbia College, New York; another was tested at Lanarkshire Steel Works, Motherwell, England; and a third at London, England. The average was 52.32 percent metallic iron.

In 1889, W. H. Ruffner did a survey for the Seattle, Lakeshore & Eastern Railway in association with the iron deposits of the Cle Elum, with the possibility of becoming the sole provider of transportation to the projected smelting mills in the Puget Sound area. He heard of well-defined ledges of iron ore two miles in

---

[36] Limonite is a mixture of hydrous iron oxides of indefinite composition, whose precise identity is not specified. Its color and luster is yellow-brown, glassy or silky to dull, with a yellowish-brown streak.
[37] Certain metallic elements, notably iron, nickel, and cobalt ore, are naturally magnetic.

length, said to be rich in magnetic ore assaying from 55 to 66 percent iron. The iron outcropped as high as 3,000 feet in elevation, 200 feet above water level. Peter Kirke owned the property. Ruffner got his information from a Mr. Whitworth and Mr. Burch.[38] Burch informed Ruffner about an iron ore claim he held four miles below Kirke's. Burch's property extended from the Cle Elum River, east up Boulder Creek, to the head of the flow and into the mountains beyond. Burch said the ore body was 20 feet wide and contained gray iron ore, some standing out as 80- to 100-foot outcrops.

In 1890, Peter Kirke had partially constructed an iron and steel works at Kirkland near Lake Washington. The facility would have been the nearest mill able to process the iron ores of Snoqualmie Pass and the Cle Elum Mining District. The enterprise was nipped in the bud, owing to the looming economic depression of 1893. Kirke had spent $300,000 by the time the plant was abandoned and finally removed. During this same period, the Pacific Investment Company, an English syndicate, purchased 18 claims between Camp Creek and Boulder Creek from the original locator. Pacific Investment did nothing in the way of production development for a number of years. James Bell, a Roslyn resident and Pacific Investment representative, did state that the company had a crew of 15 miners taking out iron ore from its Fish Lake holdings, in addition to developing the company's Big Creek iron claims south of Easton. Pacific Investment Company was in possession of the iron claims where the most interest would be focused in future iron, nickel, and chromium exploration, long after it had abandoned its holdings.[39] The group of claims forms an "L" starting at Camp Creek, following south along the west side of the Cle Elum river, to Boulder Creek, where the claims head east into the hills and mountains.

In the winter of 1892, James Bell was involved in a claim relocation race. The Monitor (later the Iron Monitor) Claim was situated in the midst of Pacific Investment's group of properties. The Monitor had been originally located in 1889 by H. Walters and two local boys, the Livingston brothers. They kept current on their assessment work for the first two years, but then got careless and were delinquent on the third year's maintenance, which left the dig open to first claimant relocation.

James Bell had been watching the Monitor for some time with the notion of acquiring it for Pacific Investment. George Elliott of Ellensburg was also interested in it. Just before New Year's, George arrived at Roslyn with John Burke and Jim Muldoon[40] in tow. Elliott had offered the two $100 to relocate the Monitor in the names of Elliott, Burke, and Muldoon should the trip be a success. Bell caught wind of this, and the race was on.

Bell left Roslyn on horseback, while Burke and Muldoon headed out on snowshoes. The snow was 12 to 15 feet deep. Bell got as far as the south end of Cle Elum Lake, where he had to abandon the horse. He used a boat to get to the upper end of the lake, where his cabin was located. There he picked up a pair of snowshoes and took off for the iron mines. He brought no food, clothes, or blankets, concerned that the extra weight would slow him down. Eventually Bell got lost because the deep snow had covered the blazes on the trees. Add to this the dense cloud cover to hinder route finding, and you have a formula for disaster. Nightfall caught him stranded in the snow with no idea of where he was, no food, no blankets, and not even matches to start a fire. He had to stomp around in a small circle most of the night to keep from freezing. Near exhaustion toward morning, he finally dug a snow tunnel and stayed there until daylight. Fortunately, the sun was out, and using it to keep a true course, he found his way. He found the Monitor around noon. Ten hours later, Burke and Muldoon arrived, and to their tired dismay found that the Monitor was in the hands of the Pacific Investment Company. This probably made the trip back seem much longer than it would have had they won the prize.

---

[38] Ben Burch was a former partner/owner of the "Robber's Roost" trading post/store at Ellensburg.
[39] These claims are shown on L. K. Hodges' Cle Elum Mining District map, in *Mining in the Pacific Northwest*, but there is no data about the maps. The information here is from claim holders and surveys taken after Hodges wrote about the area.
[40] Jim Muldoon was a miner who worked in the Cle Elum Mining District. He was also known to prospect or to have been involved in producing mines in other districts of Washington State.

Belfour-Guthrie Iron Claims (North and South Deposits)

Not rated. There are 30 properties on and around the Belfour-Guthrie iron claims. Eleven are patented or presently on private land (as of 1999). They are located in Sections 26, 34, and 35, T23N, R14E, and in the southeast ¼ and northwest ¼ of Section 1, in the north ½ of Section 2, and the east ½ of Section 3, T22N, R14E, as shown on the USGS 7.5 Minute Series Davis Peak map. Elevations in the upper valley where iron occurs are between 2,900 and 3,500 feet. In the southern outcrops on the divide south of Boulder Creek, iron appears at elevations of 3,500 to 5,000 feet.

History of Activities, 1900–1960

Some prospecting and sampling via the construction of tunnels, shafts, trenches, and pits along outcrops were done prior to 1903. Other exploration occurred later. Early drill core sample records were lost in the San Francisco earthquake and fire of 1906. Four known drill holes from 1903 were 70, 106, 397, and 448 feet deep. The estimated amount in the ore bodies varied with each survey. Examples of early figures are 300,000, 3 million, and 12 million tons of ore. More recent and accurate numbers showed five million tons of possible ore deposits. This discrepancy might be due to promotional agendas as opposed to an urgent need to locate strategic metals for World Wars I and II.

Because of the war demands for nickel in 1942, the Cle Elum iron-nickel deposits underwent more tunneling and diamond drill holes. There was talk of constructing an ore treatment plant in the region to process 1,000 tons per day. P. E. Pesonen, a mining engineer for the Bureau of Mines, conducted the examination. The major drawback was the heavy rain and snowfall that made the deposits inaccessible during winter months. Development amounted to 10 tunnels totaling 1,300 feet in length, six shafts, 60 shallow cuts and trenches, three pits, one winze, and four drill holes. Most of these are now unreachable due to flooding and caved ground.

In 1943, the Iron Monarch, Bessemer Iron #2, Iron Boss, Iron Boss Fraction, and Iron King were selected for restudy from the large Belfour-Guthrie group of 20 claims. The Iron Boss, Iron King, and Iron Monarch dominated the report. Nothing noteworthy stood out from any of the previous studies, except the end conclusion suggesting that an incline shaft be used to work the dip of the formation, which had been deemed the only workable method to access the lode in such extreme topographic and physiographic conditions. Working depths would be 1,000 to 2,000 feet.

As of 1944, there had been no commercial production of iron-nickel ore from any of the iron deposits, only small shipments for testing purposes.[41] One study in 1944 did add new data about areas identified as Cle Elum Iron Ore Zones 1, 2, 3, and 4, as follows.

Zone 1

Located on the north and south sides of a ridge about a half mile south of Boulder Creek, in the southeast ¼ and southwest ¼ of Section 1, T22N, R14E, as seen on the USGS 7.5 Minute Series map of Davis Peak. Development consisted of several old, open tunnels and two caved adits. Iron exposure occurs on the east side of the ridge between 4,900 to 5,000 feet in elevation. The iron bed has a total length of 1,000 feet and a thickness of three to six feet.

Zone 2

Zone 2 is about 1,800 feet west of Zone 1, in T22N, R14E. It extends from the top of Magnetic Ridge (located right of center in Section 2), at an elevation of 5,000 feet, down the west slope to 4,000 feet. Development consists of several open cuts in and around 14 outcrops of fine-grained iron. It is possible that 144,000 tons of iron ore lies in Zone 2.

---

[41] From 1892 through 1944, 23 separate reports were written about iron ore in the Cle Elum, Teanaway, and Blewett Mining Districts.

Zone 3

This area extended off Zone 2's west boundary, and it varies in elevation from 4,000 to 3,200 feet. It is located in the southwest ¼ of the northwest ¼ of Section 2 and southeast ¼ of the southeast ¼ of Section 3, T22N, R14E. Development consists of several open cuts, one caved adit, and a 500-foot tunnel. Zone 3 has seven outcrops of fine-grained iron ore. The 500-foot adit is at the western/lowest end of the iron bed. It cuts Swauk peridotite a short distance from the portal and follows it to the face, the end of the tunnel, which is 180 feet below the surface. There is no sign of iron in any part of the tunnel. This proves that the surface depth of the iron is shallow, only about six feet deep, on the surface above the adit.

Zone 4

This area is located on the east bank of the Cle Elum River in the southeast ¼ of the northeast ¼ of Section 3, T22N, R14E, at elevations that range from about 2,700 to 2,800 feet. This places the area about 1,000 feet west and a little north of Zone 3. Development amounts to one caved shaft and several old, open cuts. Three outcrops of fine-grained iron are on the property. There is a bed of iron 310 feet long with an exposed thickness of two to five feet.

The bottom line is that mining the Cle Elum iron beds to great depth below the river might be prohibitively expensive given the excessive pumping costs that would be required. The ore lies in a valley bottom that routinely gets major drainage in a region of heavy precipitation. High pumping costs, narrow mining widths, structural complexity, expensive transportation, plus somewhat low-grade ore doesn't leave much room for profit.

A 1960 report shows that Burlington Northern Inc. owned the original Belfour-Guthrie Claims. One last survey from 1960 ended further exploration in the area. This survey was done in Section 26, T23N, R14E, as seen on the Davis Peak map. The zones tested were on the River, Bessemer #2, Iron Boss, Iron King, and Iron Duke Claims. It concluded that under normal and current economic, technologic conditions, it would be too costly to develop the deposits.

For the Rockhound

Although we offer no hiking data in this section, if you have the urge and the necessary skills to locate some of the iron outcrops, you might find some of the following:
- Hematite: Occurs in different colors, including steel-gray, red, reddish-brown, black, metallic, cherry-red, and brownish-red with a dark red streak.
- Magnetite: Iron black in color, with a metallic, black streak. When in crystal form, octahedrons are the shapes you'll most likely find.
- Limonite: Yellowish, brown, glassy or silky to dull in color and texture, with a yellowish-brown streak.

Little Boulder Creek Area

Hardscrabble and Mattie Claims

Rated at B-3. These claims are located on the section centerline, near the west line of Section 2, T22N, R14E, on the USGS 7.5 Minute Series map of Davis Peak.

William "Cascade Bill" McKasson (mentioned in the Red Mountain property report) had a six-foot ledge on his Hardscrabble workings that carried iron pyrites under gossen-stained rock. A claim with an ore-bearing vein crosses the ledge and is owned by John Corbin, who also prospected Red Mountain.

Asphaltum A report on long-forgotten asphaltum (asphalt) beds in the upper Cle Elum indicates they were discovered in 1882 by an Olympia pioneer, locally known around Cle Elum as "Old Uncle Billy." The old pioneer found the beds but never filed a claim, not knowing what he had discovered. He thought it was coal because of its resemblance to the bituminous fuel. Uncle Billy had samples assayed and found the substance to be asphaltum, a non-event in his estimation. Years passed before the old guy decided to go back to the spot, but he died without locating it. Before he passed away, he had drawn a rough map of the area where he thought the deposit was located. His nephew, M. Barnett of Seattle, inherited the map and got some local entrepreneurs to help him search for the mineral pitch.

Three separate attempts to find the deposit were unsuccessful, and the matter was taken over by two mining men, E. M. Dickson and a Mr. Price. Together with Barnett, they went in search once more. Inclement weather drove them back, but not before they found evidence of asphaltum in the area. In May 1900, Dickson headed up a party of paid company representatives on a systematic expedition, and they finally found the deposit in June.

The location was filed on a blanket deposit covering 140 acres, comprising seven full-size claims. The layers varied from a few inches to several feet in thickness. Dickson and Price then attracted the attention of eastern parties by advertising in The Seattle Times. J. J. Hohman of Seattle had business contacts, and he sent samples east for an asphalt pavement company to test. We don't know what, if anything, came of this deposit. There are no claim records, nor have we come across any news reporting on the property.

These two claims are near or within the iron claims area east of the Cle Elum River, but their exact location is not given. The two digs seem to be prospects because no development is in evidence. A possible route travels up an unnamed feeder stream, near Section 3. Bushwack along the gully or high-bank until you find a place to explore. A shallow shaft and some building sites from the old Yankee Iron Claim lie near the north side of a secondary road, where there is a hairpin turn to the south, east of the center in Section 3. This might serve as an alternative to trudging up the mountainside to unlocated prospects. The ore primarily contains iron.

Princeton Bar and Illinois Quartz Claims

Rated at B-3. These claims are located in the southeast ¼ of Section 35, T23N, R14E, as seen on the USGS 7.5 Minute Series map of Davis Peak.

In 1889, L. F. McConihe (also owner of a Red Mountain claim) was in possession of the Princeton Bar and Illinois Quartz digs. The claims area is simple to find on the map, but getting there involves a very steep hike. A road follows the course of Little Boulder Creek, but it is badly washed out. Hiking is the only way to go. Start your search at the end of the road, where the digs are located. Check the creek bed for signs of ore samples in the float. Find rusty rocks that are abnormally heavy and break them with a hammer to see if any is a "keeper." The ore contained gold.

Big Boulder Creek History

The first copper mining claims were made in 1881 at the headwaters of Big Boulder Creek, by A. F. York (Kittitas County surveyor) and a mining district claims recorder, Judge E. P. Boyles. Three hundred locations were listed for gold, silver, copper, and other minerals that same year.

James Grieve and E. P. Gassman made an attempt to establish the Boulder City Mining Camp at the confluence of the Cle Elum River and Big Boulder Creek in 1891. These mining and prospecting partners had been in the Cle Elum area since 1880. They later displayed ore samples of gold- and silver-bearing quartz from outcrops at their properties on Paddy-Go-Easy Pass, while traveling to and when in Cle Elum.

The English-owned Pacific Investment Company, holders of the promising iron claims along the Cle Elum River, challenged Gassman and Grieve over this well-situated site from Camp Creek and south for two miles. Pacific Investment had also filed on Boulder Creek for its town site. Litigation ensued, and the judicial system eventually eliminated the chance of a town developing on that location.

The year before this squabble, a huge forest fire caused by careless campers or miners burned the trees and land around Scatter, Silver, and Fortune Creeks. Damaged timber, plus the demand by miners for lumber to build winter quarters, created an opportunity for the sawmill that filled the voided land of the town site.[42]

Big Boulder Creek Claims

We will examine the Big Boulder Creek Prospects, beginning at the mouth of the creek at the Cle Elum River, to southwest and south of Hawkins Mountain, including some of the Gallagher Head Lake area. Use the USGS 7.5 Minute Series maps of Davis Peak and Mount Stuart, and Green Trails maps for Kachess Lake #208, and Mount Stuart #209.

Bertha Prospect

Rated at A-2. This site is located in the gulch of Big Boulder Creek east of the Cle Elum River. This could be a gold placer or lode property. The ore contained gold.

Boulder Creek (Burke) Prospect

Rated at B-3. This property is in the southeast ¼ of the northeast ¼ of Section 35, T23N, R14E, at an elevation of 2,700 feet. The ore contained chromium.

During World War I, the Burke brothers mined small, lens-shaped deposits of chromium and shipped them by horse-drawn ore sled to the Cle Elum River Road. In 1942 (World War II era), Frank Bryant, the new owner from Cle Elum (of Swauk Creek-dredging notoriety), also mined chromium from areas of serpentinized peridotite. He worked two short adits and some open cuts. About a carload of ore was shipped.

To find this area, use the USGS Davis Peak map. Locate the start of the 4×4 road/pack trail at the Cle Elum River Road about 750 feet north of Boulder Creek, indicated by United States Mineral Monument (USMM) #1 on the map. This is where the trail starts. It is blocked by recently placed boulders, so look carefully. When reaching 0.7 mile on the trail, head for the creek bank ridge. Search until you see an open cut with a caved tunnel. At creek level, 250 feet below, there is a 30-foot tunnel in a solid serpentine mass. This is the claim site. We discovered that there was no longer an ore dump when we visited, contrary to what was stated in a property report.

Denny Prospect[43]

Rated at C-3 to the Denny cabin site, and D-4 if you are seeking the open cuts and ledges on the southwest slopes of Hawkins Mountain. It is located in the northeast ¼ of Section 36, T23N, R14E, at an elevation of from 5,200 to 5,500 feet. It sits on the nose of a ridge, situated southwest of Hawkins Mountain on the north side of Boulder Creek. The country rock of the region is serpentinized peridotite, from which chromium is mined.

---

[42] Another commercial opportunity initiated by the fire involved mine timbers of varying sizes and types. Only red fir (douglas fir) would do; pine and white fir rotted too fast (even red fir rots). Rotting wood causes unattended mine tunnels to cave in and portals driven in loose earth to collapse.

[43] We found two spellings for Denny, that already mentioned and "Denney." The "Denny" version is correct, per the family name affiliation with A.W. (Dick), Joseph N. Denny (Roslyn fireman in 1888, a barber in 1885, and mayor of Roslyn in 1897), David, Phil, Charles, and Victor Denny. All had mining connections throughout the state (plus other connections alluding to the Denny Clan's expansion into many areas of commerce).

The Fred Denny cabin site is 0.4 mile from the Boulder Creek Claim. The cabin site is marked as a square on the Davis Peak USGS map. Only the charred remains of the cabin are now at the site. In the 1940s, Denny was looking for chromium deposits. Some of the deposits were leased early on from the Burke brothers by W. A. (Dick) Denny (Fred's father). Eventually, Fred Denny ran all the properties. Fred, his wife, Viola, and Ben Kelly lived in the cabin on Boulder Creek. Other residents of the Boulder Creek area were a prospector, Mr. Nathan A. Batchelder, and his wife, Fran Batchelder[44] (Fred Denny's aunt). Forest Ranger Jenkins was stationed at the Salmon La Sac Headquarters, which served the district.

During World War II, the search for needed strategic metals was carried on throughout the area. Massive deposits of serpentine rock characterize practically all the sections around Hawkins Mountain. Chromium is exposed high on the ridges in small, eroded drainage cuts, and shows in the serpentine as disseminated pieces and blebs. Prospect work was limited but encouraging. Fred had planned to bulldoze the light overburden away, down to the chromium lenses (there is no information to show that he did, though). Some serpentine is black and quartzy-looking, with manganese crystals and a high occurrence of iron that colors it cherry-red in some locations. Low on the hill just above Denny's cabin site, there is a zone with a dike of light-colored manganese-chromium silicate rock, containing traces of nickel-chrome. The way to help distinguish the plain black serpentine from the chromite-carrying ore is by weight (chromium is heavier).

The mining must have been very selective given the lack of massive chromium deposits. These open cuts were mined as small deposits and were important only as occurrences of chromium in serpentine. They were considered unimportant commercially.

In 1942, geologists W. Carthers and Bennett reported examining several hand-casted samples of fairly pure manganese oxide at Fred Denny's cabin. Fred stated that the samples had come from a deposit about five miles north of the cabin.[45] A chemist from Los Angeles was hired to extract the mineral from the ore using an acid process unknown to Denny. Shavings on ignited paper produced sparks, indicating the promise of manganese (which is combustible). The ore contained mostly chromium.

For the Rockhound

Chromite can be found in masses, disseminated as grains in serpentine, among placer material, or (the best place) in prospect pits. Chrysolite is common olivine, but it can be found in a gemstone state as pale-yellowish crystals (if good fortune graces one's search).

Washington Quicksilver Company/Elsner/Nickelodeon

Rated at D-3 to D-4. This property is located in the southeast ¼ of Section 6, T22N, R15E, at an elevation of 5,600 feet. Its adit symbol is printed on the USGS 7.5 Minute Series map of Davis Peak.

History of Owners

The first mention of Adolph Elsner Sr. is as a joint owner in the late 1880s of a property south of what became the Washington Quicksilver Company by 1904. General Manager Gerritt D'Ablaing ran the operation until sometime before 1922, when the Ben Nevis Quicksilver Mining Company is listed as operating the only producing mercury mine in the area near Hawkins Mountain. There is a time gap in the records, ending when Elsner Sr. is found in possession of 16 claims (six of which might have once been in the Keystone Group). By 1939, O. F. Fry owned the Elsner digs, naming them Nickelodeon #1 and #2. These two claims are either part of, or lie north of, the boundary line of the Keystone Group of 10 claims.

---

[44] Fran Batchelder (N.A.'s first wife) died in the early 1930s in childbirth. Fran was the first to be buried at Boulder Creek Camp. Other upper Cle Elum residents laid to rest there were Charles Denny, Mrs. Nathan Batchelder, Fred and Viola Denny, and Phil Denny. Phil's body was found on August 15, 1961, under a hemlock tree after he had disappeared from his cabin. It was assumed he had gone to look over his claims on the north slopes of Hawkins Mountain.

[45] This is the area of Fred's antimony mine at the base of Goat Mountain, in the northeast ¼ of Section 10, T23N, R14E. Conflicting data has the location at the northwest part of T19N, R15E, putting it 17 miles south at Cle Elum. W. Carthers' field notes contain the correct information.

Geology of the Nickelodeon

Calcite shows in the fault vein, but on a very irregular basis. These occurrences are visible at the adits' portals. Schist, which outcrops north of the fault vein, has quartz stringers a half inch to one inch wide that traverse the rock in all directions. A basalt outcropping 200 feet south of the adit forms a dike along the south contact of the vein. Five hundred feet east of the tunnel, there is a massive outcrop of serpentine containing quartz or calcite stringers throughout. The one 30-foot adit doesn't merit the number of cabin sites and the ore-cooking oven in the meadow west of it, leaving open the possibility that there are more developments in the area.

Assay reports from 150 feet below the adit, in the tailing pile, carried 0.3 ounce of gold per ton and a trace of silver, indicating the spotty nature of the ore present in the area. In the meadow below the adit, we discovered a cinnabar-roasting oven, which was used to retort mercury from the ore. The oven stood four feet high, 15 feet long, and six feet wide. Seven 12-inch by 6 feet–long steel roasting tubes, each with access doors at one end and exit pipes to their rear, are situated in the retort. A four-foot–high brick base supports them. Beneath the tubes, a one-foot space allows for heat to pass through from the wood-burning chamber at the far end. The circulating heat cooked the ore, releasing the mercury as vapor, which then rose and escaped through three-inch pipes at the back of each roasting tube. The three-inch pipes are tapered and empty into flask containers[46] positioned at the end of each tube. The mercury vapors entered and condensed into liquid mercury when cooled. The ore consisted of cinnabar that contains mercury, along with some nickel and cobalt.

Getting There

Take the same route that goes to the Denny cabin from the mouth of Big Boulder Creek, or start on the pack trail (Trail #1392 on the Green Trails map for Kachess Lake, #208) that begins off Camp Creek Road #138.[47] Trail #1392 contours along the slope of Hawkins Mountain to the Denny cabin cutoff (the pack trail is about one mile long). There is a caved adit (it is open according to the USGS Davis Peak map) 0.3 mile from the Denny cabin cutoff. The tunnel was inundated with rock in 1996. From the caved adit, go south on the trail for 0.6 mile. An unnamed feeder stream crosses the trail here. Three walls, four logs high, are all that remain of a cabin that lies southwest of the trail but north of the creek.

There are no known digs that we could find near the site, or visible paths leading away to mineralized areas. But the spot seems strategically placed, indicating mine workings are close by, probably within a ¼-mile radius. Six-tenths of a mile up the trail, two cabin sites appear on the wayside by Big Boulder Creek. An adit is located about 100 yards south and off the trail. It is a snub

This tunnel at the Nickelodeon Mine followed a fissure vein into the hillside. Apparently it pinched out, because the tunnel is only 30 feet in length. (Victor Pisoni photo)

---

[46] The commercial weight for a flask of mercury was 55 pounds at that time (today it is 76 pounds). A flask is the standard type of measure used for this purpose.

[47] Trail #1392 is a scenic hike. After passing the Denny cutoff, and beyond the caved adit on the south-trending trail, the hike breaks out into the open, revealing the lower flanks of Hawkins Mountain. Outcrops of serpentine, Swauk sandstone, and iron-capped ridges are a treat to see. This is a good spot to bring out the binoculars. Trees become prominent at a cabin site farther on and remain till the Nickelodeon Mine cutoff. You get occasional glimpses of the surrounding mountain and ridge views along this section.

The Nickelodeon Mine produced cinnabar, the ore of mercury. Rather than try to transport the ore, the mine's owners built this mercury retort at the site. Heat was supplied by a firebox on the righthand side of the structure. The flue gases conducted across the outside of the tubes seen here and then vented from the left, presumably through a stack. The crushed ore would be loaded into the cylinders and the ends seen here would be sealed. The mercury vapor would discharge through smaller tubes on the opposite end of the cylinders. The vapor would then be conducted through water traps, where it would condense into the liquid metal and be contained in the water. (Victor Pisoni photo)

tunnel, now caved. Trek 0.3 mile farther, and locate Trail #1392G (on the Green Trails map for Kachess Lake). This leads to the Nickelodeon #2 Claim area, and is the long way to get to the interesting part of the mining goodies.

Conserve your energy by going beyond #1392G for another 0.4 mile on south-bearing Trail #1392H. The main Nickelodeon #1 cabin site is 0.4 mile from the main trail. The cabin shows evidence of modern additions to the older part of the structure. This is either a hunter's camp or maybe represents renewed interest in prospecting (up to the 1950s?). Go past the cabin site, and high-bank east on a streambed for about 100 yards. This is a vague path, so watch carefully. As you approach the meadow, look among the trees and bushes on the north perimeter for ground impressions of four other cabin sites (no structures remain). On the eastern edge of the open slope lies a cinnabar ore-roasting oven that was used to extract mercury. The tunnel is about 200 feet higher in elevation and east of the oven, as indicated by the adit symbol printed on the USGS map for Davis Peak.

Dolphin/Bonanza Claims

Rated at E-3 to E-4. These claims are located at an elevation of 5,800 to 6,000 feet in the right center of Section 33, T23N, R15E, as shown on the USGS 7.5 Minute Series map of Mount Stuart. The ore contains copper, silver, gold, and cobalt.

Claim Geology

The Dolphin Properties are west of Gallagher Head Lake[48] (formerly Ennis Lake). Regional host rock had developed from the Ingalls formation complex. The country rock is mainly made up of serpentinized peridotite and greenstone. This peridotite belt runs north to the southern side of Mount Stuart. Surrounding ridge crests are capped with remnants of felsitic lava rock.[49] Leached and weathered outcrops of iron oxide stain (iron cap) indicate where the copper values are often found. The non-ore, or gangue minerals, consisted of serpentine and quartz.

There is magnetite in almost every area of the Dolphin Claims, but its occurrence is spotty and irregular. Copper and nickel-bearing magnetite was found in a small shear zone on a west ridge. A minimal amount of chromite appears in the magnetite but is of little importance. There are scattered nickel dikes that are extensively veined with calcite and other carbonates, and a few that are iron-stained.

---

[48] The lake and the prominent ridge extending southeast off Hawkins Mountain were renamed to honor an earlier prospector/settler, C. E. Gallagher. He also organized the Gallagher Mining and Milling Company.
[49] Felsitic is an omnibus term for fine-grained igneous rock. This type of lava contains patchy mosaics of quartz and feldspar throughout.

Hematite, an altered product of the magnetite, is found disseminated in the open cuts of the Dolphin #2 East Extension. Limonite, also derived from altered magnetite, is present in most of the deposits.

Dolphin/Bonanza History

The Gallagher Mining and Development Company bought the Dolphin Property in 1905.[50] In 1907, it evolved into the Gallagher Head Mining and Milling Company, with its 25 claims operated as one. The names of the claims are Fortune; Dolphin East and West Extensions; Copper Queen #1 and #2; Pay All; Mountain View; Mammoth; W. J., Uncle Sam; Copper King; Madie; Sadie; Copper Star; Legal Tender; Copper Prince; Jenny; Loraine; Zana; Golden Eagle #1 and #2; and Copper Glance #1, #2, #3, and #4.

To process these various claims, ore was transported to a completely water-powered reduction mill. An upslope crib dam held water, which was piped to a Pelton wheel down the mountain slope that ran a five-stamp mill, using 1,500-pound stamps. Mining expert E. J. Rice ran this operation, employing five men to handle the equipment. Two thousand tons of ore was on the dump, and 24 tons of ore had been run through the mill, returning $65.00 per ton. Two tons of concentrates (predominantly gold, silver, and

The opposite side of the mercury retort at the Nickelodeon Mine showing the smaller tubes through which the mercury vapor would flow on its way to being condensed in the water traps. (Victor Pisoni photo)

copper) were taken from each day's work. Two carloads of ore were treated in an eastern state reduction works, netting good profits despite the expense of transportation. The company projected a continuation of volume in ore output, if the deposits carried to depth (uh-oh). Five buildings, a storehouse, bunkhouse, cook house/dining room, office building, and mill building served the needs of the company.

Between 1905 and 1908, five tons of ore, containing six percent copper, was shipped from the main Dolphin adit. When the ore deposits failed in December 1908, the company went into receivership. There were 15 tons of ore on the dump and 15 tons of concentrates stashed away in a mine tunnel at that time. In Washington State Superior Court, the Halliday [sic] (possibly Hallidie) Machinery Company went up against the Gallagher Mining and Milling Company. The sale of the mining company went to Lee A. Johnson of Sunnyside, Washington, a representative stockholder who bought it for $2,800.00. The company was reorganized, and Johnson appointed G. W. Gallagher as manager. Gallagher then hired workers to mine and run the mill.

---

[50] Brothers G. W. Gallagher and Ed D. Gallagher were also involved in the Howson Creek Group of claims, which they bought and renamed the Golden Gate Mining Company in 1906.

In the records, Gallagher is shown as owning the claims in 1920[51] when the Bonanza Mining Company acquired the property. After 1920, Bonanza failed to refile on the claims. The minerals lay undisturbed, except for a flurry of prospecting activity that took place during the war years. Phil Denny[52] became involved in the Dolphin Properties, as company president, in a mineral properties sales promotion in 1952.

The five unpatented claims on the property were the Dolphin, Dolphin #2 East Extension, Dolphin #3 West Extension, Last Chance, and Legal Tender. The two westernmost claims, the Dolphin (which crosscuts the main outcrop) and the Dolphin #3 West Extension (which paralleled the main outcrop) had the best ore deposits. A 100-foot shaft was said to have bornite at the bottom. The shaft is now caved.

Dolphin Claim

Copper was the predominant ore, and silver and gold were minimal byproducts at best. Some cobalt was found in the main tunnel on a 25-foot ledge, paying $41.00 per ton.

The 925-foot adit crosscut a mineralized outcrop. At 201 feet and 252 feet into the tunnel, there are two drifts of unknown length. A cave-in occurred[53] 50 feet from the portal, and a shaft was sunk from the surface to bypass the unstable area. The caved portion was reopened and timbered for 64 feet through the unstable rock to the portal. Elsewhere, the adit was timbered wherever rock was prone to shatter or shift.[54] So much of the area is caved, with filled-in shafts, tunnels, and trenches, that it is difficult to locate these claim workings, even using the company's old mining map.

Dolphin #3 West Extension

The claim comprises an 18-foot open cut on the west bank of De Roux Creek, with a caved 20-foot adit south of it. Both are on an outcrop. A 40-foot adit was driven west of De Roux Creek on the south face of a ridge. It has collapsed, and now looks like nothing more than a trench. Another sloughed-in trench lies farther west, on the ridge between De Roux Creek and Big Boulder Creek. On the remaining claims, there are several open cuts and other caved tunnels and shafts. We couldn't determine whether they were connected with the Dolphin Mining Company properties, mainly because of overlapping exploratory work done over the years by several interested parties.

About 400 feet north of the main Dolphin adit, we located an old reservoir/crib dam site, fitted with four-inch pipe that left the dam and pointed directly toward the Dolphin milling area. Evidently, it served to bring water to a Pelton wheel/electrical generator set that was probably the mill's source of power. The

An ore wagon lies in ruins, with its cargo still on board in 1922 along the road near the Gallagher Mine. In 2000, it was still there, but the surface level was almost flush with the top of the wagon's sides. (Grace Browitt Elkins collection)

---

[51] What transpired between 1909 and 1920, we don't know.
[52] Documents show the Denny family was related to the Gallagher family. *The Cle Elum Echo* newspaper obituary, under "Death of a pioneer" (July 10, 1909), stated that James M. Gallagher died of a heart attack. Born in 1834, he served in the Civil War, Company "K" 20th Wisconsin Regiment, until the war's close. He arrived in Roslyn, Washington, in 1892, and lived there until 1902, when he moved to Seattle due to illness, and lived with relative J. N. Denny until he died in 1909.
[53] This was caused from the Dolphin adit crosscutting into a slight to steeply dipping, faulted, sheared, and fractured zone of serpentinized peridotite; a common occurrence in weak rock formations such as this.
[54] We found the caved Dolphin portal and about 50 feet of collapsed tunnel using the tunnel map. If you came across the portal and didn't know what you were looking at, you might think it was nothing more than a trench.

To gather precious water for operations at the Dolphin Mine, this masonry dam was constructed to collect snowmelt. Esmeralda Peak forms the backdrop. (Victor Pisoni photo)

dam's dimensions are 150 feet long by 10 feet high (a road crosses the length of the structure) and 8 to 10 feet wide. Tightly placed interlocking rocks and boulders, sealed with mortar or concrete, hold it together. The mill site, 400 feet below the dam, is just north of the road that goes to the ridge where the Big Boulder Creek Trail heads downslope. About 0.2 mile past Gallagher Head Lake, take the second fork in the road (south), in Section 33, as shown on the USGS map of Mount Stuart. About 50 yards from the road, in a meadow southwest of the main Dolphin adit, there is an old, narrow-bed ore-hauling wagon. Its wagon tongue and front axles are still visible; the rest is buried in dirt. Just above it is the mill site, with telltale artifacts strewn about the area.

For the Rockhound

The massive deposits of serpentine allow for an abundant variety in many altered mineral forms. Chrysotile is common to serpentine. It is fibrous, forming as small veins in the rock (also called Canadian Asbestos). Quartz fills fractures throughout the region, and calcite usually occurs with it. At some locations, the serpentine is so black it could be mistaken for obsidian by the inexperienced eye. Weathered, grainy slabs of serpentine, colored brown and green, resemble petrified wood. Some specimens are stained bright green to blue by malachite and azurite.[55] Pits and trenches (when they can be found) contain different types of collectible pyrites. Chalcocite appears as a grayish-black sulfide. It congregates within unweathered parts of shear zones, veins, and beds with other copper ores. Chalcocite (also called copper glance or redruthite) is uncommon, and is hard to identify.

We found several crystals of pyrite in the oxidized outcrop on the slope above the Dolphin adit and directly above the collapsed tunnel/portal. The region is constantly exposed to erosion and caving of sulfide material into and over past mining efforts so that it is difficult to locate most of the main workings. Any shafts or adits that escaped nature's erosive effects were most likely closed by the Forest Service. Due to concerns about public mishaps, this area is easy to access by road or trail, in case emergency response vehicles are required to rescue foolish amateurs or to fight forest fires.

Getting There

Use Green Trails maps of Kachess Lake #208 and Mount Stuart #209. Take Camp Creek Road #138 to Trail #1392. Hike about 2.5 miles, where Trail #1392 becomes #1392.1 for the remainder of this one-way, five-mile hike to the Gallagher Head Lake area. Or hike the Fortune Creek Road #160 to #161 to the lake/mines area. There is a good logging road, #171, that starts about one mile north of #161, but it is gated at three places. Contact the Forest Service in Cle Elum for current gate status. Big Boulder Creek Trail #1392/1392.1 is without a doubt one of the most scenic hikes in the Upper Cle Elum.

---

[55] Malachite and azurite are secondary products of chalcopyrite and other copper sulfides that have come in contact with carbonated waters, forming a hard, colorful green and blue glaze on the surfaces.

Silver Bow, 1892

Not rated. Ben Kelly and Judge Boyles owned this claim, which is situated on Hawkins Mountain. The property has a four-foot vein in a 30-foot incline shaft or tunnel. The ore contained copper and gold.

Mount Hawkins Chrome Properties

Crowe/Skipper Chrome Mining Company

Rated at E-3 to E-4.[56] This area is located in the southwest ¼ of the northwest ¼ and the lower ½ of Section 33, T23N, R15E, at an elevation of 6,000 feet.

History, Geology, and Rockhounding

These claims overlap with and lie adjacent to the Gallagher Head/Bonanza properties. Gallagher leased his digs to Jack Crowe of Cle Elum, who leased to H. W. Hansen of Seattle. The Skipper Chrome Mining Company was the result of that exchange. Bill Lunsden of Roslyn also had an interest in the area. No record verifies this, though he is mentioned as having prepared ore for shipment. Richard Denny expressed interest in the property in 1920, but his offer to buy in was declined. This mine was most recently named the Crown Copper. New adits (now caved) and exploratory prospecting were done on the property relatively recently.

The geological area is the same for Crowe/Skipper and Gallagher Head/Bonanza. They all worked the same land at one time or another. The ore was mined primarily for its chromium content.

Rockhounding in the region is similar to that in the Gallagher Head/Bonanza area.

This 1922 picture of a cabin located at the Gallagher (Dolphin) Mine, shows a structure that is typical of the mining buildings of the day. It is propped up to counter the downhill pressure of the heavy winter snows that fall in the region. A side ridge of Esmeralda Peak rises in the distant right of the photo. (Grace Browitt Elkins collection)

Crowe Property

The Crowe workings extend from southwest of a small, unnamed drainage lake down to the head of De Roux Creek. In the summer of 1941, Jack Crowe of Cle Elum worked a U-shaped open-cut trench that exposed chromite. It was 25 feet long by 10 feet wide, in sheared and slabby serpentine, which was covered by 10 feet of till (boulder clay). This open cut was located on the southwest bank of a shallow gully, which drains southeast into De Roux Creek. (It was probably a deeper reworking of a Gallagher Head/Bonanza dig.) The essentially solid body of chromite measured three feet wide by 10 to 12 feet long. The deposit was massive, consisting of a mix of olivine, serpentine, or chlorite.[57]

---

[56] Use the same route-finding directions for Gallagher Head Lake/Mining area to get to the Crowe/Skipper Claims.
[57] A group of minerals, such as hydrated silicates of aluminum, iron, and magnesium.

Crowe found other deposits, but they were on Northern Pacific Railroad Land[58] and ore could not be mined or shipped from them without a lease. At that time, the Northern Pacific's policy was to lease at $50 the first year and $100 the second year. The price of a lease later increased to $100 the first year and $200 the second. Moreover, depending on the value of the ore developed, Northern Pacific could grant or reject the following year's lease request at will. Much of the prospecting done on the railroad's property was a total loss.

Skipper Chrome Mining Company

When H. W. Hansen formed the Skipper Chrome Mining Company, it consisted of nine claims: the Chrome Compass, Don, Scoop, Last Wagon, Hope, Mary Ann, Homesite, Vision, and June. A report from 1942 showed that the company shipped 22 tons of ore.

Upper Cle Elum Mining District

In 1881, major attention was drawn to and serious prospecting began in the Cle Elum Mining District. The first event of note was a trip up Camp Creek and around the Hawkins Mountain area by A. P. Boyles, S. S. Hawkins, and Mose Splawn. They traced two parallel ledges containing ore and also found bits of coal. The three men knew there was coal in that part of the Kittitas—it had been commonly known for years that travelers and cattle drivers used the black lumps to build small fires—but they were not interested.

The first mine claim locations were found by S. S. Hawkins and Mose Splawn. They were the Cle Elum Lode, Iias, Hawk, and Ida Elmore. A. F. York (the county surveyor) and E. P. Boyles (the district claims recorder) located the first copper properties. Twenty more claims were added to the district in 1883 by P. J. Flint, E. W. Wilson, S. S. Hawkins, H. C. Walters,[59] and others. That same year, Hawkins, Joe Stevenson, and Mose Splawn claimed the Silver King Mine. Others listed are the Mammoth Copper Lode (found by James Grieve), Aurora Gold Quartz Lode (found by John and T. J. Lynch), Bald Eagle (found by E. P. Gassman and Hodges), the Vidette (found by E. P. Boyles), and the Bronco (found by Phil A. Stanton and James Grieve).

These early prospectors and mines figure all through the district's two economic mining booms, and they helped to create interest in the area. A census conducted in 1890 (a significant part of the data from which is missing) showed 13 gold mines as producing gold, with only two declaring more than $1,000 profit, out of a total of $10,822 worth of gold produced in the Kittitas area that year.

The upper Cle Elum Mining District caught the attention of several Montana copper mine entrepreneurs who came to check out the reports of minerals at the head of Camp Creek and the upper end of the Teanaway Valley. Early on, they gave glowing reports, but nothing was heard from them later when the deposits proved not to be massive.[60]

The name McConihe, familiar throughout the Swauk and Cle Elum Mining Districts, reappears in the records in 1889 when he served as representative for a company claiming placer ground along the section of Camp Creek, which flows through the Galena town site to the Cle Elum River.

A search for the right spot to build a major mining camp was being conducted in the district in the late 1800s. By 1890, rumors were circulating about a railroad that would run up into the mining district, but a good reason and a destination were needed. The district had no major mining camp, only a string of minor ones that stretched out along the main road from Cle Elum Lake up to Fish (or Tucquala) Lake. There were two camps east of Cle Elum Lake, Newport and Davis, and the Welsh and Preachers Camps were a little north of the lake. Dewitt was located at the mouth of Howson Creek; Galena City (the proposed site for the

---

[58] Fred Denny provided the following information to field geologist W. Carthers in 1942.
[59] Walters let his claim, the Iron Monitor, expire in 1892. The result was the race to relocate the property, in which James Bell won out over John Burke and Jim Muldoon.
[60] These men understood the scrambled nature of the district's geology. When they investigated the ledges and veins, they realized that the ledges were unpredictable, dipping, twisting, and pinching out, caused by the earth's crust-building episodes. Attractive assay reports were also often a result of the prospector high-grading the assay ore, but frequently the samples were the only good ore on the claim. The inexperienced buyer or investor was usually the prime target of a sales pitch that consisted of such misleading reports.

main camp) sat by the mouth of Camp Creek; and two others, Dunlap and Lynch, were northeast of Fish Lake. Camp Stanley was treating ore from the Cle Elum Mining District at this time using a cyanide process, but the records don't specify its location.

Galena

In May 1890, A. F. York, the Kittitas County surveyor, platted the 35-block town site of Galena near the mouth of Camp Creek at the Cle Elum River, which was considered a government site. The Northern Pacific Railway had surveyed a railroad route to the Galena site, the proposed terminus. It was to have exclusive rights to serve the upper Cle Elum. Of the blocks platted, most were sold, but Galena never became the mining metropolis it was intended to be, although it did remain a name place and focal point for the mining district. In 1897, Paul Hopkins of Seattle supervised the placing of an engine and boiler for a smelter at Galena.[61]

We visited Galena in 1997 and found a mill site on the river side of the main road. We saw a variety of ores around the structure, which indicates that it processed ore for several of the district mines. Leading from the mill site toward the river, there is a trail (about 150 feet long) that switchbacks past three cabin sites. We discovered the remains of a group of cabin sites on the east side of the road across from the mill site—the now-defunct town site of Galena.

The Miner's Social Life

Galena was large enough to serve as a center for social gatherings, including prospectors from the town and its outlying areas. The gatherings relieved the monotony so often associated with mining. There were also meetings to attend, business transactions to perform, supplies to buy, and saloons (primitive as they might be) to patronize, complete with gambling, which was par for the course in a mining community. Women dancers, if present, provided much appreciated amusement as well. There was boxing for prize money, wrestling, horse racing, and always singing. Admission was free, so the only price to pay was an exaggeratedly free hangover. Whenever miners met a music maker in the wilderness they'd throw a "shindig." It was a great excuse to cut loose and make life more bearable. Some musicians were miners or prospectors by day, and entertainers on the dance floor (or campfire, depending on how developed the camp was) by night. Most of this entertainment was of a rough, and sometimes crude, nature. For more refined activities, such as attending the theater, church, literary clubs and joining fraternal orders, inhabitants of the district had to go to Roslyn or Cle Elum.

But life in the mining camps was also dangerous. All too often a fire would sweep away a camp. And no wonder, considering the flammability of the haphazard collection of tents, shacks, lumber-framed structures, and log cabins—a testament to the impermanence of some of the camps.

Mines in the Camp Creek Area

Ruby Group

Rated at A-1 to A-3. This group is located approximately in the northwest ¼ of Section 25, T23N, R14E, on the USGS 7.5 Minute Series map for Davis Peak.

The Ruby Group consisted of two claims on three parallel ledges. One crosses the Cle Elum River and extends westward up Goat Mountain. At river level, a 50-foot tunnel showed fine-grained arsenical iron and iron sulfides containing gold and silver. Another small tunnel had similar ore. When we visited in 1997, there were three adits, all flooded. This is the John Burke Silver Mine, developed in more recent times in

---

[61] On April 18, 1905, the Galena Post Office was established, but it was closed on October 30. For several years afterward, Jack Greaser had a small store (which he had bought from Adolph Elsner) at Camp Creek, and he provided mail service to the settlers in the area as a courtesy. Greaser died at Camp Creek, in the late 1930s, at the ripe old age of 93.

the same area. The extended workings in the adits belong to Burke. An ore cart axle, with wheels attached, was visible, buried and frozen (below the high-water level) into the riverbed, about 40 yards upstream from the Ruby tunnels. Gold and silver were the metals sought here.

For the Rockhound

There are two heaps of ore at river level outside the Ruby digs. The two piles contain different types of ore. It is worth the effort to break open some chunks. The black and white banded rock inside is ore with a silver and lead mix. The other heap is a less impressive type of pyrite.

Brown Bear[62]

Information about this claim originated in an 1897 report. Rated at A-1 to A-3. This property is located in approximately the northwest ¼ of Section 25, T23N, R14E.[63] The property extends west, off the Ruby Group and up Goat Mountain. The best ledge outcrops in a gully that has a 25-foot waterfall. Galena shows in a 10-foot tunnel. We explored the slopes of Goat Mountain and found nothing, mostly because of the thick underbrush and vine maple. The overburden has also had plenty of time to do its dirty work by sloughing over what remained of the digs. There are other short adits at the river level, but their identities are uncertain. Gold and silver were sought here.

Silver Dump

Rated at A-2. The Silver Dump is located in the southeast ¼ of Section 23, T23N, R14E, as seen on the USGS 7.5 Minute Series map for Davis Peak. At 0.4 mile north of Camp Creek, there is a small, old, deteriorating cabin on the left (west) side of the main road. Near an outcrop of rock behind the cabin, there is a cable extending across the river that was used to transfer mining goods to the other side, where a cabin site now exists. Find the path down the steep riverbank. The Silver Dump tunnel is across the river. If you search around the area under the cable, you'll see a large, iron-stained mass of ore rock in and along the river. It was blasted with explosives at one time, creating obvious holes in the river bottom, to determine the quantity of the ore-bearing rock. You can see these holes only when the river is low. The ore that was sought here contained gold and silver.

Beaver Claim

Rated at A-1. The site is located in the northeast ¼ of Section 26, T23N, R14E, as found on the USGS 7.5 Minute Series map for Davis Peak. Three-tenths of a mile north of Camp Creek, an old secondary road heads east off the main road. Go about 200 feet on this road, look right, and walk south into the trees. When a hill appears, watch for a tailing pile and the adit. The tunnel is caved, but the top is visible above the debris on the floor. Roots extend from the ceiling. Do not enter the adit. It is in a constant state of collapse and unsafe. Instead, walk 300 feet east of the Beaver adit and check out the cabin site. The ore contains gold, silver, and copper.

For the Rockhound

There are some ore samples in the tailings, but from the looks of it you might have to do some digging to turn up a decent one.

---

[62] Another Brown Bear Group of claims appears on record, located at the headwaters of creeks flowing south into the North, South, and Middle Forks of the Teanaway Rivers. It is included in the Teanaway Valley mineral information.
[63] Owner George Koppen sold the property to Weise and Smith.

Maud-O, 1889 / Modog Claims

Rated at C-2 to C-3. These claims, currently known as the Modog Claims, are located in the top ¼, and center, of Section 25, T23N, R14E, as seen on the USGS 7.5 Minute Series map for Davis Peak, at an elevation of 4,400 feet.

The owners were A. D. Olmstead, C. O. Swayne, and A. W Haight[64] from Roslyn and E. W. Wilson and S. W. Sill of Seattle. The property has an 18-inch vein containing free-milling gold on a ledge, exposed by a 147-foot incline tunnel.[65] A very dry summer in 1889 prevented the Maud-O from doing anything beyond blocking out ore and stacking the blasted rock until waterpower would allow machinery to complete the final steps of ore concentration. Swayne and Haight purchased a five-stamp mill and concentrator from the Donahue Mine in the Blewett Mining District, which was moved to Roslyn for repairs. Meanwhile, the miners continued adding to the growing heap of high-grade ore waiting to be crushed and processed. The processing included a new cyanide ore treatment that Swayne had been formulating. When the time came to move the repaired mining machinery to the Maud-O, three four-horse teams were required to haul the massive machine parts. This mine continued to produce into the 1930s.

Geology

The gold was extracted from mineralized quartz (free gold) and in zones of crushed serpentinized peridotite, where gold was produced from pyrite and arsenopyrite.

When we were there in 1996, the adit had been inundated by rock debris and hillsides were eroded from snow and rain. We did notice recent signs of prospecting activity. In a few areas, hammered rock samples lay scattered here and there. We didn't see any high-grade ore, however.

Getting There

Use the USGS 7.5 Minute Series map for Davis Peak. Take Camp Creek Road to its end, and cross Camp Creek (the bridge is out). Start up the 4WD road[66] on foot, passing a private residence to the left. After the fifth switchback (at 0.7 mile), go 0.2 mile and watch carefully for the Maud-O Trail leading off to the right (east). Hike 0.3 mile to the mine.

Ida Elmore, 1883/Melade, 1948/Hughes-Wayman

Rated at C-4, this one mine has had three different names at different phases of its history. Originally named the Ida Elmore, in 1948 it was renamed the Melade, and it's currently known as the Hughes-Wayman. This property is in the southeast ¼ of Section 24 and northeast ¼ of Section 25, T23N, R14E, as seen on the USGS 7.5 Minute Series map for Davis Peak, at an elevation of 5,275 feet.

Geology

The prevailing rocks are chiefly peridotite, altered to serpentine. Large peridotite bodies with dikes expose several high-grade ore shoots. A dike-like mass of serpentine about 200 feet thick cuts across areas of the Hawkins lava formation located on the property. The dark green lavas are the greenstone of the area. The Ida Elmore's shear zones vary from a few inches to 50 inches in width, and are filled mainly with kaolin (a gray, clayish material), quartz, and talcs. Gold and silver were the metals of value sought here.

---

[64] Swain and Haight owned and ran a general merchandise store in Roslyn.

[65] Anthony Stoves Jr. was sole owner of the Maud-O at some point in the mine's history. He also bought stock in several of the mineral properties in the Cle Elum Mining District. At Roslyn, he operated a fish market and drug store, was undertaker, served as city treasurer (from 1898 to 1907), and then owned and operated the town telephone system around 1900. By the mid-1920s he had 200 phone subscribers. The Stoves family resided in Roslyn up to 1955, according to old-timers in the town.

[66] This is the mine-to-market road that served the mines along and around the Camp Creek area. Though the road passes through private land, it is a public thoroughfare. Respect *all* private land. Enter private property *only* with the owner's permission.

Mineralogy

The principal ores are of the sulphide types, mostly arsenopyrite, pyrrhotite, chalcopyrite, and pyrite that contain gold and silver, while the gangue is quartz. A 50-pound sample was sent to the Tacoma smelter in 1950, and it showed values of $26.25 per ton.

Ida Elmore History

In 1898, S. S. Hawkins, James Grieve, and a person named Dunlap, all from Cle Elum, discovered and started the Ida Elmore.[67] These miners drove a tunnel toward the deposits that had been exposed by discovery pits 125 feet above the Ida Elmore adit. They worked through most of the winter to develop the tunnel, during which time there was just one mishap: one day, something frightened Hawkins' valuable packhorse, and it plunged down the mountainside, breaking its neck in the fall.

By 1892, the adit was in over 200 feet, with good prospects in sight. All work on this mine was apparently done prior to 1913, because no written evidence was found to show production beyond that date. In 1913, the two claims were patented as the Ida Elmore, and the name Apex appears in place of the Valinia.

History of the Melade

M. S. Pechet formed the Melade Mine from the leasing of the Ida Elmore/Apex Claims in 1948.[68] The property occupied by the claims totaled 35 acres. Ida Elmore was the usual 1,500-by-600–foot claim. Apex was a short claim, or fraction, measuring 1,500 feet by 400 feet. Eight unpatented claims were staked and recorded by Pechet in 1950. This brought the total acreage to 160. A two-mile–long tractor road to the mine was put in the same year. While Pechet was in control of this property (there is no data showing he developed the ore deposits), it included three tunnels on the west slope of Huckleberry Mountain in the south ¼ of Section 24, T23N, R14E. At that site, we found two lower snub tunnels (one 20 feet long and the other 50 feet long). The shorter adit had a vein of arsenopyrite showing that was about five feet long by one foot wide, and very hard to work samples from. Farther up and at trailside, there is a caved adit. At the end of the trail lies a tunnel about 100 feet long. A cabin site located 100 feet south of the upper tunnel seemed to be a barren dig. These are not part of the original Ida Elmore Claims; Pechet added them to the Melade Mine's unpatented properties.

Hughes-Wayman Prospect[69] History

We have investigated and sampled the property. It looks like development during recent years has significantly altered the site's original configuration; it now consists of two open adits, two caved adits, and five prospect pits. The deposits at the Ida Elmore Mine/Melade Mine/Hughes-Wayman Prospects reportedly have potential for additional resources.

When we visited this spot in 1996, Adit #1, which lies at the end of the road, was ankle deep in iron-stained mud and flooded with water caused by overburden building up at the portal. The wood base, steel-strip–topped ore-cart tracks were still visible past the floodwater area. The drift with the best high-grade ore is now completely caved, with about 100 tons of rock and dirt reaching to the floor of the main tunnel. The portal is well on its way to being sloughed over and covered by overburden. Adit #2 is 150 feet down and on the south side of the road from the #1 tunnel. This 50-foot tunnel is open and dry. It follows a 6 to 18–inch quartz vein containing disseminated pyrite crystals.

---

[67] A second claim listed with the Ida Elmore was the Valinia property.
[68] Nine people owned shares in the Ida Elmore/Apex Claims. Charles Larsen of Sioux Falls, South Dakota (spokesman, and one of the nine who owned the properties), authorized a 25-year lease to Pechet for a 10 percent royalty based on smelter returns.
[69] The latest name for the old Ida Elmore Mine/Melade Mine.

For the Rockhound

At one time, there was a large pile of high-grade ore in front of and across the road from Adit #1. You can find samples by digging. The ore, when hammered open, reveals various pyrites. In the surface prospect pits, 125 feet above Adit #1, look for arsenopyrite, chalcopyrite, quartz, and rocks stained green by malachite.

Getting There

Use the USGS 7.5 Minute Series map for Davis Peak. This will be a 2 to 2½–hour (2.4 mile) hike on a steep 4WD road. Take the Camp Creek Road to its end at Camp Creek (the bridge is out). As the hike starts up the 4WD road, notice the house on the left (west). Continue to the fifth switchback (0.7 mile), and head onward. Watch for a trail (going east) in another 0.2 mile. (Do not take it; it goes to the Maud-O.) Keep on truckin' ahead for one mile to a fork in the road, and go northwest (left) for 0.4 mile to the end of the road, where you'll see Tunnel #1. A log along the north bank of the portal marks the tunnel entrance (if it happens to be caved). Across from the portal is where the ore was piled. Backtrack 150 feet down the road to the Adit #2 (west) side of the road (the downhill slope). From the Ida Elmore #1, you can enjoy a view of Hawkins Mountain and the Cle Elum River valley on a clear day. The Copper Queen Claims are visible to the left (on the southeast slope of Hawkins Mountain, about one mile away), if you know the vicinity of the claim site. Look for the rust-colored tailing piles that mark the Copper Queen Adits.

Olmstead Mine

Not rated. Olmstead was one of the Maud-O original owners. He later obtained sole possession of the property, which was located near the Maud-O and Ida Elmore. Olmstead was working a 150-foot tunnel containing free gold in a decomposed quartz vein. The tunnel's exact location is unknown.

Silver Claim

Not rated. This is another of the Ida Elmore's neighbors. A 70-foot incline tunnel is in the general area in the southwest ¼ of Section 24, T23N, R14E. The exact adit location is unknown.

Cle Elum and Hawk Mines

Not rated. These mines are located near the southwest ¼ of Section 24, but we weren't able to find them. The original owners, Ben Kelly and A. W. Boyles, had four claims on two ledges of ore that were two to five feet wide, exposed in a 70-foot incline shaft. A 120-foot crosscut was driven to tap the shaft. The other ore ledge had a 30-foot incline shaft showing 8 to 10 feet of ledge. The gold value from the three claims varied, high to low, with a showing of silver.

Edna R.

This property was located in the same area as the Cle Elum and Hawk. The ore that was sought here contained gold. Free gold was found in a quartz vein, which ran through granodiorite near a serpentine contact.

Iias, 1881/Williams, 1949

Rated at D-5. The site is located in the southwest ¼ of Section 29, T23N, R15E, as seen on the USGS 7.5 Minute Series map for Mount Stuart, at an elevation of 5,900 feet. In 1881, Mose Splawn and S. S. Hawkins were the first to locate this claim. John Flint was the recorded owner in 1887. There is an absence of data until 1948, when Riley Williams of Yakima took ownership. The Iias/Williams had two claims: the Iias (patented) and the Iias Extension (unpatented). The ore sought here contained copper, silver, and gold.

Geology/Mineralogy/Development

Adit #1

There is a 17-foot shaft on the north boundary of the Iias (patented) Claim. It is 200 feet north of caved Adit #1. Adit #1 is the northmost tunnel. This 51-foot–long working is now caved. A two-foot-wide quartz vein is exposed in the altered volcanic rock at the portal. The quartz is rusty and vuggy, showing euhedral crystals.[70] No sulfides are present. A recent grab sample assayed for gold came out negative.

Adit #2

This adit is 130 feet south of Adit #1. It has a two-foot–wide white quartz vein in an outcrop above the adit (the same type of quartz as Adit #1), with little or no iron stain showing. The vein pinches out before reaching the tunnel level, which is 50 feet below the quartz outcropping. Adit #2 is only 28 feet long and caved. A gold assay was taken here, but it turned out negative.

Adit #3

The longest tunnel, at 112 feet, is located 80 feet south of Adit #2. Adit #3 is at the edge of a slide, next to the tree line on the slope. It is also caved. You can find chunks of rusty quartz with chalcopyrite speckled throughout the old tailing pile and dump. The tailings are the only way to identify the hidden portal. An assay showed only a trace of gold.

Riley Williams reported the presence of bornite stringers when he was working in Adit #3. Fifty feet north of Adit #3, there is an old open cut. Before it sloughed in with rock and dirt, it measured 10 feet wide by 22 feet deep and 33 feet long. What remained of the dump showed no indication of quartz or altered material. This claim was in a zone 500 feet long and 20 feet thick, which had been hydrothermally altered. Quartz is deposited along fractures that are scattered throughout. Pods of sulfides, which could be an indication of low copper values, lie in serpentine along lenticular shear zones at drainage-creek level in a gulch south of the claims.

Getting There

Use the USGS 7.5 Minute maps of Davis Peak and Mount Stuart. Follow the same instructions for getting to the Ida Elmore turnoff. At 0.3 mile past that turnoff, take the road/trail that leads downhill (south), where it will become indistinct at the meadow area (0.4 mile from the last south-trending turn). Walk to the southwest area of the trees, at the meadow's edge. A very good road all the way to the claims area (about a half mile long) can be found within 300 feet (you'll find it if you search around). Backtrack and try a more southerly route if your first attempt fails. The tunnels are in the area below the road level, downslope, and another is in the drainage to Big Boulder Creek.

> **Caution** All decisions to continue at any point in the "How To Get There" guidelines are entirely your responsibility.

Epha Claim

This claim was an eastern extension of the Iias Property in 1887. Owners Mose Emerson and John O'Neil worked it as a surface vein. This could be the open cut on the Iias extension that Williams added to the Iias Claims in 1948.

---

[70] Rock minerals that are bounded by crystal faces.

Mining with a Goat According to an article in the Cle Elum Tribune from the 1890s, an old miner named Joe Bourke discovered that a considerable amount of blasting powder was mysteriously missing from his supplies. While searching for his purloined goods on the mountain where he lived, he spotted three sticks of dynamite on the trail ahead. Just as he started for them, a large mountain goat emerged from some bushes and started to eat the dynamite. Joe stopped and stared in disbelief until the last stick disappeared down the goat's throat. Joe began shouting, and the startled goat bolted down the trail, exploding after several leaps. The roar from the explosion was heard by miners at camp a mile away. It seems the billy goat had swallowed a blasting cap along with the rest of his dangerous meal. The explosion dug a shaft into the mountainside seven feet deep, exposing a rich vein of fine copper ore. Joe landed unhurt in a snow bank 40 feet away. Makes a person wonder whether Joe was smiling or looking serious when he told this tale.

Silver Bullion

Not rated. The Silver Bullion is located in the west ½ of Section 32, T23N, R15E, at about 1,000 feet elevation, south of the Iias Claims. In 1949, Riley Williams was listed as owner of the Silver Bullion. Its 168-foot shaft was blasted into a serpentine slide area near a drainage to Big Boulder Creek. The shaft's tailing pile was said to be heavily copper-stained, the rock containing magnetite with scattered specks of chalcopyrite. The material contained less than three percent copper and was not considered good ore. We haven't visited this property.

Blue Bonnet, 1952

Not rated. The Blue Bonnet is located in the southeast ¼ of Section 25, T23N, R14E. Riley Williams owns this claim. The ore contains copper, nickel, gold, and silver.

Boyles, 1881

Not rated. This property is located in Section 31, T23N, R15E, as seen on the USGS 7.5 Minute Series map for Davis Peak. The Boyles Property was made up of eight claims. The largest ledge (#1), had 40-, 70-, 90-, and 200-foot tunnels, all in ore. A smaller ledge (#2) was opened by 30-foot and 100-foot tunnels. Its copper ore was assayed at from 10 to 48 percent. Another ledge, 18 to 36 inches wide, assaying high in free gold, crossed through Ledges #1 and #2 at a right angle. This area is very steep and high-ridged, and there are slopes of slide debris throughout. It is not accessible by trail. The ore contained copper, silver, and gold.

Bobtail Mine, 1900

Not rated. The location of the Bobtail is unknown. Washington Copper Preferred Company of Cle Elum, and mine manager W. F. McNalt, are mentioned only once in printed information about the property. The workings consisted of three shafts and a tunnel driven toward a four-foot vein of high-grade black oxide of copper ore. The miners were lucky enough to cut three blind veins of ore while working the tunnel to the main vein on the Bobtail lead. At the time, the *Cle Elum Tribune* ran a story reporting that three shifts of miners had been at work continuously for four months and had driven the tunnel in 500 feet. The claim could have changed hands, and property names may have changed, which would explain the loss of further details on the mine's development under the title of Bobtail. The ore contained copper.

Copper Queens

Rated at D-4. This property is located in the center of Section 30, as seen on the USGS 7.5 Minute Series map for Davis Peak.

Geology

Elongated granitic rock bodies intrude into the serpentinized peridotite of the claim area country rock. The granitic intrusion, stained by iron oxide, can be seen for 600 feet on the surface. The rock has narrow veins and pods of quartz, with stringers of calcite containing disseminated chalcopyrite and pyrite. Some of the surface areas and joints contain azurite and malachite coatings.

We haven't uncovered any turn of the last century claims that can be cross-referenced to workings of the Copper Queens. These are digs of older origin, and more than likely some of Hawkins and Splawn's earliest locations. Because some claim data is so convoluted, this one has given us the slip.

When we visited the property in 1996, the 300-foot crosscut adit (printed on the USGS Davis Peak map) was caved. Follow the indistinct road, passing under the caved adit, through the meadow, and up a steeply graded switchback road (not on the map). Then bear left (north to northeast) when other trails radiate off in different directions. It will end at the two upper Copper Queens tunnels. The 20-foot adit was open; the 10-footer was caved. The view west and north of these adits is worth the effort to gain this world-surveying perch. On a clear day, Goat Mountain is visible to the west on the other side of the Cle Elum River valley. The Ida Elmore area and ridges to the west comprise a natural portrait of scenic grandeur.

For the Rockhound

There are rocks among the tailings and around the upper tunnels area that contain various pyrites. Find the heavy ones, hammer them open, and enjoy the prize.

Getting There

This is a mostly steep, three-mile hike, one-way. Take along the USGS Davis Peak map; it will save you from lapses of memory when you make unplanned detours. The time it takes to reach the property will depend on your physical condition and hiking experience. Use the same route guide given up to the Iias Claims turnoff, but instead go straight ahead on the level road toward the meadow area. Rest here, because after the meadow the remaining half mile to the upper adits is the steepest.

Huckleberry

Not rated. This property was located in the southwest ¼ of Section 24, T23N, R14E, south of a stream that flows to the Cle Elm River.

Geology

The Huckleberry Mountain area consists mainly of greenstone and serpentinized peridotite, with intrusions of granodiorite. Some of the high elevations have areas of bedded silicified volcanic breccia. There are sparse surface exposures of gold, silver, and copper. Most of the prospects were located along shear zones, with quartz veins in serpentine lying within the brecciated volcanics. The ore contained copper, silver, and gold.

History of Ownership/Mineralogy/Development

The original owners were Swain and Haight of Roslyn. Assays of the ore showed 39 percent silver, three percent gold, and 22 percent copper. The projected tunnel would tap the vein at a distance of 200 feet below the outcropping ore.

The year 1887 found R. Montague, O. R. Johnson, Andrew Jackson, and Simon Justhand with a ledge of ore that crossed three claims. Tunnels 20 and 40 feet long were driven in an effort to extract gold, silver, and copper.

In 1889, Simon Justhand and the Jackson brothers partnered up to work the adit into a four-foot ledge of ore. The minerals sent for assay turned out to be 76 ounces of silver, one-tenth ounce gold, and 30 percent lead per ton. The installation of a 10-ton water jacket smelter was planned for the following spring.

Prior to 1935, four cars of ore were sent to the Tacoma Smelter. By 1943, Justhand added another property and became the sole owner of the four claims. Copper was the main ore mined, and silver and gold were the lesser values. The four-foot vein had been worked by a 600-foot tunnel at that point in time. There was no mention of development for the other adit in the 1887 report.

Camp Creek Mine/Bob Canson Mining Company, 1938/ White Cat/Three Crosses

Rated at B-3, this property was located in the northeast ¼ of the northeast ¼ of Section 26, on the dividing line between Sections 25 and 26, T23N, R14E, about 0.3 mile north of Camp Creek, as seen on the USGS 7.5 Minute Series map for Davis Peak. The elevation is 3,200 to 3,800 feet.

Geology

Four unpatented claims were located on shear zones that cut silicified rocks with calcite stringers. Pods and lenses in the shear zones show occurrences of pyrite, arsenopyrite, chalcopyrite, sphalerite, and galena. The common gangue minerals are calcite and quartz. The ore carries silver, gold, copper, lead, and zinc.

Adit #1

This tunnel is 100 feet long. At 3,100 feet elevation, the lowest adit had random lenses and sulfide minerals in shear zones from 1 to 1½ feet wide.

Adit #2

At 175 feet in length, this tunnel is located up a switchback trail that starts above Adit #1, at an elevation of 3,800 feet, on the south side of a snow melt and rain runoff gulch. Adit #2 cuts a sulfide mineral zone 4½ to 6 feet wide, with a 20-foot stope area, 95 feet from the portal.

Adit #3

This tunnel is 150 feet long and is the uppermost Camp Creek Mine dig. It is also south of the gulch and 50 feet above Adit #2. Number 3 follows a shear zone, whose width was 3 to 3½ feet. The lenses and pods have sulfide minerals from 5 to 20 percent in high-grade ore. A modern survey reports a possible resource of 15,000 tons in ore. The assay (an average of many samples) showed 2.63 ounces of silver per ton, 0.07 percent in copper, 0.34 ounce in lead, 0.03 in zinc, and gold from 0.14 to 0.27 ounce per ton. A total of 15½ tons of this ore was shipped to the Tacoma smelter in 1927 and 1956.

Ownership History

It's not clear who the owners and locators of this property were from the late 1880s to the turn of the century. Bob Canson Mining Company (1938) and Camp Creek Mining Company, Inc., of Seattle (1929–1940) both claimed to own it at the same time, followed by Phil Denny of Seattle (1951) and Cle Elum River Mining Company (1952–?). This mine is also listed as the White Cat Mine (1989). In 1998, Art Baydo was involved with the Three Crosses Property (White Cat), but exploratory drilling was the only activity recorded. The commodities sought were copper, gold, and silver.

Getting There

Three-tenths of a mile north of Camp Creek, there is an eroded dirt road on the east side of the Cle Elum River Road that goes about 300 feet, runs steeply to the northwest for another 300 feet, and ends at the lower tunnel (Adit #1). This tunnel shows some signs of deterioration, as do the other adits. A switchback trail begins just above Adit #1 to the southeast, and winds its way up for a 600-foot elevation gain. Near the upper two tunnels and just off the trail, you'll notice an ore car missing its wheels, with three white crosses painted on it.

For the Rockhound

Below Adit #3, in the gulch, there are various sizes of high-grade ore. They are iron-stained, so hammer the heavy ones to break them open and find a sample. The different types of pyrites show themselves well when released from their rusty, camouflaged coating.

> **Attention** These claims could still be actively held by the Three Crosses Mine folks, so respect any signs posted. Get permission before entering posted property.

Claims Between Huckleberry Mountain and Fortune Creek

No rating is given for these mines. All the properties are in the north ½ of Section 24, the south ¼ of Section 13, T23N, R14E, the north ½ of Section 19, and the south ¼ of Section 18, T23N, R15E, south of Fortune Creek as seen on the USGS 7.5 Minute map of Davis Peak. The following has been compiled from sparse data and should be used only as a general information guide. We haven't visited these sites.

Family Group

Consisting of four claims, this property is assumed to be on the east bank of the second feeder stream from the mouth of Fortune Creek. That would place it near the upper ½ of short-platted Section 19, and the lower ½ of Section 18, south of Fortune Creek. The claims start from the mouth of the feeder stream at Fortune Creek and extend south to the northernmost summit of a two-peaked, unnamed 6,031-foot mountain. They lie east of the stream on a sloping gulch bank. The four claims cover a massive body of low-grade ore 80 feet wide at the summit and 225 feet wide at the lower elevation, where the property is cut by the feeder stream. The minerals of the ledge are talcose quartz in a talc gangue, with fine-grained sulfides distributed throughout. A 33-foot tunnel follows a syenite hanging wall and a granite foot wall, which crosses a zone of hard, dark quartz. A 10-foot crosscut works through ore at an angle headed toward the hanging wall. Assays showed some gold and silver.

Don Tom

Consisting of two claims, this offshoot claim runs northeast from the Family property. It follows a spur ridge downslope near the east line of Section 19. As a surface dig, it assayed gold and a trace of silver.

Mountain Whistler[71]

This two-claim property is located on the same gulch as the Family Claims, but on the opposite bank (west). The Whistler properties are at the bottom of the gulch (near the south bank of Fortune Creek) and run up the mountain. The ledge of ore was 14 feet wide, exposed by an open cut 20 feet long by 20 feet deep, similar to the ore of the Family Group.

Piper Hiedseck

The single claim on this property runs south off Fortune Creek and extends west from the Mountain Whistler's western claim boundary.

St. Paul

Consisting of one claim, the property starts off Fortune Creek and east of the last (westernmost) feeder stream flowing into Fortune Creek. It is located about 500 feet west of the Mountain Whistler.

Silver Queen

These two claims situated on parallel ledges are on the next (westernmost/last) feeder stream gulch west of the Family Group of claims and Mountain Whistler Properties. The Silver Queen Claims angle off the feeder stream in a southeast direction, near 4,600 feet in elevation, east of center in Section 24.

Ole Olehamer Claim

The location of this claim is unknown. Ole drove a 50-foot tunnel following a ledge 3½ feet wide; the sulfides carrying gold and silver assayed from $20 to $30 per ton. An ore house had 70 tons of ore stored in it at the time of the report.

Morning Star Mining and Milling, 1889

This property extends northeast, off the northeast corner of the Silver Queen.

    This mining company was headquartered in Seattle, and had been incorporated for $1 million, with one million shares at $1.00 each. William Campbell was president, and J. McDonald served as secretary and treasurer. Both were from Seattle. Work was underway on buildings to accommodate the mining crew that was expected that spring.

Gold Bug/Midway

These two claims lie southeast of the Silver Queen, about 1,500 feet away and at an elevation of between 5,400 and 5,800 feet on the east side, near the head of the same feeder stream/gulch as the Silver Queen. Eighteen feet of open cut revealed free gold on a four-foot ledge.

Fortune Creek

Geology

Numerous prospects and mine sites are scattered along Fortune Creek and up the mountain slopes containing the properties. The rock generally consists of underlying serpentinized peridotite, with intrusions of granodiorite. The individual claim's geologic ore is of a more specific nature. Where the rock is sheared,

---

[71] Once more, William McKasson and John Corbins appear on the property roll call, this time as co-owners with the mayor of Roslyn, H. P. Fogh.

slickensides (created when fault rock slides against each other) appear in the serpentine. Fractured shear zones can be found filled with arsenopyrite, chalcopyrite, and pyrite. The dominant mineral in the veins is chalcopyrite, while the most abundant vein materials are quartz, talc, and carbonates.

Fortune Creek Mining Development

This area is located on the USGS 7.5 Minute Series map for Davis Peak.

Numerous placer mines operated along the Cle Elum River from its headwaters to Cle Elum Lake and to the Yakima River, but most placer miners barely made a living here. These mines were located at about the same time that the quartz lodes were being discovered in the nearby hills. Fortune Creek, its north and south branches, and all feeder streams were prospected and claimed for gold content. In some instances, the miners began to focus on silver and copper, which eventually became the dominant ores produced.

Two miners, Mr. Hicks and Mr. Jones of Ellensburg, worked the placers of Fortune Creek[72] for four years with varying success. They reportedly found coarse gold and nuggets. The largest nugget was worth $16.00 (by the 1896 gold standard). On one prospecting trip, they struck an old river channel, in which the character of the gravel changed and the gold became coarser.

Fortune Creek Placer, 1887

Rated at A-1, this placer, also owned by Hicks and Jones, produced gold. It is located on the Cle Elum River, near the mouth of Fortune Creek, in the southeast ¼ of Section 14, T23N, R14E, 1½ miles north of Camp Creek.

Fortune Creek Mill Site

Rated at A-1. The mill site was located in the southeast ¼ of Section 14, T23N, R14E.

By 1889, Hicks and Jones had formed the Fortune Creek Smelting and Refining Company, which consisted of a building with a 15-ton–capacity and a water-jacketed silver and lead smelter. They ended the season on a prosperous note. Hicks and Jones expanded their operation again in 1895, renaming it the Fortune Creek Mining, Milling, and Smeltering Company. They added a two-stamp mill that sported 600-pound stamps, and special coil springs to increase its efficiency. It was powered by a 10-foot–high dam on the Cle Elum River that produced enough flow to push a waterwheel. The damn dam soon fell down from the force of the fall floods, which caused a flow of fast-moving flotsam (and jetsam). During the winter the dam was rebuilt, and by spring of 1896 Hicks and Jones had added a cyanide plant to the reopened mill.

Fortune Mining & Smelting Company

Organized in Spokane on April 5, 1899, this company had 19 claims in the Cle Elum and Leavenworth Mining District, which included property from the mouth to the divide at the head of Fortune Creek. Eleven distinct ledges from 1 to 300 feet wide were located. A very favorable and unproven statement was made about the Jackson, Golden Chariot, and Silver Tip ledges.

Fortune Creek Mine

A 1903 report referred to this mine as equipped with up-to-date amenities, a bunkhouse, business and assay offices, and so on. Tom Collier was superintendent and G. D. Davis manager. These two individuals were also linked to the Sure Thing Gold & Copper Mining Company.

The McPhail Engineering Company of Tacoma reopened the mine, and was in the process of developing the Fortune Creek to Van Epps Pass road. The company invested $70,000 in the mines and roadwork and was taking out several tons of ore. McPhail reported its intention to invest $100,000.00 in further development, including a proposed mill if all went well, but the endeavor failed.

---

[72] Miners Jim Muldoon and Curt Homer owned two cabins near this area.

Getting There

Fortune Creek is a popular area among modern prospectors, and the creek is in a constant state of claims possession and activity. Always ask permission to enter on posted land. When you do visit one of these historic sites, remember to leave it clean. Also, respect the property boundaries of the owners. Their land is private and off limits to the public.

The map that we use shows the mill site to be south of Fortune Creek on the east side of the road, though others have said it's on the north side of the creek due to a flood that altered the creek's course. Go just past the Fortune Creek Bridge, and take the road that goes west to the river.

A group of Ballard community miners and investors from Seattle were supposed to have constructed their own stamp mill on Fortune Creek, but we haven't found any records supporting this. Apparently, their claims furnished ore to the Fortune Creek Mill, since their property is adjacent to it on a mountain slope to the east.

Fortune Creek Mines

Golden Eagle

Not rated. This single-claim property is located in the southwest ¼ of Section 13, T23N, R14E, as seen on the USGS Davis Peak map.

This claim extends north from the St. Paul Claim's previously described north boundary to 0.8 mile up the 4WD road that winds north of and east along Fortune Creek.

Mountain Belle

Not rated. This site, consisting of one claim, is located in the center of Section 13, and extends northwest off the Golden Eagle, one mile from the mouth of Fortune Creek. This property belonged to the Fortune Creek Mining and Milling Company. An open cut showed ore valued mostly in copper and gold.

Mountain Chief Mining Company/Mayflower

Not rated. These properties consisted of one claim each, and were owned by S. C. Emery and H. F. Weise. Emery and Weise later sold to a group of Ballard/Seattle men. The properties are located in the center of Section 13, one mile from the mouth of Fortune Creek.

The Mountain Chief cuts east/west across the north end of the above-mentioned Mountain Belle Claims. It had a 1½-foot ledge of talc between black quartz and granite walls.

The Mayflower was a gold dig with two short adits in crystalline quartz. It runs northwest off the middle-north boundary of the Mountain Chief. These two claims belonged to the group of aforementioned Scandinavian miners from Ballard, Washington, who were thought to have had their own mill site.

Water rights were of great importance and worth at this time. If the Mountain Chief and Mayflower owners had them, which they didn't, they could have built a log dam with a penstock and diverted water via a line ditch or flume to the property. The creek generally flows about 10 cubic feet per second during the driest part of the season (600 cubic feet per minute). The fall gradient is about 10 percent or more. All the necessary ingredients were present to run a mill.

Rocky Point Mining Company

Not rated. This company held two claims in the northwest ¼ of Section 13 and southwest ¼ of Section 12 as indicated on the USGS 7.5 Minute Series map for Davis Peak. They were owned by two men from Tacoma, Mr. Sidney and Mr. King.

These two claims have three fissure veins of pyritic ore following up an unnamed 5,121-foot mountain slope. A ledge showed in a 50-foot tunnel. The full width of the adit indicates ore from one wall to the other, with an 18-inch sulfide streak. Two open cuts showed three feet of ore in one and three feet in the other. Gold was the primary metal sought.

Big Bug

Not rated. This property consisted of two claims and is located in the northwest ¼ of Section 13 on the Davis Peak map.

The Big Bug extends off the northernmost Rocky Point Claim in a northwesterly direction, downslope to Silver Creek, approximately 0.8 mile from the main Cle Elum River Road.

Ole Olehamer and the Terwilliger brothers dug free gold from an 18-foot open cut that ran through the middle of a four-foot–wide ledge.

Grizzly Bear #1 and #2

Not rated. The claims run northwest to southeast through the center of the southwest ¼ of Section 27, T23N, R15E, about one mile northeast of Gallagher Head Lake. Use the USGS 7.5 Minutes Series map of Mount Stuart.

S. S. Hawkins located this claim in the early 1890s. He was looking for copper deposits at that time and believed that a 100-foot tunnel would tap the ore ledge on his claim. However, he did not do more than the required assessment work. In 1897, Hawkins got around to pulverizing a piece of decomposed quartz ore in a mortar and washed out a streak of gold. He repeated the process several times, and the results were the same. The old miner was set in his ways and determined to find a rich ledge of copper. The show of gold added to the value of his property, but he did not consider it of great importance.

In 1900, he had the long-ignored rotten quartz assayed in Spokane. The return showed $234.00 in gold and $1.20 in silver per ton. When Hawkins drove two tunnels, trying to locate the sought-after copper lead, he had to blast through a massive deposit of the dark red decomposed rock.

Hawkins bonded the Grizzly Bear to A. O. Hellen[73] of Cle Elum for $70,000. Hellen thought it was a steal. There was nothing written on the subject until 1914, when the Dover Mining Company listed the Grizzly Bear as a gold, silver, lead, and antimony claim.

Gold Mountain

Not rated. Consisting of a single claim, this property was located in the center of Section 13. It cuts across a south-flowing feeder stream at a northwest-to-southeast angle on the south slope of a 5,121-foot unnamed mountain in T23N, R14E, as seen on the USGS 7.5 Minute Series map of Davis Peak.

The Ballard Gold Mining Company worked free-milling gold from a short tunnel located near the head of the feeder stream. Gold was thought to be the metal of value on this property.

Just In Time

Not rated. This free-gold mining property, consisting of one claim, extends northwest from the north end of the Gold Mountain Claim. Six feet of free-milling gold ore was exposed in a 10-foot shaft.

Queen of the Hills

Not rated. The single claim on the Queen of the Hills leads off the Just In Time Claim at a 90-degree angle to the northeast, near the summit marked 5,121T on the Davis Peak map. A 15-foot tunnel driven into a five-foot ledge exposed free-milling gold.

---

[73] A. O. Hellen also had nine claims in the Swauk Mining District.

Big Dome Prospect

Rated at E-3, this property is located near the north borderline at the center of Section 13 on the USGS 7.5 Minute Series map for Davis Peak, at an elevation of about 4,450 feet. Also see Green Trails Map #208 for Kachess Lake. Officers of the Big Dome Prospect were Oscar Johnson, president, and Mr. Petroberg, secretary (1954).

Big Dome is situated in the middle of the area once occupied by the Queen of the Hills, Just in Time, and Gold Mountain Claims. A 30-foot tunnel was driven into serpentine, which could be a later extension of the 15-foot tunnel driven on the Queen of the Hills Claim. The tunnel walls show chalcopyrite in the joints and contact zones. There are several pits and an open cut, with sulfides showing. We found a 12-inch outcrop of white quartz in serpentine, on a ridge west of a drainage gulch in the area. It was traced down the side of the gulch for about 40 feet. The ore found here contains copper, silver, and gold. Samples assayed at 0.44 percent copper.

Getting There

Drive north from Fortune Creek 0.8 mile to Road #170. There is a gate 1,000 feet up the road. If the gate is locked, park 100 yards back where the road forks. Use the USGS Davis Peak map to track your progress on this hike. Walk one mile from the gate, turn north up the mountain slope (or go until you reach a drainage gulch), and high bank upward 1,000 feet. It's a strenuous, straight-up hike and scramble. From any part of the ridge area, you will see a top-of-the-world view.

Red Bird Prospect

Rated at A-3, this single-claim property is located in approximately the southeast ¼ of the northeast ¼ of Section 13, T23N, R14E, as seen on the USGS 7.5 Minute Series map of Davis Peak.

The claim cuts Road #170 about 1.7 miles from the Cle Elum River Road, where the gully runoff crosses Road #170 over a concrete drain slab. The Red Bird runs up the gulch from the road. We found evidence of a collapsed pit, some very old timbers, and indications of more recent prospecting within 200 yards of the road.

Fountain of Gold

Not rated. Consisting of a single claim, this property is located in approximately the northeast ¼ of Section 13, T23N, R14E (determined from the general vicinity of the Red Bird), on the USGS 7.5 Minute Series map of Davis Peak. The Fountain of Gold extends to the northeast, off the north end of the Red Bird Claim.

Ballard Prospect

Not rated. This single-claim prospect is located in the northeast ¼ of Section 13, T23N, R14E, as seen on the USGS Davis Peak map. It lies 500 feet west of the Red Bird Claim, extending at 90 degrees, and south downslope off the end of the Fountain of Gold.

Red Eagle

Not rated. This one-claim property is located in the northeast ¼ of Section 13, T23N, R14E, on the USGS Davis Peak map. It runs south, off the south end of the Ballard Claim.

Sherman/Wisishin

Not rated. Consisting of a single claim each, these two properties are located in the northeast ¼ of Section 17, T23N, R15E, on the Mount Stuart map. They are situated between two feeder streams, at 4,200 to 5,400 feet elevation (according to a vague map reference). Lying northwest to southeast, the Sherman is to the northeast, and the Wisishin is to the southeast.

Fortune Creek Gold Placers

Nugget Placer

Rated at A-1, this single claim is located in the south ½ of Section 17, T23N, R15E, as seen on the USGS Mount Stuart map, and Green Trails Map #208 for Kachess Lake.

The Nugget Placer is west of where the south fork of Fortune Creek flows into Fortune Creek. It includes the area where the two feeder streams enter the creek. This was an active placer claim in 1998 under a different name.

Trio Placer

Rated at A-1. This single claim is located in the south ½ of Section 17, T23N, R15E, on the USGS Mount Stuart map.

The Trio is the connecting claim west and downstream from the Nugget and, as of this writing, is active.

Mountain Placer

Rated at A-1. Consisting of only one claim, this placer is located in the south ½ of Section 17, T23N, R15E, on the USGS 7.5 Minute Series map of Mount Stuart. The claim runs upstream on the South Fork Fortune Creek at its confluence with Fortune Creek. It was an active claim in 1998 and has been renamed.

Helm Placer

Rated at A-2. This single claim is located in the south ½ of Section 17, T23N, R15E, on the USGS Mount Stuart map. It is joined to the Mountain Placer's east end, and it runs up the south fork of Fortune Creek. It was active in 1998 under a new name.

Lake City Placer/Prospect

Rated at A-2 to A-3 and inaccessible by trail, reaching these two claims requires a high-bank creek hike. Use the creek bed in the dry season. Find these claims in the south ½ of Section 17, T23N, R15E, on the USGS Mount Stuart map.

The Lake City property lies along Fortune Creek. Its two claims run upstream from where South Fortune Creek and Fortune Creek meet. Somewhere on the property, there was a 24-inch ledge of sulfides that crossed into the Ruby King Claims at the upstream end of the Lake City Claim.

Getting There

These placer claims can be reached by driving on the Cle Elum River Road 0.8 mile north of Fortune Creek to Road #170. If the first gate you see is locked, find a place to park on the side of the road. Walk Road #170 for 2½ miles to the confluence of Fortune Creek and South Fork Fortune Creek. This is the placer claim area. When the gate is open, obey any cautionary or instruction signs posted. We suggest a more scenic, historic, and shorter hike along the Fortune Creek 4WD road/Trail #160 when the Road #170 gate is closed.

Tree Prospecting While the basic procedures for prospecting were generally observed, a more unconventional mode of prospecting gained a little status for a time as well. Tree prospecting was promoted for a short period, only to sink into obscurity again soon afterward. The discovery of minerals, as revealed by leaves from bushes, trees, and pine needles nearby, was briefly considered an open book to the presence of gold and other minerals. At the time this information was released to the world, it was claimed that tests had located gold, silver, copper, zinc, lead, manganese, and so on. The leaves and pine needles not only assayed correctly from foliage above known metal deposits, but they also indicated new mineral locations.

The tree miner would set a line along the projected mineral surface to be tested and pick leaves off the greenery at 50-foot intervals, about one pound from each at the same height above the ground, while also bagging and labeling the samples.

The testing process involved burning the leaves in front of a spectroscope (an instrument for revealing chemical composition by analyzing the rainbow, or spectrum makeup, of the light from the burning chemical). This procedure revealed even the slightest traces of metals or minerals in the burning leaves and gave their concentration. We could find no other data pertaining to this method of prospecting and concluded that the only mother lode was economic, enjoyed solely by spectroscope manufacturers.

Black Bear Prospect Tunnels, 1989

Rated at A-3, this property is located in the south ½ of Section 17, T23N, R15E, about 1,000 feet up Fortune Creek from Road #170, within the original Lake City Claim area. While not a placer, these tunnels are located so close to the placers listed in this section that we include them here for the sake of continuity.

The two adits are 25 feet apart, and 50 to 100 feet up the north bank of Fortune Creek. They are on the same vein, driven north, and both are about 50 feet long. Adit #1 (the west tunnel) was driven on a 50-foot vein along the hanging wall where the ore seems to be arsenopyrite. Adit #2 (the east adit) also runs its entire length along a hanging wall. The ore contains gold, silver, and copper.

For the Rockhound
We noticed on a 1996 visit that the adit walls were coated with moist dirt. A hammer and chisel were required to define and remove samples from the hard ore.

Getting There
From the Cle Elum River road, take Road #170 by foot or vehicle for 2½ miles. This is the junction of Fortune Creek and South Fortune Creek. Road #160 starts at this junction and follows the creek course for about a mile; then it heads northeast toward Van Epps Pass. The most direct route to the Black Bear adits is to walk, hike, and scramble about 0.25 mile from Road #170 upstream on Fortune Creek. Watch to the left (north) for indistinct traces of tailings high on the creek bank. Use caution when following the creek bed—the rocks are very slippery except during the dry season. Even dry rocks in the creek can be a challenge. There is a cabin site somewhere in this area.

Mine Accidents With all the mining that went on in Washington State, many incidents involving occupational accidents and deaths occurred. Most went unreported, but the following stands out as worthy of recognition.

On a Friday afternoon in the year 1900, two young miners, George Gray and Herbert Maycock, finished putting in four shots of dynamite (one had three sticks in one hole) prior to quitting work for the day. They were short on fuse and decided to divide what they had into four pieces. The fuse was damp and difficult to light. Three fuses ignited successfully, but the fourth took a few more seconds to start. Gray headed quickly toward safety with Maycock close behind. He got to the ladder and started up. Maycock lingered a few seconds at the bottom. Gray was 25 feet up the ladder when the first and heaviest blast (the result of three sticks of dynamite) went off. Maycock, still at the base of the ladder, was knocked senseless, and Gray was nearly shaken loose from his position above. The other three shots went off in quick succession, throwing rocks up the shaft and filling the hole with a thick cloud of dust and suffocating smoke. Some of the flying rocks struck Gray, inflicting painful but not serious injuries. Gray started back down at the immediate risk of suffocation by the dynamite's poisonous gases, discovering that Maycock was almost completely covered by rocks and dirt. A shroud of smoke swirled around him, and he lay motionless. With great effort, Gray extricated Maycock, whose body was limp and covered with bleeding cuts and abrasions. Then came the herculean task of climbing the 65-foot ladder with Maycock in tow.

Gray was not a large man, but his exceedingly strong 165-pound frame, plus a good rush of adrenalin, got them to the top of the shaft. With Maycock across his back, Gray hiked over 2½ miles to the miners' cabin. During the trek, Maycock recovered consciousness, but could not see or hear, and every part of his body had been injured. His eyes, ears, and nostrils were packed full of earth and bits of rock. Sharp, flinty particles of rock were stuck in his face, neck, chest, and hands. Blood oozed from numerous wounds.

Once they arrived at the cabin, Gray dispatched two other men the 12 miles to fetch the doctor, George Wright. The doctor found no broken bones, only cuts and bruises. Patiently, he picked out all the pieces of splintered, shattered rock and sewed up the larger gashes. Maycock regained sight in one eye within a few hours, but it took three days before he could see out of the other. He stayed with a fellow named Reddick while he recovered. Maycock was scarcely recognizable for some time, hobbling around town with contusions and dramatic discolorations on his face.

It was noted that Maycock's watch, which he wore in the left-hand pocket of his vest, was a total wreck after the explosion. The hands had stopped at 5:50 P.M., the exact instant of the blast. Amazingly, Maycock had a stick of dynamite in his pants pocket at the time of the explosion, yet it was not set off.

George Gray deserves recognition for his heroism and courage in the display of almost superhuman efforts to rescue his companion. Had Gray hesitated a few moments before descending into the deadly pit, Maycock would have been asphyxiated.

North Fortune Creek

Jacobson Cabin

Not rated. This property is located in the southeast ¼ of the northeast ¼ of Section 17, along North Fortune Creek, in T23N, R15E, as seen on the USGS 7.5 Minute Series map of Mount Stuart. Its original name is unknown.

Prospect pits are located from about 5,000 to 5,200 feet elevation along the trail following the north fork. The trail starts somewhere near the creek as it cuts south across Road #160. The trail is difficult, and its condition is not known.

The Jacobson Cabin digs is 5,300 to 5,400 feet in elevation. Workings consist of prospect pits and a caved adit on a 60-foot–wide iron-stained shear zone in serpentine. Pyrite and marcasite show in a 15-inch–wide talcose vein on the southeast wall of the shear zone. Gold, silver, and copper were sought here.

Silver Treasury Prospect

Not rated. This prospect is located in the southeast ¼ of Section 17, T23N, R15E, which can be found on the USGS Mount Stuart map. The prospect is on the upstream claim of the two old Lake City properties, 2,000 feet east from the Black Bear property and south off Fortune Creek.

Development consists of a cribbed shaft in serpentinized rock with iron stains in the fractures.

Ruby King,[74] 1896/Silver Bowl Prospect, 1989

Rated at B-3, these two claims are located in the southwest ¼ of Section 16, T23N, R15E, and can be found on the USGS 7.5 Minute Series map for Mount Stuart. From the aforementioned Black Bear Prospect, go 0.4 mile up the 4WD road where it crosses the North Fork Fortune Creek. Off-trail experience is a must, along with a warped kind of affection for bushwhacking.

In 1897, owners George Terwilliger, president of the Ballard Mining and Milling Company, his brother Ed, and R. E. Miles reported an ore sample that assayed 1,025 ounces of silver and $118.00 in gold, per ton. The ore was extracted from a six-foot ledge between granite walls and contained gold, silver, copper, lead, and antimony.

There was a cabin on the property, but we didn't find it. Development on the claim consists of two trenches on the north side of Fortune Creek: a caved 40-foot shaft sunk in serpentine with stringers of quartz showing dolomite and gypsum. A 125-foot caved adit was also driven southward on a vein. During early development, the ore was reportedly transported from the claim on packhorses.

Rushing Water and White Water

Not rated. These two claims are located in Section 16, T23N, R15E, as seen on the Mount Stuart map.

The claims were owned by the Terwilliger brothers, and they cut across either North Fortune Creek or Fortune Creek upstream from the Ruby King and above a feeder stream that flows southeast into the creek. The written data, and especially the physically misleading map (in distance and placement), makes only a general location possible. Gold was said to be present in a 40-foot ledge.

Standard and Olehamer

Not rated. These two claims are located in Section 16, T23N, R15E, as shown on the Mount Stuart map. The owners were three Ballard men, Ole Olehamer and George and Ed Terwilliger.

These digs run through the feeder stream just below the Rushing Water and White Water Claims, and are joined together where a stream turns, running through both properties. The workings were on three ledges, varying from two to three feet wide, where several open cuts were made. Gold, silver, and copper were found in the sulfides, plus a 20-foot streak of native lead one inch wide. Fifty tons of ore sat on the property dump. Gold was the major value sought here.

Twin Mining Company (two claims) and Jumbo (one claim)

Not rated. These claims are located in Section 16, T23N, R15E, as seen on the Mount Stuart map. Written data puts these claims 600 feet east of the Ruby King digs, which is completely inconsistent with the map's location. Road #160 runs through the general area.

---

[74] The Owner in 1914 was the Dover Mining Company.

George and Ed Terwilliger owned these digs in 1896. There were five separate and distinct veins within the boundary of the properties. Outcroppings from the veins could be traced for over 1,000 feet. The ore created much interest in its day. A 15-foot tunnel exposed two inches of copper sulfides, and an eight-foot crosscut into a 30-foot–wide outcrop showed galena and sulfides in quartz. Assays averaged $9.75 in gold, $6.00 in silver, $26.01 in copper, and $7.72 in lead per ton.

Eureka and King of Sweden

Not rated. Consisting of two claims, the location of this property is uncertain due to conflicting information sources. The claims were owned by Thomas McNutly of Tacoma. They were staked in 1891 and were listed as near Fish (Tucquala) Lake. The properties' rich gold and silver ore, taken from a four-foot ledge, was identified as similar to that of the Aurora Claim. The Aurora workings are east of Fish Lake. The mention of ore comparison could be an example, not an indication, of property adjacency. We mention the King of Sweden Claim because it extended off the Eureka Property to the northwest.

Tip Top #1

Not rated. This single claim is located in the northeast ¼ of Section 8, T23N, R15E, at the head of North Fork Fortune Creek as seen on the Mount Stuart map. John Berg and John Kelly of Roslyn had a 15-foot shaft driven into a 30-foot ledge. Sulfides carrying gold and silver were mined. The ore contained gold, silver, and copper.

Van Epps Pass Area Mines

Geology

There are numerous metal deposits in the Van Epps Pass area, and copper is the most dominant ore. Copper and other base metals occur as sulfide minerals in weakly developed shear zones. Some of the digs show only a copper carbonate stain. Mount Stuart granodiorite intrudes Paleozoic and Mesozoic ultramafic, metasedimentary, and metavolcanic rock. Shear zones parallel the contacts of the granitic rocks, while other shear zones cross the contacts.

The ore mined was pyrite, chalcopyrite, arsenopyrite, and sphalerite, which produced gold, silver, copper, molybdenum, and zinc. The areas worked are commonly iron-stained. Mineral deposits appear in ultramafic rock that is altered, or in shear zones and joints. Metallic ore is in veinlets in shear rock or quartz veins, or it is disseminated throughout the rock.

Only minor production has occurred even though the area was intensely prospected from the 1800s up to the present. In 1896, the existing claims were mostly in the Van Epps drainage, with some extending to the Fortune Creek side of the ridge. These were taken over by the Pickwick Mining and Development Company. Eighteen mining claims cover most of the mineralized area from the northeast ¼ of Section 16, T23N, R15E, the area in Section 9 west of 4WDR Road #160 to the west boundary of Section 9, and north in Section 9 to the last feeder stream above Van Epps Creek. These were patented in 1904. Prospecting continued off and on until the 1950s.

Benita Prospect

Rated at E-2 (E-3 for off-trail exploring), this prospect is located in the northeast ¼ of Section 15, as seen on the USGS 7.5 Minute Series map of Mount Stuart, 0.3 mile southeast of Van Epps Pass. It is at an elevation of 5,800 to 6,400 feet. The adit and shaft areas are printed on the map.

Extensive prospecting has resulted in several pits and trenches. There are four adits (two are caved), and a road cut near one tunnel has covered it with dirt and rocks. There are also two shafts (the incline shaft is caved). When we visited the site in 1996, the incline tunnel was eroded and open enough to see that it was flooded. We also saw water in the open shaft. These digs are aligned with a silicified zone enriched with sulfides. The Benita shear zone is reported to be 1,500 feet long, extending into the workings between serpentine, with rock walls to a width of 8 to 15 feet. In the center section of the zone, a quartz vein about five inches wide is 5 to 10 percent pyrite, chalcopyrite, and galena. Elongated pyrite-rich sulfide lenses, near some faults, average six inches to six feet long.

For the Rockhound

Hammering iron-stained rock from the available tailing piles can produce samples of mixed quartz and talc showing pyrite, chalcopyrite, and arsenopyrite in masses three to four inches wide.

Getting There

The Benita Claims are 4 to 4½ miles from the Cle Elum River Road if you hike or drive (as of 1998, three gates might have eliminated the driving option). The USGS 7.5 Minute Series Mount Stuart map lays out the route; all you need is stamina, good weather, and an early start. This is a good morning-to-dusk day hike, including side trips for rockhounding. There are good camping spots in the area near and on Van Epps Pass too. Water from feeder streams sometimes flows late into the hiking season.

Several main trail systems serve the region. The area is such that you need four maps to plot a course. Use Green Trails maps of Stevens Pass, #176; Chiwaukum Mountains, #177; Kachess Lake, #208; and Mount Stuart, #209. These maps give you the opportunity to put together hikes to and around these mining digs, with their memorable mountain scenery.

HHY Prospect

Rated at E-2 and progressing to E-3. It is located in the top and center of Section 16, T23N, R15E, north of the Scatter Creek Trail.

The serpentine of the HHY workings is fractured and weakly mineralized, and small fractures in the country rock are filled with disseminated pyrite. The adit[75] on the claim has a surface vein exposed along a strike zone for 24 feet. Samples from the vein assayed 2.9 ounces of silver and 4.2 percent copper per ton.

For the Rockhound

We haven't been to this site, but the geological picture indicates the possibility of finding samples from the vein.

Getting There

The directions to the Van Epps Pass/Benita Prospect apply here. Use Green Trails Map #209, Mount Stuart. From Van Epps Pass, take Trail #1226 (Scatter Creek Trail) west for a half mile. The HHY Prospect digs are north of and near the trail. Two pits or trenches are upslope from, and on either side of, the adit. They are the closest digs to the trail.

Van Epps Pass/Spirit Lake Prospects

This property is located in the northwest ¼ of Section 15, T23N, R15E, on the USGS Mount Stuart map.

There are several workings near Spirit Lake. A steep trail, about 200 yards south of Van Epps Pass, leads off the ridge to the lake. The trail is vague and hard to find from the ridge down. On our trip, we dropped over the ridge to the lake basin, located the trail there, and followed it on the return trip back up to the ridge. A search south and west of Spirit Lake revealed the debris from a few old cabin sites. The only open tunnel was southwest of the lake, 300 feet up the trail. It was in dangerous condition, because of its semi-caved portal, and more rock was ready to fall. The other adits and pits in the talus slopes, east and southeast of the lake, were visible using binoculars. They appeared to be caved, and we didn't visit them.

---

[75] The length of this adit is unknown.

Unnamed Adit #1

Rated at C-3 from Van Epps Pass Road #160, this adit is located in the northeast ¼ of the southeast ¼ of Section 8, T23N, R15E, as seen on the USGS 7.5 Minute Series map for Mount Stuart, and the Green Trails Map #209, Mount Stuart.

Follow the Scatter Creek Trail (#1226) from Van Epps Pass for 1.3 miles. High bank east of the eastmost, south-flowing feeder stream of North Fork Fortune Creek for 0.3 mile. The adit is between 5,800 and 6,000 feet elevation, and about 500 feet east of the feeder stream.

There is a 20-foot tunnel, driven into a lightly mineralized zone of serpentinized peridotite, in which a small pod of pyrite is exposed. Copper and silver were sought here.

Mines East of Van Epps Pass

These mines and prospects are in Chelan County's Leavenworth Mining District, up to one mile east of the Kittitas/Chelan County boundary line (the Cle Elum Mining District's east border). Access is shorter and easier via the Cle Elum Mining District side, and will be dealt with in the Cle Elum Mining Area data.

Goldie Mine

Rated at A-2 to A-3 from Road #160. The Goldie is located in the northeast ¼ of Section 16, T23N, R15E, as seen on the USGS Mount Stuart map. Go 500 feet north and down Road #160 from Van Epps Pass, and then 300 to 350 feet southwest off Road #160 up the hillside.

The two tunnels, 37 and 68 feet long, are driven into serpentine, felsite, and diorite, with disseminated pyrite and shear zones to 12 inches wide showing pyrite. The values sought here were in silver and copper.

Meadow Adit

Rated at B-3 from Road #160. This property is located in the northeast ¼ of the southeast ¼ of Section 9, T23N, R15E, as shown on the USGS Mount Stuart map.

From Van Epps Pass, go 0.5 mile to the second Van Epps Creek feeder stream that cuts across Road #160. Scramble up the stream bank to a large meadow. The adit is along the northern edge, blasted into a large outcrop of rock at the base of one of the ridge peaks. The huge tailing pile will be the first and most obvious indicator of the workings. The tunnel was caved enough to dam water, partially flooding the adit. Using the proper gear, we gained access and explored the digs. The 1,500-foot tunnel was driven toward the center of an iron-stained peak of felsite, felsite prophyry, and serpentinized peridotite. Several blind veins were intersected when the adit was driven.

About 200 feet from the portal, there is a drift that goes northwest (right side of the tunnel). It starts four feet off the tunnel floor, and is caved 150 feet into the drift. The remainder of an arsenopyrite vein, three to four inches thick, still shows on the footwall. The vein was very hard, making it difficult to extract samples. Many of the tunnel walls are rust colored, while a light greenish-gray color appears in places. Some areas are a mottled pattern of both. An area where the ore was stoped extends 150 feet past the northwest-bearing drift. Two drifts lie 150 feet past the stope, one to the right and the other to the left; both are about 50 feet long. The drift on the right (north) is uninteresting. The left-trending drift (south) more than makes up for the other. A rusty accumulation of iron oxide has thickly layered itself beneath several inches of water. It crunches like ice-glazed snow when you walk on it. At the end of the drift, there is a wet box containing six decomposing sticks of dynamite. Since we didn't know whether the dynamite was still dangerous, we terminated the exploration in favor of a return to sunlight and lunch.

This tunnel could be the extensive development work done by Charles McPhail in 1957.[76] Reports indicate that this tunnel was one of the original King Solomon Group of claims. There were 26 claims in the King Solomon Group at one point. As claims from the group were fractioned off via sales, lack of interest,

---

[76] The failure of mines in this area to become large producers was due to several factors: the high cost of transportation, the high cost of smelting because of arsenic and sulphur content, and the fact that very few high-paying veins remained intact for any significant distance.

assessment work, or for other reasons, they showed up under different owners who did different types of physical development in separate locations with varying results. Thus, some confusing data is related to the King Solomon name. Gold, silver, and copper were sought here.

Unnamed Adit #2

Rated at B-2 to B-3 from Road #160. Showing ore containing gold and silver, this adit is located in the southeast ¼ of Section 9, about 600 feet south of the Meadow Adit. The rock is mafic and pyritized silicified felsite, into which a 20-foot adit was run.

Unnamed Adit #3

Rated at B-2 to B-3, with ore values in gold and silver, these adits are located about 1,000 feet northwest of the Meadow Adit, at an elevation of 6,400 feet. One tunnel is 32 feet long; the other is 56 feet in length. They were driven into serpentine-showing veins of magnetite and chromite up to 12 inches in width.

Unnamed Adit #4

Rated at A-2, with ore containing silver and copper, this adit is located in the northwest ¼ of the southeast ¼ of Section 9, as seen on the USGS Mount Stuart map. The adit is about 75 feet up the west side of the road cut on Road #160, 250 feet past the northernmost feeder stream in the southeast ¼ of Section 9.

This tunnel is in a sheared contact between serpentine and silicified felsite. A caved adit (east and below the road from the upper tunnel) is in a vein six inches wide containing pyrite and arsenopyrite. Gold, silver, and copper were found in samples taken from the lower adit.

King Solomon #1, 1947/Blackhawk, 1989

Rated at A-1 to A-3 from Road #160. There are three separate references to the King Solomon Claim areas. They are all physically, geologically, and developmentally different, including ownership. The data used here matches closely with that of the Blackhawk Prospect.

John Gray owned a King Solomon claim (1947), with statistics paralleling those of the Blackhawk. The similarities are location (Section 9); ore (copper, silver, gold, zinc, and cobalt); ore minerals (pyrrhotite, chalcopyrite, pyrite, sphalerite, and arsenopyrite); deposit (in hydrothermally altered zones of granite/gneiss, two to six feet wide; solid sulfide lenses in the zone are two to eight feet wide, mostly pyrrhotite); and development consisted of an 832-foot adit, two caved adits each about 200 feet long, and a 10-foot adit. The #1 designation distinguishes this individual King Solomon claim from the other King Solomon properties.

This property is located in the southwest ¼ of the northeast ¼ of Section 9, T23N, R15E, 800 feet down (north) from 4WD Road #160 and Adit #4. The lower tunnel's tailing pile is large and easy to see, because it lies at the road's edge. We visited all four adits. They represent about 1,000 feet of tunneling work. The lower adit had two piles of nearly solid sulfides near the caved portal area. A mix of pyrite, pyrrhotite, and chalcopyrite are in one heap, and arsenopyrite is in the other. The three caved adits upslope are unimpressive and not worth bushwhacking to.

For the Rockhound

At the time we visited the Blackhawk, there was still lots of high-grade ore on the pile to choose from.

Van Epps Creek/Solomon Creek Area

Geology

Metavolcanic and metasedimentary ultramafic rock is intruded by granodiorite. The contacts of granodiorite are paralleled by shear zones, while other shear zones cross the contacts. The most plentiful minerals in shear zones are quartz, talc, and carbonates. Distributed throughout the rock are pyrite, pyrrhotite, arsenopyrite, chalcopyrite, sphalerite, stibnite, and galena, with accessory minerals in the form of chromite and magnetite.

Pickwick Shaft/Copper King/King Solomon/Nelson/Van Epps Copper

Rated at A-1 from Road #160. Consisting of seven unpatented claims, and showing ore containing copper, gold, and silver, this property is located in the northeast ¼ of Section 9, T23N, R15E, on the USGS 7.5 Minute Series map of Jack Ridge, at the end of 4WD Road #160. There are two shafts at road level, south of but still close enough to the road to be mistaken for part of the thoroughfare. Both of these deep shafts are open, although on our visit bright warning tape had been placed around the shaft collars in an effort to alert the unwary. Stay away from them. There is nothing to see by peering down into the shaft except the timbers you would pass by if you fell.

Serpentine, diorite, and shear zones were encountered when the Pickwick Mining Company shaft was sunk to a depth of 110 feet in 1897. Pickwick drifts, off the shaft are at the 50-, 80-, and 110-foot levels. Others who developed these claims were the Vanno Mining Company (1921), Frank Sontag of Wenatchee (1942), and S. J. Holden and Associates (1946), who leased to the Phantom Creek Copper Company of Tacoma (1953). Studies on the economical geology of the area were done in 1911 and 1955 for the Defense Minerals Exploration Administration.

In 1924, the Van Epps Adit was blasted to a point where it was connected to the bottom of the shaft by a raise. The drift at the 50-foot level of the shaft once extended to the surface early in the development of the digs. Stoping at the 110-foot level was done to a minor degree.

Sulfide minerals consisting of bornite, chalcopyrite, pyrite, copper carbonate, and pyrrhotite were taken from lenticular concentrations along the shear zones. The gangue was decomposed quartz. Early indications pointed to the possibility of the ore body widening to 120 feet. Nothing more was reported about that projection. A majority of the deposits were mined out before 1957. Early workings around the shaft area have long since been obscured by later development.

Van Epps Adit/Copper King/Nelson

Rated at B-2 from the shafts at Road #160, and carrying ore of copper, gold, and silver, this property is located in the center of the east line of Section 9 and the center of the west line of Section 10, T23N, R15E, at an elevation of 5,070 feet, 2,500 feet southeast of the Pickwick Shaft, and south of Van Epps Creek. This adit was part of the original King Solomon Group of 26 claims. Use the USGS 7.5 Minute Series maps of Jack Ridge and Mount Stuart.

The easiest way to the portal[77] is to stay west of the creek gully originating west of the shafts and go south. Eventually, the tailing pile will appear. The distance from the shafts to the Van Epps portal is about 2,500 feet. The tunnel was started around 1900, to connect to the Pickwick shaft via a raise. It was driven through glacial deposits, serpentine, and diorite. Sulfides were found mostly in the first 700 feet from the portal in tunnel rock. The remainder is disseminated throughout the rest of the adit. Several carloads were reportedly taken out by packhorse around 1912. A conflicting source of information gives credit for these shipments to one of the unspecified King Solomon Claim tunnels.

---

[77] The Van Epps Adit was caved in 1996 when we visited. An investigation of the tunnel in 1942 included a report of bad air near the face of the adit. This could be an ongoing situation. If the portal and tunnel happen to be accessible, the only safe thing to do is stay out.

For the Rockhound
Dig in the very large tailing pile, where sulfides and ore can be found.

Gold and Silver #2, 1936/Porcupine, 1989

This 71-foot tunnel is located 300 feet upstream, and on the east bank of Van Epps Creek in the same gully as the Van Epps Adit. The claim was recorded on March 14, 1936, by Oscar Erlandsen and Ernest Johnson. The portal was open and the tunnel accessible in 1996. The adit was mostly barren, except for a little pyrite showing at the portal and in some of the rock debris nearby.

Solomon-Jack Creek Tunnel and Shaft

Rated at D-3 from the Van Epps Adit and containing ores of copper, lead, and vanadium, this property is located in the southeast ¼ of Section 34, T24N, R15E, on the USGS 7.5 Minute Series map of Jack Ridge, two miles down the Van Epps Creek pack trail, west of the trail and east of the creek, about 1,500 feet south of where Solomon Creek and Jack Creek meet. The prospect consists of an adit of unknown length and a caved shaft in weathered, banded dolomitized rock and serpentine rock.

Van Epps #1

Not rated. With ore containing silver and copper, the Van Epps #1 is located approximately in the center of the northern ½ of Section 9, T23N, R15E, at about 5,600 feet elevation, as shown on the USGS Jack Ridge map.

There is a one-foot wide, 90-percent–rich sulfide vein exposed in pits dug into serpentine at the base of a cliff. The adit is lower, near the bottom of the slope. It is driven into the overburden and country rock, and its portal is under a tree. Some of the portal roof had sloughed down, exposing the root system, when we visited. We didn't notice any minerals.

Snook/Ellen Prospect

Rated at C-3 from the Pickwick Shaft on Road #160, this property consisted of 15 claims. This is a one-mile, 800-foot elevation gain trail hike along Trail #1594 on the Green Trails map of Chiwaukum, #177,[78] and Mount Stuart, #209. It is an enjoyable and scenic trip, with several off-trail slopes to scramble up, and opportunities to photograph the grandeur at the trail's end, where a picture is worth a thousand breathless words.

The values sought were in gold, silver, nickel, antimony, zinc, and lead, which are contained in the minerals arsenopyrite, chalcopyrite, galena, stibnite, sphalerite, and bethierite.

It is located in the southeast ¼ of Section 4, T23N, R15E, at the west end of the twin-peaked mountain (6,023 and 6,821 feet). Solomon Mountain lies in a northeast-southwest direction through the west half of Section 3, and into the southeast ¼ of Section 4, on the USGS 7.5 Minute Series map of Jack Ridge.[79]

Starting at the divide/pass that separates Solomon Creek (on the north) and Van Epps Creek (on the south), the claims are located between 4,400 to 6,000 feet elevation and are found east, west, and north of the pass area.

Snook Property

In 1949, when B. F. Harrison of Seattle owned the Snook, it comprised six claims that were separate from the Ellen. In a later report (1989), the Snook's six claims and the Ellen's nine claims were combined as the Ellen Prospect. Here they will be dealt with according to their property status as recorded in 1949.

---

[78] Trail #1594 starts 50 yards east of the shafts, and north of some more recent cabin site debris.
[79] These properties were once part of the original King Solomon Group of 26 claims.

A miner loads an ore car with pay dirt that has been placed in the chute somewhere up a stope in the 1890s. The shoring above the tunnel is typical of that often used in the Cle Elum mines of central Washington State. (The Engineering and Mining Journal, July 1897)

The Snook is the western group of six claims. The main digs outcrop between diorite on the north and serpentine on the south. The outcrop occurs across the steep-sided northward-trending ridge (centered at the southeast ¼ of Section 4, T23N, R15E), and rises to a point 100 feet above the pass near the 6,821-foot southwest peak of Solomon Mountain.

The 220-foot–long contact zone has an average thickness of 15 feet. The Snook Prospect is on the west side of the steep, northward-lying ridge 200 to 300 feet beyond a cabin site. Located here is the trail that goes through the pass to the east and crosses a boulder-strewn area. The trail is nonexistent along this stretch. Explore the area east and past this obstacle to find the workings.

In 1996, the dig's 210-foot adit was caved. According to the records, it followed the strike of the contact northeast via five crosscut tunnels at right angles that exposed the entire 15-foot–thick contact zone. B. F. Harrison (1949) assayed chip samples that were worth $15.00 per ton in gold, with some stringers as high as $1,100.00 per ton in gold. In an open cut (which appeared to be a 12-foot caved adit) above the caved tunnel, we saw a 10-foot–thick exposed contact zone. It contained a three-foot–wide white quartz vein, which appeared to have been worked as recently as the year of our visit. Chunks of the quartz lay scattered around the area. The vein is poorly mineralized, showing blebs of galena in some samples and pyrites in others.

At this dig, the diorite to the north and the serpentine on the south of the contact are easy to see. Prospectors are attracted to these workings and surrounding outcrops by their tan-to-buff/rusty–looking rock spotted with dark green. Dikes in the area appear to be of a silica-carbonate composition. Three-inch quartz veins speckled with galena were also in evidence in the area.

Ellen Group

This group of nine claims is located on the west side of the southeast ¼ of Section 4, T23N, R15E. The claims are situated in the same silica carbonate formation as the Snook. Explore existing trails (that pass at tunnel level) in a west-to-northwest direction from the Snook, in the steep-sloped Solomon Creek headwaters area. About 1,000 feet west of the Snook digs, there is a 28-foot tunnel bored to the south with a 10-foot drift driven to expose a six-foot–thick quartz vein. The vein is divided into three equal parallel slip strikes. There is a 10-inch deposit of antimony along the highly brecciated footwall. A well-defined six-inch quartz vein on the hanging wall has been intruded by stringers of stibnite.

We saw several caved prospects in the rocky slopes of the Solomon Creek Basin. Mining artifacts in advanced states of deterioration have been sighted downslope, including slag, firebricks, and a cabin site. They could indicate some kind of a smelting or assaying setup.

More mining camp debris lies west of the pass that separates Solomon and Van Epps Creeks. To the southwest, in the cirque area, there are two cabin sites. We also saw a broken duck nest forge among fragmented stove parts at one of the campsites. A duck nest forge is a piece of blacksmith equipment. Its size allows it to be used in the field, and it can be easily transported to the claim site. The forge is similar in shape to a 16-inch–diameter doughnut with a handle. The middle holds charcoal to heat the drill and chisel points that were to be resharpened, or to custom-make mining tools and any other item needed. The depth from top to bottom of the inner cup shape is about three to four inches. The 10-inch–long, two-inch–diameter outer handle-shaped part of the forge is hollow to allow the nozzle end of a four-foot bellows to be inserted. The bellows is used to blow air into the nest-shaped forge, which has a built-in separation circling the base plate so that air can get to the charcoal at the bottom of the fuel-burning cup. The blacksmith controls the forging temperature in this manner.

King Solomon/Silver Fiend/Humbug/White Star/Last Chance/Three Unnamed Claims

This group of eight claims lies west of the Ellen/Snook Claims. All are located in the east ½ of Section 5, T23N, R15E, as seen on the USGS 7.5 Minute Series maps for The Cradle and Jack Ridge. Records show the eight claims lie north to south along or near the Kittitas/Chelan County line, on the peaks and ridges of the Wenatchee Mountains. The Wenatchee Mountain Range separates the Cle Elum River Valley from the headwaters of Solomon Creek, and these claims, which are in Section 5.

Some of the mineral geology and property development data between the eight claims of the King Solomon area and the Ellen/Snook prospects are similar, but not identical. This means that the two areas could be related by a common alignment of some ore ledges from one claim area overlapping into the neighboring digs.

King Solomon (The Original)

Rated at C-4, from the Pickwick shaft on Road #160, this property consists of a single claim. It has ore that contains gold, silver, lead, and copper. The property is located in the southeast ¼ of Section 5, starting at the south line (from the 7,031-foot peak) at the head of West Fork Solomon Creek. Use the USGS 7.5 Minute Series maps for The Cradle and Jack Ridge.

The earliest record of any King Solomon claim in the Cle Elum Mining District was this claim in 1882. That year, a Native American guided prospectors William Splawn and George Carey of Yakima to the area. They staked out a claim on a ledge of galena ore.

By 1889, James Grieve, August Sasse[80] of Cle Elum, and Ken W. Dunlap (an English businessman)[81] owned the digs. They had two shifts of miners driving a 300-foot tunnel located 300 feet down from the summit of a sharp peak. Their purpose was to drive the tunnel to a large body of ore in white quartz eight feet wide, running north to south through the peak. An experimental smelter was completed and ready to start up on the ore, but it was unsuccessful because it could not raise sufficient heat to smelt the lead in the ore. After two days, the smelter was abandoned. Reports said the quartz carried gold, silver, copper, galena, and antimony. The ore that was assayed averaged $133 per ton (1889 scale), mostly in gold. Some of the richer streaks ran as high as $180 in gold, 60 ounces in silver, and 22 percent lead. Most of the ore came from a 22-foot raise in the 300-foot tunnel.

We found a Y-shaped snub tunnel at 6,400 feet elevation in the southeast ¼ of Section 5, and about 1,000 feet north of the 7,031-foot peak that the Chelan/Kittitas County line runs through (see the Jack Ridge map). We located it by hiking west of the Ellen/Snook Cirque area through a low pass into Section 5 for 1,500 feet. On the higher north slopes, an iron-stained outcrop causes the eye to focus on what appears

---

[80] August Sasse was one of the founding industrial and commercial settler/businessmen from Cle Elum, who also got involved in mining. Mr. Sasse ran a cookhouse for the railroad crews when the line was being built through the Cle Elum area. Mrs. Sasse operated a boarding house, which included the feeding of miners, loggers, and Native American tenants. Later Sasse managed the Reed House and in 1887 built the Cascade House.
[81] Gassman replaced Dunlap as a partner in 1892.

to be a large tunnel opening. One of the misleading attractions was a huge talus slope and tailings scattered from the top to the bottom, 300 feet in length. Convinced it was worthy of exploring, we scrambled to the digs of snub dimensions (15 feet per cut). Our reward for the effort was some unimpressive rock with pyrite disseminated through it, and a three-foot–long steel rock bar.

A strong wind, blowing icy rain, put an early end to the day's plan for this visit. With the information we gained and knowledge of other claims in this iron-capped area, future trips will be arranged.

Rated at E-5, the original access to the King Solomon Claim area was up the Cle Elum River/Scatter Creek side of the Wenatchee Mountain Range. This is a 9.2 mile (round trip) hike, not including exploring.[82] We recommend staying overnight.

Use the Green Trails maps for Stevens Pass, #176, Chiwaukum Mountains, #177, and USGS 7.5 Minute Series maps for The Cradle and Jack Ridge. Scatter Creek is located 0.3 mile south of Tucquala Lake, from which the Cle Elum River flows. The Scatter Creek trailhead is 0.4 mile south of Scatter Creek. This is another of the upper Cle Elum River Valley's most scenic hikes. The higher the elevation gained, the better the view.

Start on Trail #1328.[83] At 3.4 miles, the trail splits. Go northwest on Trail #1328 and continue 1.4 more miles to the trail's end. Expert cross-country skills are needed from here, as indicated by the seriousness of the hike rating. The responsibility of matching your ability to the task at hand is up to you.

Silver Fiend

Not rated. With showings of gold, silver, and copper, this property is located in the southeast ¼ of Section 5, T23N, R15E. It is the next claim extending north from the north end of the King Solomon Claim.

The Silver Fiend is on the same ledge as the King Solomon, but it is over the summit on the north side of the peak, and it runs down the gulch. There it outcrops to eight feet wide between granite walls 100 feet high. James Grieve once started a 20-foot crosscut on the property in an attempt to tap the ledge 200 feet in, close to the King Solomon Claim line.

Humbug Claim

Not rated. Containing gold, silver, and copper, the Humbug is located in the southeast ¼ of Section 5, as seen on the USGS map of Jack Ridge.

Grieve, E. P. Gassman, and Ken W. Dunlap had an eight-foot–wide ledge running parallel to the Silver Fiend. The tunnel length is unknown.

The shoring in this mine tunnel on Silver Creek indicates that loose or fractured rock had been dug into and the extra support was needed to prevent collapse. (Victor Pisoni photo)

Last Chance

Not rated. The ore contains both gold and lead. The property is located in the southeast ¼ of Section 5, on the USGS map of Jack Ridge, in the gulch to the east and parallel to the Silver Fiend. The owners were Grieve, Gassman, Sasse, and a Mrs. Churchill. The property had a six-foot ledge with a 30-foot crosscut and a 25-foot shaft.

---

[82] This area includes possibly some of the most trying off-trail bushwhacking, shin-skinning, rock-cursing, lonely looking (but extremely beautiful), lip-parching terrain ever to be encountered. Pursuit of this dig depends on good or so-so fortune. Plot your course well, mates.
[83] Trail #1328 follows the original mine-to-market course (of 1882) taken by the prospectors who first found the King Solomon Claims and other properties. The distance from the trailhead to the trail's end in the mining claims area is 4.8 miles, one way.

White Star

Not rated. With ore containing gold, silver, and copper, this site is located in the northeast ¼ of Section 5, as seen on the USGS map for Jack Ridge, directly north of the Silver Fiend Claim. In 1897, John Stewart had run a 20-foot tunnel on a six-foot ledge of ore similar to that of the Silver Fiend.

Silver Creek Area

Silver Creek was a Native American campground located between the flat west side of the main road and the Cle Elum River. Teepees would be spread north toward Fish Lake during the late summer or fishing, hunting, and huckleberry season. Until 1910, Fish (Tucquala) Lake was large and scenic. A huge population of rainbow, cutthroat, and Dolly Varden trout thrived there. In 1910, a big snow slide came roaring down Goat Mountain onto the lake. The pileup left more of a marsh than its namesake suggests.

Anthony Stoves had a cabin on the east side of the lake by the main road. Civil War veteran Jack Clark also kept a cabin near the lake, occupying it when he trapped for furs around the Fish and Hyas Lakes area. Phil Stanton's large cabin was just north of Jack's place. The John Lynch homestead was located north of Stanton at the trailhead leading to his mining property. Jack Kelly (known as Paddy-Go-Easy) had a cabin and claim on top of Mammoth Mountain next to Lynch's property. When Kelly sold his claim, he traveled to town with a barrel of whisky in a wheelbarrow, and went up and down the streets of Roslyn, giving a drink to anyone who wanted one.

A miner named E. P. Gassman had a cabin near Fish Lake as well, and Billy Clark (no relation to Jack) had a place 100 feet away from him. Other lake residents included James Grieve, Old Dad Spence (a trapper), Mose Emerson, and Charley Holt.

Silver Creek Mining Company, 1937/Cle Elum Mining Company, Inc., 1952/Peter Tu Claim, 1971–72

Rated at A-2, and containing ore with showings in gold and silver, this property is located in the northwest ¼ of the southwest ¼ of Section 12, T23N, R14E, on the USGS 7.5 Minute map of Davis Peak.

History of the Claim

By 1937, owner W. A. Hoage of Tacoma had done the majority of the development on the Silver Creek Mining Company claims. The lower tunnels were on the White Elephant Claim, one of a group of four claims. They ran in a southwest/northeast direction. The other three claims were unnamed. Another group of four claims is located upstream, upon which the upper tunnels and workings are situated on the Silver Tip Claim. The Rambler Chief Claim extends south off the Silver Tip. We found two unrecorded, caved tunnels at the dig located 200 feet southeast up the steep creek bank, its vein striking northwest in line with the vein in the caved tunnel of the Silver Tip. The remaining two unnamed claims were undeveloped. This group ran southeast to northwest, joined to the middle of the lower claims to form a "T."

About 800 feet up Silver Creek from the upper property, and separate from all other development, there is a newly exposed four-foot–thick quartz vein that is 300 feet long. We saw it from an opposing ridgeline. It is halfway up the creek's unclimbable 300-foot bank. The quartz vein dips down into a west-flowing feeder stream to Silver Creek. This very low-value white quartz vein ran from six inches to 20 feet wide. Phil Denny of the Cle Elum River Mining Company (1952) had possession of the claim as part of a multiple property promotion. No development was recorded for this latter company.

In 1971 and '72, Tom Lloyd held the property as the Peter Tu Claim, with no indication of development on record.

Getting There

Take the Cle Elum River Road to Fortune Creek, go north 0.8 mile on the river road (unnumbered) and pass Road #170. At 0.2 mile, there is a dirt road heading east. Take it for another 0.3 mile to where the road is washed out by Silver Creek. Park off the road, and hoof it.

Victor Pisoni, a member of Northwest Underground Explorations, examines the ruins of the Silver Creek Mill in 1995. A mine dump is visible at the right side of the picture. Many small mills were constructed throughout the Cle Elum region. (Victor Pisoni photo)

What to See

The three lower adits, 220 feet directly north of the road washout, were part of the Silver Creek Mining Company. Serpentine outcrops, some with white quartz veins, dominate the dig's entire area. Two of the lower adit's tailing piles are visible to the north, across from the road washout. These lower tunnels are printed on the USGS map of Davis Peak.

On the other side of the washout, the road passes west of the three lower tunnel workings. The adit nearest the creek is plugged with bulldozed dirt and is not accessible. Mining camp artifacts, plus general debris, can be found just south of the caved adit around the cabin site areas. We went into the tunnel before it was blocked. It was well timbered from the portal to halfway through. Solid, untimbered serpentine runs from there to the face. The adit is about 125 feet in length. It is headed for a serpentine outcrop, but we didn't notice any important vein or amount of ore.

The other two lower claim's tunnels, north and 150 feet away from the sealed adit, are accessible. The upper adit has a six to eight–inch white quartz vein centered at the top of the portal. Viewing from the portal is the only safe feature of this tunnel. Rotten timbers and loose rock make the dig entirely too hazardous for exploring. A 15-foot–deep winze was worked from the portal inward, about 20 feet in length. It was then boarded over to make a floor,[84] from which the vein and tunnel were dug for 20 feet more, where the tunnel turns south, keeping the remainder of its length from view.

Upper Adits

Rated at A-2 from unnumbered Road. At the upper Silver Creek Mining Company digs, there are four adits (three caved), a collapsed mill, debris at a powerhouse site, and a caved shaft. All are located 1,500 feet east (upstream) from the lower digs at the unnumbered Road. A vague trail starts from the road, 150 feet south of the washout, and parallels the south side of Silver Creek for 1,000 feet. In this spot, parts of an old footbridge lie scattered around both sides of the creek bed. Rocks have been placed in the water (probably during the dry season) like stepping stones, so the trail can be picked up on the opposite bank of the creek. The collapsed mill site is 500 feet up the trail, along with a tailing pile. There are varying sizes of white quartz chunks from the vein in the open tunnel lying all around the mine area. Also, several mining artifacts are visible, mainly machinery parts.[85] One hundred feet north of the mill site is where the powerhouse remains

---
[84] Most of the board flooring has rotted and fallen into the winze, exposing its dimensions and revealing danger.
[85] This site is identified, on the USGS map of Davis Peak, as "X Prospect."

are located. A noticeable tailing pile can be seen here, with an intact surface ore chute that carried ore from the top of the tailings (of the open adit) down to the quartz-processing equipment site. Five tons were shipped between 1937 through 1940, at $12.00 per ton.

Scramble straight up, or switchback up the tailings, to the open tunnel. The adit is driven into a serpentine outcrop and follows a one-foot–wide vein of white quartz. We reached the 125-foot mark where we encountered a cave-in at the beginning of an unstable and heavily timbered area.[86] The blockage in this tunnel seemed to be from a natural collapse. A vein of white quartz two feet in width is visible in the roof going into the caved portion, and it also dips upward toward the surface. Rock was cleared along the side of the upward-trending vein to a length of four feet, defining its size and direction.

The quartz that was mined was of very low value, with mineralization seen in a widely dispersed pattern. None of the samples we examined showed any concentrations of sulfides or minerals in the form of pockets or blebs. The deposits that had been worked and shipped out must have been few and far between, but there had to be encouragement at the start to justify the amount of time and development put into this claim. We had to use a magnifying eyepiece to pick out the minerals in the white quartz.

For the Rockhound
It is easy to find a chunk of white quartz in this dig for display or perhaps to decorate your garden.

Goat Mountain (Denny Claim)

Rated at B-3. The ore in this claim, also known as the Denny Claim, contains antimony, and the minerals are stibnite, pyrite, magnetite, chromite, and nickeliferous carbonate. The gangue consists of quartz, calcite, and sericite. The property is located in the northeast ¼ of Section 10, T23N, R14E, at an elevation of 3,700 feet (300 feet above the Cle Elum River). Use the USGS 7.5 Minute Series map of Davis Peak.

Fred Denny held this property until 1948. It was an open claim in 1998 when we visited the workings. The adit dump is on the east slope of Goat Mountain, and can be seen from the Cle Elum River Road in the northeast ¼ of section 11. Park in this area.

To start this trek, you have to ford the river, because there is no footbridge or trail. Stay to the north of the feeder stream, and bushwhack a course to the tailing pile. Go through the trees to avoid having to fight with the tangled brush.

Three open cuts and a 178-foot adit are on the north side of the seasonal feeder stream that flows into the river. The uppermost open cut is 110 feet directly above the adit. It exposes a six-inch quartz vein with scattered stibnite throughout. Serpentine comes in contact with the Swauk formation's white, medium-grained sandstone in the mine area. The vein can be seen for 15 feet up the creek beyond the open cut. Thirty-five feet below the upper open cut, there is another opening in the creek bank in the same mineral formation. A fault contact between sedimentary breccia and serpentine overlaid with sandstone lies 50 feet below this cut. In the breccia, there is a lean stibnite vein 4 to 12 inches wide. Stibnite fills vugs in the quartz, and contacts between breccia and serpentine show a ledge mineralized with nickel. The nickel also originated in the serpentine.

The 178-foot adit was driven to intersect the stibnite vein defined by the prospect development. Serpentine is visible for the first 125 feet into the tunnel, where it cuts across the main fault. Swauk sandstone is what the remaining 53 feet of tunnel runs through. No mineralization is noticeable. The vein was not reached, because the portal was started 70 feet below the point where the fault dips from one angle to another. The developers of the adit weren't aware of this, and the tunnel ran too far under, missing the vein.

---

[86] Serpentine, while being mined, sometimes has a tendency to shift or burst explosively as a result of unsupported downward pressure, sending razor sharp shards of rock flying through the air at high speed. This can cause injury, or worse, to anyone near the fracturing zone.

For the Rockhound

Reportedly, there are small vugs lined with quartz crystals in these workings, along with rare occurrences of vugs filled with stibnite in association with highly silicified Swauk material. Stibnite, as very fine blades, also appears in part of a discontinuous lens a half inch thick. It seems that the stibnite is a filling rather than a replacement. The view from the adit toward the valley bottom and eastern mountain slopes is interesting.

Paddy-Go-Easy Pass Mines

This 1½-mile–long area of ridges in the Wenatchee Mountain Range was mined and prospected into a geology that is underlain by ultramafic rock, which is intruded by small bosses of granitic rock and serpentine. Between the granite and serpentine there are mineralized fractured zones. These mineral deposits are of a discontinuous nature. Vein deposits in the Sprite Lake area were consistent in silver and gold values, while arsenopyrite was the main source. The deposits were found in the mid-1880s. Fifteen claims cover most of the Paddy-Go-Easy and Sprite Lake workings. Several digs were completed by 1886 on the American Eagle and Aurora Group of claims. Their ore, along with the ore from other claims on Mammoth Mountain, were hauled down the mountain slope in containers and treated by a small mill near Fish (or Tucquala) Lake.[87] This was a three-mile trip from the pass to the trailhead (notice the 1880s mill site cabin south of the parking lot).

Bronco Mining and Improvement, 1892 and Elsner, 1989 (two claims)

Rated at D-5. The values sought here were in gold. Situated at an elevation of 5,600 feet, this property is located in the southwest ¼ of Section 26, T24N, R14E, as seen on the USGS 7.5 Minute Series map of The Cradle. The area can also be found on the Green Trails map of Stevens Pass, #176.

The steep 1.8-mile hike, plus 0.3-mile sidetrail[88] to the workings, starts at a trailhead. This can be found in the corner of Section 34, on the USGS 7.5 Minute Series map of The Cradle. It is also shown as Trail #1595 on the Green Trails map of Stevens Pass, #176. The elevation gain is 2,200 feet. At 1.8 miles up the trail, there is a vague path that forks right (east). The Bronco (Elsner) workings are at 0.3 mile on the slope trail you will pass the lower Aurora Portal.

Two mine dumps belonging to the Peter Tu Mine are visible in this picture looking down toward the bottom of the valley. (Victor Pisoni photo)

---

[87] In the spring of 1891, several old California prospectors were in the upper Cle Elum Mining District examining the mineral potential at claim sites that had been put up for sale by earlier prospectors.

[88] Aside from the mining history and rockhounding possibilities, the hike up this steep mountain slope affords scenery of the most memorable kind. Like all Upper Cle Elum high-elevation hikes, vast, worthy, photographic vistas abound. The Paddy-Go-Easy area is a top-of-the-list hike, and from the pass eastward the trail continues into wilderness backcountry, which too is visually gratifying terrain.

This photograph, taken in one of the lower Silver Creek mines, graphically illustrates the hazards that are present in all mines. The floor of the mine drops away in a winze, while another tunnel is bored ahead past the woodwork. (Victor Pisoni photo)

Phil Stanton of Cle Elum and James Grieve owned the Bronco Claim in 1892. It was located 1,000 feet across the west slope from the Aurora, Mountain Sprite, and Blue-Eyed Nellie Properties on Mammoth Mountain, which is the present-day, unnamed 6,566-foot peak in Section 26. It's located 0.4 mile south of Sprite Lake.

In 1896, Judge Turner of Spokane was president of the Bronco Mining Company, with Phil Stanton as secretary; James Grieve as treasurer; and a fourth partner, Fred Parker. In 1897, the Bronco was reported to have cleaned up $150 per ton from a strong lead of rich, decomposed quartz in a vein of free-milling gold ore and sulfide ore. The two to four–foot vein was located in a six-foot–wide ledge. An 80-foot tunnel ran between granite and serpentine walls. In one report, assays were said to run as high as $690 to the ton.

This same year, the residents of Cle Elum and Roslyn raised $200, and the county commissioners produced $400, to improve and finish the Cle Elum River Valley Road through to Fish Lake. Phil Stanton[89] ran a through-stage service (two round trips per week) from Cle Elum to the upper Cle Elum Mining District, where he also owned and operated a hotel. James Grieve became postmaster at Fish Lake. It was reported that around 1,000 people were living in the valley along and above Lake Cle Elum at this time.

After further development, the Bronco Claim grew to comprise a 30-foot adit, located 100 feet above a 110-foot tunnel that was driven into a four-foot–wide ledge of free-milling gold on a 26-inch feeder vein. Arsenopyrite was also present, carrying sulfides in paying quantities.[90] Bronco Claim workings seem to match some of the geological and mineral data of the Elsner Adits report of 1989, suggesting that they are the same property. Both also have common elevations and locations.

The difference at the present time is the amount of added workings. The three Elsner adits are now caved, but like the Bronco, they were driven into a mineralized zone with serpentine wall rock on one side and granitic material on the other. Sporadic deposits of narrow quartz pods in the fault zone were enough to discourage additional work.

For the Rockhound

Samples of the mineralized, vuggy, quartz-rich material can be found at the upper adit on the dump pile.

---

[89] Phil Stanton later owned and operated the Red Front Livery Stable in Cle Elum up to 1908.
[90] A third tunnel was driven later. No data is available other than a reference to its physical presence.

A group of folks pose for a picture at the portal of the Bronco Mine near Paddy-Go-Easy Pass, high above Tuquala Lake. (*A pictorial History of Kittitas County, Volume I,* 1989)

Aurora #1 Lode, 1902 (Lower Adit, 1989)

Rated at D-5, the ore consists of free-milling gold and deposits of arsenopyrite. This property is located in the northwest ¼ of the southwest ¼ of Section 26, T24N, R14E, at an elevation of 5,700 feet.[91] This is about 0.1 mile east of Trail #1595 on the Bronco/Elsner Adits' turnoff path (note the distance hiked). Neither adit tailings nor a side trail are visible from the main trail, so determine where to turn upslope in search of the workings.

In the spring of 1902, a drill and compressor plant were installed to drive the tunnel through Mammoth Mountain to an area 20 to 30 feet under the bottom of Sprite Lake (located on the east side of the mountain ridge). This would have drained the lake's water, thus ensuring that the Aurora and most other upper workings would be dry mines. In the construction of the tunnel, several ledges were crosscut. Development ended at 1,700 feet, but it was intended to go 2,000 feet. Why this objective was not reached is not mentioned in the mine's documentation.

Of the several blind ledges that were crosscut, the only one mineralized enough to be valuable was a vein in a fault zone. It was located about 1,095 feet from the portal. A 160-foot drift ran east along the vein until it became a hairline stringer at the drift's end. Samples of the ore at the intersection of the main tunnel and drift showed 0.37 and 0.02 ounce of gold per ton, and 0.2 ounce of silver to the ton. The stability and air quality (which were bad) of the adit may have changed since we visited.

Aurora Group of Five Claims

The area of Mammoth Mountain where the Aurora Group was situated was called Lynch's Mountain[92] by the owners of this group of claims and nearby property holders. These five claims were established in 1886. The aforementioned Aurora Tunnel #1 lode was the southernmost claim on the south slope of the mountain. The Argonaut lode continues north off Aurora Tunnel #1. Sharing south/north property lines, the next claim up is the Aurora lode, and north on its boundary is the Mountain Sprite lode. On the Mountain Sprite's east line lies the Mountain Sprite #2 lode. A later addition to this group of five claims was the Flanker lode. It is on the claim line south of Mountain Sprite #2 and is connected to the Aurora lode's east line.

Development reports on the Aurora Group were taken from those printed in 1897 and 1989. Names and developments for 1897 were found in text but were not specifically assigned, giving us only a general overview of what took place.

---

[91] At this elevation, the scenery in all directions is worth stopping to look at.

[92] Mammoth Mountain is the area of ridges and peaks ranging from the southwest ¼ of Section 25, through Section 26 from its southeast ¼ to the northwest ¼; continuing on through Section 22, at the southeast ¼ and following the county's border for Kittitas and Chelan, which ends near Section 22's center line area. Lynch Mountain is a peak or prominent ridge on the Aurora Group mining property (a mountain on top of the mountain, if you will).

Within the Aurora Group's five claims, there were fissure ledges of quartz containing high-grade gold and silver. These ran east and west through dikes of granitic rock, which cut diagonally into Mammoth Mountain's mainly metamorphic structure. One of the ledges was reported to be five feet wide and 2,000 feet long. It carried free gold and was heavily oxidized, with sulfides reaching a depth of 50 feet.

In the area presently named the Snow Workings and Cabin Adit (within the Aurora Group of claims), there is a steeply inclined shaft. This caved dig ran along a vuggy, limonite-stained quartz hanging wall that fills fractures at a contact of serpentine and granodiorite. An 1880s assay averaged $40.00 in gold per ton. At the Cabin Adit's workings, there was a five to eight–inch vein with a stringer of arsenopyrite and quartz. A winze was also in the adit. Open cuts and pits can be found on the surface area.

Elsewhere at unspecified locations in the Aurora Group, there were a 20-foot tunnel showing sulfides; a 70-foot tunnel, with ore showing the full width of a four-foot ledge; a 60-foot tunnel into a three-foot–wide ledge that had been traced for 1,000 feet; a 115-foot tunnel driven into slate, carrying pyrite; and a 20-foot tunnel showing good minerals. Shipments from these workings totaled 20 tons and averaged $56.00 in gold and some silver per ton.

Aurora, Argonaut, Mountain Sprite, Mountain Sprite #2, and Flanker, 1882

Rated at D-5. The owners of these claims were John and Timothy Lynch.[93] With ore carrying gold, silver, and copper, this property lies south and southwest of Sprite Lake in the upper ½ of the southwest ¼, and in the center of Section 26, about 1,000 to 1,500 feet above the Aurora Tunnel #1 lode. From Paddy-Go-Easy Pass, head southeast cross-country for 1,700 feet to the Sprite Lake area. Numerous workings sit west and southwest of the lake.

The Lynch brothers started with the Aurora Claim and speedily expanded their property holdings and development. The vein on the Aurora lode was three feet wide and was loaded with free-milling gold quartz, which assayed at $50 to $200 per ton. The surface equipment comprised a bunkhouse, blacksmith shop, and arrastre, which was erected to test the ore. It worked well enough to extract gold in quantities that covered expenses.

By 1889, the Aurora was expanded into a group of five claims, one of which had an incline shaft bored into free-milling gold. A stamp mill with four 320-pound stamps was built at the head of the trail beside a small, swift stream, the water from which was used to power the plant. The stamp mill was used for sampling purposes, but it also ran ore for a fee from other claims. The ore was packed down from the mines on horses, at the rate of $4.00 per ton.

The Aurora Claims cleaned up $150 in gold for each working day the mine was run that season. Another report lists $30.00 per ton in free gold, besides concentrates, for the summer run. Future plans were made to build a cyanide plant with a high-pressure waterwheel to treat tailings and concentrates, but it was never constructed.

By 1902, the properties were well developed and incorporated. The Lynches of Yakima owned the principal stocks. By 1940, there were reportedly 16 patented claims in the Aurora Group,[94] owned by John Lynch. In 1940, Lynch leased to Paramount Mines, Inc., which didn't record any specific development.

Paddy-Go-Easy Lode and Golden Rule, 1897/Pass Workings, 1989

Rated at D-5. The original owners of this property were John and Timothy Lynch. It lies at an elevation of 4,000 feet, in the northwest ¼ of Section 26, T24N, R14E, on the USGS map of The Cradle. The ore contained gold and silver.

---

[93] John and Timothy Lynch came into the mining industry after raising livestock at Lynch Coulee on the Columbia River. They had a group of six claims called the State Properties, five miles above the mouth of Ingalls Creek, and the Nickel Plate Group of 12 claims near Cascade Creek in the Negro Creek headwaters (both in the Blewett Mining District).

[94] Only 15 claims can be accounted for and verified from old claim maps. They are the Golden Rule, Paddy-Go-Easy, Barbed Wire, Wonder, Pickett, Rear Guard, Grand Skidhue, Blue-Eyed Nellie, Skirmisher, Mount Sprite, Mount Sprite #2, Aurora, Argonaut, Aurora Tunnel #1, and the Flanker Lode.

The hiking distance from the trailhead to Paddy-Go-Easy Pass is 2.3 miles one way. All the developments from the beginning of the group's claims to the latest report in 1989 are located here. There is no data to determine exactly who did the later work or when it was done. What is known is that the digs are in or near a contact of granodiorite and serpentine. About 100 feet from the contact there is a 150-foot vertical shaft in serpentine rock. Several pits and trenches exposing limonite-stained fractures were dug on the surface near and on the contact. The best values found (in 1989) of three samples taken from the area's workings were 0.21 ounce of gold per ton and 0.10 ounce of silver. The scenery from these ridges is excellent.

Grand Skidhue, 1897 (from the Aurora Group of 16 claims)/#5 Adits, 1989

Rated at D-5, and with ore containing gold and silver, this property is located in the northeast ¼ of the northwest ¼ of Section 26, T24N, R14E, at an elevation of 5,600 feet.

The workings are north of Sprite Lake, about a half mile east of Paddy-Go-Easy Pass. Two adits lie on the north side of the trail; a third adit is 500 feet east of these two tunnels on the south side of the trail. The westernmost adit was open in 1989; the middle and east adits were caved. The vein on which the middle and west adits were driven was two to three feet wide, in a vuggy quartz vein that filled the fault zone with sporadically deposited gold. Some of the gold might have come from the one foot of gangue on the hanging wall. The vein crossed from the workings of one adit to the other.

On this claim, the discontinuous deposit of gold and silver was probably mined selectively over the option of processing high- and low-grade ore together in bulk amounts. This would account for the higher assay values reported by the original miners and prospectors.

Blue-Eyed Nellie and Skirmisher, 1897 (two of the Aurora Group of 16 claims)/Lake Adit and North Workings, 1989

Rated at D-5 to Paddy-Go-Easy Pass, and B-2 from the pass to the claims area. This area is located in the southeast ¼ of the northwest ¼ of Section 26, T24N, R14E, on the USGS map of The Cradle. The adit and open cuts are 450 to 500 feet west of Sprite Lake. The pits and trenches are 600 to 700 feet northwest of Sprite Lake. Both are south of Trail #1595. The Blue-Eyed Nellie had a 60-foot shaft and a 400-foot tunnel (from 1880s information).[95] One carload of ore was shipped to the Tacoma Smelter, and it paid values of $36.00 per ton. The Skirmisher Claim was a northeast extension off the Blue-Eyed Nellie. No specific development is recorded for the Skirmisher. Grab samples showed unimpressive amounts of gold and silver.

The Barbed Wire, Wonder, Pickett, Rear Guard, and Flanker Claims (the remainder of the Aurora Group of 16 claims) were not included in this report. We couldn't find their locations or any developmental data, which leads us to doubt whether they were worked beyond the pit-prospecting stage.

This mine tunnel along Silver Creek cuts a clearly identifiable vein of quartz, seen at the top of the picture. It was usually in these quartz veins that gold was found. (Victor Pisoni photo)

---

[95] When we cross-referenced our data, we realized that more shafts were reported than we have located. This suggests some of the reported pits and trenches might be caved shafts. We have verified these workings on or near the Blue-Eyed Nellie Claim: the caved adit ran on a zone of shattered and altered rock parallel to a diorite dike, and the strike of the shattered zone above the adit was defined by a line of pits.

For the Rockhound

Arsenopyrite can be found in the rock piles of the adit dump and lower pit. The arsenopyrite is thought to be from the pods and stringers in the shattered zone. We didn't see any other sulfide minerals here. Of the five pits and trenches located 500 feet north of the adit area, a 40-foot trench exposes a limonite-stained fracture. Samples taken from this nearby pile of rock contained 3.2 ounces of silver and 4 percent copper. A sharp eye and a rock hammer could turn up some nice high-grade ore.

East of Paddy-Go-Easy Pass

Great Scott Group, 1909

This unknown number of claims adjoined the north and east lines of the Lynch brothers' Aurora Group of claims. The headwaters of French Creek, and a mountain known as The Cradle, are in their probable vicinity. Boston entrepreneurs had bonded the properties for $190,000.00, with the stipulation that $30,000.00 would be expended on development within three years.

Roy A. Barry[96] was the work superintendent and representative for easterners who were persuaded by the mineral showings that there was an immense deposit of precious metal in the Cle Elum Mining District. They expected to make the area a beehive of industry, drawing up plans to erect a smelting mill at the Galena site to work on the custom ore, along with other companies' ore in the district that required smelting. Barry worked for six additional months obtaining options and arranging to purchase more claims for the company. The last mention of Barry in the records says that he was headed back to the East Coast to report to company financiers, and that he planned to put a crew together that would work all winter developing the various properties.

Meadow Creek Placers (two, located in the Leavenworth Mining District)[97]

Rated at E-4. These two placers were located in the northwest ¼ of the northwest ¼ of Section 27, and the northeast ¼ of Section 28, T24N, R15E, on the USGS 7.5 Minute Series map of Jack Ridge. Green Trails map for Stevens Pass #176 also covers this area.

This 6.8-mile hike (one way) to the placer area starts at the Paddy-Go-Easy Pass trailhead. Hike 0.3 mile on Green Trails Map Trail #1595 (from the trailhead to Paddy-Go-Easy Pass). From the pass, go 4.5 miles on Green Trails Map Trail #1559 to the digs. These three placer claims end two miles upstream from the Meadow Creek confluence with Jack Creek. Reports of samples taken from Meadow Creek showed trace amounts of gold from the surface, but no bedrock was exposed to sample. Various sizes of stream gravel are common, and boulders as much as two feet in diameter abound.

Skookum Group

Rated at C-3 from the Meadow Creek placers downstream to Ben Creek (1.6 miles), at its confluence with Jack Creek. This property is located in the Leavenworth Mining District. Up Ben Creek a half mile and in a draw north of the creek, there are a caved 300-foot adit and cabin site ruins. The elevation gain to this site is 400 feet at the 4,400-foot level. The tailing dump has vuggy, limonite-stained quartz from the mine's three-foot–wide vein, which was in serpentinized peridotite country rock. Copper was found in the samples taken from the tailing pile.

---

[96] R.A. Barry, a miner turned developer, was involved in the promotion of the Mother-in-Law Group of claims (Swauk Mining District) in 1901.
[97] This property can be accessed more easily from the Cle Elum Mining District side via Paddy-Go-Easy Pass, and will be included within its data.

South of Paddy-Go-Easy Pass

Fish Eagle

Not rated. Consisting of a single claim, this copper prospect is in the general area of the center of Section 35, T24N, R14E, on the USGS map of The Cradle. Old mine property maps show a trail running off Paddy-Go-Easy Pass to the southeast into and across the northeast ¼ of Section 35. Here the Fish Eagle Claim trail heads south toward the digs on the west side of a feeder stream (between the 4,800 and 5,400 feet elevation contour lines).

James Grieve and K. W. Dunlap[98] located a prominent outcrop stained red, black, and blue (azurite) from oxidized iron and bromide or oxide of copper. The copper ore showed 40 feet in width. A report indicated that there was a 262-foot tunnel driving to strike the ledge at a depth of 190 feet below the surface.

North of Paddy-Go-Easy Pass

American Eagle, 1891 (four claims)/North Workings, 1989

Rated at D-5, these claims had ore that contained gold and silver, and the primary ore mineral was arsenopyrite. The location of this property is in the southeast ¼ of the southeast ¼ of Section 22, T24N, R14E, about a half mile northwest of Paddy-Go-Easy Pass on Eagle Mountain, a 6,573-foot peak (unnamed on current maps) on the same series of high, iron-stained ridges running along Mammoth Mountain northwest of the pass. Mammoth Mountain is higher in elevation than the rest of the ridges in the area. Use the USGS map of The Cradle.

This is a cross-country situation. We accessed the area by leaving the trail just before gaining the pass. We then headed northwest for a half mile along the rust-colored, boulder-strewn west slope of Mammoth Mountain. A pile of gray tailings marked the portal of an adit that went in 45 feet to a caved area.

E. P. Gassman was sole owner of the four claims in 1891.[99] The American Eagle started out with a 60-foot tunnel on a six-foot vein, with a 1½-foot pay streak. An incline shaft in the vein also exposed high-grade ore. Assays for the ore showed $30.00 in gold per ton and $15.30 in silver.

Sales of the American Eagle's other three claims occurred the same year, 1892, creating the Boss, Ledger, and Silver Bull Properties. All were on the same line of ridges at the northern end of Mammoth Mountain. They extended off the American Eagle and each other in a northwesterly direction.

The claim areas at present show a caved adit, a shaft of unknown depth, an open adit, and two known trenches or open pits. These workings were developed along outcrops of veins and zones that are mineralized. Most of the digs are in serpentine, intrusive granitic, and porphyritic rocks in small, irregular bodies. Dike-like masses are also in close proximity to these serpentinized areas. The workings farthest south show evidence of sulfide veins.

Artifacts such as a boot, shovels, and an empty dynamite box lie in the area. Assays, in 1989, gave values of 0.12 ounce per ton in gold and 6.80 ounces per ton in silver.

Mammoth Claim, 1892 (one claim)

Not rated. With ore carrying gold, silver, and copper, this claim is located in the southeast ¼ of Section 22, T24N, R14E, east of Eagle Mountain. James Grieve and Phil Stanton[100] developed a 75-foot crosscut into a six-foot vein on this property.

---

[98] A. Stoves later became sole owner of the claim.
[99] E. P. Gassman and a Mr. Hodges are listed as joint owners of the American Eagle Claim in 1892.
[100] The original owner was E. P. Gassman, who sold to Colonel C. Bell.

Boss Lode, 1892 (one claim)/North Working Area, 1989

Rated at D-5. The ore produced showings of gold and silver, and the ore mineral was arsenopyrite. The property is in the southeast ¼ of the southeast ¼ of section 22, T24N, R14E, on the USGS map of The Cradle.

The Boss Claim was an extension of the American Eagle, a continued working of the Mammoth's six-foot vein, with an 18-inch pay streak. Listed value per ton in 1892 was $25.00 in gold and 22 ounces per ton in silver.

Silver Bull, 1890 (one claim)/Ledger Lode, 1892 (one claim)/Skeeter Workings, 1989

Rated at D-5, with ore showing gold and silver, this property is located in the southeast ¼ of Section 22, in Stevenson's Gulch,[101] about 0.4 mile northwest of the American Eagle Claim. Use the USGS map of The Cradle.

Reports list E. P. Gassman as owner of the Ledger Claim, but its location is not given. The Silver Bull was jointly owned by E. P. Gassman, James Grieve, and August Sasse. The American Eagle, Ledger, and Silver Bull ledges were worked all winter in 1891. Extra miners and work shifts were put to the task of finishing a projected plan set for the three claims. Tunnels and shafts were driven systematically in hopes of having the ore ready for further development, or perhaps to sell shares of mining stock to investors after they had examined the prepared properties. The rich, white quartz veins, carrying free-milling gold and pyrite, were mined to pay for expenses during this phase of development. While work was in progress, Gassman coordinated the Silver Bull project, along with the other two claims. The Silver Bull ledge was reported to have been 14 feet wide, with a five-foot–wide vein. The main workings were 40, 70, 90, and 130 feet long. The 130-foot adit tapped the ledge 600 feet below the surface.

August Sasse went to Seattle and Tacoma to form a stock company to officially inaugurate the business. Gassman and James Grieve made trips to Cle Elum with specimens from their high-grade vein of gold- and silver-bearing quartz, which were taken from the Silver Bull's ledge outcropping in a formation of slate and granite. The ore assayed at $100.00 per ton in gold and silver.

Vedette Claim, 1892 (one claim)

Not rated. The ore produced gold and silver. Its general location is north of the Silver Bull Claim, on the same northwest-bearing ridge as the Kittitas/Chelan County line, somewhere northwest of Section 22, as seen on the USGS map of The Cradle.

Owner Judge E. P. Boyles had a shaft on ore similar to that of the adjoining Silver Bull Properties.

Topping Claims, 1892 (two claims)

Not rated gold and silver. The general location is in the north ½ of Section 21, as seen on the USGS map of The Cradle.

The owner, J. H. Topping, had a crosscut and a 33-foot incline shaft run into a six-foot ledge of free-milling gold and concentrating ore that was said to show good values in gold and silver.

Prince Group of Five Claims, 1892

Rated at D-2 to the lower claim area. The ore lay in a sulfide ledge running the length of the five claims, from high up the mountain slopes between the creeks flowing from Tuck Lake and Robin Lake to the valley bottom. The uppermost claim had a short adit. The general location is in Section 8, between 3,200 to 6,000 feet elevation, as seen on the USGS map of The Cradle. The owners were J. H. Topping, J. A. Johnson, and Mrs. J. F. Cummings, all from Seattle.

---

[101] Joe Stevenson is reported to have owned the Silver King Claim in 1892 (location unknown). The exact location of Stevenson's Gulch is undetermined. This is just one more missing piece of the puzzle to ponder.

Getting There

Travel to the end of Road #4330 on Green Trails Map #176, Stevens Pass. Also use the USGS map of The Cradle. A half mile past Tucquala Lake, you'll come to the Tucquala Meadows Campground and trailhead parking area for Trail #1376. It is an easy 2½-mile valley-bottom hike to the Prince Group's lower claim area. Anything beyond this point is purely exploratory.

The Declining Years of the Cle Elum Mining District

White and Yellow Group/Climax Group of Claims #1 and #2

In 1927, mild interest in the few remaining active—and abandoned—mining claims was boosted by mine property promoters. The first attempt to attract attention was a sales report on the White and Yellow Group, and the Climax Group of claims, #1 and #2, which comprised a total of 135 claims. Gilbert A. Salisbury distributed promotional information for the 16 unnamed people holding these claims. The main sales pitch showcased the properties' potential for mining ore in commercial quantities.

The claims ranged in location from Kittitas County in the upper Cle Elum Mining District to the east into Chelan County. The vein and ore reports were repeats of the highest assay information obtained from past owners, usually from limited ore deposits. A map of the claims placed them in an area covering Sections 15 and 17 on the USGS 7.5 Minute Series map for Davis Peak in T23N, R14E, and Sections 9, 10, 15, 16, 17, 18, 20, 21, and 22, on the USGS 7.5 Minute Series map for Mount Stuart in T22N, R15E. These areas and mining properties have been covered in previous chapters. They are located mostly on or around the Fortune Creek region.

The promotional report suggested that the buying party or parties have a competent mining engineer open the property (via blasting and mineral assay). It also recommended that investors install water pipes and penstock for a Pelton wheel, air compressor, and receiver, and that roads and tunnels be constructed at specific locations.

The Black Bear, Climax Group, White Metals Group, and a wide vein that cut from the bottom to the top of Bald Knob Mountain (Peak 5924T in the north ½ of Section 21, one mile east of South Fork Fortune Creek) were the most heavily promoted properties.

Specifically, the report instructed that the rich ore be shipped to the mill and smelter at Selbys, in California, exclusively. There was a reference made to 1,000 tons of high-grade ore on the Climax ore dump, of which samples were said to be en route to San Francisco for proof through assay. The end of the sales boost contained a report on a "Mysterious White Metal."

Early in the history of the Cle Elum Mining District, miners had a fascination for a mysterious white metal they had come across that they could not identify. Much discussion and difference of opinion arose over this metal, which came from serpentine deposits running well into the billions of tons in size. The white metal was easily recovered from the serpentine via low-degree roasting. For years, prospectors would throw a few pounds of serpentine into the cooking stove firebox or campfire for three or four days, panning out the ashes to recover a number of small pieces of metal. The same ore/rock was taken to assayers in Cle Elum, who claimed it carried no metal. The assayers accused the prospectors of salting their sample with flux, but the miners insisted that wasn't true.

Calvin H. Barkdull,[102] a consulting engineer, conducted an analysis of the metal and concluded that it could be one of the following substances:

Metal	Melting Point (degrees Celsius)
Tellurium	452.0
Lead	327.0
Cadmium	320.09
Thallium	302.0

---

[102] Barkdull had mining claims in the Negro Creek area in the Blewett Mining District.

Lanthanum	286.0
Bismuth	271.0
Tin	231.85
Selenium	220.0

No one appeared interested in the metal until the war years, when iron, manganese, and chromium were found in serpentine. This proved to the doubting assayers that serpentine does indeed contain metal.[103] This mysterious "white metal" later proved to be magnesium.

Ten years passed, and the White and Yellow Group, plus the Climax Group, faded out of the picture.

Camp Creek Mining Company

Officers for the Camp Creek Mining Company included President Phil Denny of Seattle, Vice President Kenneth Bartlett of Seattle, and Secretary-Treasurer Gary Kelly of Tacoma. The company was incorporated on October 23, 1937, for the purpose of mining gold and silver in the Fish Lake Mining District. Stock was sold as nonassessable.[104] Nonpar values, in 1937, were common stock $100,000.00, consisting of a million shares at 10 cents each (authorized capital stock). The company's real estate was worth $100,000.00 and its equipment $100.00. Nothing was ever produced.

Thirteen mines were listed as real estate. They were merely old claims offered from the Cle Elum Mining District properties that had no more developmental potential than when the minerals were first discovered. In 1955, a Camp Creek Mining Company stockholder (in possession of 7,000 shares of stock) wrote to the Division of Mines and Geology to request information about the status of the company. Supervisor Sheldon L. Glover wrote back that the company had been automatically dissolved on July 1, 1941, for nonpayment of annual license fees. This marked its end.

Cle Elum River Mining Company, Inc.

Founded in Seattle in 1952, the company prospectus gave full warning of the speculative nature involved in the venture. Investors were advised not to buy stock in excess of what they could lose without creating financial hardship. Like the Camp Creek Mining Company, all stock was common, fully paid, and nonassessable.[105] Company officers included President Phil Denny, Vice President Don W. Denny, and Secretary/Treasurer Fred Denny.

The Cle Elum River Mining Company was incorporated with two million shares, each at a par value of 10 cents. Capital stock was issued on May 10, 1953, for 860,000 shares. The prospectus was for the purpose of offering 350,000 shares at 10 cents per share.

The financial statement for the company stands out in that its several assets were offset by the same monetary total in liabilities, $86,954.50. This was also the case with the proposed budget from the expenditures column. The amount from stock sales received was $35,000.00 total, the exact amount listed as spent on mine development. This included a jeep, tram work, extracting and shipping ore samples, stock sales commission, and a former working agreement for stock, which was not explained. The amount of cash needed to cover the expenses was $35,000.00.

The 10 unpatented claims were on three separate mining properties. These included four silver claims, five copper claims, and a gold ledge. The new offering was promoted via repeated, glowing assay reports from the late 1880s to early 1900s. These assays, along with developmental projections, were used to stir up interest, but they failed. There was no revival of mining to any noticeable degree. Now, as then, buyer beware.

---

[103] For every 20 pounds of mineralized serpentine crushed to 60 mesh, 20 ounces of white metal could be produced. The metal does not corrode or rust when submerged in saltwater or soft water. It never tarnishes, but rather remains bright.

[104] Meaning all stockholders will either share in the profits together or be left holding useless paper.

[105] In 1970, Vaughn E. Livingston Jr., assistant supervisor with the State Division of Mines and Geology, responded to an inquiry about claims in association with the Cle Elum Mining Company, Inc. Livingston stated that the records showed that the Cle Elum River Mining Company was a rearranged version of the Camp Creek Mining Company, Inc.

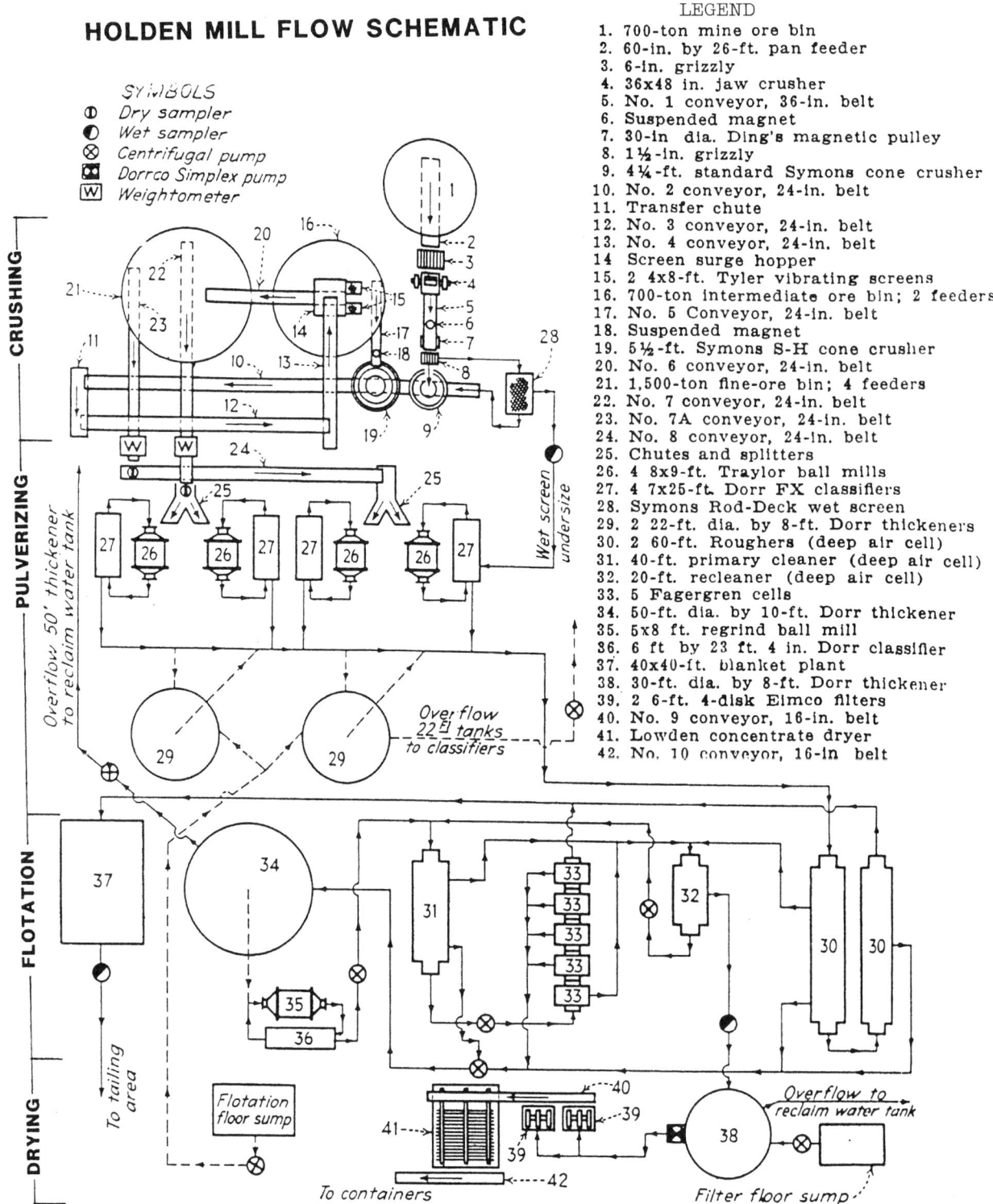

HOLDEN MILL FLOW SCHEMATIC

SYMBOLS
- ① Dry sampler
- ◐ Wet sampler
- ⊗ Centrifugal pump
- ⊠ Dorrco Simplex pump
- Ⓦ Weightometer

LEGEND
1. 700-ton mine ore bin
2. 60-in. by 26-ft. pan feeder
3. 6-in. grizzly
4. 36x48 in. jaw crusher
5. No. 1 conveyor, 36-in. belt
6. Suspended magnet
7. 30-in. dia. Ding's magnetic pulley
8. 1½-in. grizzly
9. 4¼-ft. standard Symons cone crusher
10. No. 2 conveyor, 24-in. belt
11. Transfer chute
12. No. 3 conveyor, 24-in. belt
13. No. 4 conveyor, 24-in. belt
14. Screen surge hopper
15. 2 4x8-ft. Tyler vibrating screens
16. 700-ton intermediate ore bin; 2 feeders
17. No. 5 Conveyor, 24-in. belt
18. Suspended magnet
19. 5½-ft. Symons S-H cone crusher
20. No. 6 conveyor, 24-in. belt
21. 1,500-ton fine-ore bin; 4 feeders
22. No. 7 conveyor, 24-in. belt
23. No. 7A conveyor, 24-in. belt
24. No. 8 conveyor, 24-in. belt
25. Chutes and splitters
26. 4 8x9-ft. Traylor ball mills
27. 4 7x25-ft. Dorr FX classifiers
28. Symons Rod-Deck wet screen
29. 2 22-ft. dia. by 8-ft. Dorr thickeners
30. 2 60-ft. Roughers (deep air cell)
31. 40-ft. primary cleaner (deep air cell)
32. 20-ft. recleaner (deep air cell)
33. 5 Fagergren cells
34. 50-ft. dia. by 10-ft. Dorr thickener
35. 5x8 ft. regrind ball mill
36. 6 ft by 23 ft. 4 in. Dorr classifier
37. 40x40-ft. blanket plant
38. 30-ft. dia. by 8-ft. Dorr thickener
39. 2 6-ft. 4-disk Eimco filters
40. No. 9 conveyor, 16-in. belt
41. Lowden concentrate dryer
42. No. 10 conveyor, 16-in. belt

Appendix A

Holden Mill

Mines were usually quite far from smelters, so cost wise it made sense to separate as much worthless rock from the metal-bearing ore as possible before shipment. This meant the base rock, or gangue, had to be removed. This process, called concentration, would occur in a mill located on the mine site.

The mine at Holden, Washington was most definitely remote. To get to the smelter, the Holden ore had to be trucked to the shores of Lake Chelan, barged 40 miles to Chelan, and then shipped by truck and train to the smelter. Shipping only the "pay dirt" was critical to the mine's economic survival, so a large concentrating mill was built nearby.

Concentrating mills are distinct from pulverizing mills, which serve free-milling gold mines. The gold mills would simply break up the ore to allow the gold to be more easily extracted from the base rock. The concentrating mills, on the other hand, process sulfide or oxide ores that contain metal chemically combined with sulfur, oxygen, or other elements or radicals (blends of elements such as phosphates). Once concentrated, the ore still has to be sent to a smelter to allow the metal to be reduced, or separated from the chemical compound. In the case of the Holden Mine, the metal sought was copper, although other metals such as gold and silver were also processed.

Concentrating mills, or concentrators were designed specifically for the mines they served. The design of the Holden concentrator was fairly straightforward. The ore was reduced in size before it left the mine. It was then transported to the mill where it was stored in a bunker. From the bunker it was carried by conveyor to a jaw crusher that reduced the size of the ore particles even further. This ground ore was carried by conveyor beneath a set of powerful magnets to remove any "tramp iron" before being run through a cone crusher to again reduce its particle size. It was transported by another conveyor and stored in a second bunker. From the second bunker the ore was run through another cone crusher. It was then called "fine ore" and stored in a bunker. The fine ore was delivered by conveyor to the ball mills where it was mixed with water and tumbled in a large drum containing iron balls of various sizes.

The resulting product was a slurry containing ore that had been pulverized to the consistency of flour and water. This material was mixed with chemicals and introduced to the sets of flotation tanks. Air forced into the bottom of the tanks through perforated pipes created tiny bubbles. As the bubbles rose through the slurry, the fine particles of metallic ore attached themselves to them, assisted by certain chemicals. The gangue material was more easily wetted and sank to the bottom. The concentrated ore material was skimmed off the top of the tank in the resulting froth. For this reason, the term "froth flotation" is often used to describe this process.

This cavity—referred to as a stope—was once solidly filled with copper ore. After the ore was blasted down from the roof, it dropped into pre-constructed bulldozer rooms at the bottom of the stope. (Chadebourn collection, North Central Washington Museum, Wenatchee, Washington)

The floors of the bulldozer rooms were constructed with a grizzly screen, and had enough headroom to accommodate workers. The ore dropped from the stope was often too coarse to fit through the grizzly's bars and had to be jack hammered into smaller pieces. Below the grizzly screen was a reception chamber for the ore. The ore was loaded from these chambers into large cars that were hauled by compressed air–powered engines to the surface. (Chadebourn collection, North Central Washington Museum, Wenatchee)

The resulting concentrates were skimmed off the top and sent to a classifier or thickening vat. Large particles were removed from the vat and sent to a different ball mill for additional pulverizing. Once most of the water had been drawn off, the concentrates were run through drying filters that removed the remainder of the water. The processed, concentrated ore was then ready to be loaded into tubs for shipment to the smelter, while the slurry material that had fallen to the bottom of the flotation tanks was piped to the tailing pile, or returned to the process for additional concentration.

The tailing pile at the Holden Mine became so large that small aircraft used it as a landing field. The concentration process, while fairly efficient, was not perfect, and a fair amount of metallic material ended up in the tailing pile. Silver and gold are among the metals that passed through the system and ended up in the pile. When the mining company tried to reprocess the tailings using cyanide, the Forest Service forbade it, fearing that the cyanide would get away from the mine, flow into Railroad Creek, and end up in Lake Chelan.

The ore cars at the Holden Mine were large in comparison to those for smaller mines in the region. This scene shows a train of cars ready to be hauled across the automatic dumpers. (Chadebourn collection, North Central Washington Museum, Wenatchee)

A schematic flow diagram of the Holden Mill is on page 304. This was printed in *Modern Mining and Milling Practice,* which was a compilation of articles from the *Engineering & Mining Journal* in 1940. Recovery of copper at the mill averaged around 94 percent. Gold recovery presented some technical problems due to the ore's super-fine nature, and was limited to around 85 percent. A total of about 40 men were employed at the mill, and they ran three shifts around the clock.[1]

An ore car at the Holden Mine is shown dumping as it is pushed over the camel back rail in the tipping building. (Chadebourn collection, North Central Washington Museum, Wenatchee)

Once the ore had been tipped from the ore cars, it traveled via conveyor to the holding bins, where it was stored until ready to be processed. The large devices suspended above the conveyor are powerful electromagnets used to remove the tramp steel and iron from the ore prior to crushing. (Chadebourn collection, North Central Washington Museum, Wenatchee)

The first stage of processing the ore at the Holden Mine was to run it through the large jaw crusher seen in this picture. The jaws would reduce the size of the ore in preparation for the next stage of processing. (Chadebourn collection, North Central Washington Museum, Wenatchee)

---

[1] Wages were $4.60 per day for miners, laborers were paid $4.00, and room and board was $1.20 a day. Were these the good old days?

In the first week of April 1938, the mill began operating.[2] By the end of May, production had exceeded all expectations and the mill's capacity was increased from 1,100 tons per day to over 2,000 by the addition of another ball mill, classifier, flotation cell, and filter.

During the mill's operation it concentrated ore that resulted in the production of 212 million pounds of copper, 40 million pounds of zinc, 2 million ounces of silver, and 600,000 ounces of gold.

Once the jaw crusher had reduced the size of the ore, it was run through two cone crushers and stored in "fine ore" bins. Then, the ore was transported via conveyor to the ball mills to be further reduced in size. (Chadebourn collection, North Central Washington Museum, Wenatchee)

This bank of four ball mills pulverized ore to the consistency of fine flour. The mills consist of the cylinder seen here, filled with iron balls about eight inches in diameter. The ore, along with water, was fed into the mills and reduced to a fine slurry that was then transported to the flotation tanks. (Chadebourn collection, North Central Washington Museum, Wenatchee)

The flotation tanks skim the concentrated mineral from the slurry and drop it into receiver troughs at the edge of the tanks. The gangue, or base rock material, sinks to the bottom of the tanks and is dredged out to be reprocessed or sent to the tailings pile. (Chadebourn collection, North Central Washington Museum, Wenatchee)

---

[2] The mine and mill operated three shifts, 24 hours a day. Day shift lasted from 7:00 A.M. to 3:00 P.M.), swing from 3:00 P.M. to 11:00 P.M., and graveyard 11:00 P.M. to 7:00 A.M. The crews worked 12 days on and had two days off, giving them time to make a trip to the "outside world" Chelan.

In the classifier vat, the ore slurry was thickened. Ore particles that were too large were returned to the ball mills to be further pulverized. The water was finally removed by the dewatering vacuum filters visible at the rear of the vat—the eight disk-shaped devices. The dewatered ore concentrates were then ready for shipment out of the mountains to a smelter. (Chadebourn collection, North Central Washington Museum, Wenatchee)

Once processed, the concentrated ore was loaded into these tubs. Each loaded tub weighed five tons. The tubs were then hauled by truck to the shore of Lake Chelan to be loaded onto barges for the 50-mile trip to the town of Chelan. (Chadebourn collection, North Central Washington Museum, Wenatchee)

Loading the tubs of ore concentrates onto the barge for the journey down Lake Chelan to the smelter. (Chadebourn collection, North Central Washington Museum, Wenatchee)

References

Adams, Nigel B., *The Holden Mine: Discovery to Production, 1896–1938.* World Publishing Company, 1981.

Alt, David D. and Hyndman, Donald W., *Roadside Geology of Washington.* Mountain Press Publishing, 1984.

American Geological Institute, *Dictionary of Geological Terms,* Dolphin Books, 1962.

An Historical Overview of the Wenatchee National Forest, Wenatchee National Forest Archaeological and Historical Services, Report 100-80, Eastern Washington University, Cheney, Wash. (no date).

Anderson, Arthur L., *The Nickelodeon Claims of Kittitas County.* Unpublished thesis, University of Washington, 1939.

Anderson, Burton, *Petrography and Ore Genesis of the Holden Ore Deposit.* Unpublished thesis, University of Washington, 1938.

Anderson, Eva, G., *Pioneers of North Central Washington.* Reprinted articles from the *Wenatchee Daily World.*

Arno, Steven F. and Hammerly, Ramona P., *Northwest Trees.* Mountaineers Books, 1977.

Asamera Minerals, United Mining Company. Tunnel maps and company records, Lovitt Mining Company.

Bailey, Kate, taped interview by Al Hopkins, early 1960s.

Barlee, N. L., *Gold Creeks and Ghost Towns of Northeastern Washington.* Old Okanogan Publishing Company, 1988.

Barquist, William Swan, *Test of Ore from the St. Francis Vein,* Phelps Ridge, Chelan County, Wash. Unpublished thesis, University of Washington, 1927.

Bell, Chris, one of our prolific information gatherers and companion hiker/bushwacker, and in memory of his dad, Dan, who passed away on one of our history gathering hikes.

Bethune, George A., "Mines and Minerals of Washington Annual Report," 1890.

Brochure, *North Cascades Highway,* GPO 796-036.

Broughton, W. A., "Blewett–Cle Elum Iron Ore Zone, Chelan and Kittitas Counties," Wash. Report No. 12, Department of Natural Resources 1944.

Bryant, Sandy K., *Mountain Air,* Webco Publications (no date).

Burchfiel, B. Clark, Foster, Robert J., Keller, Edward A., Melhorn, Wilton N., Brookins, Douglas G., Mintz, Leigh W., and Thurman, Harold V., *Physical Geology, the Structure and Processes of the Earth.* Charles E. Merrill Publishing Company, 1982.

Byrd, Robert, *Lake Chelan in the 1890s,* 1972. (Revised in 1992.)

Cameron, Donald E., *The Cannon Mine and its Surface Outcrop, Wenatchee, Wash.*, 1994.

Cannon Mine and Cyprus Mining's records, maps, and files, Washington State Department of Natural Resources, Olympia, Wash.

Cannon, Bart, *Minerals of Washington,* Cordilleran, 1975.

Cannon Mine visit in 1991 and underground tour, courtesy of Asamera Minerals.

Carl, Joe, interviews with.

Carlson, Terry and Todd his son, matching step for step in the slopes, and at data gathering. They were constantly coming up with discoveries in the field and finding informative print materials. Thanks for the years.

Case, Matthew H., Northwest Frontier, B.S.C. Educational Aids Inc., 1982.

Chelan Butte gold rush, articles dealing with, *Chelan Leader* newspaper, 1907.

Chesterman, Charles Wesley, *National Audubon Society Field Guide to North American Rocks and Minerals.* Random House, 1979.

Chin, Art, self published, *Golden Tassels,* 1992.

Chinese Exclusion Act, University of Washington Law Library.

The Cle Elum Tribune, various articles and dates.

Coal and Metal Miner's Pocket Book. International Text Book Company, 1907.

Coast Magazine (Wilhelms Magazine), March 1904.

Coates, Robert, *Nature of the Ore Deposit of the Chelan Copper Mining Company at Chelcop, Chelan County.* Unpublished thesis, University of Washington, 1931.

Compton, Mike, interviews with.

The Quarterly Publication of the North Central Washington Museum, Wenatchee, Washington. Confluence, summer 1990.

Crowder, D. F. and Tabor, R. W., *Routes and Rocks.* Mountaineers Books, 1965.

Culver Gulch miners; Clint Black, Tom Richardson, Rob Polley and others. Great interviews, now great friends.

Curtis, Edward S., *The North American Indian: The Indians of the United States and Alaska.* Johnson Reprint Corporation, 1962.

Dana, Edward Salisbury, and Ford, William E., *A Textbook of Mineralogy.* John Wiley and Sons, Inc., 1932.

Daniel, J. R., technical paper, date unknown.

Davidson Report, Swauk Creek Placer Mines, Kittitas County, Wash., 1923.

Dealing with Remembrances of the Black Warrior and the Horseshoe Basin Mine. The Wenatchee World newspaper, September 17, 1997.

Deeson, A. F. L., *The Collector's Encyclopedia of Rocks & Minerals.* Clarkson N. Potter, Inc., 1973.

Denny vs. Holden Lawsuit. Courtesy of Sorrels and Wans law firm, Edmonds, Wash.

Derkey, Robert E., Joseph, Nancy L., Lasmanis, Raymond, *Metal Mines of Washington.* Washington Department of Natural Resources, Division of Geology and Earth Resources, Open File Report 90-18, November 1990.

Dow, Edson, *Passes to the North.* Wenatchee Bindery and Printing Company, 1963.

Duncan, W., *Mineralogy of the Holden Ore Body.* Unpublished thesis, University of Washington, 1939.

Elkins, Grace (Browitt) interviews with. Thanks for the great historic photographs.

Ellensburg Capital, various articles and dates.

The Ellensburg Dawn, December 28, 1900.

Engineering and Mining Journal, February 1988.

Engstrom, Wes and Carole, interviews with.

Fackler, Ralph, interviews with.

Flodin, John and James, interviews with. May, 2001

Gaspers, Joseph, interviews with.

Gaspers, Ann McDowall, interviews with.

Weis, Norman D., *Ghost Towns of the Northwest.* Caxton Printers Ltd., 1988.

Guenther, Ben: Mine information sheets, technical data, drawings, and studies of the Wenatchee ore deposits, 1997.

Guenther, Ben, interviews with.

Handbook of Mining Details by the editorial staff of *Engineering and Mining Journal.* McGraw-Hill, 1912.

Heit, Paul, interviews with.

Helland, Maurice, *They Knew Our Valley,* Helland, 5309 Crest Drive, Yakima, Wash. 98908, 1975.

Henderson, Eugene M., *The Pine Tree Express: A History of the Cascade Lumber Company's Pine Hauling Railroad,* 1990.

Hill, Thomas B. and Melrose, J. W., Division of Mines and Geology, *The Dolphin Mining Claims.* Information Circular No. 7, Olympia, Wash., March 1941.

Hodges, L. K., *Mining in the Pacific Northwest. Seattle Post Intelligencer,* 1897. Reprinted by Shorey's Book Store, Seattle.

Holden, Cathy, interviews with.

Holden Miner newsletters, courtesy of Patty Tappan.

Hometown Heritage: A Remembered History of Ellensburg/Cle Elum. Unpublished manuscript, 1910–1950.

Huntting, Marshall T., *Inventory of Washington Minerals, Part II, Metallic Minerals Vol. 1.* Department of Conservation and Development, Division of Mines and Geology, State of Washington, Bulletin 37, 1956.

Huntting, Marshall T., *A Geologic Trip Along Snoqualmie, Swauk, and Stevens Pass Highways.* Department of Conservation and Development, Division of Mines and Geology, State of Washington, Information Circular 38.

Idaho, an Illustrated History, 1976

Jackson, Bob, *The Rockhound's Guide to Washington, Vol. 4.* Jackson Mountain Press, 1987.

Jim, Negro Creek, ongoing conversations with prospector; Negro Creek Jim (name omitted by request).

Johnson, Toby, *Perspectives on Liberty, Washington: From Controversy to Compromise. Self published,* 1996.

Johnson, Harold, *The Geology of the Copper King Mine, Safety Harbor Creek, Chelan County.* Unpublished thesis, University of Washington, 1938.

Johnson, W. P., *Geologic Report for the North American Exploration Property, Blewett Mining District,* Mining company report, 1958.

Jordan, Josie, *You're at Liberty Here, Mines and Minerals of the Swauk.* Franklin Press, Inc., 1967.

Kenney, Nathaniel T. and Blair, James P., *New National Park Proposed: The Spectacular North Cascades. National Geographic Magazine,* p. 650, May 1968.

Ketchum, Liza, *The Gold Rush,* 1996

King family, interviews with, owners and operators of the Mineral Springs Resort. Great stories and great food. We highly recommend.

Kirch, Jack, interviews with.

Kirk, Ruth and Alexander, Carmela, *Exploring Washington's Past, a Road Guide to History.* University of Washington Press, 1991.

Kittitas Historical Society, thanks to Erin Black and her staff for all the help in pursuing all aspects of our research.

Kittitas Localizer, various articles and dates.

Koschmann, A. H. and Berhgendahl, M. H., *Principal Gold Producing Districts of Washington.* U. S. Department of the Interior, 1966.

Landes, Henry, Thyng, William S., Lyon, D. A., and Roberts, Milnor, Washington Geological Survey, Vol. I, Part II, *The Metalliferous Resources of Washington, Except Iron,* 1902.

Landes, Henry, Washington Geological Survey Annual Report, Part I, 1901.

Lasmanis, Raymond and Cheney, Eric, *Regional Geology of Washington State,* 1994.

Lasmanis, Raymond, et al., Washington Geology article, Vol. 25, No. 3, September 1997.

The Leavenworth Echo, various dates.

Lewis, Robert S., *Elements of Mining.* John Wiley and Sons Inc. 1933, 1941

Liberty Coalition, *Liberty is in Danger* pamphlet, April 1975.

Liberty visits, 1997, 1998, 1999, 2000 and 2001.

Lilly, Frank, Gold Bond Report and Analysis. (No date available.)

Lindsay, F. W., *Cariboo Yarns,* 1963

Livingston, Vaughn E. (revised by) and the University of Washington geology department staff, *A Geologic Trip Along Snoqualmie, Swauk, and Stevens Pass Highways.* Department of Conservation, State of Washington, Information Circular No. 38, 1963.

Lovitt, Edward Jr., interviews with.

Lovitt Mine visits, 1997.

Lynch, Leonard, interviews with.

MacFall, Russell P., *Gem Hunters Guide, How to Find and Identify Gem Minerals.* Bell Publishing Company, 1969.

Marr, James Jr., interviews with.

Marr, James Jr., *The Life Times of the Holden and Lovitt Mines.* Design and layout by W. P. Wanm, printing by Craftsman Printing, 1994.

Martin, Ken, Martin, Vida, editors, *Gold Mining in Washington State.* Golden Treasures Publishing, 1995.

Mason, Charles L., *A Geologic History of the Wenatchee Valley and Adjacent Vicinity.* Self published, no date.

Mayo, Roy F., *Liberty Gold.* Self published, 1994.

McDowall, Vere, Handwritten notes provided by Ann Gaspers.

Meschter, Daniel Y., *History of the Blewett Mining District, Chelan County, Washington, Part II, Lode Mining Discovery and Development, 1874–1900.* Unpublished manuscript, no date.

Meschter, Daniel Y., *History of the Blewett Mining District, Chelan County, Washington, Part I.* Unpublished paper, Ellensburg Public Library.

Mine Safety and Health Administration accident reports.

The Miner, Chemist, and Engineer, various articles and dates.

Miner-Echo, various articles and dates.

Mineral Resources of the Alpine Lakes Study Area and Additions, Chelan, King, and Kittitas Counties, Washington. United States Geological Survey and United States Bureau of Mines, U.S. Geological Survey, Bulletin 1542, 1989.

The Mineralogist, Portland, Oregon.

Mining and Engineering World, March 16, 1912.

The Mining Journal-Press, 1925

Mining Truth Magazine, 1925–1927, November 1928.

Modern Mining and Milling Practice, compiled by *Engineering and Mining Journal,* various authors, 1940s vintage. Article by H. A. Pearse, Mill Superintendent and V. A. Zanadvoroff, Metallurgist for Howe Sound Company, Chelan Division, Holden, Wash.

Moen, Wayne S., *Silver Occurrences of Washington,* Department of Natural Resources, Bulletin 69, 1976.

The National Amateur Mineralogist, 1942.

Newletters from the Swauk Mining District, 1904.

North Central Cascade Miners Association, conversations with. Liberty, Washington.

The Northern Miner, articles, March 10, 1983.

Northwest No Name Prospectors Club, for history input and good old B.S. story conversations everywhere we meet.

Northwest Underground Explorations library and files.

Notenboom, Gayle, *Resurrection of a Ghost Town, Liberty, Washington.* Unpublished thesis, Ellensburg City Library, 1981.

Operation Cooperation, Community Development Study, Cle Elum, Wash., May 1955.

Osgoodby, Bruce and Joyce, for historic information and acquainting us with Ralph Fackler, who launched us on our quest for the colorful history of the Swauk Mining District.

Ott, Larry, *Exploration and History of the Wenatchee District.*

The Pacific Mining Journal, various articles and dates.

The Pacific Quarterly, various articles and dates.

Patton, Thomas Charles, *Economic Geology of the L and D Mine, Wenatchee, Wash.* Unpublished thesis, University of Washington, 1967.

Patty, Ernest N., *The Metal Mines of Washington.* Washington Geological Bulletin, No. 23, 1921.

Paull, Gary, *Reflections of Lake Chelan.*

Pechet, M. S., *Melade Gold Mine, Cle Elum, Wash.,* November 8, 1948.

Pioneer Days in British Columbia, 1977

Priestly, Bill, interviews with.

Priestly, Bill, video tape, Corbaley collection.

Ramsey, Guy Reed, *Postmarked Washington, Chelan, Douglas, and Kittitas Counties.* The Wenatchee World, 1973.

Ream, Lanny, *Gems and Minerals of Washington.* Jackson Mountain Press, 1990.

Rex Mine and mill visit in September 1997.

Roberts, Milnor, Dean, Bulletin of the University of Washington, University of Washington Extension series No. 21, Gen. Sr. No. 110, University of Washington College of Mines Series.

Roe, JoAnne, interviews with.

Roe, JoAnne, *Stevens Pass.* Mountaineers Books, 1995.

Rose, Ric, several informative conversations with Swauk area miner/resident Ric Rose, February and March 2000.

Ruby, Robert, *Indians of the Pacific Northwest*. University of Oklahoma Press, 1988.

Ruffner, W. H., *A Report on the Washington Territory*, 1889.

Saunders, Edwin J., *The Coal Fields of Kittitas County, Washington*, Geological Survey, Bulletin No. 9.

Schuster, Helen H., *The Yakimas: A Critical Bibliography*. Indiana University Press, 1982

Scofield, William E., *Northwest Heritage*. Amsco School Productions Inc., 1978.

Seattle Times, various dates.

Seattle Post Intelligencer, various articles and dates.

Shedd, Solon, Jenkins, Olaf P., Cooper, Herschel H., *Iron Ores, Fuels, and Fluxes of Washington*, Division of Geology, Bulletin No. 27, 1922.

Shedd, Solon, *Mineral Resources of Washington*. Division of Geology, State of Washington, Bulletin No. 2, 1922.

Siever, Raymond, *Earth*. W. H. Freeman and Company, 1986.

Smith, Clareta Olmstead, sketches by Smith, Leta May, *Campfires in the Valley*. History report, 1976, (reprinted 1986).

Snyder, Jerry, owner and great cook of the Liberty Café. Thanks for all the introductions to local miners, and bearers of local Swauk mining history, and all the home style food.

Spawn of Coal Dust, History of Roslyn, Washington...1886 to 1955. A Project of Operation Uplift, community development program, Roslyn, Wash., 1955.

Spring, Ira and Manning, Harvey, *100 Hikes in the North Cascades*. Mountaineers Books, 1985.

Spurr, Josiah Edward, *Ore Deposits of Monte Cristo Washington*, USGS 22nd Annual Report, 1902.

Tappan, Patty, interviews with.

The Miner, Chemist, and Engineer, August 1940 and 1942.

The Night the Mountain Fell. K P Q Publishing, 1973.

The Pacific Northwesterner Magazine, Vol.17, No. 3, summer 1973.

The Yakimas, Treaty Centennial, 1855–1955. Published and authorized by the Yakima Tribal Council, The Republic Press, Yakima, Wash., 1955.

Thompson, Oscar, interviews with.

Thomson, John Prentiss, *Ellensburg Blue*. Acme Printing Company (Now only available at the Kittitas County Historical Society), 1961.

Thomson, John Prentiss, *Genesis of Swauk Placer Gold, Swauk Mining District, Wash.* Unpublished thesis, Washington State College, 1932.

Torgerson, Ronald T., *Treatment of Gold and Copper Ore from the Malade Gold Mine, Cle Elum, Washington*. Unpublished thesis, University of Washington Mining Engineering, May 18, 1951.

Tozer, Warren Wilson, *The History of Gold in the Swauk, Peshastin, and Cle Elum Mining Districts of the Wenatchee Mountains*, 1853–1899; Unpublished thesis, Washington State University, 1965

Trails and Tales of the Early Day Settlers of Northeast Okanogan County. Compiled by Wauconda and surrounding area Historical Committee, Wauconda, Wash., 1982.

Trinity town site visits, underground exploration of the tunnels.

U.S. Geological Review, 1998, *International California Mining Journal,* January 2000.

U.S. Department of the Interior Geological Survey joint bulletin describing gold mining in the U.S.

Valentine and Huntting, *Inventory of Washington Minerals Parts I and II, Metallic Minerals and Nonmetallic Minerals.* Division of Mines and Geology, State of Washington, Text Bulletin 37, 1956.

Valley of the Strong: Stories of Yakima and Central Washington. Kit Publishing Company, December 1974.

Van Voorhis, Ford, *The Homesteaders of Chelan Butte*. Binford and Mort Publishing, 1984.

Vincent, Will Pierre, *Test on a Low-Grade Copper Ore from the Royal Development Company, Leavenworth, Wash.* Unpublished thesis, University of Washington, 1927.

Von Bernewitz, M. W., *Handbook for Prospectors and Operators of Small Mines*. McGraw-Hill, 1935.

Von Bernewitz, M. W., *Handbook for Prospectors and Operators of Small Mines, 4th Edition, 9th Impression,* Revised by Chellson, Harry C., 1943

War Minerals Report, U.S. Department of the Interior, Bureau of Mines, War Minerals Report 27-Nickel, iron, November 1942.

Washington State Department of Natural Resources unpublished data files.

Washington State Historical Society, Tacoma, Wash.

Weaver, Charles E., *Geology and Ore Deposits of the Blewett Mining District.* Washington State Geological Survey Bulletin No. 6, 1911.

Wenatchee Chamber of Commerce.

Wenatchee Daily World, various dates.

Western Miner and Oil Review Magazine, March 1954.

Western Trail Magazine, December 1899

Wood, Charles, *Lines West.* Superior Publishing Company, 1967.

Yakima Herald Republic, various articles and dates.

The Yakima Nation Museum.

Zim, Herbert S. and Shaffer, Paul R., illustrated by Perlman, Raymond, *Rocks and Minerals, a Guide to Familiar Minerals, Gems, Ores, and Rocks.* Golden Press, 1957.

Maps

USGS 7.5 Minute Series Washington Quadrangle Maps:

Ardenvoir	Liberty
Blewett	Polallie Ridge
Blowout Mountain	Mount Stuart
Chelan	Quartz Mountain
Chikamin Creek	Red Top Mountain
Chikamin Peak	Reecer Canyon
Cle Elum	Ronald
Cle Elum Lake	Stehekin
The Cradle	Swauk Prairie
Mount Clifty	Swauk Pass (or Blewett Pass)
Davis Peak	Teanaway
Easton	Teanaway Butte
Enchantment Lakes	Trinity
Frost Mountain	Thorp
Holden	Wenatchee
Jack Creek	Wenatchee Heights
Jack Ridge	Winesap

Green Trails Maps of Washington:
- Chiwaukum Mountains #177
- Kachess Lake #208
- Liberty #210
- Lucerne #114
- Prince Creek #115
- Stehekin #82
- Stevens Pass #176
- Mount Stuart #209
- Thorp #242

Geologic Map of Washington, State of Washington Department of Natural Resources, Division of Mines and Geology, 1961.

3D TopoQuads, Washington, Delorme, Yarmouth, Maine, 1999 (computer mapping program).

Asamera Mining tunnel maps.

U.S. Forest Service Map of the Wenatchee National Forest, 1997.

Glossary

adit A horizontal mine tunnel of any length that enters from the surface. Other special types of tunnels include crosscuts, drifts, and inclines.

aerial tramway A device for transporting materials by means of buckets that travel over a suspended cable.

agate A form of cryptocrystalline (hidden crystals) quartz.

alluvium Loose rock, gravel, soil, sand, and silt that have been washed onto lower terrain by water.

amalgam A mixture of any metal with mercury. Mercury was often used to amalgamate free-milling gold and silver away from the fine rock dust in which it was dispersed.

amethyst The lavender to purple form of quartz crystal. The color is the result of a slight amount of iron in the crystal structure.

andesite A reddish type of lava, named for the Andes Mountains in which it was first identified.

anorthosite Igneous rock that exhibits a whitish-to-dark-gray color.

arkose A type of sedimentary rock that results from the rapid disintegration of granite or gneiss with no alteration by weathering.

arrastre (arrastra) An early device for crushing ore consisting of a flat or dished, circular, horizontal stone floor up to 20 feet in diameter. A vertical axle in the center rotated by a long, horizontal arm attached to a mule, horse, or other beast of burden, or operated by waterpower, if available. Attached to another arm was a stone or stones that were dragged or rolled around the circular floor as the animal was driven in a circle around the axle. The ore was positioned on the floor of the device, and was gradually crushed by the action of the rolling or dragging rocks.

arsenopyrite A mineral containing arsenic, iron, and sulfur.

assay Chemical analysis of an ore to determine its metal composition.

assessment work The minimum amount of work required by the U.S. government as proof that a mine is not lying idle; $100 per year is usually considered adequate. Assessment work is only required on unpatented claims.

azurite An ore of copper that exhibits a brilliant blue color.

bad ground Any area with unstable ground conditions either overhead or underfoot.

ball mill A grinding machine that consists of a large, horizontal cylinder filled with cast-iron or steel balls. The cylinder is rotated, and the ore is mixed with water and admitted into the mill. The action of the tumbling balls grinds the ore into a powder as fine as cooking flour.

barring down For safety reasons, using a crow bar or pry bar to loosen and drop cracked rock located overhead or on the side wall of a mine.

basalt A dark-colored igneous rock that is very fine-grained in texture.

batholith A large mass of igneous rock that was forced, under great pressure, into cooler rock layers. This normally happens deep below the Earth's surface, which causes the mass to cool very slowly, giving rise to a moderately coarse rock structure similar to common granite. These structures can be very large, sometimes many miles across.

bethierite A mineral that occurs in granular to fibrous masses and contains iron, antimony, and sulfur.

blind vein, or blind drift A vein that doesn't outcrop on the surface and is usually discovered by tunneling.

block cave Another term for shrinkage stoping, where the entire roof of the stope is blasted down in a single shot and then mucked out of the bottom.

bonded In mining, a term similar to "leased." Bonders must pay to lease the mine and agree to make certain improvements to it. There is also usually a provision for the bonders to share the proceeds from the property with the owners.

bornite Also called peacock ore. A mineral containing copper, iron, and sulfur. It is similar to chalcopyrite but is composed of a higher percentage of copper. The mineral is the color of shiny brass when first broken open, but it quickly tarnishes to an iridescent peacock color.

breast of the tunnel The far end, or blasting face, of a mine tunnel.

breccia (pipe) A formation of material that has been extruded from deep inside the upper mantel or lower crust of the Earth. Because of the forces involved in this extrusion, the material in the pipe is usually severely broken (brecciated). The minerals in the pipe have formed under extraordinary pressure and heat, so they are not often found in surface or near-surface rock structures. Many exotic minerals, such as diamond, are found in breccia pipes, which leads to great excitement among prospectors when uncovered.

bucket tramway An aerial tramway usually consisting of a single bucket and a haulback cable or rope.

bulldozer chamber In mining, the chambers created at the base of a block cave or shrinkage stope, into which the ore being blasted down from the stope ceiling is deposited.

calcite A mineral composed of calcium carbonate, which can form in many different crystal types.

carbonaceous Containing carbon in its structure. This term sometimes describes organic carbon as well as inorganic.

carbonate Any compound that contains the CO_3 radical.

Carboniferous A period of the late Paleozoic era during which many of the world's coal deposits were formed.

cassiterite Also called stannite, the principal ore of tin, consisting of tin and oxygen.

Cenozoic A major geologic interval, called an era, which began about 66 million years ago and encompasses the present time.

chalcedony A mixture of crystalline and hydrated silicas exhibiting a cryptocrystalline structure.

chalcocite Copper sulfide that also contains small amounts of silver or iron.

chalcopyrite A mineral containing iron, copper, and sulfur.

chlorite Any of the hydrous-ferrous iron-magnesium aluminosilicates. These may also contain ferric iron, chromium, or manganese.

chromite An iron chromate containing chromium, iron, and oxygen.

chrysotile A hydrated magnesium silicate, often found in the fibrous form called asbestos.

cinnabar Mercury sulfide, a mineral containing mercury and sulfur and exhibiting a brick red color.

classifier A device that separates crushed ore into its different sizes. This usually consists of a trough set at a slant and shaken, causing the crushed ore to move downward. The bottom of the trough is perforated by holes that are graduated from very fine at the top to very coarse at the bottom. The various sizes are routed to different areas of the processing plant for further treatment.

concentrator A plant that uses a number of processes to separate the heavier ore from the lighter gangue (waste) rock.

conglomerate A rock that is made up of various smaller rocks that have been cemented together by a matrix, usually deposited out of solution.

contact zone The zone in which the rock has been altered by contact between the country rock and an igneous intrusion. If the zone is near the surface and cools rapidly, it is very narrow, whereas if it was created at great depth and took a long time to cool, the zone can be very wide. The minerals that occur within such a zone get their constituents from both contacting rock types.

core drilling Also called hollow stem drilling, drilling using a hollow stem diamond bit that allows samples of the rock to be withdrawn from hundreds of feet inside a rock mass.

coyote holing In shrinkage stoping, the boring of the narrow holes above the roof of the stope into which explosives are to be packed in order to blow the roof down.

Cretaceous The geologic time period that began about 144 million years ago and continued until about 66 million years ago.

cribbing A form of shoring in which the timbers are laid in a pattern similar to that of a log cabin, with the main timbers periodically interlocked by cross timbers.

crosscut tunnel A tunnel that is not run along a vein, but rather is driven to intersect a vein at some point.

crusher, cone A crusher in which a large cone-shaped mortar contains a solid, smaller cone-shaped pestle. The annular space between the mortar and the pestle tapers from small at the bottom to large at the top. The coarse ore is admitted to the top, and the inner cone is gyrated by an eccentric cam so that the ore is gradually crushed as it moves downward toward the annular gap at the base of the mortar. Also called a gyratory crusher.

cuprite Copper oxide, containing copper and oxygen. Forms cubic crystals.

cyanide plant A mineral treatment facility that uses potassium cyanide or other cyanide compounds to dissolve gold away from the gangue rock.

Dacite The extrusive equivalent of quartz diorite, often call tonalite.

decline A tunnel that descends at a nonvertical but not horizontal angle from the surface.

diabase A dark-colored igneous rock of the gabbro clan that is generally of a medium-grained texture.

diamond drilling Similar to core drilling, in which the annular cutting bit is embedded with industrial diamonds that serve as the cutting medium.

dike In geology, a rock structure caused when magmatic material is extruded into vertical or near-vertical cracks in the country rock. When cooled, a vertical "fin" can form on the surface after the softer country rock has eroded away.

diorite An igneous rock that is similar to granite, except that it lacks quartz.

dip The vertical angle that a mineral vein makes with the Earth's surface.

drift A horizontal tunnel driven along a mineral vein.

druse A fine crust of very small crystals, such as drusy quartz.

duck nest forge A small, cast-iron air distributor, about 8 to 10 inches in diameter, that can be set in the center of a bed of coals. Air is introduced through a pipe radiating from one side and is directed out of ports around the circumference. This allows the bed of coals to reach a high temperature. Duck nest forges were popular among miners and prospectors because they are relatively lightweight and were easy to carry to remote spots.

Eocene A geologic time epoch that existed between 57 and 378 million years ago.

euhedral Exhibiting strong, fully developed crystal grains with well-formed facets.

exploratory work In mining, the work involving tunneling, surface trenching, and so on intended to determine the extent of an ore body.

fault A feature of the Earth's surface where slippage has occurred or is underway between two rock structures. There are various types of faults, such as upthrust, overthrust, lateral, etc.

felsite Igneous rock similar to granite, exhibiting medium-grain size and a gray-to-pinkish color.

fissure vein A mineral vein that has been formed by the forcing of hydrothermal liquids into cracks in country rock.

float Scree that contains minerals that have descended from an exposed vein located somewhere up the slope from the point of discovery.

flotation A process for separating ore from gangue, or base rock. The ore is first crushed and milled as fine as cooking flour. It is then mixed with water and chemicals and introduced as a slurry to a large vat with perforated piping at the bottom. Air is forced through the pipes to create bubbles to which the metallic grains attach themselves and float to the surface to be skimmed off. The gangue rock drops to the bottom as slime. There are other flotation processes that work opposite, where mineral sinks and gangue floats.

foot wall The lower wall of a slanted stope or tunnel.

fortification agate Agate that forms by the depositing of successive layers of silicate on the interior surface of a vesicle, or entrained air bubble. As the layers are deposited, they form concentric shapes that mimic the irregular shape of the bubble wall. When the resulting agate nodules are broken open, the patterns inside often resemble an aerial view of a medieval fort, hence the name.

fossiliferous Containing or composed of fossils.

free milling A mineral deposit in which the metal of value is not chemically attached to country rock, or sulfides, and can be easily removed from the gangue rock by panning, flotation, or other mechanical processes not requiring smelting.

frue vanner A type of shaker table that consists of a wide rubber belt arranged at a shallow angle to the horizontal. The belt is slowly moved over two rollers, one at each end. Finely ground ore is introduced at the top of the belt as a slurry. As the belt moves, it is shaken. The heavier components of the slurry descend the sloping belt and fall off the bottom into a trough. The lighter gangue material tends to remain on the belt and falls off the end into a different trough.

gabbro A type of igneous rock that consists mostly of plagioclase feldspar.

galena The principal ore of lead, lead sulfide, consisting of lead and sulfur.

gangue The material in a vein structure that has no value. The host or country rock.

geode A mineral nodule that usually has euhedral crystals protruding from its outer walls toward its center.

glaucophane A hydrated sodium-magnesium, aluminum, and ferrous-iron silicate. Consists of sodium, magnesium, aluminum, iron, oxygen, silicon, and hydrogen.

glory hole The hole opened when a stope that is being dug upward along a mineral vein breaks out onto the Earth's surface.

gneiss A high-grade, coarse-grained, and banded metamorphic rock.

granitic rocks Rocks that exhibit the characteristics of granite; i.e., medium- to large-grain size and consisting of quartz, feldspar, and biotite (black) mica.

granodiorite An igneous rock similar to granite that is coarse-grained and contains quartz, feldspar, and biotite (black) mica.

greenstone A rock containing a high percentage of chlorite and other green minerals that has metamorphosed from igneous rocks.

grizzly A coarse screen that separates the chunks of ore that are too large to be sent to the first crusher. The chunks that are larger than the screen must first be broken up until they pass through.

Hallidie aerial tram An aerial conveyance similar to a ski lift in which the material-carrying buckets are permanently attached to the cable. The single cable serves to both carry and move the buckets.

hanging wall The upper wall on a sloping stope or tunnel.

haulage (tunnel) A tunnel bored at the lowest possible elevation to tap an ore body at its base. Boring upward into the ore body allows gravity to be used in dropping the ore to the haulage tunnel.

hematite A primary ore of iron, consisting of iron and oxygen.

high banking In placer mining, the acquisition of soils or gravels from high on a water course's bank and panning it or running it through a riffle box near the stream.

high grading 1. The hand selection of ore before shipment to market. 2. The theft of high-grade ore or nuggets by miners before the mine boss was aware of what had been uncovered in the mine.

homestead A plot of land amounting to 160 acres awarded individually to pioneers to be farmed or otherwise productively used. Once in production for a period of time, the land was deeded to the pioneer by the federal government.

hydrothermal Mineral solutions in water that are at an elevated temperature. Hot springs are hydrothermal in nature.

igneous Molten rock that has subsequently cooled.

ilmenite Titanium iron oxide.

incline A tunnel that ascends at a nonvertical angle, often called a decline.

intrusive rock Any igneous rock that has been forced under pressure into the country rock, thus "intruding" into the area.

jasper A red form of agate.

Jurassic A geologic time period that extended from 208 until 144 million years ago.

kimberlite An ultrabasic igneous rock that is usually brecciated (broken) and highly altered. It is classified as a hypabyssal rock, meaning that it was formed at a great depth below the Earth's surface.

lagging The wooden planks that are placed behind shoring timbers to prevent granular or gravelly rock from entering a tunnel.

laterite A sedimentary rock consisting of hydrated aluminum iron oxides and usually exhibiting a white-to-cream-red color.

lenticular In the shape of a lens, thick in the center and tapering to very thin at the periphery.
lignite A very soft, low-grade coal, one step above peat and a step below bituminous.
limonite A hydrated iron oxide containing iron, oxygen, and water.
lode A mass of ore that is embedded in the country rock.
long-hole drilling The act of drilling a series of long diamond drill holes over the area of a proposed shaft, with the goal of sinking the shaft quickly. The holes around the periphery are filled with sand, and the interior holes are filled with sand to within five or six feet of the surface, the remainder with explosives. The holes around the periphery are then charged with explosives and fired. The loosened rock is removed, and the process is continued until the bottoms of the drill holes are reached.
mafic Silicate minerals that are based in iron and/or magnesium.
magnetite An iron oxide that forms cubic crystals and may exhibit a magnetic nature. A lodestone.
malachite A hydrated copper carbonate exhibiting a brilliant green color. The hard variety is considered a semiprecious gem.
marcasite A type of iron pyrite characterized by a silvery color.
metasedimentary A sedimentary rock that has been metamorphosed.
metavolcanic A metamorphosed igneous rock.
Mesozoic A major geologic era that extended from roughly 245 million to 66 million years ago, spanning the Cretaceous, Jurassic, and Triassic periods.
metamorphic Rock that has been altered from its original form by heat, pressure, or other agents.
migmatic Exhibiting coarse grains and a banded structure. Rocks that exhibit these characteristics are called migmatites.
mine dump The unwanted rock debris that has been dumped at the adit of a mine.
mine claim A plot of land usually consisting of 20 acres on which the claimant has rights to the minerals contained therein.
MSHA The Mine Safety and Health Administration.
monazite A phosphate containing lanthanum, thorium, and cerium.
monzonite A plutonic igneous rock containing roughly equal amounts of the orthoclase and plagioclase feldspars.
muck The material remaining in a mine tunnel after blasting the rock down. Mucking consists of the removal of muck from the mine.
olivine A silicate with magnesium, iron, and manganese and with or without calcium.
oölite Any number of minerals that form in masses consisting of spherical or near-spherical grains up to several millimeters in diameter.
Ordovician A geologic period that existed from 505 to 438 million years ago.
ore chute A structure positioned in a vertical tunnel down which ore is transported by gravity to a lower tunnel. The term "ore shoot" is sometimes used to describe a nearly vertical vein of ore.
outcrop The area where a mineral vein reaches the surface.
overshot water wheel A water wheel in which the water is conducted by pipe or trough and discharged at the top of the wheel, allowing the weight of the water to rotate it.
Paleocene A geologic epoch that lasted from 66 million years ago to 57 million years ago.
Paleozoic A major geologic era that lasted from about 570 million years ago until about 245 million years ago.
patent In mining, the document that conveys the title of a claim to the claimant. A patented claim is owned by the claimant, who must pay taxes on the property and follow all of the local county and state laws. In the case of an unpatented claim, the claimant has rights to the minerals only, and the land remains in the ownership of the government.
penstock A pipe or trough that conducts water to a water wheel or a water turbine for the production of power.
peridotite A fine- to coarse-grained ultrabasic igneous rock containing olivine, amphibole, pyroxene, and biotite. Often exhibits a greenish color.

Phenocryst Large crystals of one mineral embedded in a finer matrix. Usually created by differential cooling of igneous rocks.

placer A water-borne or glacial deposit of gravel or sand containing heavy metal ore minerals such as gold, platinum, etc., which have eroded from their original bedrock and concentrated as small particles that can be washed out.

placer claim A mining claim located over a placer deposit.

placer mining The mining of placer deposits by washing, dredging, or other hydraulic methods.

Pleistocene An epoch during the Cenozoic era, which began about 1.6 million years ago and lasted until about 10,000 years ago.

Pliocene An epoch during the Cenozoic era that began 5.3 million years ago and lasted until 1.6 million years ago.

pluton Any of a number of differently shaped and sized bodies of rock created when magma intruded into country rock far below the Earth's surface and (usually) cooled very slowly.

porphyry Hypabyssal igneous rock that contains primarily orthoclase feldspar. Often exhibits phenocrysts in its structure.

portal The entrance to a tunnel.

prospect A mine claim where minerals of value are being sought but few have been located.

pull the pillars When a large body of ore has been removed, pillars of ore are often left in place to support the roof of the cavity. The last act in mining the cavity is to remove the pillars to extract their mineral content. This is risky business, because usually the roof of the mine collapses during the process.

pyrargyrite An ore of silver containing silver, antimony, and sulfur.

pyrite Any of a number of minerals containing iron and sulfur as their principal constituents, also known as fool's gold.

pyrrhotite A form of pyrites that develops flat, platy to tabular crystals exhibiting a hexagonal structure.

Quaternary The most recent geologic period that began about 1.6 million years ago and includes the recent time period.

quartz Silicon oxide, containing silicon and oxygen. A major constituent of the Earth's surface and often found in common beach sand.

quartzite Grains of quartz that have been cemented together by another mineral, often calcite.

quicksilver Common name for mercury, a metal that is liquid at room temperature.

raise In mining, a shaft that is bored vertically upward from a horizontal tunnel.

range (R) In the standard geographical mapping scheme used in the United States, the east-west measurement of a township from an established north-south meridian. Each township consists of a square of land roughly six miles on a side. The first range to the east of the designated meridian is called R1E, the second R2E, and so on.

reef In the Wenatchee, Washington, region, the large dike structures that are roughly vertical and often stand above the softer country rock.

retort A vessel in which a material is heated in the absence of air to drive off a volatile mineral. The act of heating an ore in the absence of air to drive off a volatile component.

rhyolite An extrusive igneous rock similar in composition to granite. Contains phenocrysts of quartz and other minerals.

rock bolting A technique for retaining the roof of a mine by drilling long holes upward and placing expansion bolts into them. Once the bolts are secured, metal plates or mesh is bolted tightly against the roof.

rod mill Similar to a ball mill, in which iron or steel rods are used in the rotating cylinder instead of balls. The coarse ore enters the mill as a water slurry, and the outer cylinder is rotated until the ore is finely crushed. A rod mill can't pulverize as finely as a ball mill, and is often used to reduce the ore grain size prior to passing it through a ball mill.

roof pendant When a pluton is formed by igneous rock intruding into country rock, pendants of the country rock are often surrounded on three sides by molten magma. There is usually a greater amount of mineral alteration in the roof pendant than in the wall contact zones, so prospectors seek them out.

schist A metamorphic rock whose grains have been altered by enormous pressure into flat platelets arranged along the same plane.

section Each of the approximately 36 square miles contained in a geographic township range is called a section. Each is numbered according to a consistent plan from 1 to 36.

sedimentary Rocks that have been formed from sediments. The sediments can be sand, soil, or carbonates (the residue of the shells of sea creatures). Once buried miles below the Earth's surface, pressure and heat, along with cementing minerals, fused the sediments into rock.

sericite A scaly, fibrous form of muscovite (clear) mica.

serpentine A hydrous magnesium silicate mineral containing magnesium, silicon, hydrogen, and oxygen. The color of serpentine ranges from black to green, and it has a slippery feel.

shaft A vertical mine tunnel driven downward from the surface.

shaker table A trough that is slightly tilted to the horizontal and contains slats or riffles to entrap the heavier components of a finely divided ore. As the ore is admitted with water to the upraised portion of the trough, the device is shaken to help the lighter component wash to the lower end, while the heavier metallic minerals collect in the slats or riffles.

shear zone A geologic feature in which two adjacent rock structures slide against each other, causing an alteration of the rock along the zone of contact.

shoring Beams erected in a mine tunnel or stope to prevent collapse.

shotcrete A concrete mixture that is shot from a nozzle onto the application area.

shrinkage stoping A method of mining in which the roof of a stope is drilled and blasted down. The resulting debris serves as the platform for the next episode of drilling and blasting, until there is a large amount of loose ore that can be withdrawn with relative ease. A variation uses coyote holes bored above the roof of the stope to be packed with explosives, and the entire block of the roof is blasted down in one act. In neither case is shoring used in the mining of the stope.

silicified Altered to a silicate from its original form.

silicosis A disease caused by the persistent breathing of silicate dust often present in mine tunnels.

sill A flat and roughly horizontal igneous intrusion.

skip Also known as a hoist, a mine hoist that is used to raise the ore from a mine.

slurry A suspension in liquid of finely-divided particles of a solid.

Slip strike Also call a slip plane. Closely-spaced surfaces along which differential movement takes place in rock. Similar to the movement of shuffling playing cards.

smelter A processing plant in which the metallic content is extracted by melting the ore in a reduction furnace.

snub tunnel A short tunnel, usually less than 20 feet in length, driven from the surface.

sphalerite Zinc sulfide, a common ore of zinc containing zinc and sulfur.

stamp mill A device used to pulverize ore by repeatedly dropping heavy weights, or stamps, on it.

stibnite Antimony sulfide, an ore of antimony, which forms sometimes spectacular bladed crystals.

stope The cavity created as ore is removed from a vein.

streak The color left by scraping a piece of ore on a rough, white, ceramic plate. The color of the streak is often different from that of the actual sample and gives a hint of its composition.

strike The angle of a vein with true, or magnetic, north.

stringer A very thin vein of ore.

sulfide Any mineral that has sulfur as one of its major components but does not contain oxygen.

syenite Igneous rock that contains between 55 and 66 percent silica. Igneous rock rarely contains free quartz.

tailing pile The pile of slag that remains after the milling or smelting process.

talc A hydrous magnesium silicate. Talc is very soft and may be slippery to the touch.

tarn A mountain lake formed in a cirque by glacial action.

Tertiary A geologic period that began 66 million years ago and continued until 1.6 million years ago.

township (T) In the township-range method of geographical subdivision, the measurement that designates how far north a 36–square-mile piece of land is from a designated parallel.

tram Any conveyance used to carry supplies, personnel, or equipment to and from a mine site. Trams can be aerial or surface devices.

tuff A rock that consists of fused volcanic ash.

ultrabasic rock Igneous rock that contains less than 45 percent silica and has no developed quartz or feldspar.

ultramafic rock Igneous rock that contains a great amount of iron or magnesium.

underhanded stope A stope that is driven downward from a tunnel to tap a vein of ore. This process is not generally done because water usually floods this type of stope.

unpatented In mining, a claim in which the claimant has rights only to the minerals on the land, but the government retains the land itself.

uplifting The raising of portions of the Earth's crust by enormous pressures within.

vein A roughly linear body of mineral ore situated between two blocks of country rock.

vesicle A hole left in igneous rock by expanding gases as the magma cooled and the pressure on it was released.

vug, or vuggy Containing holes of various sizes often filled with crystalline minerals.

water-jacketed smelter A smelting oven whose sides are cooled by means of a water jacket.

winze A vertical shaft that is bored downward from within a horizontal tunnel.

zeolite Hydrated aluminosilicates that contain alkali metals such as calcium and sodium.

Resources

Chelan Ranger District
428 West Woodin Avenue
Chelan, WA 98816
(509) 682-2576

Cle Elum Ranger District
803 West 2nd Street
Cle Elum, WA 98922
(509) 674-4411

Ellensburg Public Library
209 N. Ruby
Ellensburg, WA 98926

Entiat Ranger District
2108 Entiat Way
P.O. Box 476
Entiat, WA 98822
(509) 784-1511

Forest Service Campground Information
(800) 280-CAMP

Forest Service Back Country Avalanche Forecast
(206) 526-6677

Gold Prospectors Association of America (GPAA)
43445 Business Park Drive
Temecula, CA 92590
(909) 699-4062

Golden West Visitors Center at Stehekin
(360) 856-5703, Ext. 14

Registrar, Holden Village
H C 00 Stop 2
Chelan, WA 98816-9769

International Prospecting Supply
6169 4th Avenue South
Seattle, WA 98108
(206) 762-6900

International California Mining Journal
P.O. Box 2260
Aptos, CA 95001

Lady of the Lake (Lake Chelan boat trips)
1418 West Woodin Avenue
Chelan, WA 98816
(509) 682-4584
www.ladyofthelake.com

Lake Chelan Chamber of Commerce
(800) 4CHELAN

Lake Wenatchee Ranger District
22976 State Route 207
Leavenworth, WA 98826
(509) 763-3103

Leavenworth Ranger District
600 Sherbourne
Leavenworth, WA 98826
(509) 548-6977

Mountain Pass Report
(206) 434-7277

North Cascades National Park Headquarters
2105 U.S. 20
Sedro Woolley, WA 98284-1799
(360) 856-5700

North Central Cascade Miners Association
Email: nccminers@yahoo.com

North Central Washington Museum
127 South Mission Street
Wenatchee, WA 98801

Northwest Mining Association
10 North Post Street
Spokane, WA 99201
(509) 624-1241

Northwest No Name Prospectors Club
P.O. Box 2872
Woodinville, WA 98072

Northwest Treasure Supply
(800) 845-5258

Northwest Underground Explorations
P.O. Box 386
Monroe, WA 98272
nwuemines@cs.com

Stehekin Lodge
(509) 682-4494

Stehekin Visitors Center
(360) 856-5703

U.S. Bureau of Land Management
P.O. Box 2965
Portland, OR 97208

Washington Department of Wildlife
16018 Mill Creek Boulevard
Mill Creek, WA 98012
or
600 Capitol Way
Olympia, WA 98501

Washington State Historical Society
1911 Pacific Avenue
Tacoma, WA 98042

Washington State Department of Natural Resources
Natural Resources Building
1111 Washington Street
Olympia, WA 98501

Washington Prospector's Mining Association
10002 Aurora Avenue North
Seattle, WA 98133

Index

A
A Reef, 97, 108–9, 127
Accident Claim, 198
accidents, mine, 280
Ace of Diamonds Claim, 183, 185
adits, defined, 317
aerial tramways, 151, 154, 317
agates
    Ellensburg blue agate, 227–28
    Frost Mountain agates, geodes, 224, 226
    glossary definition, 317
    overview, 224
    Red Top Mountain agates, geodes, 216
    Yellow Hill red agate and jasper, 228–29
Allen, Ed, 228
alluvium, 220, 317
Alta Vista Mining Company, 154
altimeters, xxvii
Amalgamated Gold Mines Company, 136
amalgamation, xii
Ambers, Tom, 219
American Eagle Claims, 300
American Nickel and Copper Company, 186
American Nickel Mine, 186
American Smelting and Refining Company, 100
Anaconda, 101, 108, 109, 110, 112
Anderson, Joe, 210
Anderson, Pete, 159
Anderson, William, 182
Anna May Claim, 185–86
Arabian Knight Claim, 198
arachnids, dangerous, xviii
arrastres, 172, 188, 193, 194, 317
artifacts, ix
Asamera Minerals, xvii, 109, 112, 114, 123, 127
asphaltum, 253
Augonaut Claim, 297
Aurora #1 lode, 296
Aurora Group, 296–99

B
B Reef, 97, 105–6, 111, 112, 114, 124, 127
Bailey, Kate, 138, 139
Bainard, Gerald, 111
Baker Creek area claims, 209–12
Ball Eagle Prospect, 240
ball mills, 119, 308, 317
Ballard, Miles and Minnie, 229
Ballard Gold Mining Company, 235, 276
Ballard Mining and Milling Company, 235, 281
Ballard Prospect, 277
Barkdull, Calvin H., 302
Barkdull Mine, 142
Barnett, M., 253
Barry, Roy A., 210, 299
Bartlett, Kenneth, 303
Bartolet, Matt, 186
basalt, 221
Batchelder, Fran, 255

Batchelder, Nathan A., 255
bats, xviii, 244
Baydo, Art, 272
Bean Creek iron deposits, 238
Bear Creek, 219
Beautiful Snow Prospect, 234
Beaver Claim, 264–65
Belcher Prospect, 39
Belfour-Guthrie iron claims, 251–52
Bell, Cornelius, 219
Bell, James, 219, 250, 262
Bell Creek, 219
Benita Prospect, 282–83
Benson, Mr. and Mrs., 212
Berg, John, 282
Bertha Claim, 199
Bertha Prospect, 254
Betty Lou Two Group, 186
Big Antoine's tunnel, 143
Big Bear/Little Bear Claim, 210
Big Boulder Creek area claims, 253–55
Big Boy Claims, 192, 193
Big Bug Mine, 276
Big Creek Claim, 223
Big Creek Mining District, 223
Big Dome Prospect, 277
Big Salmon La Sac Creek, 246
Big Z Mine, 202
Bigelow, Mr., 107
Bigney, Charles, 180, 182
Black, John, xxi, 182, 207
Black and White Mines, 161
Black Bear Prospect, 279
Black Warrior Mine, 35–36
black widow spiders, xviii
Blackhawk Claim, 285
Blackjack Mine, 160, 161, 183
Blankenship Prospect, 40
Blewett, Edward, 132, 133
Blewett Gold Mining Company, 132
Blewett mining area
    description, 129
    exploring mill site, 146–49
    geology, 137–38
    getting there, 137
    history, 129, 131–37
    list of mines, 138–65
    map, 130
    town site, 133, 134, 135, 146, 147
    what to see, 137
Blewett workings, 158
Blinn Claims, 135, 158
Blissett, Miss Allie, 198
block caving, 55
Bloomquist, Frank, 212
Bloomquist, G.A., 192
Bloomquist Brothers Mine, 205
Blue Bonnet Claim, 269
Blue-Eyed Nellie Claim, 298–99
Blue Jay Claimns, 62
Bob Canson Mining Company, 271–72
Bob Tail Claim, 209

Bobtail mines, 153, 269
Bollman, Mose, 160, 164
Bonanza Claims, 141
Bonanza Mining Company, 259. *See also* Dolphin Claim
Boss Claim, 301
Boston Group, 140
Boulder Creek Claims, 199
Boulder Creek Placer, 200
Boulder Creek Prospect, 254
Bourke, Joe, 269
Boxall, James, 210
Boyles, A.W., 267
Boyles, E.P., 262, 301
Boyles property, 269
Brand, Sullivan, and Carson Company, 135
Breakwater Resources, Ltd., 112, 114
breccia pipes, 73, 318
Brighton, Larry, 203
Bronco Claim, 294–95, 296
Brown, E.K. (Sonny), 191, 196, 236
Brown, John, 219
Brown, N.W.L., 96
Brown, R.S., 54
Brown Bear Claim, 264
Brown Bear Group, 186
Brown Bear Mining Company, 233–34
brown recluse spiders, xviii
Brusha, Jack, 131
Bryant, Frank, 190, 254
Buckeye Claim, 198
Buel, Clarence M., 242
Buhrn, Ed, 219
bulldozer chambers, 55, 306, 318
Bunker Hill Mine, 195
Burbank Valley gold panning, 227
Burch, Ben, 250
Burke, John, 250, 262
Burke brothers, 254, 255
Burke Prospect, 254
Butte Mine, 87
Butte Prospect, 40

C
C Reef, 97, 109–10
Cain, J.B., 241
Caldo Mine, 142
California Gold Rush, xx–xxi, xxii, xxiii, 93, 94
Camp Creek area claims, 263–72
Camp Creek Mining Company, 271–72, 303
Campbell, William, 241, 273
Cannon, Donald G., 111
Cannon Mine
    closure, 127
    cost to open, xvii
    description, 96, 110
    development, 114–15
    fatalities, 124, 125, 126
    geology, 96–97
    getting there, 110–12
    history, 112–14
    isometric drawings, 119, 122, 124

main adit photos, 116, 120
mill, 25, 119–20
mysteries, 121–23
operations, 115–18
production, 119, 126–27
underground, 115–19
Carey, George, 289
Carkeek, V., 95
Carthers, W., 255
Cascade Chief Mine, 195–96
Cascade Consolidated Company, 37
Cascade Copper Company, 35
Cascade Mining Company, 226
Cedar Grove Campground, 141
Cedar Valley Gold Mining Company, 169
Chapman, Mrs. M.A., 186
Charlotte Prospect, 107, 109
Chelan Butte mining area
description, 83
geology, 84
getting there, 84
gold rush, 83
history, 83
list of mines, 84, 86–88
map, 85
what to see, 84
Chelan Consolidated Copper Company, 67, 69
Chelan Copper Company, 51
Chelan Copper Mining Company, 51
Chelan Mining and Milling Company, 134, 135
Chelan mining area
description, 43
geology, 46
getting there, 45–46
history, 43, 45
Holden Mine, 48–61, 62, 63
list of mines, 47–66
map, 44
what to see, 45
Chelan town site, 45
Chief Joseph, 94
China Camp Claim, 247–49
Chinese miners
in Cle Elum Mining District, 247–49
history, 93, 94–95
illustrations, xiii, xvii, 93, 100, 131
in Negro Creek area, 143
treatment, xxi, 94–95
work along Columbia River, 94–95
work in D Reef area near Squilchuck Creek, 95, 100
Chiwawa mining area
description, 67
geology, 72–73
getting there, 72
history, 67, 69–71
list of mines, 73–90
map, 68
what to see, 71
Chiwawa Mining Company, 80
Chung Yune, 248
Churchill, Mr., 290
cinnabar, 257, 318
Clagstone Prospect, 37

claims
filing and retaining, xvii, xx
glossary definition, 321
Clark, Billy, 291
Clark, Jack, 291
Cle Elum iron claims, 249–52
Cle Elum mining area
background information, 221–22
declining years of district, 302–3
description, 217
geology, 220–21
getting there, 220
history, 217, 219–20
list of mines, 222–302
map, 218
trails and roads, 222
what to see, 220
Cle Elum River Mining Company, 271–72, 291–92, 303
Climax Group, 302–3
coal mining, 96–97
Cockle, C.E., 101
Cole, W.R., 175
Collins Placer, 176
Columbia River, and Chinese miners, 94–95
concentrators
Cannon Mill, 119–20, 125
glossary definition, 318
Holden Mill, 304–9
illustrated, 125
Condon, H.C., 195
Connell, E., 236
Conrad, John, 111
Consolidated Gold Mines and Refining Company, 137
contact zones, 221, 318
Cooper, Harbin M., 131, 229, 244
Cooper, Theodore, 229, 248
copper. See Holden Mine
Copper King Claim, 286
Copper King Mine, 65–66
Copper Queen properties, 245–46, 270
Copper Queen Prospects, 144
Corbins, John, 240, 241, 252, 273
Corey, R.C., 236
Cougar Claim, 186
Cougar Gulch Mining Company, 186
Cover, Sylvester, 131
coyote holing, 55, 318
critters, dangerous, xviii
crosscut tunnels
glossary definition, 318
mucking operation photo, 59
on Peshastin ore, 135, 150, 151
Phipps tunnel, 158
Royal Development Mine, 70, 72, 73–74, 79
Stoner tunnel, 158
Crowe, Jack, 261
Crowe property, 261–62
Crown Point Mine, 47
Crystal Mountain hike, 214–15
Culver, Samuel, 131
Culver Gold Mining Company, 132, 169

Culver Mines, 158
Culver Springs Gulch Creek, 162–65
Culver Springs Mining Camp Claim, 162–63
Cumby, William, 228–29
Cummings, J.F., 301
Cyprus Mines Corporation, 112, 127

D
D Reef, 95, 97, 100, 106–7
D'Ablaing, Gerritt, 230, 255
Dandy Claim, 194
Danport Mine, 35
Davenport, C.P. (Cliff), 135, 136, 144, 159
Davis, Cap, 219
Davis Creek, 219
Davison, J.B., 241
Day, Henry L., 103, 106
De Roux, August, 233–34
Deadwood Claims, 141
declines, 106, 108, 114, 115, 126, 319
Deer Gulch dredge pond, 179, 184, 212
Defender Prospect, 40
Dennett Placer tunnels, 176–77, 184
Denny, A.W. (Dick), 219, 254, 255
Denny, Charles, 255
Denny, David, 48
Denny, Don W., 303
Denny, Fred, 254, 255, 262, 303
Denny, Phil, 255, 272, 291, 303
Denny, Richard, 261
Denny, V.C. (Victor), 48, 49, 51, 226, 227, 254
Denny Claim, 293–94
Denny Prospect, 254–55
Dewitt, R., 246
diabase, 172
diamonds, 176
Dick, Condi, 90
Dick Mine, 89–90
Dickson, E.M., 253
Discovery Mine, 169, 170
Dixie Claim, 183
Dodge, Ella I., 133
Dolphin Claim, 257–60, 259–60
Don Tom Claim, 272
Doubtful Prospect, 38
Draw tunnel, 150
dredge mining, 179, 184, 187, 212, 214, 215
Driscoll, Joe, 243
Duncan, George C., 124
Dunlap, Ken W., 186, 266, 289, 290, 300
Durrwachter, Charles and Ernest, 245
Durrwachter property, 244–45
Durst Creek lode, 205

E
E Reef, 97, 107, 109
Earnest, Frank S., 137
Earnest, John, 137
earthquakes, 43, 45, 203
Edna R. property, 267
Elinor tunnel, 155
Ellen Group, 287, 288–89
Ellensburg Improvement Company, 223
Elliott, George, 250

Elliott Claim, 185
Ellis, Arthur H., 136
Elsner, Adolph, Sr., 230, 232, 255
Elsner Claims, 294–95
Emerson, Mose, 268, 291
Emery, S.C., 275
Emma Lee Prospect, 62
Entiat mining area
    description, 83
    geology, 84
    getting there, 84
    list of mines, 88–90
    map, 85
    what to see, 84
Epha Claim, 268
Erlandsen, Oscar, 287
Ernest, Henry, 159
Esther Gold and Silver Mine, 48
Etienne, Antoine, 129, 143
Eureka Claim, 282
Eureka Mine, 160
Evens, Jesse, 228
Ewell, William, 187
Ewell Claim, 187
Eyler, Earl, 202

F
Fackler, Karl, 135, 156, 159
Fackler, Ralph, 175, 203
Fackler #2 Adit, 156
Fairy Queen Mine, 197
Falleto, John, 48
Falls Prospect, 38
Family Group, 272
Fanny Edell Claim, 211
federal lands, laws and regulations that
    govern prospecting, xix, xx, xxv–xxvi
First Creek hike, 21
Fish Eagle Prospect, 300
Flamingo Prospect, 39
Flanker Claim, 297
Fletcher, Clinton, 242
Flint, P.J., 262
Flodin, Andrew, 182, 193, 194
Flodin, John, 174, 193
Flodin Mine, 193–94
flotation, 119, 305, 308, 319
Flummerfelt, Charles, 230
Ford, W.A., 206, 210
Fortune Creek area
    Fortune Creek Mine, 274
    geology, 273–74
    getting there, 274–75
    list of gold placers, 278
    list of mines, 275–78
    mill site, 275
    mining development, 274
    North Fortune Creek, 280–82
Fortune Creek Smelting and Refining
    Company, 275
Fortune Mining and Smelting Company, 275
Fountain of Gold, 277
Fowler, William H., 192
Fraction Placer, 174, 180, 182

Francis Girard quartz lode, 186
Franklin Prospect, 38
free-milling gold, xvi, xxii, 84, 97, 319
French, Ben, 220
French Cabin Creek, 220
Frost Mountain agates and geodes, 224, 226
Fry, O.F., 189, 232, 255
Funkhouser, Frank, 36

G
gabbro, 221
galena, xxiii, 320
Galena Prospect, 38
Galena town site, 263
Gallagher, Ed D., 242
Gallagher, G.W., 242, 258
Gallagher Mining and Development Company,
    258
gangue, 173, 305, 320
Gannon, T.F., 226, 227
Garnierite Claims, 140
Gaspers, Ann, 102
Gassman, E.P., 253, 262, 290, 291, 300, 301
Gaston, Paul, 236
Gayre, D.H., 201
Gem Claim, 62, 162
geodes, 224, 320
geology
    Blewett mining area, 137–38
    Cannon Mine area, 96–97
    Chelan Butte mining area, 84
    Chelan mining area, 46
    Chiwawa mining area, 72–73
    Cle Elum mining area, 220–21
    Entiat mining area, 84
    Fortune Creek area, 273–74
    Holden Mine, 48
    Lovitt Mine, 96–97
    Solomon Creek area, 286
    Stehekin mining area, 35
    Swauk mining area, 171–73
    Teanaway Valley and headwaters area,
    228
    Van Epps Creek area, 286
    Washington State, xxii–xxiv
    Wenatchee mining area, 96–97
George Markle Mining Co., 36
Georgie Smith Mine, 80
"Ghost" photo, 80
glaucophane, 245, 320
Glover, Sheldon L., 303
goat, exploding, 269
Goat Mountain Claim, 293–94
Godwin, J., 203
gold
    Cannon Mine production, 126–27
    characteristics, xii
    consumption and value, xii, xiii–xiv
    costs in developing lode deposits, xvi–xvii
    free-milling vs. non-free-milling, xvi, 176
    history, x–xi
    locating lode deposits, xvi–xix
    and mercury, xii
    mining, xii–xiii, xiv

    placer mining vs. lode mining, xvi, xvii
    prospecting as hobby, xix
    theft of high-grade ore, xiv–xvi
    in Washington State, xiv, xvi–xvii, xxii, xxiii
Gold and Silver Claim, 287
Gold Bond Mining Company, 135–37, 158
Gold Bug Claim, 273
Gold Bug Mine, 86
Gold Finger Claim, 156
Gold King Mine, 101
Gold Knob Prospect, 108–9
Gold Leaf Mine, 197
Gold Mine Gulch, 84, 86
Gold Mountain Claim, 276
Goldbeldt Mines, 112
Golden Bar Placer Claim, 200
Golden Chariot Mine, 160
Golden Cherry Mine, 160
Golden Crown Mine, 153
Golden Eagle Mine, 151, 275
Golden Eagle Placer Claim, 199
Golden Fleece Mine, 196
Golden Gate Mining Company, 242–44
Golden King Claim, 95
Golden Rule Claim, 297–98
Golden Thunderbird Mining Company, 175
Golden Wedge Mine, 163
Goldie Mine, 284
Goodwin, Newton and Benton, 167, 169
gossem. See iron cap stains
government agencies
    and early mining law, xx–xxi
    and hobby prospectors, xix, xx, xxv–xxvi
Grace Mine, 62
Graham, F.M., 201
Grand Entry Mine, 223
Grand Skidhue Claim, 298
Grandby Company, 51
Grandview Copper Claim, 235–36
Granger, Walter, 243
Graves, O.M., 194
Gray, George, 280
Gray, John, 285
Gray Eagle Prospect, 41
Greaser, Jack, 341
Great Scott Group, 299
Great Western Group, 195
Great Wonder Claims, 195
Green Horn Claim, 209
Green Tree Mining Company, 182
Grieve, James, 253, 262, 266, 289, 290, 291,
    295, 300, 301
Griffin, Jack, 236
Grizzly Bear Claims, 276
grizzly screens, 107, 306, 320
Grosso, John, 230
Groves, Thomas, 107
Guenther, Ben, 122–23

H
H-O-M-E Mining Company, 227
Hackney, Hadley, 136
Haight, A.W., 265, 271
Hall, E.H., 111

Halverson, Lars, 210
Hamlin, J.T., 236
Hampton, George, 187
Hansel, John, 138, 139
Hansen, H.W., 261, 262
Hard Hat #1 Mine, 203
Hardman, Mr., 233
Hardscrabble Claim, 252–53
Harrington, Mr. and Mrs., 219
Harrison, B.F., 287
Hart, W.R., 199
Hatley, J.W., 135
haulage tunnels, 49, 98, 99, 101, 320
haunted claims, 81
Hawkins, S.S., 262, 266, 267, 276
Hawks, Bill, 202
H.C. Dennett Placer Claim, 176–77, 184
Hellen, A., 211, 276
Helm Placer, 278
hematite, 252, 320
Henzer, Mr. and Mrs., 217
HHY Prospect, 283
Hicks, Mr., 274
Hidden Treasure Prospect, 64
Higgins Mine, 84
high-grading, xiv–xvi
Higson, Jacob, 249
hikes, rating, xxix
Hill, D.W., 223
Hoage, W.A., 291
Hocking, J.F., 135
Hodges, L.K., 221, 241
Hohman, J.J., 253
Holden, John Henry, 48–51
Holden, S.J., 286
Holden Mine
    cleanup, 60–61
    closing, 59
    concentrator, 304–9
    cost to open, xvii
    development, 51–52
    geology, 48
    getting there, 48
    history, 48–61
    isometric drawing, 56–57
    mill flow schematic, 304, 307
    mining and milling, 52–55
    mining methods, 55–59
    ore deposit geology, 48
    production, 60
    today, 60–61
    town site, 52, 56–57, 60, 61
Holland, Bill, 115
Holt, Charley, 291
Homestake and Star Prospect, 39
Homestake Claims, 178
Homestake Hill Mine, 177, 178
Homestake Mine (Blewett mining area), 164
Homestake Mine (South Dakota), xiii
Homestead Lode Claim, 178
homesteads, 229, 320
Hood, Harry J., 140
Hope Claim, 235
Hope Quartz Claim, 198

Hopkins, Paul, 263
Horseshoe Basin Mine, 36–37
Horseshoe Basin Mining and Development Company, 35, 36
Howe Sound Mining Company, 51, 54, 59, 61
Howson Creek Claims, 241–42
Huckleberry Mountain area, 270–71
Hughes-Wayman Prospect, 265, 266
Humbug Claim, 289, 290
Hunt, Harry H., 65
Hunter Claims, 62
Hurley, George J., 197
Hurley, Pat, 197
Hurley Creek Claim, 197
Husband, John T., 124
hydraulic mining, 188, 189

I
Ida Elmore Mine, 265–66
Idaho Prospect, 64
Iias Claim, 267–68
Illinois Quartz Claim, 253
Indians. See Native Americans
Ingalls, Ben, 138–39, 140
Ingalls, Dewitt Clinton, 139
Ingalls Creek
    lost gold mine story, 138–40
    mines, 140–41
    Teanaway River area, 235–36
insects, dangerous, xviii
iron cap stains, xviii, xxii
iron deposits
    Bean Creek deposits, 238
    Cle Elum claims, 249–52
    iron cap stains, xviii, xxii
    Iron Peak deposits, 236–38
    Negro Baby lode, 223
    Stafford Creek deposits, 238–39
    Taneum lode, 224
    Upper Cle Elum deposits, 249
    upper Teanaway Valley claims, 236–38
    what to look for, 252
Iron King Mine, 164
Iron Peak deposits, 236–38
Isoletta Prospect, 39

J
Jackson, Andrew, 271
Jackson, Henry M., 175
Jacobson Cabin, 280–81
Jennifer Ann (Taft) Mine, 186–87
Joe J. Morris Claim, 235
John C. Claim, 240–41
Johnson, A.W. (Billy), 207, 208
Johnson, Ernest, 287
Johnson, J.A., 301
Johnson, O.R., 271
Johnson, Thomas, 132, 134, 223
Johnson, Will, 236
Johnson pocket, 209
Johnson property, 145–46
Jones, H.C., 182
Jones, Mr., 274
Jones brothers, 241

Jordan, Jack, 189
Jordin, Amos and Mae, 191
Jordin, A.R. (Amos), 185, 191, 192, 236
Jordin, Clarence, 185, 190, 197
Jordin, Ollie, 198
Josie Claim, 199
Jumbo Claim, 281–82
Just In Time Claim, 276
Justhand, Simon, 271
Jutzy, J.J., 136

K
Kalma, Don, 111
Kaup, William, 206
Keefer Brothers Mine, 78
Keegan, J.J., 100, 101, 108
Kelly, Ben, 255, 261, 267
Kelly, Gary, 303
Kelly, Grover, 48
Kelly, Jack, 291
Kelly, John, 282
Key Note tunnel, 160
Keystone Group, 230
Killson, Ben, 180
Kineth, Charles, 195
Kineth, O., 195
King, Mr., 275
King, Pat, 164
King Creek area claims, 162
King of Sweden Claim, 282
King Solomon Claim areas
    east of Vap Epps Pass, 285
    original, 289–90
King Solomon Mine, 64
Kingman, Morrison M., 35, 36, 86
Kingman Prospect, 41
Kirch, Jack, 183, 190, 208
Kirke, Peter, 250
Kittitas Gold Mining Company, 187
Knob Hill Mining Company, 100
Koppen, George, 230, 233

L
La Bonn, John, 220
La Caff, Pete, 219
La Rica Mining Company, 135
Lake Ann Prospect, 235
Lake Chelan, 43, 45, 46, 51–52
Lake City Placer, 278
Lake Ennis Prospect, 234–35
Lake Shyall Prospect, 40
Lamar, Bill, 159
Lamb, E., 187
Lancaster, Bill, 105
Lannigan, Ed, 189
Last Chance Claim, 289, 290
law
    early mining law, xx–xxi
    filing and retaining claims, xvii, xx
    legal aspects of prospecting, xix, xx, xxv–xxvi
L&D Mining, 103
Lechman, Andrew M., 201
Ledger lode, 301

lenticular veins, 138, 321
Leschi (Nisqually chief), 93
Lewis, George H., 135
Lib Group, 206
Liberty Mine, 191–93
Liberty (town), 171, 173–75, 176, 177, 178, 179, 180, 181
Liggett, Irvine, 209
Lilne, Roy, 198
Lily, Frank, 136
limonite, 252, 321
Lind, John, 248
Linston Mine, 79
Little Boulder Creek area claims, 252–53
Little Gem Claim, 197
Little Salmon La Sac Creek, 246
Little York Claim, 208
Livingston, Dave, 177, 178
Livingston, Jim, 177, 178
Livingston, Tom, 177, 178, 189
Livingston, Vaughn E., 303
Livingston brothers, 250
Livingston Placer tunnels, 177
Lloyd, Tom, 291
Lockwood, E.W., 131
Lockwood, James, 131
lode, defined, 321
lode mining vs. placer mining, xvi, xvii
log buildings, 34, 131, 132, 134, 226
Logan Prospect, 40
Lone Rock Mine, 160
Lonergan, Phillip, 69
Lost Vein, 84
Lottie S. Prospect, 39
Love, J.R., 197
Lovitt, Ed, 101–2, 103, 104, 105, 106, 112, 114, 127
Lovitt Mine
    description, 96, 97–99
    development, 101–5
    geology, 96–97
    history, 100–101
    isometric drawing, 98, 99
    production, 107
    tunnels, 98–99, 101, 103
Lower Hummingbird Mine, 151
Lucky Queen Mine, 159
Lunsden, Bill, 261
Lynch, John, 141, 262, 297
Lynch, Leonard, 58–59
Lynch, Timothy, 262, 297
Lynch, William, 141
Lynch Group, 140–41
Lyon, Jack, 227

M
magnetite, 252, 321
Magpie Canyon, 227
Mammoth Claim, 300
Manastash Creek Claim, 224
Manastash Ridge Pack Trail mineral sites, 226
maps
    Blewett mining area, 130
    Chelan Butte mining area, 85
    Chelan mining area, 44
    Chiwawa mining area, 68
    Cle Elum mining area, 218, 223
    Entiat mining area, 85
    mines overview, vi
    Stehekin mining area, 32
    Wenatchee mining area, 92
Marcus Stein Mine, 47
Marlin Prospect, 40
Marr, Charles E., 136
Marr, James, Jr., 58, 104, 107, 109
Maryellen Claim, 209–10
Mason, J.B., 195
Masterson, Bat, 229
Masterson, Harry, 229
Masterson, James, 229
Mattie Claim, 252–53
Matwick Mine, 149
Maud-O Claims, 265
Maycock, Herbert, 280
Mayflower and East Side Prospect, 41
Mayflower Claim, 275
Mays, D.W., 111
McAulay, George F., 243
McBeth Claim, 95
McClellan, George, 91
McConihe, L.F., 197, 241, 253, 262
McCormick, Mike, 175
McCurdy, E.H., 243
McDonald, John, 241, 273
McDowall, Vere, 101, 102, 103
McGuire, L. H., 111
McIntire, J.D., 159
McKasson, William, 240, 252
McManimie, J.S., 242, 243
McNalt, W.F., 269
McNutly, Thomas, 282
McPhail, Charles, 284
McPhail Engineering Company, 275
McSherry, Jack, 175
Meadow Adit, 284–85
Meadow Creek mining area, 61, 62, 64–66
Meadow Creek Placers, 299
Meagher, Thomas, xxi, 173, 180, 182, 199, 244
Medicine Creek Claims, 205–6
Medill, J.D., 243
Melade Mine, 265, 266
Melrose, T.W., 193
Mercer, A.L., 192
Mercer, George, 192
Mercer, Ted, 192
mercury, xii
Meschter, Daniel, 138
metal detectors, xix
Meteor tunnel, 149–50, 152, 153
Meyer, Mrs. Marle, 136
Michals, Mr., 223
Midway Claim, 273
Miles, R.E., 281
Mill Creek, 217
Mill Creek Claim, 210
Mill Gulch Claim, 210
mine accidents, 280
mine claims, defined, 321
Miner, Ed, 198
Mineral Creek area claims, 244–46
miners, xxi, 52, 54, 263, 307. See also Chinese miners
mines. See also specific mining areas
    Accident Claim, 198
    Ace of Diamonds Claim, 183, 185
    American Eagle Claims, 300
    American Nickel Mine, 186
    Anna May Claim, 185–86
    Arabian Knight Claim, 198
    Asamera Minerals, 111, 112, 123
    Augonaut Claim, 297
    Aurora Group, 296–99
    Ball Eagle Prospect, 240
    Ballard Prospect, 277
    Barkdull Mine, 142
    Beautiful Snow Prospect, 234
    Beaver Claim, 264–65
    Belcher Prospect, 39
    Benita Prospect, 282–83, 282–83l
    Bertha Claim, 199
    Bertha Prospect, 254
    Betty Lou Two Group, 186
    Big Bear/Little Bear Claim, 210
    Big Boy Claims, 192, 193
    Big Bug Mine, 276
    Big Chief Claim, 192
    Big Creek Claim, 223
    Big Dome Prospect, 277
    Big Z Mine, 202
    Black and White Mines, 161
    Black Bear Prospect, 279
    Black Warrior Mine, 35–36
    Blackhawk Claim, 285
    Blackjack Mine, 160, 161, 183
    Blankenship Prospect, 40
    Blinn Claims, 135, 158
    Bloomquist Brothers Mine, 205
    Blue Bonnet Claim, 269
    Blue-Eyed Nellie Claim, 298–99
    Blue Jay Claimns, 62
    Bob Tail Claim, 209
    Bobtail mines, 153, 269
    Bonanza Claims, 141
    Boss Claim, 301
    Boston Group, 140
    Boulder Creek Claims, 199
    Boulder Creek Placer, 200
    Boulder Creek Prospect, 254
    Bronco Claim, 294–95, 296
    Brown Bear Claim, 264
    Brown Bear Group, 186
    Buckeye Claim, 198
    Bunker Hill Mine, 195
    Burke Prospect, 254
    Butte Mine, 87
    Butte Prospect, 40
    Caldo Mine, 142
    Cannon Mine, xvii, 96–97, 110–27
    Cascade Chief Mine, 195–96
    Charlotte Prospect, 107, 109
    China Camp Claim, 247–49

Clagstone Prospect, 37
Claim, 187
Cle Elum iron claims, 249–52
Climax Group, 302–3
Collins Placer, 176
Copper King Claim, 286
Copper King Mine, 65–66
Copper Queen Prospects, 144
Cougar Claim, 186
Crown Point Mine, 47
Culver Mines, 158
Culver Springs Mining Camp Claim, 162–63
Dandy Claim, 194
Danport Mine, 35
Deadwood Claims, 141
Defender Prospect, 40
Denny Claim, 293–94
Denny Prospect, 254–55
Dick Mine, 89–90
Discovery Mine, 169, 170
Dixie Claim, 183
Dolphin Claim, 257–60, 259–60
Don Tom Claim, 272
Doubtful Prospect, 38
Ellen Group, 287, 288–89
Elliott Claim, 185
Elsner Claims, 294–95
Emma Lee Prospect, 62
Epha Claim, 268
Eureka Claim, 282
Eureka Mine, 160
Fairy Queen Mine, 197
Falls Prospect, 38
Family Group, 272
Fanny Edell Claim, 211
Fish Eagle Prospect, 300
Flamingo Prospect, 39
Flanker Claim, 297
Flodin Mine, 193–94
Fraction Placer, 174, 180, 182
Franklin Prospect, 38
Galena Prospect, 38
Garnierite Claims, 140
Gem Claim, 62, 162
Georgie Smith Mine, 80
Goat Mountain Claim, 293–94
Gold and Silver Claim, 287
Gold Bug Claim, 273
Gold Bug Mine, 86
Gold Finger Claim, 156
Gold Knob Prospect, 108–9
Gold Leaf Mine, 197
Gold Mountain Claim, 276
Goldbeldt Mines, 112
Golden Bar Placer Claim, 200
Golden Chariot Mine, 160
Golden Cherry Mine, 160
Golden Crown Mine, 153
Golden Eagle Mine, 151, 275
Golden Eagle Placer Claim, 199
Golden Fleece Mine, 196
Golden King Claim, 95
Golden Rule Claim, 297–98

Golden Wedge Mine, 163
Goldie Mine, 284
Grace Mine, 62
Grand Entry Mine, 223
Grand Skidhue Claim, 298
Grandview Copper Claim, 235–36
Gray Eagle Prospect, 41
Great Scott Group, 299
Great Western Group, 195
Great Wonder Claims, 195
Green Horn Claim, 209
Grizzly Bear Claims, 276
Hard Hat #1 Mine, 203
Hardscrabble Claim, 252–53
H.C. Dennett Placer Claim, 176–77, 184
Helm Placer, 278
HHY Prospect, 283
Hidden Treasure Prospect, 64
Holden Mine, xvii, 48–61, 62, 63, 304–9
Homestake and Star Prospect, 39
Homestake Claims, 178
Homestake Hill Mine, 177, 178
Homestake Mine (Blewett mining area), 164
Homestake Mine (South Dakota), xiii
Homestead Lode Claim, 178
Hope Claim, 235
Hope Quartz Claim, 198
Horseshoe Basin Mine, 36–37
Howson Creek Claims, 241–42
Huckleberry Claims, 270–71
Hughes-Wayman Prospect, 265, 266
Humbug Claim, 289, 290
Hunter Claims, 62
Hurley Creek Claim, 197
Ida Elmore Mine, 265–66
Idaho Prospect, 64
Iias Claim, 267–68
Illinois Quartz Claim, 253
Iron King Mine, 164
Isoletta Prospect, 39
Jennifer Ann (Taft) Mine, 186–87
Joe J. Morris Claim, 235
John C. Claim, 240–41
Josie Claim, 199
Jumbo Claim, 281–82
Just In Time Claim, 276
Keefer Brothers Mine, 78
Keystone Group, 230
King Creek area claims, 162
King of Sweden Claim, 282
King Solomon Claim, 285, 289–90
King Solomon Mine, 64
Kingman Prospect, 41
Lake Ann Prospect, 235
Lake City Placer, 278
Lake Ennis Prospect, 234–35
Lake Shyall Prospect, 40
Last Chance Claim, 289, 290
Lib Group, 206
Liberty Mine, 191–93
Linston Mine, 79
Little Gem Claim, 198
Little York Claim, 208

Livingston Placer, 177
Logan Prospect, 40
Lone Rock Mine, 160
Lottie S. Prospect, 39
Lovitt Mine, 96–97, 107
Lower Hummingbird Mine, 151
Lucky Queen Mine, 159
Lynch Group, 140–41
Mammoth Claim, 300
Manastash Creek Claim, 224
Marcus Stein Mine, 47
Marlin Prospect, 40
Maryellen Claim, 209–10
Mattie Claim, 252–53
Matwick Mine, 149
Maud-O Claims, 265
Mayflower and East Side Prospect, 41
Mayflower Claim, 275
McBeth Claim, 95
Meadow Creek Placers, 299
Medicine Creek Claims, 205–6
Melade Mine, 265, 266
Midway Claim, 273
Mill Creek Claim, 210
Mill Gulch Claim, 210
Minneapolis Prospect, 39
Modog Claims, 265
Monte Cristo Mine, xviii, xxiii
Morning Claim, 194
Morning Star Mine, 243
Morrison Gold Quartz Mine, 195–96
Morrison Mine, 193–94
Mother-in-Law Group, 210
Mountain Beaver Placer Claims, 201
Mountain Belle Claim, 275
Mountain Placer, 278
Mountain Sprite Claims, 297
Mountain Whistler Claim, 273
Nairn Claim, 197
Naneum Creek Placers, 201
Negro Creek (Davenport) Claim, 144
Nelson Claim, 286
New Discovery Placer, 174, 182
Nickel Plate Group, 141
Nickelodeon Claims, 255–57, 258
Nilson Hill, 190–91
North Star Claim, 199
Nugget Placer, 200, 278
Ollie Jordin Mine, 198
Olmstead Mine, 267
Olympia Claims, 158
Ombompo Prospect, 40
Orion Claim, 204–5
Oro Grande Claim, 192, 193
Orphan Boy Mine, 64
Panama #2 Prospect, 38
Pangborn Mine, 89
Peshastin Mine, 134, 150
Peter Tu Claim, 291–92, 294
Phoenix Claim, 208, 209
Piper Hiedseck Claim, 273
Pole Pick Mines, 135, 136, 153–54
Porcupine Claim, 287
Potato Patch Mine, 207, 210

Prince Group, 301–2
Princeton Bar Claim, 253
Prospect Claim, 163
Queen Bee Mine, 142
Queen of the Hills Claim, 276
Quien Sabe Prospect, 38
Raymond Mine, 47
Red Bird Prospect, 277
Red Eagle Claim, 277
Red Hook Claim, 211–12
Red Jacket Mine, 201
Red Mine, 187
Red Rock Mine, 223
Rex Mine, 86, 88
Rouse Prospect, 39
Royal Development Mine, 70–71, 72, 73–78, 79
Ruby Group, 263–64
Ruby King Claim, 281
Rushing Water Claim, 281
Safety Harbor Mine, 65–66
Sandell Mine, 150
Savage Mine, 89
Settler Claim, 208
Sherman Claim, 278
Silver Bow Claim, 261
Silver Bowl Prospect, 281
Silver Bull Claim, 301
Silver Bullion Claim, 269
Silver Claim, 267
Silver Fiend Claim, 289, 290
Silver Jack Prospect, 39
Silver Queen Claims, 273
Silver Tip Mine, 226–27
Silver Trail Mine, 47
Silver Treasury Prospect, 281
Skirmisher Claim, 298–99
Skookum Group, 299
Skookum Mine, 230–33, 234
Snook Prospect, 287–88
Sonny Brown Mine, 191
South Fork Manastash Creek Placers, 224
South Mount Stuart Prospect, 235
Southern Star Mining Claim, 196–97
Sperry/Iverson Mine, xvi
Spirit Lake Prospect, 283
Spokane Boy and Girl Prospect, 39
Spring Pheasant Claim, 162–63
St. Francis Mine, 69, 73–74
St. John Mine, 240
St. Luke Mine, 240
St. Paul Claim, 273
Standard Claim, 281
Starlite Prospect, 240
State Group of claims, 140–41
Summit Prospect, 39
Sunday Morning Mine, 64
Sunset and Mountain Sheik Prospects, 40
Sunset Mine, 67
Sunshine Mine, 88–89
Sylvanite Mine, 201–2
Texas Jack Prospect, 41
Thorp Claim, 240–41
Tiger Prospect, 41

Tillicum Gold Prospect, 162
Tip Top Claim (Gold Creek Basin), 143–44
Tip Top Claim (North Fortune Creek area), 282
Tip Top Mine (Blewett area), 160–61
Tip Top Mine (Mount Stuart area), 235
Tommy Jack Prospect, 40
Topping Claims, 301
Trail Creek Prospect, 246–47
Trio Placer, 278
True Fissure Gold Mine, 193–94
Twin Falls Prospect, 41
Una Claims, 78
Upper Hummingbird Mine, 153
Van Epps Pass Prospect, 283
Vap Epps Copper Claim, 286
Vedette Claim, 301
Velma Claim, 140
Virden Mine, 187–88
Wall Street Mine, 188–90
Wheelbarrow Mine, 158
White and Yellow Group, 302–3
White Star Claim, 289, 291
White Water Claim, 281
Wilder Mine, 135
Williams Claim, 267–68
Williams Creek Placer, 183–84
Wind Fall Claim, 212
Winesap Canyon Prospect, 90
Winesap Nickel Prospect, 90
Wisishin Claim, 278
Wye/Amber Glee Mine, 153
Yellow Hill Claim, 228–29
Zerwekh Mine, 202
mining. *See also specific mining areas*
    early law, xx–xxi
    entering mines, xxvii–xxviii
    explosives and chemicals, xvii
    filing and retaining claims, xvii, xx
    gold, xii–xiii, xiv
    high-grading, xiv–xvi
    history, ix–x
    laws and regulations that govern prospecting, xix, xx, xxv–xxvi
    locating lode deposits, xvi–xix
    placer *vs.* lode, xvi, xvii
    regulating, xxv–xxvi
    salting of mines, xvi
    silver, xiv, xx
    theft of high-grade ore, xiv–xvi
mining districts. *See also specific mining areas*
    Big Creek District, 223
    vs. mining areas, xx
    overview, xx–xxi
    Swauk District, xxi
    Upper Cle Elum District, 262–63
Minneapolis Prospect, 39
Modog Claims, 265
molybdenite, 47
Montague, R., 271
Monte Cristo Mine, xviii, xxiii
Moore, J.R., 64
Morgan Creek, 219–20

Morning Claim, 194
Morning Star Mine, 243
Morning Star Mining Company, 241, 242, 273
Morrill, J.K., 180
Morris, Frank, 95
Morrison, A.B., 193
Morrison, Archie, 174
Morrison, Daniel, 193
Morrison, J.B., 199
Morrison Gold Quartz Mine, 195–96
Morrison Mine, 193–94
Mother-in-Law Group, 210
Mount Hawkins chrome properties, 261–62
Mountain Beaver Placer Claims, 201
Mountain Belle Claim, 275
Mountain Chief Mining Company, 275
mountain goat tale, 269
Mountain Placer, 278
Mountain Sprite Claims, 297
Mountain Whistler Claim, 273
mucking, 55, 59, 117, 118, 321
Muldoon, Jim, 250, 262

N
Nairn Claim, 197
Naneum Creek Placers, 201
Native Americans, 91, 93–94, 204, 248
Naughten, Francis J., 67, 69
Naughten, James, 69
Navaho Peak area prospects, 239–40
Negro Baby iron lode, 223
Negro Creek, 129, 131, 141–45
Negro Creek (Davenport) Claim, 144
Negro Creek milepost four cabin and tunnel, 144–45
Nelson, Gus. *See* Nilson, Gus
Nelson, Peter, 223
Nelson Claim, 286
Neubauer, Anton, 136, 159
Neubauer, Thaddeus, 158, 159, 182
New Discovery Placer, 174, 182
Newberry, Charles, 141
Newman, John, 203
Newport Creek, 219
Newstrum, William, 188, 189
Nez Perce, 94
Nickel Plate Group, 141
Nickelodeon Claims, 255–57, 258
Nilson, Gus, 169, 173, 190, 195, 210
Nilson Hill, 190–91
Nisqually Indians, 93
North Fortune Creek area claims, 280–82
North Star Claim, 199
North Star Mining Company, 67
Northwest Oil Research Corporation, 96
Nugget Placer, 200, 278
NW Mining Ventures, 136

O
Olden, John, 131, 164
Olehamer, Ole, 273, 276, 281
Ollie Jordin Mine, 198
Olmstead, A.D., 265
Olmstead Mine, 267

Olmsted, E.B., 192
Olympia Claims, 158
Ombompo Prospect, 40
O'Neil, John, 268
Oregon Territory, 91
Orion Claim, 204–5
Oro Grande Claim, 192, 193
Orphan Boy Mine, 64

P
Paddy-Go-Easy Pass, 294–302
Panama #2 Prospect, 38
Pangborn, Percy, 161
Pangborn Mine, 89
panning for gold. See placer mining; prospecting
Parker, Fred, 295
patents, defined, 321
Patton, Thomas Charles, 127
Peak 4047T Adit, 204–5
Pearsall, Joe, xviii
Pearshall, William, 36
Pease, Roy T., 192
Pechet, M.S., 266
Pechiney Corporation, 60
Pelland, C.A., 192
Pennell, William, 178
peridotite, 138, 221, 273
Perish, T.A., 134
Perry, Crooker, 65
Pershall, Lloyd, 35, 86
Peshastin Mine, 134, 150
Pesonen, P.E., 251
Peter Tu Claim, 291–92, 294
Peterson, Ole, 208
Peterson, W.F., 141
Phipps, Harve, 135
Phipps tunnel, 158
Phoenix Claim, 208, 209
Pickwick Mining Company, 282, 286
Pike, J.C., 210
The Pinnacles, 157
Piper Hiedseck Claim, 273
Pisoni, Victor, 195, 292
placer, defined, 322
placer claims, defined, 322
placer mining
    in Blewett area, 129, 131
    finding gold, xvii, xviii–xix
    glossary definition, 322
    vs. lode mining, xvi, xvii
    photos, xv
    rules for federal lands, xxv–xxvi
    rules in Washington State, xxvi
pocket hunting, xviii
Pole Pick Mines, 135, 136, 153–54
Pool, Mrs. M.A., 198
Porcupine Claim, 287
porphyries, xxii, 46, 322
Porter, George, 161
Porter, John M., 124
Potato Patch Mine, 207, 210
powder drifting, 55
Powles, charles H., 198

Price, C.E., 242
Price, John H., 188
Price, Mr., 253
Priestly, Bill, 156
Priestly, Willis R., 136
Prince Group, 301–2
Princeton Bar Claim, 253
Prospect Claim, 163
prospecting
    filing claims, xvii, xx
    as hobby, xix
    legal aspects, xix, xx, xxv–xxvi
    and metal detectors, xix
    preparations, xix, xxvii–xxviii
    retaining claims, xx
prospects, defined, 322
Pruyn, Edward, 241
pulling the pillars, 106, 322

Q
quartz
    Crown Point Mine area, 47
    glossary definition, 322
    in Swauk area, 172–73
Queen Bee Mine, 142
Queen of the Hills Claim, 276
Quien Sabe Prospect, 38
Quietsch, Louis, 178, 194

R
Rabicharid, Peter, 65
Radabaugh, George, 188, 210
Railroad Creek, 49, 51, 53–54
rating of hikes, xxix
rattlesnakes, xviii, 90, 96
Raymond Mine, 47
Red Bird Prospect, 277
Red Bluff, 215–16
Red Eagle Claim, 277
Red Hook Claim, 211–12
Red Jacket Mine, 201
Red Mine, 187
Red Rock Mine, 223
Red Top Mountain agates and geodes, 216
reefs
    A Reef, 97, 108–9, 127
    B Reef, 97, 105–6, 111, 112, 114, 124, 127
    C Reef, 97, 109–10
    D Reef, 95, 97, 100, 106–7
    E Reef, 97, 107, 109
    glossary definition, 322
Reeves, Clarence, 105, 111
Reeves, Don, 111
Reeves, J.A., 111
Reeves, Robert, 111
Rex Mine, 86, 88
riffle boxes, xvii, 170, 183
Ripsaw Ridge, 33
Robertson, Mortimer, 129
Robinson, W.P., 49
Robinson Gulch, 201, 203
Rock Creek "Ghost" photo, 80
Rockefeller, John D., xxiii

rockhounding, xxv–xxvi, xxvii. See also geology
Rocky Point Mining Company, 275–76
rod mills, 119, 198, 200, 322
Rogers, A.B., 91
Rogers Mine. See Rex Mine
Rooster Comb, 109
Roseland, Oscar, 192
Ross, J.J., 67
Rouse Prospect, 39
Royal Development Mine
    closing, 77–78
    history, 69–71
    mill, 74, 75, 77
    mine production, 75
    overview, 73–75
    St. Francis ore, 73–74
    today, 78
    Trinity town site, 69, 76, 78, 79
    tunnels, 70, 72, 73–74, 79
Rubin, Ernie, 163
Ruby Creek, 145–46
Ruby Group, 263–64
Ruby King Claim, 281
Ruby tunnel, 163
Ruffner, W.H., 249
Runnels, H.B., 209
Rupert, R.R., 201
Rushing Water Claim, 281
Rutherford, Wallace, 208

S
Saddle Rock, 108
Safety Harbor Mine, 65–66
St. Francis Mine, 69, 73–74
St. John Mine, 240
St. Luke Mine, 240
St. Paul Claim, 273
Salisbury, Gilbert A., 302
Salmon La Sac, 246–49
salting of mines, xvi
Sandell Mine, 150
Sasse, August, 248, 289, 290, 301
Savage Mine, 89
Sayers, Dave, 202
Scheble, F.M., 107
scorpions, xviii
Scotty Creek area, 164, 165
Searles, H.A., 163
Seaton, W.A., 197, 198
serpentine, 138, 221
Settler Claim, 208
Sexton, K.P., 54
Shafer, John, 131
Shafer tunnel, 158
Shaser Creek area, 164–65
Sherman Claim, 278
shrinkage stopes, xxiii, 101, 118, 323. See also bulldozer chambers
Sides, George, 188
Sidney, Mr., 275
Sill, S.W., 265
silver, xiv, xx
Silver Bow Claim, 261

Silver Bowl Prospect, 281
Silver Bull Claim, 301
Silver Bullion Claim, 269
Silver Claim, 267
Silver Creek area, 290–94
Silver Creek Mining Company, 291–93
Silver Dump, 264
Silver Fiend Claim, 289, 290
Silver Jack Prospect, 39
Silver Queen Claims, 273
Silver Tip Mine, 226–27
Silver Trail Mine, 47
Silver Treasury Prospect, 281
Simmons, Ed, 230
Sims, N.E., 54
Skamow (Wenatchee chief), 93
Skeeter workings, 301
Skipper Chrome Mining Company, 261, 262
Skirmisher Claim, 298–99
Skookum Group, 299
Skookum Mine, 230–33, 234
Sloan, George, 236
Sloan, Newton, 111
slurry, 119, 305, 308, 323
Smith, Tommy, 156
Smith, T.W., 206
snakes, dangerous, xviii
Snook Prospect, 287–88
Snyder, Vestal, 186
Solomon Creek area, 286–91
Solomon Creek-Jack Creek tunnel and shaft, 287
Somers, John, 230
Sonny Brown Mine, 191
South Fork Manastash Creek Placers, 224
South Mount Stuart Prospect, 235
Southern Star Mining Claim, 196–97
Sperry/Iverson Mine, xvi
spiders, xviii
Spirit Lake Prospect, 283
Splawn, Andrew, 129, 248
Splawn, Charles, 139
Splawn, Mose, 244, 262, 267
Splawn, William, 289
Spokane Boy and Girl Prospect, 39
Spring Creek, 219
Spring Pheasant Claim, 162–63
Spurr, Josiah E., 70
Stafford Creek iron deposits, 238–39
stamp mills, 86, 132, 134, 146, 148, 149, 150, 152, 323
Standard Claim, 281
Stanton, Phil, 200, 262, 291, 295
Starlite Prospect, 240
State Group of claims, 140–41
State of Washington Mining Company, 186, 196
static electricity, 117
Stehekin mining area
   description, 31
   geology, 35
   getting there, 34
   history, 31, 33
   list of mines, 35–37

   list of prospects, 37–41
   map, 32
   what to see, 33–34
Stevens, Isaac Ingalls, 91
Stevens, John, 91
Stevens Pass, 91
Stevenson, Joe, 262
Stewart, Mrs. Corliss, 136
Stewert, Archie, 136
Stoner, H.B., 135
Stoner tunnel, 158
stopes, xxvii, 72, 98, 99, 100, 103, 115, 117, 122, 124, 288, 305, 323. *See also* shrinkage stopes
Stoves, Anthony, Jr., 265, 291
Strander, E., 195
Stucky, H.A., 192
Stumpf, Chuck, 100, 105, 111
Stumpf, Dick, 100
Summit pockets, 159
Summit Prospect, 39
Sunday Morning Mine, 64
Sunset and Mountain Sheik Prospects, 40
Sunset Mine, 67
Sunshine Mine, 88–89
Sure Thing Gold & Copper Mining Company, 274
Swain, C.O., 265, 271
Swauk mining area
   description, 167
   diamonds, 176
   District boundaries, xxi
   District history, xxi
   District mining laws, xxi
   geology, 171–73
   getting there, 170–71
   hiking and touring, 212–16
   history, 167, 169–70
   list of mines, 176–216
   what to see, 170
Sylvanite Mine, 201–2

T
Table Mountain hike, 213–14
Taneum iron lode, 224
Taylor, William, 246
Teaghers, T.I., 170
Teanaway River area, 235–36
Teanaway-Swauk Prairie Cemetery, 228
Teanaway Valley
   geology, 228
   and headwaters area, 228
   mineral claims, 228–29
   settlers, 229
   upper iron claims, 236–38
   upper mine claims, 230–35
Tenneco Minerals, 113, 114
Terwilliger, Ed, 276, 281, 282
Terwilliger, George, 276, 281, 282
Texas Jack Prospect, 41
theft of high-grade ore, xiv–xvi
Thompson, Oscar, 103, 109
Thomson, J.N.O., 227
Thomson, John Prentiss, 227

Thorp, Elvin A., 241
Thorp Claim, 240–41
Three Crosses Mine, 272
Tibbs, Shorty, 114
ticks, xviii
Tiffany, Ross, 243
Tiger Prospect, 41
Tillicum Gold Prospect, 162
Tip Top Claim (Gold Creek Basin), 143–44
Tip Top Claim (North Fortune Creek area), 282
Tip Top Mine (Blewett area), 160–61
Tip Top Mine (Mount Stuart area), 235
Tommy Jack Prospect, 40
Topping, J.H., 301
Topping Claims, 301
Trail Creek Prospect, 246–47
trams. *See* aerial tramways
transcontinental railroad, 93
tree prospecting, 279
Trinity town site, 69, 76, 78, 79. *See also* Royal Development Mine
Trio Placer, 278
True Fissure Gold Mine, 193–94
tunnels
   Black Bear Prospect, 279
   construction photo, 41
   crosscut, 59, 135, 150, 151, 158, 318
   Dennett Placer, 176–77, 184
   haulage, 49, 98, 99, 101, 320
   Holden Mine photos, 49, 58, 59, 60, 61
   Livingston Placer, 177
   Lovitt Mine, 98–99, 101, 103
   Royal Development Mine, 70, 72, 73–74, 79
   Williams Creek Placer, 183–84
Turner, Judge, 294
Turton, R.H., 223
Tweet, Torkel (Tom), 207, 208
Twin Falls Prospect, 41
Twin Mining Company, 281–82
Twiss, Ben, 210
Twomey, Patrick, 223, 236

U
Una Basin Mining and Milling Company, 67
Una Claims, 78
uplifting, 221
Upper Cle Elum iron deposits, 249
Upper Cle Elum Mining District, 262–63
Upper Hummingbird Mine, 153
Upper Negro Creek, 143–45
U.S. 97 tourist tunnel, 179

V
Van Epps adits, 86, 287
Van Epps Creek area, 286–91
Van Epps Pass area mines, 282–85
Van Epps Pass Prospect, 283
Vanderbilt, Cornelius J., 230
Vap Epps Copper Claim, 286
Vauthiers, Jon, 185, 198
Vedette Claim, 301
Velma Claim, 140

Vinton, T.J., 160
Virden, George, 187–88, 228
Virden Mine, 187–88

W
Waddell, Earl, 228–29
Wall Street Mine, 188–90
Walters, H.C., 262
Warner, Mr., 133
Warrior General Company, 134
Washington Copper Preferred Company, 269
Washington Gold Mining Company, 186
Washington Meteor Company, 135, 136, 154
Washington Quicksilver Company, 255–57
Washington State. *See also specific mining areas*
    geology, xxii–xxiv
    gold in, xiv, xvi–xvii, xxii, xxiii
    laws and regulations that govern prospecting, xix, xx, xxv–xxvi
    mines overview map, vi
    mining districts, xx–xxi
    mining history, xxii–xxiv
    ore deposits, xvi, xxii–xxiv
Watson, F.N., 209
Weise, H.F., 275
Welsh, Dick, 217
Welsh, Jacob, 241
Welsh, Joe, 217
Wenatchee Indians, 93
Wenatchee mining area
    Cannon Mine, xvii, 96–97, 110–27
    description, 91
    geology, 96–97
    getting there, 96
    Lovitt Mine, 96, 97–110
    map, 92
    mining history, 95
    and Native American history, 91, 93–94
    what to see, 95
Wenatchee Mining Company, 101
West, L.H., 236
Western States Uranium Company, 65
Wheat, Ernest, 210
Wheelbarrow Mine, 158
Whitaker, C.C., 199
White, John, 161
White and Yellow Group, 302–3
White Star Claim, 289, 291
White Water Claim, 281
Wilder, Peter, 131
Wilder Mine, 135
Williams, Riley, 267, 268, 269
Williams Claim, 267–68
Williams Creek Placer tunnels, 183–84
Wilson, E.W., 262, 265
Wilson, F.D., 210
Wind Fall Claim, 212
Winesap Canyon Prospect, 90
Winesap Nickel Prospect, 90
wire gold, 85
Wisishin Claim, 278
Woeppel, Fred F., 136
Wright, George, 280

Wright, James, 248
Wye/Amber Glee Mine, 153

Y
Yellow Hill Claim, 228–29
York, A.F., xxi, 199, 208, 228, 253, 263
Young, E.J., 210

Z
Zeran, Isaac, 209
Zerwekh Mine, 202
Zude, Howard, 102